ORLANDO

WALT DISNEY WORLD

2009

Simon & Susan Veness

foulsham
LONDON • NEW YORK • TORONTO • SYDNEY

foulsham
The Oriel, Thames Valley Court, 183–187 Bath Road,
Slough SL1 4AA

Foulsham books can be found in all good bookshops or direct from www.foulsham.com

ISBN: 978-0-572-03489-4

A CIP record for this book is available from the British Library

Dedication: To our special three-boy research team – Ben, Anthony and Mark – who help make our work fun!

SPECIAL THANKS
Special thanks for this edition go to: Orlando/Orange County Convention and Visitors Bureau, Kissimmee Convention and Visitors Bureau, Daytona Beach Area Convention and Visitors Bureau, St Petersburg/Clearwater Convention and Visitors Bureau, Tampa Bay & Company, Walt Disney Theme Parks, Universal Orlando, Anheuser Busch Entertainment Corporation, The Sandpearl Resort Clearwater Beach, Allan Oakley at Alexander Holiday Homes, Nigel Worrall at Florida Leisure, Andy James and James Brown at Florida Dolphin Tours, Nina and Pete Dew, Margie Long and Michelle Peters at Boggy Creek Airboats.

Our sincere thanks also go to all the hard-working people at Foulsham who help to bring our work to life every year.

Printed in Dubai

CONTENTS

FOREWORD

Simon says... Once again, we're looking at another exciting year in Excitement Central, otherwise known as Orlando. This place never ceases to amaze us – after a year (2008) that saw the opening of the fabulous Aquatica water park and major new attractions for Walt Disney World, Universal Studios and Busch Gardens, there is even more to look forward to! And yet again it goes to show why you need a really good guide – the *Brit Guide*, now in its 15th record-breaking edition. This portion of Central Florida is an utterly unique destination but making the most of your time there requires a level of planning and organisation unlike anywhere else in the world. For newcomers and repeat visitors alike it is a serious challenge – which is why we started this guidebook in the first place. Stick with us and you'll have the very best possible preparation for this amazing holiday, plus a tried and trusted 'friend' to take with you while you're there. We'll help you avoid the pitfalls and circumvent (most of) the queues, and save you money while you relish the trip of a lifetime. It's all here waiting for you to discover and enjoy – just come on inside!

Susan says... With even more to enjoy in Orlando in 2009, savvy veterans and well-prepared first-timers will understand the need for a plan of action that provides the greatest value for money without making everyone collapse in a heap at the end of the holiday. Central Florida's focus has always been on the family, but this year sees an increase in offerings specifically for adults, teens and pre-schoolers, making for exciting times for visitors of all ages while also emphasising the need to make informed decisions. And that's where the *Brit Guide* comes in. Do your homework and make the right choices for this holiday – and bear in mind that there will almost certainly be another one (Orlando is nothing if not addictive!). Once you have narrowed down your must-do list, rest assured that you are travelling with the best, most comprehensive information resource (that's us), geared toward making your visit the most magical holiday yet. Overwhelmed? Let us help with our *Itinerary Planner Service.* And now, on with the planning!

Simon and Susan Veness
(visit us at **venesstravelmedia.com** or email **britsguide@yahoo.com**)

1 Introduction

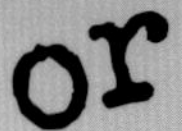

or Welcome to the Holiday of a Lifetime

Get ready for the most exciting holiday experience in the world, bar none, guaranteed! The area of central Florida we call 'Orlando' is a vast mix of adventure rides, thrills, fun and fantasy with no equal anywhere else on earth. And we're not just talking about the amazing *Walt Disney World Resort.*

First off, this is a BIG venture in every sense of the word and you must be aware of the extensive and complex nature of this tourist wonderland. Disney is the leading attraction, but there is a strong supporting cast, led by Universal Orlando and SeaWorld. There's something for all tastes and ages – young and old; families, couples and singles – but it exacts a high toll. You'll walk a lot, queue a lot and probably eat a lot. You'll have a fabulous time, but you'll be exhausted, too. It's not so much a holiday as a military campaign!

The Brit Guide *research team*

Eight theme parks

In simple terms, there are 8 essential major theme parks, and at least one will require 2 days to make you feel it has been well and truly done. Add a day at one of the water parks, a trip to see some of the wildlife or other nature attractions, and the lure of the nearby Kennedy Space Center, and you have 12 days of pure adventure mania. Then mix in the night-time attractions of *Downtown Disney*, Universal's CityWalk and a host of dinner shows, plus some world-class shopping, and you'll have an idea of the awesome scope of the place. Even with 2 weeks, something has to give – just make sure it isn't your patience, wallet or sanity!

So, how do you get full value from this truly magical holiday? The basic answer is Good Planning – read, reflect and prepare. At the back of this book is a handy outline guide for all that you might want to do. Be aware of the time demands of the parks and make sure you build in a quiet day or two by the pool or at one of the smaller attractions. With SO much on offer, it just isn't possible to 'do it all', so try to ensure you get full value from your choices. Also, don't under-estimate the vast scale involved. Everything is well spread out and it takes time even to get from park to park. But do stop to admire the clever detail and imagination of what's on offer as it is simply world class.

BRITTIP

All website addresses in this book are preceded by 'www.' unless they begin with 'http'.

Orlando

Orlando itself is a relatively small but bright young city that has become synonymous with *Walt Disney World* in its south-west corner. When Walt's dream of a vast resort opened in 1971 with the *Magic Kingdom* park (sadly, he never saw it realised as he died in 1966), it led to a massive tourist expansion that has never stopped. New attractions pop up all the time and it's easy to get carried away by the sheer volume on offer, which varies from terrific to tacky.

The name 'Orlando', however, has grown to encompass much of Central Florida and it is more accurate to detail the area by its 7 counties: **Orange County** is home to the city of Orlando, but part of *Walt Disney World* is in **Osceola County** to the south, with Kissimmee its main town; **Seminole County**, home of Orlando Sanford International Airport, is north-east of Orange County; **Lake County** is to the north and west, with Mount Dora its principal town; **Polk County** lies to the south-west and is home to many vacation villas; **Brevard County** and **Volusia County** are on the east (Atlantic) coast, home to the Kennedy Space Center and Daytona Beach. The local population of Greater Orlando (Orange, Seminole, Osceola and Lake counties) numbers 1.9 million, of which some 375,000 are employed in the tourist business. And, in 2008, some 50 million people were expected to make Orlando their holiday choice, spending more than $30 billion. Britain accounts for 40% of foreign visitors, and in 2007 that was just over a million of us. Orlando International Airport has seen traffic boom from 8 million passengers in 1983 to a record 36.5 million in 2007. In addition, the Metro Orlando area boasts around 115,000 hotel rooms, 26,000 vacation homes and more than 4,000 places to eat. Shopaholics also have the choice of some 250 shopping centres, including 30 malls. Here's a taste of the main attractions.

Walt Disney World Resort in Florida

This is where the 'magic' really starts – and the effect is vividly real. This vast resort actually consists of 4 separate theme parks, 20 speciality hotel resorts, a camping ground, 2 water parks, a sports complex, 4 18-hole golf courses, 4 mini-golf courses and a huge shopping and entertainment district (*Downtown Disney*). It covers 47sq mls/122sq km. The likes of Alton Towers and Thorpe Park would comfortably fit into its car parks! Indeed, Alton Towers, Britain's biggest theme park, is 60 times smaller. On average, there are estimated to be 200,000 visitors at any one time. The Disney organisation does things with the most style, and there are always new projects on the drawing board. It maintains an extremely high level of customer service, where everyone who works for them is officially a Cast Member, not just staff, and they take that ethic to heart. Here's a quick rundown of what's on offer.

Magic Kingdom Park: This is the essential Disney, including the fantasy of its wonderful films, the adventures of the Wild West and Africa, the excitement of thrill rides like Space Mountain (a huge indoor roller-coaster), the 3-D film fun of Mickey's PhilharMagic and splendid daily parades and fireworks.

Epcot: Disney's 2-part park, with the technology-inspired Future World, plus a potted journey around the globe in World Showcase. Though more educational than adventurous, it still has some memorable rides, including Test Track, Mission: SPACE and the superb Soarin', along with excellent dining.

Florida

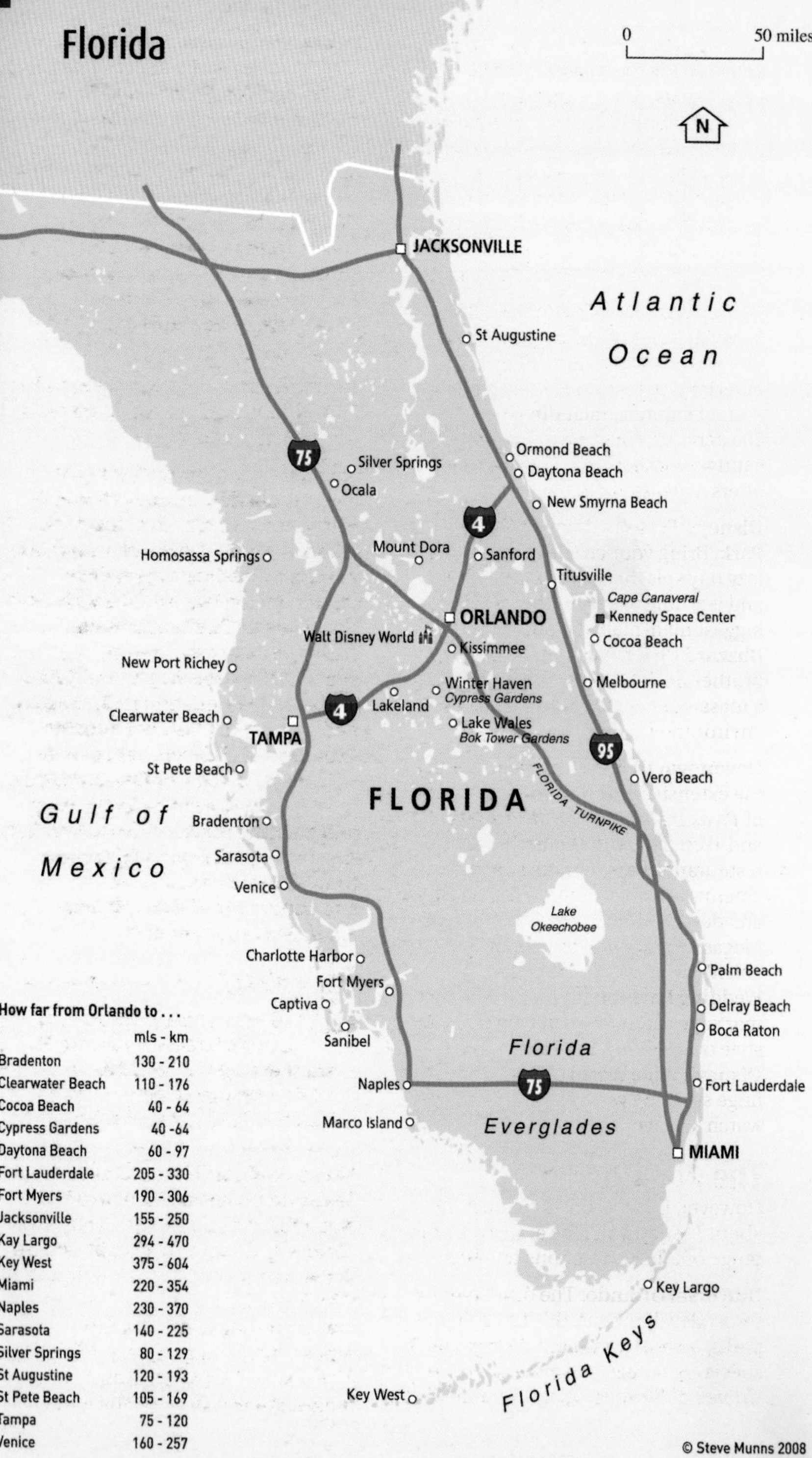

How far from Orlando to . . .

	mls - km
Bradenton	130 - 210
Clearwater Beach	110 - 176
Cocoa Beach	40 - 64
Cypress Gardens	40 -64
Daytona Beach	60 - 97
Fort Lauderdale	205 - 330
Fort Myers	190 - 306
Jacksonville	155 - 250
Kay Largo	294 - 470
Key West	375 - 604
Miami	220 - 354
Naples	230 - 370
Sarasota	140 - 225
Silver Springs	80 - 129
St Augustine	120 - 193
St Pete Beach	105 - 169
Tampa	75 - 120
Venice	160 - 257

Disney's Hollywood Studios: Here you can ride the movies in style, meeting Star Wars™, the Muppets and Indiana Jones; drop into the fearsome Tower of Terror or the high-speed Rock 'n' Roller Coaster Starring Aerosmith; and learn the tricks of the trade at the likes of the epic Lights, Motors, Action!™ Extreme Stunt Show, plus try the new Toy Story Mania ride.

Disney's Animal Kingdom: Billed as 'a new species of theme park', this delivers another contrasting and entertaining scenario. With realistic animal habitats, including a 100 acre/40.5ha safari savannah, captivating shows and terrific rides, it offers a pleasant change of pace.

Disney's Typhoon Lagoon Water Park: Bring your cozzie and spend a lazy day splashing down waterslides and learning to surf in the world's biggest man-made lagoon. **Disney's Blizzard Beach Water Park:** The big brother of all the water parks, this has a massive spread of rides in a 'snowy' environment.

Downtown Disney: This incorporates the extensive entertainment district of *Pleasure Island, The Marketplace* and *West Side* with themed restaurants, bars, unique stores, a cinema multiplex, the DisneyQuest arcade of interactive games, Virgin Megastore and the famous Cirque du Soleil® company. There is even a **Wedding Pavilion** for picture-perfect marriage ceremonies in true fairytale style overlooking Bay Lake, while **Disney's Wide World of Sports** is a huge sporting venue to both play and watch top events.

The other parks

However, if you think Orlando is all about Disney, you'll be amazed by the range of other attractions on offer.

Universal Orlando: The other big resort development, this has 2 theme parks, an entertainment district and 3 speciality hotels. The parks are **Universal Studios** where you Ride The Movies as you encounter The Simpsons, Jaws, the Men In Black and ET, the Shrek 4-D show and Revenge of the Mummy ride, plus Woody Woodpecker's KidZone and the amazing Terminator 2: 3-D show; and **Islands of Adventure**, a superb blend of thrill rides, family attractions, shows and eye-catching design, with some of the world's most advanced hardware (like the Amazing Adventures of Spider-Man).

Wet 'n Wild: Although on International Drive, this water park is Universal-owned and offers plenty of fun rides and slides.

SeaWorld: Don't think this is just another dolphin show; SeaWorld is *the* place for creatures of the deep, with killer whales the main attraction, a bright, refreshing atmosphere (check out the Waterfront district and the amazing Blue Horizons and Believe shows) and a serious ecological approach, plus thrill rides Journey to Atlantis and Kraken and a dedicated area for rides and other activities for children. Its exclusive neighbour, **Discovery Cove**, offers the opportunity to swim with dolphins, among other things, and the stunning new water park **Aquatica** provides even more fun and animal encounters in a vividly colourful South Seas environment.

BRITTIP

Beware travel-agent pressure to buy more tickets than you need. You simply won't get full use out of, say, a 14-day Disney ticket and the Orlando FlexTicket Plus in a 2-week holiday.

Busch Gardens: The sister park to SeaWorld (in nearby Tampa) offers creatures of the land, with a good mix of rides and shows. Highlights are the SheiKra mega-coaster, the Rhino Rally ride, Myombe Reserve, a close-up look at the endangered central African highland gorillas, the Edge of Africa 'safari' experience and the new Jungala 'village' of rides and animal exhibits. A real family treat, plus a must for coaster fans.

Other key attractions

These include the **Kennedy Space Center**, the dramatically upgraded home of space exploration, with the Shuttle Launch Experience; **Cypress Gardens**, Florida's oldest 'theme park' reborn in 2004 with coasters and other rides, plus wonderful gardens; **Silver Springs**, a close look at Florida nature via various boat journeys on the crystal-clear Silver River, plus animal exhibits; and **Fantasy of Flight**, an aviation museum experience that includes the world's largest private collection of vintage aircraft, plus fighter-plane simulators.

Disney tickets

Most people buy one of the multi-day passes that allow you to move between the theme parks on the same day and grant unlimited access to the transport system. Make no mistake, you cannot walk between the parks (except for a long haul between *Epcot* and *Disney's Hollywood Studios*), and trying to do more than one a day is hard work. The choice of tickets is bewildering, so be sure to buy ONLY what you need.

Disney's basic ticket system is called Magic Your Way and is horribly complicated for the first-timer. Happily, it also has simplified tickets sold in advance for the UK visitor. All multi-day passes offer savings against 1-day tickets but unused days DO expire unless you buy an upgrade at the parks.

Magic Your Way: If you just turn up at the ticket booths, you must choose from the Magic Your Way menu:

- The number of days you need (1–10).
- Whether you want *Park Hopping* (the ability to visit more than 1 park on the same day for a $50 flat rate).
- Whether you want the *Water Park Fun & More Option* (1–10 visits to the water parks, *DisneyQuest* and *Disney's ESPN World of Sports*™) for $50. NB: With the closure of clubs of *Pleasure Island* (previously included on the More Options), Disney now offers 1 free round of golf at its 9-hole Oak Trail course (book in advance on 407 939 4653); club hire NOT included.
- Whether you want the *Non-expiration Option* (at $15–180, depending on the number of days of ticket). This option can be added *after* the initial purchase, but what you pay is still based on the original length of the ticket; e.g., if you buy a 7-day ticket and decide after 5 days you won't use the rest of it on this visit, you can add non-expiration for $95 and save the remaining 2 days for the future. You *must* upgrade within 14 days of first use.

> **BRITTIP**
> Buy your theme park tickets in advance, NOT at the park gates. You will save time AND money as there is a built-in advance purchase discount.

Per-day ticket savings increase with the more days you buy: 1 day = $71 plus tax; 10 days = $225 plus tax, or $22.50/day.

> **BRITTIP**
> To avoid the queues at the Disney park ticket booths, you can also buy tickets in advance from the Guest Services office at *Downtown Disney*.

UK tickets: The bonus of coming from the UK means there are really only 4 tickets to consider, sold in advance (2 exclusively in Britain), and all good value. They are the 5- and 7-Day Premium Ticket, and the 14- and 21-Day Ultimate Ticket (see chart on page 11). The 1-, 2-, 3-, 4- and 6-day Disney tickets can be bought *only* in the US.

Other tickets

When it comes to Universal Orlando, SeaWorld and Busch Gardens, the choice can be equally complicated, and there are often periodic special offers (check with Attraction Tickets Direct, below).

- There are **1-** and **2-Day Tickets**.
- The **Orlando FlexTicket** remains the best value, providing 14 consecutive days' access to both Universal parks, Wet 'n Wild, SeaWorld and Aquatica; or those 5 plus Busch Gardens with the **FlexTicket Plus**.
- The **2-Park Unlimited Admission** ticket (online only from **universal orlando.com**) offers 7 days at Universal Orlando's 2 parks.
- The **2-Day 2-Park Ticket** with 3rd day free.
- And a **3-Park Bonus Ticket**, which is unlimited admission to both Universal parks and Wet 'n Wild for 14 days.
- SeaWorld and Busch Gardens also now have **2-** and **3-Park Tickets**, combining SeaWorld and Busch Gardens, or SeaWorld and Aquatica, or all 3, for a full 7 days.
- A day at exclusive **Discovery Cove** includes a **7-Day Pass** for SeaWorld or Busch Gardens, but the new **Discovery Cove Ultimate Ticket** includes SeaWorld, Busch and Aquatica for 14 consecutive days for an additional $35.
- For CityWalk, there is also a **CityWalk Party Pass** ($11.99 plus tax) or a **Party Pass with Movie** ($15.40 plus tax), as the centre has a 20-screen cinema.
- Another choice is the **Go Orlando Card**, which offers 1, 2, 3, 5 or 7 days of visits in the space of 14 days to more than 50 Florida attractions, including Kennedy Space Center, Gatorland, Cypress Gardens, airboat rides, mini-golf, dinner shows and more ($60–260 adults, $54–200 3–12s). You'd have to work hard to get full value for the 7-day card, but the 3- or 5-day ones are a good catch-all for some of the smaller attractions. It also comes with a handy guidebook to the attractions. Look up more on **goorlandocard.com**.

BRITTIP

Save money on some of the smaller attractions, dinner shows, restaurants, shops and more with the FREE Orlando Magicard from the Orlando Tourism Bureau at **orlandoinfo.com/uk**. Download online, order it directly, or call in to the Official Visitor Center on International Drive.

With price hikes every year, it's worth buying your tickets as soon as you book. We recommend shopping around, as many ticket outlets have periodic sales and special offers, but stick with a reputable agent and always use your credit card where possible for added security. These all come well recommended.

Attraction Tickets Direct: Britain's top direct-sell Florida ticket broker, with a sharp bookings team, has no credit card fees, free delivery in 7 days and a promise to beat any other brochure price (plus a full range of dinner shows, excursions and sports, many of them theme park backstage tours and a keen online Florida Forum and info centre). It also offers Disney hotels, with the same price-match guarantee as its attraction tickets (0845 130 3876, **attraction-tickets-direct.co.uk**).

Keith Prowse Attraction Tickets: Also offering the full range of theme parks, with new 1- and 2-week Passports that group various tickets together (e.g. a Disney 7-Day Premium, Orlando FlexTicket and Arabian Nights dinner show), plus a number of excursions, notably to the Kennedy Space Center, Silver Springs, Clearwater, Orlando Shopping and a Real Florida Experience tour (08701 232425, **keithprowsetickets.co.uk**).

Orlando Ticket Deals: A keenly priced and extremely helpful broker that also issues real tickets (not vouchers), offers a 'Next Day' delivery service and has a significant Price Promise for all its attractions, including all the

Choosing a ticket

Ticket type	Park	Allowance
1-Day Ticket	Any Disney park, Universal Orlando parks, SeaWorld or Busch Gardens	Access to 1 park ONLY for 1 day; not available in advance
5-Day Premium Ticket	*Magic Kingdom, Epcot, Disney's Hollywood Studios, Disney's Animal Kingdom*	Access for 5 days, with multiple parks on same day; plus 4 water park visits, *Disney's ESPN World of Sports™* and *DisneyQuest,* plus 1 free round at *Disney's Oak Trail Golf Course*; valid for 14 days after first use; non-expiration option available
7-Day Premium Ticket	*Magic Kingdom, Epcot, Disney's Hollywood Studios, Disney's Animal Kingdom*	Access for 7 days, with multiple parks on same day; plus 6 water parks visits, *Disney's ESPN World of Sports™* and *DisneyQuest,* plus 1 free round at *Disney's Oak Trail Golf Course*; valid for 14 days after first use; non-non-expiration option available
14-Day Ultimate Ticket	All Disney parks	Unlimited access to all attractions, inc. water parks, *DisneyQuest* and *ESPN World of Sports™* for 14 days after first use, plus 1 free round at *Disney's Oak Trail Golf Course*; NO non-expiration option; available only in advance in the UK
21-Day Ultimate Ticket	All Disney parks	Unlimited access to all attractions, inc. water parks, *DisneyQuest* and *ESPN World of Sports™* for 21 days after first use, plus 1 free round at *Disney's Oak Trail Golf Course*; NO non-expiration option; available only in advance in the UK
Annual Pass	*Magic Kingdom Park, Epcot, Disney's Hollywood Studios, Disney's Animal Kingdom*; inc. discounts for shops,dining,tours	Unlimited admission and free parking for 365 days after purchase date. If ordered online, you get a voucher which must be activated at a park; the 365 days start on the first day you activate the pass
Premium Annual Pass	All Disney parks; inc. discounts for shops, dining, tours	Unlimited admission and free parking for 365 days after purchase date; plus discounts on sports, recreation
1-Day 2-Park Ticket	Universal Studios, Islands of Adventure	Access to both Universal parks for 1 day
2-Park Unlimited Ticket	Universal Studios, Islands of Adventure, CityWalk	7 consecutive days' access to both Universal parks and CityWalk clubs (Universal online exclusive only)
2-Day 2-Park Ticket with 3rd Day Free	Universal Studios, Islands of Adventure, CityWalk	Access to both Universal parks for 3 days in a 14-day period; access to CityWalk for all 14 days
3-Park Bonus Ticket	Universal Studios, Islands of Adventure, Wet 'n Wild, CityWalk	Access to both Universal parks, plus Wet 'n Wild with multiple parks on same day, plus CityWalk for 14 days
Orlando FlexTicket	Universal Studios, Islands of Adventure, SeaWorld, Wet 'n Wild, Aquatica, CityWalk	Access to all 5 parks, with multiple parks on same day, for 14 days from first use, plus CityWalk clubs
Orlando FlexTicket Plus	All the above, plus Busch Gardens	Access to all 6 parks, with multiple parks on same day, for 14 days from first use, plus CityWalk clubs
SeaWorld 2- and 3-Park Tickets	SeaWorld, Aquatica and Busch Gardens	7 consecutive days' access to either SeaWorld and Aquatica; SeaWorld and Busch Gardens; or SeaWorld, Aquatica and Busch Gardens

parks, dinner shows and many excursions (0845 678 1682, **orlando-ticket-deals.co.uk**)

Theme Park Tickets Direct: Another well-priced Orlando specialist (part of Theme Park Holidays Ltd, 0870 040 0210, **themeparkticketsdirect.com**).

Tickets 4 Fun: Offers all the main attractions and tours, plus its Freedom Ticket, which combines Disney's Ultimate Ticket with the Orlando FlexTicket for maximum flexibility, as well as villa rentals, insurance and car hire (0870 890 3402, **tickets4fun.com**).

There are others, but beware of the lure of 'free' tickets as these are usually timeshare scams. Stick with one of these main brokers, who offer good products, service and local knowledge. Don't forget to plan with the benefit of our Busy Day Guide on page 361. You'll end up exhausted if you do the parks in one big chunk!

BRITTIP

For all your theme park tickets, be sure to check out *Brit Guide* partner **Orlando Ticket Deals** first, as it features an exclusive money-saving offer for our readers (see inside back cover).

The climate

The next question is when to go. Florida's weather varies from bright but cool winter days from November to February, with the odd drizzly spell, to furiously hot and humid summers punctuated by torrential tropical downpours.

The most pleasant option is to go between the two extremes, in spring or autumn – and you also avoid the worst of the crowds. However, as most families are governed by school holidays, Easter and July–August remain the most popular months for British visitors, so we have plenty of advice on how to stay ahead of the high-season crush. If you do need to take your holiday in summer, opt for late August as some US schools have resumed by then.

BRITTIP

The humidity levels – up to 100% – and fierce daily rainstorms in summer take a lot of visitors by surprise, so carry a lightweight, rainproof jacket or buy a cheap plastic poncho locally.

The mood

Orlando is big, brash and fun, but above all it's American and that means everything is well organised, but with a few cultural differences such as tipping (see below). It's clean, well maintained and eager to please: Floridians generally are an affable bunch, but they take affability to new heights in the theme parks, where staff are almost painfully keen to make sure you 'have a nice day'.

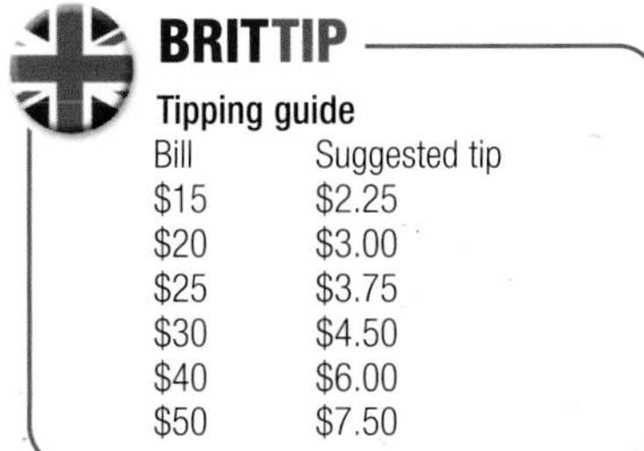

BRITTIP

Tipping guide

Bill	Suggested tip
$15	$2.25
$20	$3.00
$25	$3.75
$30	$4.50
$40	$6.00
$50	$7.50

Tipping

Close to every American's heart is the custom of tipping. With the exception of fast-food restaurant servers, just about everyone who serves in hotels, bars, restaurants, buses, taxis, airports and other public amenities will expect a tip. In bars, restaurants and taxis, the usual rate is 15% of the bill, while porters expect $1/bag and chambermaids $1/day per adult. It's important to know and remember that all service industry workers are taxed on the basis of receiving 15% in tips, whether they're given it or not.

Visa requirements

Holiday visitors to America do not need a visa providing they hold a valid machine-readable passport

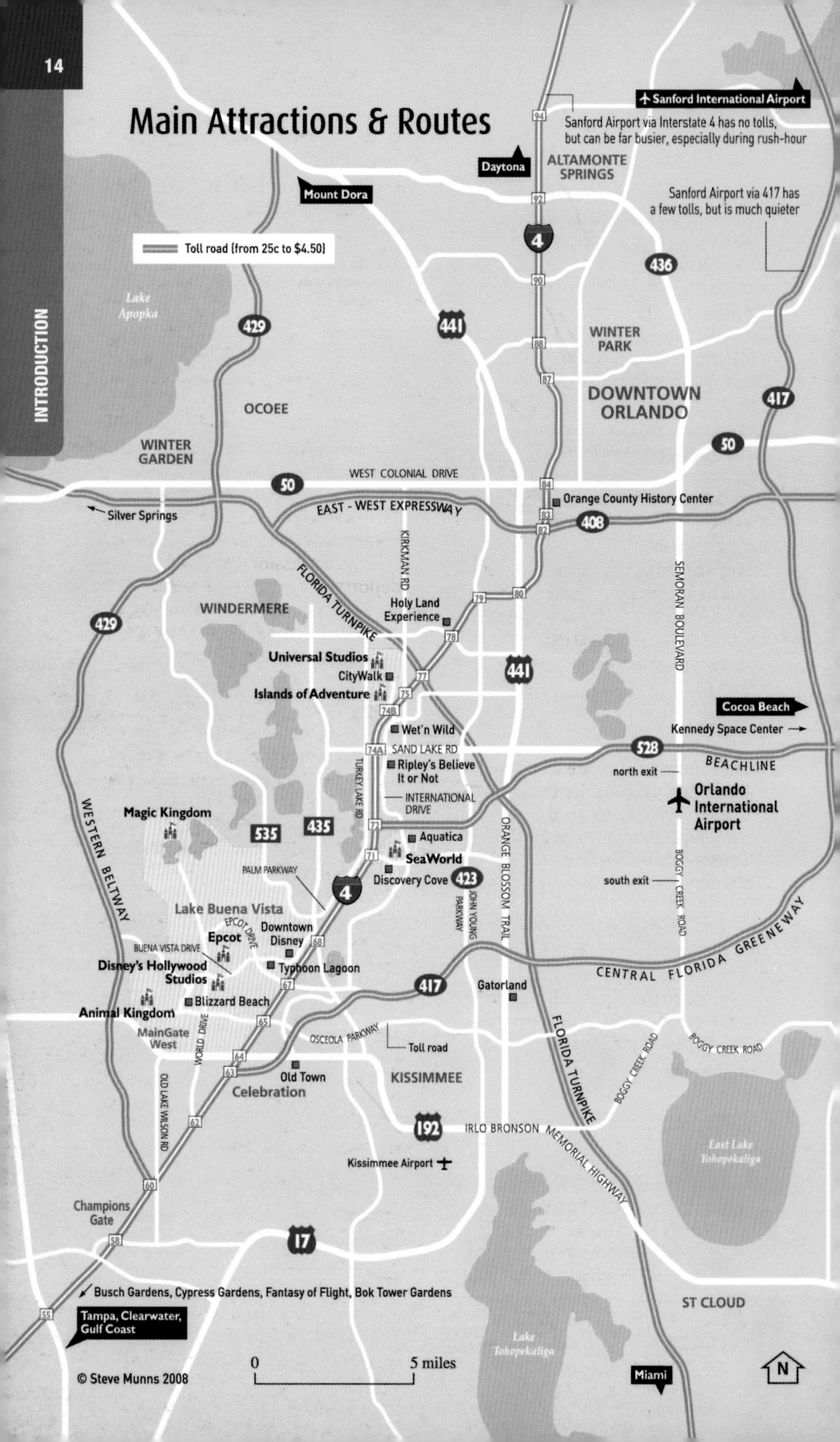
Main Attractions & Routes
Sanford International Airport
Sanford Airport via Interstate 4 has no tolls, but can be far busier, especially during rush-hour
Sanford Airport via 417 has a few tolls, but is much quieter
Daytona
Mount Dora
ALTAMONTE SPRINGS
Toll road (from 25c to $4.50)
Lake Apopka
WINTER PARK
DOWNTOWN ORLANDO
OCOEE
WINTER GARDEN
WEST COLONIAL DRIVE
Silver Springs
EAST - WEST EXPRESSWAY
Orange County History Center
KIRKMAN RD
FLORIDA TURNPIKE
SEMORAN BOULEVARD
WINDERMERE
Holy Land Experience
Universal Studios
CityWalk
Islands of Adventure
Wet'n Wild
Cocoa Beach
Kennedy Space Center
SAND LAKE RD
TURKEY LAKE RD
Ripley's Believe It or Not
INTERNATIONAL DRIVE
BEACHLINE
north exit
Orlando International Airport
Magic Kingdom
WESTERN BELTWAY
ORANGE BLOSSOM TRAIL
Aquatica
SeaWorld
Discovery Cove
PALM PARKWAY
JOHN YOUNG PARKWAY
BOGGY CREEK ROAD
south exit
Lake Buena Vista
EPCOT DRIVE
Epcot
Downtown Disney
BUENA VISTA DRIVE
Disney's Hollywood Studios
Typhoon Lagoon
CENTRAL FLORIDA GREENEWAY
Gatorland
Blizzard Beach
Animal Kingdom
MainGate West
WORLD DRIVE
OSCEOLA PARKWAY
Toll road
FLORIDA TURNPIKE
OLD LAKE WILSON RD
Old Town
Celebration
KISSIMMEE
BOGGY CREEK ROAD
BOGGY CREEK ROAD
IRLO BRONSON MEMORIAL HIGHWAY
Kissimmee Airport
East Lake Tohopekaliga
Champions Gate
Busch Gardens, Cypress Gardens, Fantasy of Flight, Bok Tower Gardens
ST CLOUD
Tampa, Clearwater, Gulf Coast
Lake Tohopekaliga
0
5 miles
© Steve Munns 2008
Miami
N
94
92
4
436
90
429
441
88
87
417
50
50
84
83
408
82
80
79
78
429
441
77
75
74B
528
74A
535
435
72
71
423
4
68
67
417
65
64
63
192
62
60
17
58
55

Immigration forms

En route to the US, you will need to fill in 2 forms – your Immigration details and a Customs form (these are given to you on the plane or at check-in; there are also plenty available on arrival but it's better to have completed them in advance). If travelling under the visa waiver programme, you fill in a green I-94W form (both sides) with your personal details, flight number and holiday address. An Immigration form must be completed for every member of your group or family. Those with a US visa need a white I-94 form (fill in the front only). Every family group must then fill out one white Customs form, which asks for some of the same info but also the value of any goods that will stay in the US (put $0 unless you are arriving with gifts for family or friends). Hand both documents with your passports to the Immigration official who checks you through and takes the fingerprints and photo. The Customs form will be handed back to you to present to another official when you exit the baggage hall.

(MRP) showing they are a British citizen. Any passport issued from 26 October 2005 must include a digital photograph (not glued or laminated). All passports issued from 26 October 2006 must include the new biometric data. Each family member must have his or her own passport that does not expire for 90 days from the time of entry. Provided your passport conforms to the above, all you do is fill in a green visa waiver form and hand it in with your passport to the US immigration official after landing.

BRITTIP

US immigration now requires that ALL visitors aged 14–79 give fingerprint and photo ID on arrival. It slows things down but the process is simple – first, left index finger then right index finger on the glass panel, then stand still for the camera. Some US gateways will require a full 10-finger scan in 2009.

However, British subjects, those without a MRP or those who fail to meet the photo/ biometric data criteria DO need a visa ($131), and should apply at least 2 months in advance to the US Embassy.

Some travellers may NOT be eligible to enter under the visa waiver programme and will have to apply for a special restricted visa or they may be refused entry. This applies to those who have been arrested in the past (even if it did not result in a conviction), have a criminal record (the Rehabilitation of Offenders Act does not apply to US visa law), have a serious communicable illness (and the US includes AIDS sufferers in this category), or have previously been refused admission into, been deported from, or have overstayed in the US on the visa waiver programme. Minor traffic offences that have not resulted in an arrest and/or conviction do not count.

In England, Scotland and Wales, write to the Visa Office, US Embassy, 24 Grosvenor Square, London W1A 1AE (020 7499 9000). In Northern Ireland, write to US Consulate General, Danesfort House, 223 Stranmillis Road, Belfast BT9 5GR (028 9038 6100). You can call 09042 450 100 (£1.20 per minute; 8am–8pm Mon–Fri, 9am–4pm Sat) for more detailed advice, or visit **usembassy.org.uk**.

Cinderella Castle

US travel information

From 12 January 2009, anyone flying to the US on the Visa Waiver Program must register online via the new **Electronic System for Travel Authorization** (ESTA) no later than 3 days before departure. This simply requires the input of all the basic information on the I-94W visa waiver form and is then valid for any visits in the next 2 years. This is effectively a pre-authorisation process prior to arriving at US immigration and should provide an almost immediate response of *Authorization Approved* or *Pending*. However, it will also indicate if a traveller must get a Visa in advance if the response is *Travel Not Authorized*. You can apply for ESTA at **http://esta.cbp.dhs.gov**. Remember to have your holiday address details available both for the ESTA and for your flight check-in. Ask your tour operator if you don't have a specific address (e.g. for a villa allocated on arrival) as it will have a formula for this.

BRITTIP

Cabin baggage restrictions often change, so check with your airline in advance for up-to-date info.

Luggage: This is now liable to random searches (especially in the US) and you are advised NOT to lock your suitcases or bags at check-in for the flight home as TSA officials have the authority to break into them. Using zip-lock seals that can easily be snipped open is permissible and some airlines provide them free. Leave any gifts unwrapped in case screening requires them to be opened; don't put film in checked bags as screening equipment will damage it; and put scissors, tweezers, pocket-knives and other sharp items in checked bags, never in your carry-on.

Encounters at the Florida Aquarium

BRITTIP

Complete your Immigration form carefully in block capitals. Mistakes are often sent to the back of the queue. Please be courteous with the immigration officials – they do a difficult job in demanding circumstances, and jokes about terrorism do not go down well.

Central Florida festivals

Here are some major – and unusual – annual events worth keeping an eye out for in 2009.

Blue Spring Manatee Festival: 24–25 Jan. Beautiful Blue Spring State Park is home to the wonderful manatee, and special celebrations are staged around their seasonal migrations, with craft shows, park tours and interpretive programmes. This park in Orange City is worth seeing at any time of year (off exit 118 of I-4) (**themanateefestival.com**).

33rd Annual Arts Festival: 7–8 Feb. The charming town of Mount Dora, north-west of Orlando, hosts 17 festivals each year, of which this is one of the best – a nationally ranked fiesta with artists from all over the world (take Florida Turnpike, the Western Beltway 429 and Highway 441 to Mount Dora) (**mountdora.com**).

Florida State Fair: 5–16 Feb. This 105-year-old fair just outside Tampa (right on I-4) draws big crowds to its fairground rides, arts, crafts, livestock and live entertainment, with a variety of contests and competitions (**floridastatefair.com**).

Silver Spurs Rodeo: 20–22 Feb, 11–13 Jun (TBC). A twice-yearly celebration of an original American sport at Osceola Heritage Park in Kissimmee, it features top-quality events, plus associated crafts and activities (just off the eastern end of Highway 192) (**silverspursrodeo.com**).

What's new?

In keeping with Orlando's tradition of an ever-changing profile, there's always much that is new.

Walt Disney World: New attractions at *Disney's Hollywood Studios* include the **High School Musical 3: Senior Year** street show (in late 2008) and the **American Idol Live** show (from January 2009), hot on the heels of the **Toy Story Mania** ride and **Block Party Bash** parade. We also anticipate a long-expected upgrade for the **Space Mountain** ride (with new lighting and on-ride audio) at the *Magic Kingdom*, though this may result in it being closed for part of 2009. At the *Epcot* park, the **Storm Struck** attraction (putting guests at the heart of a hurricane) is new in Innoventions East. Big changes are also afoot at *Downtown Disney*. On the Marketplace side, look for the latest restaurant experience at **T Rex: A Prehistoric Family Adventure** and a new covered area at the Marketplace Stage for more live entertainment. In *Pleasure Island*, all the nightclubs have closed to make way for a complete rebuild, with more restaurants and shops. The first will be a high-energy Latin American venue, with live music and a waterfront terrace. A new 300ft-high **Tethered Balloon** ride will also be added in 2009. And there will be much to hear about in **Kingdom Tower**, the newest resort, next to *Contemporary Resort* by the *Magic Kingdom*.

Universal Orlando: Expect to see a LOT of new work here as the **Universal Studios** park gets ready for **Hollywood Rip, Ride, Rockit**, its biggest ride to date and one of the most ambitious roller-coasters ever built – this at a park that also opened the fab new **Simpsons Ride** in summer 2008. Over at its **Islands of Adventure** park, construction is now well advanced for **The Wizarding World of Harry Potter** – a completely new land dedicated to JK Rowling's young wizard, due to open in early 2010. This 'theme park within a theme park' adds rides, shops, restaurants and original theming, including a Hogwarts Castle and Hogsmeade Village. However, it may also mean a few closures in the Lost Continent area of the park as the work continues.

SeaWorld: And talking of major roller-coasters, SeaWorld will add another 'big splash' here with the opening of **The Manta** in spring 2009. This amazing new ride features some animal encounters as well as a 'flying' style coaster and will sit right in the middle of the park, with a couple of water 'splashdowns' for good measure! It will be its second major addition following the opening of its dramatic water park **Aquatica** in 2008.

Elsewhere: The big shopping expansion in Orlando continues with the opening in late 2008 of a major 39-store extension to the **Orlando Premium Outlets** centre. That will be followed by an even bigger development in 2009 to expand into the site left by the Dixie Stampede dinner show. The full opening of **Prime Outlets International** (in spring 2008) added still more shopping choice, while, down in Kissimmee, **The Loop West** also finished construction in 2008, and the **Winter Garden Village** shops should also be fully open.

Accommodation: Among the hotel choices due to open in 2009 are the magnificent new **Waldorf-Astoria** and **Hilton at Bonnet Creek**, a joint resort centre right in the *Walt Disney World* area that promises to provide some of the most luxurious accommodations in Orlando.

Florida Strawberry Festival: 26 Feb–8 Mar. One of the most unusual and fun events, a country fair in Plant City based on the local produce but with concerts, shows, exhibitions and parades (off exit 19 of I-4) (**flstrawberryfestival.com**).

Daytona Beach Bike Week: 27 Feb–8 Mar. A lively celebration of all things 2-wheeled and mechanical, with races at Daytona Speedway, concerts, parades and street festivals (**officialbikeweek.com**).

Daytona Beach

Sidewalk Arts Festival: 20–22 Mar. Winter Park hosts one of America's most prestigious arts festivals, with arts, food, music and children's events (exit 87 of I-4) (**wpsaf.org**).

Village Antique Festival: 28–29 Mar. A unique fiesta of boats, antiques and more in the second of Mount Dora's major festivals. Almost a 3-day street party and well worth sampling (**mountdora.com**).

Fun 'n Sun: 21–26 Apr. Annual aviation spectacular in Lakeland, with museums, vintage planes, aerobatics and more; one of America's biggest (off exit 27 of I-4) (**sun-n-fun.org**).

Zellwood Corn Festival: 23–24 May. Another offbeat but fun offering, with the festival featuring corn-eating contests, carnival rides, concerts, games, arts, crafts and live entertainment (25mls/40km north-west of Orlando on Highway 441; follow directions for Mount Dora) (**zellwoodcornfestival.com**).

Independence Day: 4 July. A huge US national holiday, but watch out for big special events at Lake Eola (downtown Orlando), Lakefront Park (Kissimmee), Mount Dora, Celebration and Winter Park, plus most of the theme parks.

Mount Dora Craft Fair: 24–25 Oct (TBC). Some of the best national crafters line up for this annual competition featuring a huge range of arts and crafts (**mountdora.com**).

Great Outdoor Festival: 7 Nov (TBC). At the end of Kissimmee's annual 8-week Anglers' Challenge (a huge local fishing festival), try this celebration of family fun, races, live music and outdoor recreation exhibits at the Osceola Heritage Park (**floridakiss.com**).

Plan your visit

The next few chapters will tell you all you need to know to plan the ideal holiday. Make a rough itinerary and then fine tune it with this book. You can also take advantage of our unique *Itinerary Planner Service* (see page 49). Now read on and enjoy…

Incredible Hulk Roller Coaster at Universal

2 Planning and Practicalities

or How to *Almost* Do It All and Live to Tell the Tale

Getting the most out of your Orlando holiday is down to one simple factor – good planning. This is not a place where you can 'make it up as you go along', and frustration and exhaustion lie in wait for all those without a sound plan of campaign!

Nowhere is more complex and demanding on your time and money than Orlando; nowhere pulls you in a dozen different directions at once; and nowhere is so difficult to negotiate at times. So, do your homework first: work out WHEN you want to go; decide WHERE in this vast area is best for you; consider WHAT sort of holiday you're looking for; WHO you want to book with; and finally HOW MUCH you want to try to do.

When to go

To avoid the worst of the crowds, the best times to go are October to December (but not during Thanksgiving week in November or 20 December to New Year); early January to mid-March (avoiding President's Day in February); and the week after Easter to the end of May.

BRITTIP

Thanksgiving is the 4th Thurs in Nov; George Washington's birthday, or President's Day, is the 3rd Mon in Feb, and both make for above-average crowds.

Orlando is busiest at **Easter**; from **Memorial Day** (the last Monday in May, the official start of the summer season) to **mid-August** (plus the Labor Day weekend at the start of September and the last holiday of summer); and over the **Christmas** period. It peaks at the week of Easter itself; the big Fourth of July national holiday; and (massively so) from just before Christmas to 2 January. At these times, it is not unknown for some parks to close to new arrivals by mid-morning. The best combination of good weather and smaller crowds is in April (after Easter) and October. However, few attractions are affected by rain (roller-coasters and water rides close only if lightning threatens) and you'll be one jump ahead if you have waterproofs as the crowds noticeably thin out when it rains. All

Journey to Atlantis at SeaWorld

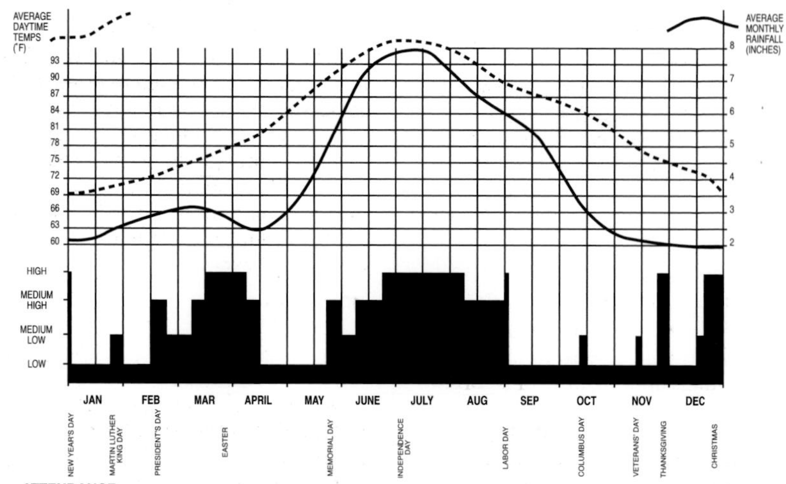

Temperature, rainfall and attendance figures

the parks sell cheap plastic ponchos (even cheaper at Wal-Mart or other supermarkets). In the colder months, take a few warm layers for early morning queues then, when it heats up, leave them in the park lockers. When it gets hot, take advantage of the air-conditioned attractions (and drink LOTS of water).

Where to stay

Where to stay is equally important. Inevitably, there is a huge choice of locations and prices. As a rough guide, 4 main areas make up the great Orlando tourist conglomeration.

Hard Rock Hotel

Walt Disney World Resort in Florida: Some of the most sophisticated, convenient and fun places to stay are Disney's own hotels. The same imagination that created the theme parks has been at work on the likes of Disney's Polynesian Resort and Disney's Animal Kingdom Lodge. They all feature free transport to the parks, your own resort ID card (so you can charge meals and souvenirs to your room, and have purchases delivered to the hotel), free parking and the BIG bonus of **Extra Magic Hours**. This allows Disney resort guests entry to 1 theme park each day, either a full hour before the official opening time or 3 hours after closing, meaning you can do many of the main attractions with only a fraction of the crowds (though the evening magic hours can still be busy). Many resorts also have great kids' clubs and babysitting services. The drawback here is, with the exception of Disney's All-Star and Pop Century Resorts, its hotels are among the most expensive, especially to eat in, and are a fair way from other attractions you may wish to visit. They make a good 1-week base, though.

Lake Buena Vista: Around the eastern fringes of *Walt Disney World Resort*

BRITTIP

Beware the holiday homes (and some hotels) that insist they are just 'minutes from Disney World'. This is often a gross exaggeration, and you may be 30 minutes or more from the parks. Try to get the exact address of the property and then do a location check on **mapquest.com**.

and along Interstate 4 (I-4), this features a good mix of hotels. It is also handy for all the Disney fun, with most hotels offering free transport to the parks, plus there is excellent dining and shopping. Still a bit pricey, but its proximity to I-4 makes it convenient for much of Orlando.

International Drive: The ribbon development known as I-Drive lies midway between Disney and downtown Orlando and is an excellent central location. Running parallel to I-4, it's about 20 minutes' drive from Disney, closer to Universal and SeaWorld. It is also a well-developed tourist area in its own right, with great shops, restaurants and attractions like Wet 'n Wild, Ripley's Believe It Or Not, WonderWorks and SkyVenture. The downside is it gets heavily congested in peak periods, especially the evenings. But it does represent good value and is one of the few areas with extensive pavements, making it easy to explore on foot. A sub-district off I-Drive is the Universal area of Kirkman Road and Major Boulevard.

Kissimmee: Budget holiday-makers can be found in their greatest numbers along the tourist sprawl of Highway 192 (the Irlo Bronson Memorial Highway), an almost unbroken 20ml/32km strip of hotels, motels, restaurants and shops. It offers some of the best economy accommodation and is handy for Disney, though it is further from Universal and downtown Orlando. A car is most advisable here, though there is now extensive pavement, landscaping, bus shelters, benches and water fountains, which makes it better for getting around on foot or by bus. **Highway 27** is often referred to as 'Kissimmee' but is actually either in Lake County (on the northern stretch) or Polk County (to the south). This is prime holiday home territory, with numerous community developments along its 13ml/21km (and ever-increasing!) extent.

BRITTIP

The junction of I-4 and Highway 408 in downtown Orlando will be an ongoing major roadwork project until mid-2009 and can cause some nasty snarl-ups. The Beachline Expressway (Highway 528) is also likely to be a problem until early 2009, with major construction between the airport and the Florida Turnpike.

Split holidays

Florida has so much to offer, many people opt to split their holiday by having a week or two in Orlando and a week elsewhere, such as the Gulf Coast, Miami or the Florida Keys. The Atlantic coast has some great beaches only an hour's drive to the east, the magnificent Florida Everglades are 3–4 hours to the south, and there are more wonderful beaches and pleasant coast roads to the west. There's great shopping almost everywhere, while Florida boasts some stunning golf courses and there

Beach cottage at St Pete's

are plenty of opportunities to play or watch tennis, baseball and basketball, or go fishing, boating or canoeing. The main tour companies offer a huge variety of packages, with some popular cruise-and-stay options. If you can afford the time (and expense), the best option is to have 2 weeks in Orlando then a week relaxing on one of Florida's fabulous beaches. A 2-week, half-and-half split is a regular choice, but can make your time in Orlando rather hectic, unless your additional week is somewhere like Cocoa Beach (near the Kennedy Space Center), which gives you the chance for day trips back to Orlando. Some companies offer a worthwhile 10/4-day Orlando/coast split, which is a better idea for 2 weeks. Fly-drives offer the greatest flexibility, but there is a lot to tempt you in 2 weeks and you may find it better to book a 2-centre stay that includes a car and accommodation so you can still travel but avoid too much packing and unpacking (see also Chapter 9, The Twin Centre Option).

Travel companies

There is serious competition for your hard-earned holiday money but the travel companies work hard to keep Florida costs down, whether you fly-drive, book your own flights or take a package. Shop around to get the best value but make sure the company you book with has some kind of bonding,

Tchoup-Chop restaurant at Universal's Royal Pacific Resort

either with ABTA in the case of travel agents or ATOL for flights, in case anything goes wrong. At the last count, there were more than 60 tour operators offering holidays to Florida. They divide roughly into the Big Boys; the Specialists; and the Online Agents.

The big boys

Airtours: Now part of the Thomas Cook Group but still operating its tried-and-trusted brand of reliable package holidays, Airtours has a wide range of choice from 6 UK airports (just Manchester and Gatwick in winter), including Newcastle, Glasgow and Cardiff, with some good 2-centre combos, including a week at a Disney resort or the Gulf Coast and a week on I-Drive. Airtours also has an extensive range of Florida fly-drives for great flexibility and a time-saving off-airport check-in for the return flight. Look out for early-booking 'kids go free' deals and a wide choice of Disney hotels, along with an extensive villa selection.

Info: 0871 664 7988, **airtours.co.uk**.
Airlines: Thomas Cook and Monarch.
Airport: Orlando Sanford International.

British Airways Holidays: BA benefits from its own direct, scheduled air service (10 flights a week to Orlando and 5 to Tampa), offering great flexibility with almost any duration and combination possible, from budget to luxury 5-star accommodation (its impressive Prestige collection), plus 45 hotels with 'free night' bonuses. Beach add-ons, 2 centres (a wide selection of both coasts plus Tampa and the Florida Keys), and an extensive choice of private homes are all available, plus many pre-bookable tours and excursions. BA also flies to Miami, opening up plenty of fly-drive and multi-centre possibilities, while its online check-in option can save valuable time at the airport.

Info: 0844 493 0759, **ba.com/florida**.
Airline: British Airways.
Airports: Orlando International, Tampa, Miami International.

Cosmos: With a long history in Florida, Cosmos focuses on the key resort areas in Orlando and the Gulf Coast (with an excellent range of properties in the likes of Clearwater, St Pete Beach, Sarasota, Newport Richey and Naples). With a full range of hotels (including Disney and Universal), suites and villas, it offers 7-, 14- and 21-night holidays on a package, fly-drive and flight-only basis, and is particularly well priced for car hire. There are early booking offers and kids' prices from just £99. Early off-airport check-in is available on I-Drive for £7/person, as is the Royal Palm Lounge at Orlando Sanford International Airport (£10/adult, £7.50/child).

Info: 0871 423 8422, **cosmos.co.uk**. *Airline:* Monarch. *Airport:* Orlando Sanford International.

First Choice: A complete programme from 7 UK airports (Birmingham, Bristol, Gatwick, Manchester, Nottingham East Midlands, Glasgow and Newcastle) using the newly-merged Thomson Airways 6 days a week, means First Choice remain a great family-friendly choice. Its flights feature all seat-back entertainment, more leg-room, wider seats and all meals included, plus Premier upgrades with a 92cm/36in pitch and leather seats, a 9in TV screen (with stop/start function), 30 channels to choose from and a choice of meals. Other First Choice brands selling Florida are: **First Choice Villas** for a selection of 5-star hotels and **Skytours**, the budget operator featuring mainly 2- and 3-star hotels.

Info: 0871 200 7799, **firstchoice.co.uk/florida**. *Airline:* Thomson Airways. *Airport:* Orlando Sanford International.

Thomson: Another of the large, mass-market operators, parent company TUI merged with First Choice in 2008 but the two main brands kept their separate identities, though now with just one shared airline. There is a strong emphasis on its villa and Disney hotel selection, plus twin-centre options, including an I-Drive/Disney combo and a 9-day/5-day Orlando/coast split. Like several other package holiday operators, Thomson has stopped its winter programme but still offers 7 departure airports (including Birmingham, Newcastle, Glasgow and Manchester), with good in-flight entertainment and attractive kids' packs. Like First Choice, there is a day-before check-in service at both Gatwick and Manchester and a new in-resort check-in for the return flight (for a fee).

Info: 0870 165 0079, **thomson.co.uk**. *Airlines:* Thomson Airways and other charters. *Airport:* Orlando Sanford International.

Travel City Direct: The UK's largest direct-sell Florida operator, with more than 170,000 customers a year. It is part of the XL Leisure Group, which provides its own in-house airline, plus sister companies Kosmar, Freedom Flights and Aspire Holidays. It offers a huge range of packages at ultra-competitive prices (because you book direct), including fly-drives, 1- and 2-centre holidays (including the Florida Keys, New Smyrna Beach and Fort Myers), private pool villas and Caribbean cruise-and-stay holidays (notably with the fun Carnival Cruises), all of 14 days, and featuring all Disney's resorts. A Florida

Red Coconut Club at CityWalk

Attractions brochure was also new for 2009. Its valuable *Freetime Check-In* service (at its Welcome Lounge at Lake Buena Vista Factory Stores) allows guests to make the most of their last day by checking in luggage early on the final morning – and reduces the time needed at the airport. Most flights year-round are with XL Airways (with no charge for meals and headsets), but it also has a tailor-made service featuring scheduled airlines. A new fleet of Airbus A330-200 aircraft for summer 2009 will include state-of-the-art touch-screen seat-back TVs.

Info: 0871 911 4180, **travelcitydirect.com**. *Airlines:* XL Airways, plus BA, Virgin, US Airways, American and Continental. Airports: Orlando Sanford International (XL Airways), Orlando International (scheduled airlines).

Virgin Holidays: Offering the most extensive programme to Florida, Virgin has a vast variety of combinations – more than 180 properties and twin-centres including Miami, Daytona Beach, the Keys, New York, Boston, Mexico and the Caribbean, plus some tempting cruises with Disney, Royal Caribbean and Carnival. With Virgin's non-stop scheduled service to Orlando (up to 14 times a week from Gatwick and 8 a week from Manchester, plus Glasgow, and Heathrow to Miami), it offers free drinks, kids' packs, meals and games. It has a wide choice of accommodation (including most Disney resorts and a value section) and is popular for fly-drives, flying into Orlando and out of Miami, and vice versa. Its Platinum collection features deluxe resorts like Reunion in Orlando and Little Palm Island in the Florida Keys. Virgin also has a valuable Downtown Disney check-in service for return flights, allowing guests to check in on the morning of departure, freeing up the rest of the day to enjoy at leisure. New is the V-Room at Gatwick, a special premium lounge for families and adults only at £15 per adult and £10 per child (2–11).

Info: 0844 557 3875, **virginholidays.co.uk**. *Airline:* Virgin Atlantic. *Airports:* Orlando International, Miami.

Shamu Express at SeaWorld

The specialists

Continental Airlines Vacations: An attractive new brand in 2007 with flights to 11 destinations in Florida from 7 UK airports, offering daily scheduled services for great flexibility of holiday choice. Its Glasgow and Edinburgh routes are particularly popular, while it also features a huge range of multi-centre options, including a New York stopover.

Info: 0844 557 4040, **covacations.co.uk**. *Airline:* Continental. *Airport:* Orlando International.

Funway Holidays: The sister company of America's largest tour operator and a leading US specialist, Funway offers a tailor-made service to match Orlando with any option, providing total flexibility from 16 UK airports. Its private villas are a big feature but it also serves up a wide array of Florida hotels, including all Disney's resorts. It features a 'Boutique Collection' of hotels too, all with added style, and well-priced fly-drive deals.

Info: 0844 557 3333, **funway holidays.co.uk**. *Airlines:* various scheduled, including Virgin Atlantic, BA and Continental. *Airport:* Orlando International.

Jetsave: This Florida specialist with more than 30 years' experience puts the accent on flexibility, with a wide choice of flights with scheduled

John's Pass Village at Clearwater

airlines. You have the full selection of hotels, apartments and an exhaustive choice of holiday homes, with simple, accurate star ratings given for each property and plenty of opportunity to mix-and-match.

Info: 0871 231 2271, **jetsave.co.uk**. *Airline:* Virgin Atlantic. *Airport:* Orlando International.

Style Holidays: One of the UK's top Florida specialists, Style offers a huge selection of villas with private pools, self-catering apartments and a wide range of hotels, as well as fly-drive options. All properties are in named, well-described locations and can be booked on an accommodation-only basis or as a package with a hire car.

Info: 0870 442 3661, **styleholidays.co.uk**. *Airlines:* various charters. *Airport:* Orlando Sanford International.

Thomas Cook Signature: Here's another quality-conscious and selective offering using only scheduled flights (though still with competitive prices). It tends to suit repeat visitors especially, ticketing info and material are first class, and there is a strong tailor-made element. The holiday home selection is particularly good and there is a 'kids eat free' offer for under-11s. The Group's upmarket **Tradewinds** brand (0871 664 7964) also offers fully tailor-made holidays (and a free Planet Hollywood meal).

Info: 0870 443 4440, **tcsignature.com**. *Airlines:* Virgin Atlantic, BA, American. *Airports:* Orlando International, Miami, Tampa.

Other specialists: Try **Jetlife** (0870 787 7877, **jetlife.co.uk**); the high-quality style of **Kuoni** (01306 747002, **kuoni.co.uk**); **USAirtours**, tailor-made US itineraries, many with villas in Orlando (0800 0350 149, **usairtours.co.uk**); and **Premier Holidays**, more tailor-made choice and seasonal specials (0844 4937 085, **premierholidays.co.uk**).

The online agents

The growth of online travel agents has been huge in recent years, and you will find some great deals in this group, for packages, flights only or accommodation. Some are familiar names that have grown online, others are internet-only.

eBookers, originally the travel agent arm of Flightbookers (now part of the international Orbitz Worldwide group, including the Orbitz and CheapTickets agencies in the US), this is another big company with a good reputation for flights, hotels, insurance and more (0871 223 5000, **ebookers.com**); **Expedia**, one of the biggest companies worldwide, with simple, easy-to-use booking, e-mail updates and a useful Deals section (0871 226 0808, **expedia.co.uk**); **LastMinute**, an online company set up purely to offer late deals has now become a major mainstream agent, with the full range of holidays, flights, hotels, etc. (0871 222 5969, **last minute.com**); **Travel Supermarket**, a service that instantly searches multiple online travel sites, and gives you the best price match it can find, plus it also has Fare Alert and Bargain Hunters features, weekly e-mails and various travel forums (0845 345 5708, **travelsupermarket.com**); **Trailfinders**, the UK's largest independent travel firm and tailor-made specialists (0845 054 6060, **trailfinders.com**); **Travelbag** (0800 804 8911, **travelbag.co.uk**); and **Opodo** (0871 277 0090, **opodo.co.uk**).

Other online search engines:

- **Kelkoo** (**http://travel.kelkoo.co.uk**), **Kayak** (**kayak.co.uk**), **Travel Jungle** (**traveljungle.co.uk**) and **Sidestep** (**http://uk.sidestep.com**), though its package holiday choice can be limited.
- Highly rated **Attraction Tickets Direct** is now selling Disney hotels (with a Price Match Guarantee), so you can book accommodation and tickets at the same time (020 7350 4544, **attraction-tickets-direct.co.uk/hotels/**).
- For flight only, try **Flight Centre** (0870 499 0040, **flightcentre.co.uk**), **Dial A Flight** (0870 333 4488, **dialaflight. com**) and **NetFlights.com** (0844 493 1234, **airline-network.co.uk**).
- For flight price comparison services, **Sky Scanner** (**skyscanner.net**) and **Cheap Flights** (**cheapflights.co.uk**) are both also worth a visit.

Scheduled flights

Apart from the charter airlines, there are only a handful of direct flights to Orlando, notably with **Virgin Atlantic** (Gatwick and Manchester), **British Airways** (from Gatwick) and **Aer Lingus** (from Dublin), but you can often save money on indirect flights. Choose from **Delta** (from Gatwick via New York, Atlanta or Cincinnati; Heathrow via Atlanta or New York; Manchester via New York or Atlanta; or Edinburgh via Atlanta); **American Airlines** (from Heathrow via New York, Boston, Dallas, Raleigh-Durham, Miami or Chicago; or Manchester via New York); **Continental** (from Gatwick, Manchester, Birmingham, Bristol, Belfast, Dublin, Glasgow and Edinburgh via Cleveland, Houston or New York); **Northwest** (from Gatwick or Heathrow via Detroit or Minneapolis); **United** (from Heathrow via Washington or Chicago); **US Airways** (from Gatwick via Charlotte or Philadelphia; Heathrow, Manchester or Glasgow via Philadelphia); and **bmi** (from Manchester via Chicago). The obvious drawback is the extra journey time, and you may arrive in Orlando late in the evening after the connecting flight. However, it does give you the chance to break the journey, and places like Detroit and Atlanta often process international passengers quicker than Orlando, meaning less hassle when you arrive in Florida. **Icelandair** (from Heathrow, Glasgow and Manchester; 0870 787 4020, **icelandair. co.uk**) offers a scheduled transatlantic route to Orlando Sanford Airport via Reykjavik in Iceland. Also worth a look is **flyglobespan**, Scotland's low-cost specialist, with direct flights from Glasgow and Belfast to Orlando Sanford as well as some package holidays and an online discount (0870 556 1522, **flyglobespan.com**). Another alternative is low-cost carrier **Zoom Airlines**, which started in easyJet style with a Gatwick–New York route and added twice-weekly flights to Fort Lauderdale in May 2008 (with some tempting prices), providing an alternative route into Florida (0870 240 0055, **flyzoom.com**).

The Star Wash at Islands of Adventure

Direct flights to Orlando

All flights are to Orlando Sanford International Airport unless specified; 'Orlando' means Orlando International.

Airline	Flying from (to)	Economy seat pitch	Premium seat pitch	Aircraft used	In-flight entertainment	Baggage allowance
British Airways ba.com or 0844 493 0787	Gatwick (to Orlando and Tampa); Heathrow (to Miami)	31in/78.7cm	38in/96.5cm (World Traveller Plus); 73in/185cm (Club World)	Boeing 777	Seat-back TVs	2 x 23kg; 3 x 23kg (Club)
Thomson Airways firstchoice.co.uk/florida or 0871 200 7799/ thomson.co.uk or 0870 165 0079	Bristol, East Midlands, Gatwick, Glasgow, Manchester, Newcastle	33in/83.8cm	36in/91.4cm	Boeing 767	Seat-back TVs	1 x 20kg; 1 x 23kg (Premier)
Flyglobespan flyglobespan.com or 0871 271 0415	Belfast, Glasgow (summer only)	32in/81.2cm	50in/127cm (Business)	Boeing 767, Boeing 757	Seat-back TVs Business only	1 x 25kg; 2 x 20kg (Business)
Monarch flymonarch.com or 01582 398036	Belfast, Gatwick, Glasgow, Manchester, Newcastle	31in/78.7cm	34in/86.3cm	Airbus A330, Boeing 767	Seat-back TVs Premium only	1 x 15kg; 1 x 25kg (Premium)
Thomas Cook Airlines flythomascook.com or 0870 750 0512	Belfast, Cardiff, Gatwick, Glasgow, Manchester, Newcastle	33in/83.8cm	35in/89cm	Airbus A330	Seat-back TVs	1 x 15kg; 1 x 30kg (Premium cabin)
Virgin Atlantic virgin-atlantic.com or 0870 380 2007	Gatwick, Manchester and Glasgow (to Orlando); Heathrow (to Miami)	31in/78.7cm	38in/96.5cm (Premium) and 79.5in/202cm (Upper)	Boeing 747 (Orlando), Airbus A340 (Miami)	Seat-back TVs	2 x 23kg; 2 x 32kg (Premium); 3 x 32kg (Upper)
XL Airways xl.com or 0871 911 4220	Cardiff, Gatwick, Glasgow, Manchester	32in/81.2cm (08/09); 33in/ 83.8cm (summer 09)	45in/114cm (XL One); 38in/96.5cm (summer 09)	Boeing 767; Airbus A330-200	In-cabin TVs; all seatback TVs in new Airbus	1 x 20kg; 2 x 20kg (XL One)

What to see when

Once you arrive, the temptation is to head for the nearest theme park, then the next, and so on. Hold on! This is the best recipe for theme park indigestion. Some days at the parks are busier than others, while it is inadvisable to attempt 2 of the main parks on successive days at peak times. So here's what you can do.

With the aid of the Holiday Planner on pages 360–1 (or the *Brit Guide* Itinerary Planner service (see page 49), make a note of all the attractions you want to see over the length of your stay. The most sensible strategy is to plan around the 8 'must-see' parks – *Magic Kingdom Park, Epcot, Disney's Hollywood Studios, Disney's Animal Kingdom Theme Park,* Universal

Studios, Islands of Adventure, SeaWorld and Busch Gardens. If you have only a week, drop Busch Gardens and focus on Disney, Universal and SeaWorld. Space travel fans would be foolish not to include the Kennedy Space Center, but it would probably bore young children.

As a basic rule, the *Magic Kingdom Park* is the biggest hit with children, and families often find it requires 2 days. The same can be said for *Epcot*, but there are fewer rides to amuse the younger ones. Only the most fleet of foot with the benefit of relatively low crowds would be able to negotiate *Epcot* in a day. The *Animal Kingdom Park* is also a little short on attractions for the youngest visitors, but it still requires nearly a whole day. *Disney's Hollywood Studios* is usually possible to do in a day (not forgetting the evening Fantasmic! show), while SeaWorld occasionally needs rather longer and Universal Studios can be a 2-day park at its busiest. Islands of Adventure will almost certainly keep everyone (except possibly under-5s) busy all day, too. Busch Gardens, extremely popular with British families, is another full-day affair, especially as it is a 75-minute drive away in Tampa to the south-west.

All the attractions are described in detail in Chapters 5–8, so it's best to get an idea of time requirements before you pick up your pencil.

Sunset over Clearwater Beach

Smaller attractions

Of the other, smaller-scale attractions, the nature park of Silver Springs is a full day out as it also involves a near 2-hour drive to get there, and the revamped Cypress Gardens will certainly keep you occupied all day, but everything else can be fitted around your Big 8 itinerary. The water parks make for a relaxing ½-day, as does the quieter Bok Tower Gardens. Gatorland is a unique look at some of Florida's oldest inhabitants and is a good combination with Boggy Creek Airboats. Aviation fans must not miss a trip to Fantasy of Flight (further down I-4) for a novel experience. Then there are the likes of Ripley's Believe It Or Not museum and the WonderWorks house of fun, both offering several hours' entertainment, the thrills of Sky Venture (an indoor 'sky-diving' wind tunnel) and the lure of old-fashioned go-karts and other fairground-type rides at Fun Spot, Magical Midway and Old Town. Many stay open after the major theme parks close.

Disney also has *DisneyQuest*, an imaginative interactive 'arcade' that guarantees several hours of fun (especially for older children) in its *Downtown Disney* area, while each main area is also well served with creatively designed mini-golf courses for that spare hour or two.

Evenings

The evening entertainment features a similarly wide choice. By far the best, and worth at least one evening each, are *Downtown Disney* and Universal's CityWalk. Both will keep you busy until the early hours. Dinner shows provide a lot of fun; 2-hour cabarets based on themes like medieval knights, pirates, Arabian Nights and murder mysteries that all include a hearty meal. Rounding it up is the huge variety of nightclubs and bars, many offering live music.

Our must-do experiences

Soarin' and IllumiNations show (*Epcot*)

Cirque du Soleil® (*Downtown Disney*)

The Amazing Adventures of Spider-Man and The Hulk rides (Islands of Adventure park)

Boggy Creek Airboats (Kissimmee)

Expedition Everest and Festival of The Lion King (*Animal Kingdom*)

Wishes fireworks and Pirates of the Caribbean ride (*Magic Kingdom*)

Fantasmic! show and Star Tours ride (*Disney's Hollywood Studios*)

Shrek 4-D and The Simpsons Ride (Universal Studios)

Orlando Premium Outlets (shopping)

Believe and Blue Horizons shows (SeaWorld)

KaTonga show and SheiKra coaster (Busch Gardens)

Shuttle Launch Experience (Kennedy Space Center)

A Disney character meal

A day at a water park

Shopping

Shopping in Orlando is world class (see Chapter 12). Your battle plan should include at least a day to visit the spectacular malls and discount centres, like the excellent Orlando Premium Outlets or Prime Outlets International, Mall at Millenia and the Florida Mall.

What to do when

There are several general guidelines for avoiding the worst of the tourist hordes, even in high season. The vast majority are Americans, who often arrive at weekends and head for the main theme parks first. That means Monday is generally a bad time to visit the *Magic Kingdom Park*, as is Sunday, while Tuesday is usually also humming at *Epcot*. New rides like Toy Story Mania (*Disney's Hollywood Studios*) also create longer queues here, too, notably at weekends.

Disney's Extra Magic Hours programme, which allows its hotel guests entry to 1 park a day either an hour early or 3 hours after regular closing time, creates a greater build-up of crowds, too. So, if you are NOT staying at a Disney hotel, you need to avoid these EMH days. For much of the year, they keep to the following regular weekly pattern (where you should avoid the parks on those days, unless you are a Disney hotel guest): *Magic Kingdom*, Tues and Thurs in peak season, Thurs only off-peak; *Epcot*, Sun in peak, Tues off-peak; *Disney's Hollywood Studios*, Mon and Fri in peak, Sat off-peak; *Animal Kingdom*, Wed and Sat in peak, Mon off-peak. However, the EMH days can change from month to month, and we are able to reflect this on our **website** by regularly updating the essential Busy Day Guide (see page 361), which shows at a glance the busiest and quietest days at each Orlando park. The *Animal Kingdom* is also the hardest to get round when crowded, while *Epcot* handles the crowds best of all. *Disney's Blizzard Beach* and *Typhoon Lagoon* water parks hit high tide at the weekend, and Thurs and Fri in summer.

At Universal Orlando, the picture is different as there are no early entry days, and the busiest days are usually the weekends when locals visit. This often means Monday is quietest at both Universal and Islands of Adventure, getting busier through the week, with the former being slightly

Serengeti Safari at Busch Gardens

more crowded (especially with the opening of the new Simpsons attraction). If Walt Disney World is humming early in the week, that makes it a good time to visit SeaWorld, Busch Gardens, Silver Springs or the Kennedy Space Center. Avoid Wet 'n Wild at weekends, when the locals come out to play. SeaWorld's new Aquatica water park also tends to fill quickly at weekends, and Wed–Fri in peak season.

Ensuring you get the most out of your days at the main parks is another art form, and there are several practical policies to pursue. The official opening times seldom vary from 9am but arriving early is highly advisable. Apart from being near the head of the queues (and you will encounter some SERIOUS queues, or 'lines' as the Americans call them), sometimes the parks open earlier than scheduled if the crowds build up quickly. So, you can be a step ahead of the masses by arriving at least 30 minutes before opening time, or an hour early during the main holiday periods. Apart from anything else, you will be better placed to park in the huge car parks and catch the tram to the main gates (anything up to ½ mile away).

BRITTIP

If your hotel is not far away, take a mid-afternoon break from the park and return for a siesta or a swim. Your car park ticket is valid all day, and the evening is often the best time to be in the parks.

Once you've put yourself in pole position, don't waste time on the shops, scenery and other frippery that will lure the unprepared first-timer. Instead, head straight for some of the main rides and get a few big-time thrills under your belt before the main hordes arrive. You will quickly work out where the most popular attractions are as the majority of other early birds will flock to them. Use Chapters 5 and 6 to help plan your park strategies.

You can also benefit from doing the opposite of what the masses do after the initial rush has subsided. Try not to have all your meals in the parks, too. Eating here is becoming a touch expensive and it can be $10/person for even a basic counter-service meal. Eating as much as you can at a buffet breakfast somewhere like Golden Corral means you can skimp on lunch and save $$$s!

BRITTIP

The water IS safe to drink in the US but it may not taste great as it's heavily fluoridated. Bottled water is cheap at supermarkets – and you'll save big time on buying it in the parks.

Pace yourself

Another word of warning: Disney's parks, notably the *Magic Kingdom*, stay open late for the main holidays, until midnight at times, and that can be a l-o-n-g day for children. It's vital to pace yourself, especially if you have been among the first through the gates. There are plenty of options to take time off for a drink or a sit-down somewhere air-conditioned, and you can benefit from the American propensity to take mealtimes seriously by *avoiding* lunchtime (noon–1.30pm) and dinnertime (5.30–7pm). So, after you've had a couple of hours of park-going, it pays to take an early lunch (before noon), plunge back into it all for another 3 hours or so, have another snack mid-afternoon and then return to the main rides as the crowds ease off a little in late afternoon.

Comfort and clothing

You may feel jet-lagged for the first day or two after your arrival, but this can be reduced by avoiding alcohol and coffee on the plane and drinking plenty of water.

Top things to do for FREE!

While Orlando has a magnificent array of paid-for attractions, there are still many things you can do that don't cost a cent.

Disney's Boardwalk Resort: Free nightly entertainment includes jugglers, comedy skits and live music. Time your visit to coincide with the 9pm IllumiNations fireworks extravaganza at nearby *Epcot*.

Fort Christmas Historical Park: 20mls/32km east of Orlando in the town of Christmas is this replica of an 1837 US Army fort from the Seminole Indian Wars, with tours, exhibits, video presentations and restored homes, and special events during some weekends; 8am–8pm summer, 8am–6pm winter (**nbbd.com/godo/FortChristmas**).

Lake Eola Park: Take a walk on the mild side in downtown Orlando. The kids can play or feed the swans and there is live entertainment in summer at the Walt Disney Amphitheater (see Familes, Parks & Recreation on the 'Departments' link at **cityoforlando.net**).

Lake Tibet-Butler Preserve: Just 5 minutes from Disney but light years from the theme park hustle-bustle (CR 535, Winter Garden-Vineland Road) is this local nature preserve, with quiet trails, lake overlook and interpretive centre. Open 9am–dusk (not public holidays), it is on the Great Florida Birding Trail and is a minor gem of native wildlife (**http://myfwc.com/viewing/sites/site-c07.html**).

Lakeridge Winery and Vineyards: Join a free wine-tasting tour and you'll know why Lakeridge (in nearby Clermont) has won more than 300 awards. But designate a driver as sample sizes are generous! 10am–5pm Mon–Sat, 11am–5pm Sun (**lakeridgewinery.com**).

Leu Gardens: Just north of downtown Orlando, this sanctuary of peace and quiet, with wildlife, nature trails and the 1880s' Leu House Museum is free 9am–noon every Mon (**leugardens.org**).

Morse Museum of American Art: This superb little museum in tranquil Winter Park, dedicated to American paintings, ceramics and representative arts from the 19th and 20th centuries, is free 4–8pm every Fri Nov–Apr (see **morsemuseum.org** and page 254).

Old Town, Kissimmee: The biggest vintage car parade in the US every Saturday, with cars on display from 1pm and the parade at 8.30pm, a Friday Night Cruise (classic cars from 1978 to 1985) at 9pm and Bike Nites at 6pm every Thurs, with up to 700 motorbikes each week, plus live music nightly (see **old-town.com** and page 241).

Peabody Duck March: Turn up at 11am or 5pm at the Peabody Hotel to see the resident mallards get the red carpet treatment as they either arrive or leave their lobby fountain 'home' (**peabodyorlando.com**).

Pianoman Bob Jackson: Disney's Port Orleans Riverside Resort hosts some excellent free entertainment on Wed–Sun evenings with Pianoman Bob, who gets everyone doing the Chicken Dance and singing along with old favourites in a family-friendly atmosphere.

Sanford Museum: Some quaint local history is well presented through the personal collections of city founder Henry S Sanford (11am–4pm Tues–Fri, 1–4pm Sat). Combine a visit with a walking tour, including the new Riverwalk (**ci.sanford.fl.us/cf03.html**).

PLUS – just watching the participants in action at **SkyVenture** on International Drive (page 239); the **Cornell Fine Arts Museum** at Rollins College in Winter Park (page 254); the many hiking trails and scenic points of **Ocala National Forest**, north of Orlando (**fs.fed.us/r8/florida/recreation/index_oca.shtml**); and the beautiful little **Maitland Art Center**, in the northern suburb of Maitland (9am–4.30pm Mon–Fri, noon–4.30pm Sat and Sun; **maitlandartcenter.org**).

Marvel Superhero Island at Islands of Adventure

BRITTIP

Don't be tempted to pack a lot of smart or formal clothing – you really won't need it in hot, informal Florida.

The most important part of your holiday wardrobe is your footwear – you will spend a lot of time on your feet, even at off-peak periods. The smallest of the parks is 'only' 100 acres/40ha, but that is irrelevant to the amount of time you spend queuing. This is not the time to break in new sandals or trainers! Comfortable, well-worn shoes or trainers are essential (many rate Crocs shoes as ideal park footwear). Otherwise, you need dress only as the climate dictates. T-shirts and shorts are appropriate in all the parks and nearly all restaurants will accept casual dress. However, swimwear is not acceptable away from pool areas.

If, after a long day, you feel the need for a change of clothes or a sweater for the evening, take advantage of the handy lockers (unlimited use all day, even if you change parks). All the parks are also well equipped with pushchairs (or 'strollers') for hire, and baby services are located at regular intervals. It is *vital* to use high-factor sun creams at all times, even during the winter when the sun may not feel strong but can still burn. Nothing can be quite so guaranteed to ruin your holiday as severe sunburn. Orlando has a sub-tropical climate and you need to use higher factor creams than you would in the Mediterranean. Use sun block on sensitive areas like nose and ears, and splash on the after-sun lotion liberally at the end of the day. You'll also need waterproof sun cream for swimming. Skincare products are widely available and usually inexpensive (at the likes of Wal-Mart, Publix and Target). Wear a hat during the day, and avoid alcohol, coffee and fizzy drinks until the evening as they are dehydrating and make you liable to heatstroke. You must increase your fluid intake significantly in the summer, but stick to still soft drinks such as Gatorade, an energy squash, and lots of water.

BRITTIP

One of the best ways to keep cool in the Florida sun is to visit a supermarket and buy a simple mist spray fan (about $7.99), which you carry with you and just refill with water.

Want to see more?

If, like us, you want to make the most of every holiday opportunity, you could travel further afield in America with the help of its efficient low-cost airline system. Orlando is an excellent base from which to explore city destinations like New York, Chicago, Boston, Dallas, Washington, Baltimore and Memphis, and great states like Georgia, South Carolina, Virginia and Pennsylvania, plus the Caribbean and Mexico, all of which are only 2 hours' flight away; or go even further to glittering Las Vegas, Los Angeles, San Francisco or San Diego. With the benefit of cheap hotel deals (check out **hotels.com** and **orbitz.com**), you can seriously spread your wings (ahem!) by using the likes of **AirTran Airways**, Florida's leading low-cost carrier, which is based at Orlando International Airport and also flies from 9 other Florida airports, including Tampa, Miami, West Palm Beach and Fort Myers. Skip ahead to page 355 for more on how to extend your holiday. Repeat visitors may like to consider this, and it's only a small additional investment after going all the way to Florida (look up **airtran.com** for its timetable, fares and frequent fare sales).

BRITTIP

Look after your feet and avoid the onset of blisters by buying some moleskin footpads from a supermarket.

Medical aid

Should you require medical treatment, whether for sunburn or other first aid, consult your tour company's info about local hospitals and surgeries. In the event of a medical or other emergency, dial 911 as you would 999 in Britain. It cannot be over-stressed, however, that you should take out comprehensive travel and health insurance (see pages 34–6) for any trip to America, as there is NO National Health Service and ANY form of medical treatment is expensive and must be paid for. Keep all the receipts and put in a claim on your return home.

BRITTIP

The summer is mosquito time and a spray-on or roll-on insect repellent is highly advisable. Brands to look for locally are Cutter, Repel and Off!.

Emergency outpatients: These can be found with **Centra Care** at Florida Hospital Medical Center in 16 Central Florida locations and can provide hotel in-room services (407 238 2000) and free transport (407 938 0650; **centracare.org**). Open from 8am daily, Centra Care centres are at: 12500 S Apopka-Vineland Road near the Crossroads shopping centre and *Downtown Disney* at Lake Buena Vista (until midnight on weekdays, 8pm Sat and Sun; 407 934 2273); 7848 West Irlo Bronson Memorial Highway (192), in Formosa Gardens Village (until 8pm Mon–Fri, 5pm Sat and Sun; 407 397 7032); 6001 Vineland Road, near Universal Studios (7am–7pm Mon–Fri, 8am–6pm Sat and Sun; 407 351 6682); on Sand Lake Road, between John Young Parkway and Orange Blossom Trail (8am–8pm Mon–Fri, 9am–5pm Sat and Sun; 407 851 6478); and 4320 West Vine Street, near

Airtran

BRITTIP

If you take regular prescription drugs, check with your doctor or pharmacist to see if they have a different name in the US. Many do (e.g. adrenaline is known as epinephrine) and it is worth finding out and carrying the drug with both names in case of an emergency. The US name for paracetamol is acetaminophen.

Medieval Times (until 8pm Mon–Fri, 5pm Sat and Sun; 407 390 1888). **Dr P Phillips Hospital** on 9400 Turkey Lake Road has an emergency outpatient department (407 351 8500). The **East Coast Medical Network** (407 648 5252, **medicalconcierge.com**) makes hotel 'house calls' 24 hours a day.

Chemists: The two largest chemists ('drug stores' in the US) are **Walgreens** (**walgreens.com**) and **CVS** (**cvs.com**), and the Walgreens at 12100 S Apopka-Vineland Road (near Downtown Disney), 5935 W Irlo Bronson Memorial Highway (Highway 192 in Kissimmee), 6201, 8050, 8959 and 12650 International Drive (among others) are open 24 hours a day.

Travel insurance

Having said you shouldn't travel without insurance, you shouldn't pay more than you need to either. Your travel agent may imply that you need to buy its policy (which can be expensive, and you should be free to buy elsewhere). In all cases you should make sure you are covered in the USA for the following.

- **Medical cover** of at least £2m.
- **Personal liability** up to £2m (this won't cover driving abroad; you would still need Supplementary Liability Insurance with your car hire firm).
- **Cancellation** or **curtailment** cover up to £5,000.
- **Personal property cover** up to £1,500 (but check on expensive items, as most policies limit single articles to £250).
- **Cash and document** cover, including your passport and tickets.
- **24-hour emergency helpline**.

If you want to go horse riding, check that your policy includes **dangerous sports** cover.

Downtown Disney

American-speak

Many words and phrases have a different meaning across the Atlantic. For instance, when Americans say the first floor, they mean the ground floor, the second floor is really the first, and so on. (NB: NEVER ask for a packet of fags; 'fag' is a crude, slang term for a homosexual.) Here are a few everyday words to help you:

American	English	American	English
Appetiser	Starter	Fender	Car bumper
Band aid	Plaster	Freeway	Motorway
Bathroom	Private toilet	Fries	Chips
Biscuit	Savoury scone	Gas	Petrol
Broiled	Grilled	Graham cracker	Digestive biscuit
Cellphone	Mobile phone	Hood	Car bonnet
Check	Bill	Intersection	Junction
Chips	Crisps	Nickel	5 cents
Collect call	Reverse charge phone call	No standing	No parking OR stopping
Cookie	Biscuit	'Pound sign'	The # on a phone keypad
Cot/rollaway	Fold-up bed	Purse	Handbag
Crib	Cot	Quarter	25 cents
Diaper	Nappy	Ramp	Slip road
Dime	10 cents	Restroom	Public toilet
Divided highway	Dual carriageway	Seltzer	Soda water
Eggplant	Aubergine	Shrimp	King prawn
Eggs 'over easy'	Eggs fried both sides but soft	Soda	Fizzy drink
Eggs 'sunny side up'	Eggs fried on just one side (soft)	Stroller	Pushchair
Entrée	Main course	Trunk	Car boot
Facecloth/washcloth	Flannel	Turn-out	Lay-by
Faucet	Tap	Yield	Give way
		Zucchini	Courgette

Shop around at reputable dealers like **American Express** (0800 028 7573, **americanexpress.com/uk**); **AA** (0845 492 0606, **theaa.com**); **Direct Travel** (0845 605 2700, **direct-travel.co.uk**); **Club Direct** (0800 083 2466, **clubdirect.com**); **Columbus** (0870 033 9988, **columbusdirect.com**); **Egg** (08451 222 888, **http://new.egg.com**); **Norwich Union** (0808 101 4991, **norwich union.com**); **Worldwide Travel Insurance** (0870 112 8100, **worldwide insure.com**). **Money Supermarket** also compares different travel

Orlando Convention & Visitor Bureau on I-Drive

insurers at **moneysupermarket.com/insurance**.

Florida with children

We are often asked what we think is the right age to take children to Orlando, and there is no set answer. Some toddlers take to it instantly, while some 6- or even 7-year-olds are overwhelmed. Very often, the best attractions for young children are the hotel swimming pool or the tram ride to a park's front gates! Some love the Disney characters instantly, while others find them frightening. There is no predicting how they'll react but, at 4½, Simon's oldest boy loved just about every second of his first experience (apart from the fireworks – see opposite) and still talks about it. A 3-year-old may not remember much, but WOULD have fun and provide you with some great memories, photos and videos. Here are some top tips for travelling with youngsters:

BRITTIP

Look out for the *Kids Eat Free* card for Orlando, which offers a free child's meal with every adult meal or entrée purchased for children 11 and under. It features more than 50 local restaurants – from standard choices like Chick-fil-A and Dunkin' Donuts to the upmarket Taverna Opa and Bergamo's – with potential savings of $350. See more at **kidseatfreecard.com**.

The flight: Try to look calm (even if you don't feel it) and relaxed. Small children soon pick up on any anxieties and make them worse. Pack a bag with plenty of little bits for them (comics, sweets, colouring books, small surprise toys, etc.) and keep vital 'extras' like Calpol (in sachets, if possible), a change of clothes, a small first-aid kit (plasters, antiseptic cream, baby wipes), sunglasses, a hat and sunscreen in your hand luggage.

BRITTIP

Pushchairs ('strollers') are essential, even if your children are a year or two out of them. The walking wears kids out quickly and a pushchair can save a lot of discomfort. You can take your own, hire them at the parks or, better still, buy one at a local supermarket for as little as $20.

Once you're there: Take things slowly and let your children dictate the pace to a large extent. In hot, humid summer, only the most placid children (and few under 5s, in our experience) will happily queue for an hour or more at a ride, so use Disney's FastPass system (see page 106) judiciously. The heat, in particular, can result in grizzly kids in no time, so take breaks for drinks and splash zones or head for attractions with air-conditioning. Remember to carry your small first-aid kit. Baby wipes

Kids can have an amazing experience at Disney

On the beach at St Pete's

always come in handy, and it's a good idea to take spare clothes, which you can leave in the lockers at all the main parks. Going back to the hotel for an afternoon snooze is a good idea – you will also dodge the worst of the heat and crowds.

In the sun: Carry sun cream and sun block at all times and use it frequently, in queues, on buses, etc. A children's after-sun lotion is also advisable. And make sure they drink a lot of water or non-fizzy drinks. Tiredness and irritability are often the signs of mild dehydration.

Dining out: Look for 'kids eat free' deals in many places, as they can apply to children up to 12, and take advantage of the many buffet options (see Chapter 11, Dining Out) to fill up the family or for picky eaters. Many restaurants do Meals To Go if you want a quiet meal in your own accommodation without the worry of the kids playing up. And try to let your children get used to the characters and the size of them before you go to one of the many wonderful Disney character meals.

Having fun: Let your children do some of the decision-making and be prepared to go with the flow if they find something unexpected (the many squirt fountains and splash zones in the parks are an example – bring swimsuits and/or a change of clothes!). The Orlando rule of 'You Can't Do It All' applies especially with kids. And be aware that the evening fireworks are loud and youngsters can get distressed (Simon's 4-year-old had to be taken out of *Epcot* in a hurry). The resort hotels around the *Magic Kingdom* offer safe ways to view the fireworks – at a distance.

BRITTIP

Avoid making phone calls from your hotel room – they're hugely expensive. It's cheaper to buy a local phonecard and use a normal payphone. British tri-band mobiles are also costly to use in the US. To call the UK from the US, dial 011 44, then drop the first 0 from the UK area code.

Baby centres: All the parks have facilities for nursing mothers and can provide baby food and nappies on request (check the park map for the locations). The centres can even provide spare children's underpants for those little accidents. All Disney's hotel gift shops stock baby food and nappies. Expectant mothers are strongly advised not to ride some of the more dynamic attractions and coasters, and there will be clear warnings on park maps and at the rides. Basically, the rides to avoid are: *Magic Kingdom:* Space Mountain,

Woody Woodpecker's Kidzone

Treetops Trails at Busch Gardens

Splash Mountain; *Epcot:* Test Track, Mission: SPACE; *Disney's Hollywood Studios:* Tower of Terror, Rock 'n' Roller Coaster Starring Aerosmith, Star Tours; *Disney's Animal Kingdom:* Dinosaur!, Primeval Whirl, Kali River Rapids, Expedition Everest; *Universal Studios Florida:* The Simpsons, Men In Black – Alien Attack, Revenge of the Mummy, Jimmy Neutron ride (unless you use the static seats); *Islands of Adventure:* Incredible Hulk Coaster, Dr Doom's Fearfall, Popeye and Bluto's Bilge-Rat Barges, Dudley Do-Right's Ripsaw Falls, Jurassic Park River Adventure, Dueling Dragons; *SeaWorld:* Wild Arctic (avoid the simulator ride), Journey to Atlantis, Kraken; *Busch Gardens:* SheiKra, Gwazi, Kumba, Montu, The Scorpion, Congo River Rapids, Stanley Falls Log Flume, Tanganyika Tidal Wave, The Phoenix, Sandstorm, Cheetah Chase.

Babysitting: Available through many Disney resorts and some of the bigger hotels elsewhere, while **Kids Nite Out** is a service providing parents with a chance to have an evening out on their own. It offers in-room sitters or helpers during your stay at a rate of $14/hour for the first child, $16.50 for 2, $19 for 3 and $21.50 for 4, with an additional $2/hour after 9pm (children 2 years and older only). There is a 4-hour minimum and reservations are required (1800 696 8105 or 407 828 0920; **kidsniteout.com**).

Hurricane alert?

Florida was hit by an unprecedented 4 hurricanes in 2004, 3 of which affected Orlando, with a lot of resultant publicity and worry. But the simple fact is this was the worst weather in more than a century and big storms are rare in central Florida. The hurricane 'season' is June–Nov, with Aug–Sept the most storm-prone. However, even the extremes of 2004 caused no significant damage to the theme parks and the biggest inconvenience for tourists was losing electricity for a few days. In the unlikely event of a major storm, switch your TV to the Weather Channel and local news station WESH 2 and follow their advice.

Travellers with disabilities

The parks pay close attention to the needs of visitors with disabilities and Florida in general is extremely disabled-friendly (though Americans tend to use the word 'handicapped' as we use 'disabled'). Though there are few rides that cannot cater for them, wheelchair availability and access is almost always good. For hearing-impaired guests, there are assistive listening devices and reflective captioning at attractions where a commentary is part of the show. Braille guidebooks are available, plus rest areas for guide dogs. Disney hotels all have disabled-accessible rooms (407 939 7807, **disneyworld.com**) and Disney publishes a *Guidebook for Disabled Guests* (as does Universal), available in all 4 main parks (and online). Life-jackets are always on hand at the water parks, and there are special tape cassettes for blind guests. If you require help while queuing or have children with special needs, call in at any Disney guest relations office to ask what provisions are available. Walt Disney World also has a Disabled Guests Special Requests Line on 407 939 7807 and can produce a Guest Assistance Card (GAC) tailored to your specific needs. It doesn't provide front-of-the-line access (which many people believe) but it can make the waiting more comfortable. Universal, SeaWorld and Busch Gardens provide similar assistance through their Guest Services offices.

Please note, the rules for disabled drivers using their blue UK disabled parking permits in Florida have changed. To use any of the plentiful designated parking areas in all public areas (including the parks), drivers must obtain a **Temporary Disabled Parking Permit**, which costs $15 locally. You can either go to a local tax collection office, with your UK blue badge and a form of ID when you arrive (but bear in mind most open 8.30am–4pm Mon–Fri only), or apply by mail at least 4 weeks in advance. You need to send a photocopy of your Blue Badge (both sides), a copy of your passport ID page, and a money order for $15 (or your credit card details, for which there is a $2 surcharge; please do NOT send cash) to: Tag Department, Osceola County Tax Collector, 2501 E Irlo Bronson Memorial Highway, Kissimee, Florida 34744, USA (407 742 4000 or fax 407 742 3995 8am–4.30pm Mon–Fri). For a list of tax collection offices in Orange County (for the Orlando area), call 407 836 4145 (**octaxcol.com**, and click on Office Locations), or in Osceola County (for Kissimmee), call 407 742 4000 (**osceolataxcollector.com**).

Orang Outpost at Busch Gardens

The temporary permits are issued for 90 days so it's best to apply no sooner than 5–6 weeks before travelling to ensure it will be valid for the duration of stay. Include an email address where possible for the Tax Office to query any details. However, Disney has said it WILL still honour the British blue badge at its 4 main theme parks.

Local company **Suntastic Tours** can help travellers with both physical and mental disabilities in many different areas, including travel, arranging tours of the parks and many other accessibility issues (1877 226 6750, **suntastictours.com**). For other local assistance, **Walker Medical & Mobility Products** specialises in 3-wheeled electric scooters and wheelchair rentals, with free delivery and pick-up even from holiday villas (407 518 6000, **walkermobility.com**). **Rainbow Wheels**, with three locations in central Florida, hires out full-size or mini vans equipped for wheelchair users (1800 303 4545, **rainbow wheels.com**). The discussion forums on **wdwinfo.com** also include a board geared to visitors with disabilities, while the excellent **AllEarsNet** website has a big section on advice for a whole range of concerns, from children with ADD to vegetarian and vegan food. Visit **allearsnet.com**, click on Planning, then For Travelers With Special Challenges.

Orlando for grown-ups

You don't need to have kids in tow to enjoy Orlando. There is so much clever detail and imagination, it is usually the grown-ups who get the most out of the holiday experience. In fact, as many couples and single people visit the parks as do families with children.

Certainly, when you look at the entertainment on offer at *Downtown Disney* and CityWalk, downtown Orlando and the great range of bars and fine restaurants, with a good number of romantic offerings, it is easy to see the attraction for those aged 21 and over. As well as Florida being a key honeymoon destination, its friendly, sociable atmosphere provides an ideal place for singles, while couples without children can also take advantage of late opening at the parks and clubs like Jellyrolls and Atlantic City Dance Hall at *Disney's Boardwalk Resort.*

BRITTIP

If you have a fridge in your hotel, put drink cartons in the freezer overnight and they will be cool for much of the next day in your back-pack. Better still, buy a cheap coolbag, freeze it with some water bottles in, and leave it in the car – great after a day in the parks.

bluezoo

Top 10 romantic restaurants

1 Tchoup Chop, Universal's Royal Pacific Resort
2 California Grill, Disney's Contemporary Resort
3 Todd English's bluezoo, Walt Disney World Dolphin Resort
4 Zen, Omni Orlando Resort at Champions Gate
5 Jiko, Disney's Animal Kingdom Lodge
6 The Boheme, Grand Bohemian Hotel
7 Seasons 52, Sand Lake Rd, Orlando
8 Old Hickory Steakhouse, Gaylord Palms Resort
9 Cala Bella, Shingle Creek Resort
10 Capital Grille, The Pointe Orlando

Orlando for seniors

The more mature traveller can also benefit from a healthy dose of the Sunshine State. And, if our parents (all in their senior years) are any guide, they will have just as much fun, within slightly different parameters. For the older person, staying in a Disney hotel is highly recommended as it removes the stress of driving. The extra cost is offset, Simon's parents feel, by the beauty and convenience of their surroundings. They still find plenty to do in the parks, even if they aren't keen on most of the thrill rides (though just watching can be entertainment enough!). *Epcot* and *Disney's Animal Kingdom* both have much to engage the older visitor, while the shows of *Disney's Hollywood Studios* make that a popular choice, too, and the *Magic Kingdom Park*, while 'probably the noisiest of all the parks', still represents one of the essential experiences.

The *Downtown Disney* area can feel a bit frenetic for the senior crowd, but the *Boardwalk Resort* is popular and the whole of the *Epcot* resort area offers much in the way of fine dining and relaxation. In fact, this is often a prime area for seniors, notably the quieter *Disney's Yacht and Beach Club Resorts*, and the superb Swan-Dolphin complex.

Simon's parents highlight the following for their age group: Jim Henson's Muppet Vision 3-D and Fantasmic! at *Disney's Hollywood Studios*; Kilimanjaro Safaris, the Maharajah Jungle Trek and Festival of the Lion King at *Disney's Animal Kingdom Theme Park*; Spaceship Earth, Soarin', Universe of Energy, Test Track and IllumiNations at *Epcot* (plus the superb gardens and architecture); The Haunted Mansion, Jungle Cruise, Pirates of the Caribbean and the monorail ride to the *Magic Kingdom*; watching the children at the many parades and

There are no age limits!

The Amazing Adventures of Spiderman at Islands of Adventure

character greetings; dinner at the California Grill in *Disney's Contemporary Resort*; shopping at Orlando Premium Outlets; most of Universal Studios, but less of Islands of Adventure (though, like most, they were wowed by the Amazing Adventures of Spider-Man).

In terms of the weather, March was just about ideal for them, but they wouldn't be keen to visit in summer. Seniors can also take advantage of numerous discounts and special deals for their age group at the attractions as well as at many restaurants and hotels. The official Visitor Center on I-Drive (see page 50) publishes a brochure of all the deals (**orlandoinfo.com**).

BRITTIP

Looking for essential travel accessories and useful knick-knacks, like TSA-approved locks, plug adapters and luggage scales (essential for the trip home to avoid excess baggage!)? Check out **tripneeds.com**. Asda supermarkets also sell a good travel range.

Repeat visitors

Repeat visitors create a large part of the Orlando market and are always on the lookout for something new after they have done all the main parks. To that end, Chapter 8, Off the Beaten Track, is largely designed with them in mind. Listed here are 10 things worth doing once you have Been There and Done That:

1 Behind the scenes tours at the Disney parks.

2 Dolphin watch cruise from Dolphin Landings at St Pete Beach.

3 Daytona Beach Aqua Safari.

4 The scenic boat ride and Morse Museum in Winter Park.

5 Bok Tower Gardens and lunch or dinner (plus a visit to the soup cannery!) at the eclectic Chalet Suzanne in Lake Wales.

6 A picnic in Lake Louisa State Park in Lake County.

7 Boggy Creek Airboats.

8 The amazing SkyVenture on I-Drive.

Two-way radio rentals

Two-way radios have taken on a popular new role in Orlando, in terms of both safety and convenience. Many families buy these 'walkie-talkies' to keep in touch around the parks and it is common to see them in use in preference to mobile phones. You can pick them up locally for as little as $35 in stores like Wal-Mart, Best Buy, Circuit City, Radio Shack, Office Depot and Staples. However, they cannot be used back home as they use the same frequency as the UK emergency services.

9 Merritt Island National Wildlife Refuge at Titusville.

10 A visit to Mount Dora, north-west of Orlando.

Measurements

American clothes sizes are smaller than ours, hence a US size 12 dress is a UK 14, or an American jacket sized 42 is a 44. Shoes are the opposite: a US 10 should fit a British size 9 foot. The measuring system is also still imperial, not metric.

You've got mail

Sending postcards and letters home is easy but the American postal system can be hard to understand. You won't find postboxes in many locations and some post offices don't seem to know the fees for postage to the UK. So here's what you need to know: all the parks DO have postboxes and you can get stamp books from most stamp machines and City Hall at the *Magic Kingdom*; a standard postcard costs 84c; a birthday or other greetings-type card in an envelope requires a 94c stamp; standard postage within the US is 42c; the main post office for the Disney area is at **10450 Turkey Lake Road** (just north of the junction with Palm Parkway and Central Florida Parkway; 8am–7pm Mon–Fri, 9am–5pm Sat); in Kissimmee, try **2600 Michigan Avenue** (8am–6.30pm Mon–Fri, 9am–4pm Sat) or **1415 W Oak Street** (8.30am–5pm Mon–Fri, 9am–2pm Sat). You will also find a full-service post office inside the **Mall at Millenia**, off the lower level of the Grand Court.

Wedding bells

Florida is an increasingly popular choice for couples looking to tie the knot (some 20,000 couples a year at the last count). Its almost guaranteed sunshine and lush, natural landscape make it a huge hit as a wedding backdrop. Orlando also has some terrific services, wedding co-ordinators and scenic venues like Magnolia Acres, Southport Park, Winter Park, Leu Gardens and the many resort hotels (like the Buena Vista Palace, Walt Disney World Swan and Dolphin, Wyndham Resort and the Orlando Marriott World Center) and even the pristine golf courses (like Celebration Golf Club). More unusual ones include getting married in a hot-air balloon or a helicopter, on the beach or a luxury yacht, in the pit-lane of the Richard Petty Driving Experience at *Walt Disney World* or even at 145mph/233kph around the speedway itself! All the main tour operators feature wedding options and co-ordinated services, and offer a variety of ceremonies, or you can pick a local specialist like Get Married In Florida (see below). Prices vary from around £300/couple (for a basic civil ceremony) to more than £2,000.

Wedding at Fort Harrison Hotel in Clearwater

Walt Disney World's Wedding Pavilion: True fairytale romance, with the backdrop of Cinderella Castle, you can opt for traditional elegance in this Victorian setting with up to 260 guests or the full Disney experience, arriving in Cinderella's coach with Mickey and Minnie as guests. Disney's wedding planners can tailor-make the occasion for you (407 828 3400) but at a price – rates *start* at $3,000/couple for the basic ceremony and can easily top $20,000.

Licence: To obtain a marriage licence you can visit one of the local courthouses, which include the Osceola County Courthouse, Courthouse Square, Suite 2000, Kissimmee (just off Bryan Street in downtown Kissimmee) 8am–4pm Mon–Fri (407 343 3500); the Orange County Courthouse, 425 North Orange Avenue (downtown Orlando) 7.30am–4pm Mon–Fri (407 836 2067); Clermont Courthouse, 1206 Bowman Street, Clermont (in Sunnyside Plaza) 8.30am–4.30pm (closed for lunch noon–1pm; 352 394 2018). All courthouses are closed on US bank holidays. Both parties must be present to apply for the marriage licence, which costs $93.50 (in cash, travellers' cheques or by credit card) and is valid for 60 days, while a ceremony (equivalent to a British register office) can be performed at the same time by the clerk for an extra $20 (times vary according to courthouse). Passports and birth certificates are requested, and if you have been married before you should bring your decree absolute. After acquiring a licence, a couple can get married anywhere in Florida. Neither witnesses nor blood tests are necessary and there are no residence qualifications. It is also possible to obtain a licence *before* arriving in Florida (see **floridamarriage licencebypost.com**).

Get Married in Florida: An internet business dedicated to organising weddings for couples from the UK, this is run by Briton Lorraine Ellis, who has specialised in Orlando marriages for many years and is ideally placed to deliver the ultimate personal service. She offers the complete package for the perfect wedding – as we can personally vouch for (407 226 3383, **getmarriedin florida.com**)!

Recommendations: We can also add our recommendation for caterers **Levan's** (**levans.com**) and the amazing **andreacheesecake.com**. Another wedding specialist is harpist **Christine MacPhail**, who can provide

Cinderella wedding at Walt Disney World Resort

an elegant touch to the occasion (407 239 1330, **orlandoharpist.com**). For photographers, try **Abba Photography** (407 672 1121, **abba photography.com**) or **Broadway Fotographics** (by Bill Otten, 407 339 5542, **broadwayfoto.com**).

Religious ceremonies: If you would prefer to get married in a church or place of worship, contact the **Center of Light Church & Spiritual Center** on East Robinson Street (407 228 0101), the **First Baptist Church** on John Young Parkway (407 425 2555), **St Nicholas Catholic Church** on Sand Lake Road (407 351 0133) or **Trinity Lutheran Church** on East Livingston Street downtown (407 422 5704, **trinitydowntown.org**). Another church worth noting for general worship (8.30 and 11am Sun and 7.30pm Thurs) is the **Community Presbyterian Church** in the town of Celebration (near Kissimmee) at 511 Celebration Avenue (407 566 1633, **commpres.com**).

Disney special occasions

Birthday badges: Free badges can be found at City Hall in the *Magic Kingdom Park* and Guest Services at *Epcot, Disney's Hollywood Studios* and *Disney's Animal Kingdom Theme Park.* Cast Members like to make a fuss over children (and adults!) wearing a birthday badge.

Birthday cakes: Contact room service at your resort or Guest Services at one of the parks. All Disney restaurants can offer cakes (from $12.50 at each restaurant, or $25–120 pre-ordered at least 24 hours in advance on 407 827 2253). Be sure to tell the Cast Member at check-in (or when you make your reservation) as well as hostesses and/or servers in restaurants if someone in your group has a birthday. While not guaranteed, Disney staff often go out of their way to make the day special. If characters know it's a birthday when they sign a child's autograph book, they may add a special birthday wish in it.

Birthday cruise: The IllumiNations Birthday Cruise (to *Epcot*) provides cake, drinks, streamers and balloons for a 90-minute tour from *Disney's Yacht and Beach Club Resort* marina for $275 (call 407 939 7529).

Birthday parties: *Disney's Polynesian Resort* will arrange themed birthday parties with various lunch options at its Never Land kids' club for ages 4 and up. A themed 2-hour Premium party with cake, pizza, drinks, party activities and one Disney character is $56.45 per person, while the Basic version (without a Disney character) is $26.63/person (at least one week's notice required on 407 939 7529).

Winter-Summerland Miniature Golf: 2-hour birthday parties for 10 or more, including pizza, soda, cake and a round of mini-golf at $16.95 a head, plus tax (407 939 7529, call at least a week in advance).

Disney's Pirate Cruise: this 2-hour adventure for kids 4–12 sails (on pontoon boats) from 4 of the resorts (Grand Floridian, Yacht/Beach Club and Caribbean Beach at 9.30am and Port Orleans at 11.30am) to find pirate 'booty' at different ports of call, with a final stop for lunch at $30.01 per child (407 939 3463, up to 180 days in advance).

International Drive

Safety first

While crime is not a serious issue in central Florida, this is still big-city America so don't leave your common sense at home. International Drive has its own dedicated police unit (a division of the Orlando City Police), with several dozen officers patrolling purely this long tourist corridor, arranging crime prevention seminars with local hotels and generally ensuring I-Drive takes good care of its visitors. You will often see these police out on mountain bikes, and they are a polite, helpful bunch should you need assistance. Tourism is such a vital part of the economy, the authorities have a highly safety-conscious attitude. However, it would be foolish to ignore the usual safety guidelines when travelling abroad.

BRITTIP

Don't want to take your mobile with you for fear of high charges? Hire a phone for your holidays from **Adam Phones** and take advantage of its special local rates for the US (0800 123 000, **adamphones.com**).

Emergencies

Emergency services: For police, fire department or ambulance, dial 911 (9-911 from your hotel room). Make sure your children are aware of this number.

General: For smaller-scale crises (mislaid tickets or passports, rescheduled flights, for instance) your holiday company should have an emergency contact number in the hotel reception.

Independent travellers: If you run into passport or other problems that need the assistance of the British Consulate, its office is at Suite 2110, Sun Trust Center, 200 South Orange Avenue, Orlando, Florida, 32801, with walk-in visitors' hours 9.30am–noon and 2–4pm, or call 407 254 3300 (**britainusa.com/orlando/**).

BRITTIP

Phonecards, which you need to make a call from a local payphone (much cheaper than using your hotel room phone), are available from most 7-Eleven stores or from your tour rep.

Hotel security

While in your hotel, always use door peepholes and security chains when someone knocks at the door. DON'T open the door to strangers without asking for identification, and check with the hotel desk if you are still not sure. It is stating the obvious, but keep doors and windows locked at all times and always use deadlocks and security chains. Always take cash, credit cards, valuables and car keys when you go out (or put them in the room safe), and don't leave the door open at any time, even if you just pop down the corridor to the ice machine. Most hotels now have electronic card-locks for extra security and can offer deposit boxes in addition to the standard in-room mini-safes. Don't be afraid to ask reception staff for safety advice for the surrounding areas or if you are travelling somewhere you're not sure about.

BRITTIP

If your room has already been cleaned before you go out for the day, hang the 'Do Not Disturb' sign on the door. Always keep your valuables out of sight, whether in the hotel or the car.

Safety is a major issue for the Central Florida Hotel/Motel Association and hotel staff are usually well briefed to be helpful. A bumbag (Americans say 'fanny pack'!) is a better bet than a handbag or shoulder bag. And try not to look too obviously like a tourist! The map over the steering wheel is a giveaway, but other no-nos are wearing masses of jewellery and carrying lots of camera equipment. The biggest giveaway is leaving a camera or camcorder on view in the car (and the heat may ruin them).

Finally, and this is VERY strong police advice, in the unlikely event of being confronted by an assailant, DO NOT resist or 'have a go', as this can often make a bad situation worse.

BRITTIP
For your journey to the US, use a business address rather than your home address on all your luggage. It is less conspicuous and safer should any item be stolen or misplaced

Money matters

It is useful to know that dollar travellers' cheques can be used as cash almost everywhere (though a few places will no longer accept them, like the Wal-Mart superstores and Golden Corral restaurants) and can be readily replaced if lost or stolen, so it is not necessary (as well as not advisable) to carry large amounts of cash. However, sterling travellers' cheques can be cashed only in major banks. You'll need to carry ID in many cases, though, even for credit card purchases (the new UK driving licence card is useful for this).

BRITTIP
Want the best exchange rate for your holiday cash? Check out **comparetravelmoney.co.uk** for the best deals on a day-by-day basis.

Having a credit card is almost essential as they are accepted everywhere and provide extra buying security. In some cases, notably car hire, you can't operate without your flexible friend. Visa, Mastercard and American Express are all widely accepted. It is worth separating the larger notes from the smaller ones in your wallet to avoid flashing all your money in view. Losing £300 of travellers' cheques shouldn't ruin your holiday – but losing $600 in cash might. All of the theme parks have cash dispensers (called 'ATM machines' in the US) at which you can use your credit card to withdraw cash. Some UK banks (notably

The Barn at the Grand Cypress Equestrian Center

BRITTIP

Take note: all Orlando prices, both in this book and on every price tag you see, do not include the 6–7% Florida Sales Tax. There is also a 4–5% Resort Tax on hotel rooms.

Nationwide and Chase Bank) have no currency conversion charges for using their credit card in the US.

Car safety

Car crime has led to some lurid headlines in the past, especially in the Miami area in the mid-1990s. Once again, it pays to make basic safety checks before you set off. The first thing is to familiarise yourself with the car's controls BEFORE driving away – which button is the air-conditioning, which control operates the indicators, where the windscreen wiper switch is, and so on. Also, try to memorise your route in advance, even if it's only a case of knowing the road numbers. Most hire firms now give good directions to all the hotels, so check them before you set off (or, better still, hire a GPS system). Make sure the fuel tank is well filled and never let it get near empty. Running out of 'gas' in an unfamiliar area holds obvious hazards. If you stray off your pre-determined route, stick to well-lit areas and ask for directions only from

BRITTIP

American banknotes are all the same size and predominantly green, with just the occasional splash of colour in the newer notes. The only real difference is the picture of the president and the denomination in each corner.

Simon and Susan

Simon and Susan can plan a Personalised Itinerary Planner for your holiday. You'll find all the details on the *Brit Guide* website: **britguideorlando.co.uk**. They also write a *Brit Guide to Disneyland Resort Paris.*

Discovery Cove

official businesses like hotels and petrol stations or the police.

You will find THREE kinds of police locally. The **State** police (in khaki uniforms) drive beige-and-black cars with circular blue badges with 'State Trooper' and 'FHP' (Florida Highway Patrol) on and are mainly found on the motorways. Each **County** then has its own police force, which drives white vehicles with gold stars marked 'Orange County Sheriff', or 'Osceola County Sheriff', and similar (both Orange and Osceola County deputies have green uniforms). Bigger cities also have **City** police, and Orlando's drive white cars with blue and yellow stripes and have dark blue uniforms. Learn more at **fhp.state.fl.us**, **ocso.com**, **osceola.org** and **cityoforlando.net/police**.

Always try to park close to your destination where there are plenty of lights and DO NOT get out if there are suspicious characters around. Always keep windows closed (and air-conditioning on), and don't hesitate to lock the doors from the inside if you feel threatened (larger cars have

Let us plan your holiday …

… with our unique personalised *Itinerary Planner Service*

In conjunction with the *Brit Guide* website – **britguideorlando.co.uk** – our Itinerary Planner Service (IPS) will help you get the very most out of your time in central Florida. This is a service no other agency can offer. We will design an itinerary tailored to your individual plans for the parks and attractions of central Florida. In your planner (which usually runs to 30-plus pages for a 2-week itinerary), we will indicate the best days to visit the parks to avoid the crowds; all the main show and parade times; any rides that may be closed for refurbishment; and provide a detailed touring plan for each park, a shopping guide, updates on new rides, etc., as well as up-to-the-minute advice right from the source of the fun, plus a host of additional Brit Tip Extras and Brit Picks (our special favourites) that we can't fit into this book.

All you have to do is visit the *Brit Guide* website and click on the **Itinerary Planner** link. Fill out the online form with your travel dates, hotel and family details, the tickets you have bought (or are buying) and what you would like to fit into your visit. Submit the form, along with your payment, and you will receive an acknowledgement of your requirements. A few days before you go, you will receive, by email, your unique Itinerary Planner, which will consist of:

1. An official *Brit Guide* welcome from Simon and Susan Veness.
2. A full day-by-day plan for the length of your holiday.
3. A touring strategy for ALL 8 main parks, the water parks and shopping centres, avoiding the crowds and taking advantage of the latest developments.
4. An alternative plan in case of bad weather.
5. All the main parade and fireworks times with your daily plans.
6. A note of any rides/shows that are closed during your visit.
7. A special selection of Brit Tip Extras and local advice specifically for you.
8. Our Brit Picks – a guide to a range of personal favourites from restaurants to shops – that we feel may appeal to you most.
9. The ultimate insider knowledge, as both Simon and Susan are based in the heart of the Orlando magic and are fully up to date on all developments.
10. Our special bonus – an exclusive Platinum VIP Passport for Orlando Premium Outlets (not available to the general public), providing extra savings at select upmarket stores at this fabulous shopping venue (in addition to its free VIP Coupon Book we offer to all readers – see inside back cover).

All in all, it adds up to the most comprehensive package of specialised holiday info anywhere, and it represents the secret to the most fun, in the most hassle-free way, in the most exciting place on earth. What more could you ask for? Just check us out on **britguideorlando.co.uk** and we'll do the rest for you.

Please note: There is a minimum order period, so do check the website and make sure you apply for your IPS in good time before your holiday (usually at least 2 weeks). We are not a travel agency or ticket service and you MUST know your ticket requirements in advance.

doors that lock automatically as you drive off). Don't forget to lock up when you leave the car. Not all rental cars have central locking, so double-check! It is comforting to know that Orlando does not have any no-go areas in the main tourist parts. The nearest is the portion of the Orange Blossom Trail south of downtown Orlando (a selection of strip clubs and 'adult bars' that can be downright seedy at night) and the Parramore area south-west of downtown. For more info on safety, contact the Community Affairs office of Orange County Police (407 836 3720) or the International Drive police team office (407 351 9368).

BRITTIP

You'll find masses of info on all things Orlando on the fun-packed discussion forums at **wdwinfo.com** and **attraction-tickets-direct.co.uk**, to which we also contribute. They also have features, theme park info, restaurant advice, news, weather, facts and tips.

Know before you go

You can contact these organisations for advance info. **Visit Florida** offers a free Vacation Guide (0870 770 1177, **visitflorida.com/uk**). The **Orlando Tourism Bureau** in London has a 24-hour info line or website where you can request or download its free holiday planning pack and **Preferred Visitor Magicard** (see Brit Tip, page 11; 0800 018 6790, **orlandoinfo.com/uk/**). You can also visit the **Kissimmee Convention & Visitors Bureau** (**floridakiss.com**).

It's worth checking Orlando's ONLY official **Visitor Center**, 8.30am–6.30pm daily at 8723 International Drive (407 363 5872 or email **info@orlandocvb.com**) for discounted attraction tickets, free brochures and accommodation advice, free info pamphlets and maps. The **Kissimmee Visitor Center** (8am–5pm Mon–Fri) is at 1925 E Irlo Bronson Memorial Highway, or Highway 192 and also offers free maps, discount coupons and brochures (407 847 5000 or toll-free in the US on 1800 333 5477).

The official sites aren't bad, though Disney's can be hard work: **disneyworld. co.uk** (for opening hours, rides, parades, etc. and bookings). Then see **seaworld. com, universal orlando.com**, and **buschgardens.com**. The online service of the local newspaper (**orlandosentinel. com**) is packed with info (especially for shopping, dining and nightlife), while the free *Orlando Weekly* is also worth checking (**orlandoweekly.com**). Among the many useful fan-based websites are **thedibb.co.uk** ('Disney with a British accent'), the well-designed **wdisneyw. co.uk** (with more pages for UK visitors), the comprehensive **allearsnet.com** (notably the Disney dining section) and **orlandorocks.com** (for the true theme park addict).

Now, on to the next step of the holiday, your transport…

The Disney-inspired town of Celebration

© Disney

3 Getting Around

or The Secret of Driving on the Wrong Side of the Road!

Arriving and driving in Orlando are two of the biggest concerns for visitors, especially first-timers, but there's really no need to worry. Although most people begin their holiday by leaving the airport in a newly acquired, automatic, left-hand-drive hire car on roads that appear quite bewildering at first, driving here is a lot easier and more enjoyable than in the UK. Anyone who is familiar with the M25 should find Florida FAR less stressful.

Before you get to your hire car, though, you need to be aware of your arrival details at either Orlando International Airport or Orlando Sanford International Airport.

Orlando International Airport

This is one of the most modern and enjoyable airports in the world, but it can be confusing for newcomers. All flights arrive at one of 4 satellite terminals and you then take a shuttle tram (like a mini monorail) to the main terminal.

International arrivals: If you arrive with British Airways or Virgin Atlantic, you disembark at the satellite for Gates 60–99, where you first need to go through Immigration and Customs. There are individual queues for each of the Immigration kiosks, and you need to get in any of the queues marked 'Visitors' and wait for the official to call you forward (the queues on the right tend to move a bit quicker as they are next to the US Citizens lanes, which are often not too busy). Once through Immigration, collect your baggage from the carousel and go through the Customs check. Then you have a choice (new in 2008!): *either* deposit your checked luggage on a second conveyor belt to take it to the main terminal while you go upstairs to the shuttle with your hand luggage only; *or* (if you can manage it all without a trolley), take it with you on the (new) escalator straight up to the shuttle itself. If you did the former, once in the main terminal you are on Level 3 and you follow signs down to Baggage Claim B (NB: **Virgin** flights now need to cross over to Baggage Claim **A**) on Level 2. If you brought all your luggage with you on the shuttle, you can proceed straight to pick up your transport on

BRITTIP

Make sure you fill out your Immigration form accurately. The official will send you to the back of the queue if there are errors or crossings out. For country of residence put 'UK', and you must give a valid US address for your first night's accommodation.

Level 1 (or, if a specific driver is meeting you, Level 2). Allow at least an hour from landing to reach ground transportation.

Domestic arrivals: For anyone arriving on a US domestic flight (from another US gateway), you disembark at the satellite terminal and proceed straight to the main terminal on the shuttle to collect your baggage on Level 2 (either A or B side, depending on arrival gate). Once at the main baggage claim, porters can help you to Level 1 (for a $1/bag tip) for all car hire, shuttles and buses. Trolleys need $3 in change (or you can use a credit card) to operate – they are not free as at UK airports.

Transfers: Kerbside pick-up is just outside the doors on Level 2. If a driver is meeting you, he or she will wait on Level 2, either at the bottom of the escalators or by your baggage reclaim. Several tour operators have help desks here, too, while Virgin has a big reception desk on Level 1. The public bus system, Lynx (see page 54), operates ONLY from the A side of Level 1, in spaces 38–41. Links 11, 41 and 51 depart every ½ hour (less often on Sundays and bank holidays) for Orlando city centre (about 45 minutes away), while Link 42 serves International Drive (about a 1-hour journey). Fares are $1.75.

BRITTIP

Visit **orlandoairports.net** for a photo preview of the arrival process at Orlando International Airport (click on Passenger Terminal, then Arrival Walkthrough) and other handy info.

Car hire: The hire companies with check-in desks at the airport are Dollar, National, L&M, Budget, E-Z, Avis and, of course, *Brit Guide* partners **Alamo**, and all offer a full service (look out also for Alamo's new automated self-service kiosks, as these are being introduced to its busier locations and can save queuing time.) A phone desk on Level 1 connects to another 17 off-airport companies, including Hertz, Thrifty and Enterprise. Off-airport firms have a free shuttle on Level 1 to take you to their depots, but obviously this takes longer. Dollar is used for packages with Thomson, Airtours, Virgin, Style Holidays, Travel City and First Choice; Alamo is the main client for Funway, Jetsave, Kuoni, BA Holidays and Thomas Cook. After completing your paperwork with the one-site companies, simply walk out of Level 1, across the road to the multi-storey car park to collect your car. If you arrive late, consider staying overnight at the **Hyatt Regency** hotel inside the airport itself or the recently revamped **Orlando Airport Marriott** nearby (see pages 80–1), rather than driving tired. You will be far more ready to drive next day (and the car hire queues will be shorter).

BRITTIP

If you are hiring a car from one of the on-airport companies, save time by sending the driver to complete the paperwork BEFORE collecting your luggage on Level 2.

Leaving the airport: When you drive out of the airport, DON'T look for signs to 'Orlando'. The main tourist areas are south and west of the city proper, so follow the respective signs for your accommodation. For International Drive (or I-Drive), take the North Exit and the Beachline Expressway (Route 528) west until it crosses I-Drive just north of SeaWorld. Most hotels on I-Drive are to the north, so keep right at the exit.

For Kissimmee, Disney and villas in Clermont/Davenport, take the South

BRITTIP

The Martin Andersen Beachline (formerly Beeline) Expressway (528) and Greeneway (417) are both toll roads, so make sure you have some US currency before leaving the airport. Toll booths hate to change notes above $20, while some auto-tolls take ONLY coins.

Exit for 3mls/5km and pick up the Central Florida Greeneway (Highway 417) west. For most Disney resorts, take exit 6 and follow the signs; for *Animal Kingdom* resorts, use exit 3 and take Osceola Parkway west. For eastern Kissimmee, come off Highway 417 at exit 11, the Orange Blossom Trail (Highway 17/92), and go south. For west Kissimmee and Clermont/Davenport (Highway 27), take exit 2, turn right on Celebration Avenue and left on to Highway 192, which runs west all the way to Highway 27.

Orlando Sanford International Airport

Arriving at Sanford (in Seminole County) couldn't be easier. The list of airlines visiting this easy-to-use airport currently includes XL Airways, Thomson Airways (from May 2009), Monarch, Thomas Cook Airlines, Flyglobespan and Icelandair. It generally takes only 30–40 minutes from arrival to leaving the baggage hall, but there may be delays in peak season when several planes arrive at once as its handling capacity is limited. It's a short walk from the plane to the immigration hall (where there are just 2 queues that feed through to the kiosks); you then collect your baggage, pass through Customs and walk straight out to car hire, shuttle or taxi pick-up.

BRITTIP

Don't want to drive? Consider a multi-centre stay within Orlando itself, staying first at, say, I-Drive or Universal Orlando and then a Disney resort, to get the best of the free or cheap transport options.

Car hire: You will find the tour operator welcome desks and Dollar car hire offices immediately in front of you, while our *Brit Guide* **Alamo** partner has a large welcome centre that is reached via a covered walkway and boardwalk behind this, and its British-dedicated operation is pretty smooth. National, Avis, Budget, Enterprise, Thrifty and Hertz are also on-airport (turn right out of Customs then take the first door on the right). Look up more on **orlandosanford airport.com**.

Leaving the airport: It may be 35mls/56km to the north and involve more driving (and taxis and shuttles are more expensive – a town car service would be around $110 one-way to I-Drive and a taxi $85), but you usually save time by your quicker exit. There is just one main road out, on to Lake Mary Boulevard, and you then take the Seminole Expressway (Highway 417, which becomes Central Florida Greeneway in Orange County) south. The slip road to this toll motorway is just under the flyover on your LEFT, and you need $5.25 to reach Disney or Kissimmee or $4.50 for I-Drive (via the Beachline Expressway). You can avoid the tolls by staying on Lake Mary Blvd for 6mls/10km until you get to I-4, but you're likely to hit heavy traffic through the city centre. The Expressway/Greeneway is an excellent, easy-driving introduction to Orlando, even if it does cost a few dollars. For traffic news and reports, tune to 660AM (WORL) or 580AM (WDBO). Dial 511 on a tri-band mobile phone for traffic info on I-4.

I-Ride trolley bus

ORLANDO WITHOUT A CAR

Although being mobile is advisable, it is certainly possible to survive without a car. However, few attractions are within walking distance of hotels, and taxis can be expensive. You also need to plan with greater precision to allow for extra travelling time (and with children, taking buses can be tiring). For non-drivers, your best base is either *Walt Disney World* itself (free transport throughout, but harder to get to the rest of Orlando) or International Drive for its location, 'walkability' and the great I-Ride Trolley. Many hotels have free shuttles to some of the parks or a cheap, regular mini-bus service. There are basically 4 main options: public transport; shuttle services; town cars and limousines; and taxis.

Public transport

Lynx bus system: Reliable, cheap but slightly plodding, this covers much of Orlando. Its online system map shows all its routes (or 'links') and the main attractions (407 841 5969, **golynx.com**). Worth noting are **Link 42** from Orlando International Airport to I-Drive; **Link 56** from Kissimmee to Disney (from Osceola Square Mall, along Highway 192 via Old Town and Celebration to Disney's Transportation & Ticket Center (TTC) by the *Magic Kingdom*); **Link 304** to Disney from the I-Drive area (Oak Ridge Road to *Downtown Disney*, via Sand Lake Drive and Vineland Road); **Link 18** from Kissimmee to downtown Orlando (from Osceola Square Mall, east on Highway 192 and north on Boggy Creek Road, Buenaventura Boulevard and Orange Avenue); **Link 55**, Kissimmee's Highway 192 from Osceola Square Mall west to Four Corners via the Summer Bay Resort; **Link 38**, I-Drive to downtown Orlando (from the Convention Center via Wet 'n Wild, Kirkman Road and I-4); and **Link 50** (from the TTC via SeaWorld and I-4) and **Link 300** (from *Downtown Disney* via I-4), from Disney to downtown Orlando.

BRITTIP

Lynx buses use the Downtown Disney West Side Transfer Center as their Disney hub, with Links 301, 302 and 303 spreading out from there to the theme parks and resorts.

Lynx fares are $1.75 a ride (transfers are free) or $14 for a weekly pass (children 6 and under go free with a full-fare passenger). The service is every 30 minutes in the main areas, every 15 minutes 6–9am and 3.30–6.30pm, but you must have the right change. Lynx stops are marked by pink paw-print signs and all buses are wheelchair accessible. There can be long queues for buses at Disney at closing time, so you could take Disney transport to *Downtown Disney* (via one of the resorts or the TTC), then get a taxi back to your hotel (about $30 to I-Drive).

I-Ride Trolley: Great-value service for the I-Drive area, this operates 2 routes along a 14ml/23km stretch of this tourist corridor. The *Main Line* has 41 stops and runs from the new-look Prime Outlets International shopping centre at the top of I-Drive, to SeaWorld and Aquatica via Westwood Boulevard and Sea Harbor Drive, and on to Orlando Premium Outlets. The *Green Line*, with 26 stops, goes from the Universal resort area (Windhover Drive and Major Boulevard) south to Orlando Premium Outlets Boulevard via Universal Boulevard, the Convention Center and SeaWorld. Running every day, 8am–10.30pm at roughly 20-minute intervals (30 minutes on the Green Line), it costs $1/trip (25c for seniors) – please have the right change – or you can buy Unlimited Ride Passes for 1, 3, 5, 7 or 14 days at $3, $5, $7, $9, $16. If you need to transfer between routes, ask for a transfer coupon when you board (not required with Unlimited Ride Passes). Kids 12 and under go free with an adult, and all trolleys have hydraulic lifts for wheelchairs. Passes are sold at more than 100 locations in the I-Drive area, including the Official Visitor Center and most hotel desks but NOT on the trolleys (407 248 9590 or US freephone 1866 243 7483, **iridetrolley.com**).

BRITTIP

Cheapest way to get from I-Drive to Disney? Take the $1.75 Lynx bus Link 50 from SeaWorld – 6600 Sea Harbor Drive – to the Transportation & Ticket Center next to the *Magic Kingdom Park*. All Disney transport then operates from here. You can use the I-Ride Trolley to get to SeaWorld.

Busch Shuttle Express: Another regular service worth noting is from SeaWorld to Busch Gardens in Tampa, with 6 departure points, 8.15–9.30am daily. It costs $10/person but is FREE if you have bought Busch tickets in advance (included in the 5-Park FlexTicket). For more details, see page 12 or call locally on 1800 221 1339 toll-free.

Shuttle services

An alternative to public transport are the well-organised firms offering set-fee shuttles to the attractions that pick up at hotels. There are more than a dozen, with everything from Hummer limos to buses.

Mears: The most comprehensive service, with a 1,000-vehicle fleet from limousines to town cars and coaches. Typical round-trip shuttle fares would be: airport to *Walt Disney World*, round-trip $32 adults, $24 under-12s, under-4s free ($19 and $15 one way); airport to I-Drive, $28 and $21 ($17 and $13 one way); airport to Highway 192 in Kissimmee $44 and $35 ($25 and $21 one way); *Walt Disney World* to Universal Orlando, $16 round trip; I-Drive to *Walt Disney World*, $16; I-Drive or *Walt Disney World* to Kennedy Space Center, $30. You can book a Mears shuttle on arrival at one of its desks in the luggage halls, but be aware it can be a longish journey if it has a full van making several hotel drop-offs before yours (407 423 5566, **mears transportation.com**).

Several shopping malls also have their own shuttle service.

- **Lake Buena Vista Factory Stores:** Collects guests free each day from 49 hotels in the Orlando and Kissimmee areas. Ask at your hotel (407 363 1093, **lbvfs.com**).
- **Orlando Premium Outlets:** Provides a free shuttle from 15 Lake Buena Vista area hotels or for $10 a round trip from Kissimmee hotels (call at least 2 hours in advance on 407 390 0000).
- **Florida Mall:** Free shuttle service twice daily from hotels on I-Drive and in Lake Buena Vista (check with your hotel concierge or call 407 851 6255).

There are also excursion services offered by the likes of *Brit Guide* partners **Florida Dolphin Tours** (407 352 5151, **floridadolphintours.com**) and **Gator Tours** (see pages 269–70).

Town cars and limousines

When it comes to limousine, town car and other transport services, there is again a wide range of choice (more than 300 at the last count!). The following trio have all earned a *Brit Guide* recommendation:

A 'town car' is an American term for a deluxe saloon, such as a Cadillac or Lincoln.

Quick Transportation: A good bet for airport transfers and tailor-made transport packages, its town cars comfortably cope with a family of 4, while luxury vans cater for larger parties and all offer a ½-hour grocery stop, if required, for an extra $20.

Luxury van rates (for up to 7) one-way from the airport range from $54.75 to the I-Drive area up to $81.50 for the farthest parts of *Walt Disney World.* Up to 11 can use a van for a small additional fee per person. Larger parties may need a luggage trailer for $20 extra each way. Town car rates are $104 from the airport to anywhere in Greater Orlando and $207 for a round trip, while stretch limos are $175 and $350. It serves all the parks and attractions and offers online quotes for all services, while it can also supply vehicles for the disabled and will quote for Orlando Sanford International Airport pick-ups, too (407 354 2456 or 1888 784 2522, **quicktransportation.com**).

Skyy Limousine: Not only a dynamic, well-run company, it also has one of the largest selections of vehicles in Orlando, from Lincoln town cars and executive vans to the amazing Hummer limo and its Limo bus. One-way airport transfers at $65 (plus a 20% driver gratuity), and vehicles can also be hired by the hour from $50/hour. Other options cover much of central Florida, with cruise transfers, a night-on-the-town, all-day services, beach trips, concerts and tailor-made excursions (407 352 4644 or **skyylimousine.com**).

FL Tours: This well-established and popular company specialises in both airport–Disney routes and Port Canaveral transfers. One-way trips start from $60 and round trips from $109 ($119 and $229 from Orlando Sanford International Airport), plus gratuity; it also offers a free ½-hour grocery stop, free kids' booster and car seats, 24-hour online reservation access, and no charge for late pick-ups (407 857 9606, **fltours.com**).

Mears town car

You can look up the full airport list at **orlandoairports.net/ops/vfh.htm**.

Taxis

For groups of 4 or 5, taxis can be a more cost-effective option than the shuttles. Orlando International Airport to I-Drive would be around $35 (plus tip), making it around $7 each for 5; $45–55 for the Kissimmee area; $60 to *Magic Kingdom* resorts and $55 for the *Epcot* resort area; $10–15 from I-Drive to Universal Orlando; and $25 from I-Drive to *Downtown Disney*. You will find plenty of taxis waiting in ranks at the parks, hotels and shopping centres, but they don't cruise around looking for fares, so it is usually best to book one in advance. You also need to ensure you choose a reliable, fully insured company (Orlando has what are known as 'gypsy' cab drivers, who appear to be with reputable firms but often do not have full passenger insurance). Check that the name and phone number of the cab company is clearly displayed on the side, the driver's ID and insurance are visible and the rates are shown on the window or inside the car. 'Gypsy' drivers look for fares in the airport baggage hall, which is strictly illegal; all legitimate taxis should be in the rank on Level 1.

Mears: A group of 3 firms – Checker Cabs, Yellow Cabs and City Cabs (407 422 2222) – all of which are reliable. Mears is the main taxi company for Orlando Sanford International Airport, and you can pre-book its cabs for around $78 to I-Drive, $93 to Lake Buena Vista and $98 to Disney hotels. Most taxis are metered but it is also acceptable to ask in advance what the fare will be.

Other reputable firms: Ace Metro/ Luxury Cab (407 855 1111), **Star Taxis** (407 857 9999) and **Diamond Cab Co** (407 523 3333). Several hotels have town cars at their ranks, and these will not have meters, so you can either ask for the fare or call one of the companies listed above.

BRITTIP Double check you have your driving licence BEFORE you leave home (both parts of it with the new photo-card type). Without it you will simply NOT be given a hire car.

THE CAR

Ultimately, having a car is the key to being in charge of your holiday and, on a weekly basis, car hire tends to work out quite reasonable.

BRITTIP The boot (trunk) size of American cars tends to be slightly smaller than the British equivalent. And you will not get 7 adults PLUS all their luggage in a 7-seat people carrier ('van')!

Weekly rental rates can be as low as $100 for the smallest car, an **Economy** (or sub-compact), usually a Vauxhall Corsa-sized hatchback; next up is the **Compact**, a small family saloon like a Ford Focus; the **Midsize** (or Intermediate) is a more spacious 4-door, 5-seater like a Mondeo; and the **Fullsize** would be a larger-style executive car like a Peugeot 407. You can go up the scale further, with **Premium**, **Luxury** and **Convertible**, plus the **Minivan** (a Ford Galaxy or Renault Espace type). The car models, will, of course, be mainly American – Chevrolet, Dodge, Pontiac, Buick, Chrysler, Ford, Mercury and Lincoln. But beware of the low starting rates – there are essential insurances, taxes and surcharges that can take the weekly rate to $300 or more. However, all the big rental companies now offer all-inclusive rates, which can work out significantly cheaper if booked in advance in the UK, and you also benefit from easier processing at the Orlando end, making the whole business quicker.

BRITTIP Be firm with the car hire company check-in clerk; some can push you into having extras, like car upgrades, you don't need.

The scale of the car hire operation is huge, with as many as 1,000 visitors arriving at a time. Most holiday companies offer 'free car hire', but that doesn't mean it won't cost you anything. Only the rental cost is free and you must still pay the insurances, taxes and other extras (which makes the all-inclusive packages much more attractive).

BRITTIP Your first call for car hire should be to *Brit Guide* partners Alamo. See inside the front cover for our special readers' offer.

Car rental companies: Alamo is our *Brit Guide* partner and offers excellent rates and service (see inside front cover). For other companies, you can try **Dollar** (0808 234 7524), **Avis** (0844 581 0147), **Budget** (0844 581 9998), **Thrifty** (01494 751 540), **Hertz** (0870 841 5161), **National** (0870 400 4581) or **Suncars** (0871 664 9680).

BRITTIP Unless you have accepted the SunPass pre-pay auto-toll option from the car rental firm, you cannot drive through the toll booths marked 'Sunpass' or 'E-Pass' only. You must stop at the booths marked 'Change Given' (in green) or 'Exact Change Only' (in blue).

Insurance: Having a credit card is essential, and there are two main kinds of insurance, the most important being the Loss or Collision Damage Waiver (LDW or CDW). This costs $23–25 a day and covers you for any damage to your hire car. You can do without it, but the hire company will insist on a deposit in the order of $1,500 on your credit card (and you are liable for ANY damage). You will also be offered Supplemental Liability Insurance (SLI) or Extended Protection at around $13 a day, which is not essential but does cover you against being sued by any litigious American you may bump into. Relatively new and again optional is the Underinsured Motorists Protection (in case somebody with only minimal cover runs into you) at around $6 a day. Drivers must be at least 21, and those under 25 have to pay an extra $25 a day. Other costs include local and Florida state taxes, which can add $20 a week to your bill, and an Airport User Fee at $6–7 a day. Many companies also try to get you to take out Roadside Plus (around $5/day), which covers any breakdowns or locking your keys in the car, but this really is a bit steep to our mind (why should you have to pay if *their* car breaks down?).

Then there is **fuel**, though this is much cheaper than in the UK. You can either *pre-pay* for a full tank (so you bring it back empty; the charge is usually slightly under the local rate/gallon for this); *fill it up yourself* so you have a full tank on return; or pay a *fuel surcharge* at the end for the company to re-fill the tank (the most expensive option).

You can even accept the new SunPass auto-pay system (Dollar calls it Pass24) for the area's toll roads, so you don't have to stop at the toll booths (where some serious queues can build up) but just drive through and have all your tolls auto-recorded for payment when you return the car (along with a $4–6/day 'convenience fee').

Those on a budget can cut costs by taking travel insurance through specialists like **Extrasure** (01242 518300, **extrasureonline.co.uk**), whose Americasure policy offers both LDW and SLI at around £14 a day. You may still need to leave a credit card imprint with the hire firm, but it should accept these policies (but check in advance).

Controls

Most people soon find driving in America is a pleasure, mainly because nearly all hire cars are automatics and nearly new. And, because speed limits are lower (and rigidly enforced), you won't often be rushed into taking a wrong turn. Keep your foot on the brake when you are stationary as automatics tend to creep forward, and always put the gear lever in 'P' (for Park) after switching off.

All cars have air-conditioning, which is essential for most of the year. Turn on the fan with the A/C button or it won't work! Don't worry if a small pool of liquid forms under the car – it's condensation from the A/C unit. Power steering is also universal and larger cars have cruise control, which lets you set the desired speed and take your foot off the accelerator. There will be 2 buttons on the steering wheel, one to switch on cruise control, the other to set the desired speed. To cancel cruise control, either press the first button again or simply touch the brake. The handbrake may also be different. Some cars have an extra pedal to the left of the brake, and you need to push this to engage the handbrake. To release it, you pull the tab just above it, if there is one, or give a second push on the pedal. The car probably won't start unless the gear lever is in 'P'. To put the car in 'D' for Drive, depress the brake pedal. D1 and D2 are extra gears for steep hills (none in Florida!). Not all cars have central locking, though, so make sure you lock ALL the doors before leaving it.

BRITTIP

With an automatic, you won't be able to take the keys out of the ignition unless you put the gear lever in the 'Park' position first.

Getting around

Your car hire company should provide you with a basic map of Orlando, plus directions to your hotel. Insist it gives you these, as all the hire companies make a big point of this in their literature. Try to familiarise yourself with the main roads in advance and learn to navigate by the road numbers (as it's mainly those that are given on the signposts) and the exit numbers of the main roads.

BRITTIP

Be organised – get your directions in advance off the internet at sites like **mapquest.com** or use Google Earth to source maps, directions and even check out the lie of the land in advance. Download it free from its website at **http://earth.google.com**.

The signposting and road-naming systems can be confusing. For instance, you can't fail to find the main attractions, but retracing your steps can be tricky as the exit road may be different from the way in. It's vital to learn the road numbers (and directions, east–west or north–south) around the attractions so you know where you're heading, and if you want I-4 east or west or 192 as you exit *Walt Disney World*. Exits off motorways can be on EITHER side of the carriageway, not just on the right, but you can overtake in ANY lane on multi-lane highways. Therefore, you can sit in the middle lane until you see your exit. You don't get much advance notice of turn-offs, though.

Orlando has yet to come up with a comprehensive tourist map of its streets, and the maps supplied by the car rental companies are pretty basic. It helps that none of the main attractions are off the beaten track, but the support of a front-seat navigator can be useful. Around town, road names are displayed at every junction, hung underneath the traffic lights but suspended ABOVE the road. This road name is NOT the road you are on, but the one you are CROSSING. Once again there is little advance notice of each junction and the road names can be hard to read as you approach, especially at night, so keep your speed down if you think you are close to your turn-off to allow time to get into the correct lane. If you do miss a turning, most roads are on a grid system, so it is easy to work your way back.

Occasionally you will meet a crossroads where no right of way is obvious. This is a 4-way stop, and the priority goes in order of arrival. So, when it's your turn, you just indicate and pull out slowly (America doesn't have many roundabouts, so this may be the closest you get to one).

BRITTIP

Disney is notoriously poor at signposting to help find your way out. Ask for a copy of its Transportation Guide/Map from Guest Services.

Tolls and traffic lights

For the toll roads, have some change handy in amounts from 25c to $2. They all give change (in the GREEN lanes), but you will get through quicker if you have the correct money (in the BLUE lanes). On minor exits of Osceola Parkway and the Greeneway, there are auto-toll machines only, so keep some loose change in the car. As well as the obvious difference of driving on the 'wrong' side of the road, there are several differences in procedure. The most frequent British errors occur at traffic lights (which are hung above the road, not on posts). At a red light it is still possible to turn RIGHT, providing there is no traffic coming from the left and no pedestrians crossing, unless otherwise specified (occasionally signs will indicate 'No turn on red'). Turning left at the lights, you have the right of way with a green ARROW, but you have to give way to traffic from the other direction on a SOLID green.

The majority of accidents involving overseas visitors take place on left turns, so take extra care here. There is also no amber light from red to green, but there IS from green to red. A flashing amber light at a junction means proceed but watch for traffic joining the carriageway, while a flashing red light indicates it is okay to turn if the carriageway is clear.

BRITTIP
The Osceola Parkway toll road that runs parallel to Highway 192 is a better route in to *Walt Disney World* from eastern Kissimmee and costs only $1.50. Use Sherberth Road for Disney access from west 192 or the new Western Beltway (Highway 429).

Restrictions

Speed limits are always well marked with black numbering on white signs and the police are pretty hot on speeding, with steep on-the-spot fines. Limits vary from 55–70mph/88–113kph on the Interstates (where there is also a 40mph/64kph minimum speed limit) to just 15–20mph/24–32kph in built-up areas. Seat belts are compulsory for all passengers, while **child seats** must be used for under-4s and can be hired from the car companies at $10–15 a day (better still, bring your own or buy one locally for $70–80). Children aged 4 or 5 must use a seat belt, in the front or back, or have a child seat fitted.

It is illegal to park within 3m/10ft of a fire hydrant or a lowered kerb, and never park in front of a yellow-painted kerb – they are stopping points for emergency vehicles and you will be towed away. Never park ON a kerb, either. Park bonnet first – reverse parking is frowned upon because number plates are only on the rear of cars and police then can't see them. If you park parallel to the kerb, you must face the direction of traffic. Flashing orange lights over the road indicate a school zone; school buses must NOT be overtaken in either direction when they are unloading and have their hazard lights on. U-turns are forbidden in built-up areas and where there is a solid line down the middle of the road. You must pull to the side of the road to allow emergency vehicles to pass, in either direction, when they have lights and/or sirens going. Also, on multi-lane highways in Florida, the recent Move Over law means you must pull out into an adjacent lane if you see a police car on the hard shoulder, or slow down if you can't move over. And you must put on your lights in the rain.

BRITTIP
On the Greeneway (417) heading south, just after exit 34, it appears to split into two where it meets Highway 408. Stay in the RIGHT lane to stay southbound. Be aware also on the 471 and 429 that at the manned toll booths you have to pull in to a slip road on the right as it is SunPass/E-Pass *only* on the main carriageway.

Finally, DON'T drink and drive. Florida has strict laws, with penalties of up to 6 months in prison for first-time offenders. The blood-alcohol limit is lower than in Britain, so it is safer not to drink at all if you are driving. It is also illegal to carry open containers of alcohol in the car.

Bonus for AA members: Your membership is recognised by the equivalent AAA in the US and you also benefit from a number of special offers. Take your AA card and, where you see the AAA 'Show & Save' signs in hotels, shops and restaurants, just produce it to enjoy the same money-saving benefits as the locals. Visit **aaasouth.com** and click on Savings for the full low-down (use the zip code 32819 when prompted).

Accidents

In the unlikely event of an accident, no matter how minor, you must contact the police before the cars can be moved (except on the busy I-4). Car hire firms will insist on a full police report for the insurance. If you break down, there should be an emergency

The SatNav Solution

Of course, the best way to navigate these days is by a GPS or SatNav system. All car hire companies now offer this as an extra (at $50–70/week), or you can bring your own. If your system has only the base-level (i.e. UK) maps loaded, you can download the necessary maps for south-east USA for around £35. If you are thinking of buying a GPS system, the likes of Wal-Mart offer new systems, fully loaded for the US, for less than $200.

number for the hire company in its literature or, if you are on a main highway, raise the bonnet and wait for one of the frequent police patrol cars to stop (or dial *FHP on your mobile). Always carry your driving licence (*both* parts with the new card type) and hire agreement forms in case you are stopped by the police.

Key routes

Interstate 4: I-4 is the main route through Orlando, a 4-, 6- or 8-lane motorway linking the coasts. Interstates are always indicated on blue shield-shaped signs. For most of its length, I-4 travels east–west but, around Orlando, it swings north–south, though directions are still given east (for north) or west (for south). All main motorways are prefixed I, the even numbers going east–west and odd numbers north–south. Federal Highways are the next grade down, numbered with black numerals on white shields, while state roads are called Routeways and are prefixed SR (black numbers on white circular or rectangular signs). All the attractions of *Walt Disney World*, plus SeaWorld and Universal Orlando are well signposted from I-4. Bok Tower Gardens and Cypress Gardens are a 45-minute drive from central Orlando west (south) on I-4 and Highway 27, while Busch Gardens is 75–90 minutes down I-4 to Tampa. I-4 is regularly affected by roadworks, and you can check the latest up-dates on **trans4mation.org**.

All American motorways have their junctions numbered in mileage terms, which makes it easy to calculate journey distances. I-4 starts at exit 1 in Tampa and goes all the way to exit 132 at Daytona. In Orlando, the main junctions run from exit 55, at Highway 27, to exit 83 (downtown Orlando) and exit 101, for the Seminole Expressway (417) and Sanford International Airport.

International Drive: I-Drive is the second key local roadway, linking a 14½ml/24km ribbon of hotels, shops, restaurants and attractions like Wet 'n Wild, The Pointe Orlando and Festival Bay (I-Drive South, from Highway 192 in Kissimmee north to Route 535, is NOT the main stretch and the 2 sections are linked via Route 535 and World Center Drive). From I-4, take exits 71, 72, 74A or 75A going east (north), or 75B, 74A or 72 going west (south). To the north, I-Drive runs into Oak Ridge Road and the South Orange Blossom Trail, which leads to downtown Orlando (junctions 82C–84 off I-4). I-Drive is also bisected by Sand Lake Road and runs into World Center Drive (536), to the south, also convenient for Disney. I-Drive is a major tourist centre and makes an excellent base, especially around the Sand Lake Road junction, as it is fully pedestrian-friendly. It's a 20-minute drive to Disney and 10 minutes from Universal. However, at peak times, heavy traffic means it's best to avoid the stretch from the Convention Center north. Use Universal Boulevard instead.

Kissimmee: The other main tourist area, south of Orlando and south-east of Disney, its features are grouped along a 20ml/32km stretch of the Irlo Bronson Memorial Highway (192), which intersects I-4 at junction 64B, and is close to *Walt Disney World* (though a good 20–25 minutes from SeaWorld and Universal). The downtown area of Kissimmee is off Main Street, Broadway and Emmett Street and is ideal for walking. A handy visual along Highway 192 is the Marker Series from Formosa Gardens (number 4) to just past Medieval Times (number 15). These highly visible signs are good locators for hotels, restaurants and attractions, and much of this stretch is also walkable (though few places are close together). The unique Disney-inspired town of **Celebration** is also here (just south of *Walt Disney World*). At the west end of **Highway 192**, you find **Highway 27**, which runs north to Clermont and south to Davenport (and Haines City). Highway 27 is a major area of holiday home developments that are, generally, quite convenient for Disney. However, many home owners claim they are only '5 minutes from Disney', which is extremely misleading. It is usually a good 15 minutes from Highway 27 to the edge of Disney property. The area is also starting to add shops and restaurants, notably in the Cagan Crossings junction (just north of where 192 meets 27), where there's a new outlet of the excellent Sherlock's restaurant group, plus some boutique shops and a large Wal-Mart.

Western Beltway: The new 429 provides a western Orlando 'by-pass', avoiding the often-crowded I-4 and linking with the Florida Turnpike and Apopka to the north. More importantly, it offers an alternative west gateway to *Walt Disney World* at Exit 8 (Western Way), which is handy for the Davenport/Clermont areas. This junction is also set to see much new development in the next 4 years.

Fuel

All local petrol, or 'gas', stations are self-service and most require you to pay before filling up. However, the pumps should allow you to pay by credit card without having to visit the cashier (some stations ask for a local zip code with a credit card swipe, and this means you DO need to go inside). To activate the petrol pump, you may need first to lift the lever underneath the pump nozzle. Race Trac and Hess petrol stations are often the cheapest. The two Hess stations in *Walt Disney World* are, surprisingly, among the cheapest in the area, while the Wal-Mart on SR535 (Vineland Road) is also a cheap option. Petrol stations in Lake Buena Vista just outside Disney are the MOST expensive.

Local maps

The best of the free maps is the bright orange *Welcome Guide Map* (also full of discount coupons), available in the main tourist areas, and the pull-out map inside the *Kissimmee-St Cloud Visitors' Guide* (from the Official Visitor Center on East Highway 192, 407 847 5000). You can also download some useful maps from its website **floridakiss.com** (under Travel Tools). AA members are also well catered for (see page 60).

Enter Mapman

By far the best and most up-to-date (fully updated in 2008) map of the area is a British production, created by Disney fan and cartographer Steve Munns, at £6.95 (plus 78p p&p). It is magnificently detailed for the I-4 corridor, Highway 192 and *Walt Disney World*, with special sections on I-Drive and villa locations. All the main attractions, hotels and even many restaurants are clearly indicated and there is accompanying text and photographs. The website provides regular updates to important landmarks and other insider tips. The latest edition is also on a heavier-grade paper and is far more robust. We think it's the perfect companion to the *Brit Guide* and you won't go wrong with it. Just visit **orlandomaps.co.uk** (online orders only). Happily, Steve is also now our resident 'mapman' for the 2009 *Brit Guide*!

Now, let's go on to the next vital step – your holiday accommodation…

4 Accommodation

or Making Sense of American Hotels, Motels and Condos

To list all the accommodation in this area would fill a book much larger than this. Metro Orlando has the second highest concentration of hotels in the world (after Las Vegas) and more are being built all the time – with 115,000 rooms (plus some 26,000 villas for rent) and counting. Therefore what follows is a general guide to the bigger, better and budget types.

HOTELS

American hotels, particularly in the tourist areas, tend towards the motel type. The service and facilities are fine but are not necessarily all located in one main building. Your room may be in one of several blocks sited round the pool, restaurant or other amenities. Room size rarely alters, even from 2- to 4-star hotels; their amenities and services form the basis of their star ratings. A standard room usually has 2 double beds and will accommodate a family of 4 (couples should ask for a king room, with an extra-size bed). All hotels should offer non-smoking rooms. Motel-type accommodation often lacks a restaurant as American hotels operate on a room-only basis, so you may have to drive to the nearest restaurant (of which there are many – see Chapter 11, Dining Out) just for breakfast. Check the dining facilities before you book.

Most hotels are big, clean, efficient and great value. You'll find plenty of soft-drink and ice machines, with ice buckets in all the rooms (though it's cheaper to buy drinks from a supermarket). All accommodation will be air-conditioned and, when it is really hot, you have to live with the drone of the A/C unit at night. If you need a more spacious room, look for one of the many suite hotels, which provide sitting rooms and mini-kitchens, as well as 1, 2 or even 3 bedrooms.

Hotels are also the most expensive places from which to make a phone call. Most add a 45–70% surcharge to every call (Disney resorts even add a connection fee), while you can even be charged for an unanswered call, if

Disney's Beach Club Resort

it rings 5 or more times. Buy a phonecard instead (see pages 37 and 46). Remember, too, hotel prices (in this book and in Orlando) are always per *room* (not per person). They will be cheaper out of the main holiday periods but can vary from month to month, with special deals at times. Always ask for rates if you book yourself and check if any special rates apply during your visit (don't be afraid to ask for their 'best rate' at off-peak times, which can be lower than published or 'rack' rates). There may be an additional charge ($5–15/person) for more than 2 adults sharing the same room, plus there is a per night state tax and, sometimes, a resort fee that can add $10–20/day to the rate.

BRITTIP

Buy soft drinks at the supermarket, and a polystyrene cooler for about $4 that you can fill from your hotel ice machine to keep drinks cold.

If you've just arrived and need a hotel, visit one of the official Visitor Centers: International Drive just north of The Pointe Orlando (on the corner of Austrian Court, 8.30am–6.30pm daily; 407 363 5872); or on east Highway 192 in Kissimmee (8am–5pm Mon–Fri; 407 847 5000), where they have brochures and info on all the latest deals. If you're keen on auction websites like **priceline.co.uk**, you may land a bargain. Other useful agencies are **Expedia** (0871 226 0808, **expedia.co.uk**), **Hotel Anywhere** (01444 410 555, **hotelanywhere.co.uk**), the multi-search facility **Travel Supermarket** (**travelsupermarket.com**), and, in the US, **Hotels.com** (0800 547 6561 in the UK, or 1800 346 8357 in the US, **hotels.co.uk**) and **Orbitz** (1888 656 4546 in the US or 001 312 416 0018 from the UK, **orbitz.com**).

There is no widely accepted star rating, so (with the exception of Disney's resorts), we group hotels into 4 ranges: Budget, Standard, Superior and Deluxe, where the rough price groups per night will be:

* Budget	=	up to $50
* Standard	=	$51–99
* Superior	=	$100–160
* Deluxe	=	$161 plus

Our price guide is only a rough reckoner as rates can vary from month to month. The main factor to bear in mind is the extra facilities involved. Hence, a Deluxe grading will include the highest level of facilities and service, while a Budget grade will be a basic motel-type. A key factor in price, though, is your location – the closer to Disney and the other parks, the higher the price. So, you can save money if you don't mind a longer distance between the parks and your accommodation.

Suite things

Suites hotels, virtually unknown in the UK, provide a combination of hotel and apartment, with extra value for large families or groups. Typically, a suites room gives you a living room and kitchenette, including microwave, coffee-maker, fridge, cutlery and crockery, while many offer a complimentary continental breakfast (or better). All have pools and grocery stores or snack bars and several have restaurants. They vary only in the number of bedrooms and can usually sleep 6–10 people.

Disney hotels

Our review of Orlando's hotels starts with Walt Disney World Resort. Conveniently sited for all its attractions – and linked by an excellent free transport system of monorail, buses and boats – Disney's hotels, suites and campsites are all magnificently appointed and maintained. It also groups them into 4 types: Value (equal to our Standard category), Moderate (our Superior), Deluxe (the same) and Home Away From Home (with a strong element of self-catering – Wilderness Lodge Villas, Old Key West, Boardwalk Villas,

Kidsuites = happy families!

Orlando has pioneered a new type of family accommodation in recent years, and these are worth seeking out if you have kids who enjoy bunk beds. Basically, a kidsuite is a separate area within the hotel room that gives kids their own 'bedroom' (with bunks), usually also with their own TV and games console.

Saratoga Springs Resort & Spa and Fort Wilderness cabins). They range from the Deluxe Grand Floridian Resort & Spa to the Value but still fun style of the Pop Century Resort – and Disney's imagination and attention to detail here are as good as at the theme parks. There are some 28,000 rooms, while Fort Wilderness Resort & Campground has 1,190 sites.

Grand accommodation comes at a price, though. A regular room at the Grand Floridian can be $700 a night in high season (suites can top $2,000) and even the Moderate Caribbean Beach Resort can be $160 a night. Dining at resort hotels is not cheap either, and you'll find few fast-food outlets on site. However, staying with the Mouse is one of the great thrills, for the style, service and extras. The 19 resorts (20 later in 2009) offer a superb array of facilities, and children especially love being a part of Disney full-time. The benefits are:

- Resort ID card: Every guest receives a card with which to charge to their room account almost all food, gifts and services bought while on site.
- Package delivery: In conjunction with your ID card, you can have park purchases sent back to your hotel gift shop.
- Free parking: With your ID card, there is no charge at any of the Disney car parks.
- Free transport: Leave the car behind and use the monorail-bus-boat network.
- Refillable mugs: All Disney resorts sell collectable drinking mugs, which are well worth buying ($13 each) as you can then get free refills at their self-service cafés.
- Dining priority: Many Disney restaurants hold tables for resort guests, while you can also book 180 days in advance *plus* the length of your stay (i.e. 194 days if you are going for 2 weeks). Call 407 939 3463 or dial *88 on any Disney phone or press the Dining button on your resort phone (non-Disney hotel guests can book only 180 days in advance).
- Priority golf: The best tee times are reserved for resort guests and can be booked 90 days in advance on 407 939 4653.
- Children's services: All resorts have in-room or group babysitting (subject to availability, so book in advance on 407 827 5444) and 8 of the 9 Deluxe resorts have supervised activity centres and dinner clubs (around $11/child per hour), usually open until midnight.
- Mickey on call: What better way to wake than with an alarm call from the Mouse himself?
- Extra Magic Hours: This is the BIG bonus, the chance to get into one of the parks each day either 1 hour early or for 3 hours after regular park closing, and enjoy many rides with reduced crowds.

Disney's All-Star Movies Resort

Value resorts

Disney's All-Star Resorts: These were Disney's first foray into the more modestly priced market in 1994. Here you can stay in one of the 5 *Sports*-themed blocks (surfing, basketball, tennis, baseball and American football) centred around a massive food court, 2 swimming pools, a games arcade and shops; the *Music*-themed version (Jazz, Rock, Broadway, Calypso and Country); or the *Movies* complex (Mighty Ducks, 101 Dalmatians, Fantasia, Love Bug and Toy Story). The latter is possibly the most imaginative, with its Fantasia pool and kids' play areas, and the most popular blocks are Toy Story and 101 Dalmatians (both non-smoking). All 3 centres, with 5,760 rooms, have pool bars, shops, laundry facilities, video games rooms and a pizza delivery service. The All Star Music Resort has also recently been converted to 192 impressive 2-room suites sleeping up to 6. Each suite has 2 bathrooms, a well-stocked kitchenette, a lounge and private master bedroom, making the accommodation choice here more flexible. Standard rooms are bright and compact (if a little tight for families of 4 with older children), but well designed for those who want all the Disney conveniences but not the price tag. Close to the entrance is a large McDonald's if the resort's food court doesn't appeal. All resort transport is provided by an efficient bus service.

BRITTIP

To make a reservation at any Walt Disney World Resort, call 407 934 7639. For further information, visit **disneyworld.co.uk**.

Disney's Pop Century Resort: In a similar vein, themed round the decades of the 20th century, there are 10 blocks with giant icons – such as yo-yos, Rubik's cubes and juke-boxes – and a riot of period sayings and visual gags. The first half of the resort (the Classic Years, 1950s–90s) opened in December 2003 and features a pool fashioned like a huge 10-pin bowling lane (the other 2 are shaped like a computer and a flower), a huge table football set-up and open-air Twister mats. Blocks are grouped around a main building housing a spacious check-in area (with a large-screen TV showing Disney films), an imaginative food court, a lounge (with quick-breakfast bar), a Disney store and games arcade. The 177 acre/72ha complex also features a central lake and lots of bright landscaping. It all adds significantly to Disney's budget-orientated offerings and has a well-organised bus service to the parks. The drawbacks? Long queues to check in for much of the afternoon and a rather hectic feel, even late in the evening. You need to request a hairdryer from reception and rooms are, again, rather small.

Moderate resorts

Disney's Caribbean Beach Resort: Opened in 1988 with 2,112 rooms spread over 5 Caribbean 'islands' (with an inter-island bus service), rooms are still relatively plain but comfortably sleep 4, and the food court, main restaurant Shutters, and outdoor activities (with a lakeside recreation area with themed waterfalls, slides and games arcade) are a big hit with children. The 6 counter-service outlets in the food court at Old Port Royale Town Center (the hub of this pretty resort) can get busy in the morning, and the Trinidad South and Barbados 'islands' are a fair walk from the centre. But it is an action-packed resort with some imaginative touches, like Parrot Cay Island Playground with its tropical birds and play area. Transport to all the parks is solely by bus.

Disney's Coronado Springs Resort: Possibly the best value of this trio as it is newer (built in 1997) and has slightly more facilities for its 1,921 rooms spread over 125 acres/50ha: 4

pools (including the massive Lost City of Cibola), 2 games arcades, a boating marina, bike rentals, restaurant, food court and convenience store, lounge bar, gift shop, beauty salon and health club, business centre and 2 guest launderettes. New in 2008 was the chic and very upscale Rix Lounge, a combination bar/nightclub serving unique cocktails and appetisers. Constructed on a scenic Mexican/ Spanish theme in 3 'villages' (Casitas, Ranchos and Cabanas), Coronado is an often-overlooked treasure. Check out the Maya Grill and its New Latino cuisine. Coronado Springs is also only 5 minutes from *Disney's Animal Kingdom* and is well served by the bus network.

Disney's Port Orleans Resort: Opened in 1991, this is a 2-part complex (formerly Port Orleans and Dixie Landings) split into the 2,048-room *Riverside* – with a steamboat reception area, a great Riverside Mill food court, Boatwright's full-service restaurant, the River Roost lounge (with live entertainment on certain nights) and an old-fashioned general store (the gift shop) – and the 1,008-room *French Quarter*, which has the Sassagoula Floatworks and Food Factory court, 2 bars, a games room and shopping arcade. The Riverside includes Ol' Man Island, a magnificent 3½ acre/1.5ha playground with swimming pool, kids' area and a fishing hole, while the French Quarter has Doubloon Lagoon, with Mardi Gras dragon slide, alligator fountains and a play area. The eye-catching landscaping and design vary from rustic Bayou backwoods to turn-of-the-century New Orleans. Transport for both sections is by bus to the parks and bus or boat to *Downtown Disney.*

BRITTIP

Disney resort restaurants can (and we think should) be visited even if you aren't staying there. Advance book at any of the parks from any Disney phone (dial *88) or call 407 WDW DINE.

Deluxe resorts

More than anything, Disney specialises in high-quality hotels with all manner of grand design features, amenities and restaurants. All 9 offer a Concierge level, which adds an exclusive, personalised service, and a private lounge with meals and snacks.

Disney's Animal Kingdom Lodge: This stunning private game lodge (which opened in 2001) is on the edge of a 33 acre/13ha animal-filled savannah, which many rooms overlook. The pervasive African theme is almost overwhelming, and the effect of opening your curtains to a vista of giraffes and zebras is immense. This wonderful creativity comes before you consider the amenities of this 1,293-room resort (which adds a new wing, Kidani Village, in 2009): 2 restaurants, café, bar, elaborately themed 'watering-hole' main pool (with waterslide) and kids' pool, massage and fitness centre, large gift shop, children's play area and an awesome 4-storey atrium. The main restaurant, Jiko, is spectacular, but there is also the buffet-style Boma, a 'marketplace' restaurant featuring African-tinged dishes from a wood-burning grill and rotisserie for breakfast and dinner.

Disney's Port Orleans Resort

The lavishness and detail are superb, right down to the guides who can tell guests about the 200 animals and their habitats, the African folklore stories around the outdoor firepit and the chance for children to become junior safari researchers while Mum and Dad do some wine-tasting (the hotel boasts the largest collection of South African wines in America).

BRITTIP

Jiko at Disney's Animal Kingdom Lodge offers an imaginative, New World cuisine menu, attentive service and authentic ambience, and is a wonderfully romantic choice.

Rooms range from standard doubles to 1- and 2-bedroom suites, some of which have bunk beds. Simba's Cubhouse is for 4–12s (4.30pm–midnight), and all transport is by bus (with the *Animal Kingdom* barely 5 minutes away). Part of the main building of the Lodge (now called Jambo House) has been converted into studios and 1- and 2-bed villas (the latter of which boast full kitchens) for Disney Vacation Club guests, sleeping 4–12, but these will also be available to regular guests when not in use for the DVC programme. New in 2009 will be the Kidani Village wing (also for DVC), with similar 1- and 2-bed villas, plus 16 2-storey Grand Villas. Additional features will be a 120-seat fine-dining restaurant, Sanaa (for breakfast and dinner), an extensive pool with slide, bar and Jacuzzis, and a huge kids' water play area, plus extended animal savannahs.

Disney's Animal Kingdom Lodge

© Disney

Disney's BoardWalk Inn and Villas: One of the Crescent Lake resorts next to *Epcot*, completed in 1996 is this 45 acre/18ha extravagant Inn and entertainment 'district'. It features a 372-room hotel, 520 villas, 4 themed restaurants, a TV sports club and 2 nightclubs, plus an array of shops, sports facilities and a huge, free-form swimminuteg pool with a 200ft/60m waterslide, all on a semi-circular boardwalk around the lake. The effect is stunning, and the in-room attention to detail excellent. Highlights are the 'summer cottage' villas, tapas-style restaurant Spoodles (breakfast and dinner) and the Big River Grille Brewing Company (lunch and dinner) for a great range of beers from its own micro-brewery. Top of the lot is the expensive but superb seafood of the Flying Fish Café (dinner only). You can try the Boardwalk Bakery for a snack, while Spoodles has a quick-service window for takeaways. It is a delightful place to visit for a meal, the nightlife (especially Jellyrolls piano bar and ESPN Club) or just to wander along the boardwalk. Transport is by boat to *Epcot* and *Disney's Hollywood Studios* and by bus to the other parks.

Disney's Contemporary Resort: Situated on the monorail, right next to the park, opened with the *Magic Kingdom Park* in 1971, the 15-storey resort has 1,008 remodelled rooms, a cavernous foyer, 5 shops, 4 restaurants, 2 lounges, a real sandy beach, a marina, 2 pools (1 with waterslide), 6 tennis courts, a video games centre and health club – and fabulous views, especially from the superb, hotel-top California Grill (one of the most romantic settings in Orlando; try to get a reservation to coincide with the park's fireworks). Don't miss Chef Mickey's for a breakfast or dinner buffet with your favourite characters, while the monorail runs right *through* the hotel – fascinating for kids. Rooms are some of Disney's largest and were all renovated in 2005/06, adding elegant new decor, dark-wood furniture and ultra-comfy duvets. New in 2008 was the ultra-chic restaurant/lounge The Wave, featuring a modern bar and dining area with a highly varied menu. Within walking distance of the *Magic Kingdom*, transport to other parks is by bus.

Disney's Grand Floridian Resort & Spa: This true 5-star hotel (which opened in 1988) is built like an elaborate Victorian mansion, with 867 rooms, an impressive domed foyer and staff in period costume. Again on the monorail, 1 stop from the *Magic Kingdom*, the rooms and facilities are truly luxurious – hence the mega prices, though it's worth a look even if you are not staying. Its 6 restaurants include the top-of-the-range Victoria and Albert's (where the set 6-course dinner with wine costs $185), the chic seafood-based Narcoossee's (one of our favourites), with its excellent view over Seven Seas Lagoon, and Mediterranean-styled Citricos. You will also find 4 bars and impressive sporting and relaxation facilities, notably the fabulous Spa and Salon. There's a wonderful second pool area, complete with zero-depth entry and waterslide. The Mouseketeer Club caters for 4–12s (4.30pm–midnight) and the 1900 Park Fare restaurant is hugely popular for character breakfasts and dinners, plus the children's Wonderland Tea Party with Alice and friends (1.30–2.30pm Mon–Fri, $28.17/child) and Disney's Pirate Adventure (9.30–11.30am, Mon, Wed, Thurs and Sat, $30/child).

For young princesses, the Garden View Lounge hosts My Disney Girl's Perfectly Princess Tea Party (10.30am–noon daily except Tues and Wed), featuring Princess Aurora from Sleeping Beauty and with storytelling, singalongs and a princess parade, plus a princess doll and gifts for each child (3–11). The cost for 1 adult and child is a whopping $250 ($165 each additional child, plus $85 for an additional adult), but reservations are still advisable on 407 WDW DINE. The Garden View Lounge also serves a variety of traditional Afternoon Teas 2–4.30pm daily, $9–25/head. Transport to the *Magic Kingdom* is by boat and monorail; by bus to the other parks.

BRITTIP

Watch out for the free nightly Electrical Water Pageant on Bay Lake and Seven Seas Lagoon, which you will be able to see from all the Magic Kingdom resorts.

Disney's Grand Floridian Resort & Spa

Disney's Polynesian Resort: The other 1971 original is a South Seas tropical fantasy with modern sophistication and comfort. Beautiful beaches, lush vegetation and architecture are home to 853 rooms built in wooden long-house style, all with balconies and superb views. Also on the monorail line opposite the *Magic Kingdom*, it boasts a lovely 3-storey atrium, with 75 varieties of tropical plants, parrots and a waterfall. The Polynesian's large rooms, like those of the Contemporary Resort, have been extensively refurbished to revive the Pacific isles theme, with custom-made furniture, tapestries and warm, earth colours. The resort offers excellent eating: 'Ohana is an entertaining and stylish dinner venue that also offers lively character breakfasts, while the Kona Café is slightly less formal but still with an extensive menu, and Captain Cook's Snack Company offers more basic counter-service fare. Then there are canoe rentals, a beautiful pool area with waterslide, a games room, shops and children's playground. The Neverland Club caters for 4–12s (4pm–midnight). Catch the monorail or a boat to the *Magic Kingdom*, and buses to the other parks. The Poly is also home to the nightly *Spirit of Aloha* dinner show (see page 306), which is open to non-resort guests and makes a great evening among the torchlit gardens. The Resort's beach is also a great area from which to view the nightly *Magic Kingdom* fireworks.

BRITTIP

Dine in superb South Seas style at 'Ohana's but don't even think of asking for salt – unless you want to spark an amazing reaction…!

Disney's Wilderness Lodge: Opened in 1994 and one of the most picturesque resorts, this is also a great romantic destination. It is a detailed re-creation of a National Park lodge,

© Disney

Disney's Wilderness Lodge

from the stream running through the massive wooden balcony-lined atrium into the gardens, past the swimming pool (with hot and cold spas) to a geyser that erupts each hour. Offering authentic backwoods charm with true luxury, the resort is connected to the *Magic Kingdom* by boat and bus (and buses to the other parks). Rooms are all spacious with some lovely furniture, while the Courtyard View rooms are the best of the regular rooms (though at a slight premium). Deluxe rooms sleep up to 6 and the suites (at up to $815 a night) are truly sumptuous. It also has 2 restaurants: the brilliant Artist's Point (lunch and dinner) and the Whispering Canyon Café (lively breakfast and huge all-you-can-eat buffets) – plus a snack bar and pool bar. The Cubs' Den is for 4–12s (4.30pm–midnight). The Villas at Wilderness Lodge is a Home Away From Home development of 136 studios and 1- and 2-bed villas. Facilities include living areas, kitchens, private balconies and whirlpool baths. There is a quiet pool area, a spa and health club.

Disney's Yacht and Beach Club Resorts: Refined and almost intimate, Disney added more quality when these opened in 1990 with 630 and 583 nautical-themed rooms respectively. Set around Crescent Lake next to the *Epcot* park, they help to form one massive resort area that is a delight to walk around at any time but especially at night. For dinner, the Yachtsman Steakhouse offers friendly, polished and elegant dining at the Yacht Club, while the sister hotel features Cape May Café for lovely character breakfasts and a nightly New England-style clambake buffet. Beaches & Cream can also be found here, a classic 1950s-style diner for burgers, shakes and sundaes. Both resorts are set along a white-sand beach like a tropical island paradise and share water fun at Stormalong Bay, a superb 2½ acre/1ha recreation area with waterslides and a sandy lagoon. You can go boating or catch a water-shuttle to *Epcot* or *Disney's Hollywood Studios*; other park transport is by bus. The Sand Castle Club here caters for youngsters aged 4–12 (4.30pm–midnight).

BRITTIP

Look out for the nightly Disney film shows on the big outdoor movie screen by the beach at the Yacht and Beach Club Resorts.

Walt Disney World Swan and Dolphin: These unmistakable hotels also went up on Crescent Lake in 1989 and, while not actually owned by Disney, they conform to the same high standards. They have some of the most extensive facilities of all the resorts, a wonderful location, fabulous restaurants and a night-time view second to none, while they are usually slightly cheaper than most Disney Deluxe resorts. They're within walking distance of *Epcot* and *Disney's Hollywood Studios, Disney's Boardwalk Resort* and the Fantasia Gardens Miniature Golf Courses, but also have a boat service to both parks (and bus to the others). The unique architecture is extensive, with the Swan featuring a 45ft/14m statue on top, as well as 756 large rooms (including 55 suites), while the Dolphin (1,509 rooms, 136 suites) is crowned by 2 even bigger statues. Both were extensively redesigned in 2004 to feature the popular Westin Heavenly Bed® and add high-speed in-room internet. The Dolphin also boasts the Balinese-inspired Mandara Spa, including a relaxing tea garden and authentic Meru Temple. This resort boasts 17 restaurants and lounges, 4 tennis courts, 5 pools (1 an amazing grotto pool with hidden alcoves and waterslide), a kids' pool and white-sand beach, 2 health clubs, bike and paddle boat rentals, a great range of shops, a video arcade and the Camp Dolphin centre for 4–12s (6pm–11pm, $10/hour).

Even for non-guests, Shula's Steak House and celebrity chef Todd English's bluezoo (both Dolphin) are worth seeking out. New in 2007 was Il Mulino Trattoria, New York's top Italian restaurant (in the Swan). Fresh, the Dolphin's Mediterranean-style market, serves breakfast and lunch, featuring all made-to-order menu items and both à la carte and tableside dining. At the Swan, the Garden Grove Café makes guests feel they have been transported to the tranquil gardens of Central Park with its decor and atmosphere. It serves à la carte or buffet breakfasts, with Disney character dining at the weekend. Those who like authentic sushi will enjoy the intimate ambience of Kimonos, in the Swan,

Disney's Yacht and Beach Club Resorts

which also features a karaoke bar. Picabu Buffeteria in the Dolphin is open 24 hours with all-American favourites. With its ideal location and amenities, this is very nearly the perfect resort (407 934 3000, **swandolphin.com**).

Home from home resorts

Disney's Fort Wilderness Resort & Campground: Opened in 1971, possibly the best value of all the Disney properties can be found here. Situated on Bay Lake, almost opposite the *Magic Kingdom*, it offers impressive camping facilities and chalet-style homes that can house up to 6 in a 750 acre/304ha spread of Florida countryside. Two 'trading posts' supply fresh groceries and there are 2 bars and cafés plus a range of on-site activities, including 2 swimming pools, the thrice-nightly Hoop-Dee-Doo Musical Revue, Mickey's Backyard Barbecue (a character buffet dinner), campfire programme, open-air films, sports, games and a prime position from which to view the nightly Electrical Water Pageant. You can rent bikes or boats or take horse rides around the country trails, while the Tri-Circle D ranch has a small petting zoo. There is even a new Segway Tour (the amazing 2-wheeled personal transports), the *Wilderness Back Trail Adventure*, which provides a unique 2-hour trundle around the many trails of the resort ($85/person, Tues, Fri and Sat, over-15s only). The Trails End restaurant (sit-down and takeaway) offers a great value buffet breakfast, lunch and dinner, while Crockett's Tavern serves pizza and appetisers (dinner only). Buses and boats link the resort with other areas (and the short boat ride to the *Magic Kingdom* is a great start to the day). If you need a lunch or afternoon break from the *Magic Kingdom*, hop on the boat to Disney's Fort Wilderness Resort and try the family-friendly Trail's End Buffet – only $11.99 for adults and $7.99 for 3–9s.

Fort Wilderness Resort and Campground

Disney's Old Key West Resort: Disney's first Vacation Club resort in 1992, this is primarily a 5-star holiday ownership scheme (one of 6 such 'timeshare' properties), but the 1-, 2- or 3-bed studios in a Key West setting can also be rented nightly when not in use by members. Facilities include 4 pools, tennis courts, games room, shops and fitness centre, plus the lovely Olivia's restaurant. Transport to all parks is by Disney's bus service.

BRITTIP

Most Disney hotel rooms will accommodate only 4, with the exception of *Port Orleans Riverside* (which will accommodate an extra child on a trundle bed). For larger groups, consider *Old Key West, Saratoga Springs*, the *Boardwalk Villas*, the new 1- and 2-bed villas at *Animal Kingdom Lodge, Wilderness Lodge Villas, Fort Wilderness cabins* or the 2-room suites at the *All Star Music Resort*.

Disney's Saratoga Springs Resort & Spa: The newest member of the Disney Vacation Club line-up, a 65 acre/26ha apartment complex opposite Downtown Disney has some wonderful views over the lake and is next to the beautiful Lake Buena Vista Golf Course. It boasts 828 units, from standard 2-bed hotel-style studio rooms to huge 2-storey, 3-bed apartments sleeping 12. The first phase opened in 2004 and the theme is the 1880s' New York resort of the

Walt Disney World and Lake Buena Vista Accommodation

Magic Kingdom
Grand Floridian Resort & Spa
Seven Seas Lagoon
Polynesian Resort
Transportation & Ticket Center
Car Park
Contemporary Resort
Bay Lake
Wilderness Lodge
Fort Wilderness Resort & Campground
BAY LAKE
monorail
Walt Disney World
Perri House Bed & Breakfast
Big Sand Lake
PALM PARKWAY
APOPKA - VINELAND ROAD
Cypress Pointe Resort
Staybridge Suites
Hawthorn Suites
Avista Resort
Extended Stay America Deluxe
Residence Inn
Embassy Suites
Hampton Inn
Quality Suites Lake Buena Vista
Celebrity R
Comfort Inn
Courtyard Orlando
Holiday Inn Express
Country Inn & Suites
Sheraton Safari
Venturella Resort
Floridays
Hilton Grand Vacations Club (I-Drive)
Crossroads Center
Radisson Lake Buena Vista
Marriott Village
Courtyard by Marriott, Fairfield Inn, Springhill Suites
Hyatt Regency Grand Cypress
Orlando Vista
LBV
Doubletree Guest Suites
Best Western
Royal Plaza
Holiday Inn
Regal Sun Resort
The Hilton
HOTEL PLAZA BLVD
Buena Vista Palace
Saratoga Springs Resort & Spa
DOWNTOWN DISNEY
BUENA VISTA DRIVE
Holiday Inn Sunspree
Blue Heron Beach Resort
Vistana Resort
Bryan's Spanish Cove
Embassy Vacation Resort
Caribe Royale
Embassy Suites
Marriott Vacation Club
Buena Vista Suites
Orlando World Center Marriott Resort
Nickelodeon Family Suites
WORLD CENTER DRIVE
INTERNATIONAL DRIVE SOUTH
Toll road
Port Orleans Riverside Resort
Port Orleans French Quarter Resort
Old Key West Resort
Typhoon Lagoon
EPCOT CENTER DRIVE
Waldorf-Astoria and Hilton Orlando Bonnet Creek
Caribbean Beach Resort
Pop Century Resort
Epcot
Car Park
Beach Club
Boardwalk
Yacht Club
Dolphin
Swan
Victory Way
Disney's Hollywood Studios
OSCEOLA PARKWAY
WORLD DRIVE
Blizzard Beach
Coronado Springs Resort
All-Star Resorts
WESTERN WAY
Animal Kingdom
Animal Kingdom Lodge Resort
N

same name, with a peaceful, gracious look and a great array of facilities, from the free-form, zero-depth entry main pool (with waterslide and squirt-fountains), a smaller quiet pool, the health-conscious dining room (the Artist's Palette, offering breakfast, lunch and dinner, plus groceries), a large video arcade, tennis courts and a wonderful full-service spa and gym. This is spacious, elegant accommodation for large groups. The standard 1-bed apartment can sleep 4; the 2-bed sleeps 8 and there's a 3-bed, 3-bath villa for 12. All but the hotel-style studios have a kitchen (with dishwasher and microwave), washer-dryer, whirlpool bath and DVD player, with TVs in the living room and each bedroom. The resort includes room service, babysitting and childminding services plus a water launch to the shops and entertainment at *Downtown Disney*. Rates for the 3-bed villas top $1,000 a night, but the 1-bed units are more modestly priced and, although it is a Vacation Club property, some rooms are available to the general public. Transport to all parks is by bus.

A new DVC resort, **Disney's Kingdom Tower** is under construction next to the Contemporary Resort but isn't likely to be finished until late 2009. It will also be on the monorail and feature its own pool, waterslide and tennis courts, and will connect to the Contemporary via a 5th floor bridge.

Best Western Lake Buena Vista

Disney Hotel Plaza

In addition to the official hotels, there are another 7 'guest' hotels on Disney property at the Disney Hotel Plaza on the doorstep of *Downtown Disney* (where we now revert to our ratings of Budget, Standard, Superior and Deluxe). There's a free bus service to the attractions, guaranteed admission to the parks (even on their busiest days), and you can make reservations for shows and restaurants before the general public, but they tend to be more expensive than similar hotels outside Disney property (though the convenience of being able to walk to *Downtown Disney* and the Crossroads shopping plaza is worth a lot).

Best Western Lake Buena Vista: This 18-storey, tropically themed hotel has 325 rooms (all with high-speed internet access) with views over the Marketplace, in-room coffee-makers and hairdryers, while the huge top-floor suites are magnificent. Garden-themed Traders Island Grill is pleasant for breakfast or dinner, plus there is a Pizza Hut Express and the deli-style Parakeet Internet Cafe, as well as a large pool, video arcade and small gym, with a Garden Gazebo for special occasions, including weddings (407 828 2424; Standard).

Buena Vista Palace Hotel & Spa: Arguably the outstanding property here, this has been extensively renovated (at a cost of $50m), with an all-new lobby area, including bar and lounge, totally remodelled rooms (with chic decor, flatscreen TVs, ergonomic chairs, new bathrooms and plush bedding) and extra amenities. The elegant 27-storey cluster offers 1,012 rooms and suites (in 8 categories, many with a view over much of *Walt Disney World*), plus an enhanced (and quite blissful!) European-style spa, 3 heated pools, tennis court, jogging track, basketball and sand volleyball court and no fewer than 5 restaurants. The Australian-themed Outback Restaurant (not part of the Outback

Steakhouse chain) is an ideal venue for a memorable meal, while Kook Sports Bar has a network of 38 TVs. The smart Watercress Café will undergo a complete overhaul late in 2008, meaning a change of venue for the hotel's buffet breakfast and lunch and Sunday breakfast with Disney characters (407 827 2727; Superior).

Doubletree Guest Suites: For extra space with your accommodation, these contemporary suites offer 229 family suites with every convenience, from in-room safe to cookies, high-speed internet access, wet bar, 2 TVs, fridge and microwave. There are excellent kids' facilities, with their own check-in area, pool, playground and video arcade, and a casual restaurant, lounge and bar (Streamers), plus a large main pool (albeit right next to noisy I-4), an exercise room and tennis court (407 934 1000; Superior).

Regal Sun Resort: More upmarket and also just off a $23m renovation, this has 619 rooms and 7 suites, all remodelled with bright, crisp decor and furniture. There are 2 main pools, a large hot tub and a children's pool with playground, as well as a fitness centre, volleyball, tennis and basketball courts. There is a Disney character breakfast 3 days a week at the graceful LakeView Restaurant, plus an English-style pub (Moriarty's), poolside bar and grill and 24-hour café, Sundial 24/7. There are also the fun MurderWatch Mystery Theater dinner shows here on Saturdays (407 828 4444; Superior).

Hilton Orlando Resort: Top of the list (for service, mod cons and price) is this 10-storey, 814-room hotel, with 2 excellent pools, 7 restaurants and lounges and a superb state-of-the-art health club. It is also the only 'outside' hotel to enjoy Disney's Extra Magic Hours feature, while there's a babysitting service and Disney character breakfast on Sundays. The rooms all offer high-speed wireless internet and ultra-plush decor. The dining choices feature the superior Benihana restaurant for sushi, sashimi, chicken and great steaks; Covington Mill for a casual breakfast and lunch; Andiamo Italian Bistro; the 24-hour Mainstreet Market deli; a pool bar and grill; and a coffee/wine bar (407 827 4000; Deluxe).

Royal Plaza Resort: This spacious 394-room hotel (in 5 categories of rooms and suites accommodating up to 5) features the plush new Royal Beds and excellent personal amenities. There is a full-service diner-restaurant (the Giraffe Café and Lounge, with an excellent breakfast buffet; free for under-11s), Grab 'n Go deli-café, landscaped pool area and pool bar, 4 tennis courts, a health club

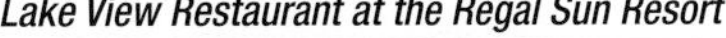

Lake View Restaurant at the Regal Sun Resort

and fitness centre and Disney gift shop. Standard rooms include a sitting area and balcony, while the magnificent 2-room suites have oversized private patios (407 828 2828; Superior).

For more info on these 6 hotels, go to **downtowndisneyhotels.com**. The seventh, the 323-room **Holiday Inn in the Walt Disney World Resort**, is due to re-open in March 2009 after a long-overdue $25m rebuild that will dramatically upgrade guest rooms.

Beyond Disney

Once you move away from *Walt Disney World*, your hotel choice becomes more diverse. The Budget and Standard types are the most common, and the area you stay in also has an effect on price: the further you go from Disney on Kissimmee's Highway 192, the cheaper the hotel/motel, while parts of International Drive are more expensive than others (generally, north of Sand Lake Road is cheaper). Facilities vary little and what you see is usually what you get. All the chain hotels can be found here, with rates as low as $30/room off-peak (but remember the local sales tax). Some also have rooms with a kitchenette (an 'efficiency'). Be prepared to shop around, especially on Highway 192, where many hotels advertise their rates on billboards, and feel free to ask to see a room before you book (some motels can be pretty basic).

Howard Johnson Maingate East

Looking from the price perspective, here is a guide to the main options.

Budget hotels

Chain hotels can be found at their most numerous in this category and you'll find few frills from what is an identikit bunch. All will have pools but not many have restaurants and none will have bars or lounges (though quite a few provide a free continental breakfast). Conversely, many offer fridges and microwaves that add real value.

Choose from: The **Days Inn** chain, which varies widely, from tatty older hotels to smart relatively recent ones, and with free continental breakfast (1800 329 7466, **daysinn.com**); **Econo Lodge**, also with a free continental breakfast (1877 424 6423, **econolodge.com**); **Howard Johnson**, which tends to have older properties, many with a 'kids eat free' option, but rooms are often more spacious (1800 446 4656, **hojo.com**); **Knights Inn**, a smarter choice in this area (1800 843 5644, **knightsinn.com**); **Masters Inn**, another to offer a free continental breakfast (1800 633 3434, **masters inn.com**); the **Microtel Inn & Suites** chain, with much newer properties (1800 771 7171, **microtelinn.com**); the bargain basement **Motel 6** (1800 466 8356, **motel6.com**); **Red Roof Inn**, which has several newly renovated properties in Orlando (1800 733 7663, **redroof.com**); the **Rodeway Inn** chain has slipped from Standard to more Budget territory in recent years (1877 424 6423, **choicehotels.com**); the **Super 8 Motel** chain varies a lot but has several newer motels (notably on American Way, near Universal Orlando; 1800 800 8000, **super8.com**); and **Travelodge**, also having a smart new hotel on American Way, (1800 578 7878, **travelodge.com**).

BRITTIP

Hotels designated Maingate East or Maingate West should be close to Disney's main entrance on Highway 192, though it is wise to check.

Our Budget recommendations

In this range, the ones we rate among the best include the **Magic Castle Inn & Suites Maingate** in Kissimmee (good range of amenities – free continental breakfast, free Disney transport, in-room fridge, microwave, safe, kids' playground and guest laundry; 1800 446 5669, **magicorlando.com**); The **Inn at Summer Bay** at the Clermont end of Highway 192 (the budget part of the big Summer Bay complex, just across the Highway, but still benefiting from the many facilities; 863 420 8282, **summerbayresort.com/inn.html**); **Knights Inn Maingate**, also in Kissimmee (reliable, cheap option in a great location, with free Disney transport, daily breakfast and fridges in all rooms; 407 859 5410, **knightsinn.com**); the **Howard Johnson Enchanted Land** offers some fun frills for kids with their 'treehouse' rooms, plus free breakfast and ice-cream; **Wynfield Inn**, on International Drive, remains a perennial budget favourite, with well-furnished rooms, free continental breakfast and a pleasant pool and bar, plus excellent location; and **Econo Lodge Inn & Suites International Drive**, recently converted from the Best Western Plaza, so above average for this chain (407 345 8195, **econolodge.com**).

There are also dozens of smaller, independent outfits that offer special rates periodically, especially a battery of cheap and cheerful motels along Highway 192 in Kissimmee.

Standard hotels

At first glance there may not seem much difference here, as some of these are still firmly in motel-style territory. They should have generally smarter facilities but not all will have their own restaurant. Again, they are dominated by the big chain hotels:

AmeriHost Inns have some newer motels here, with a free breakfast bonus (1800 434 5800, **amerihostinn.com**); **AmeriSuites** (the Hyatt budget brand) is another good name, with large, well-fitted rooms and free hot breakfast (1877 877 8886, **amerisuites.com**); the **Comfort Inn** chain is equally identikit but offers a valuable free breakfast, while sister brand **Comfort Suites** has some smart, newer properties, and the **Clarion Inn** (and Suites), also in the Choice Hotels group, often includes restaurants, though properties vary considerably in age (all 3, 1877 424 6423, **choicehotels.com**); for pure no-frills, clean and consistent chains with more space than many in this category (and kitchens in most hotels), look for **Extended Stay America**, which also has **Extended Stay Deluxe** properties; sister brand **StudioPLUS** offers extra facilities (all 3, 1800 804 3724, **extendedstayamerica.com**); **Fairfield Inns** is the budget version of the Marriott chain and usually has newer hotels, many with gyms and most with free breakfast (0800 221 222 in the UK, **marriott.com**); **Hampton Inns** (and Suites) are also usually above average in this category, with a free breakfast bar and tea/coffee in the lobby 24 hours a day (1800 426 7866, **hamptoninn.com**); **Ramada** hotels represent good value at this level as some have complimentary breakfast (1800 272 6232, **ramada.com**); and **Quality Inns** are a popular choice, with a reputation for value, while some hotels boast an exercise room (1877 424 6423, **choicehotels.com**).

At the upper end of the Standard category, you have the **Best Western** group, all with good facilities, family-orientated but large (0800 393 130 in the UK, **bestwestern.com**); the **Holiday Inn** (and Holiday Inn Express) chain varies a bit but provides some great-value (and well-equipped) hotels in Standard/Superior territory as kids eat free (with their parents) at all properties and many include sophisticated pools and extra facilities like games rooms (0800 405 060 from the UK, **holidayinn.com**); and the smart **La Quinta Inn** (and Suites), which has some notable newer hotels

Kissimmee Accommodation

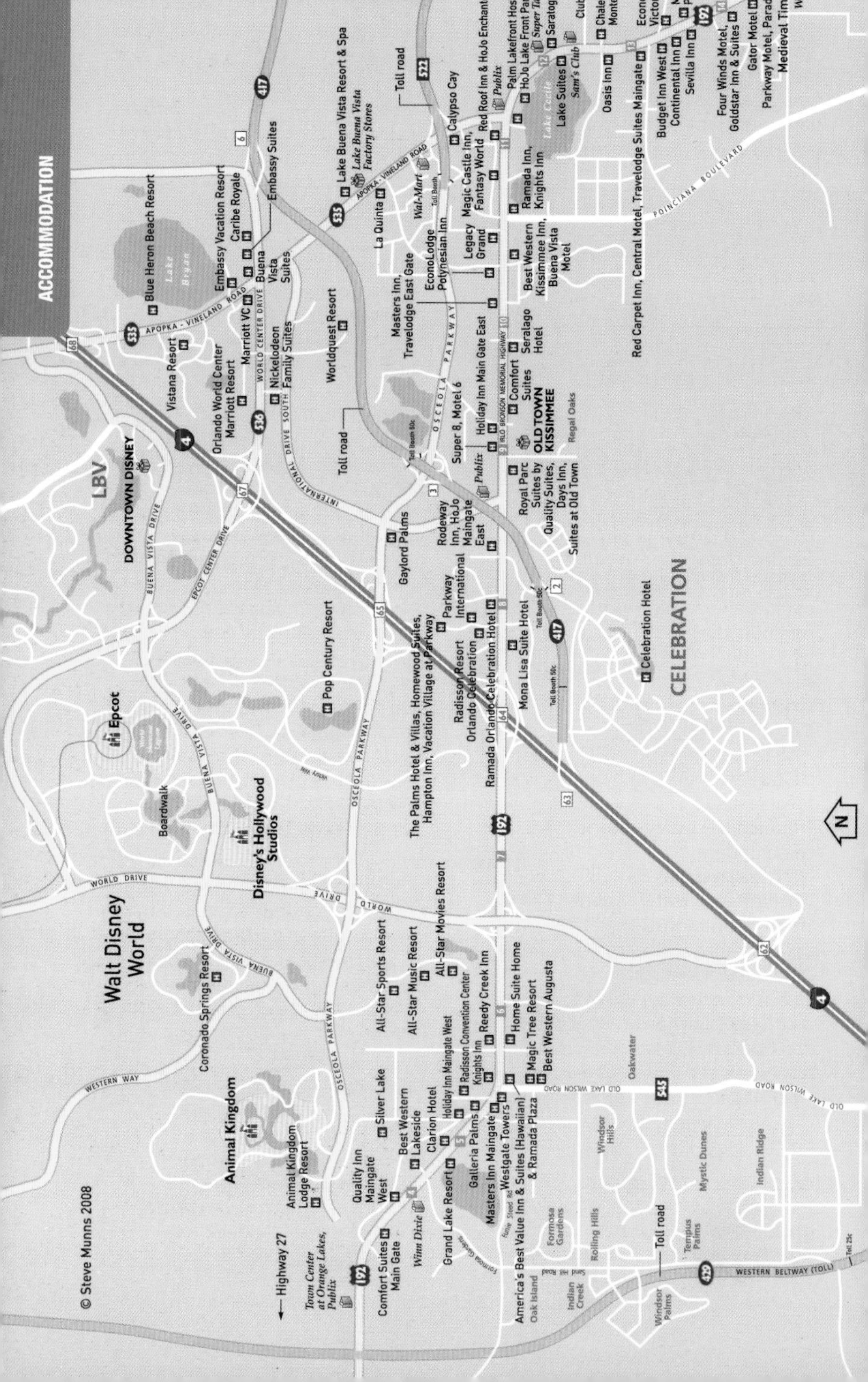

Walt Disney World
LBV
DOWNTOWN DISNEY
Epcot
Boardwalk
Disney's Hollywood Studios
Animal Kingdom
Animal Kingdom Lodge Resort
Coronado Springs Resort
Pop Century Resort
All-Star Sports Resort
All-Star Music Resort
All-Star Movies Resort
Blue Heron Beach Resort
Lake Bryan
Embassy Vacation Resort
Caribe Royale
Embassy Suites
Marriott VC
Buena Vista Suites
Vistana Resort
Orlando World Center Marriott Resort
Nickelodeon Family Suites
Worldquest Resort
Lake Buena Vista Resort & Spa
Lake Buena Vista Factory Stores
La Quinta
Wal-Mart
Masters Inn, Travelodge East Gate
EconoLodge Polynesian Inn
Legacy Grand
Magic Castle Inn, Fantasy World
Calypso Cay
Red Roof Inn & HoJo Enchanted Land
Publix
Palm Lakefront Hostel, HoJo Lake Front Park, Key Motel
Super Target
Saratoga Resort Villas
Club Cortile
Chalet Motel, Monte Carlo Motel
Econo Lodge, Victoria Inn
Maple Leaf Inn, Parkside Inn
Rodeway Inn
Ramada Inn, Knights Inn
Lake Cecile
Lake Suites
Sam's Club
Oasis Inn
Budget Inn West
Continental Inn
Sevilla Inn
Four Winds Motel, Goldstar Inn & Suites
Gator Motel
Parkway Motel, Paradise Inn
Medieval Times
Wal-Mart
Red Carpet Inn, Central Motel, Travelodge Suites Maingate
Best Western Kissimmee Inn, Buena Vista Motel
Seralago Hotel
Holiday Inn Main Gate East
Comfort Suites
OLD TOWN KISSIMMEE
Regal Oaks
Super 8, Motel 6
Publix
Royal Parc Suites by Quality Suites, Days Inn, Suites at Old Town
Rodeway Inn, HoJo Maingate East
Gaylord Palms
Parkway International
The Palms Hotel & Villas, Homewood Suites, Hampton Inn, Vacation Village at Parkway
Radisson Resort Orlando Celebration
Ramada Orlando Celebration Hotel
Mona Lisa Suite Hotel
Celebration Hotel
CELEBRATION
Toll road
Toll Booth 50c
Toll Booth 25c
Quality Inn Maingate West
Silver Lake
Best Western Lakeside
Clarion Hotel
Holiday Inn Maingate West
Radisson Convention Center
Knights Inn
Reedy Creek Inn
Home Suite Home
Magic Tree Resort
Best Western Augusta
Galleria Palms
Masters Inn Maingate
Westgate Towers
Grand Lake Resort
Winn Dixie
America's Best Value Inn & Suites (Hawaiian) & Ramada Plaza
Comfort Suites Main Gate
Town Center at Orange Lakes, Publix
Highway 27
Oakwater
Windsor Hills
Mystic Dunes
Indian Ridge
Formosa Gardens
Rolling Hills
Tempus Palms
Oak Island
Indian Creek
Windsor Palms
APOPKA - VINELAND ROAD
WORLD CENTER DRIVE
INTERNATIONAL DRIVE SOUTH
OSCEOLA PARKWAY
IRLO BRONSON MEMORIAL HIGHWAY
POINCIANA BOULEVARD
BUENA VISTA DRIVE
EPCOT CENTER DRIVE
WORLD DRIVE
WESTERN WAY
OLD LAKE WILSON ROAD
WESTERN BELTWAY (TOLL)
Sand Hill Road
Formosa Gardens Blvd
Funie Steed Rd
Victory Way
N

© Steve Munns 2008

in Orlando (1800 642 4271, **lq.com**). Possibly the best overall value here, though, is provided by the **Radisson** group, which has some excellently priced hotels in the area, all with above-average amenities and services and most well situated for the parks (0800 374 411, **radisson.com**).

BRITTIP

Not all hotels provide hairdryers, though they can often be ordered from the desk. For your own, you will need a US plug adaptor (with 2 flat pins). Their voltage is 110–120 AC (ours is 220) so appliances will be sluggish.

There are also a handful of individuals in this category. Look out in particular for the **Seralago Inn Hotel and Suites Maingate East**, which boasts deluxe suites, 2-room suites and kidsuites, plus great kids' facilities (including free films in their own cinema), making it an outstanding family resort. Its proximity to Old Town is also handy, while under-13s eat breakfast and dinner free (1800 411 3457, **seralagohotel.com**). The reliable 2-bed **Enclave Suites** (on Carrier Drive, just off I-Drive) are excellent value as 'kids eat free' with parents, there's free breakfast and a good array of facilities – though the resort could do with some updating in places (1800 457 0077, **enclavesuites.com**). Similarly, the rebuilt **Palms Hotel & Villas** right on Parkway Boulevard off Highway 192 in Kissimmee (close to I-4), features spacious 2-room suites (with fully equipped kitchens), large pool, sports court, free shuttle to the Disney parks and free continental breakfast but no restaurant (407 396 2229, **thepalmshotelandvillas.com**).

BRITTIP

It is usual to tip hotel chambermaids by leaving $1/adult each day before your room is made up.

Superior hotels

This is a category where there are fewer of each brand, so we highlight a few worthy individuals as well as the chain details. All properties provide a good pool (often with extra facilities like a waterslide, kids' pool and/or playground), at least 1 restaurant, bar and café, and extra in-room amenities, such as tea/coffee-makers.

Main chains: A relative newcomer but highly worthwhile is **Baymont Inn & Suites** group, which boasts several properties in the area (1866 999 1111, **baymontinns.com**), while the **Country Inn & Suites** are almost identical, newer hotels with spacious rooms and a pleasant country-house style lobby, serving an extensive free breakfast (1888 201 1746, **countryinns.com**); the **Doubletree** chain offers smart, modern properties with fewer frills than most but more spacious rooms (1800 222 8733, **doubletree.com**); **Residence Inns** tend to be newer and feature free breakfast and exercise rooms but still with microwave, fridge and tea/coffee-making facilities; equally, the **Springhill Suites** (also part of the Marriott group, along with the more upmarket Courtyard hotels) offer reliable and comfortable value for money in this range (1888 236 2427 in the US, 0800 221 222 in the UK, **marriott.com**).

More upmarket: Here you have **Crowne Plaza Hotels**, which has made a mark for itself in recent years with some fabulous new properties (**ichotelsgroup.com**). They feature great pool areas, whirlpools, good-quality restaurants, fitness centres and ultra-comfortable rooms. The **Crowne**

They've got the lot

The **Marriott Village complex** in Lake Buena Vista features a Fairfield Inn, Courtyard and Springhill Suites (**http://orlando2stay.com/village/**), with 24-hour gated security, free Walt Disney World transport and a great a range of facilities.

Our standard recommendations

Standout properties in this range include the **Galleria Palms Hotel & Suites**, also in Kissimmee at Maingate West just off Highway 192, a completely refurbished ex-Hampton Inn which now has a smart, contemporary look (more like a Superior class hotel), ultra-comfy rooms, a great location close to Disney, free shuttle to the main theme parks, free buffet breakfast and a relaxing pool area; there is no restaurant but plenty of choice nearby (1800 391 7909, **galleriapalmsorlando.com**); **Holiday Inn and Suites Maingate East** in Kissimmee (between Markers 8 and 9), which underwent a complete rebuild in 2007/08 to refurbish its 446 rooms (including kidsuites) in 2 high-rise towers; there's an oversized pool, kids' pool, waterslides, gym, children's theatre, food court and lobby lounge, plus a 'kids eat free' programme (1800 337 1128, **holidayinnmge.com**); **Radisson Hotel Lake Buena Vista** is a dramatically remodelled property extremely convenient for Disney and the Crossroads area, with some sleek rooms and furnishings (including large flatscreen TVs), the Liquid Bar & Grill, poolside bar and a Starbucks coffee shop (407 597 3400, **radisson.com/lakebuenavistafl**); and the **Radisson Resort Orlando-Celebration** in Kissimmee (on Parkway Boulevard, close to the Highway 192 junction with I-4), in 20 tropical acres/8ha and with 3 landscaped swimming pools, a state-of-the-art fitness centre, comfy rooms and great dining choices, all in a great location (407 396 7000, **radisson.com/kissimmeefl**).

Plaza Orlando Universal is a fine example, with 398 rooms and suites in 2 distinct, stylish blocks and a spectacular circular atrium. Two restaurants, a cocktail lounge, guest laundry and fitness centre, plus a huge heated pool add up to top quality and value in an ideal location on Universal Boulevard's junction with Sand Lake Road (407 355 0550, **cporlando.com**). The Hilton chain is notable here for its **Hilton Garden Inn** brand, with a number of attractive, modern hotels (1877 7829 444, **hiltongardeninn.com**). The **Hyatt** group is rare in tourist territory, but one prime example is the **Hyatt Regency at Orlando International Airport**, especially if you arrive late and could benefit from a first-night rest. It has 2 excellent restaurants and a smart pool deck, plus a fitness room, lounge and business centre. Rooms are superbly spacious, particularly the corner rooms, and many feature internal balconies overlooking the 6-storey airport atrium. Surprisingly, there is no noticeable aircraft noise and none of the bustle you would expect of an airport hotel. Staying there gives the distinct advantage of collecting your hire car in the morning rather than straight after a long flight (407 825 1234, **http://orlandoairport.hyatt.com**). **Marriott** is another well-represented group here, with some of the smartest hotels in this category, often providing extra facilities and more landscaped grounds, with a choice of restaurants and some of the largest standard rooms. Recent enhancements include stylish features like its signature Revive beds for a guaranteed good night's sleep. The **Orlando Airport Marriott** has recently undergone major renovations to its public rooms and guest rooms and is a great choice for either your first night (especially if you are arriving late) or the final day,

Cycling is a popular way to get around

© Disney

Suite choice

To our mind the best suites hotels here are the **Embassy Suites**, with smart interior courtyards, good restaurants and relaxing pool areas (1800 362 2779, **http://embassy suites1.hilton.com**). But other worthwhile choices include the **Homewood Suites**, which provide extra room for larger families in 1- and 2-bed suites with full kitchens, a free hot breakfast daily and a more upmarket feel with mid-range pricing (1800 222 4663, **homewoodsuites.com**). Equally, **Hawthorn Suites** and **Staybridge Suites** both feature spacious 1- and 2-bed suites that sleep up to 6 and fully fitted kitchens, plus a hearty free breakfast and free local phone calls (1800 527 1133, **hawthorn.com** and 1800 225 1237, **staybridge.com**). For a more individual choice, try the well-appointed **Buena Vista Suites** (1800 537 7737, **bvsuites.com**) or the stylish **Caribe Royale Resort** (1800 823 8300, **cariberoyale.com**), both on World Center Drive just off the lower end of I-Drive. The former is the more basic type, with spacious 2-room suites, a free full breakfast, heated pool, whirlpool, tennis courts, gift shop, mini-market and the Vista Bistro. The **Caribe Royale** is more luxurious, with a choice of 1-bed suites and 2-bed villas, a super pool area with waterslide, tennis courts, 2 fitness rooms and one of the best free breakfast buffets in town. Its Venetian Room is a real treat for lovers of fine continental cuisine, and there are 4 other cafés and lounges. Finally, not so much a hotel as a theme park in resort form, **Nickelodeon Family Suites by Holiday Inn** on I-Drive South provides a wonderfully striking and kid-friendly holiday choice. Characters from the Nickelodeon TV station adorn strategic points and there is plenty of live interaction (notably at breakfast). A huge range of daily activities include scavenger hunts, arcade tournaments and pirates, while Studio Nick stages shows in its mini-theatre. There is also an evening programme and babysitting to allow parents some free time! Suites come complete with bunk or twin beds and a TV and video console. The water features form 2 huge play areas, complete with all manner of sprays, showers, pools, slides and flumes, and there are poolside games, a video arcade, mini-golf and a large shopping arcade. Suites come in 1, 2 or 3 bedrooms, with a living room and bathroom, microwave and fridge (and full kitchen with some). The Nicktoons Café offers buffet dining (plus à la carte in the evening), with 'kids eat free' at all times. Plus there is a food court, pool bar and grill, along with the Nick@Nite Lounge. It all adds up to a striking (if somewhat raucous) holiday base in an excellent location conveniently close to Disney (1866 462 6425; **nickhotel.com**).

letting you relax around the tropical indoor/outdoor pool area and indulge in some fine dining at its excellent steakhouse, Porterhouse (1800 380 6751, **marriott.com**); **Sheraton** hotels are well represented in Orlando and boast a smart, revamped look in recent years (as part of the Starwood group). Several are themed and feature extra facilities and good dining (1888 625 5144, **starwoodhotels.com**). A novel choice is the African-themed **Sheraton Safari Hotel** in Lake Buena Vista, which offers a waterslide, heated pool and kids' pool, free transport to Disney parks and 'kids eat free' with parents. Its rooms are large and well equipped, and there's a good selection of restaurants and shops nearby (407 239 0444, **sheratonsafari.com**).

One last group is **Rosen Hotels & Resorts** of Florida. Four of its hotels are budget-minded properties on I-Drive (including the Brit-popular Quality Inn Plaza and Quality Inn International), but it also has the **Rosen Plaza Hotel**, a distinctive 800-room property with excellent resort facilities – including 2 restaurants, a pizza shop, deli, fitness centre and nightclub – and spacious, recently redecorated accommodation (1800 627 8258, **rosenplaza.com**).

Notable individuals: there are only a few non-chain properties in the Superior category. The recently remodelled **International Plaza Resort and Spa** condo-hotel (formerly the Sheraton World Resort) is just off the main I-Drive area and makes a good choice. Set in 28 acres/11ha, it offers 3 pools, 2 kids' pools, a playground and mini-golf, well-furnished rooms and extra-large suites. Dining options are more limited, but the tropical grounds give it an upmarket feel (407 352 1100, **internationalplazaresortandspa.com**).The recently refurbished and fun-styled **Orlando Vista Hotel** (formerly the Doubletree Club) on Apopka-Vineland Road in Lake Buena Vista is located at the entrance to *Downtown Disney*, and, as well as featuring highly popular kidsuites, it has a pleasant bar and café, large pool deck and spacious, airy rooms, which all make this a bit of a bargain (1800 521 3297, **orlandovistahotel.com**). The **Wyndham Orlando Resort**, in the heart of I-Drive, offers a formidable line-up of facilities (3 pools, a full-service restaurant and bar, a deli and ice-cream shop, 2 pool bars, a pool restaurant, tennis courts, a kids' club and games arcade, and a health club) in beautifully landscaped grounds but without the high price tag you would expect. The resort covers 42 acres/17ha and takes some getting around, but it is one of the best hotels all round for the money (407 351 2420; **wyndham.com**).

Deluxe hotels

When it comes to the best hotels, it is very much a question of individuals. There is only a handful of genuinely deluxe properties in this area, and they are all highly distinctive, with excellent facilities, outstanding

Hard Rock Hotel

service and, usually, at least one 5-star restaurant. We have already detailed Disney's luxury offerings (see pages 67–72), so we'll start here with Universal's counterparts.

When Universal decided to build its own hotels, it teamed up with the Loews group and consequently ended up with 3 of the best. They also come with a rare bonus – *Universal Express,* front-of-line access to the main attractions of both parks just by showing your key card. All Universal resort guests also benefit from a number of other privileges: resort ID card (for buying food, merchandise and other items throughout Universal Orlando); free water taxi transport; priority seating at most restaurants (show your room key card); package delivery to your room; and the chance to buy a special Length of Stay pass (for unlimited park access while you are at the resort). For all Universal hotels, call 1888 273 1311 or go to **universal orlando.com**.

Hard Rock Hotel: Possibly the coolest hotel in Orlando, this icon of rock chic is themed as a former rock star's home, with 650 rooms and suites in California mission style. High ceilings, wooden beams, marble floors and eclectic artwork give an eye-catching style, with a rock-star theme to most public areas, music memorabilia, black-suited foyer staff and fairly constant music. The 14 acre/6ha site includes 3 bars (including the ultra-cool Velvet Bar), 2 restaurants (the full-service The Kitchen and the 5-star, dinner-only Palm Restaurant), plus a take-away café, fitness centre, gift shop, kids' club (for 4–14s) and games room. The lido area that is the hotel's focus is terrific, with a large, free-form pool and 240ft/73m waterslide, two jacuzzis, a beach and volleyball court, shuffleboard and life-size chess and draughts. The pool even has an underwater sound system! The rooms (including 14 kidsuites) are big, beautifully furnished in the hotel's chic style and superbly comfortable.

Our superior recommendations

The 21-storey **Four Points Sheraton Studio City Hotel** is an I-Drive icon near Universal Orlando and features a 1950s' film theme throughout. Facilities include a heated outdoor pool and paddling pool, games room, mini-golf, fitness room and free shuttle to Universal, Wet 'n Wild and SeaWorld. All 301 well-appointed rooms have coffee makers and Nintendo games, plus superb views over the surrounding area (ask for a Universal view if possible). The Starlight Grille restaurant is a minor gem, with a fun ambience for breakfast, lunch or dinner, and an imaginative dinner menu, while you can also grab a drink at Oscar's Lounge and enjoy being a 'movie star' (407 351 2100, **starwoodhotels.com**). The **Embassy Suites Hotel International Drive South** consistently gets good reader feedback and is exceedingly smart, with excellent service and spacious rooms (either standard 2-room suites sleeping 4 or double-doubles for 6) providing 2 TVs, coffee maker, fridge and microwave. There's a great outdoor pool deck, kids' splash pool and indoor pool, plus a sauna, steam room and gym. The Sedona Café and Hurricane's Lounge give it a real edge in dining options and it also has a free Disney shuttle service and transport to the other parks (407 352 1400, **embassysuitesorlando.com**). Finally, the spectacular 24-storey **Rosen Center Hotel** is a real star property and one of the largest in the area. It caters mainly for the convention trade (it's next door to the massive Convention Center), but also offers excellent facilities with 1,334 rooms and 80 suites. It has a huge swimming grotto, tennis courts, exercise centre, 2 top-quality restaurants (the excellent seafood-orientated Everglades and casual all-day choice Café Gauguin, plus a handy 24-hour deli) and 2 smart bars. The overall style is distinctly luxurious, yet the prices aren't (1800 204 7234, **rosencenter.com**).

Portofino Bay Hotel: The jewel in Universal's crown is a splendid re-creation of the famous Italian port and a stunning resort with every facility. The elaborate porticos, genuine trompe l'oeil painting, harbourside piazza and faithful ornamentation of the waterfront make it one of Florida's most memorable settings. The 750 rooms are impeccably appointed, with lashings of Italian style. Standard rooms are sumptuous, with huge beds, spacious bathrooms, mini-bar and coffee facilities, ironing board and hair-dryer, while the exclusive Villa rooms feature butler service and private pool. There are 18 kidsuites with separate themed rooms that include TV, CD player and Sony Playstation. The resort facilities are equally breathtaking – a Roman aqueduct-style pool with waterslide (and poolside films on Saturday evenings), an enclosed kids' play area and wading pool, a separate quiet pool, jacuzzis, the beautiful Mandara Spa and fitness centre, business centre, gift shops and video games room. There is also the Campo Portofino activity centre for kids 4–14 (5–11.30pm, $12 hour/child, $12/meal). The Portofino also has 8 restaurants and lounges, including the 5-star (and very romantic) Bice Ristorante, the boisterous Trattoria del Porto (with family-themed

Portofino Bay Hotel

High Velocity bar at the Orlando Marriott World Center

entertainment, including a magician, character dining or clown balloonist 6.30–9.30pm Thurs–Sat), Mama Della's, an authentic Italian family dining experience (watch out for Mama herself!), an aromatic deli, a pizzeria and gelateria. It is only a short boat ride from Universal, but it feels light years away in terms of its tranquil ambience.

BRITTIP

For some wonderful gift shopping, check out the Portofino Bay's Galleria Portofino where you'll find magnificent art and jewellery.

Royal Pacific Resort: This 53 acre/21ha, 1,000-room resort has an exotic South Seas feel, transporting you back to a 1930s hotel in the tropics, and you really feel as if you have stepped into another world as you cross the bamboo bridge into the elegant lobby, faced by the splendid Orchid Garden courtyard. Extensive use of rich, dark woods, cool stone floors and masses of greenery (58,000 plants and 2,500 trees) give the place an opulent, colonial feel, while the rooms and facilities are equally impressive. Standard rooms feature hand-carved Balinese furniture, among many refined touches, and there is also a Club level, with separate lounge and extended facilities, and some superlative suites. Islands Dining Room offers breakfast, lunch and dinner in a setting of oriental simplicity (children have their own buffet area with TV screen), while fine dining is taken to a new dimension by a magnificent restaurant run by American celebrity chef Emeril Lagasse called Tchoup Chop (possibly the best in Orlando, see page 336). There is a pool snack bar and luau garden area, with the *Wantilan Luau* buffet on Saturdays and Tuesdays from 6pm ($52 adults, $29 under-13s), featuring a Polynesian feast and dinner show. The huge free-form pool is ideal for kids, with zero-depth entry at one end and a boat-shaped interactive play area of squirting fountains. Add a health club (with jacuzzi, sauna and gym), kids' club (with computer games, TVs and organised activities), video arcade and 2 shops and you have superb value, even at this end of the scale.

The largest Marriott on earth!

A firm *Brit Guide* Deluxe favourite over the years that never seems to lose its lustre is **Orlando World Center Marriott**, a hugely impressive landmark on Disney's outskirts, set in 200 landscaped acres/810ha and surrounded by a beautiful golf course. With 2,000 spacious rooms (most of them boasting fabulous views up to 28 storeys high), 10 restaurants and 6 pools (holding a million gallons of water), it is a monumental prospect, set among landscaped tropical foliage and with fabulous facilities, including a Bill Madonna Golf Academy, tennis courts, volleyball, basketball, spa and state-of-the-art gym. Highlights are the Mikado Japanese Steakhouse, Ristorante Tuscany and the new High Velocity Sports Bar – one of the largest in Florida – while there are also excellent children's amenities and programmes – plus the whizziest glass-fronted lifts in Orlando! It gets busy with convention business, but the picturesque main pool area offers true relaxation bliss (407 239 4200, **marriottworldcenter.com**).

International Drive Area

Stepping back outside Universal, there are a number of excellent offerings on I-Drive.

Floridays Resort Orlando: One of the newest and smartest of the area's condo-hotels, this is extremely well situated in a quieter part of I-Drive but close to Orlando Premium Outlets and with a free shuttle service to the parks. The full site consists of 6 condo blocks (each with 72 rooms), 2 pools (including the elaborate main zero-depth entry pool and water-play area), a Pool Bar and Grill, fitness centre, stylish Welcome Center, kids activity centre and games room, plus a small grocery store. With concierge services, a business centre and meeting facilities, it is also highly versatile. The water-jet play area will probably keep kids amused for hours without having to set foot outside the resort! The 2- and 3-bed grand suites are beautifully furnished and will easily sleep 6–10, and have either a balcony or patio. Living rooms include large-screen plasma TVs, high-speed internet, games console and stereos, while each bedroom also has a TV. And, if you don't fancy cooking, you can use the delivery service from the Marketplace, which also serves Starbucks coffee. All rooms are wheelchair-accessible and some are specifically adapted for the disabled with roll-in showers (407 238 7700, **floridaysresortorlando.com**).

Hilton Orlando: Due to open in summer 2009 is this impressive new 1,400-room hotel right next to the big Convention Center and set in 26 acres/10.5ha. It will feature an upscale steakhouse (Spencer's), along with David Club's bar and grill, a 24-hour Marketplace, smart lobby lounge-bar and a pool bar and grill. A full-service spa, fitness centre, 2 pools, lazy river (in a wonderful 'tropical island' setting), tennis and basketball courts and a 9-hole pitch-and-putt golf course complete the amenities. Rooms feature the latest Hilton 'Serenity' bedding, flatscreen TVs and high-quality bathroom toiletries (407 313 4300, **hilton.com**).

Peabody Orlando: Classy and conventional, this luxurious 891-room tower block on I-Drive has an Olympic-size pool, health club, 4 tennis courts and some superb

Floridays Resort

International Drive Accommodation

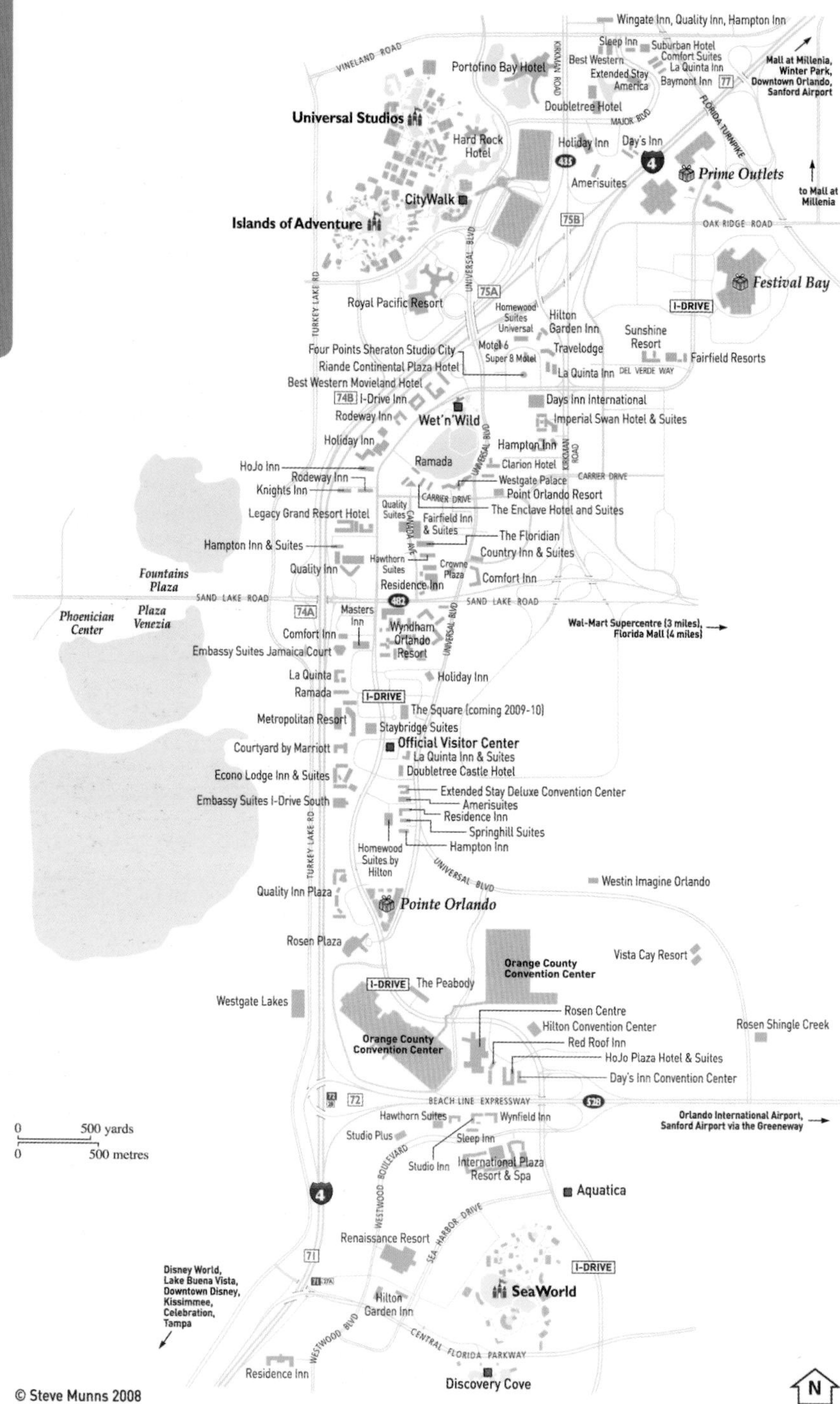

restaurants, notably the gourmet Dux (jacket advisable), classy Italian Capriccio, and the amazing B-Line Diner (see page 327). Service is superb and the style is a cut above normal tourist fare – just check out the Royal Duck Palace! Larger-than-average rooms and huge suites add to the quality, but conference business can make it a bit hectic. Real English afternoon tea is served daily 3–4.30pm (407 352 4000, **peabody orlando.com**).

BRITTIP

Don't miss Peabody's twice-daily red-carpet Duck March at 11am and 5pm, when its trademark ducks take up residence in the lobby fountain.

Pointe Orlando Resort: This chic new condo-hotel on Universal Boulevard just off I-Drive (behind Wet 'n Wild) features some exceedingly smart and very spacious 1- and 2-bed units with fully equipped kitchens in 4 12-storey buildings around extensive resort facilities, including clubhouse, pool, sauna, shop and bistro restaurant with a free daily continental breakfast (1866 956 2015, **thepointorlando.com**).

Renaissance Orlando Resort: This superb resort (788 rooms on Sea Harbor Drive, behind SeaWorld) is highly notable for its style, service and genuine hospitality. It boasts a massive 10-storey atrium lobby and some equally enormous rooms and suites, an extensive (recently remodelled) pool area with bar and grill, tennis courts, fitness centre with sauna and steam room, plus kids' play areas and activities. There's a choice of bars and shops, and all rooms have recently been renovated to a high standard as part of a $31m makeover in 2007, which added extra bathroom amenities, flatscreen TVs and the Marriott company's Revive bedding. The new dining line-up includes the Mist Sushi Lobby Bar, the Boardwalk Sports Bar, the upscale but casual Tradewinds for breakfast, lunch and dinner, The Deli and a Starbucks café. The hotel offers some great packages in conjunction with SeaWorld, which is a 2-minute walk across the car park, and its rates are often the best in the Deluxe category (1800 327 6677, **marriott.com**).

Rosen Shingle Creek Hotel: This 230 acre/93ha hotel opened in September 2006 and ranks among the grandest. In the middle of the award-winning Shingle Creek Golf Club (with its acclaimed Brad Brewer Golf Academy), just to the east of I-Drive behind the Convention Center, it boasts 1,500 rooms and suites, all with immaculate furnishings and comfort, as well as a full-service spa and state-of-the-art fitness centre. Rooms vary from standard doubles to presidential suites, but all with fabulous flatscreen TVs, wireless

Rosen Shingle Creek Hotel

internet access, fridges and first-class toiletries. Amenities include 5 restaurants, 4 bars, a lounge, coffee house, deli and ice-creamery, plus 3 outdoor pools, tennis, basketball and volleyball courts and nature trails. There is also a neat kids club, The Swamp, for 4–14s (5–11pm Thurs, 5pm–midnight Fri–Sat; $12/hour first child, $8/hour each additional child). The whole resort is built in a 1900s' Spanish revival style, and it provides immaculate service (especially at concierge level). Look out in particular for the exquisite A Land Remembered, its upscale steakhouse (one of the best in the state and named after a famous Florida novel) in the Golf Clubhouse, and Cala Bella, a spectacular fine-dining Italian restaurant, with truly out-of-this-world desserts from its renowned pastry chef (407 996 9939, **shingle creekresort.com**).

BRITTIP

Don't miss the 1.5ml/2.4km nature trail at the Rosen Shingle Creek Hotel, among the cypress trees, creeks and lush natural vegetation, where you might spot some local wildlife.

Westin Imagine Orlando: Also on Universal Boulevard, this is another new condo-hotel property, the first part of an extensive residential and hotel/shopping community that will build up in the next 2–3 years. The hotel features 315 1- and 2-bed suites, with either kitchenettes or full kitchens, and the trademark Westin Heavenly bed, plus other distinctive decor and furnishing touches. There is also a signature Italian restaurant, a lobby lounge and pool Tiki Bar, in addition to a modern fitness centre (407 233 2200, **starwoodhotels.com**). When completed, the full development will encompass 30 acres/ 12ha with 1,000 homes, and condo-hotel units (**westinimagine.com**).

Blue Heron Beach Resort

Lake Buena Vista

Moving to the next major resort area, there is a growing range of deluxe choice here, too.

Blue Heron Beach Resort: Not quite the full 'beach' experience (it is set on the edge of Lake Bryan), this brand new condo-hotel complex on SR-535 features 140 beautifully furnished 1-, 2- and 3-bed condos, all with a balcony and fully equipped kitchen. There is a huge 6,000sq ft/557sq m pool, kids' pool, video game room, pool bar, fitness centre and a wetlands lakeside walk, but no restaurant of any kind (though there are plenty within walking distance). And, as a 'self-catering' resort, daily housekeeping service is available only for a separate charge. The second phase (of 4) is due to open in early 2009 (407 387 2910, **blueheronbeach resort.com**).

Hilton at Bonnet Creek Resort: Due to open in September 2009, this is a rare and extensive development in a unique position inside *Walt Disney World* but privately owned (the only piece of land that Walt was unable to buy from the original landowners back in 1966). It is also part of a twin 480 acre/194ha resort complex with a new Waldorf-Astoria (see page 90) and hence shares some of the same deluxe facilities. The Hilton itself features 1,000 rooms, 4 restaurants, a lagoon pool complex with lazy river and waterslide, an ultra-modern fitness centre, 18-holf golf course, tennis courts and the adjoining full-

Condo-hotels

Many of Orlando's newer developments are of the condo-hotel variety, a cross between a villa and a hotel. Instead of a villa, people buy hotel 'rooms' in these big properties (which look, to all intents and purposes, like regular resorts), which they then own – unlike timeshare, where you just 'own' a time period for a resort. All the rooms are identically furnished, unlike villas, but tend to include kitchens and separate bedrooms. They are then rented out by a management company on behalf of the owners. For guests, they are booked as you would for any hotel. Some are owned and run by hotel groups like Starwood and Four Seasons, while others are just managed by hotel specialists to ensure they are maintained to the right standards. They are usually built in tower blocks around communal facilities with a club house and guest check-in, and include pools (often with elaborate water features and play areas), restaurants, fitness centres and even luxury spas. They will be more expensive than a typical hotel, but they do provide more style and amenities.

service European spa. Fine dining will be provided by the Italian-themed La Luce restaurant, while the chic Pomegranate Restaurant will offer the main alternative, along with the Mojo Coffee Bar, Zeta bar/lounge and Blue Beech pool bar and grill. One of its prime draws, though, is that it is just minutes from the Disney parks and attractions, and benefits from the full Hilton package of stylish accommodation and an entertaining children's activity programmes (407 722 3456, **hilton.com**).

Hyatt Regency Grand Cypress: The area's first genuine Deluxe resort is also still one of the best. Opened in 1984, it is a mature 1,500 acre/608ha resort with a unique mix of facilities, including a rare 9-hole pitch-and-putt golf course, 27 holes of regular golf (designed by Jack Nicklaus), a golf academy, boating lake and even an equestrian centre. It is also due to undergo a carefully phased \$50m/£25.5m refurbishment in late 2008/09 that will add significantly to its upmarket appeal. The elegant lobby will be enhanced with a new lounge-bar area and an enlarged sushi bar, while a modern, full-service spa will be added on the lower level. There will also be alterations to both the La Coquina gourmet restaurant and the main Cascade dining room. The 750 guest rooms will be extensively refurbished to provide a contemporary European design ambience with some beautiful finishing touches like large flatscreen TVs, larger shower units and elaborate lighting. The hotel is also perfectly situated, almost on the doorstep of Disney and yet blissfully self contained (on Winter Garden-Vineland Road, just around the corner from the Crossroads Plaza at Lake Buena Vista). The huge free-form swimming pool comes complete with jacuzzis, waterfalls and slide, while the white sand beach and magnificent array of restaurants make for a sumptuous stay, especially Hemingway's, its Key West-styled dinner spot, and La Coquina, with a novel Chef's Table inside the kitchen 3 evenings a week and a sensational Sunday Brunch. There is also a sports bar and grill, pool bar, a deli-style café and a general store. Once among its richly landscaped grounds, you could easily be light years away from the theme park hustle-bustle (407 239 1234, **http://grandcypress.hyatt.com**).

Hyatt Regency Grand Cypress

Lake Buena Vista Resort Village & Spa: This stylish condo-hotel opened in 2006 with the first of five current tower blocks (there will eventually be 14) of 2-, 3- and 4-bed condos, right next to Lake Buena Vista Factory Stores on Highway 535. The current phase includes a magnificent free-form swimming pool, complete with pirate play-ship for the kids, a second quiet pool, a fitness centre, video games room, convenience store and gift shop, plus a Pizza Hut Express, a specialist pub-restaurant (Frankie Farrell's Irish Pub & Grille) and a truly superb spa. The rooms themselves (all with full kitchens, jacuzzi tubs, digital TVs and internet) are comfortable and stylish, with the 4-bed condos incredibly spacious. The fully completed village will eventually feature 4 pools, jacuzzis, children's play areas, tennis courts and clubhouse, plus more restaurants and shops. The Reflections Spa & Salon in particular is a 5-star facility offering some wonderfully relaxing treatments (407 597 0214, **lbvorlandoresort.com**).

BRITTIP

Visiting the Lake Buena Vista Factory Stores? Relieve aching limbs by popping next door to the Resort Village & Spa for a soothing pedicure, or some of its blissful massage and other spa treatments (407 597 1695).

Waldorf-Astoria: The second part of the 480 acre/194ha Hilton Bonnet Creek development, this 498-room hotel is the first Waldorf outside New York and should add a whole new level of luxury to the Orlando scene when it opens in September 2009. Stately, distinguished and serene, the historic Waldorf will feature 313 standard rooms with Italian marble bathrooms and 42-inch high-definition flatscreen TVs, and 185 suites ranging from 945sq ft/88sq m to a humongous 3,300sq ft/306sq m, with a grand foyer, 2 bathrooms and butler service. The zero-entry pool boasts cabanas and waiter service, and then there is the dining choice, from the poolside grille and Bull and Bear Steakhouse to the small-plate cuisine of Peacock Alley and gourmet style of signature Oscar's brasserie. The Spa by Guerlain will also be unashamedly 5-star in its scope. Other amenities include floodlit basketball and tennis courts, jogging trails, free bike rentals, a state-of-the-art fitness centre (with personal trainers), yoga and aerobics classes and a range of boutique shops that are all on a par with the Waldorf's deluxe cachet. Even children are not forgotten, with the Young Explorers activity programmes for creative and educational fun (407 722 3863, **waldorfastoriaorlando.com**).

The Waldorf-Astoria will be finished in September 2009

Kissimmee

The more budget-oriented area of Osceola County also now has its share of upmarket properties.

Celebration Hotel: In the Disney-inspired town of Celebration just off Highway 192, the Central Florida Greeneway and I-4, this unique hotel offers a refreshing small-town America style. It has an elegant lounge and 2 reception desks, and you are a long way from the usual tourist hurly-burly. With just 115 rooms in its 1920s' wood-frame design, the Celebration has a classy ambience and a wealth of high-quality touches, notably in the ultra-comfy rooms. These come in a choice of an attic-like Retreat, Traditional (with either a king or 2 queen-size beds), Studio or a 2-room suite and are all beautifully furnished. Lovely artwork, courteous staff and a good array of facilities – pool, jacuzzi and fitness centre, plus the Plantation Room Restaurant (excellent buffet breakfasts and a range of 'new Florida' dishes) – mark out this hotel as a real gem. In addition, it is within a short stroll of the town's shops, restaurants and lakeside walks. It is also ideal for a romantic stay (407 566 6000, **celebrationhotel.com**).

Gaylord Palms Resort: One of the most dramatic hotels, with 1,406 rooms, is on the junction of I-Drive South and Osceola Parkway (ideal for Disney). A cross between a convention centre and a vast turn-of-the-century Florida mansion, it features 4½ acres/2ha of indoor gardens, fountains and 'landscaped' waters under a glass dome, with live entertainment nightly. Three themed indoor areas bear witness to great creativity and the resort offers every creature comfort, with an array of restaurants and bars, full-service spa, children's centre and 10 shops. Its imaginative Recreation Park has 2 full-size pools (1 family-orientated, with octopus waterslide and kids' splash area; the other a sophisticated

BRITTIP

The Gaylord Palms features the truly stunning Christmas celebration ICE!, a wonderland of ice sculptures, snow scenery and ice slides, plus skating. Early Nov–3 Jan, tickets $20 adults, $16 over-55s and $10 4–12s, or combo tickets (ICE! plus skating) for $25, $20 and $14.

adults-only area), bocce court (a type of boules), volleyball, croquet lawn and a realistic 9-hole putting challenge. Standard rooms are some of the smartest and most spacious in the area, while the suites are enormous. There is even a hotel-within-a-hotel, as the central Emerald Tower offers an even more upmarket room choice and concierge facilities. One area is landscaped like the Everglades, with native plants, trees and animals; another copies St Augustine's old-world charm, with replica Spanish fort; and the third reproduces the offbeat style of Key West, with a mock-up marina and sailboat. To walk into the resort's marbled lobby and cavernous interior at night is like entering a future world. Then there is the resort's signature fine dining, with the choice of Old Hickory Steakhouse (naturally aged Black Angus beef a speciality), Sunset Sam's (for fine seafood) and the Spanish buffet-style Villa de Flora, plus the new Sora sushi bar. The Canyon Ranch Spa Club is one of the area's largest, with a state-of-the-art

Gaylord Palms Resort

spa, fitness facilities and beauty salon. There are an amazing 13 shops, plus the Java Coast coffee shop, Auggie's Jammin' Piano Bar and H2O Sports Bar and Grille. The hotel stages regular special events and it is also a great venue for weddings (407 586 2000, **gaylordhotels.com**).

Mona Lisa Suite Hotel: Another of the area's new condo-hotels, right at the entrance to the town of Celebration on Highway 192, this is a luxury 5-storey, 240-unit property set around a spectacular 'vanishing edge' swimming pool and boasting up-scale dining (breakfast, lunch and dinner at The Galerie Restaurant & Bar). The suites feature beautifully furnished living areas, full kitchens and ultra-comfy bedrooms, with Egyptian cotton linens, down pillows and duvets, and L'Occitane toiletries. All have balconies that overlook either the infinity pool or lush landscaping. There is a complimentary shuttle service to Disney's theme parks and privileged use of the Celebration Day Spa and Golf Club (1866 404 6662; **http://monalisasuitehotel.com**).

Further afield

Beyond the main tourist areas is a further selection of high-quality offerings.

Grand Bohemian Hotel: Sister property to the Celebration, this adds a touch of class to the downtown scene. It features an early 20th-century Austrian theme, with the accent on fine art, fine dining and good service. Its 14 storeys make it a major landmark and it boasts the wonderful Boheme restaurant and über-stylish Bösendorfer Lounge – with great live entertainment nightly – plus a 14th-floor concierge suite, heated pool, spa, fitness centre, Gallery of Fine Art and Starbucks lounge. The rooms are superbly appointed: all with high-speed internet access, mini-bars, CD players and interactive TVs, plus there are 36 superb suites. Every room features the ultra-comfy Sumptuous Bed (407 313 9000, **grandbohemianhotel.com**).

Bösendorfer Lounge at the Grand Bohemian

Grande Lakes Orlando: You'll find mega-luxury at this 500 acre/200ha combination of a 584-room, 5-star Ritz-Carlton Hotel, a 1,000-room JW Marriott Hotel, 40,000sq ft/3,700sq m spa, an 18-hole Greg Norman-designed golf course, tennis centre and a range of shops and 11 restaurants, including the outstanding Norman's, featuring the 'new world' cuisine of celebrity chef Norman Van Aken. Located on the edge of a forestry preserve, it feels secluded and remote – quite a feat in this area. It is slightly off the beaten track – at the junction of John Young and Central Florida Parkway – yet only 2mls/3km from SeaWorld, 7mls/11km from Universal Orlando and 10mls/16km from Disney and Orlando International Airport.

The **JW Marriott** is the flagship hotel for the Marriott group, with Spanish-Moorish design, a formal Italian restaurant, French brasserie, Starbucks coffee lounge and a pool bar and grill. It also has a wonderful 'lazy river' mini-water park, plus a children's zero-depth entry pool and splash fountain. And, while the Marriott is more convention-orientated, it is well geared for families with all its own facilities plus the option to use the Ritz Kids programme and dining options next door. Rooms are plush and ultra-comfortable; 70% have balconies and there are 64 grand suites. The golf course is immaculate and every foursome is assigned a free caddie (virtually unknown for a public course in Florida). The beautiful citrus-tinged Health Spa boasts a huge fitness centre and aerobics studio, lap pool (all free to guests at both hotels), lovely spa-cuisine restaurant and a huge array of massages and therapies. The pricing is suitably upscale, but it is a rare holiday treat (407 206 2300, **http://jw-marriott.grandelakes.com**).

BRITTIP

Head for the Ritz-Carlton's lobby lounge for afternoon tea or drinks in style with a magnificent view, especially at sunset.

The **Ritz-Carlton** is the first of the brand's properties in central Florida, and the scale and detail are wonderful: lush gardens, abundant lakes and streams, Venetian-inspired architecture and a wealth of genuine antiques. It has a large, sloped-entry pool, kids' pool, 3 floodlit tennis courts, a signature shop and 5 restaurants, plus a separate children's check-in and the excellent Ritz Kids Club (5–12s), while all the restaurants offer child menus. The rooms are gorgeous – beautifully furnished, with high-quality products in the marbled bathrooms – and feature plasma-screen TVs, radio/CD, mini-bar, hair-dryer, slippers and robes, and all have balconies. There are 66 spacious suites and 92 Club rooms on the top 2 floors, with concierge and butler service, food and drink presentations in the Club Lounge and Bvlgari amenities. Two kidsuites feature a separate bedroom and bathroom, with toys, games, TV and video games for 100% child appeal (407 206 2400, **http://the-ritz-carlton.grandelakes.com/**).

Omni Orlando Resort at Champions Gate: A real golfing paradise, this offers 720 rooms and suites overlooking a superb golf set-up with 2 Greg Norman-designed courses. An imposing hotel with impressive facilities, including the HQ of the renowned David Leadbetter golf academy, main swimming pool and activity pool (including a 'lazy river' feature, fountains and waterslide), 4 restaurants (notably the superb Asian cuisine of Zen and the chic David's Club bar-restaurant), coffee bar, deli, 3 lounge bars, state-of-the-art health club and full service spa. Just 10 minutes south of Disney and right off I-4, this is well situated yet slightly off the beaten track for those looking for something different (especially golfers). Set in 1,500 landscaped acres/607ha and with a magnificent vista as you walk in the front doors, it suits both business traveller and leisure-seeker alike. It also has 59 superb 2- and 3-bed villas, affording a more private stay, with full kitchens and an amazing array of specialised services in addition to opulent furnishings (407 390 6664, **omnihotels.com** and **championsgate golf.com**).

Holiday resorts

This accommodation type combines the best of hotels, suites and villas, though some of the purpose-built complexes double as timeshare resorts (or vacation ownership) and the new condo-hotel type. Resorts have the advantage of a greater variety of facilities. They tend to be fairly spread out and don't necessarily feature any signature restaurants, but they represent a very flexible choice.

Champions Gate

Bahama Bay Resort: A wonderful place on Lake Davenport in Davenport (at the west end of Highway 192, then south on Highway 27, or enter off of Westside Blvd), this opened in 2003 and is spread over 70 acres/28ha, with 498 condos in 38 buildings, 2 and 3 storeys high. The community is woven with tropical landscaping that includes water features, a recreation centre and clubhouse, restaurant and snack bar, internet café, fitness centre, sauna and spa (the fabulous Eleuthera Spa & Salon), tennis, basketball and volleyball, 4 heated pools and kiddie pools. You can fish in the lake, which has a sandy beach, plus there is a video arcade and small cinema. A regular shuttle goes to and from the theme parks for a small charge. The 4 types of condo offer 2-bed, 2-bath (sleeping 6, with a sofa-bed in the lounge) and 3-bed, 2-bath (sleeping 8, again with sofa-bed), with fitted kitchen, laundry room/washer-dryer, living room and dining area. The Grand Bahama 3-bed condo has 1,739sq ft/162sq m of space and is one of the most elegant (0870 160 9632 in the UK, 1866 830 1617 in the US or **bahamabay.com**).

Barefoot'n in the Keys: This boutique little timeshare development of 40 1-bed self-catering condos is nicely tucked away next to Old Town in Kissimmee and will be dramatically enhanced in 2009 with another 50 1- and 2-bed units. On-site is a main pool, children's pool and whirlpool, while the facilities of sister property Liki Tiki Village (see below) are also available (407 589 2127, **barefootn.com**).

Cypress Pointe Resort: Tucked away in Lake Buena Vista (just off Apopka-Vineland Rd north of the Crossroads area) but convenient for all the attractions is this well-established timeshare resort offering a terrific spread of facilities as well as comfy 1- and 2-bed rooms. There is a large main pool, kiddie pool and whirlpool, fitness centre, games room and gift shop, and all rooms feature whirlpool baths, full kitchen and satellite TV (407 238 2300, **cypress-pointe.com**).

Liki Tiki Village: On the western fringe of Highway 192, this timeshare set-up often has good-value apartments to rent on a weekly basis. Its newest blocks offer huge 2-bed apartments, with well-equipped kitchens (all with coffee and ice makers), while the 64 acre/26ha complex boasts 2 pools, a mini water park, tennis courts, paddle boats, bikes, pool-bar and grill and free continental breakfast Mon–Fri when timeshare presentations are held – but you don't have to attend the timeshare hard-sell (407 239 5000, **islandone.com**).

The beach at Bahama Bay

Our deluxe recommendations

It's hard to go wrong with your choice in this area, but our personal favourites would be:

Gaylord Palms

Hyatt Grand Cypress

Orlando World Center Marriott

Portofino Bay Hotel

Rosen Shingle Creek Resort

Mystic Dunes Resort and Golf Club: Formerly the Wyndham Palms Resort and tucked away in a quiet corner of Kissimmee, this is primarily a holiday ownership property but it also offers hotel rentals, often at terrific rates. It is a truly luxurious resort with just about every facility you could think of, plus an impressive array of beautiful 1-, 2- and 3-bed villas that sleep up to 12 (1800 463 7256, **mystic-dunes-resort.com**).

Orange Lake Resort: A hugely extensive resort 4½mls/7km west of Maingate on Highway 192 with a mixture of well-furnished 1-, 2- and 3-bed villas and suites (sleeping 5–12), golf, water sports and cinema. Then there are kids' activities, exercise classes, tennis, racquetball, mini-golf and a Village Marketplace of general store, pizzeria and golf shop. The amazing 12 acre/4.8ha water park River Island boasts a lazy river, 2 zero-depth entry pools, mini-golf, whirlpool tubs and waterfalls, and a new Clubhouse, arcade and fitness center opened in 2008. The Water's Edge entertainment complex was due to open later in 2008, adding two restaurants, poolside bars, cabanas and gift shop, along with an Olympic-size pool with feature beach-style entry (407 239 0000, **orangelake.com**).

Regal Oaks at Old Town: Newly opened in 2008 is this mix of luxury townhomes, from 3-bed, 2-bath units to grand 4-bed, 3-bath villas. The second resort opened by British-owned Superior Group, it follows the successful blueprint of accommodation set around an elaborate clubhouse, with water features, restaurant and other facilities, including a smart spa. Situated right next to all the fun and shopping of Old Town in Kissimmee, it all adds up to terrific value (407 997 1000, **regaloaksresort.com**).

Regal Palms Resort: This development set the style for the popular Superior Group developments. Next door to the Highlands Reserve vacation home community on Highway 27, it offers a pleasing mix of 3- and 4-bed townhomes and 4- to 6-bed private pool homes, all set around a beautiful Clubhouse that includes a mini water park (with lazy river and waterslides), pools, jacuzzis and extensive sun terraces. It also features a pub that shows live UK sports, a business centre, gym and gift shop/grocery store, plus an indulgent Spa & Health Club (863 424 6141, **regalpalms orlando.com**). A third Superior property, Oakmont Resort & Spa, is under construction. Check out **superiorus.com**.

Reunion Resort & Club: Arguably the grandest of all the resorts, this will be of keen interest to golfers who appreciate the 5-star touch. On Highway 532 in Kissimmee, just off exit 58 of I-4 south of Disney, this fledgling 'community' will have 6,000

Reunion Resort

units when complete in 2012, but it already boasts a vast line-up of condos, townhomes and luxury homes set around 3 superb golf courses (designed by Arnold Palmer, Tom Watson and Jack Nicklaus). The choice is deluxe in every way: 1-, 2- and 3-bed immaculate condo villas (many with stunning views over the golf courses); a range of private homes, from modest 3-beds to mansion-style 8-beds (costing upwards of $1.8m/£918m), but all available for rent (and some for sale); a stylish golf clubhouse with excellent bar and restaurant; a full-service spa, with a superb array of beauty and health treatments; the scenic Seven Eagles pool, complete with Pavilion Bar & Grille, jacuzzis, fitness room and children's activity centre; 5 floodlit tennis courts with professional instruction; an amazing water park consisting of lazy river, slides, pools, waterfalls and interactive kids' area; and miles of biking and hiking trails. Its first high-rise condo, the Reunion Grande, opened in 2007, with 82 luxurious 1- and 2-bed suites, magnificent fine-dining chophouse Forte, a state-of-the-art fitness facility and, uniquely for central Florida, a rooftop pool and bar, serving up tapas, cocktails and panoramic views. It all comes with concierge service and even private in-room dining that marks this out as one of Florida's most upmarket resorts. Much is still to be finished, but all the golf courses are operating, and the clubhouse also benefits from the supervision of outstanding executive chef Shawn Kane, who has made a name for himself with Disney and others. Only those staying here or members can play on the courses, but the scale and imagination of the resort make it quite awesome. There is even an activity programme for children, Kids Crew (8am–5pm Sun–Fri, 8am–11pm Sat) at $12/hour per child and $6 for lunch (1888 418 9611, **reunionresort.com**). Reunion is also home every April to the LPGA Ginn Open, one of the richest women's golf tournaments. Reunion guests can improve their technique at state-of-the-art facility Annika's Academy of Golf and Fitness, created under the careful supervision of top golfer Annika Sorenstam.

Windsor Palms Resort villa

Sheraton Vistana Resort: This sprawling family-friendly timeshare property in Lake Buena Vista, close to Walt Disney World, features roomy 1- and 2-bed/2-bath villas (sleeping 4–8) with fully equipped kitchens, 7 giant pools, 13 tennis courts, a food court, restaurant and convenience store. There is a free shuttle to Disney parks and lots of family-orientated activities, including cookouts and storytelling (407 239 3100, **sheraton.com/vistanaresort**).

Sheraton Vistana Villages: A sister property, located on International Drive south of SeaWorld, this upscale family resort offers spacious 1- and 2-bed/2-bath villas with fully equipped kitchen, dining area, washer/dryer and more. Less than 6mls/9.9km from Disney, guests enjoy resort amenities like free scheduled shuttles to the theme parks, a large pool, fitness centre, games room, basketball, tennis courts and 2 restaurants (407 238 5000, **sheraton.com/vistanavillages**).

Summer Bay Resort: Out on west Highway 192 is a mix of Budget motel (The Inn at Summer Bay), Standard hotel (Holiday Inn Express), some

Tuscana

3-bed vacation homes and new 1-, 2- and 3-bed villas and condos. The 700 rooms spread over 64 acres/26ha are all smart, while the facilities include outdoor heated pools and kiddie pools, an elaborate children's water-play area, mini-golf, clubhouse with volleyball, tennis, basketball, shuffleboard and fitness room, video arcade, gift shop and snack bar. The lake provides jet-skis, paddleboats, waterskiing and more, plus daily kids' activities and organised sports. Even those in The Inn and Holiday Inn (which has its own pool and breakfast area) benefit from the clubhouse facilities, while there is a Denny's diner and Publix supermarket next door. It represents great value in this area, with wonderful accommodation in the condos, and is still only 15 minutes from Disney (1888 782 9847, **summerbayresort.com**).

Tuscana: Bordering the Champions Gate golf courses, this Mediterranean-inspired condo-resort offers 288 oversize 2- and 3-bedroom condos, each with 2 full baths, balcony, fully equipped kitchen, washer and dryer. The $2m/£1m clubhouse boasts a Café and Tiki Bar, elegant pool, kiddie pool, cabanas, exercise facilities and a 35-seat movie theatre (407 787 4800, **tuscana.net**).

Windsor Palms Resort: Just off West Highway 192 in Kissimmee, this popular gated community has a mix of 2-bed condos, 2- and 3-bed townhomes, and 3- to 6-bed pool homes. Amenities include a large clubhouse and fitness centre, tennis courts, an Olympic-sized pool, a kiddie pool and spa, basketball, billiard room, volleyball court, video arcade, playground and a 58-seat cinema showing recent films. Similarly, the (slightly newer) sister resort of **Windsor Hills Resort** on Old Lake Wilson Road offers the same spread of accommodation choice and impressive amenities, like its huge lagoon-style pool with waterslide and state-of-the-art fitness centre (1800 503 1127, **globalresortshomes.com**).

B&B choice

Bed-and-breakfast in Orlando is offered in a more upscale, almost boutique style than we know it in the UK. The Lake Eola district in downtown has two fine choices: **The Veranda** has 12 individual, cottage-style rooms, ranging from Queen Studio and King Suites to a lovely honeymoon suite in landscaped gardens with a private courtyard, pool and spa area. Breakfast consists of fresh pastries, seasonal fruits, juices, tea and coffee, and it's a quiet spot, though an easy walk to some good restaurants and shops (407 489 0321, **theverandabandb.com**); and the nearby **Eo Inn and Urban Spa**, a genuine boutique hotel and spa (with a huge range of treatments), featuring 17 deluxe rooms. The lush grounds, rooftop terrace and lake vistas provide a refreshing alternative to the usual hotel experience (407 481 8485, **eoinn.com**).

Perri House B&B: Beautifully tucked away in a quiet location yet only 5 minutes from Disney property, this has a genuine country-house charm and semi-rural setting (on a voluntary bird sanctuary). Its 8 rooms and Villa de Perri, which has a full kitchen and sleeps up to 6, are a true delight and the whole property is a real one-off in this rare location (on Winter Garden-Vineland Road). It makes a wonderfully romantic little hideaway as all rooms have king 4-poster or queen canopy beds and some sweet individual touches. There is also a pool and jacuzzi, plus a hearty continental breakfast buffet (407 876 4830, **perrihouse.com**).

Wonderland Inn: A restored, 11-room Historic Registry property off the beaten track in Kissimmee but only 10 minutes from the Highway 192 area. Each of its rooms has a delightful, individual touch, and several are designed for singles as well as doubles, and there's also a honeymoon suite. The staff are wonderfully attentive and even the lovely gardens have an old-fashioned charm, with their gourmet continental breakfast served amid the flowers and birdhouses (407 847 2477, **bnblist.com/fl/wonderland_inn/**).

HOLIDAY HOMES

This is in many ways the biggest area of accommodation in Orlando, especially for UK visitors. There has been a huge development of holiday homes in the last 20 years, and it shows no sign of stopping. Generally speaking, vacation homes provide a valuable way for large families and groups to stay together and cut costs by self-catering. The homes (or 'villas'), whether individual houses, collections of houses, resorts or condominiums (apartment blocks), often have access to other communal facilities like large pools and recreation areas, and are always equipped with microwaves, multiple TVs and washer-dryers. For these, a hire car is usually essential, but the savings can be significant. Prices can be as low as $450/week off-peak, but expect to pay at least $1,500/week for a 5- or 6-bed villa in high season.

Wonderland Inn

Holiday homes to rent are big business in central Florida and now account for a huge slice of the European market as they are ideal for repeat visitors, large groups and those who like their privacy and own facilities. They tend to be grouped in newly built estates and some are gated communities for added security. Nearly all offer a private pool and the largest can sleep 16. Some are classed as 'executive' homes, and this usually means more facilities (games rooms, barbecues, jacuzzis, etc.) rather than an increase in size. If you book independently, there are several key questions to ask:

Do you need to go to an office some way away to pick up the keys or is there a combination lockbox at the house? Is there a local contact if anything goes wrong (most owners do not live in Florida) and is the property maintained by a local company? Does it offer a security bonding for your booking, and is it a member of a reputable organisation like the Better Business Bureau of Central Florida? In winter, is the pool heated, and what is the charge for heating? Finally, is it as close to Disney as it says – some homes can be down in Polk County, which can be 40 minutes' drive away.

A word of warning, though – once you've experienced pool-at-home life, you may never go back to a hotel!

There are some 26,000 homes on offer these days, spread right across Kissimmee and out in Polk, Lake and Orange Counties to the west and south-west of Disney. Some are brand new and still suffer from ongoing

Rental Accommodation

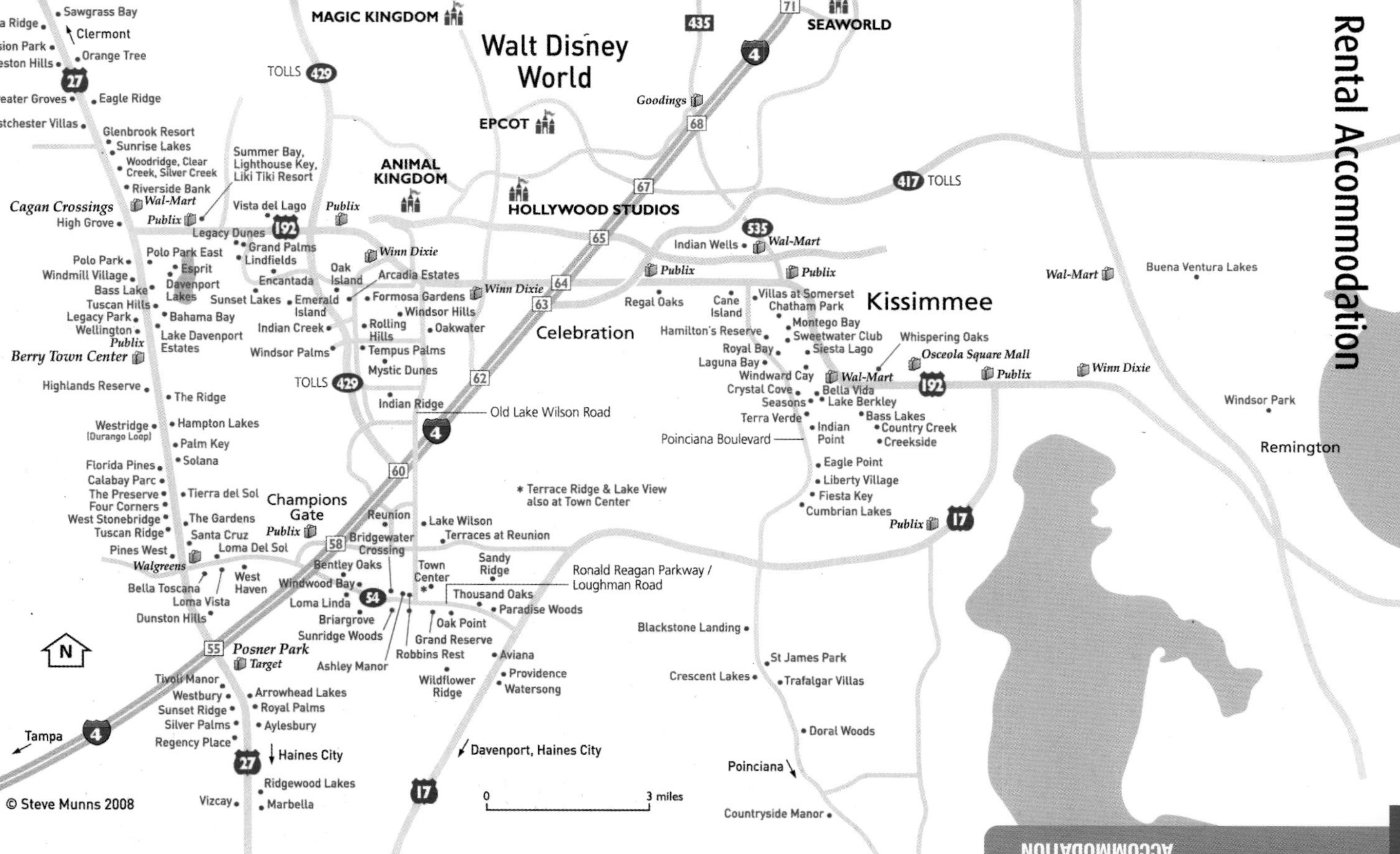

construction, others are now well established and mature (Highlands Reserve is a good example), while others may be in need of repairs. You can rent either direct from the owners (on sites like **vrbo.com** and **lastminutevillas.net**) or from a property management company, which will look after multiple villas. Ironically, there is also a move to 'townhomes', which are a more British style of terraced house (so developers can fit in more!); for a 'detached' house, ask for a 'single family home'.

The bottom line is you must do your homework and shop around as you would for any significant purchase, and check with organisations like the Central Florida Vacation Rental Managers Association. This is the only generally acknowledged umbrella organisation for the holiday home business and helps to provide a level of credibility and weed out some of the rogue operators we've seen in the past. The following companies all pass the *Brit Guide* credibility test.

Advantage Vacation Homes: In the villa rental business for 20 years and one of the largest companies, none of its 2–6 bed homes (the majority are on West Highway 192 and Highway 27 in Clermont and Davenport) are more than 7 years old, while many are 3–4 years at most. It also manages an increasing portfolio of condos (in the Bahama Bay and Sun Lake resorts) and townhomes. It offers 24-hour management, with courteous and efficient staff at its office just off west Highway 192 (plus an attraction ticket service), open 9am–10pm daily. Its

Check them out!

The Central Florida Vacation Rental Managers Association has a new website designed to promote villa rentals and make booking easier. Look it up at **www.vacationwith confidence.com**. There is also another general website that sets out the advantages at **www.discovervacationhomes.com**.

Advantage Vacation Homes

holiday homes are rated Silver, Gold or Platinum, with the difference measured in the extras rather than size (larger-screen or plasma TVs, tiled floors rather than carpeting and perhaps a jacuzzi or games room). Newer properties on Highway 27 usually have communal playgrounds and tennis courts (0871 711 9531 in the UK, 1800 527 2262 in the US, **advantagevacationhomes.com**).

Alexander Holiday Homes: Family-owned, Alexander manages some 260 properties in Kissimmee, from standard condo-villas to luxury executive homes sleeping 14, all with pools and immaculately furnished, within 15–20 minutes of Disney. This company was the first of its kind in Orlando (in 1981) and still offers a highly personable, efficient service. It was only the third management company in Florida to earn the distinguished AAA (American Automobile Association) 3 Diamonds rating and definitely gets our approval. It also shows prices in UK and US currency and even offers an airport meet-and-greet service to ensure you get to your home. Its informative website also provides photo tours of all its homes (0871 711 5371 in the UK, 1800 621 7888 in the US, **floridasunshine.com**).

Executive example

A good example of the newer homes on offer are provided by typical UK owners Nina and Pete Dew, who have 3 Orlando properties on their website **floridavipvacationhomes.com**. Set in 2 new communities – Sandy Ridge and Terrace Ridge – just to the south of Disney (but still barely 15 minutes' drive away), they are representative of the more upmarket, 'executive'-style homes.

Florida Choice Vacation Homes: Provides townhouses (3–4 beds with communal pools and recreation facilities), standard and executive homes (3–7 bed private properties) in Orlando and Naples, some with heated pools and with free local phone calls. There is optional maid service and cot and highchair rentals (407 397 3013, **floridachoice.com**).

Florida Leisure Vacation Homes: Another company we know well and can recommend, it is British-owned and pays great attention to detail. With almost 100 homes (3–7 beds) in the Kissimmee area, most just a few years old, it prides itself on a personal touch (even down to providing personal chef, massage and concierge services) and offers some of the biggest and newest properties, as well as a fully automated online booking system. Many are in the Executive range, with the fullest array of amenities in addition to their private, screened pools, and often in gated communities. All homes have lockboxes, so you don't need to visit the management office to check in. You can see all its homes online (in extended photo and video) plus lots of local info, especially for restaurants and golf, while its new testimonial sections provide first-hand feedback. Its office is on Highway 192 in Kissimmee, at the junction with Apopka-Vineland Road, SR 535 (407 870 1600; **floridaleisure.com**).

FRO Group: Another local British specialist also involved in creating a villa community of homes that are purpose-designed for the disabled (Monticelli at Tower Lake), it already features a select range of new homes in some of the smartest local developments. Options include Formosa Garden Estates, Emerald Island Resorts and a rare twin-centre opportunity with some lovely beachfront villas on the Gulf Coast at Indian Shores (near St Pete Beach). Its concierge service offers the chance to arrange many other services in advance (like dining), while its website features a Last Minute Deals section (a great money-saver), and you can rent things like barbecues and cots on a weekly basis. It is also building an advice centre for people looking to expand their businesses or simply relocate to sunny Florida (1866 394 2583; **fro-group.com**).

Loyalty Homes: For a luxury touch, all these homes (2–7 bedrooms) are no more than 4mls/6.5 km from Disney and all offer the true 'executive' style, with the likes of digital door locks (so no key collection required), cable TV and many with games rooms. The website offers video tours, too (407 397 7475, **loyaltyusa.com**).

Premier Vacation Homes: A good range of spacious properties with 2–6 bedrooms, sleeping up to 14, in secure residential communities within a 15-minute drive of Disney. All are privately owned and have been

Florida Choice Vacation Homes

purchased and furnished as holiday homes, with screened pools, 2 TVs, fully equipped kitchens (including dishwasher, washer-dryer, microwave and coffee maker), at least 1 king or queen bed, and free local phone calls. Maid service can be added for a fee. The Luxury homes (2–4 beds) are the standard accommodation, while Executive homes (3–6 beds) are bigger, with an extra TV, VCR and barbecue, and there is also an expanded townhome and condo choice (407 396 2401, **pr-vacation.com**).

BRITTIP

You'll find Marmite, Ribena, McVities etc., at all local Publix supermarkets, at the new Wal-Mart on Turkey Lake Road or the 24-hour Goodings stores at Crossroads and on I-Drive. Just look in the store for the 'international' aisle.

Prestige Vacations Direct: Another British-owned and run company, this agency specialises purely in renting out a wide variety of vacation homes, from 3- to 7-bed homes, most within a short drive from Disney. They can provide special month-long rates and even UK sterling prices, as well as having periodic special offers, and feature as many as 26 different villa communities, from the Windsor Palms resort to Westridge and Highlands Reserve out on Highway 27 (1877 462 4424, **prestigevacations direct.com**).

Sun Villas Florida Direct

Sun Villas Florida Direct: An alternative UK-based company providing bespoke holidays offering villa accommodation, flights, attraction tickets and car hire. Its variety of properties in Orlando and all the along the Gulf Coast maintain consistently high standards (01926 336 611, **sunvillasfloridadirect.com**).

Villa Direct: Another major Orlando specialist, and one of the biggest, with an extensive range of some 600 properties in the area, from 2-bed condos to luxury 7-bed villas, and a good user-friendly website, plus an excellent range of guest services, including arrival groceries and even mobility equipment rental. Its office is handily located on Highway 192, 2mls/3.2km from Disney (1877 259 9908, **villadirect.com**).

BUYING A HOLIDAY HOME

The quality of life, the favourable exchange rate, an attractive 'buyer's market' and fabulous weather are all compelling reasons to consider acquiring a vacation home, for holidays, investment, a winter retreat or as a retirement home. But, apart from the fact that it's easy to be starry-eyed on holiday, there are companies willing to exploit naive tourists and investors alike, so be sure to do your homework, especially to understand the terminology of US property buying.

If you've looked in the window of a 'realtor' (a US estate agent), you will know the big price difference compared with the UK. New homes are still popular, but there are also an increasing number of re-sales on the market which can represent great value.While buying new remains the most popular option, quality can vary, so you need to find a proven builder. **Meritage Homes** (formerly Greater

Five basic buying tips

1 Get references from UK owners and check management company references.

2 Try to stay in the community on holiday before you buy. Walk through it and talk to people there

3 Make sure the home meets requirements for short-term rentals, such as emergency exit lighting, smoke detectors and a keyed, locked owners' closet.

4 Ensure the builder offers a warranty and the property regulations allow you to let on a short-term basis.

5 Make sure you have all the proper US fees, registrations and taxes.

Homes) has an unimpeachable reputation and gets full *Brit Guide* approval. It is a quality-conscious company that has been building here since 1965 and has sold more than 3,000 homes to British owners. Both its latest vacation homes developments, **The Overlook at Lake Louisa** and **Aviana**, are resort-style communities with many necessary holiday amenities. **Lexington Green** at Providence is a collaborative development that is currently offering sites within Providence, a golf and country club community (407 869 0300, **meritagehomes.com**).

All the above are zoned for short-term rentals (which is important to check), plus they are within easy reach of Orlando International Airport and the area's top attractions. The highest recommendation we can offer is that we bought a Greater Home in 2004 and could not have been more satisfied with our purchase and after-sales care. Other builders worth considering are **Beazer Homes**, **Lenar Homes** and **KB Homes**, all rated above average for build quality. More useful home-buying info can be found from Alexander Holiday Homes (**floridasunshine.com**) and Florida Leisure (**floridaleisure.com**), a registered realtor. UK magazines *International Homes* (**international-homes.com**) and *Homes Overseas* (**homes overseas.co.uk**) both have big Florida sections and are worth picking up.

Owning a piece of the magic is tempting, but you *must* get all the facts first, then look for a company that specialises in assisting British buyers. Many firms primarily offer vacation-style properties, and several deal mainly with the British. Consider investigating one of the firms that enables you to fund your mortgage in sterling, dollars or euros through a UK bank, rather than a US one. If you live in the UK, dealing with a US lender can be costly and inconvenient. For instance, US mortgage companies often 'sell' new mortgages to another lender after closing a loan, making it hard to track. Repayment of a dollar mortgage with sterling can also be subject to fluctuating exchange rates. In this instance, a company we've come to know well through our contacts with the British American Chamber of Commerce, and which we have been happy to recommend for almost 10 years now, is the **British Homes Group Florida** (**britishhomes group.com**). Its British-staffed, Orlando-based team recently completed a market test in Orlando of a new multi-currency mortgage designed for UK, Irish and international residents buying investment properties in Florida. The test was a great success and multi-currency mortgage is now the most

Lake Louisa

popular product for overseas buyers purchasing properties anywhere in the Sunshine State.

BRITTIP

Good legal advice for house-buying, business and (especially) immigration matters is absolutely essential. Contact Orlando firm **LaVigne, Coton & Associates** (407 316 9988, **lavigne law.us**) for the best advice on all these matters.

It allows Brits to purchase buy-to-let villas and second homes using the Florida property (rather than the buyer's UK home) as security for the mortgage (irrespective of currency chosen), which removes the potential of putting the primary UK home at risk and still provides the interest deduction on US tax returns. **British Home Sales Florida**, the group's estate agency, has relationships with the some of the State's top builders and developers and can help search for the ideal property anywhere from the Keys to the Panhandle and, with online access to more than 20,000 properties in Central Florida alone, there is definitely a lot to choose from. Add in BHG's useful Florida

British Homes Group have many Florida properties

Downtown St Petersburg

Advisory Panel, free Florida rental booking and listing services, and a Florida Blog for the latest local info, and it's easy to see why it's a great one-stop-shop for British investors in Florida. It has a UK freephone number (0800 096 5989) and can provide a starting point for your property search, an evaluation of a proposed purchase, or an assessment of your existing mortgage position, all free and without obligation (see inside back cover for current promotion). Call (in Florida) 407 396 9914, email **info@britishhomesgroup.com** or visit its offices at 2960 Vineland Rd, Kissimmee, above the Edwin Watts Golf Shop at the junction of Routes 535 and 192, just minutes from Walt Disney World.

But, whoever you go with, ensure it can refer you to experts in UK and US taxation, immigration, hazard insurance, structural warranties and other issues essential for hassle-free ownership in Florida. Property in Orlando has increased substantially in value over the last 10 years, but there is never any guarantee, and rates fluctuate.

OK, that's enough accommodation advice. Now it's on to the parks…!

5 The Theme Parks: Disney's Fab Four

or Spending the Day with Mickey and the Gang

By now you should be prepared to deal with the main business of any visit to Orlando: *Walt Disney World.* This is the heart of all the excitement and fun in store (along with the other theme parks of Universal Orlando, SeaWorld and Busch Gardens).

In our opinion, two weeks is barely enough to see all that this vast resort has in store. So, when you add in the other 4 theme parks and the array of smaller-scale attractions, you start to realise the awesome scope of an Orlando holiday!

Buying your tickets in advance is highly advisable (it often adds up to better value and saves time), but work out your requirements first – you wouldn't get full use out of, say, a 7-Day Premium ticket AND an Orlando FlexTicket Plus in just a fortnight. Once you're ready to buy, check what measure of security the ticket outlet offers (ABTA bonding etc.) and what it does in case of lost or stolen tickets during shipping. Try to use your credit card for all purchases – there is built-in additional security (for our list of recommended ticket outlets, see page 11). You will also find a welter of **discount coupons** in tourist publications distributed in Orlando for many of the smaller attractions (or from the Guest Services desk at your hotel – it's often worth asking), while the **tour operators'** welcome meetings usually have special offers and tickets for the latest excursions.

> **BRITTIP**
> Offers of 'free' Disney tickets usually mean timeshare firms, which also claim to have 'official' visitor centres. I-Drive has the only genuine Official Visitor Center.

The **Official Visitor Center** at 8723 International Drive in the Gala Center on the corner of Austrian Row (407 363 5872, **orlandoinfo.com/uk**, see map on page 86) is also worth checking out for discounts. Equally, the Universal Attractions booths at several shopping malls have great deals (3 days for the price of 2, 2-for-1 drinks etc.) from time to time. Yes, it IS possible to bag free tickets by

Mad Tea Party

© Disney

attending timeshare presentations, but they can easily take half a day of your precious holiday and do you really want the hard-sell hassle?

BRITTIP

If you DO want to check out timeshare options, look first at Disney Vacation Club for the guaranteed way to secure memorable holidays. A tour (for which you will be picked up) will take around 3 hours, but you will be given some Disney FastPasses in return to save time back at the parks. Call 407 566 3300, 1800 500 3990 or visit **http://dvc.disney.go.com/dvc/index**.

Ratings

We judge all the rides and shows on a unique rating system that splits them into **thrill rides** and **scenic rides**. Thrill rides earn T ratings out of 5 (hence a TTTTT is as exciting as they get) and scenic rides get A ratings out of 5 (an AA ride is likely to be over-cute and missable). Obviously, it is a matter of opinion to a certain extent, but you can be sure a T or A ride is not worth your time, a TT or AA is worth seeing only if there is no queue, a TTT or AAA should be seen if you have time, but you won't miss much if you don't, a TTTT or AAAA ride is a big-time attraction that should be high on your 'to do' list, and a TTTTT or AAAAA attraction should not be missed! The latter will have the longest queues, so you should plan your visit around them. Some rides have height restrictions and are not advisable for people with back, neck or heart problems or for expectant mothers. Where this is the case we say, for example, 'Restrictions: 3ft 6in/106cm'. Height restrictions (strictly enforced) are based on the average 5-year-old being 3ft 6in/106cm tall, those aged 6 being 3ft 9in/114cm and 9s being 4ft 4in/132cm.

BRITTIP

Smoking is not permitted in the parks, apart from in a handful of designated areas. Check park maps for their exact locations. All restaurants are strictly non-smoking.

Disney's FastPass

One essential aid to queuing is **Disney's FastPass** system. Most of the main attractions have this wonderful service that allows you to roam while you wait for an allotted time to ride. How it works: insert your main park entrance ticket into the FastPass (FP) machine (to the side of the attraction's entrance) and you get another ticket giving you a period of time in which to return for your ride with only a minimal wait (NB: you need a FP ticket for every person who wants to ride, not just 1 per group). You can hold only 1 FP ticket per 2-hour period, though once you've used it you can get another. If you start by going to one of the FP rides, collecting

Magic Carpets of Aladdin

Character dining

Having a meal with Mickey and Co (or Winnie the Pooh, Cinderella or Mary Poppins) is one of the great Disney experiences – even if you don't have children! It is also often the best way to meet your favourite characters without a wait as they come to YOU. All reservations can be arranged up to 180 days in advance by phoning 407 WDW DINE (939 3463), calling at any Guest Services desk in a hotel, or by touching *88 on a Disney resort phone.

Some meals are difficult to get. Breakfast at **Cinderella's Royal Table** at the *Magic Kingdom* usually sells out within minutes of the 180-day window being open. **Chef Mickey's** and the **Princess Storybook** meals also go quickly. If you cannot book in advance, try calling the day you'd like to dine or, as a last resort, show up to see if there have been any cancellations. You must check in at the podium 10 minutes prior to your time and you will be given the next available table. Some characters don't enter the restaurant so, if they are in the lobby, you'll want to meet them before you are seated. Dining is all-you-can-eat, served buffet, pre-plated or family-style. Inside the restaurant, characters circulate among the tables giving attention to each group (particularly when children are holding the camera!). Character interaction is top-notch, especially if you dine off-hours when the restaurant is quieter. Be sure to bring your autograph book, a fat pen or marker (easier for the characters to hold) and plenty of film or an extra digital card for your camera. Some characters are huge, and children may be put off by them. If you aren't sure how they'll react, see how they are with the characters in the park before booking a character meal. Price range: breakfast $18.99–36.99 adults, $10.99–24.99 children; lunch $20.99–39.99 and $11.99–25.99; dinner $27.99–44.99 and $12.99–27.99 (NB: beware the peak season price rises – Disney has started the dubious practice of raising its restaurant rates in high season).

The meals

MAGIC KINGDOM: Crystal Palace for breakfast, lunch or dinner with Winnie the Pooh and Co – especially good for smaller children; **Cinderella's Royal Table** for the (expensive) *Once Upon A Breakfast*, with Cinderella and her Princess Friends; *Fairytale Lunch* (Cinderella and Friends); and *Dreams Come True Dinner* (Fairy Godmother only). Payment in full on your credit card is required to book, $10/person may be charged for no-shows (photo package included in price, additional photos available for a fee); **Liberty Tree Tavern** for dinner with Chip 'n' Dale, Meeko, Minnie and Pluto.

EPCOT: Garden Grill for lunch or dinner with Farmer Mickey, Pluto, Chip 'n' Dale; **Princess Storybook Dining** for breakfast, lunch and dinner; an alternative to Cinderella's, with some of Belle, Jasmine, Snow White, Pocahontas, Mulan, Sleeping Beauty and Mary Poppins (but NOT Cinderella). Credit card needed to book, $10/person charged for no-shows.

DISNEY'S HOLLYWOOD STUDIOS: Hollywood & Vine for breakfast or lunch with the Playhouse Disney Pals, including JoJo and Goliath from JoJo's Circus and June and Leo from Little Einsteins.

DISNEY'S ANIMAL KINGDOM: Donald's Safari Breakfast at Tusker House with Donald, Goofy, Pluto and sometimes Mickey.

DISNEY RESORTS: Chef Mickey's at *Contemporary Resort*; breakfast or dinner with Mickey, Minnie, Goofy, Pluto, Chip 'n' Dale – peak times book up quickly; **1900 Park Fare** at *Grand Floridian*; breakfast with Alice and her Wonderland Friends; dinner with Cinderella, Perla, Suzy, Fairy Godmother and, sometimes, Prince Charming – again, book early; **Wonderland Tea Party** at *Grand Floridian*; 1.30–2.30pm Mon–Fri, 3–10s only, $28.17, lunch, activities and storytelling with Alice and friends ($10 no-show); **'Ohana** at *Polynesian Resort*; breakfast with Lilo, Stitch, Pluto and Mickey; **Cape May Café** at *Beach Club Resort*; breakfast with Goofy, Chip 'n' Dale and Pluto; **Mickey's Backyard Barbecue** at *Fort Wilderness*; $44.99 and $26.99, games, storytelling, live entertainment, music and dancing with Mickey, Minnie and Co; unlimited beer, wine, iced tea and lemonade (6.30pm, Mar–Dec); *Garden Grove Café* at **Walt Disney World Swan**; Sat and Sun breakfast with Goofy and Pluto; dinner nightly with Timon and Rafiki or Goofy and Pluto.

BRITTIP

Purchase a lanyard for your park tickets if you plan to use FastPass often. This keeps your tickets together and easily accessible.

your ticket and returning later, you can by-pass a lot of standing in queues. You can also get another FP as soon as your 'window' opens: if your time slot for Space Mountain in *Magic Kingdom Park* is 10–11am, you could get another FP for, say, Buzz Lightyear's Space Ranger Spin at 10.01 and then go and ride Space Mountain! Many people still miss out on this, but it is FREE (FastPass rides are indicated by FP in descriptions). If you miss your FP time, you will still be allowed to ride, but you cannot ride before your time period.

With young ones

All Disney's parks offer pushchair ('stroller') hire, and you can save \$2/day by purchasing a multi-day rental at your first park. Children of ALL ages seem to get a big thrill from collecting autographs from the various Disney characters, and most shops sell handy **autograph books**.

Pal Mickey

If you want the ultimate theme park friend to help you queue, offer tips, play games and help find the characters, just ask Mickey – Pal Mickey, that is. This is a high-tech 10½in/27cm tall cuddly toy that talks to you around the parks (using wireless communication) as a kind of tour guide, with hints (e.g. in *Disney's Hollywood Studios*: 'Fantasmic! will be starting in about an hour'), insider info (on Main Street USA: 'See the names written on those second-storey windows? Those folks helped Walt build his Magic Kingdom!') and interactive games while you queue (which still work when you get home). Sounds fun? Wait for the price – Pal Mickey costs a whopping \$65.

PhotoPass

This unique and worthwhile scheme is available in all Disney's parks and (occasionally) in *Downtown Disney*. Disney photographers take photos of guests and, instead of receiving a paper claim ticket, they receive a *Disney PhotoPass* that links together all their photos on one online account for easy viewing. There is no charge

Smiles are guaranteed!

it's a small world

for obtaining a *PhotoPass* or for viewing or sharing photos online (though there is if you want to download and print them), while each photo can be enhanced with Disney characters and special borders. Guests typically have 30 days after their photos were taken to decide if they want their photos (visit **disneyphotopass.com**), or you can view them at one of 3 PhotoPass shops – at the *Magic Kingdom*, the *Epcot* park or *Disney's Grand Floridian Resort.* Collect as many as you want (up to 300!) and have them all burned on to one CD for a bargain $124.95.

Cast Members

Disney employees are called Cast Members or CMs (never 'staff' as they all play a 'role' in the entertainment) and they are renowned for their helpful and cheerful style, always willing to assist, offer advice or just stop and chat. Interaction with CMs often provides some of the best memories of a visit. So, if you've had exceptional service or a CM has gone out of their way to help, let Disney know as it values such feedback (plus CMs get credit for it). Call in at Guest Relations (or City Hall at the *Magic Kingdom Park*) to record your thanks.

Child Swap

Where families have small children, but Mum and Dad still want to try a ride with height restrictions, you DON'T have to queue twice. When you reach the entrance to the queue, tell the operator you want to do a Child Swap. This means Mum can ride while Dad looks after junior in a quiet area and, on her return, Dad can have his go. You may also be given a Child Swap ticket while you wait.

Park security

All visitors with bags are required to go through a security bag-check before reaching the turnstiles at all parks. This is a fairly cursory (but compulsory) inspection and there is a separate lane for those without bags. When you put your ticket through the turnstile, you are also required to give a finger scan (which stops others from using your ticket).

Magic Kingdom Park

The starting point for any visit has to be the *Magic Kingdom,* the park that best embodies the genuine enchantment Disney bestows on its visitors. It's the original development that sparked the Orlando tourist boom in 1971. In comparative terms, the Magic Kingdom is similar to the *Disneyland Park* at *Disneyland Resort Paris®* and *Disneyland California.* Outside those, it has no equal as a captivating day out for all the family. However, although superficially some rides are the same as those in Paris or Los Angeles, there are key differences, notably on Pirates of the Caribbean, Big Thunder Mountain Railroad and Haunted Mansion. And Space Mountain is a completely different ride from the one in Paris.

And, even if a couple of attractions are closed for refurbishment, you won't be short of things to do! We will now attempt to steer you through a typical day at the park, with a guide to the main rides, shows and places to eat; how to park, how to avoid the worst of the crowds and how much you should expect to pay. The *Magic Kingdom* takes up just 107 acres/ 43ha of Disney's near 31,000 acres/ 12,555ha but attracts almost as many visitors as the rest put together. It has 7 separate 'lands', like slices of a cake, centred on Florida's most famous landmark, Cinderella Castle. More than 40 attractions are packed into the park, not to mention numerous shops and restaurants (though the eating opportunities are less impressive than in *Epcot* and *Disney's Hollywood Studios*). It's easy to get overwhelmed by it all, especially as it gets so busy (even the fast-food

Magic Kingdom Park at a glance

Location	Off World Drive, Walt Disney World	
Size	107 acres/43ha in 7 'lands'	
Hours	9am–7pm off peak; 9am–10pm President's Day (see Brit Tip, page 19), spring school holidays; 9am–11pm high season (Easter, summer holidays, Thanksgiving and Christmas)	
Admission	Under-3s free; 3–9 $63 (1-Day base ticket), $287 (5-Day Premium), $293 (7-Day Premium); adult (10+) $75, $322, $328. Prices do not include tax.	
Parking	$11	
Lockers	Next to stroller and wheelchair hire $7 and $12 ($5 deposit refunded)	
Pushchairs	$15 and $31 (Stroller Shop to right of main entrance); length of stay price varies	
Wheelchairs	$10 or $65 ($20 deposit refunded) at Main Ticket Centre	
Top Attractions	Splash Mountain, Space Mountain, Mickey's PhilharMagic, Big Thunder Mountain Railroad, Pirates of the Caribbean, most rides in Fantasyland	
Don't Miss	Disney Dreams Come True Parade, SpectroMagic Parade (certain nights) and Wishes fireworks (most nights)	
Hidden Costs	**Meals**	Burger, chips and coke $9.40 3-course dinner (Cinderella's Table) $44.99 and $27.99 (kids) Kids' counter service meal $4.49
	T-shirts	$19.95–30.95
	Souvenirs	$1–25,000
	Sundries	Chalk colour portraits $17.95–35.95, or silhouettes $8, with oval frame $15.95

restaurants have big queues in high season), so plan around what most takes your fancy.

Location

The *Magic Kingdom* is situated at the innermost end of *Walt Disney World*, with its entrance Toll Plaza ¾ of the way along World Drive, the main entrance off Highway 192. World Drive runs north–south, while the Interstate 4 (I-4) entrance, Epcot Drive, runs east–west. Unless you are staying at a Disney resort, you must pay the $11 parking fee at the Toll Plaza to bring you into the massive car park.

BRITTIP

For the smoothest entry by road from Highway 192, take Seralago Boulevard opposite the Seralago Hotel & Suites next to Old Town, turn left on to a non-toll stretch of Osceola Parkway and follow the signs to your chosen park. On West 192, turn off on Sherberth Road, go north to the first traffic lights and turn right, then pick up the Disney signs.

The majority arrive from 9.30–11.30am, so the car parks are busiest then, which is another good reason to get here EARLY. If you can't make it by 9am during peak periods, you might want to wait until after 1pm, or even later when the park is open as late as 11pm. Remember to note *exactly* where you park, e.g. Mickey, Row 30, otherwise you'll be struggling because many hire cars look the same!

A motorised tram takes you from the car park to the Transportation and Ticket Center at the heart of the operation. Unless you already have your ticket (which will save you valuable time), you have to queue up at the ticket booths. From here, the monorail or ferryboat will bring you to the doorstep of the *Magic Kingdom* itself. The monorail (straight ahead) is quicker if there isn't a queue, otherwise bear left and take a slower ferryboat. If you are staying at a Disney hotel, the resort buses deliver you almost to the park's front door (or the monorail or boat will if you are staying at one of the *Magic Kingdom* resorts). Finally, the *Magic Kingdom* is the only 'dry' park – that is, there's NO alcohol on sale.

BRITTIP

An easy way to remember where you parked is to take a picture of the Section and Row number on your digital camera or your phone. Then simply delete it when you get back to your car.

Main Street USA

Right, we've finally reached the park itself… but not quite. Hopefully, you've arrived early and are among the leading hordes aiming to swarm through the main entrance. The published opening time may say 9am, but the gates can open up to 45 minutes earlier.

BRITTIP

Save paying up to 3 times more for your drinks by bringing your own bottled water to all the parks and use the many drinking fountains dotted about for refills.

This is the first of the 7 'lands' and, at opening time, there is an informal Welcome Parade, with costumed singers and dancers, and the Character Train then arrives at Main Street Station to bring a variety of

Main Street USA

© Disney

MAGIC KINGDOM PARK

FRONTIERLAND
LIBERTY SQUARE
FANTASYLAND
MICKEY'S TOONTOWN FAIR
TOMORROWLAND
ADVENTURELAND
MAIN STREET, U.S.A.
MONORAIL STATION
BUS STATION
FERRYBOAT LANDING

ADVENTURELAND
1 Swiss Family Treehouse
2 Jungle Cruise
3 Magic Carpets of Aladdin
4 The Enchanted Tiki Room (under new management)
5 Pirates of the Caribbean

FRONTIERLAND
6 Splash Mountain
7 Big Thunder Mountain Railroad
8 Country Bear Jamboree
9 Raft to Tom Sawyer Island

LIBERTY SQUARE
10 Liberty Tree Tavern
11 Liberty Square Riverboat
12 The Haunted Mansion
13 The Hall of Presidents

FANTASYLAND
14 'It's a Small World'
15 Cinderella's Golden Carrousel
16 Mad Tea Party
17 The Many Adventures of Winnie The Pooh
18 Snow White's Scary Adventures
19 Dumbo The Flying Elephant
20 Mickey's PhilharMagic
21 Peter Pan's Flight
22 Castle Forecourt Stage
23 Cinderella's Royal Table
24 Ariel's Grotto
25 Fairytale Garden (Storytime with Belle)
26 Pooh's Playful Spot

MICKEY'S TOONTOWN FAIR
27 Mickey's Country House
28 Minnie's Country House
29 Toontown Hall of Fame
30 The Barnstormer at Goofy's Wiseacre Farm
31 Donald's Boat

TOMORROWLAND
32 Space Mountain
33 Tomorrowland Indy Speedway
34 Tomorrowland Transit Authority
35 Walt Disney's Carousel of Progress
36 Astro Orbiter
37 Stitch's Great Escape!
38 Buzz Lightyear's Space Ranger Spin
39 Monsters Inc. Laugh Floor
40 Galaxy Palace Theater

TRANSPORT
41 Walt Disney World Railroad
42 Boat Dock
43 Monorail Station
44 Bus Station

Find the characters

Can't find Mickey and Co? This is often one of the main laments of those who arrive unprepared. Check in at City Hall and they can tell you where the characters can be found. In fact, City Hall is your best friend for a variety of queries, from the location of baby facilities to meal bookings (but there are NO baby facilities at City Hall). Character meet-and-greets are also shown on all park maps with a Mickey's glove icon.

characters for a meet and greet in Town Square (get those autograph books ready!). A family is then chosen at random to sprinkle some 'pixie dust' to open the park officially for the day. Immediately on your right is **Exposition Hall**, a photographic centre featuring archive film material, interactive games, a mini cinema showing Disney classics and some cartoon photo opportunities. On your left is **City Hall**, where you can pick up a park map and daily schedule (if you haven't been given them at the Toll Plaza) and make bookings for restaurants (highly advisable at peak periods). You can also find out where and when the characters will appear. Ahead of you is **Town Square**, where you can take a 1-way ride on a horse-drawn bus or fire engine, or visit the **Car Barn** mini museum. The Street itself houses the park's best shopping (check out the massive Emporium), plus the **Walt Disney World Railroad** (AAA), a Western-themed steam train that circles the park and is one of the better attractions when queues are long elsewhere (though Town Square station is often the busiest).

Dining: The Italian-style **Tony's Town Square Restaurant** serves lunch and dinner, **The Plaza Restaurant** offers salads and sandwiches (lunch and dinner), and **The Crystal Palace** (breakfast, lunch and dinner) is buffet-style food with Winnie the Pooh, Tigger and Co. Quick bites can be bought from **Casey's Corner** (hot dogs, chips and soft drinks), **Main Street Bakery** (coffee and pastries), **Main Street Cinema** and **Main Street Confectionary** (chocolate and sweets) and the **Plaza Ice Cream Parlor**. Disney characters also appear periodically throughout the Square.

BRITTIP

For the best chance of being chosen to march in the Family Fun Day Parade, be in the Castle Forecourt area at least 15 minutes before the parade starts.

Look out for the **Guest Information Board** at the top of Main Street (on the left) as it gives waiting times for all the attractions. The **Baby Center** (for nursing mothers) is also at the top of Main Street, to the left next to the Crystal Palace, along with the park's **First Aid** station.

Unless you are a late arrival, give Main Street no more than a passing glance and head for the end of the street to the real entrance to the park. This is where you await the official opening hour for the famous **'Rope Drop'**, and you should adopt 1 of 3 tactics here, each aimed at doing some of the most popular rides before the queues become substantial (wait times of 2 hours for Splash Mountain are not unknown). **One:** If you fancy the 5-star, log-flume ride Splash Mountain, keep left in front of the Crystal Palace with the majority of the crowd, who will head for the same

Space Mountain

place. **Two:** If you have young children who can't wait to have a ride on Cinderella's Golden Carrousel or the other Fantasyland rides, stay in the middle and pass around the Castle. **Three:** If the thrills of indoor roller-coaster Space Mountain appeal first, move to the right by The Plaza Restaurant and you'll get straight in to Tomorrowland. Now you'll be in pole position for the initial rush (and it will be a rush; take care with children).

Other Entertainment: Watch out for the **Family Fun Day Parade** up to 3 times daily, from Main Street USA to Town Square, as Disney characters lend a hand in making this decidedly American parade a real flag-waving, Yankee Doodle dandy! The **Main Street Trolley Parade** also appears in the morning, with more musical fun, while the fun barbershop quartet the **Dapper Dans** and brass band **Main Street Philharmonic** add more lively musical interludes.

Adventureland

If you head to the left (effectively going clockwise around the park), you will enter Adventureland. If you're going to Splash Mountain first, you pass the Swiss Family Treehouse on your left and bear right through an archway (with toilets on your right) into Frontierland, where you turn left and Splash Mountain is right in front of you. However, stopping in Adventureland, these are the attractions.

Jungle Cruise

© Disney

Swiss Family Treehouse: This imitation Banyan tree is a clever replica of the treehouse from Disney's 1960 film *Swiss Family Robinson*. It's a walk-through attraction where the queues (rarely long) move steadily if not quickly, providing a fascinating glimpse of the ultimate treehouse, complete with kitchen, rope bridges and running water! AA.

Jungle Cruise: It's not so much the scenic, geographically suspect boat ride (where the Nile suddenly becomes the Amazon) that is so amusing here as the patter of your boat's captain, who spins a non-stop yarn about your adventure that features wild animals, tropical plants, hidden temples and sudden waterfalls. Great detail but long queues, so visit either early morning (opens 10am) or late afternoon (evening queues are shortest, but you'll miss some of the detail in the dark). AAAA (FP).

BRITTIP

When you are faced by more than one queue for an attraction, head for the left-hand one. Almost invariably this moves slightly quicker.

Pirates of the Caribbean: One of Disney's most impressive attractions that involves its pioneering work in audio-animatronics, life-size figures that move, talk and, in this instance, lay siege to a Caribbean island! Your 8-minute underground boat ride takes you through a typical pirate adventure and into the world of Captain Jack Sparrow and his nemesis Captain Barbossa as they search for buried treasure. It's terrific family fun (though perhaps a bit spooky for young children, with one small drop in the dark) and the 2006 addition of the *Pirates of the Caribbean* film characters and some new special effects means this is again highly popular. Queues are longest from late morning to mid-afternoon. AAAAA.

The Enchanted Tiki Room: A bird-laden, audio-animatronics show, Iago (from *Aladdin*) and Zazu (from *The Lion King*) lead a colourful 16-minute revue that will especially appeal to younger children. Queues are rare (and it is air-conditioned!). AAA.

Magic Carpets of Aladdin: Here, in an Agrabah-themed area, this ride spins you up, down and around as you try to dodge the spitting camel! Your 'flying carpet' tilts as well as levitates, but it is basically simple stuff geared for younger children (virtually identical to the Magic Carpets of Agrabah in the *Walt Disney Studios in Disneyland® Resort Paris*). TT (TTTT under-5s).

Shrunken Ned's Junior Jungle Boats: This costs an extra $2 for kids to try their hand at steering rather tame toy boats. T.

Other Entertainment: Outside the Pirates of the Caribbean ride (and a must for young swashbucklers) **Captain Jack Sparrow's Pirate Tutorial** runs up to 7 times daily. Captain Jack and his sidekick Mack invite youngsters to join them in sword fights and treasure hunting, ending with the Pirate Oath as children become honorary buccaneers. **Disney characters** also turn up near Pirates of the Caribbean and Magic Carpets rides and on the Adventureland Veranda.

Shopping and dining: The best shopping is in the **Pirates Bazaar**. For food, you have **Aloha Isle** (yoghurt and ice-cream), **Sunshine Tree Terrace** (fruit, snacks, yoghurt, tea and coffee), and the more substantial tacos, empanadas and taco salads of **El Pirata y el Perico Restaurante**.

Frontierland

Passing through Adventureland brings you to a popular target for many of the early birds. This Western-themed area is one of the busiest and is best avoided from late morning to late afternoon.

Splash Mountain: Based on the 1946 classic Disney cartoon *Song of the South*, this is a watery journey into the world of Brer Rabbit, Brer Fox and Brer Bear. The first part is all jolly cartoon scenery and fun with the main characters and a couple of minor swoops in your 8-passenger log boat. The conclusion, a 5-storey plummet at 45° into a mist-shrouded pool, seems like you are falling off the edge of the world! A huge adrenalin rush, but busy almost all day (try it first thing or during one of the parades to avoid the longest queues). You also get VERY wet! Restrictions: 3ft 4in/101cm. TTTTT (FP).

Big Thunder Mountain Railroad: When Disney does a roller-coaster it will be one of the classiest, and here it is – a runaway mine train that swoops, tilts and plunges through a mock abandoned mine filled with clever scenery. You have to ride it at least twice to appreciate all the detail, but again queues are heavy, so go first thing (after Splash Mountain) or late in the day. Restrictions: 3ft 4in/101cm. TTTT (FP).

Country Bear Jamboree: Now here's a novelty: a 16-minute musical revue presented by audio-animatronic bears! It's great family fun with plenty of novel touches (watch for the talking moose-head). Crowds are rare here, so it's a good one when it's busy elsewhere. AAA.

Big Thunder Mountain Railroad

Frontierland Shootin' Arcade: The only other attraction in the park to cost extra ($1 for 35 shots), as you take aim at a series of animated targets. TT.

Tom Sawyer Island: Take a raft over to an overgrown playground of mysterious caves, grottos and mazes, rope bridges and Fort Sam Clemens, where you can fire air guns at passing boats (opens 10am). A good get-away in the early afternoon when the crowds are at their biggest, while **Aunt Polly's Dockside Inn** is a refuge within a refuge for snacks and soft drinks. TT.

Other Entertainment: Get ready up to 6 times daily for **Woody's Cowboy Camp**, where a posse of youngsters are rounded up to join in the fun outside Country Bear Jamboree. Sam the Singin' Cowboy leads the hoedown while Woody, Jesse and Bullseye kick up their heels for some rootin'-tootin' interactive fun (AA, or AAAA under-6s). Other musical interludes are provided by the comic trio of **The Notorious Banjo Brothers and Bob**, and the **Frontierland Hoedown**, with the Country Bears.

Shopping and dining: Frontierland shops sell cowboy hats, guns and badges as well as Native American and Mexican crafts. Look out for the nicely themed **Briar Patch** and **Prairie Outpost** for interesting gifts. For food, try **Pecos Bill Tall Tale Inn & Café** (salads, sandwiches and burgers), **Frontierland Fries** (fries and drinks) or **Turkey Leg Cart** (massive, smoke-grilled turkey legs).

Liberty Square Riverboat

Liberty Square

Continuing the clockwise tour brings you next to a homage to post-independence America. A lot of the historical content will go over the heads of British visitors, but it still has some great attractions.

Liberty Square Riverboat: Cruise America's 'rivers' on an authentic paddle steamer, be menaced by Native Americans and thrill to the stories of How the West Was Won (opens 10am). This is also a good ride at the busiest times of the day, especially early afternoon. AAA.

The Haunted Mansion: A clever delve into the world of ghost train rides that is neither too scary for most kids nor too twee for adults. Not so much a thrill ride as a scenic adventure. Watch out for the fun touch at the end when your car picks up an extra 'passenger'. Longish queues for much of the day, however, so try to visit late on. AAAA (TTTT under-6s).

The Hall of Presidents: This is the attraction likely to mean least to us, a 2-part show that is first a film about the history of the Constitution and then an audio-animatronic parade of all 43 American presidents (opens 10am). Technically it's impressive, but dull for youngsters (though it is another air-conditioned haven). AAA.

Shopping and dining: Shopping here includes **Ye Olde Christmas Shoppe** and **The Yankee Trader**, while eating options are the full-service **Liberty Tree Tavern** (hearty soups, steaks and traditional dishes like meatloaf and pot roast, plus dinner with Mickey and Co), **Columbia Harbor House** (counter-service fried chicken or fish and some excellent soups, salads and sandwiches, notably for vegetarians) and Sleepy Hollow (a picnic area serving snacks, fruit and drinks).

BRITTIP

Get more value for your money at the parks by ordering sodas 'without ice' to get a full cup.

Fantasyland

Leaving Liberty Square, you walk past Cinderella Castle and come into the park's spiritual heart, the area with which young children are most enchanted. The attractions are designed with kids in mind, but the shops are pretty sophisticated.

'It's a Small World': This could almost be Disney's theme ride, a family boat trip through the different continents, each represented by hundreds of dancing, singing audio-animatronic dolls in delightful set-piece pageants. If it sounds twee, it actually creates a surprisingly striking effect, accompanied by an annoyingly catchy theme song that young children adore. Crowds peak in early afternoon. AAAA.

Cinderella's Golden Carrousel: The Fantasyland centrepiece shouldn't need any more explanation other than it is a vintage carousel ride that kids adore. Long queues for much of the day, though. T (TTT under-5s).

Mad Tea Party: The kids will insist you take them in these spinning, oversized tea cups that have their own 'steering wheel' to add to the whirling effect. Actually, they're just a heavily disguised fairground ride. Again, go early or expect crowds. Characters from Alice in Wonderland also visit periodically. TT (TTTT under-5s).

The Many Adventures of Winnie the Pooh: Building on the timeless popularity of Pooh, Piglet and Co, this family ride offers a musical jaunt through Hundred Acre Wood with some clever effects (get ready to 'bounce' with Tigger!) and another original soundtrack. AAA (AAAAA under-5s) (FP). In front of the ride is **Pooh's Playful Spot**, a themed Hundred Acre Wood play area with slides, climbs and the ever-popular pop-jet fountains (which are guaranteed to get youngsters wet!), plus character appearances from Pooh, Tigger and Eeyore.

Snow White's Scary Adventures: This lively indoor ride tells the cartoon story of Snow White with a few ghost train effects that may scare young children. Good fun, though, for parents and kids. Again, you need to go early or late (or during the main parade) to beat the queues. TTT (TTTTT under-5s).

Dumbo the Flying Elephant: Parents hate it but kids love it and all want to do this 2-minute ride on the back of a flying elephant that swoops in best Dumbo style (even if the ears don't flap). Ride early or expect a long queue. TT (TTTT under-5s).

Mickey's PhilharMagic: This utterly fun-tastic 10-minute 3-D film show has a host of in-theatre special effects as Donald tries to conduct the Enchanted Orchestra – to comic effect. It features a 150ft/46m wide screen to immerse guests in the 3-D world of *Beauty and the Beast, The Little Mermaid, The Lion King, Peter Pan* and *Aladdin,* with hapless Donald surviving a string of adventures before Mickey brings him back to earth. The lavish theatre, artistic new animation, special effects (you can 'smell' the food!) and all-round family entertainment add up to one of the most enjoyable attractions.

Mickeys PhilharMagic

There is no scare factor here (though the sudden plunge into darkness at one point and noise of the 'orchestra' can spook young children), while you'll be enchanted when Tinker Bell seems to fly out of the screen in front of you. AAAAA (FP).

Peter Pan's Flight: Don't be fooled by the long queues; this is a rather tame ride, though still a big hit with kids. Its novel effect of flying with Peter Pan quickly wears off, but there's a lot of clever detail as your ship sails over London to Neverland. AA (AAAAA under-6s; FP).

Other Entertainment: The superb **Dream Along With Mickey** show is staged up to 6 times a day on the Castle Forecourt Stage, a 20-minute fantasy featuring Donald, Mickey, Minnie, Goofy and various Princesses and their Princes. Peter Pan and Wendy join the battle against the evil Maleficent and Captain Hook to help Donald remember the power of believing in your dreams (AAA). The **Fantasyland Woodwind Society** plays up to 5 times daily, while Cinderella's **Fountain Meet and Greet** happens twice a day. Other character opportunities are **Ariel's Grotto**, a chance to meet The Little Mermaid (which draws a queue at peak periods), and **Storytime with Belle** in the Fairytale Garden, on the corner of the Castle facing Tomorrowland.

Cinderella's Golden Carousel

Shopping and dining: Shop at **Tinker Bell's Treasures**, the excellent **Sir Mickey's, Fantasy Faire** and **Pooh's Thotful Shop**. There is also an outlet of the **Bibbidi Bobbidi Boutique** here (the other is in *Downtown Disney*), where 'little princesses' can choose from three makeover packages ($44.95–255), and three different hairstyles – the Disney Diva, Pop Princess or Fairytale Princess. The salon is open 9am–7pm and children must be 3 or older. Eating opportunities are at **The Pinocchio Village Haus** (pizza and Italian fare), the **Enchanted Grove** (iced drinks and juices), **Scuttle's Landing** and **Mrs Potts' Cupboard** (for ice-creams and sundaes). **Cinderella's Royal Table** is a fine setting for the hugely popular character breakfast and lunch (dinner is also served, but with the Fairy Godmother only). The majestic hall, waitresses in costume and well-presented food – salads, seafood, roast beef, prime rib and chicken – provide a memorable experience. It's pricey, though ($124 for a family of 4 for breakfast; $132 for lunch).

Mickey's Toontown Fair

In the top corner of Fantasyland (just past the Mad Tea Party) is the shrub-lined entrance to **Mickey's Toontown Fair** (opens 10am). It is easy to miss, but it does have a station on the railroad. Its primary appeal is to young children as they can meet their favourite characters. Exceptionally kid-friendly and well landscaped, there is also the **Toon Park** playground to give youngsters the chance to let off some steam.

Mickey's Country House: Here is a walk-through opportunity to see Mickey at home and have your picture taken with him in the Judge's Tent. AAA (plus TTTTT for the photo opportunity!).

Minnie's Country House: This is a chance to view Minnie's home and unique memorabilia, all designed in a country and western style. AAA.

Toontown Hall of Fame: 3 'rooms' of classic Disney characters for photo meet and greets with Minnie, Daisy and Pluto; Chip 'n' Dale and Goofy; and the Storybook Princesses (including Snow White, Cinderella and Aurora). TTTTT.

The Barnstormer at Goofy's Wiseacre Farm: A mini roller-coaster just for the young 'uns, its masterful design features a swoop right through the barn itself (though it is a pretty short ride after the slow-moving queue). Restrictions: 3ft/91cm. TTT (TTTTT 4–8s).

Donald's Boat: Parents beware, youngsters get seriously wet here! If you've seen the pavement fountains at *Epcot*, prepare for more watery delights as this boat-themed playground spouts off in all sorts of wonderful ways. Ideally, bring a change of clothes or swimsuit for kids. It's also a great place to revitalise tired or irritable children. AAAA under-10s.

Shopping and dining: The huge merchandise area of **County Bounty** will test your wallet; **Toontown Farmers Market** offers fruit, snacks and drinks.

Tomorrowland

The last of the 7 lands, this has a cartoon-like space-age appearance that has guaranteed appeal for youngsters, while it also boasts some original shops.

Space Mountain: One of the 3 most popular attractions in the park, its reputation is deserved. It's a fast, tight-turning roller-coaster completely in the dark save for occasional flashes as you whiz through the galaxy. Don't do this on a full stomach! The only way to beat the crowds is to go either first thing, late in the day or during one of the parades (or, of course, get a FastPass). Restrictions: 3ft 8in/111cm. TTTTT (FP). Children are also likely to gravitate towards the **Tomorrowland Arcade** as you exit.

Tomorrowland Indy Speedway: Despite the long queues, this is a rather tame ride on supposed race tracks that just putt-putts along on rails with little real steering required (children must be 4ft 4in/132cm to drive alone). T (TTTT under-6s).

Astro Orbiter: A jazzed-up version of Dumbo in Fantasyland, this ride is a bit faster and higher and features rockets. Large, slow-moving queues are another reason to give this a miss unless you have young children. TT (TTTT under-10s).

Walt Disney's Carousel of Progress: This will surprise, entertain and amuse. It is a journey through 20th-century technology with audio-animatronics in a revolving theatre that reveals different periods in history. Its 22-minute duration is rarely threatened by crowds (open only at peak periods). AAA.

Tomorrowland Transit Authority: A neat 'future transport system', this offers an elevated view of the area, including a glimpse inside Space Mountain, in electro-magnetic cars. Queues are usually short. AAA (TTT under-8s).

Stitch's Great Escape!: This 15-minute experience receives mixed reviews – some like it for the audio-animatronic prequel to Disney's *Lilo & Stitch*, with visitors being recruited into the madcap Galactic Federation prison

Barnstormer at Goofy's Wiseacre Farm

service (where things go hilariously wrong as Stitch arrives and proceeds to cause havoc), while others find it rather puzzling. Young children can also be scared by the complete darkness at times. There are 2 pre-show areas before recruits are ushered into the sit-down chamber (with shoulder restraints) where Stitch is let loose to bounce, dribble and even belch over the unwary audience. Restrictions: 3ft 2in/101cm. AA (FP).

Buzz Lightyear's Space Ranger Spin: Kids won't want to miss this chance to join the great *Toy Story* character in his battle against evil Emperor Zurg. Ride into action against the robot army – and shoot them with laser cannons! A sure-fire family winner, especially as you get to keep score. TTT (TTTTT under-8s) (FP).

Monsters Inc Laugh Floor: This innovative show is based on the hit Pixar film *Monsters Inc.* With 'live' animation, special effects and high-tech voice links, guests can meet and match wits with the likes of Mike, Sulley and Roz and be entertained by their patter and amusing antics. Billy Boil opens the show, introducing various comedians (including two-headed jokester Sam-n-Ella), with the objective of capturing the audience's laughter. Guest interaction is an integral part of the show. Keep an eye on the screen – you may be featured! AAA.

Buzz Lightyear's Space Ranger Spin

© Disney

Other Entertainment: Live musical productions and high-school bands appear at **The Galaxy Palace Theater** at various times of the day, while **PUSH**, the **Talking Trashcan** makes hilarious regular appearances. **Disney characters** are often on hand by the Galaxy Palace Theater and outside Carousel of Progress.

Shopping and dining: Shopping highlights are provided by **Mickey's Star Traders** and **Merchant of Venus**. For food, try the amusing **Cosmic Ray's Starlight Café** (burgers, chicken, pasta, soups and salads), the **Plaza Pavilion** (pizza, subs and salads), **Auntie Gravity's Galactic Goodies** (ice-cream and juices), the **Lunching Pad** (smoked turkey legs, snacks and drinks) or **Tomorrowland Terrace Noodle Station** (a healthier line-up of Asian stir-fry, soup and vegetarian dishes).

BRITTIP

To watch a parade, sit on the left side of Main Street USA (facing the Castle) to stay in the shade if it's hot. People start staking out the best spots an HOUR in advance.

Having come full circle, you are now back at Main Street USA and it's best to return here in early afternoon to avoid the crowds and have a closer look at the impressive array of shops.

Disney Parades

If there is one thing Disney know how to do well, it's a parade. Coupled with its range of special seasonal events, there is always much more to look forward to than just the rides. The daily highlight is the **Disney Dreams Come True Parade**, a truly enchanting multi-float presentation featuring all the favourite characters. With clever theming, lively music and non-stop (and hard-working!) dancing, the parade halts at regular intervals to reveal some eye-catching special effects. Mickey, Minnie and a host of Disney Princesses all make an

MAGIC KINGDOM PARK with children

Here is a rough guide to the attractions that appeal to different age groups (height restrictions have been taken into account):

Under-5s

Buzz Lightyear's Space Ranger Spin, Cinderella's Golden Carrousel, Country Bear Jamboree, Donald's Boat, Dream Along With Mickey, Dumbo the Flying Elephant, The Enchanted Tiki Room, 'It's a Small World', Jungle Cruise, Liberty Square Riverboat, Main Street Vehicles, Many Adventures of Winnie the Pooh, Mickey's Country House, Mickey's PhilharMagic, Monsters Inc Laugh Floor, Peter Pan's Flight, Pooh's Playful Spot, Tomorrowland Indy Speedway (with a parent), Tomorrowland Transit Authority, Walt Disney World Railroad.

5–8s

Astro Orbiter, The Barnstormer at Goofy's Wiseacre Farm, Big Thunder Mountain Railroad, Buzz Lightyear's Space Ranger Spin, Country Bear Jamboree, Donald's Boat, Dream Along With Mickey, The Enchanted Tiki Room, Haunted Mansion, Jungle Cruise, Liberty Square Riverboat, Mad Tea Party, Magic Carpets of Aladdin, Many Adventures of Winnie the Pooh, Mickey's Country House, Mickey's PhilharMagic, Monsters Inc Laugh Floor, Pirates of the Caribbean, Snow White's Scary Adventures, Space Mountain (with parental discretion), Splash Mountain, Stitch's Great Escape!, Swiss Family Treehouse, Tom Sawyer Island, Tomorrowland Indy Speedway (with a parent), Tomorrowland Transit Authority, Walt Disney World Railroad, Walt Disney's Carousel of Progress.

9–12s

Astro Orbiter, The Barnstormer at Goofy's Wiseacre Farm, Big Thunder Mountain Railroad, Buzz Lightyear's Space Ranger Spin, Country Bear Jamboree, The Haunted Mansion, Mad Tea Party, Mickey's PhilharMagic, Monsters Inc. Laugh Floor, Pirates of the Caribbean, Space Mountain, Splash Mountain, Stitch's Great Escape!, Tomorrowland Indy Speedway (without a parent).

Over-12s

Astro Orbiter, Big Thunder Mountain Railroad, Buzz Lightyear's Space Ranger Spin, Haunted Mansion, Mad Tea Party, Mickey's PhilharMagic, Pirates of the Caribbean, Space Mountain, Splash Mountain, Stitch's Great Escape!.

appearance, plus some of the classic villains, and it is sure to captivate the whole family (though it is especially popular with children). At Easter and Christmas, the parade takes on seasonal charm with appearances by the Easter Bunny and Father Christmas. AAAAA.

BRITTIP

Main Street USA closes ½ hour after the rest of the park, so you can avoid the inevitable mad rush for the car parks by lingering here to shop or enjoy an ice-cream.

And, if you think the park looks good during the day, prepare to be amazed at how wonderful it appears at night – some of the lighting effects are astounding. When the park is open into the evenings (during the main holiday periods and weekends), check out the **SpectroMagic Parade** (when

SpectroMagic Parade

there are 2 a night, the second is less crowded), which is a mind-boggling light and sound festival full of glitter and razzamatazz, with the Disney characters at the centre of a multitude of sparkling lights and fibre-optic effects. It is difficult to do it justice in words; you just have to see it. AAAA.

Most nights also finish with the stunning **Wishes** fireworks show over the Castle. With a clever soundtrack narrated by Jiminy Cricket and featuring memorable moments from various Disney classics, it is magnificently choreographed and culminates in a sequence of pyrotechnic explosions (many designed especially for this show), which truly dazzle the eyes. Starting with an appearance by Tinker Bell (from the Castle's top turret), it continues for 12 minutes of typical Disney emotional appeal; the perfect pixie-dust farewell to a memorable day. AAAAA.

Wishes Cruises: If you prefer not to fight the crowds for a fabulous view of Wishes, book one of 3 speciality cruises to view the fireworks from Seven Seas Lagoon. The *Basic Cruise* holds up to 8 guests onboard a 21ft pontoon boat and costs $225 (includes water, soft drinks and snacks); the *Premium Cruise* holds up to 10 on a 25ft pontoon boat (for $275), including water, soft drinks, snacks and an audio feed to the Wishes music; or splash out for the *Celebration Cruise*, which adds special occasion decorations to the Basic Cruise for a total of $250 and the Premium Cruise for $300.

BRITTIP

After the fireworks crowd exits, you are often allowed to take the Resort Only monorail back to the Transportation & Ticket Center, rather than queue for the main monorail.

The monorail is quicker than the ferry when you leave, but it can take up to an hour to get back to your car. Also, if the crowds get too heavy during the day, you can escape by leaving in early afternoon (your car park ticket is valid all day) and returning to your hotel for a few hours' rest or a dip in the pool. Alternatively, catch a boat to one of the Disney resorts; *Fort Wilderness* is especially fun for kids and boasts the great value **Trails End Buffet** for lunch or dinner.

Wishes fireworks show

© Disney

Fireworks at the Magic Kingdom

Halloween, Christmas – and Pirates!

Three additional annual events in the *Magic Kingdom* provide a separate, party-style ticketed event 7pm–midnight, with most of the rides open and extra themed fun and games.

Mickey's Not So Scary Halloween Party (Sept–Oct): This sees many visitors dress up for the typical American trick-or-treat fun, with plenty of treats and sweets for youngsters along the way. With special music, storytelling, parades and the HalloWishes fireworks (plus some wonderful lighting effects), tickets go on sale about 5 months in advance and sell out quickly. **Mickey's Very Merry Christmas Party** (Nov–Dec): The Christmas party sees 'snow' on Main Street and an array of magnificent festive decorations and theming. There is free hot chocolate and cookies, as well as a parade and more fireworks. The atmosphere is truly enchanting, though the evening can be prone to unfriendly weather. **Mickey's Pirate and Princess Party** (Apr–Jun): This is a newer event and dates can vary, but it is a big hit with families, with the chance to dress up in best Pirate or Princess style and enjoy some extra live entertainment, a superb parade and a special fireworks show. Once again, all the rides are open and you can really do a lot of the park this way. Don't miss the 'Treasure Spots' to fill up your free 'booty bag' with pirate swag!

Tickets for all three parties cost $56/adult and $50/child on the day (or $49 and $43 in advance on set dates). Call 407 934 7639 or visit **disneyworld.com** to book.

BRITTIP

Although the special evening parties don't start officially until 7pm, you can use the ticket to gain entry to the park from 4pm, which gives you 8 full hours to enjoy all the attractions. Great value!

Park tours: Finally, one of the park's little-known secrets is the **Keys to the Kingdom**, a 4–5-hour guided tour of many backstage areas, including the service tunnel under the park, and entertainment production buildings. It's an extra $60 (including lunch; not available for under-16s) but is a superb journey into the park's creation. **Disney's Family Magic Tour** is a 2-hour guided adventure that takes you on a search for clues throughout the park at $27/person, or you can experience the 3-hour **Steam Trains Tour** ($40/person; no under-10s) as you join the crew that prepares the park's trains each day. **Mickey's Magical Milestones Tours** is a 2-hour journey to discover the full story of the world's most famous mouse ($25/person, no under-10s). 407 939 8687 for more information.

Epcot

Epcot actually stands for 'Experimental Prototype Community of Tomorrow' but it might be more accurate to say Every Person Comes Out Tired. For this is a BIG park, with a lot to see and do, and much legwork required to cover its 300 acre/122ha extent. Actually, it is not so much a vision of the future as a look at the world of today, with a strong educational and environmental message. At almost 3 times the size of the *Magic Kingdom Park*, it is more likely to require a 2-day visit (though under-5s might find it less entertaining) and your feet in particular will notice the difference!

Location

Epcot opened in October 1982 and its giant car park is big enough for 9,000 vehicles, so a tram takes you from your car to the main entrance (though if you are staying at a Disney hotel you can catch the monorail, boat or bus service to the gates; there is a separate entrance for guests at the *Epcot* resort hotels, called International Gateway). So don't forget to note where you are parked (e.g. Create, row 78). Once you have your ticket, you pass through the turnstiles and wait in the immediate entrance plaza for Rope Drop, which

Epcot at a glance

Location	Off Epcot Drive, *Walt Disney World*
Size	300 acres/122ha in Future World and World Showcase
Hours	9am–7pm Future World (except Test Track, Mission: SPACE, Soarin'™, 9am–9pm), 11am–9pm (World Showcase)
Admission	Under-3s free; 3–9 $63 (1-Day base ticket), $287 (5-Day Premium), $293 (7-Day Premium); adult (10+) $75, $322, $328. Prices do not include tax.
Parking	$11
Lockers	Through the main entrance to the right hand side and at International Gateway $7 and $12 ($5 deposit refunded)
Pushchairs	$15 and $31 to the left after the main entrance and at International Gateway; length of stay price varies
Wheelchairs	$10 or $65 ($20 deposit refunded), with pushchairs
Top Attractions	Mission: SPACE, Test Track, Spaceship Earth, Soarin'™, 'Honey, I Shrunk the Audience', Maelstrom, Universe of Energy, American Adventure
Don't Miss	IllumiNations: Reflections of Earth, Disney Character Spot (behind Fountain View Bakery), live entertainment (including Off Kilter in Canada, JAMMitors in Innoventions plaza, Miyuki in Japan and Voices of Liberty in America), and dinner at any of the World Showcase pavilions
Hidden Costs	**Meals** Burger, chips and coke $8.38 3-course dinner $38 (Le Cellier, Canada) Kids' meal $4.49–7.49 **T-shirts** $19.95–38 **Souvenirs** $0.75–1,700 **Sundries** *Epcot* 'Passport' $9.95

is signalled by Mickey and Co arriving to greet guests.

Epcot is divided into 2 distinct parts arranged in a figure of 8 and there are 2 tactics to help you avoid the worst of the crowds. The first or lower half of the '8' consists of **Future World**, with 6 different pavilions arranged around Spaceship Earth (which dominates the *Epcot* skyline) and Innoventions. The second part, or top of the '8', is **World Showcase**, a potted journey around the world via 11 internationally presented pavilions that feature a taste of each country's culture, history, entertainment, shopping and cuisine. Once through the entrance plaza, you should aim to get the 3 big-time rides – Test Track, Mission: Space and Soarin'™ – under your belt first, then move into World Showcase for its 11am opening time. Continue around World Showcase until 4 or 5pm, then return to Future World to catch up on the other attractions there, as the majority will have moved on (apart from at the 3 main rides). As a general tactic, head first for the magnificent new **Soarin'™**, then go across to the other side of Future World and grab a FastPass for **Test Track**. While you wait for your ride time, you can queue up for **Mission: SPACE** and perhaps even take in **Universe of Energy**. Alternatively, if the rides don't appeal quite so much as a visit to such diverse cultures as Japan and Morocco, spend your first couple of hours in the Innoventions centres (busy from mid-morning), then head into World Showcase at 11am and you'll be ahead of the crowds for several hours. The other thing you should do early on is book lunch or dinner at one of the fine restaurants around World Showcase (Mexico, Canada and Japan are all highly recommended). The best reservations go fast, but check in at Guest Relations (on the left after Spaceship Earth) for advice and bookings.

Planning your visit

If you plan a 2-day visit, it makes sense to spend the first day in World Showcase, arriving by 11am and going straight there while the majority stay in Future World, booking your evening meal for around 5.30pm, then lingering around the lagoon for the evening entertainment. For your second visit, try arriving in mid-afternoon and then doing Future World in a more leisurely fashion. Queues at most of the pavilions are almost non-existent for rides like Universe of Energy, Spaceship Earth and Journey into Imagination, though Test Track, Soarin'™ and Mission: Space stay busy all day. You CAN do *Epcot* in a day – if you arrive early, put in some speedy legwork and give some of the detail a miss. But, of all the parks, it is a shame to hurry this one. In the shops (almost 70 in all), try to save your browsing for the times when the rides are busiest.

Future World

Here's what you'll find in the first part of your *Epcot* adventure.

Universe of Energy: There is just the one attraction here but it is a stunner. **Ellen's Energy Adventure** is a 35-minute show-and-ride with comedienne Ellen DeGeneres and Bill Nye the Science Guy exploring the creation of fuels from the age of dinosaurs to their modern-day usages. The film elements convince

Test Track

Future World

1 Universe of Energy
2 Mission: SPACE
3 Test Track
4 Odyssey Center
5 Imagination! (including Honey, I Shrunk the Audience)
6 The Land (including Soarin'™)
7 The Seas with Nemo and Friends
8 Spaceship Earth
9 Innoventions West
10 Innoventions East

World Showcase

11 Mexico
12 Norway
13 China
14 The Outpost
15 Germany
16 Italy
17 The American Adventure
18 Japan
19 Morocco
20 France
21 International Gateway (to Epcot resort hotels)
22 United Kingdom
23 Canada
24 Friendship Boats to Italy and Morocco
25 America Gardens Theater
26 Showcase Plaza
27 Monorail Station
K Kidcot Fun Stops

you that you are in a conventional theatre, but then your seats rearrange themselves into 96-person solar-powered cars and you are off on a journey through the prehistoric era, with some realistic dinosaurs! Queues are steady but not overwhelming from mid-morning. AAAAA.

The old **Wonders of Life** pavilion next to Universe of Energy is now permanently closed and there is no news as yet of what will take its place.

Mission: SPACE: This is more high-tech Disney imagination at work, a journey into the future to join the International Space Training Center. The space-age building prepares you for a major adventure as you enter through Planetary Plaza, with its giant replica planets (check out the model showing the Moon landings). At the main entrance you have a choice of 4 queues – FastPass Collection, Stand-by (the main queue), Single Riders and FastPass Return, and the clever organisation keeps queues to a minimum. As you enter the training facility, there are some superb models and graphics (like the giant revolving Gravity Wheel) to look at while you queue to reach Team Despatch. Here, the 4 ready rooms form you into teams of 4 for the ride itself, and you will be either Navigator, Engineer, Pilot or Commander, each with different functions to perform. You also have the choice of either the full, dynamic version of the ride (the 'orange' version) or a toned-down alternative that avoids the 'spinning' effect (the 'green' version). Once briefed (by actor Gary Sinise), you enter the Preparation Room to learn your mission – a flight to Mars. And then it is into the ride vehicle – capsules that close down tightly with outer doors, shoulder restraints and screens that move forward to just 18in/46cm from your face (this is NOT a good ride for those with claustrophobia). The sense of realism, with the control consoles, individual speakers and countdown is magnificent. For those on the full version of the ride, the blast-off feels VERY real as you experience some of the genuine forces of a rocket launch (thanks to its huge centrifuge, which is part-ride and part-simulator). Each member of the team has to perform their duties on cue (Sinise will prompt you) and you experience a simulated sling-shot around the Moon and on to Mars, where the landing is an adventure in itself. It's a truly original, aggressive ride, but you should heed the advice to keep your head still and look straight into the screen or you WILL feel sick (unless you are on the tamer version, where the capsules just tilt and turn). We think the full-on experience is much too intense for young children, and there is no backing out once you blast off (parents could try it first to check it out), while it is definitely not for expectant mothers. Restrictions: 3ft 8in/112cm. TTTTT+ (FP).

BRITTIP

Even if you don't ride Mission: Space, you (and your children) should visit the post-ride area of games and fun. Just enter through the Cargo Bay gift shop to the left of the pavilion.

As you exit the ride, there is an elaborate post-show and activities. Space Base is an excellent play area for children who can't ride (and those who just like to climb, slide and

Epcot monorail

crawl); Space Race is a great game for 2 teams of 60 players to propel a rocket back to Earth via a series of on-screen challenges; Expedition Mars is a computer game to rescue stranded astronauts; and Postcards from Space can email a space video to friends and family. There is then the inevitable (and well-stocked) gift shop. All in all, it is a mind-boggling experience and a real taste of space exploration without leaving the building!

Test Track: Another big production – a 5½-minute whirl along Disney's longest and fastest track. It starts with an elaborate queue line that demonstrates car testing techniques and quality control, and prepares riders for a taste of the ride to come. The way the cars whiz around the outside of the building (at up to 65mph/104kph) provides a glimpse of what's in store. The reality is pretty good, too, as you are taken on a tour of a General Motors proving ground, including a hill climb test, suspension test (hold on to those fillings), brake test, environment chamber, barrier test (beware the crash test dummies!) and the steeply banked, high-speed finale. Once you regain your breath, there's a post-show area with a multimedia film, an animated presentation featuring GM products and technological innovations. Along with a smart gift store and ride photo opportunity, it makes for an extremely involving exhibit. A **Kidcot** stop also adds some creative fun for youngsters. The downside is its HUGE queues, topping 2 hours at times, while the available FP service often runs out by midday. Head straight here when it opens or come back in the evening to keep your queuing to bearable levels. If you are on your own, save time by using the Single Rider Queue. Restrictions: 3ft 4in/101cm. TTTT (TTT teens) (FP).

'Honey, I Shrunk the Audience'

The Odyssey Center: Next door are baby-care and first-aid facilities, telephones and restrooms.

BRITTIP

Innoventions East and West are good places in which to spend time if you need to cool down, or if it's raining.

Imagination!: The 2-part attraction here starts with **Journey into Imagination with Figment**, an uneven but quirky ride into experiments with imagination in the company of Eric Idle (as Dr Nigel Channing of the Imagination Institute) and the cartoon dragon Figment. The sight laboratory sees Figment having fun with a vision chart, the sound lab is a symphony of imaginative melodies and Figment's house is a truly topsy-turvy world (and watch out for the skunk in the smell lab!). It's gentle fun and rarely draws a crowd. AAA. You exit into **Image Works – The Kodak 'What If' Labs**, an interactive playground of sights and sounds, which will probably amuse children more than adults (though you might be tempted to buy various cartoon images and select-your-own CDs).

'Honey, I Shrunk The Audience': Come out of the building and turn right for this fabulous 3-D experience as Rick Moranis reprises his hapless inventor character, Wayne Szalinski. A neat 8-minute pre-show is the perfect prelude to the fun and games in store. Special effects and moving seats add to the feeling that you have shrunk in size. And beware the sneezing dog! AAAA (FP). Outside, kids are always fascinated by the Jellyfish and Serpentine Fountains that send water squirting from pond to pond. Have your cameras and camcorders ready!

The Land: This pavilion combines 3 elements to make a highly entertaining but educational experience on food and nutrition – plus the spectacular new Soarin'™ ride, which is a pure thrill and a huge draw. **Living with the Land** is an informative 14-minute boat ride well worth the usually long queue. A journey through various types of food production may sound dull, but it is informative and enjoyable, with plenty to make children of all ages sit up and take notice through the 3 ecological communities, especially the greenhouse finale. AAAA (FP). Having ridden the ride, you can also take the **Behind the Seeds** guided tour through the greenhouse complex and learn even more about Disney's horticultural projects. It takes an hour ($14 adults, $10 3–9s).

The Circle of Life is a 15-minute combined live-action and animation story, featuring characters from the film *The Lion King*, which explains environmental concerns and is easily digestible for kids. Queues are not a problem here. AAA.

Soarin'™: *Epcot*'s latest and greatest, this hugely imaginative 'flight simulator' offers an exhilarating ride for all ages. A copy of the Soarin' Over California simulator ride in *Disney's California Adventure* in Los Angeles, it features a breathtaking swoop over the notable landmarks of California, complete with 'aromavision' (smell those orange groves!). An elaborate queuing area is arranged like an airport departure lounge, with the passengers embarking on rows of seats that are then hoisted into the air over a giant screen. The feeling is somewhat akin to taking a hang-glider ride as the special film, sounds and scents become all-encompassing. Feet dangling, you soar over the Golden Gate Bridge, sweep through a redwood forest and glide above Napa Valley with the wind in your hair. The finale includes a close encounter with a certain Disney theme park in LA! The ride's realism, magnificent music and superb technology ensure a 5-star experience – but also some serious, slow-moving queues. FastPasses often run out by 11am, so visit early and use FastPass for a second ride. Restrictions: 3ft 4in/ 101cm. AAAAA (FP).

Dining: The Sunshine Season Food Fair offers the chance to eat some of Disney's home-grown produce, and provides healthy alternatives to the usual fast-food fare, while the **Garden Grill** restaurant is a slowly revolving platform that offers more traditional food, including roast meats, pasta, seafood and a vegetarian selection, all in the company of Mickey, Goofy, Pluto and Chip 'n' Dale.

The Seas with Nemo and Friends: This pavilion does for the oceans what The Land does for terra firma, in the company of the characters from the Pixar film *Finding Nemo*. You start with the signature ride, **The Seas With Nemo and Friends**, which takes riders on an underwater journey in 'clamobiles' to meet Nemo and Co (who are brilliantly interwoven into the huge aquarium – to all intents and purposes swimming with the real fish!). Nemo has gone missing (again),

Soarin'™

hence the ride becomes a quest to reunite him with teacher Mr Ray and the rest of the fishy class in a rousing musical finale. AAAA. You then exit into **Sea Base Alpha**, a 2-level development offering 6 modules presenting stories of undersea exploration and marine life, including a research centre that provides a close encounter with the endangered manatee. Plenty of interactive elements and educational touch-screens are on offer, plus additional fish tanks displaying Caribbean reef fish, jellyfish and the intriguing cuttlefish, while there is also an excellent demonstration of a diving chamber. Crowds are steady throughout the day, but queues rarely get too long – with one exception. **Turtle Talk With Crush** is a splendidly interactive and original meet and greet with the cartoon surfer dude turtle and his friend Dory from *Finding Nemo*. Crush is literally the star of the show as he swims up and engages children in the audience with some genuinely fun banter. AAAA. Next door, **Bruce's Sub House** is a fun kids' play area including some great photo opportunities with more of the *Finding Nemo* characters, like friendly shark Bruce (TTT under-6s). Nemo and Friends is more hands-on fun for kids, while **Mr Ray's Lagoon** showcases some real stingrays.

The Seas with Nemo and Friends

Dining: The pavilion also includes the highly recommended **Coral Reef Restaurant** that serves magnificent seafood, as well as providing diners with a grandstand view of the massive aquarium. Dinner for 2 will be around $80, which isn't cheap, but the food is first class.

Spaceship Earth: Spiralling up 18 storeys, this attraction was extensively revamped in 2007 to become a time-travel story into various technologies. From cave paintings to the internet (with a superb depiction of Michelangelo's Sistine Chapel along the way), the gentle ride unfolds in highly imaginative historical stages, culminating in an interactive finale that invites riders to 'predict' the future. Sponsor Siemens (the electronics giant) has added a post-show interactive demonstration area (including predictive surgery and a driving challenge), which makes for an entertaining diversion after the 15-minute ride. Queues are heavy all morning but almost non-existent late in the day. AAAA.

Innoventions West and East: These 2 centres of hands-on exhibits and computer games – subtitled **The Road to Tomorrow** – include a glimpse of Disney's latest work with virtual reality entertainment and other demonstrations of current and future technologies, especially the internet and computers, by the likes of IBM, Underwriters Laboratories and Liberty Mutual. Both sides are routed like a journey into the future and will reward enquiring minds. In Innoventions East, try out the **Test the Limits Lab** and **Don't Waste It** (a recycling challenge). Other novelties include **House of Innoventions** (a 15-minute walking tour through the latest home technologies) and **Storm Struck** (experience a violent storm from a special viewing theatre). You can also take a look at the latest form of transport – the wonderful 2-wheeled Segway Human Transporter (which you can also pay to ride – see pages 136–7). In Innoventions West, kids gravitate to the free **Video Games of Tomorrow** selection by Disney Interactive and may take a bit of moving on! Worth waiting for are the 20-minute **Where's The Fire?**, an interactive game exploring home fire hazards, and the **Thinkplace**, presented by IBM and featuring a demonstration of voice recognition technology and the chance to send a 'video-card' to family and friends. More interactive stuff includes the **Rockin' Robots** exhibit, where guests can direct robotic arms to play percussive instruments, and the amusing **Slap Stick Studios** (shows every ½ hour) presented by Velcro.

Other Entertainment: Live fun is provided periodically in the Innoventions plaza with the unique **JAMMitors** percussion group, while the **Epcot Character Spot** (across from Innoventions West) offers a meet and greet with a variety of favourite Disney characters. The majestic **Plaza Fountain** choreographs to musical performances every 15 minutes.

Dining and shopping: Food outlets include the self-service **Electric Umbrella Restaurant** for lunch and dinner (sandwiches, pizza, burgers and salads) and the **Fountain View Bakery** for Edy's ice-cream and drinks. Look out also for **Club Cool** presented by Coca-Cola®, where you can check out the latest Coke-inspired products, along with various free soft-drink tastes from around the world (beware The Beverly!). For shopping, **Mouse Gear** in Innoventions East features a massive variety of *Epcot* and Disney souvenirs (and don't forget to check out the wacky ceiling architecture!).

World Showcase

If you found Future World amazing, prepare to be astounded by the equally imaginative pavilions around the World Showcase Lagoon. Each features a glimpse of a different country in dramatic settings. Several have rides or films to showcase their main features, while the restaurants offer some outstanding fare.

Mexico: Starting at the bottom left of the circular tour of the lagoon and moving clockwise, your first encounter is the spectacular pyramid of Mexico. Here you have the amusing boat ride **Gran Fiesta Tour Starring The Three Caballeros**, a 9-minute journey through the people and history of the country with Donald Duck, Panchito and José Carioca as your guides. Queues build up in mid-afternoon but are usually light otherwise. AAA. The rest of the pavilion comprises shops and cafés.

Meeting Cinderella

The San Angel Inn is a romantic restaurant offering typical Mexican fare, while the **Tequila Bar** has tempting cocktails! Outside, the counter-service **Cantina de San Angel** (nachos, burritos, tacos and salads) has a grand lagoon view. As in all the World Showcase pavilions, there is live entertainment, with music from **Mariachi Cobre**, while Donald Duck puts in character appearances.

BRITTIP

The Cantina de San Angel is a great spot from which to watch the nightly IllumiNations pyrotechnics show, but you will need to arrive at least an hour early.

Norway: Next up is the best ride in World Showcase, the Viking-themed **Maelstrom**. This 10-minute longboat journey through Norway's history and scenery features a short waterfall drop and a North Sea storm. It attracts longish queues from early afternoon, so the best tactic is to go soon after World Showcase's 11am opening. TTT (FP). There are periodical Norwegian-themed exhibits in the reconstructed **Stave Church** and twice-daily guided tours (sign up at the Tourism desk). The pavilion also contains a clever reproduction of Oslo's Akershus Fortress. The **Akershus Royal Banquet Hall** offers the Princess Storybook dining for breakfast, lunch and dinner, complete with a host of Disney Princesses, and the **Kringla Bakeri Og Kafé** serves sandwiches, pastries and drinks. **Spelmanns Gledje** provides lively Norse folk music periodically.

German pavilion

© Disney

China: The spectacular landscapes of China are well served by the pavilion's main attraction, the stunning **Reflections of China**, a 360° film in the circular Temple of Heaven. Here you are surrounded by the sights and sounds of one of the world's most enigmatic countries in an eye-catching special cinematic production. Queues build up to ½ hour during the main part of the day (but the waiting area is fully air-conditioned). AAAA. Two restaurants, the **Nine Dragons** (full-service, with a tempting Sampler for Two at $44) and the counter-service **Lotus Blossom Café** (with a tasty new menu, including Beijing barbecue chicken and a delicious sliced beef sandwich) offer tastes of the Orient, while **Yong Feng Shangdian Dept Store** is a warehouse of Chinese gifts and artefacts. Don't miss the periodic music and acrobatics shows from **Si Xian** and the stunning **Dragon Legend Acrobats** on the plaza in front of the temple. **Disney characters** from the film *Mulan* also appear in the afternoon.

The **Outpost** between China and Germany features hut-style shops and snacks, with entertainment from Africa and the Caribbean.

Germany: This provides more in the way of shopping and eating than entertainment, though you still find strolling players and a magnificent re-creation of a Bavarian **Biergarten**, with lively Oktoberfest shows featuring the resident **Musikanten** brass band at regular intervals.

BRITTIP

The lunch and dinner menus at many of the World Showcase restaurants are similar, so choose the lunch version – it's cheaper!

It also offers hearty portions of German sausage, sauerkraut and rotisserie chicken.

The **Sommerfest** is fast food German-style (bratwurst and strudel), while there are more shops than anywhere else in *Epcot*, including chocolates, wines, porcelain, crystal, toys and cuckoo clocks. An elaborate outdoor model railway is popular with children, and look out for **character appearances** from Snow White and Dopey.

Italy: Similarly, Italy has pretty, authentic architecture, including a superb reproduction of Venice's St Mark's Square, 3 tempting gift shops (including wine, chocolates, Armani collectables, fine crystal, porcelain and Venetian masks. Its full-service restaurant, **Tutto Italia**, is a temporary cover for an upscale themed restaurant that should open in 2009. And watch out for Sergio, a madcap juggler who loves to involve his audience.

America: At the top of the lagoon and dominating World Showcase is The American Adventure, not so much a pavilion as a celebration of the country's history and Constitution. A colonial Fife & Drum Corps and the wonderful *a cappella* group Voices of Liberty add authentic sounds to the 18th-century setting, overlooked by a faithful reproduction of Philadelphia's Liberty Hall. Inside, you have the American Adventure show, a magnificent ½-hour film and audio-animatronic production that details the country's struggles and triumphs, its presidents, statesmen and heroes. It's a glossy, patriotic display, featuring some outstanding technology and, while some of it will leave foreign visitors fairly cold, it is difficult not to be impressed. Avoid at midday because of the queues. AAAA. If you have some time to spare, check out the special exhibitions in the American Heritage Gallery.

Other entertainment: The America Gardens Theater, facing the lagoon, presents concerts from worldwide artists, notably during the International Flower and Garden Festival, the Sounds Like Summer series, and the Food and Wine Festival.

Shopping and dining: Antiques and handcarts provide touches of nostalgia, along with the **Heritage Manor Gifts** store, while **Liberty Inn** offers fast-food lunch and dinner.

Japan: Next up on the clockwise tour, you are introduced to typical Japanese gardens and architecture, including the breathtaking Chi Nien Tien, a round half-scale reproduction of a temple, some magnificent art exhibits (notably the Bijutsu-kan Gallery), musical shows and dazzling live entertainment (especially child-friendly **Miyuki**, a lovely lady who spins amazing candy creations out of toffee sugar). Great food is another highlight, and the restaurant line-up consists of the wonderful fine dining **Teppan Edo** (formerly the Teppanyaki Rooms, and still with its traditional chefs at each table) and **Tokyo Dining**, a new venue featuring typical cuisine and ingredients, showcasing sushi and innovative presentation. **Yakitori House** is its fast-food equivalent, with great soups, teriyaki and tempura dishes. Periodic music presentations feature the **Matsuriza** drummers. The huge **Mitsukoshi** store adds some fascinating shopping opportunities.

China pavilion

Morocco: As you would expect, this is a real shopping experience, with bazaars, alleyways and stalls selling a well-priced array of carpets, leather goods, clothing, brass ornaments, pottery and antiques. All of the building materials were faithfully imported for the pavilion, which was hand-built to give Morocco a greater degree of authenticity, even by World Showcase's high standards. Ask about its daily (free) 45-minute walking tours of the whole pavilion. **The Gallery of Arts and History** offers more historical and cultural insight into the country, while the **Fez House** depicts the style of a typical Moroccan home. **Restaurant Marrakesh** provides a full dining experience, complete with traditional musicians and a belly dancer. It's rather pricey ($41.95/person for the Taste of Morocco Marrakesh Royal Feast) but the atmosphere is lively and entertaining. However, better value can be had at **Tangierine Café**, with a healthy array of foods (hummus, tabbouleh, couscous, roast lamb, lentil salad and Moroccan breads) at more down-to-earth prices ($8.95–13.95; kids' meals $6.95).

BRITTIP

The Tangierine Café in Morocco is a peaceful haven in which to enjoy a quiet, healthy lunch, especially if you are vegetarian, while there is also a tempting coffee and pastry counter.

Morocco pavilion

© Disney

Other entertainment: Characters from Disney's *Aladdin* appear from time to time, while live musical show **MoRockin'** presents a variety of Arabic rhythms in fun style.

France: Predictably overlooked by a replica Eiffel Tower, this is clean and cheerful pre-World War I Paris, with comedy street theatre acts adding to the rather dreamy atmosphere (look out for **Serveur Amusant** for some eye-catching antics). Don't miss **Impressions de France**, another big-film production that serves up all the grandest sights of the country, accompanied by the music of Offenbach, Debussy, Saint-Saëns and Satie. Crowds get quite heavy from late morning. AAAA.

Dining and shopping: This is also the pavilion for a gastronomic experience provided by 3 restaurants, of which **Chefs de France** and **Bistro de Paris** are major discoveries. The former is an award-winning, full-service (but expensive) establishment featuring top-quality cuisine created by French chefs on a daily basis, while the latter, upstairs, offers more intimate bistro dining, still with an individual touch (and, if anything, slightly more expensive) and plenty of style (starters $12–19, main courses $29–43, Bistro 4 Course Tasting Menu $75, with wine pairings $120). The Bistro books only 30 days in advance. Alternatively, the **Boulangerie Patisserie** is a sidewalk café offering more modest fare (and wonderful pastries, as you'd expect). Shopping is also suitably chic, with a Wine Shop and **Guerlain** perfumery (ask about its free perfume tour during the *Flower and Garden Festival*). **Disney characters** from Sleeping Beauty and Beauty and the Beast also appear here.

United Kingdom: The least inspiring of all the pavilions, and certainly with little to entertain those who have ever visited a pub or shopped for Royal Doulton or Burberry goods, it is partly offset by some good live

BRITTIP

The Rose and Crown dining room in the UK pavilion is a great place from which to see the nightly IllumiNations fireworks spectacular, but outdoor seating is not guaranteed.

entertainment, led by excellent Beatles tribute band, the **British Invasion**, but that really is the sum total here. The **Rose and Crown Pub** is antiseptically authentic (complete with pub pianist), but you can get better elsewhere at these prices (roast pork $20.99, bangers and mash or fish and chips $15.99, and a pint of Bass, Harp Lager or Guinness for a whopping $8). There is also a take-away **Harry Ramsden's** fish and chippie. Other shops are the Tea Caddy, the Magic of Wales, the Queen's Table, Crown and Crest (perfumes and heraldry) and the Toy Soldier (traditional games and toys). **Disney characters** can also be found here in the shape of Mary Poppins and Friends.

BRITTIP

Best way to tour World Showcase? Start in Canada and continue anti-clockwise or jump on the Friendship Boats and go straight to Italy or Morocco.

Canada: Completing the World Showcase circle, the main features here are **Victoria Gardens**, based on the world-famous Butchart Gardens on Vancouver Island, some spectacular Rocky Mountain scenery, a replica French gothic mansion, the Hôtel de Canada, and another stunning 360° film, **O Canada!** As with China and France, this showcases the country's sights and scenery in a terrific, 17-minute advert for the Canadian Tourist Board led by comedian Martin Short. It's at its busiest in late afternoon. AAA. Resident band **Off Kilter** is also one of the most entertaining acts we've seen anywhere. Want to hear rock 'n' roll bagpipes? This is the group for you! **Le Cellier Steakhouse** is an excellent dining room offering great steaks, prime rib, seafood, chicken and several vegetarian dishes for lunch and dinner.

Kidcot Fun Stop: At 11 activity centres around World Showcase, children can play games and collect a special Epcot Passport to get stamped as they visit each pavilion. Kids will also want to pick up **Goofy's Epcot Guide** at the main entrance, which asks them to answer various questions around World Showcase and solve Goofy's dilemma.

Italy pavilion

IllumiNations: Reflections of Earth:

The day's big finale and an absolute show-stopper, this firework and special-effects extravaganza is awesome even by Disney standards. British composer Gavin Greenaway provided the original music for a 15-minute performance of vivid brilliance. Some 2,800 firework shells are launched as a celestial backdrop to a series of fire-and-water effects on the World Showcase Lagoon. The central icon is a 28ft/9m video globe of Earth that opens in a spectacular climax of choreographed pyrotechnics. Truly magnificent. However, people start staking out the best lagoon-side spots up to 2 HOURS in advance. The ultimate way to view IllumiNations is by private boat on one of 3 **speciality cruises** from *Disney's Boardwalk* or *Yacht and Beach Club Resorts* (for non-residents, too). The price range is $250–275 per boat (holding 4–10 guests) and can be used for special celebrations. The *Basic Cruise* costs $250 and the pontoon boat holds up to 10. It includes water, soft drinks and snacks. The *Celebration Cruise* costs $275 and adds a range of occasion decorations. The classic motorboat *Breathless* costs $250 (up to 6 adults). Call 407 939 7529 up to 90 days in advance to book. Be aware that cruises launch regardless of whether fireworks are taking place.

Behind-the-scenes tours

Epcot also has a big range of special behind-the-scenes tours. **Dolphins in Depth** ($150, including refreshments, souvenir photo and T-shirt) is a 3-hour dip into the backstage and research areas of The Seas with Nemo and Friends pavilion, including a chance to meet the resident dolphins (13–17s must be accompanied by an adult). **Undiscovered Future World** is a 4½-hour journey into the creation of *Epcot*, Walt's vision for the resort and backstage areas like IllumiNations ($49). **Dive Quest** ($150/person,10 and over) is a 3-hour experience, with a 40-minute dive into the Living Seas aquarium, plus a behind-the-scenes look at the facility at 4.30pm and 5.30pm every day, and you need to have scuba certification (T-shirt and certificate for all participants; theme park admission not required). The **Aqua Seas Tour** ($115/person, 8 and over; under-18s must be accompanied by an adult; inclusive of T-shirt and group photo; again, theme park admission is not required for this tour) is similar to Dive Quest but without the scuba diving element (daily at 12.30pm). **Around the World at Epcot** will appeal to those who enjoy new technology, with a World Showcase tour (7.45, 8.30, 9 and 9.30 each morning) on the innovative 2-wheeled **Segway Human Transporter**. It costs a hefty

Epcot at night

EPCOT with children

Here is our rough guide to the attractions that appeal to different age groups:

Under-5s

Circle of Life, Gran Fiesta Tour Starring The Three Caballeros, Journey into Imagination with Figment, Kidcot stops, Living with the Land, The Seas with Nemo and Friends, Soarin'™ (if tall enough), Spaceship Earth, Turtle Talk with Crush, Universe of Energy.

5–8s

All the above, plus The American Adventure, Body Wars, 'Honey, I Shrunk The Audience' (with parental discretion), Image Works, Innoventions, JAMMitors, Maelstrom (Norway), Miyuki the Candy Lady, Test Track.

9–12s

All the above, plus Dragon Legend Acrobats, Impressions de France, Matsuriza Drummers, Mission: SPACE, O Canada!, Sergio, Le Serveur Amusant, Wonders of China.

Over-12s

All the above, plus Bijutsu-kan Gallery, British Invasion (UK), Land of Many Faces (China), Off Kilter (Canada).

$95/person extra but the 2-hour tour includes full instruction and plenty of travel time on these amazing contraptions, which can reach 12.5mph/20kph. It's open to only 10 guests each day (minimum age 16), or you can try the **Simply Segway** tour, a simplified 1-hour experience, mainly indoors (at $35/person, daily except Tues). **Gardens of the World** runs only during the Flower and Garden Festival, with a 3-hour tour in the company of one of the park's horticultural experts (from 9am Tues, Thurs and Sat, $59/person, 16 and over). The most comprehensive tour, **Backstage Magic** ($199; 16 and over), goes behind the scenes of *Epcot, Magic Kingdom* and *Disney's Hollywood Studios* on a 7-hour foray into little-seen aspects, such as the backstage areas of the Studios and the tunnels below *Magic Kingdom*. Book all tours on 407 939 8687.

Annual festivals

There are 2 other annual Epcot events to watch out for. **The International Flower and Garden Festival** literally puts the whole park in full bloom with an amazing series of set-pieces, seminars and mini-exhibitions from mid-April to early June. All the exhibits and lectures are free and they add a beautiful aspect to an already scenic park. The **Food and Wine Festival** runs for 45 days from 1 October and showcases national and regional cuisines, wines and beers, with the chance to attend grand Winemakers' Dinners and Tasting Events, or just sample the offerings of more than 20 food booths dotted around World Showcase. One of our favourites! Both also offer free concerts several times a day at the America Gardens Theater.

International Food and Wine Festival

Disney's Hollywood Studios

Welcome to a journey into the world of film and TV, an epic voyage of adventure, creation – and fun. Here you will learn plenty of tricks of the trade; movie-making secrets and behind-the-scenes glimpses that have been cleverly turned into rides, shows and other attractions with guaranteed entertainment appeal.

Rather bigger than the *Magic Kingdom* at 154 acres/62ha but substantially smaller than *Epcot*, *Disney's Hollywood Studios* (renamed from Disney-MGM Studios in 2008) is a different experience yet again with its rather chaotic combination of attractions, street entertainment, film sets and smart gift shops. Like the *Magic Kingdom*, the food on offer may not win awards, but some of the restaurants (notably the Sci-Fi Dine-in Theater and '50s Prime Time Café) have imaginative settings. The park also has rather more to occupy smaller children than *Epcot*, but you can still easily see all of it in a day unless the crowds are heavy.

Location

The entrance arrangements will be fairly familiar if you have already visited the other parks. *Disney's Hollywood Studios* is located on Buena Vista Drive (which runs between World Drive and Epcot Drive) and parking is $11. Remember to make a note of where you park before you catch the tram to the main gates, where you must wait for the official opening time. If the queues build up quickly, the gates will open early, so be ready for a running start. Once through, you are into Hollywood Boulevard, a street of gift

Disney's Hollywood Studios at a glance

Location	Off Buena Vista Drive or World Drive, Walt Disney World
Size	154 acres/62ha
Hours	9am–7pm off peak; 9am–10pm high season (Easter, summer holidays, Thanksgiving and Christmas)
Admission	Under-3s free; 3–9 $63 (1-Day base ticket), $287 (5-Day Premium), $293 (7-Day Premium); adult (10+) $75, $322, $328. Prices do not include tax.
Parking	$11
Lockers	From the Crossroads kiosk through the main entrance; $7 and $12 ($5 deposit refunded)
Pushchairs	$15 and $31 from Oscar's Super Service Station
Wheelchairs	$10 or $65 ($20 deposit refunded), from Oscar's
Top Attractions	Toy Story Mania, Twilight Zone™ Tower of Terror, Rock 'n' Roller Coaster Starring Aerosmith, Star Tours, The Great Movie Ride, Voyage of the Little Mermaid, Jim Henson's Muppet*Vision 3-D, Lights, Motors, Action!™ Extreme Stunt Show
Don't Miss	Block Party Bash, Indiana Jones™ Epic Stunt Spectacular, Journey Into Narnia: Prince Caspian, Fantasmic!
Hidden Costs	**Meals** Burger, chips and coke $9.18 3-course lunch $28.97 (Mama Melrose's) Kids' meal $4.49 **T-shirts** $19.95–34 **Souvenirs** $1–4,500 **Sundries** Rock 'n' Roller Coaster Starring Aerosmith ride photo $16.95–$24.95

shops, and you have to decide which of the main attractions to head for first, as these are the ones where the queues will be heaviest nearly all day. Try to ignore the lure of the shops as it is better to browse in the early afternoon when the attractions are at their busiest.

Incidentally, if you thought Disney had elevated queuing to an art form in its other parks, wait until you see how cleverly arranged it is here. Just when you think you have reached the ride itself, there is another twist to the queue you hadn't seen or an extra element to the ride that holds you up. The latter are holding pens, which are an ingenious way of making it seem you are being entertained instead of queuing. Look out for them in particular at the Great Movie Ride, Twilight Zone™ Tower of Terror and Jim Henson's Muppet*Vision 3-D.

An up-to-the-minute check on queue times at the attractions is kept on a **Guest Information Board** on Hollywood Boulevard, just past its junction with Sunset Boulevard, where you can also book the restaurants. The **Baby Center** here is located just inside the main gates on the left, next to Guest Relations, along with **First Aid**. The park is laid out in a rather more confusing fashion than its counterparts, which have neatly packaged 'lands', so you will need to consult your map often to keep your bearings in the 7 different areas.

The main attractions

The opening-gate crowds will all surge in one of 3 directions, which will give you a pretty good idea of where you want to go. By far the biggest attraction here is the **Twilight Zone™ Tower of Terror**, a magnificent haunted hotel ride that culminates in a 13-storey drop in a lift, where queues hit 2 hours at peak periods. So, if the Tower appeals to you, do it first! Head straight up Hollywood Boulevard, then turn right into Sunset Boulevard where you'll see it at the end, looming ominously over the park. It's a FastPass (FP) ride (see pages 106–8), as is another huge draw, the **Rock 'n' Roller Coaster Starring Aerosmith** (at the end of Sunset Boulevard on the left), so you can get an FP for one and ride the other.

Star Tours, the great *Star Wars*™ simulator ride, and the new **Toy Story Mania** are also serious queue-builders and FP attractions. If you are not up for the really big thrills, grab a FP for Toy Story Mania (straight up Hollywood Boulevard, pass right of the giant Mickey Hat and into the new Pixar Studios area), then head for Star Tours (back across the main square past the Indiana Jones™ show). After Star Tours and Toy Story Mania, another gentler experience (and also worth doing early on) is the hysterical **Muppet*Vision 3-D show**, which is another big draw later in the day. It has the benefit of being air-

Rock 'n' Roller Coaster starring Aerosmith

1 Parade Route Block Party Bash
2 The Great Movie Ride
3 American Idol Live!
4 ABC Sound Studio 'Sounds Dangerous' starring Drew Carey
5 Indiana Jones™ Epic Stunt Spectacular
6 Star Tours
7 Jim Henson's Muppet*Vision 3-D
8 Honey, I Shrunk the Kids Movie Set Adventure
9 Catastrophe Canyon on Disney's Hollywood Studios Backlot Tour
10 Studio Backlot Tour
11 Meet Mickey Mouse
12 Toy Story Mania
13 Walt Disney: One Man's Dream
14 Voyage of the Little Mermaid
15 The Magic of Disney Animation
16 Playhouse Disney – Live on Stage!
17 Rock 'n' Roller Coaster Starring Aerosmith
18 The Twilight Zone™ Tower of Terror
19 Beauty and the Beast – Live on Stage
20 Fantasmic!
21 Guest Information Board
22 Toy Story Pizza Planet
23 Lights, Motors, Action!™ Extreme Stunt Show
24 Premier Theater
25 '50s Prime Time Café
26 Hollywood and Vine
27 Hollywood Brown Derby
28 Mama Melrose's
29 Sunset Ranch Market
30 Sci-Fi Dine-in Theater Restaurant
31 Journey into Narnia: Prince Caspian

conditioned, too, for when you need a rest. The park's big stunt show, **Lights, Motors, Action!™ Extreme Stunt Show**, plays 2–5 times a day and is also hugely popular, so this is another one to try to get a FastPass for.

BRITTIP

People begin queuing for the Lights, Motors, Action!™ Extreme Stunt Show a good ½ hour before seating, and the midday shows are always full. Go for the first performance, or wait until later.

Hollywood Boulevard

Moving around the park in a (roughly) clockwise direction, you start in the Hollywood Boulevard area. As with the *Magic Kingdom*, your entry here is along a street of shops and services that are best visited in early afternoon when it's busiest elsewhere. Immediately to the left through the turnstiles are the Guest Relations and First Aid offices, plus the Baby Care centre. To the right is Oscar's Station for pushchair and wheelchair hire, while locker hire is obtained at the Crossroads kiosk right in front of you.

The Great Movie Ride: This faces you (behind the Hat icon) as you walk in along Hollywood Boulevard and is a good place to start if the crowds are not too serious. An all-star audio-animatronics cast re-creates a number of box office smashes, including Jimmy Cagney's *Public Enemy*, Julie Andrews in *Mary Poppins*, Gene Kelly in *Singin' in the Rain* and many more masterful set-pieces as you undertake your conducted tour. Small children may find the menace of *The Alien* too strong, but otherwise the ride has universal appeal and features some clever live twists (there are 2 variations on this ride, a cowboy and a gangster version – ask a Cast Member if there's one you especially want to do). AAAA.

Other entertainment: Showing up to 6 times daily in front of the Sorcerer's Hat, **High School Musical 3: Senior Year** is a 20-minute song and dance act from the hit Disney TV film series. With the cheerleaders and basketball players from East High putting on an energetic display, it is sure to thrill fans of the High School Musical films (AAA). A series of **Streetmosphere** acts also enliven Hollywood Boulevard throughout the day, staging impromptu movie shoots, casting calls or even detective investigations. Have fun with them – you just might end up the star of the show! Also by the Hat, look out for favourite **Disney characters** during the morning.

Shopping and dining: Hollywood Boulevard has the best of the park's shopping (9 of the 21 stores), including **Sid Caheunga's One-of-a-Kind** (rare movie and TV items, including many celebrity autographs), **Keystone Clothiers** (some of the best apparel), **Mickey's of Hollywood** (all your souvenirs and gift items) and **The Darkroom** (for camera sales, rental, film and accessories). **The Brown Derby** is the park's signature restaurant, offering fine dining in best vintage Hollywood style (reservations usually necessary).

The Hollywood Brown Derby

Echo Lake

Turn left out of Hollywood Boulevard and you find another area that pays homage to the movie world of the 1930s and 40s.

American Idol Live!: This was due to open in January 2009, an all-new audience participation show based on the famous TV reality series. Guest performers will get to go through the full Idol experience, from audition to preparation (with a vocal coach and hair and make-up artists) to the performance, with those who score highest returning for an end-of-day Grand Finale show. The panel of judges will also be chosen from the audience, which makes us wonder just how 'amateurish' this might be, and it's hard to imagine this having much appeal for all but die-hard Idol fans. The full details were unknown as we went to press, so we suggest checking with Guest Relations for how to be in the show if it interests you (No rating – until we've seen it!).

ABC Sound Studio 'Sounds Dangerous' Starring Drew Carey: A sound FX special that features American comedian Drew Carey in an instalment of a spoof undercover police show *Sounds Dangerous*. Most of the 12-minute show is in the dark – which upsets some children – and is centred on your special headphones as Carey's stakeout goes wildly wrong. Clever and amusing – if a bit tame for older children – you exit into the Sound Works Studio to try out some well-known sound effects. AAA.

Indiana Jones™ Epic Stunt Spectacular: Consult your park Times Guide for the various times this rip-roaring stunt cavalcade hits the stage. A special movie set creates 3 different backdrops for Indiana Jones'™ stunt people to put on a dazzling array of scenes and special effects from the Harrison Ford films. Audience participation is an element and there are some amusing sub-plots. Queues for the 30-minute show begin up to ½ hour beforehand, but the auditorium holds more than 2,000 so everyone usually gets in. TTTT (FP).

Star Tours: Anyone remotely interested in the *Star Wars*™ films will enjoy just queuing for one of our favourites, a breathtaking 7-minute spin in a Star Speeder. The elaborate walk-in area is full of *Star Wars*™ gadgets and gizmos that make the long wait (sometimes up to 1 hour) pass quickly. From arguing robots C-3PO and R-2D2 to your robotic pilot, everything has a brilliant sense of space travel, and the ride doesn't disappoint! Restrictions: 3ft 4in/101cm, no under-3s. TTTT (plus AAAAA; FP).

Other entertainment: Kids should make a beeline for the **Jedi Training Academy**, on the stage outside the Star Tours ride up to 8 times a day. Here, young Jedi hopefuls get to try their light-sabre technique under the eyes of a Jedi master, before taking on Darth Vader himself. Great fun just to watch, too (TTTT for under-12s).

Shopping and dining: Shop for *Star Wars*™ goods at **Tatooine Traders** (at the exit to Star Tours) and Indiana Jones souvenirs at the **Indy Truck** and **Adventure Outpost**. There are also 3 good dining choices: the **'50s Prime Time Café** is a fun experience as you sit in mock stage sets from American TV sitcoms and eat meals 'just like Mom used to make' (the waiters all claim to be your aunt, uncle or cousin and warn you to take your elbows off the table – good fun!); the **Backlot Express** features superb burgers, hot dogs and sandwiches, while a varied buffet dinner is served up at **Hollywood & Vine** ($24.99 adults, $12.99 3–9s) in addition to the **character breakfast and lunch** with the Playhouse Disney Pals.

Streets of America

Three of the park's bigger attractions can all be found here, along with an often-overlooked gem of a restaurant.

Muppet*Vision 3-D: The 3-D is crossed out here and 4-D substituted in its place, so be warned that strange things are about to happen! A wonderful 10-minute holding-pen pre-show takes you into the Muppet Theater for a 20-minute experience with all of the Muppets, 3-D special effects and more – when Fozzie Bear points his squirty flower at you, prepare to get wet! It's a gem, and the kids love it. Queues build up through the main parts of the day, but Disney's queuing expertise makes them seem shorter. AAAAA (FP).

Honey, I Shrunk the Kids Movie Set Adventure: This adventure playground gives youngsters the chance to tackle massive blades of grass that turn out to be slides, crawl through caves, investigate giant mushrooms and more. There can be long queues here, too, so arrive early if the kids demand it (and bring plenty of film). TTTT under-10s.

Premier Theater: A brand new venue (in 2008), this fully enclosed theatre is used for the *Star Wars*™ Weekend meet and greets and other set-piece special events.

BRITTIP

If you have young children, be aware there is some (loud) mock gunfire in the Lights, Motors, Action!™ Extreme Stunt Show, which can upset sensitive ears, while the motorbike scene includes a rider catching fire, which can be frightening for them, too.

Lights, Motors, Action!™ Extreme Stunt Show: A direct import from the *Walt Disney Studios* in Paris, this is a truly amazing live stunt spectacular, featuring cars, motorbikes, jet-skis and stuntmen of all kinds. It is one of the most remarkable shows you will see anywhere, full of genuine high-risk stunts that will leave you shaking your head in amazement. Seating starts 30 minutes prior to a show, and there is some amusing pre-show chat before the serious stuff starts. The set is based on a Mediterranean village and is magnificently crafted. Once the preliminaries are completed, you are treated to a 33-minute extravaganza of daredevil stunts, with a Car Ballet sequence, a Motorbike Chase and a Grand Finale that features some surprise pyrotechnics to complete an awesome presentation (keep your eyes on the windows below the video screen at the end). Each scene – featuring a secret-agent and various baddies – is explained by a movie director and the results of each shoot are played back on screen to show how each effect was created. All the cars were specially built for the show by Vauxhall, and there are some extra tricks between the main scenes. It was all designed by Frenchman Rémy Julienne, the doyen of film car stunt sequences from James Bond films *Goldeneye* and *Licence to Kill* and other action epics like *The Rock, Gone in 60 Seconds* and *Enemy of the State*. The exit can be quite a scrum,

Lights, Motors, Action!™ Extreme Stunt Show

though, as 5,000 people have to leave together, and it can take 15 minutes to clear the auditorium, hence if you can sit towards the front, you will be out quicker. Because it involves so much genuine, live co-ordination it makes for a truly thrilling experience and you may well want to see it more than once – another reason to see it early on. TTTTT.

BRITTIP

Don't queue for the Backlot Tour when Lights, Motors, Action! Has just ended – it will be far too crowded.

Studio Backlot Tour: Before you board the special trams for a look at the off-limits part of the studios in this 35-minute walk-and-ride tour, you are treated to some special effects (involving an amusing water tank with a mock Pearl Harbor attack). The tram takes you round the production backlot and then to **Catastrophe Canyon** for a demonstration of special effects that try to both drown you and to blow you up! AAA (plus TTTT). You exit into the **American Film Institute** showcase of costumes and props from recent films.

NB: Rumour has it that the Backlot Tour's days are numbered, with the whole area due to become a Pixar Studios extension featuring a new **Monsters Inc** dark ride.

Other entertainment: Live music is provided periodically on the main street by the comedy rock band **Mulch, Sweat and Shears** (AAA), while this is also a great place to meet various **Disney characters** throughout the day – look for *Toy Story* friends by Al's Toy Barn; **Kim Possible** and the **Power Rangers** on the main street; and *Cars* friends Lightning McQueen and Tow Mater in the plaza outside the Lights, Motors, Action! show.

Shopping and dining: Shop for Christmas items at **It's A Wonderful Shop, Stage 1 Company Store** for Muppet and Sesame Street souvenirs and **Writer's Stop** for books and speciality coffees. **Mama Melrose's Ristorante Italiano** is a wonderful table-service Italian option (one of our favourites), while there are also the counter-service offerings of **Toy Story Pizza Planet** (pizza, salads and drinks) and **Studio Catering Co. Flatbread Grill** (healthier wraps, salads, grilled chicken and barbecue pulled pork).

Commissary Lane

This is just a small link between the Streets of America and the central plaza by the Sorcerer's Hat, and contains only 2 eating opportunities. **The Sci-Fi Dine-In Theater Restaurant** is a big hit with kids as you dine in a mock drive-in cinema,

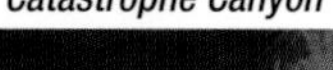

Catastrophe Canyon

© Disney

with cars as tables, waitresses on roller skates and a big film screen showing old black-and-white science-fiction clips. The menu has also been overhauled recently (now featuring gourmet burgers, ribs, chicken, pasta and sandwiches, as well as the signature milkshakes and flavoured sodas). The counter-service option **ABC Commissary** serves up a multi-ethnic choice that includes a chicken curry, Cuban sandwich and Asian salad.

Pixar Studios

This area has undergone a complete transformation from the old Mickey Avenue to the new-look Pixar Studios (styled after the Pixar Film Studios in California) after the opening of the Toy Story Mania ride.

Toy Story Mania: This is the park's latest attraction (May 2008) and is a real family fun fiesta, a 3-D ride into a fantasy fairground of games with the *Toy Story* characters. To start with you are 'shrunk' to toy-size and board special carnival vehicles (each equipped with individual spring-action shooters) to go through Andy's Bedroom, where the toys have set up a Midway Games Play Set with 5 challenges, plus a practice round. Thanks to a pair of 3-D glasses, riders can 'see' everything their shooter fires at the sequence of targets (while, with the magic of Disney's special effects, they might also 'feel' objects whirring past as they burst out of the screens; and, if you hit a water balloon, watch out!). Throw virtual eggs at barnyard targets, launch darts at balloon sheep, break plates with baseballs, land rings on Buzz Lightyear's alien friends and finish up in Woody's Rootin' Tootin' Shootin' Gallery (with a bonus roundup) before totting up your scores and comparing with fellow riders. All the while, the Toy Story characters cheer you on (and pass on hints to boost your score, so it works for all abilities) and provide some amusing commentary. At times it is a touch raucous and chaotic, but kids are sure to love the shooting game element and the whole family can enjoy the amusing ride through the toys' world. Even the queuing area is fun, with a huge animatronic Mr Potato Head acting as a fairground barker to entertain while you wait (AAA + TTTT; FP). As a new ride, it draws some HUGE queues, so you should use the FastPass option here early on.

Other entertainment: Look out for all the **Pixar characters** throughout the new-look area, including *Monsters Inc, The Incredibles* and *Cars,* plus the recent *Wall-E.*

Shopping and dining: For souvenirs and gifts from your favourite Pixar films visit the **Camera Dept** in the main courtyard, while **Studio Café** offers counter-service snacks and drinks.

Animation Courtyard

Get ready for a series of wonderful family-friendly shows in this area of the park, starting with **Voyage of the Little Mermaid**, a 17-minute live performance that is primarily for children who have seen the Disney cartoon. It brings together a mix of actors, animation and puppetry to re-create the film's highlights. Parents will still enjoy the special effects, but queues tend to be long, so go early or late. Those in the first few rows may also get a little wet. AAA (AAAAA under-9s; FP).

Toy Story Mania

© Disney

Journey into Narnia: Prince Caspian: Also new in summer 2008, this walk-through experience features a dramatic entryway that leads into a real Narnian fantasy world and multi-media show (with full surround-sound system and film screen). Set in Aslan's stone temple chamber, it tells the story of the second Narnia film and provides a couple of neat special effects touches to various re-created scenes from the Prince Caspian saga. You then exit into an exhibit of original art, props and costumes from the film itself. AAA.

Walt Disney: One Man's Dream: This interactive show-and-tell exhibit chronicles Walt himself and his lifetime of accomplishments. From archive school records to a model of the Nautilus from *20,000 Leagues under the Sea*, the story of the man behind the Mouse comes to vivid life. The homage ends with a preview of Disney's future developments, plus a 10-minute film encapsulating all Walt achieved and dreamed about. AAAA.

BRITTIP

Try to sit at least half-way back in the Mermaid Theatre, especially if you are with young children, as the stage front is a bit high.

Disney Playhouse Live on Stage

Lights, Motors, Action!™ Extreme Stunt Show

The Magic of Disney Animation: An amusing and entertaining 30-minute show-and-tour through the making of cartoons. It starts with a special theatrical performance by Mushu, the Eddie Murphy-voiced dragon from the animated film *Mulan*. From there you exit into a hands-on area of interactive fun (especially for children); Ink & Paint is a colouring challenge, at Sound Stage you can try a voice-over, and You're a Character will tell you which Disney character you most resemble. From there, you have the choice of joining the Animation Academy for a tutored class in cartoon art or stopping for a meet and greet with various Disney characters, including Sorcerer Mickey. You exit via the **Animation Gallery**, which has some fabulous gifts. Queues are rarely serious, so it's a good afternoon choice. AAAA.

Playhouse Disney – Live on Stage!: Straight out of several popular kids' TV series comes this 20-minute live show with pre-school favourites like *Mickey Mouse Clubhouse, JoJo's Circus, Rolie Polie Olie, The Little Einsteins* and *Handy Manny*. It's colourful and entertaining and children of the right age just love it. AAA (AAAAA under-5s).

Other entertainment: Look for the Playhouse Disney characters outside

Rock 'n' Roller Coaster starring Aerosmith

the Live On Stage! show, including JoJo and Goliath, The Little Einsteins and Handy Manny.

Sunset Boulevard

The final part of the park contains the two high-thrill rides, and the big night-time finale, but is also the busiest area from midday on, so try to visit here first or leave it until the last couple of hours.

Rock 'n' Roller Coaster Starring Aerosmith: Disney's first big-thrill inverted coaster is a sure-fire draw for the adrenalin ride addicts, with a magnificent indoor setting and nerve-jangling ride. It features a clever 3-D film show starring rock group Aerosmith in their recording studio. That leads to the real fun, set to specially recorded tracks from the band itself and with outrageous speaker systems, as riders climb aboard Cadillac cars for a memorable whiz through a mock Los Angeles (watch out for a close encounter with the Hollywood sign!). The high-speed launch and inversions ensure an up-to-the-minute coaster experience. Go first thing or expect serious queues. Restrictions: 4ft/124cm. TTTTT (FP).

The Twilight Zone™ Tower of Terror: This 199ft/60m landmark invites you to experience another dimension in this mysterious Hollywood Tower Hotel that time forgot. The exterior is intriguing, the interior is fascinating, the ride is scintillating and the queues are huge! Just when you think you are through to the ride, there's another queue, so spend your time inspecting the superb detail. There is a lot more to this than just the big 13-storey drop, however, as the 'Twilight Zone' theming adds a real element of curiosity and invention. Your elevator car takes several unexpected twists

Twilight Zone™ Tower of Terror

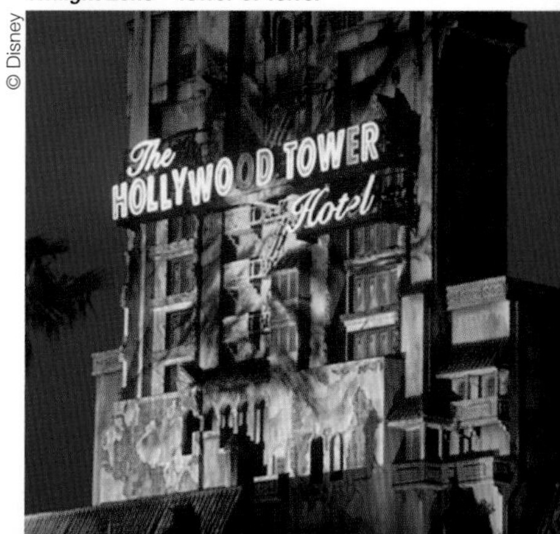

and turns before it is time to 'drop in', and the random drop sequence provides plenty of hair-raising thrills before you exit! Restrictions: 3ft 4in/ 101cm. TTTTT (FP).

Beauty and the Beast – Live on Stage: An enchanting live performance of the highlights of this Disney classic will entertain the whole family for 30 minutes in the nearby Theater of the Stars. Check the schedule for show times (and try to catch *a capella* singing group *Four for a Dollar* before each show). AAA.

BRITTIP

Beat the crowds by booking a Fantasmic! dinner package when you enter the park (or on 407 939 3463). Just reserve an early dinner at the Hollywood Brown Derby, Mama Melrose's or Hollywood & Vine, ask for the Fantasmic! package and you get VIP seating later for the show.

Fantasmic!: This special-effects spectacular is simply not to be missed. Staged every night (at peak periods; twice a week off-peak) in a 6,900-seat amphitheatre, it features the dreams of Mickey, portrayed as the Sorcerer's Apprentice, through films such as *Pocahontas, The Lion King* and *Snow White*, but hijacked by the Disney villains, leading to an epic battle with Our Hero emerging triumphant. Dancing waters, shooting comets, animated fountains, swirling stars and balls of fire combine in a breathtaking presentation – but beware of the giant, fire-breathing dragon! The 25-minute show begins seating up to 2 hours in advance and it's best to head there at least 30 minutes before (watch out for the splash zones!). AAAAA.

Other entertainment: Sunset Boulevard is also home to some of the park's **Streetmosphere** characters.

Shopping and dining: The best shopping here is provided by **Legends of Hollywood**, **Planet Hollywood Super Store** and the **Sunset Boulevard** shops (for limited edition watches, clothing and other collectibles). **Rosie's All-American Café** (chicken, burgers and salads) and **Catalina Eddie's** (pizza) are the best of Sunset Boulevard's series of 5 market-style eateries.

Daily parade

In keeping with the park's energetic style, the new daily parade (in 2008) changed to **Block Party Bash**, direct from *Disney's California Adventure* park in Anaheim. This high-energy cavalcade features 60 singers, dancers, gymnasts and Pixar movie characters – from *The Incredibles, Toy Story, A Bug's Life* and *Monsters Inc* – in a street party that stops periodically to interact with guests. With lively music, vibrant costumes and some remarkable aerial acrobatics, it's guaranteed to captivate and amuse. AAAA.

Fantasmic!

DISNEY'S HOLLYWOOD STUDIOS with children

Here is our guide to the attractions that appeal to the different age groups in this park:

Under-5s

Beauty and the Beast – Live on Stage, Block Party Bash, Fantasmic!, Honey I Shrunk the Kids Movie Set Adventure, The Magic of Disney Animation, Playhouse Disney – Live On Stage!, Voyage of the Little Mermaid.

5–8s

Beauty and the Beast – Live On Stage, Block Party Bash, Fantasmic!, Honey I Shrunk the Kids Movie Set Adventure, Indiana Jones™ Epic Stunt Spectacular, Journey Into Narnia: Prince Caspian, Lights, Motors, Action!™ Extreme Stunt Show, The Magic of Disney Animation, Muppet* Vision 3-D, 'Sounds Dangerous' Starring Drew Carey, Studio Backlot Tour, Toy Story Mania, Voyage of the Little Mermaid.

9–12s

Beauty and the Beast – Live on Stage, Fantasmic!, The Great Movie Ride, Indiana Jones™ Epic Stunt Spectacular, Journey into Narnia: Prince Caspian, Lights, Motors, Action!™ Extreme Stunt Show, The Magic of Disney Animation, Muppet*Vision 3-D, Rock 'n' Roller Coaster Starring Aerosmith, 'Sounds Dangerous' Starring Drew Carey, Star Tours, Studio Backlot Tour, Twilight Zone™ Tower of Terror, Toy Story Mania.

Over-12s

Fantasmic!, The Great Movie Ride, Indiana Jones™ Epic Stunt Spectacular, Lights, Motors, Action!™ Extreme Stunt Show, The Magic of Disney Animation, Muppet*Vision 3-D, Rock 'n' Roller Coaster Starring Aerosmith, Star Tours, Studio Backlot Tour, Toy Story Mania, Twilight Zone™ Tower of Terror, Walt Disney: One Man's Dream.

BRITTIP

We always recommend the Sci-Fi Dine-In Theater Restaurant or '50s Prime Time Café to enjoy a main meal with a difference.

Studios at Christmas

At Christmas (late Nov–1 Jan), one of the most amazing spectacles anywhere is the **Osborne Family Lights**, which are switched on every evening in the Streets of America area. This simply stunning display of 5 million twinkling, themed fairy lights draws huge crowds all evening (go during a Fantasmic! performance to avoid the worst of the throngs).

Skywalker and Co

Star Wars™ film fans will want to make a beeline for the Studios during weekends in late May and early June when the park becomes a playground for characters, film stars, photo-opportunities, competitions and other memorabilia based on anything to do with Luke Skywalker and Co. Much of the event is scheduled in and around the new Premier Theater in the Streets of America area. There is no additional fee to rub shoulders with (and get autographs from) various *Star Wars*™ personalities, and the Studios take on an extra (space) dimension each weekend (though the park is also at its most crowded).

Jedi training

© Disney

Disney's Animal Kingdom Theme Park

Disney's newest and smartest theme park opened in 1998 representing a completely different experience. With an emphasis on conservation and nature, it largely eschews the non-stop thrills and attractions of the other parks and instead offers a change of pace, a more relaxing motif, as well as Disney's usual seamless entertainment style, but still with some excellent rides, including one of its very best. The attractions are relatively few, with just 6 out-and-out rides, but there are then 2 elaborate wildlife trails, 4 shows (including 2 that alone are almost worth the admission price), an extravagant adventure playground, conservation station and petting zoo, and a Disney character greeting area. It's a far cry from the hustle-bustle of the *Magic Kingdom*, but its serious environmental message aims to create a greater understanding of many of the world's ecological problems. There are plenty of animal encounters along the way and the overall style is so creative, it positively demands you slow down to appreciate the artistry involved.

It is also outrageously scenic, notably with the 145ft/44m Tree of Life, the Kilimanjaro Safaris and the Asian village of Serka Zong (home to the gigantic Expedition: Everest™ ride), but it won't overwhelm you with Disney's usual grand fantasy. Rather, it is a chance to explore and experience; to learn and understand; and to soak up the gentler ambience of nature at its finest. It is not a zoo in the conventional sense, but it is home to 200-plus species of birds and animals (in some wonderfully naturalistic settings). The educational tone is fairly strong but children in particular may pick up easily on the

Disney's Animal Kingdom Theme Park at a glance

Location	Directly off Osceola Parkway, also via World Drive and Buena Vista Drive	
Size	500 acres/203ha divided into 6 'lands'	
Hours	9am–5 or 6pm off peak; 8am–7pm in high season	
Admission	Under-3s free; 3–9 $63 (1-Day base ticket), $287 (5-Day Premium), $293 (7-Day Premium); adult (10+) $75, $322, $328. Prices do not include tax.	
Parking	$11	
Lockers	Either side of Entrance Plaza; $7 and $12 ($5 deposit refunded)	
Pushchairs	$15 and $31 at Garden Gate Gifts, through entrance on right	
Wheelchairs	$10 or $65 ($20 deposit refunded), with pushchairs	
Top Attractions	DINOSAUR!, Kilimanjaro Safaris, It's Tough To Be A Bug!, Kali River Rapids, Festival Of The Lion King, Finding Nemo – The Musical, Expedition: Everest™	
Don't Miss	Pangani Forest Exploration Trail, Maharajah Jungle Trek, Rafiki's Planet Watch, Mickey's Jammin' Jungle Parade, dining at Rainforest Café	
Hidden Costs	**Meals**	Burger, chips and coke $8.18 3-course meal at Yak & Yeti $33.97 Kids' meal $4.49, $4.99 and $7.49
	T-shirts	$10.95–50
	Souvenirs	$1.60–20,000
	Sundries	Face painting $10, $12 and $15

DISNEY'S ANIMAL KINGDOM

The Oasis

1 The Oasis Tropical Garden

Discovery Island

2 The Tree of Life

3 It's Tough To Be A Bug

4 Discovery Island Trails

5 Flame Tree Barbecue

6 Pizzafari

Camp Minnie-Mickey

7 Character Greeting Trails

8 Pocahontas And Her Forest Friends

9 Festival Of The Lion King

Dinoland USA

10 DINOSAUR!

11 The Boneyard

12 Finding Nemo – The Musical

13 Chester And Hester's Dino-Rama!

14 TriceraTOP Spin

15 Primeval Whirl

16 Restaurantosaurus

Africa

17 Harambe

18 Kilimanjaro Safaris

19 Pangani Forest Exploration

20 Rafiki's Planet Watch

21 Tusker House Restaurant

Asia

22 Flights Of Wonder

23 Kali River Rapids

24 Maharajah Jungle Trek

25 Expedition: Everest™

26 Yak 'n Yeti Restaurant

27 Rainforest Café

© Disney

Kilimanjaro Safaris

essential conservation undertones of things like Kilimanjaro Safaris and Maharajah Jungle Trek. However, the park does get crowded, the walkways can be congested and there are also fewer places to cool down. It is definitely a good idea to be here on time and use FastPass (FP) to minimise queuing.

Getting there

If you are staying in the Kissimmee area, *Disney's Animal Kingdom* is the easiest of the parks to find. Just get on the (toll) Osceola Parkway and follow it all the way to the toll booths. Alternatively, coming down I-4, take exit 65 on to Osceola Parkway. From West Highway 192, come in on Sherberth Road and turn right at the first traffic lights. If you arrive early (which is advisable), you can walk to the Entrance Plaza. Otherwise, the usual tram system takes you in, so make a note of the row you park in (e.g. Unicorn, 67). The entrance plaza is overlooked by the **Rainforest Café**, with its 65ft/20m waterfall, which is a open for breakfast, lunch and dinner (but is busy from 12.30–3.30pm). With Orlando so hot in the summer, you need to be at the park as early as possible to see the animals before they take cover in the shade.

Expedition Everest

© Disney

BRITTIP

An early start is especially advised for Kilimanjaro Safaris. You will see far more animals in the first few cooler hours of the day than during the hotter afternoon when they seek the shade.

For the early birds, here is your best plan of campaign. Once through the gates, animal lovers should head first for Kilimanjaro Safaris, through the Oasis, Discovery Island and Africa. After the Safari, go straight to Pangani Forest Exploration Trail and you will have experienced 2 of the park's best animal encounters. Alternatively, thrill-seekers should walk straight

Primeval Whirl

through Discovery Island for Asia, where the Expedition: Everest™ ride is the big draw. With that one safely under your belt, head to Kilimanjaro Safaris or the nearby Kali River Rapids raft ride, followed by the scenic Maharajah Jungle Trek. The best combination for the first arrivals is to get a FastPass for Expedition: Everest™ then ride Kilimanjaro Safaris, and, once you have done that (and depending on your FP time), either do your Everest ride or go straight to Kali River Rapids. Check your show schedule for Festival of the Lion King and try to catch one of the first 2 performances, as the later ones draw sizeable queues. The wait time board at the entrance to Discovery Island is also helpful. Early birds can also enjoy **The Adventure Begins**, the park's official opening, featuring a welcome from Rafiki and other favourite Disney characters. Cast Members are also on hand with a variety of small critters (some furry, some not so!) as you enter through the turnstiles. Those are your main tactics – here is the full rundown.

The Oasis

The Tropical Garden is a gentle, walk-through introduction to the park, a rocky, tree-covered area featuring animal habitats and studded with streams, waterfalls and lush plant life. Here you will meet miniature deer, a giant anteater, exotic boars, macaws, iguanas, sloths and kangaroos in a wonderfully understated environment that leads you across a stone bridge to the main open park area. This is a good place to visit in early afternoon when many of the rides are busy. AAA.

Other entertainment: Look out for a host of **Disney characters** here throughout the morning and late afternoon, plus the amusing **Wes Palm** – a potted palm with attitude!

Shopping and dining: Stop at **Garden Gate Gifts** (on the right) for pushchair, wheelchair and locker hire, while **Guest Relations** is on the left. The fun **Rainforest Café** also has an entrance inside the park here. If you haven't seen the one at *Downtown Disney*, you should definitely call in to view the amazing jungle interior with its audio-animatronic animals, waterfalls, thunderstorms and aquariums. A 3-course meal costs anywhere from $28–61, but the setting alone is worth it and the food is above average. Try breakfast or an early dinner here to avoid the crowds.

Discovery Island

This colourful village is the park hub, themed as a tropical artists' colony, with animal-inspired artwork, nature trails, 4 main shops and 2 eateries. You will also find the Fist Aid station here (look for the 'ladybird' lights) and the Baby Center.

The Tree of Life: This arboreal edifice is the park centrepiece, an awesome creation that seems to have a different perspective from wherever you view it. The trunk and roots are covered in 325 carvings representing the Circle of Life, from the dolphin to the lion. **Trails** lead round the tree, interspersed with habitats for flamingos, otters, ring-tailed lemurs, macaws, axis deer, cranes, storks, ducks and tortoises. The tree canopy spreads 160ft/49m, the trunk is 50ft/15m wide and the diameter of the roots is 170ft/52m. It has 103,000 leaves (all attached by hand) on more than 8,000 branches! AAAA.

It's Tough To Be A Bug!: Winding down among the Tree's roots brings you 'underground' to a 430-seat theatre and another example of Disney's artistry in 3-D films and special effects. This hysterical 10-minute show, in the company of Flick from the Pixar film *A Bug's Life*, is a homage to 80% of the animal world, featuring grasshoppers, beetles, spiders, stink bugs and termites (beware the 'acid' spray!) as well as several tricks we couldn't possibly reveal. Sit towards the back in the middle (allow a good number of people in first as the rows are filled up from the far side) to get the best of the 3-D effects. Queues build up from midday, but they do move quite steadily. Don't miss the 'forthcoming attractions' posters in the foyer for some excruciating bug puns on famous films. AAAAA (FP).

BRITTIP

The dark, special effects and mock creepy-crawlies in It's Tough To Be A Bug! can be *extremely* scary for young 'uns. Use caution.

Other entertainment: The Island is home to live music from percussion group **Village Beatniks** and the South American sounds of **Inka Sikuri**. **Disney characters** are also on hand – Winnie the Pooh and friends at Character Landing (opposite Flame Tree Barbecue) and Lilo and Stitch next to Island Mercantile. Keep an eye (and camera) on the surrounding river for **The Adventure Continues**, a musical character boat featuring Mickey, Goofy and Co.

It's Tough to Be a Bug

Shopping and dining: This is where you will find a huge range of merchandise, souvenirs and gifts, most notably in **Disney Outfitters** and **Island Mercantile**. Counter-service restaurants **Pizzafari** (pizza, salads and sandwiches) and **Flame Tree Barbecue** (barbecued ribs, beef and pork, chicken sandwiches and salads) are both good choices. If it's not too hot, the Flame Tree is a relaxing and picturesque option, set among some pretty gardens and fountains on the bank of Discovery River; the air-conditioned Pizzafari is better in summer months.

Camp Minnie-Mickey

This is a woodland retreat featuring winding paths and more of Disney's clever scenery, plus two excellent and highly family-friendly shows, as well as a real character fest, plus the ever-popular (with kids!) squirt fountains.

Character Greeting Trails: 4 trails lead to a series of jungle encounters with Disney characters such as Mickey and Minnie (naturally), Winnie the Pooh and Tigger and Jungle Book and Lion King characters, plus Brer Rabbit and Co from *Song of the South*. AAAAA (for kids).

This is a woodland retreat featuring winding paths and more of Disney's clever scenery, plus one of their very best and highly family-friendly shows, as well as a real character fest, plus the ever-popular (with kids!) squirt fountains.

Character Greeting Trails: A series of trails lead to 4 different pavilions which are home to a variety of jungle encounters with Disney characters such as Mickey and Minnie (naturally), Winnie the Pooh and friends (plus, occasionally, Jungle Book and Lion King characters) and the Song of the South cast, Brer Rabbit, Brer Fox and Brer Bear. AAAAA (for kids).

(The old Pocahontas and Her Forest Friends show in this area closed down in late 2008 and there was no immediate word of any replacement.)

Festival of the Lion King: Not to be missed, this high-powered 25-minute production (up to 8 times a day at peak periods; 5 a day at others) brings the hit animated film to life in truly spectacular fashion, with giant moving stages, huge animated figures, singers, dancers, acrobats and stilt-walkers, plus some fun audience participation. All the well-known songs are given an airing in a fiesta of colour and sound, and it serves to underline the quality Disney brings to their live shows. However, queuing often begins a good

Tree of Life

45 minutes in advance of each high-energy show for the 1,000-seat (air-conditioned) theatre, so it is usually best to try to take in one of the earlier shows of the day. AAAAA.

Other entertainment: The kids' favourite animal songs get an airing with **Gi-Tar Dan** periodically.

Africa

The largest land in the park, it re-creates magnificently the forests, grasslands and rocky homelands of East Africa's most fascinating residents in a richly landscaped setting that is part rundown port town and part savannah. The central area, **Harambe Village**, is a superb Imagineer's eye-view of a Kenyan port town, complete with white coral walls and thatched roofs and is the starting point of your adventure. The Arab-influenced Swahili culture is also depicted in the native tribal costumes and architecture.

Kilimanjaro Safaris: The queuing area alone earns high marks for authenticity, preparing you for the sights and sounds of the 110 acre/45ha savannah beyond. You board a 32-passenger truck, with your driver/guide relaying information about the flora and fauna on view and a bush ranger/pilot overhead relaying facts and figures on the wildlife, including the dangers threatening them in the real world. Scores of animals are spread out in various habitats, with no fences in sight (the ditches and barriers are all well concealed) as you splash through fords and cross rickety bridges, and you should get good close-ups of lions, rhinos, elephants, giraffes, antelope, zebras, hippos, baboons and ostriches. Once again, the authentic nature of all you see (okay, some of the tyre 'ruts' and termite mounds are concrete and the baobab trees are fake) is truly breathtaking, with the spread of the vegetation and landscaping, and the only drawback is the lack of a photo stop or two along the way (the ride is pretty bumpy). The animals also roam over a wide area and can disappear from view. Not recommended for expectant mothers or anyone with back or neck problems. AAAAA (FP).

BRITTIP

The best (i.e. the most jolting) ride with the Kilimanjaro Safaris is at the back of the truck. There is much less to see from midday to late afternoon when many of the animals take a siesta.

Kilimanjaro Safaris

© Disney

Festival of the Lion King

Pangani Forest Exploration Trail: As you leave the Safari, you turn into a serious nature trail that showcases gorillas, hippos, meerkats and rare tropical birds. You wander the trail at your own pace and visit 'research' stations to learn more about the animals on display, including the underwater view of the hippos (check out the size of a hippo skull and those teeth!) and the savannah overlook, where giraffes and antelope graze and the amusing meerkats frolic. The walk-through aviary gives you the chance to meet the carmine bee-eater, pygmy goose, African green pigeon, ibis and brimstone canary, among others, but the real centrepiece is the silverback gorilla habitat (in fact, 2 of them). The family group is often just inches away from the plate-glass window, while the bachelor group further along can prove more elusive. Again, the natural aspect of the trail is fabulous and it provides a host of photo opportunities. Save this for late in the day and most of the crowds will have moved on. AAAAA.

Rafiki's Planet Watch: This sub-section of Africa involves a rustic train ride, with a peek into some of the backstage areas, as a preamble to the park's interactive and educational exhibits (especially for children). The 3-part journey starts with **Habitat Habit!**, where you can see cotton-top tamarins and learn how conservation begins in your own back garden. **Conservation Station** offers a series of exhibits, shows and information stations about the environment and

Kilimanjaro Safaris: the Trail

threats to its ecology. Look out for *Sounds of the Rain Forest*, the story of endangered species, at the Mermaid Tales Theater and the Eco-Heroes (who can be quizzed on-screen) trying to redress the balance, then observe the park's veterinary treatment centre, hatchery and neonatal care. You can easily spend an hour absorbing the information here, inspired by **Disney's Worldwide Conservation Fund**. Finally, the **Affection Section** is a petting zoo of (usually) lambs, goats, donkeys, sheep and guinea pigs. AAA.

Other entertainment: There's plenty more to enjoy here, with the splendid percussion of **Mor Thiam**, the pageantry and rhythms of **Tam Tam's of Congo** and energetic fun of the **Karuka Acrobats**. With luck you'll also spot the wonderful **DiVine**, a 'moving' part of the foliage! **Disney characters** can be found in Harambe and Rafiki's Planet Watch.

Shopping and dining: Harambe is home to the **Mombasa Marketplace/ Ziwani Traders**, where you can suit up safari-style, while Rafiki's Planet Watch has **Out of the Wild** for more gifts and souvenirs. **Tusker House Restaurant** (featuring *Donald's Safari Breakfast* and non-character buffets at lunch and dinner) is one of the best diners in the park, with a mouth-watering array of salads, hot carvery, rotisserie chicken, stews and vegetarian dishes ($19.99 adults, $10.99 children for lunch, $26.99 and $17.99 for dinner). There are also 4 snack and drink bars, most notably the **Kusafiri Coffee Shop & Bakery**.

Maharajah Jungle Trek®

Expedition Everest

Asia

The next 'land' is elaborately themed as the gateway to the imaginary south-east Asian city of Anandapur, with temples, ruined forts, landscape and wildlife. The element of reality is again quite startling and the architecture is full of faithful representations of genuine locations.

Flights of Wonder: Another wildlife show, this portrays the talents and traits of the park's avian inhabitants, built into a production of amusing proportions. A trainer showcases the behaviours of various birds, including macaws and hawks, before being interrupted by a bumbling tour guide – Guano Joe (groan) – who needs to be reminded of key conservation issues. This is the cue for some frolics with our feathered friends, including vultures, eagles, toucans and singing parrot Gaucho. The Caravan Stage is not air-conditioned, though, and is fiendishly hot in summer. AAA.

Kali River Rapids: Part thrill-ride, part scenic journey, this bouncy raft ride will get you pretty wet (not great for early morning in winter). It starts out in tropical forest territory before launching into a scene of logging devastation, warning of the dangers of clear-cut burning. Your raft then plunges down a waterfall (and one unlucky soul – usually the one with their back to the drop – gets seriously damp) before you finish more sedately. Queues can be long through the main part of the day, so use FastPass here. Restrictions: 3ft 6in/ 106cm (a few rafts have adult-and-child seats allowing smaller children to ride). TTT (plus AAAA; FP).

Maharajah Jungle Trek: Asia's version of the Pangani Forest Trail is another picturesque walk past decaying temple ruins and animal encounters. Playful gibbons, tapirs, Komodo dragons and a bat enclosure (including the flying fox bat, the world's largest variety) lead to the main viewing area, the 5 acre/2ha Tiger Range, whose pool and fountains are a popular playground early in the day for these magnificent big cats. An antelope enclosure and walk-through aviary complete this truly breathtaking trek (which rarely draws heavy crowds). AAAAA.

Expedition: Everest™: A major attraction, this wonderfully clever roller-coaster takes you deep into the Himalayas for an encounter with the mythical Yeti. The queuing area alone will convince you of its authentic location (try to do the main queue at least once rather than FastPass to appreciate all the fine detail) as it delivers you to an old abandoned tea plantation railway station. Here you undertake the ride to the foothills of Mount Everest, but you must first brave the perils of the Forbidden Mountain – lair of the Yeti – to get there. Will the beast be in evidence? You bet! The ride becomes a typically fast-paced whiz (though with no inversions), forwards AND backwards, as you attempt to escape the creature's domain. The final encounter with a massive audio-animatronic Yeti is truly jaw-dropping and underlines the splendidly creative nature of this massive ride. It has proved to be a fabulous attraction, but it draws equally impressive crowds all day, so make it one of the first things you do. You can also take advantage of a Single Rider

Kali River Rapids

BRITTIP

Although Expedition: Everest™ is a FastPass ride, its popularity means that FastPasses often run out, so don't leave it too late to visit here.

queue here (at the FastPass entrance) if you don't mind your group being split up. Restrictions: 3ft 8in/ 115cm. TTTTT (FP).

Shopping and dining: The retail options are pretty limited in Asia (just 2 minor kiosks) but it is also home to the fab new **Yak and Yeti** combination diner. Outside is the counter-service **Local Foods Café** (honey chicken, chow mein, egg rolls, chicken salad and sweet & sour pork), while inside the two-storey structure is the full **Restaurant**. This latter offers some of the most imaginative cuisine in any of the parks, from a Dim Sum basket to Maple Tamarind Chicken and a superb spicy Vietnamese Pho, as well as more standard Asian-fusion dishes. A good range of drinks and cocktails complement this outstanding eatery.

DinoLand USA

The final area of the park is somewhat at odds with the natural theming of the rest, a full-scale palaeontology exercise, with the accent on a 'university fossil dig'. Energetically tongue-in-cheek (the students who work the area have the motto 'Been there, dug that', while you enter under a mock brachiosaurus skeleton, the 'Oldengate Bridge' – groan!), it still features some glimpses into genuine dino research and artefacts.

DINOSAUR!: Renamed after Disney's big animated film (it was initially called Countdown to Extinction), this is a herky-jerky ride experience, rather dark and intense (and often too scary for young children). It is also a wonderfully realistic journey back to the end of the Cretaceous period, when a giant meteor put paid to dinosaur life. You enter the high-tech Dino Institute for a multimedia history show that leads to a briefing room for your 'mission' 65 million years in the past. However, one of the Institute's scientists hijacks your trip

Finding Nemo – the Musical

DISNEY'S ANIMAL KINGDOM PARK with children

Here is our guide to the attractions that appeal to the different age groups in this park:

Under-5s

Affection Section, The Boneyard, Character Greetings Trails, Discovery Island Trails, Festival of the Lion King, Finding Nemo – The Musical, Kilimanjaro Safaris, Maharajah Jungle Trek, Pangani Forest Exploration Trail, TriceraTOP Spin.

5–8s

All the above, plus Conservation Station, DINOSAUR! (with parental discretion), Flights Of Wonder, Habitat Habit!, It's Tough To Be A Bug (with parental discretion), Kali River Rapids, Primeval Whirl.

9–12s

All the above, plus Expedition: Everest™.

Over-12s

DINOSAUR!, Expedition: Everest™, Festival of the Lion King, Flights Of Wonder, It's Tough To Be A Bug!, Kali River Rapids, Kilimanjaro Safaris, Maharajah Jungle Trek, Pangani Forest Exploration Trail, Primeval Whirl.

to capture a dinosaur, and you career back to a prehistoric jungle in a 12-passenger 'Time Rover'. The threat of a carnotaurus (quite frightening for children; try to sit them on the inside of the car) and the impending doom of the meteor add up to a breathtaking whiz through a menacing environment. You will need to ride at least twice to appreciate all the detail, but queues build up quickly, so go either first thing or late in the day. Restrictions: 3ft 4in/ 101cm. TTTT plus AAAA (FP).

The Boneyard: A hugely imaginative adventure playground, it offers kids the chance to slip, slide and climb through the 'fossilised' remains of triceratops and brontosaurs, explore caves, dig for bones and splash through a mini waterfall. The amusing signage will be wasted on most kids, but it's ideal for parents to let young 'uns loose for up to an hour (though not just after the neighbouring Finding Nemo show has finished). TTTT (kids only).

Finding Nemo – The Musical: This replaced the Tarzan Rocks show in 2006 and is a first for Disney entertainment, taking a non-musical animated feature and turning it into a fully fledged all-singing extravaganza. The show combines colourful puppets, dancers, acrobats and animated backdrops with innovative lighting, sound and special effects. The basic idea remains faithful to the story of Nemo, his dad Marlin and friends Dory and Crush and features larger-than-life puppetry, plus rod,

The Boneyard

bunraku and shadow puppets, all designed by Michael Curry, who created the award-winning Broadway version of Disney's *The Lion King* show. It's a spectacular combination of music and grand staging, and performs up to 5 times a day. AAAA.

BRITTIP

Finding Nemo – The Musical is a popular addition but, although it draws long lines, the theatre seats 1,500, so most people usually get in.

Chester & Hester's Dino-Rama!: This mini-land of rides, fairground games and stalls adds a rather garish element to the park. Its main icon is a towering Concretosaurus (!), and it is designed to have a quirky, tongue-in-cheek style reminiscent of 1950s' American roadside attractions. The rides are: **TriceraTOP Spin**: another version of the Dumbo/Aladdin rides in the *Magic Kingdom*, where a flying, twirling, spinning top bounces you up and down with a surprise at the top. AA (TTTT under-5s); and **Primeval Whirl**: coaster fans will get a laugh out of this wacky offering that sends its riders through a maze of curves, hills and (quite sharp) drops that make it seem faster than it actually is. It's basically a lampoon of the DINOSAUR! ride, a mock journey 'way back in time', with plenty of cartoon frippery. Extra fun is provided by the fact that the cars spin, which gives an unpredictable element to each 3-minute ride. The queuing area is a riot of visual gags, but the ride is not recommended for anyone with back or neck problems. Restrictions: 4ft/122cm. TTTT (FP).

© Disney

TriceraTOP Spin

Primeval Whirl

© Disney

Walt Disney World at Christmas

If you can visit from the end of November to the week before Christmas, you will get the benefit of all the added decorations and atmosphere and none of the overwhelming crowds (which usually hit peak levels from around 20 December to 2 January). Each of the parks takes on a festive character, with the addition of artistic artificial snow, Christmas lights and a huge, magnificently decorated tree. *Disney's Hollywood Studios* features the signature, eye-popping **Osborne Family Lights** while, at the *Magic Kingdom*, Main Street USA is transformed into a winter wonderland, dominated by a 60ft/18m tree and lighting ceremony. The unmissable **Mickey's Once Upon A ChristmasTime Parade** replaces the main 3pm parade in December and is a positive delight for its lively music and eye-catching costumes. Another seasonal extra is the colourful **'Twas The Night Before Xmas** show at the Galaxy Palace Theater and the nightly **Castle Dream Nights** on Cinderella Castle. You can also sign up for extra festive fun at **Mickey's Very Merry Christmas Party** (see page 123). *Epcot* is the jewel in the Christmas crown, though, with 2 outstanding features. At 6pm, the daily **Christmas tree lighting ceremony** is quite breathtaking as the rest of the park lights go out and then the World Showcase bridge and the tree itself are illuminated in dramatic stages to some grand musical accompaniment. The nightly **Candlelight Processional** also draws a crowd, with a guest narrator telling the story of Christmas to the backdrop of a large choir and elaborate candle parade. It is tasteful, dramatic and eye-catching, but you should arrive early as people start queuing almost 3 HOURS in advance. However, you can get a reserved seat if you buy the **Candlelight Processional Dinner Package** ($35.99–49.99, depending on which World Showcase restaurant you select, and $15.99 3–11s), by calling well in advance on 407 939 3463 (credit card details required). But be aware that the parks are absolutely *packed* on Christmas Day itself and all the restaurants book up well in advance.

Mickey's Very Merry Christmas Parade

Other entertainment: Dino-Rama also features the **Fossil Fun Games**, 6 fairground-type stalls (each costing a rather hefty $2–6) designed to tempt you into trying to win a large cuddly dinosaur. Comic trio **Smear, Splat and Dip** perform up to 6 times a day with their brand of madcap juggling and acrobatics, while the Caribbean steel drum band **The Tropicals** can also be found here, along with a **Disney character** meet and greet.

Shopping and dining: Chester and Hester's Dinosaur Treasures (the 'Fossiliferous Gift Store' – groan!) offers a wide range of dino-related souvenirs. You can get a counter-service meal at the (you've guessed it!) **Restaurantosaurus** (burgers, hot dogs and salad) or grab a snack at **PetriFries**.

Dinosaur!

Parades and tours

Mickey's Jammin' Jungle Parade: The daily highlight is a tour de force in which the Imagineers have created a series of fanciful 'Expedition Rovers' that give various Disney characters the chance to celebrate all the animals that live here. The parade is enhanced by stilt-walkers, puppets, mobile sculptures and different 'party animals', plus live percussionists as it snakes down a narrow path from Harambe, around Discovery Island and back. With memorable musical backing, it sounds as good as it looks, while 25 park guests are chosen to take part every day, travelling on the back of amusingly designed rickshaws that follow each of the character jeeps. AAAAA.

Tours: Finally, for a behind-the-scenes look at the park, **Backstage Safari** is a wonderful 3-hour journey into the handling and care of all the animals ($70, no under-16s), while **Wild By Design** offers a 3-hour tour of the park's art, architecture and history and how it was all created ($60, no under-14s), both including lunch. Book on 407 939 8687.

Mickey's Jammin' Jungle Parade

© Disney

6 Five More of the Best

or Expanding Orlando's Universe

It's time to leave the wonderful world of Disney now, and venture out into the rest of Central Florida's great tourist attractions. And, believe us, there's still a terrific amount in store.

For a start, they don't come much more ambitious than **Universal Orlando**. The area that used to consist of just one theme park, Universal Studios, is now a fully fledged resort in its own right. A second park, Islands of Adventure, opened in 1999, hot on the heels of the CityWalk entertainment district. The first hotel, Portofino Bay, opened in 1999, followed by the Hard Rock Hotel in 2000, and the Royal Pacific Resort in 2002. And there is a LOT of exciting new development to come in 2009/10, with a major new coaster for the Studios park and the whole Wizarding World of Harry Potter at Island of Adventure!

A waterway network connects the hotels to the CityWalk hub, while the multi-storey car parks, for more than 20,000 vehicles, have done away with the need for any other transport system as it is easy to move between parks. The Orlando FlexTicket tie-up with SeaWorld and Busch Gardens, plus the purchase of the Wet 'n Wild water park, has also proved a success – not to mention great value. It's certainly a multi-day experience these days and there are periodic special ticket deals. In summer 2008,

Jaws

UK ticket retailers were offering a Universal 2-Day/2-Park ticket with an extra day free and a 3-Park Bonus Ticket (with Wet 'n Wild) with a full 2-week duration. Sadly, Universal has eliminated its free Universal Express system, now offering only the paid-for **Universal Express Plus**, a day pass that provides one-time access to the top rides with minimal queuing – for an extra $20–46 ($26–51 for both parks) per person, depending on time of year. A limited number go on sale an hour after park opening and are snapped up, but they can also be bought online for a specific day at **universalorlando.com**, or in the parks themselves for another day. It does save time but, at quieter times of the year, it can be an unnecessary expense. Universal hotel guests benefit from Express ride priority ALL DAY by producing their room key. In addition, some rides have **Single Rider** queues, which save time if you want to go by yourself or don't mind splitting up your group. Once again, any height or health restrictions are noted in ride descriptions.

The **Universal Meal Deal** ticket, which can be bought online, at either park's front gate or at any of the 8 participating restaurants (4 in each park) may be a money saver for those with a hungry brood to feed. You exchange your ticket for a Meal Deal

The Blue Man Group

wristband the first time you dine and you can 'eat all day for one low price'. Just show your wristband each time you pass through the counter-service queue, returning as many times as you like. Each time you can claim 1 main course and 1 dessert (drinks are extra – unless you buy their Meal Deal Sipper Cup for an extra $8.99 a day). The 1-Day/1-Park Meal Deal is $19.99/adult ($9.99 under-10s); the 1-Day/2-Park Deal is $23.99 ($11.99 under-10s). We reckon if you have 2 full meals and a snack in the course of the day, you will save money.

Blue Man Group joined the Universal line-up in 2007, bringing its unique brand of humour to the Orlando nightlife scene (see page 302).

Universal Studios

Universal Studios Florida®

Universal opened its first Florida park in June 1990 (its original Los Angeles site has been open since before World War II) and quickly became a serious competitor to Disney. For the visitor, it means a consistently high standard and good value (though the choice can be bewildering!). If you have been to the LA Studios, this one is very different. Universal is also a different proposition to Disney, with a more in-your-face style that appeals to teens. Younger children are still well catered for, though.

Universal parks can also need more than a full day in high season. Strategies are the same as at Disney: arrive EARLY (up to 30 minutes before opening), do the big rides first, avoid main meal times and take time out for an afternoon break (try shopping, dining or visiting the cinemas at CityWalk) if it gets too crowded.

Location

Universal Studios Florida® is sub-divided into 6 main areas, set around a huge, man-made lagoon, but there are no great distinguishing features, so you'll need your map. The main resort entrance is just off Interstate 4 (I-4 eastbound take exit 75A; westbound take exit 74B) or via Universal Boulevard from International Drive by Wet 'n Wild. Parking is in its massive multi-storey car park and there is quite a walk (with moving walkways) to the front gates. Once through, your best bet is to turn right on to Rodeo Drive, along Hollywood Boulevard and Sunset Boulevard and into World Expo for

Universal Studios Florida® at a glance

Location	Off exits 75A and 74B from I-4; Universal Boulevard and Kirkman Road	
Size	110 acres/45ha in 7 themed areas	
Hours	9am–6pm or 7pm off peak; 9am–10pm high season (Washington's birthday, Easter, summer holidays, Thanksgiving, Christmas)	
Admission	Under 3s free; 3–9 $63 (1-Day Ticket), $94.99 (2-Park Unlimited Ticket), $194.95 (FlexTicket), $234.95 (FlexTicket Plus); adult (10+) $75, $99.99, $234.95, $279.95. Prices do not include tax.	
Parking	$12 (preferred parking $17; valet parking $20)	
Lockers	Immediately to left in Front Lot $8	
Pushchairs	$11 and $17 (kiddie, with steering wheel), $14 and $19 (double, with steering wheel), next to locker hire	
Wheelchairs	$12 and $40 (with photo ID as deposit), with pushchairs	
Top Attractions	Revenge of the Mummy, Men in Black, Jaws, ET Adventure, Shrek 4-D, The Simpsons, Terminator 2: 3-D, Hollywood Rip, Ride Rockit! (summer 2009)	
Don't Miss	Universal 360: A Cinesphere Spectacular (peak season only), Curious George Playground (for kids), The Blues Brothers	
Hidden Costs	**Meals**	Burger, chips and coke $8.38 3-course dinner $28.97 (Lombard's) Kids' meal $5.49 ($6.75–6.95 in Lombard's Seafood Grill)
	T-shirts	$18.95–26.95
	Souvenirs	55c–$295
	Sundries	Face painting $8–15

Production Central

1 Guest Services

2 Shrek 4-D

3 Jimmy Neutron's Nicktoon Blast

4 Hollywood Rip, Ride, Rockit! (summer 2009)

5 Donkey's Photo Finish

6 Monsters Café

New York

7 Twister

8 Revenge Of The Mummy

9 The Blues Brothers

10 Alley Climb

11 Finnegan's Bar and Grill

12 Louie's Italian Restaurant

San Francisco/Amity

13 Disaster! A Major Motion Picture Ride … starring YOU

14 Jaws

15 Beetlejuice's Graveyard Revue

16 Central Lagoon

176 Lombard's Seafood Grille

18 Fear Factor Live

World Expo

19 The Simpsons Ride

20 Men In Black – Alien Attack

Woody Woodpecker's Zidzone

21 Animal Actors On Location!

22 Fievel's Playland

23 A Day In The Park With Barney

24 ET Adventure

25 Woodly Woodpecker's Nuthouse Coaster

26 Curious George Goes To Town

Hollywood

27 Universal's Horror Make-Up Show

28 Terminator 2: 3-D Battle Across Time

29 Lucy: A Tribute

30 Guest Services

31 Mel's Drive-In

32 Café La Bamba

Men in Black – Alien Attack

The Simpsons, followed by Men In Black – Alien Attack. From there, head across the bridge to Jaws, then go back along the Embarcadero for Disaster! and into New York for Revenge Of The Mummy. This will get most of the main rides under your belt before the crowds build up, and you can then take it a bit easier by seeing some of the shows. Alternatively, try to be among the early birds flocking to the Shrek 4-D film show in Production Central and Revenge Of The Mummy in New York to avoid the queues that build up here, then visit the likes of The Simpsons and Men in Black.

The opening of an eye-catching new roller-coaster, the tremendous Hollywood Rip, Ride, Rockit! in summer 2009, is likely to make this the hottest ride in town, so consider making this your main target (along with The Simpsons) if the thrill rides have a lot of appeal for you. Here's a full blow-by-blow guide to the Studios. For CityWalk, see Chapter 10, Orlando by Night. Watch out for the helpful mobile electronic **Wait Times** boards placed around both parks, too.

Production Central

Coming straight through the gates brings you immediately into the administrative centre, with a couple of large gift stores (have a look at these in mid-afternoon) plus **Studio Sweets**. Call at **Guest Services** here for guides for disabled visitors, TDD and assisted listening devices, and to make restaurant bookings, which can also be made at a kiosk to the right after the turnstiles, next to the Beverly Hills Boulangerie. **First aid** is available here (and on Canal Street between New York and San Francisco), while there are facilities for nursing mothers at **Family Services** by the bank through the gates on the right. In addition, Universal Studios hosts **Total Non Stop Action Wrestling** (specific dates April–July), with tickets available here on a first-come, first-served basis (call 407 224 6000 for more details). Coming to the top of the Plaza of the Stars brings you to the business end of the park.

Shrek 4-D: This adds a whole new dimension to the genre of 3-D films as the original cast of the Oscar-winning Shrek movies (Mike Myers, Eddie Murphy, Cameron Diaz and John Lithgow) return for a 13-minute prequel to Shrek 2. The evil but vertically challenged Lord Farquaad is back in ghost form to welcome visitors to his dungeons and ruin the

Shrek 4-D

honeymoon of Shrek and Princess Fiona. The amusing 7-minute pre-show leads into the 500-seat main theatre, where you don your Ogre Vision 3-D glasses and prepare to enter a new world. The film is funny enough as Shrek and Donkey have to rescue the Princess, but the addition of a host of special effects (watch out for the spiders!) and moving seats adds a startling extra element that is hugely entertaining. State-of-the-art digital projection and audio systems, lighting effects and smoke (plus a hilarious finale featuring an out-of-control Tinker Bell) ensure a real laugh-fest. A major draw, so try to go first thing or expect waits to top an hour. AAAAA+.

Jimmy Neutron's Nicktoon Blast: Anyone not familiar with the cartoon antics of Jimmy Neutron (Boy Genius) and other members of the Nicktoon stable (Rugrats, the Fairly Odd Parents and SpongeBob SquarePants) might be left bemused by this rather noisy simulator ride experience. It revolves around Jimmy tangling with the evil (but hapless) Emperor Ooblar and battling to save the world with the help of his zany inventions and cartoon friends. It's a big hit with under-10s and the ride is quite dynamic. It quickly draws a queue as it is one of the first you encounter through the gates. There is no height restriction as long as a child can sit unaided, but it is not recommended for anyone with heart, neck or back problems (though there are stationary seats). TTT.

Hollywood Rip, Ride, Rockit!: The park's iconic new ride (due to open in summer 2009) is a stunning colossus of a roller-coaster packed with the latest video and audio technology that allows you to select your own ride music and enjoy it again afterwards. The dimensions alone are daunting – at 170ft/52m it is Orlando's highest coaster – and, reaching almost 70mph, it will also be the fastest ride. And you just can't miss it as it loops out of the park itself into CityWalk, across the main waterway, and back into the park – a vivid steel monstrosity that dares you to ride it! Universal's creative gurus promise 'A true high-intensity, multi-sensory experience that is unmatched. It blends roller-coaster intensity and guest interaction in a way where no two experiences will be the same.' Other features will be 6 near-miss moments and a record-breaking loop, plus innovative concert-style lighting and other high-energy visuals. The special effects and ability to buy the video of your ride (which you can also edit and send to friends – very savvy marketing from Universal's financial department) will certainly add extra spice to the experience and we anticipate this will be a HUGE draw when it opens. Restrictions: 4ft6in/137cm. TTTTT+ (expected).

Other entertainment: Don't miss the chance to meet Shrek, Fiona and Donkey on 8th Avenue in Production Central for **Donkey's Photo Finish**, which is well worth catching for the amusing patter (mimicking the Eddie Murphy character). And look for a **SpongeBob photo opportunity** in the Nickstuff Store.

Shopping and dining: You'll find some of the best of the shops here, including **On Location** (film,

Artist's impression of Hollywood Rip, Ride Rockit!

Twister

sundries, apparel and 2-way radio rentals), **Nickstuff** (Toon merchandise with Jimmy Neutron, SpongeBob SquarePants and Dora the Explorer), the massive **Universal Studios Store** (the full range of gifts and souvenirs) and **It's A Wrap** (discounted items). The main eating outlet here is the magnificently themed **Monsters Café**, specialising in salads, pasta, ribs, pizza and chicken. The counter-service area is done up like Frankenstein's lab, with the dining areas subdivided into Swamp, Space, Crypt and Mansion Dining, all to the accompaniment of old black-and-white horror film clips.

New York

From Production Central, you head on to New York and some great scene-setting in the architecture and detail of the buildings and streets. It's far too clean to be authentic, but the façades are first class.

Twister: This experience, based on the hit film, brings audiences 'up close and personal' with the awesome destructive forces of a tornado. The 5-storey terror will shatter everything in its path (okay, it's pretty tame compared with the real thing), building to a shattering climax of destruction (watch for the flying cow!). The noise is stunning, but can be a bit much for young children (parental discretion advised for under-10s). The pre-show area is almost a work of art in itself but, unless you do it early, save this for late in the day. TTT.

Revenge Of The Mummy: This superb offering in Orlando's roller-coaster catalogue is a high-tech, high-thrill, high-fun journey into the world of the highly successful Mummy film series. It features an indoor spin into Ancient Egypt, fusing new coaster technology with space-age robotics and special effects. It starts out as a dark ride (a slow journey through the shadowy, curse-ridden interior of Hamunaptra, The City of the Dead) but before long it evolves into something far more dynamic – with a breathtaking launch.

BRITTIP

For the best ride experience on Revenge Of The Mummy, try to get a back row seat. You are not allowed to carry anything on the ride – loose items must be left in the lockers provided.

The basic premise of the film studio becoming a fully fledged archaeological discovery is a good one, and the transition from dark ride to coaster is ingenious, with a host of special effects and eye-popping audio-animatronics as you brave the Mummy's realm. The high-speed whiz into the dark (backwards to start with) doesn't involve any inversions but is still a thrill with its tight turns and

Revenge of the Mummy

sudden dips, while there are several clever twists (the front row may get slightly damp!). It is a hugely immersive experience and, with the elaborately themed queuing area, adds a real 5-star attraction to the park. However, it is probably too dark and threatening for under-8s. Be sure to preview your ride photos ($19.95–29.95) just before you enter the gift shop. Restrictions: 4ft/122cm. TTTT½. Anyone feeling energetic can then try the **Alley Climb** (rock wall) on 5th Avenue for $5.

The Blues Brothers: Fans of the film will not want to miss this live show as Jake and Elwood Blues (or pretty good doubles anyway) put on a stormin' performance on New York's Delancey Street 4 or 5 times a day. They cruise up in their Bluesmobile and go through a series of the film's hits before heading off into the sunset, stopping only to sign a few autographs. Terrific. AAAA.

Shopping and dining: Check out **Sahara Traders** for Mummy souvenirs, as well as jewellery and toys, **Rosie's Irish Shop** for all things Irish and **Aftermath** for Twister souvenirs. New York also boasts the inevitable **amusement arcade**. For dining, you have 2 main restaurants. **Finnegan's Bar and Grill** offers shepherd's pie, fish and chips, corned beef and cabbage, along with more traditional New York fare like steak, burgers, fries and a good range of beers, plus Irish-tinged entertainment and Happy Hour 4–7pm ($3.50 Bud and Bud Light; $4.50 imported beers), while **Louie's Italian Restaurant** has counter-service pizza and pasta, ice-cream and tiramisu. You will also find a new **Ben and Jerry's** store for delicious ice-cream and smoothies, and a **Starbucks** for coffee and pastries.

San Francisco/Amity

Crossing Canal Street brings you right across America to San Francisco/ Amity and 2 more serious queues.

Disaster! A Major Motion Picture Ride… Starring YOU: This hugely funny 3-part adventure (which replaces the old Earthquake attraction) gets busy from mid-morning until late afternoon and goes behind the scenes into film special effects in the mythical Disaster Studios. You go first into the Screening Room, where your tour host interacts with a wonderfully creative projection of actor Christopher Walken (playing Studios boss Frank Kincaid in high style) to set the scene for the Sound Stage (a sequence of amusing set-pieces using audience volunteers) and then the Disaster Set itself – an underground train ride into a major San Francisco earthquake, with YOU as the 'extras'.

Disaster!

Tremble as walls and ceilings collapse, trains collide, fire erupts and a seeming tidal wave of water sweeps in. Finally, check out how well you did on the screen at the end, which reveals some hilarious results! It's probably a touch scary for small children, while those with bad backs or necks or expectant mothers should not ride the final scene. Restrictions: 4ft/122cm (unless accompanied by an adult, with parental discretion). AAAA + TTT.

Jaws: The technical wizardry alone will amaze you here, and queues of an hour are common as you head out into the waters of this mini 'Amity'. This is no ordinary ride, and its 6-minute duration will seem a lot longer as your hapless boat guide steers you through an ever-more spectacular series of stunts, explosions and menace from the Great White. You WILL be impressed – and just a little scared! It can be a noticeably wet experience for those sitting on the right-hand side! TTTT.

Beetlejuice's Graveyard Revue: *Disney's Hollywood Studios* has *Beauty and the Beast* and *The Little Mermaid*: Universal goes for *Dracula, Frankenstein, The Wolfman* and *Frankenstein's Bride* in this 20-minute 'shock 'n' roll' extravaganza, compered by Beetlejuice himself. This raucous concert eschews the twee prettiness of Disney's attractions yet still comes up with a fun family show with lots of laughs, as the graveyard characters perform specially adapted rock and pop anthems (like Dancing in the Dark and Jump) with a mock-horror theme in a great setting. AAAA.

Fear Factor Live: In this live action version of the popular reality TV programme, audience volunteers are asked to take part in a series of hair-raising (and stomach-churning!) challenges, with a head-to-head competition to find the biggest daredevil. Auditions take place 70 minutes before each show, and the audience is then invited in to see the chosen few battle it out, with clips from the TV show interspersed with live action. Some of the stunts are distinctly off-colour (anyone for a maggot milkshake?) and may not be good for young children (or anyone of a weak disposition!), but it is a very well-staged production. TTT.

Shopping and dining: Visit **Quint's Surf Shack** (the latest beach apparel and other clothing), **Oakley** (sunglasses and accessories), **Amazing Pictures** (for the chance to have your photo superimposed on a variety of Universal, and other, backgrounds; $29–100) and the **San Francisco Candy Factory** (great pick-n-mix!). An added attraction is a **Boardwalk** of fairground games (which cost $2–6 to play), including a Guess Your Weight stall that is usually highly entertaining. This area also has the park's best dining choices, with **Lombard's Seafood Grill** the highlight (reservations accepted). Great seafood, pasta and sandwiches are accompanied by a good view over the Central Lagoon, and there's a pastry shop for desserts and coffee. **Richter's Burger Co** offers some tempting burger variations, while **Midway Grill** provides hot dogs and fries.

Amity

World Expo

Crossing the bridge from Amity brings you to a rather nondescript area, but home to the park's newest 5-star thrill attraction.

The Simpsons Ride: This has taken over the former Back To The Future building (since summer 2008), bringing the TV world of The Simpsons to vibrant life in a hugely colourful (and highly amusing) production, even if you're not fans of the cartoon Springfield family. It is themed as Krustyland amusement park, brainchild of the irascible Krusty the Clown, a bizarre funfair that is the setting for a hectic, breathtaking ride in the company of Homer, Bart, Lisa, Marge and Maggie. A wicked sound system and state-of-the-art motion simulator technology ensure a frantic race through outlandish attractions (watch out for the Tooth Chipper!) with the Simpsons by your side. The feel of the 'ride' is truly amazing and the huge domed screen ensures a complete sensory experience that is both breathtaking and outrageously comical. As chief designer Mike West told us: 'Your funny bone will hurt. A lot.' And it does, for a long time afterwards! All the characters have been voiced by the original stars of the long-running show and even the queuing area is a riot of gags and visual hilarity. However, this is also now the park's biggest draw, hence you need to do this early or expect to be in a LONG queue. Restrictions: 3ft 4in/101cm. TTTTT.

Men in Black – Alien Attack

The Simpsons Ride

Men in Black – Alien Attack: This combination thrill/dark ride takes up where the hit films, starring Will Smith, left off. Visitors are secretly introduced to the MIB Institute in an inventive mock-futuristic setting and enrolled as trainees for a battle around the streets of New York with a horde of escaped aliens. Your 6-person car is equipped with laser zappers for an interactive shoot-out that is like a real-life arcade game, as the aliens can also shoot back and send your car spinning. The finale features a close encounter with a 30ft/9m bug that is all mouth. Will you survive? Only your collective shooting skills can save the day, and there are numerous ride variations according to your accuracy. Will Smith and Rip Torn are your on-screen hosts, and Will returns at the end to reveal whether your score makes you Galaxy Defenders, Cosmically Average or Bug Bait! Fast, frantic and a bit confusing, this will have you coming back for more until you can top 250,000 (awarding you Defender status). Restrictions: 3ft 6in/106cm. TTTT.

BRITTIP

For a big score in Men In Black, when you meet the Big Bug – push the big red button!

Shopping and dining: To complete the Springfield effect, visit the **Kwik-E-Mart** for a range of Simpsons souvenirs (plus more trademark humour), while **MIB Gear** has more themed gifts and clothing. The **International Food and Film Festival** is a food court offering burgers, sandwiches, meatball subs and salads (in air-conditioned comfort), while **Expo Eats** offers drinks and snacks.

BRITTIP

Along the lagoon in the World Expo/KidZone area is East Green, a quiet spot where you can stop to take a break from the theme park whirl for a while.

Woody Woodpecker's KidZone

This is great place to let the kids loose for a while but it does also feature several great family attractions.

Animal Actors On Location!: An amusing mix of video, animal performance and audience interaction, several children are invited to take part and present a series of unlikely feats and stunts featuring a range of fairly tame wildlife, from a racoon to a snake, and on to cats and dogs. Many have been rescued from animal shelters and gone on to feature in films before finding a home at Universal. The big theatre also provides an escape from afternoon crowds. AAAA.

Fievel's Playland: Strictly for kids, this playground, based on the enlarged world of the cartoon mouse, offers them the chance to bounce under a 1,000-gallon hat, crawl through a giant boot, climb a 30ft/9m spider's web and shoot the rapids (a 200ft/61m waterslide) in Fievel's sardine can. TTTT (young 'uns only!).

A Day in the Park with Barney: Again strictly for the younger set (2–5), the purple dinosaur from the kids' TV show is brought to super-dee-duper life on stage in a large arena that features a pre-show before the 15-minute main event, plus an interactive post-show area. Parents will cringe but the youngsters love it. NB: check out the amazing loos! AA (AAAAA under-5s).

ET Adventure: This is as glorious as scenic rides come, with a picturesque queuing area like the pine woods from the film and then a spectacular leap on the trademark flying bicycles to save ET's home planet. Steven Spielberg (Universal's creative consultant) has added some special effects and characters, and you have an individual ET greeting at the end. The masses often overlook this corner of the park, hence it is worth saving for later in the day. There is a height restriction of 4ft/122cm to ride alone, but smaller children can ride with parents. AAAAA.

Woody Woodpecker's Nuthouse Coaster: Anchoring the excellent under-10s adventure land is this child-sized but still quite racy roller-coaster. The brilliant red 800ft/244m track reaches only 28ft/8m high and 22mph/35kph, but it seems the real deal to youngsters. However, there is still a height restriction of 3ft/91cm. TTTT (juniors only).

Woody Woodpecker's KidZone

Curious George Goes To Town: Kids of all ages love this amazing adventure playground and huge range of activities – and plenty of ways to get wet. It combines toddler play, water-based play stations and a huge interactive ball pool, and is a real bonus for harassed parents. The town theme includes buildings to climb, pumps and hoses to spray water, a ball factory in which to shoot, dump and blast thousands of foam balls and – the tour de force – two 500 gallon/2,275 litre buckets of water that regularly dump their contents on the street below. TTTTT (under-12s). Curious George himself roams the KidZone from time to time, while other characters make regular appearances.

BRITTIP

If you're planning to let your youngsters loose in the Curious George playground, it is highly advisable to bring their swimsuits or a change of clothing.

Other entertainment: Look out for the **Star Toons Show** up to 6 times a day, with music and dance from the 1980s, and a **Madagascar** meet-and-greet, with the furry stars of the cartoon film.

Shopping and dining: Shop at the **Cartoon Store**, **Barney Store** or **ET's Toy Closet and Photo Spot**. For snacks, **Kidzone Pizza Company** offers snacks such as pizza and chicken fingers.

Terminator 2: 3D

Hollywood

Finally, your circular tour of Universal brings you back towards the main entrance via Hollywood (where else?).

Universal's Horror Make-Up Show: Not recommended for under-12s, this demonstrates some of the often amusing ways in which films have attempted to terrorise us, with clips from modern additions to the genre like *Van Helsing*. It's a 20-minute show, queues are rarely long and the special effects secrets are well worth discovering. AAA.

Terminator 2: 3-D Battle Across Time: Another first-of-its-kind attraction, this is hard to describe. Part film, part show, part experience but all action, it usually leaves its audience in awe. The 'wow!' factor works overtime as you go through a 10-minute pre-show representing a trip to the Cyberdyne Systems from the *Terminator* films and then into a 700-seat theatre for a 'presentation' on its latest robot creations. The show is interrupted, though, by John and Sarah Connor and mayhem ensues, with the audience subjected to a huge array of (loud) special effects, including real actors interacting with the screen and the audience, indoor pyrotechnics and a climactic 3-D film finale that takes the *Terminator* story a step further. Arnold Schwarzenegger and other members of the original cast all collaborated on the 12-minute movie and the overall effect is dazzling, but you need to arrive early or expect queues of over an hour (parental discretion for under-12s). TTTTT.

Lucy: A Tribute: The last attraction (or first, depending on which way you go round) will mean little to all but devoted fans of the late Lucille Ball and her 1960s' TV comedy *The Lucy Show*. Classic shows, home movies, costumes and scripts are all paraded, but youngsters will find it tedious. AA.

UNIVERSAL STUDIOS with children

Our guide to the attractions that generally appeal to the different age groups.

Under-5s

Animal Actors On Location!, Curious George Goes To Town, A Day In The Park With Barney, ET Adventure, Fievel's Playland.

5–8s

All the above (minus Barney), plus Disaster! (with parental discretion), Jimmy Neutron's Nicktoon Blast, Men In Black, Shrek 4-D, The Simpsons and Woody Woodpecker's Nuthouse Coaster.

9–12s

All the above, plus Beetlejuice's Graveyard Revue, Fear Factor Live!, Jaws, Revenge Of The Mummy, Terminator 2: 3-D Battle Across Time, Twister, Universal 360: A Cinesphere Spectacular.

Over-12s

Beetlejuice's Graveyard Revue, The Blues Brothers, Disaster!, ET Adventure, Fear Factor Live, Jaws, Jimmy Neutron's Nicktoon Blast, Men In Black – Alien Attack, Revenge Of The Mummy, Shrek 4-D, The Simpsons, Terminator 2: 3-D Battle Across Time, Twister, Universal 360: A Cinesphere Spectacular, Universal's Horror Make-Up Show.

Other entertainment: The **Hollywood Character Zone** provides numerous character appearances throughout the day along Hollywood Boulevard, from Scooby Do and Shaggy to Dudley Do-Right, The Flintstones and Lucille Ball.

BRITTIP

Budding magicians should make a bee-line for the small Theater Magic shop next to Mel's Drive-In, with merchandise and some terrific small-scale magic shows several times daily.

Shopping and dining: Look for Terminator gifts and clothing in **Cyber Image**, all manner of headgear in **The Brown Derby**, Hollywood legends' jewellery in **Studio Styles** and movie memorabilia in **Silver Screen Collectibles**. If you haven't eaten by now, there are 4 contrasting eateries: **Mel's Drive-In**, a re-creation from the film *American Graffiti*, serving all manner of burgers and hot dogs (though Richter's has better burgers); **Café La Bamba** for rotisserie chicken, ribs, salad and burgers, plus margaritas and beer (Happy Hour 3–5pm); **Schwab's Pharmacy**, with old-fashioned milkshakes, sundaes and ice-cream; and **Beverly Hills Boulangerie** for a range of pastries, sandwiches, cheesecake, juices and Seattle's Best coffee.

Special programmes

Universal Studios features some brilliant extra seasonal entertainment for **Mardi Gras**, with a hectic, bead-throwing parade, plus music, street entertainment and authentic New Orleans food each Saturday at 6pm from mid-Feb to late May (and free with normal park admission). The

Mardi Gras

evening culminates in a live concert with well-known acts (like Heart, Kool & The Gang, Smokey Robinson and Earth, Wind & Fire in 2008), but it does draw HUGE crowds. Universal also throws a major party for the **4th of July**, when the park presents a stunning fireworks spectacular.

Halloween Horror Nights

Universal's massively popular Halloween celebration occurs through late September and all of October each year and is a wonderfully bloodthirsty – and thoroughly entertaining! – series of evening events. The Horror Nights have become a real trademark and add a suitably grisly touch to park proceedings (Universal has experimented with running the event in both parks in the past but in recent years it has been in Universal Studios only). The park is transformed with some highly imaginative re-creations and set pieces from various horror movies, with a parade and shows that include live (terrifyingly so, in some cases) character interaction. The general mix is 8 or so indoor Scare Houses, all with their own macabre theme (like Friday the 13th and Vampire Castle), plus several open-air Scare Zones, with atmospheric dry ice and characters lurking in dark corners, and 3 or 4 live presentations, including the signature *Bill & Ted's Excellent Halloween Adventure* (an annual comedy special that heavily satirises topical pop culture icons). All horror genres are well represented, and the Scare Houses feature some superb 'scare actors' and special effects. The rides are also all open (and often with fairly short queues), adding more novelty to the park experience, but this over-the-top (and occasionally downright gruesome) extravaganza is definitely not for kids, especially as the atmosphere can get a bit raucous late in the evening as alcohol is widely available. It goes down a treat with adults with the right sense of humour, though, and begins every evening at 7.30pm. It is a separate event costing around $65/person and it is highly advisable to book in advance at **universalorlando.com** or through Attraction Tickets Direct. There is even a Frequent Fear Pass for multiple visits on selected evenings (but not Fridays and Saturdays, when crowds are heaviest and queues for the Scare Houses can reach 2 hours). No masks or costumes are allowed, though.

Finally, **Universal 360: A Cinesphere Spectacular** brings down the curtain each evening during peak season and special events with a blaze of fireworks and 4 gigantic 'cinespheres' that allow for cinema projection. The overall effect places guests in the middle of their favourite films, with an all-new musical score (on 300 outdoor speakers), lasers and other pyrotechnics, using the spheres as video screens. It's a stunning performance, so check your park map to see if it's showing during your visit.

Cinesphere on the 4th of July

Islands of Adventure

When he officially opened the park in 1999, Universal's creative consultant Steven Spielberg insisted: 'These are not just theme park rides, these are entertainment achievements beyond anything I have seen anywhere else in the world.' And that's only the beginning. This is one of the most complete and thrilling theme parks you will find as it is a brilliantly conceived and executed concept, containing a wonderfully upbeat collection of high-adrenalin rides, shows and other entertainment (not to mention some fine dining). However, you will also notice some construction and temporary attraction closures (notably in the Lost Continent area) as Islands of Adventure prepares to unveil the eagerly awaited Wizarding World of Harry Potter (see page 17) in early 2010 as the 7th 'land', adding even more appeal to this hugely imaginative park.

It has a full range of attractions, from the real adrenaline overloads to pure family entertainment, and it even *sounds* good – with some 40 pieces of original music, you can buy the CD of the theme park! Okay, so they are not really islands (the 6 areas form a chain around the central lagoon), but that's the only illusion. And you get a lot for your money here, unless you have extremely timid children or under-5s. Seuss Landing will usually keep pre-schoolers amused for several hours, while Camp Jurassic is a clever adventure playground for the 5–12s, but the rest of the park, with its 7 5-star thrill rides and other standout attractions, is primarily geared to kids of 8 and over, their parents and

Islands of Adventure at a glance

Location	Off exits 75A and 74B from I-4; Universal Boulevard and Kirkman Road	
Size	110 acres/45ha in 6 'islands'	
Hours	9am–7pm off peak; 9am–10pm high season (Washington's birthday, Easter, summer holidays, Thanksgiving, Christmas)	
Admission	Under-3s free; 3–9 $63 (1-Day Ticket), $94.99 (2-Park Unlimited Ticket), $194.95 (FlexTicket), $233.95 (FlexTicket Plus); adult (10+) $75, $99.99, $234.95, $279.95. Prices do not include tax.	
Parking	$12, preferred parking $17, valet parking $20	
Lockers	Immediately to left through main gates; $8	
Pushchairs	$11 and $17; next to locker hire. Kiddie, with steering wheel $14; Double $19.	
Wheelchairs	$12 and $40 (with photo ID as deposit); with pushchairs	
Top Attractions	Amazing Adventures Of Spider-Man, Dueling Dragons, Incredible Hulk Coaster, Jurassic Park River Adventure, Dudley Do-Right's Ripsaw Falls, The Cat In The Hat	
Don't Miss	Eighth Voyage Of Sindbad, Jurassic Park Discovery Centre, If I Ran The Zoo playground (for toddlers), dining at Mythos Restaurant	
Hidden Costs	**Meals**	Burger, chips and coke $9.88 3-course lunch $29.94 (Confisco Grille) Kids' meal $5.49–6.99 ($4.99 at Meal Deal spots)
	T-shirts	$18.95–26.95
	Souvenirs	95c–$1,600
	Sundries	Caricature drawings; $15–36 (black and white and airbrush colour)

Port of Entry
- 1 Ocean Trader Market
- 2 Confisco Grille

Marvel Super-Hero Island
- 3 Incredible Hulk Coaster
- 4 Dr Doom's Fearfall
- 5 Café 4
- 6 Captain America Diner
- 7 The Amazing Adventures Of Spider-Man
- 8 Storm Force Accelatron

Toon Lagoon
- 9 Me Ship, The Olive
- 10 Popeye And Bluto's Bilge-Rat Barges
- 11 Dudley Do-Right's Ripsaw Falls
- 12 Comic Strip Café
- 13 Circus Amphitheater
- 14 Toon Lagoon Character Festival

Jurassic Park
- 15 Jurassic Park River Adventure
- 16 Pteranodon Flyers
- 17 Camp Jurassic
- 18 Discovery Center
- 19 Thunder Falls Terrace

The Lost Continent
- 20 Dueling Dragons
- 21 The Flying Unicorn
- 22 The Eighth Voyage of Sindbad
- 23 Poseidon's Fury
- 24 The Enchanted Oak Tavern (and Alchemy Bar)
- 25 Mythos Restaurant
- 26 The Mystic Fountain

Seuss Landing
- 27 Caro-Seuss-el
- 28 One Fish, Two Fish, Red Fish, Blue Fish
- 29 The Cat In The Hat
- 30 If I Ran The Zoo
- 31 High In The Sky Seuss Trolley Train Ride
- 32 Circus McGurkus Café Stoo-pendous
- 33 Green Eggs And Ham Cafe
- 34 Guest Services

The Wizarding World of Harry Potter

especially teenagers. There are 5 elements that look truly alarming, but don't be put off – they all deliver immense fun as well as terrific spectator value! If any one ride sums up IoA, it is the Amazing Adventures Of Spider-Man, the world's first moving 3-D simulator ride. Its jaw-dropping special effects are sure to leave you in awe and admiration!

Private nursing facilities, an open area for feeding and resting (with high chairs) and nappy-changing stations, can be found at the **Family Service Facility** at Guest Services (to the right inside the main gates), while ALL restrooms throughout the park are equipped with **nappy-changing** facilities. **First aid** is provided in Sindbad's Village in the Lost Continent, just across from Oasis Coolers and in Port of Entry.

Port of Entry

You arrive for IoA as you do for Universal Studios, in the big multi-storey car parks off I-4 and Universal Boulevard and either walk or ride the moving walkways into CityWalk, where you continue through to the entrance plaza (head for the huge Pharos Lighthouse). As with Universal Studios, you can purchase the **Universal Express Plus** pass for $20–51 (depending on time of year) at the Marvel Alterniverse Store, Toon Extra or Jurassic Outfitters. Once through the gates, the lockers, pushchair and wheelchair hire are all on your left as the **Port of Entry** opens up before you. This elaborate 'village' consists of shops and eateries, so push straight on until you hit the main lagoon. Later in the day, return to check out the extensive retail experience at places like the **IoA Trading Company** and **Ocean Trader Market**. Enjoy a snack from **Cinnabon** (cinnamon rolls and pastries) or the **Croissant Moon Bakery** (excellent coffee, croissants and sandwiches), or chill out with a soft drink or ice-cream from **Arctic Express**.

Alternatively, sit down for lunch or dinner (steak, pasta, fish, pizza, burgers and salads) at **Confisco Grille** and grab a beverage at the **Backwater Bar** (Happy Hour 4–7pm). There is also a **Character Breakfast** at Confisco Grille (9–10.30am Thurs–Sun) with various Universal characters like Spider-Man and The

Port of Entry

Cat In The Hat, plus The Grinch during the Christmas season ($15.95 adults, $9.95 children; 407 224 4012 for reservations). Above all, take in the wonderful architecture, which borrows from Middle East, Far East and African themes and uses bric-a-brac from all over the world. At the end of the street, you have 3 choices and this is where you need a plan. There are 8 attractions where the queues build up quickly and remain that way most of the day.

1 If you are here for the big thrill rides, turn left into Marvel Super-Hero Island and head straight to Spider-Man, then do Dr Doom's Fearfall and the Incredible Hulk Coaster.

2 Dinosaur fans should head straight around the lagoon to Jurassic Park, where you should be able to do the River Adventure before the majority arrives. Once you are nice and wet, head for Toon Lagoon for Ripsaw Falls and the Bilge-Rat Barges.

3 If you have younger children, turn right into the multi-coloured world of Seuss Landing and enjoy The Cat In The Hat and High In The Sky Seuss Trolley Train Ride prior to the main crowd build-up.

The Grinch at Christmas

Incredible Hulk Coaster

Marvel Super-Hero Island

Going clockwise, you arrive first in the elaborate comic-book pages of the super-heroes. As with all the islands, the experience is total immersion. The amazing façades of this world surround you with an utterly credible alternative reality that is one of the park's triumphs – and that's before you have tried the rides.

The Incredible Hulk Coaster: Roller-coasters don't come much more dramatic than this giant green edifice that soars over the lagoon, blasting 0–40mph/64kph in 2 seconds, and reaching a top speed of 65mph/105kph. It looks awesome, sounds stunning and rides like a demon as you enter the gamma-ray world of Dr David Banner, aka the Incredible Hulk, and zoom into a weightless inversion 100ft/30m up!

BRITTIP

At the Hulk Coaster, keep left where the queue splits up and you will be in line for the front car for an even more extreme Hulk experience.

Just watching is mind-boggling, and the effects are distinctly brain-scrambling! You will need to deposit ANY loose articles (cameras, sunglasses, coins etc.) in the lockers at the front of the building as the ride

Amazing Adventures of Spiderman

is guaranteed to shake anything out of your pockets. Crowds build up rapidly but the queues move reasonably quickly. Restrictions: 4ft 6in/137cm. TTTTT+.

Dr Doom's Fearfall: This is where, oh hapless visitor, you wander into the lair of the evil Dr Doom – arch-enemy of the Fantastic Four – and his sinister cohorts. His latest creation is the Fearfall, a device for sucking every iota of fear out of his victims, and YOU are about to test it as 16 riders at a time are strapped into chairs at the bottom of a 200ft/60m tower. The dry ice rolls, and whooooosh! Up you go at breakneck speed, only to plummet back seemingly even faster, with an amazing split second in between when you feel suspended in mid-air. Summon up the courage to do this and we promise an astonishing (if brief!) experience. Queues are substantial during the main part of the day. Restrictions: 4ft 4in/132cm, and we reckon this is way too scary for under-10s. TTTTT+. You exit Fearfall into the inevitable high-energy **video arcade** – as if your nerves aren't on edge already!

The Amazing Adventures Of Spider-Man: Just queuing is a novel experience as your visit to the *Daily Bugle*, home of ace reporter Peter Parker (aka Spider-Man), turns into a reporting assignment in one of the 'Scoop' vehicles. Prepare for an audio-visual extravaganza as the blend of 3-D and motion simulator takes you into a battle between Spidey and arch-villains like Dr Octopus with his anti-gravity gun, culminating in a convincing 'drop' off a skyscraper as the contest literally hots up. There are lots of eye-popping special effects and you'll need to do it at least twice to appreciate all the detail. Ride early on or leave it until late in the day – queues often top an hour. Restrictions: 3ft 4in/101cm. TTTTT+.

Storm Force Accelatron: This ride, aimed primarily at youngsters, puts you in the middle of a whirling, twirling battle between X-Men super-heroine Storm and arch-nemesis Magneto, with a range of special effects. It's basically an updated spinning-cup ride, but with some neat twists (there is a 3-way rotation where the cars look set to collide at any moment). TTT (TTTTT under-12s).

Other entertainment: Keep a lookout here for the **Marvel Super-Heroes**, who appear for photos and autographs several times a day.

Shopping and dining: Each ride has its own character merchandise, while the **Comic Book Shop** and **Marvel Alterniverse Shop** sell other souvenirs. For a bite to eat, try the Italian buffeteria **Café 4** (pizza, spaghetti, sandwiches and salads) or a burger, chicken fingers or salad at the **Captain America Diner**.

Dr Doom's Fearfall

Toon Lagoon

The thrills continue here with a watery theme and more comic-book elements as the (American) newspaper cartoon characters take a bow. Children will also love to play with the fountains, squirt pools and overflowing fire hydrants!

Popeye And Bluto's Bilge-Rat Barges: Every park seems to have a variation on the white-water raft ride, but no other is as outrageously themed and downright wet. Fast, bouncy and unpredictable, it has water coming at you from every direction, a couple of sizeable drops and a whirl through the Octoplus Grotto that adds to the fun. If you don't want to get wet, don't ride, because there is no escaping the deluge here. This is also one of the top 5 for long queues, but it's definitely worth the wait. Restrictions: 4ft/122cm. TTTTT. You can also try the Water Blasters (for 25c) on the bridge at the start of the ride to give riders a wet start!

BRITTIP

A change of clothes is often advisable after the Barges, unless it's so hot you need to cool down in a hurry. Bring a waterproof bag for your valuables or leave them in a locker.

Popeye and Bluto's Bilge Rat Barges

Toon Lagoon

Dudley Do-Right's Ripsaw Falls: Universal's designers also hit the jackpot with this flume ride that sends its passengers on a wild (and precipitous!) journey in the company of guileless mountie Dudley Do-Right, bidding to save girlfriend Nell from the evil Snidely Whiplash. The action builds to an explosive showdown at the top of a 75ft/27m abyss that drops you through the roof of a ramshackle dynamite shack and into the lagoon below. Just awesome – as are the queues from mid-morning to late afternoon. Wet? You bet! Restrictions: 3ft 8in/111cm. TTTTT. There are more Water Blasters here (25c) on the bridge overlooking the final drop to get riders even wetter.

Me Ship, The Olive: This purpose-built kids' playland is designed as a 3-storey boat full of interactive fun and games, including slides, bells and water cannons (perfect for squirting riders on the Bilge-Rat Barges below), in best Popeye style. TTTT (youngsters only).

Other entertainment: Look out for the **Toon Lagoon Amphitheatre**, which is used for seasonal live shows, and **King's Row and Comic Strip Lane**, the place to meet strolling characters like Beetle Bailey, Hagar the Horrible, Krazy Kat and Blondie. The big character meet and greet, though, is provided by the **Toon**

Comic Strip Café

Trolley Beach Bash (high season only), where you can have fun with the likes of Popeye, The Flintstones and Dudley Do-Right.

Shopping and dining: There is the usual array of character shops, like **Gasoline Alley, Boop Oop A Doop** and **Toon Extr**a, while you can grab a humongous sandwich at **Blondie's** (home of the Dagwood), a trademark burger or chicken wrap at **Wimpy's**, sample the food court variety of **Comic Strip Café** (Mexican, Chinese, American and Italian), something cool at **Cathy's Ice Cream** or a cold beverage at **Ale To The Chief**.

Jurassic Park

Leaving the comic-book lands behind, you travel back to the Cretaceous age and the credible make-believe dinosaur film world. Again, the immersive experience is first class and the extravagant scenery will have you looking over your shoulder for stray dinos.

Jurassic Park River Adventure: From scenic splendour, the mood changes to hidden menace as your journey into this magnificent waterborne realm brings you up close and personal with some seriously realistic dinosaurs. Inevitably, your passage is diverted from the safe to the hazardous, and the danger increases as the 16-person raft climbs into the heights of the main building – with raptors loose everywhere. You are aware of something large lurking in the shadows – will you fall prey to the T-Rex, or will your boat take the 85ft/26m plunge to safety (with a good soaking for all down the longest water descent in the world!)? Queues usually move quite briskly but will top an hour in mid-afternoon. Restrictions: 3ft 6in/106cm. TTTT. The ride photo comes in various packages ($22.95–29.95). The more adventurous can then try the **Rock**

Jurassic Park

Dueling Dragons

Climbing Wall (just outside River Adventure) for an extra $5. There is also a Tip Board across from the ride's entrance.

Pteranodon Flyers: The slow-moving queues are a major turn-off, especially for a fairly average ride, which glides gently over much of Jurassic Park (though it reaches a height of almost 30ft/9m at one point). It is designed mainly for kids, though, and the height range of 3ft–4ft 8in/91–142cm requires anyone OVER the upper limit (usually 11 or older) to be accompanied by a child of the right height. TT (TTTT under-9s).

Camp Jurassic: More excellent kids' fare here with the mountainous jungle giving way to an 'active' volcano for youngsters to explore, climb and slide down. Squirt guns and spitter dinosaurs add to the fun. TTTT (for kids, but parents can explore!).

Discovery Center: This indoor centre offers various interactive opportunities, including creating a dinosaur through DNA sequencing, mixing your own DNA with a dino via a touchscreen, seeing through the eyes of various large reptiles and even handling 'dino eggs', plus other fun hands-on exhibits. Being air-conditioned, this is a good place to visit when it's hot (11am–5pm). AAA.

Shopping and dining: Visit **Discovery Center** for the best shopping, while you can eat at the **Burger Digs** (some huge burger platters), visit the **Pizza Predattoria** or the **Watering Hole** bar (Happy Hour 3–5pm), or try the rotisserie chicken at the rustic **Thunder Falls Terrace** (counter service), which boasts a great view of the River Adventure.

The Lost Continent

This land is due to undergo a heavy rebuild in 2009 as part of the Wizarding World of Harry Potter expansion, which could lead to some temporary closures of rides and the occasional detour. However, it will still offer some great attractions.

Dueling Dragons: There is no disguising the intense nature of this magnificent double coaster, with its 100ft/30m drop, multiple loops, twists and 3 near-miss encounters. There is a lot more, too, as the queuing area is a real mind-boggler – 1,060yd/969m, most of it along a dark, winding path

Poseidon's Fury

through the ancient castle that is the domain of the dragons Fire and Ice. You choose which dragon to ride (the tracks differ slightly), and you can join an additional queue for the front seats. Unlike the Hulk, this is a suspended coaster, so your legs dangle free, and the initial drop is like going into free-fall! Coaster aficionados reckon the best ride is in the back of the Ice (Blue) dragon, but both offer an awesome experience. Restrictions: 4ft 6in/137cm; all loose items must be left in the lockers by the entrance. TTTTT+. *NB: This ride will close at some stage in 2009 to be incorporated, with new theming, into the Harry Potter 'island'.*

The Flying Unicorn: This junior-sized coaster is aimed primarily at youngsters and features a wizard's workshop, hidden in an enchanted wood, which is the gateway to a magical journey inspired by the Unicorn. There are no big drops, but it delivers a surprisingly fast-paced whirl. TTTTT (6–12s). *NB: This ride is also due to be closed and re-themed for Harry Potter in 2009.*

The Eighth Voyage of Sindbad: This stunt and special effects show is another marvel, as much for its elaborate staging as its performance. Mythical adventurer Sindbad and sidekick Kabob (a name that's the cue for a truly awful pun) tackle evil witch Miseria in a bid to rescue Princess Amoura, and the action springs up in surprising places. There are several loud bangs that could scare young children, but otherwise it's good family fun. There is also a great post-show feature where the cast reappears for photos and autographs. TTT/AAAA.

Poseidon's Fury: A walk-through show that puts its audience at the heart of the action as a journey in the company of a hapless young archaeologist takes a turn for the worse in the lost temple of Poseidon. The route passes through an amazing water vortex before your expedition

The Lost Continent

unexpectedly awakens an ancient demon. Again, there is an element of suspense, but the special effects showdown between Poseidon and the demon is amazing. Queuing is tedious, but at least you are inside in summer. TTT.

Other entertainment: For an extra $2–10, try the **Pitch and Skill Games** or a bit of mystic manipulation with **Psychic Readers**. But watch out for **The Mystic Fountain**. It has the ability to strike up a conversation – and soak you when you least expect it!

Shopping and dining: Find some original souvenirs at **The Coin Mint** (coins forged and struck before your eyes) and **Historic Families** (explore the history of your family name and coat of arms in a medieval armoury), **Tangles of Truth** (hand-crafted jewellery), **The Pearl Factory** (pick an oyster) and **The Dragon's Keep** (dragon apparel, games and toys). Food options include **The Fire-Eater's Grill** (sausages, chips and drinks) and **Frozen Desert** (sundaes and sodas), plus the excellent counter-service **Enchanted Oak Tavern** (inside a vast, sculpted oak tree; hickory-smoked chicken, ribs and salads) and

The Flying Unicorn

Alchemy Bar (Happy Hour 3–5pm). *NB: We believe the Enchanted Oak and Alchemy Bar will also be incorporated into the Harry Potter island, though, with full Hogsmeade Village theming.* The elaborate **Mythos Restaurant** provides the best dining in IoA, though; the food (seafood, salads, grills, pizza and pasta) is first class, but the setting (inside a dormant volcano with streams, fountains and clever lighting) is an attraction in its own right (3-course meal around $24, kids' meals $5.99–10.99).

Hogsmeade Village

ISLANDS OF ADVENTURE with children

Our guide to the attractions that generally appeal to the different age groups:

Under-5s

Caro-Seuss-el, The Cat In The Hat, High In The Sky Seuss Trolley Train Ride, If I Ran The Zoo, Jurassic Park Discovery Center, Me Ship, The Olive, One Fish, Two Fish, Red Fish, Blue Fish.

5–8s

All the above, plus Amazing Adventures Of Spider-Man, Camp Jurassic, Eighth Voyage of Sindbad, Flying Unicorn, Jurassic Park River Adventure (with parental discretion), Pteranodon Flyers, Storm Force Accelatron.

9–12s

Amazing Adventures Of Spider-Man, Camp Jurassic, The Cat In The Hat, Dr Doom's Fearfall, Dudley Do-Right's Ripsaw Falls, Dueling Dragons, Eighth Voyage Of Sindbad, Flying Unicorn, Incredible Hulk Coaster, Jurassic Park Discovery Center, Jurassic Park River Adventure, Popeye And Bluto's Bilge-Rat Barges, Pteranodon Flyers, Storm Force Accelatron.

Over-12s

Amazing Adventures Of Spider-Man, Dr Doom's Fearfall, Dudley Do-Right's Ripsaw Falls, Dueling Dragons, Eighth Voyage Of Sindbad, Incredible Hulk Coaster, Jurassic Park Discovery Center, Jurassic Park River Adventure, Popeye And Bluto's Bilge-Rat Barges, Storm Force Accelatron.

Seuss Landing

There is not a straight line to be seen in this vivid 3-D working of the books of Dr Seuss. The characters may not mean much to those unfamiliar with the children's stories, but everyone can relate to the fun here (though queues build up quickly). There is so much clever detail, from squirt ponds to beach scenes, it can be easy to miss something, so take your time.

Caro-Seuss-el: This intricate carousel ride on some of the Seuss characters – cowfish, elephant-birds and dog-a-lopes, for example – has rider-activated features that are a big hit with youngsters. AAA (AAAA under-5s).

One Fish, Two Fish, Red Fish, Blue Fish: A fairground ride with a twist as you pilot these Seussian fish up and down according to the rhyme that plays while you ride. Get it wrong and you get squirted! More fun for the younger set. TTT (TTTTT under-5s).

The Cat in the Hat: Prepare for a ride with a difference as you board these crazy 6-passenger 'couches' to meet the world's most adventurous cat and friends Thing One and Thing Two. You literally go for a spin through this storybook world, and it may be a bit much for very young children. The slow-moving queues are a bit of a drag, so try to get here early or leave it until later in the day. AAAA/TTT.

If I Ran the Zoo: Interactive playgrounds don't get much better for the pre-school brigade than with these different Seuss character scenarios, some of which can be pretty wet! Hugely imaginative and great fun to watch. TTTTT (under-5s).

Caro-Seuss-el

The High in the Sky Seuss Trolley Train Ride: This fun family adventure high above Seuss Landing was originally meant to be part of the park's opening but it took 7 years to redevelop and bring to life. It has terrific appeal to youngsters, though, as you board a special trolley to journey into the world of the Sneetches, visiting the Inking and Stamping Room, the Star Wash Room and a tour inside the Circus McGurkus Café Stoo-pendous. It is slow-paced, scenic and eye-catching, but it does draw slow-moving queues, so head here early on if your children are the requisite age (2–8). AAAA.

Other entertainment: Look out for **character appearances** by The Cat In The Hat, Thing One and Thing Two and The Grinch outside the Circus McGurkus.

Shopping and dining: If you have been captivated by the land, you can buy the books at **Dr Seuss' All The Books You Can Read Store**, Christmas-themed merchandise at **Honk Honker's**, or a full variety of character merchandise at the **Mulberry Street Store**. **Snookers and Snookers Sweet Candy Cookers** is a super sweet shop, while snacks and drinks can be had at **Hop On Pop Ice Cream Shop, Moose Juice Goose Juice** and **Green Eggs and Ham Café**

High in the Sky

(sandwiches and burgers). The **Circus McGurkus Café Stoo-pendous** is a mind-boggling eatery for fried chicken, lasagne, spaghetti and pizza – with clowns and pipe organs.

BRITTIP

For some of the park's best shopping bargains, visit Port Provisions right by the exit gates (to the left as you come through) where all the merchandise is 30–50% off.

And that, folks, is the full low-down on arguably the world's most thrilling and complete theme park. Not to be missed!

One Fish, Two Fish, Red Fish, Blue Fish

SeaWorld Adventure Park

SeaWorld is firmly established with British visitors as one of the most popular parks for its more peaceful and naturalistic aspect, the change of pace it offers and the general lack of substantial queues. Like Disney's *Epcot* park, it is large enough to handle big crowds well (though it still gets busy in peak season) and is a big hit with families in particular, but it also has some dramatic rides and imaginative attractions – including a new coaster for 2009, The Manta. It is also one of owners Anheuser-Busch's 'Worlds of Discovery', along with recent sister parks **Discovery Cove** (2000), an exotic tropical 'island' with dolphin, stingray and snorkelling adventures (see pages 203–6) and **Aquatica** (2008; see pages 250–2). These latter have added huge appeal in this area, along with new 2-, 3- and 4-park tickets that also include Busch Gardens in Tampa. Its recent new shows and enhancements means this remains a wonderfully fresh and invigorating place to visit.

Happily, this is still a park where you can proceed at a relatively leisurely pace, see what you want without too much jostling and yet feel you have been well entertained (even if the restaurants do get crowded at mealtimes). SeaWorld is also a good starting point if this is your first Orlando visit as it gives you the hang of negotiating the vast areas, navigating by the various maps and

SeaWorld Adventure Park at a glance

Location	7007 SeaWorld Drive, off Central Florida Parkway (Junctions 71 and 72 off I-4)
Size	More than 200 acres/81ha, incorporating 26 attractions
Hours	9am–6pm off peak; 9am–10pm high season (Easter, summer holidays, Thanksgiving, Christmas)
Admission	Under-3s free; 3–9 $59.95 (1-Day Ticket), $84.95 (2-Park Ticket, w/Aquatica), $89.95 (2-Park TIcket inc Busch Gardens), $124.95 (3-Park Ticket inc Aquatica and Busch Gardens), $194.95 (Orlando FlexTicket, $234.95 (Orlando FlexTicket Plus); adult (10+) $69.95, $94.95, $99.95, $134.95, $234.95, $279.95.
Parking	$11, $16 preferred parking
Lockers	Inside Entrance Plaza (next to Sweet Sailin' Candy), $6 and $8 (rent from Pushchair and Wheelchair location)
Pushchairs	$9.39 and $16.90, to right of Guest Services inside park
Wheelchairs	$10 and $38; with pushchairs
Top Attractions	Believe at Shamu Stadium, Shark Encounter, Journey To Atlantis, Kraken, Wild Arctic, Blue Horizons, The Manta (summer 2009)
Don't Miss	Mistify (high season), Manatee Rescue, behind-the-scenes tours, Odyssea show, dining at Sharks Underwater Grill
Hidden Costs	**Meals** Burger, chips and coke $10.28 3-course lunch (Sharks Underwater Grill) $39; Kids' meal $7.29, including souvenir Shamu lunchbox; $7–10 at Sharks Underwater Grill) **T-shirts** $11.99–26.99 **Souvenirs** $1.99–8,499 **Sundries** Caricatures $14.95–24.95

1 Entrance plaza
2 Key West at SeaWorld
3 Stingray Lagoon
4 Turtle Point
5 Dolphin Cove
6 Whale and Dolphin Theater
7 Blue Horizons
8 Manatee Cove
9 Journey To Atlantis
10 Kraken
11 The Manta (coming 2009)
12 Penguin Encounter
13 Pacific Point Preserve
14 Sea Lion and Otter Stadium
15 Xtreme Zone
16 Mama's Kitchen
17 The Waterfront
18 Seaport Theater
19 Seafire Inn/Makahiki Luau
20 The Tower
21 Dolphin Nursery
22 Voyager's Restaurant
23 The Spice Mill
24 Shark Encounter
25 Nautilus Theater – Odyssea
26 Sharks Underwater Grill
27 Clydesdale Hamlet
28 Anheuser-Busch Hospitality Center
29 Shamu Stadium
30 Shamu's Happy Harbor
31 Wild Arctic
32 Mango Joe's Café
33 Atlantis Bayside Stadium
34 Backstage at Believe
35 Mistify

learning to plan around the showtimes. This park has a strong educational and environmental message, plus 3 1-hour, behind-the-scenes tours (book up as soon as you enter or online), which provide a great insight into SeaWorld's marine conservation, rescue and research programme, as well as its entertainment resources.

The Polar Expedition provides a close-up of the penguin and polar bear environments; **Saving a Species** showcases the park's animal rescue and rehabilitation programme, with a chance to hand-feed exotic birds in the free-flight aviary ($1 of the tour fee also goes to the Anheuser-Busch Conservation Fund); and **Predators!** offers a backstage view of Shark Encounter and Shamu Stadium. You pay an extra $18 ($12 3–9s) for these tours, but they are worth it and, if you take one early on, it will increase your appreciation of the park. There are also discounts and special offers (like a 2nd day free and adult tickets at kids' prices) by booking online at **seaworld.com**, where you can print your own tickets and save waiting in a queue. There is also a dedicated Worlds of Discovery website for UK visitors, **floridaparks.co.uk**.

BRITTIP

The Polar Expedition tour includes a (brief) encounter with one of the park's penguins, but this tour is more about seeing the back-stage facilities than any close wildlife encounters.

Six additional programmes provide other unique insights and experiences. The 7-hour **Adventure Express Tour** offers visitors their own tour guide, with back-door access to the rides, reserved seating at shows, a lunch buffet backstage at Believe and animal feeding opportunities (an extra $120 for adults, $100 3–9s; book up first thing at the Guided Tours counter, online or call 1800 406 2244); the 5-hour **Night Adventure Tour** is similar but includes dinner and a visit to the Brewmaster's Club (peak season, adults only, $100/person); The **Marine Mammal Keeper Experience** takes 2 visitors daily (aged 13 and over) to find out about the care necessary to rehabilitate injured manatees, plus bottle-feed some of them, meet the seals and walruses and prepare meals for the beluga whales. It starts at 6.30am and lasts around 8 hours for $399/person (including lunch, T-shirt, special book, souvenir photo and 7-day SeaWorld pass); **Sharks Deep Dive** is a totally captivating experience, a chance to suit up and dive in a specially constructed cage into the huge shark aquarium, and spend ½ hour up close and personal with these amazing creatures. The 2-hour programme includes an educational induction into the world of sharks, what they are and what makes them tick (with important pointers like never wear jewellery in the sea – sharks are attracted by the glitter, mistaking it for the reflection of fish scales). Then you are equipped for the dive with wetsuit (the water IS chilly), gloves, dive belt and a special underwater helmet that also allows communication (no scuba gear needed) in the reinforced steel cage that glides slowly from one end of the 125ft/38m long tank to the other. Getting a fish-eye view of these creatures is an astounding experience, and you won't tire of the underwater panorama (which includes waving to people in the shark tunnel!). It is an eye-opening programme, but the best part is you

Dolphins at SeaWorld

get to wear a really cool wetsuit with 'Scubapro' on the front! It costs $150 (including a great souvenir T-shirt and shark book; participants must be 10 and over); the new 1-hour **Dolphin Spotlight Tour** provides a fascinating and educational glimpse backstage into the training and care of the stars of the Blue Horizons show, as well as a look into the extensive dolphin-care facilities behind the scenes. You finish up with a wide-ranging session with one of the animal trainers at the Dolphin Cove, getting a close-up of their training techniques, with the chance to touch one of the residents. It costs $50 for adults and $40 for 3–9s. Finally, the **Beluga Interactive Program** (13 and over) is unique: a chance to meet some of the park's biggest (but most benign) denizens in their own environment. Swimming isn't necessary but guests must be comfortable in the water. Touching, feeding and using hand signals are all part of this captivating and highly informative programme. It costs $179/person (including a book on whales; no expectant mothers) and runs every day, rain or shine. All tours can be booked online at **seaworld.com**.

Location

SeaWorld is located off Central Florida Parkway, between I-4 (exit 71 going east or 72 heading west) and I-Drive, and parking is $11 ($16 if you choose Shamu's preferred parking, which gets you close to the main entrance). It is still best to arrive a bit before the official opening time so you're in a good position to book one of the backstage tours or dash to one of the few attractions that draws a crowd, like Journey to Atlantis. The park covers more than 200 acres/81ha, with 6 shows (7 with the nightly **Makahiki Luau** dinner show at the Seafire Inn, $46 adults, $29 3–9s; nightly, times vary, call 407 351 3600 or book online), 3 major rides, 10 large-scale continuous viewing attractions and 7 smaller ones, plus an ultra-smart range of shops and restaurants (a notable feature of Anheuser-Busch parks). As in the other main parks, try to eat before midday or after 2.30pm for a crowd-free lunch, and before 5.30pm if you want a leisurely dinner (or better still, book Sharks Underwater Grill or Dine With Shamu). Pre-school children may also want to try **Breakfast with Elmo & Friends** (daily at the Seafire Inn at 8.30 or 10.30am), a big buffet meal featuring the stars of Sesame Street like Big Bird, Cookie Monster and Elmo himself ($16.95 adults, $14.95 3–9s; book in advance online or 407 351 3600). Non-drivers should make a note of the special daily bus service from SeaWorld (and other points on I-Drive) direct to sister park **Busch Gardens** (see pages 207–18), which you can book at Guest Relations.

Beluga Interactive Program

SeaWorld is not organised into neat 'lands' like the others, though, and it often requires a lot of to-ing and fro-ing to catch the various shows, which can be wearing. Keep a close grip on your map and entertainment schedule and try to establish a programme to allow regular breaks at the quieter spots. Taking it in a clockwise direction, here's what you will encounter:

Entrance plaza

Coming through the turnstiles brings you to the park's main business area, including the Guest Information kiosk, Lost & Found, Behind The Scenes tour desk, lockers and pushchair and wheelchair rental. You will also find some good shopping and snack options here. Look for the large **Shamu Emporium** for the full range of SeaWorld souvenirs, while **Keyhole Photos** provides all your park pictures taken by the SeaWorld photographers. You can grab a quick breakfast (tasty pastries and coffee) at **Cypress Bakery** or something colder from the adjoining **Polar Parlor Ice Cream**. This is also the place to find a colourful photo opportunity with **Shamu and friends**.

Key West at SeaWorld

A whole collection of exhibits is grouped together here under the clever Key West theme. **Stingray Lagoon**, where you can feed and touch fully grown rays, includes a nursery for newborn rays, while the park's rescued and rehabilitated sea turtles can be seen at **Turtle Point**. The centrepiece, the 2.1 acre/0.8ha **Dolphin Cove**, is a more spectacular, naturalistic development and offers the chance to feed this community of frisky Atlantic bottlenose dolphins (for $6 at specified periods through the day). There is also an excellent underwater viewing area, and park photographers patrol here ready to snap you at play with the dolphins; a 6 x 8 photo will set you back $19.99; frames are $12 and $20.

BRITTIP

If you drop your fish on the ground when feeding the dolphins, seals or sea lions you are asked to throw it away, for the animals' health and safety.

The whole area is designed in the tropical flavour of America's most southerly city, Key West, with beach huts, lifeguard chairs, dune buggies, themed shops and other eclectic elements, but it also underlines the environmental message of conservation through interactive graphics and video displays adjacent to the animal habitats, and children of all ages will find it a fun, educational experience. AAAA.

Shopping and dining: There are 5 gift shops and kiosks here, the best being **Coconut Bay Trader** (apparel and soft toys) and **Sandcastle Toys 'n Treats**. You can also grab a hot dog or chicken tenders at **Captain Pete's Island Eats**.

BRITTIP

Seek out Gulliver's store in Key West for a range of heavily discounted SeaWorld and Discovery Cove apparel and gifts.

Whale & Dolphin Theatre

The first large-scale encounter is the setting for the magnificent Blue Horizons show, plus the neighbouring Manatee rescue exhibit.

Blue Horizons: This wonderful show serves up another big helping of dramatic animal behaviour in best Broadway production style. It features dolphins, false killer whales and exotic birds (including an Andean condor), but a lot more besides as the general (and rather abstract) theme of a girl's dream about maritime wildlife is brought to life. The elaborate set design is the first eye-catching element, with a 40ft/12m sea-meets-sky backdrop that also conceals the setting for a host of additional performers, from high divers to bungee jumpers and trapeze-like aerialists. There is no obvious interaction between trainers and animals as the show moves from one scene to the next, both above and below the water, but there is plenty to admire as the stage is filled with graceful and quite daring action. The

Blue Horizons

complex staging and vivid costuming (all created by Broadway designers) is also underpinned by a stirring original score by the Seattle Symphony Orchestra and it adds up to a magnificent 25 minutes that often draws a huge ovation. AAAAA.

Manatee Rescue: Next door is an exhibit to tug at your heartstrings as you learn the plight of this endangered species of Florida's waterways. Watch these lazy-looking creatures (half-walrus, half-cow?) lounge in their man-made lagoon, then walk down the ramp to the circular theatre where a 5-minute film with 3-D effects reveals the dangers facing the harmless manatee. Then pass into the underwater viewing section, with hands-on TV screens offering more information. It's a magnificent exhibit and should invoke a strong sense of animal conservation. Try to avoid going just after a Blue Horizons show as it can get congested. AAA½.

Shopping and dining: Look to **Manatee Cove** for a kids' wonderland of cuddly toys, while there are also 2 drinks carts.

Ride Central

Continue past the Whale & Dolphin Theatre and you come to the park's serious thrill quotient.

Journey to Atlantis: Unique in Orlando, this terrific water-coaster gave SeaWorld its first 5-star thrill attraction in 1998. The combination of extra elements here ultimately makes it a one-off, with some illusory special effects giving way to a high-speed water ride that becomes a runaway roller-coaster. The discovery of Atlantis in your 8-passenger 'fishing boat' starts gently through the lost city. But evil spirit Allura takes over and riders plunge into a dash through Atlantis, dodging gushing fountains and water cannons, with hundreds of dazzling holographic and laser-generated illusions before the heart-stopping 60ft/18m drop, which is merely the entry to the roller-coaster finale back in the candle-filled catacombs. Be ready to get soaked in the course of the ride, which is great in summer but not so clever first thing on a winter morning. Restrictions: 3ft 6in/106cm. TTTTT.

The Manta

Kraken: This member of the coaster family is one of Florida's most breath-taking. Based on the mythical sea monster, Kraken is an innovative pedestal ride (you are effectively sitting in a chair without a floor – pretty exposed!) that plunges an initial 144ft/44m, hits 65mph/105kph, dives underground 3 times, adds 7 inversions (including a vertical loop, a diving loop, a zero-gravity roll and a cobra roll) and a flat spin before riders escape the beast's lair. The ride from the front row, especially down an opening drop at an angle best described as ludicrous, is positively blood-curdling, and sitting in the rear is thrilling, too. Restrictions: 4ft 6in/137cm. TTTTT+.

The Manta: Themed like a giant stingray, riders are strapped into a face-down position before being launched into a series of 4 inversions along 3,359ft/1,024m of track, reaching nearly 60mph and 140ft/43m high as well as skimming the surface of the lagoon. TTTTT+ (expected). The whole area will be themed like a mythical artisan's village, with caverns, waterfalls and floor-to-ceiling windows showcasing some 300 rays and thousands of fish. In all it should be a visual treat as well as a breathtaking ride.

Shopping and dining: Don't miss the **Sea Aquarium Gallery** as you exit Journey to Atlantis, a combination gift shop and aquarium full of tropical fish (remember to look upwards), while there are more animal-orientated souvenirs in **Kraken Gifts**.

Penguins and Sea Lions

Getting back to the animal side of the park brings you to two more outstanding natural habitats, and a hilarious show.

Penguin Encounter: Always a hit with families (and one of the more crowded exhibits), the ever-comical penguins are brilliantly presented in this chilly showpiece. You have the choice of going close and using the moving walkway along the display or standing back and watching from a non-moving position. Both afford fascinating views of the 17 different species both above and below the water. The 5 or so daily feeding times are also popular, so arrive early if you want a prime spot. There is a question-and-answer session at 2pm every day – the winner gets to pet a penguin! AAAA.

Pacific Point Preserve: This carefully re-created rocky coast habitat shows the park's seals and sea lions at their most natural. A hidden wave machine adds the perfect touch, while park attendants provide informative talks. You can also buy packs of smelt ($4 for 1 tray; $7 for 2 and $10 for 4) to throw to these ever-hungry mammals. AAA.

Sea Lion and Otter Stadium: The venue for a wonderful show, *Clyde And Seamore Take Pirate Island*, it features the resident sea lions who, with their pals the otter and walrus (plus a couple of humans as the fall guys), put on a hilarious 25-minute performance of watery stunts and gags. Arrive early for some first-class audience mickey-taking from the resident pirate 'mime'. AAAA.

Other entertainment: Xtreme Zone offers a Trampoline Jump and Rock Climbing Wall, for an extra fee (reservations required).

Shopping and dining: Pets Ahoy Gifts is the best of the shops here, along with the large **Friends of the Wild**. Grab a meal at **Mama's Kitchen** (a good range of fresh sandwiches, salads and chilli) or the **Smoky Creek Grill** (barbecue ribs, beef brisket and chicken), while there are also 3 drinks carts and an **Ice Cream** counter.

The Waterfront

Backtracking slightly (or turning right after the Entrance Plaza area) brings you to this beautiful 5 acre/2ha seafront 'village' of shops and restaurants, which is a great place to spend some time when other parts are busy, especially for lunch or dinner.

Pets Ahoy!: Just inside the Waterfront is the air-conditioned haven (during the hottest part of the day) of the Seaport Theater, which hosts this cute 25-minute giggle featuring the unlikely talents of a menagerie of dogs, cats, birds, rats, pot-bellied pigs and others, the majority of which have come from local animal rescue shelters. AAA.

Other entertainment: The Tower is the centrepiece of the Waterfront, with a 400ft/122m landmark offering (at an extra $3) slowly rotating rides for a bird's-eye view of the park and

Clyde and Seamore Take Pirate Island

surrounding areas. There are some amusing street performers, too, like the slapstick fun of **The Longshoremen** and the percussive pots-and-pans rhythms of the **Groove Chefs** (who can also be found in other areas of the park). New in 2008 was **Seafire Inn's Wild Things**, a 20-minute multi-media presentation daily from noon to 4pm, with exotic animals presented in a fun and informative set-up (plus photo opportunities!). Finally, the **Dolphin Nursery** provides close-up views with some of the park's younger dolphins.

Shopping and dining: This has some of the best in SeaWorld, starting with 4 interlinked boutique-style shops that offer a stylish range of souvenirs and other gift items (check out **Allura's Treasure Trove** and **Artisans Hall**, as well as the **Anheuser-Busch Trading Co**). The unique **Oyster's Secret** shop features resident pearl divers who can be viewed underwater as they collect the pearl-bearing oysters on request, to be incorporated into jewellery pieces by the shop's artisans. The 3 excellent eateries are: **Seafire Inn** (gourmet burgers, salads, Cuban sandwich and tropical stir-fry); **Voyagers** (wood-fired pizzas, pasta, salads and ribs, plus a low-carb option); and **The Spice Mill** (offering succulent, spicy variations on sandwiches, chilli and jambalaya). There are also 3 snack bars: **Café de Mar** for pastries, coffees, smoothies and soft drinks; **Smugglers Feast** for smoked turkey legs; and **Freezas** for frozen yoghurt and other drinks. The **SandBar** is a water's edge cocktail bar, serving snacks and speciality drinks – *the* place to watch the sun go down!

Believe!

Sharks and Co

Continuing the clockwise tour brings you towards the back of the park (which opens later than the front areas). Here you will find more animal encounters – and a wonderful show.

> **BRITTIP**
> Grab an evening meal at The Spice Mill, then head out on to its open-air terrace for one of the best seats in the house to experience the Mistify nightly finale.

Shark Encounter: Top of the bill, the world's largest collection of dangerous sea creatures can be found here, brought dramatically to life by the walk-through tubes that surround you with more than 50 prowling sharks (including sand tigers, black tips, nurse sharks and sand bars), sawfish, tropical fish and gigantic groupers. It's an eerie experience (and perhaps too intense for young children), but brilliantly presented and, again, highly informative. You can also watch the intrepid souls in the Sharks Deep Dive cage as it traverses the aquarium (see pages 193–4). Queues build up here at peak times, though. AAAA or TTTT.

Odyssea: This is one of SeaWorld's often-overlooked gems, an imaginative and often downright hilarious 30-minute show in the Nautilus Theater (great for a break when it's hot). It features some mind-boggling acrobatic feats, engaging live music, clever lighting and a host of in-theatre special effects. The show tells the spectacular, if stylised, story of a seaman who falls into the ocean and descends through various levels to the sea bed, encountering an assortment of creatures along the way. Arrive early and you'll also catch the amusing antics of the resident mime. AAAAA. The theatre is also home to various weekend events throughout the year, notably **Jack Hanna's Animal Adventure**, the **Bud**

and BBQ Country Music Festival, and the **Viva La Musica** Latin weekends.

Other entertainment: The flamingo pedal-boats on the lagoon here rent for $6 per ½ hour (for 2 people). You can also **feed the sharks** and stingrays outside the Shark Encounter at $4 per tray (2 for $7).

Shopping and dining: The 3 shops here (**Ocean Treasures**, **Shark Photo** and **Gulf Breeze Trader**) are relatively small-scale but, at the entrance to Shark Encounter is the park's top dining choice, **Sharks Underwater Grill**. Not only do you have an amazing backdrop for your meal in a clever, subterranean environment (check out the incredible bar, which is a mini-aquarium), but the upscale menu features appetising 'Floribbean' cuisine, blending local and spicy Caribbean fare. The emphasis is on seafood – and wonderful creations with scallops, jumbo shrimp (king prawns), grouper and sea bass – plus pasta, filet mignon, chicken and pork, and desserts to die for. Some refreshing (non-alcoholic) cocktails and menus for under-10s and teens complete the picture; it's a real treat on a hot day. Open from 11am to park closing, it's very busy at lunch but quieter in late afternoon, so we advise booking (at the restaurant itself) as soon as you arrive.

BRITTIP

If the main adult portions look too big at Sharks Underwater Grill – and they are pretty hefty – you can order from the Young Adults menu for smaller portions of 4 regular dishes. Check out the kids' dessert menu, too.

Clydesdale Hamlet

These massive stables are home to the Anheuser-Busch trademark Clydesdale dray horses. They make a great photo opportunity when fully harnessed and there is a life-size statue outside, which creates a good backdrop. The Hitching Barn shows how the horses are prepared for the twice-daily parade, including washing, grooming and braiding. AA.

Other entertainment: For something different, you can sign up for the free 35-minute Anheuser-Busch **Beer School** at the Hospitality Center for a glimpse into beer-making (and tasting!). The more involved **Brewmaster's Club** teaches guests how to pair Anheuser-Busch beers with various foods, to enjoy each to the full. Samples of beer (American lager to robust stout), chocolate, fruits and cheeses are free to small groups (reservations necessary; visit the Information Counter at the front of the park or the host stand in the Hospitality Center) beginning at 11.15am daily (21 and over only, with valid photo ID). The Hospitality Center also offers a daily free taste of the company's most famous product, the world's No. 1 bottled beer, Budweiser, and its cousins (try the excellent Bare Knuckle Stout for something different!). Sadly, it's only 2 small samples per visitor (21 or over only, with valid photo ID) but you can enjoy them outside on the terrace, which provides a pleasant break from all the hustle and bustle.

Shopping and dining: Good Anheuser-Busch souvenirs are on offer at **Label Stable**, while **The Hospitality Deli** restaurant is an attractive proposition for lunch, serving freshly carved turkey and beef, German sausage, sauerkraut, freshly baked breads and delicious dessert choices.

Sharks Underwater Grill

Shamu central

The other main area of the park features the iconic Shamu Stadium and a fabulous play area to entertain the kids, plus another engaging ride/ animal attraction.

Shamu Stadium: SeaWorld has long outgrown its tag as just the place to see killer whales, but the new Believe show is still one of its most amazing sights. Watch the killer whales and their trainers pull off some spectacular stunts, all set within the story of a young boy's dream of interacting with these creatures of the deep. The basic message of needing to believe in your dreams is a touch schmaltzy, but there is no doubting the brilliant choreography as animals and trainers put on a seamless display – apparently without any commands. Some dramatic staging and an original music score by the Prague National Symphony Orchestra are combined with high-tech video screens that slide and rotate in eye-catching fashion to create a truly majestic extravaganza that is way beyond the usual animal shows. And, if you think it looks good during the day, return in the evening (in high season) for an even more dramatic presentation under the lights, with the video screens coming into their own. As it is the signature element of the park, Shamu Stadium is extremely popular, hence you should try to take in one of the early shows. AAAAA+. All guests can then enjoy the backstage **Underwater Viewing** area.

Shamu's Happy Harbor

BRITTIP

The first 14 rows at Shamu Stadium get VERY wet (watch out for your cameras) – when a killer whale leaps into the air in front of you, it displaces a LOT of water on landing. In fact, the Splash Zones should be renamed the Soak Zones!

Shamu's Happy Harbor: 4 acres/ 1.6ha of brilliantly designed adventure playground and rides await youngsters of all ages here. Activities include a 4-storey net climb, 2 tented ball rooms to wade through, a giant trampoline tent, a mock pirate ship (the Wahoo Too) and a splashy water play area, **Water Works** (great on a hot day). The signature junior-sized coaster **Shamu Express** offers mild thrills over more than 800ft/245m of track. The **Jazzy Jellies** is a jellyfish-themed samba tower ride that lifts and spins, while **Swishy Fishes** features oversized seats that spin round a giant waterspout. **Flying Fiddler** (a 20ft/6.1m tower ride on a jumping giant crab), **Ocean Commotion** (a rocking tug ride) and **Sea Carousel** (a traditional carousel featuring 65 sea creatures) complete the line-up. The area gets busy from midday, but the kids seem to love it at any time. Next door is the arcade and **Games Area**, a series of fairground-type stalls ranging from $1–10 a time. TTTT. At the back of the Harbor you will also find a **Baby Care Center** and the park's **First Aid** station.

Wild Arctic: This interactive ride-and-view experience provides a realistic environment that is both educational and thrilling. It's an exciting simulator jet helicopter journey into the white wilderness arriving at a clever research base, Base Station Wild Arctic, where the passengers disembark into a frozen wonderland to meet polar bears, beluga whales and walruses. This one is not to be

SEAWORLD with children

The following gives a general idea of the appeal of the attractions to the different age groups:

Under-5s

Believe, Blue Horizons, Clyde And Seamore Take Pirate Island, Clydesdale Hamlet, Elmo Show, Manatee Rescue, Odyssea, Pacific Point Preserve, Penguin Encounter, Pets Ahoy!, Shamu's Happy Harbor, Waterfront entertainment, Wild Arctic (without the ride).

5–8s

All the above, plus Mistify, Shark Encounter, Wild Arctic (with the ride).

9–12s

All the above, plus Journey to Atlantis and Kraken.

Over-12s

Believe, Blue Horizons, Clyde And Seamore Take Pirate Island, Journey To Atlantis, Kraken, Mistify, Odyssea, Shark Encounter, Wild Arctic.

missed (but avoid just after Believe when the hordes descend). Restrictions: 3ft 6in/106cm. TTTT/AAAAA. Those who don't want to do the (quite dynamic) ride can walk through to the Base Station.

Shopping and dining: The **Wild Arctic Gift Shop** is the best of the 3 stores here, with a wide array of cuddlies. For dining, **Mango Joe's Café** offers grilled fajitas, speciality salads and sandwiches, while **Coconut Cove** offers drinks and snacks in Shamu's Happy Harbor.

BRITTIP

Any purchases around the park can be forwarded to Package Pick-up in Shamu's Emporium to collect on your way out, provided you give them at least an hour.

Two special meal opportunities are worth highlighting here: **Dine with Shamu** is a VIP experience 'backstage' with the killer whales and their trainers. A terrific all-you-can-eat dinner buffet on a covered terrace alongside the main pool gives you the chance to ask the trainers questions and watch some of their sessions (you may also get a little wet!). It is offered every day (times vary) but it's highly advisable to book in advance. We hesitate to recommend this as a must-see attraction as it's rather expensive at $39 for adults and $19 for children, but it's a great experience. **Backstage At Believe** is a similar dining experience (with an impressive lunch buffet) and the chance to see a special *Making of Believe* programme and meet the show's stage manager. There is then reserved seating for the next Believe show and a Shamu whale-tail souvenir ($24.95 adults, $9.95 children). You should book ahead for either meal, online or on 1800 327 2424.

Superb show at Believe!

Atlantis Bayside Stadium

The final part of SeaWorld is this large outdoor arena facing the central Lagoon. It's home to an array of seasonal entertainment but is most susceptible to any bad weather.

Elmo and Abby's Treasure Hunt: Each spring and summer sees a special Sesame Street live show on stage here, from late May to 1 Sept. Guaranteed to appeal to the pre-school set, the musical presentation features Elmo, Cookie Monster, Rosita, Grover, Abby Cadabby and others in a 25-minute song and dance fest, encouraging youngsters to use their imagination in a mock treasure hunt. There is also a post-show character meet and greet. AA (or AAAA, depending on age). **Bayside Ski Jam**: This is a new night-time show (summer only) that adds fun and funky music to some fast-paced water-ski and jet-ski action. AAA.

Summer extras

During the official summer season, SeaWorld has extended hours to 10pm and an array of extra live entertainment as part of its **AfterDark** programme (which includes the Night Adventure Tour; see page 193). The 'rock 'n' roll' party atmosphere is generated by live DJs and other entertainers and features 3 extra shows, notably Bayside Ski Jam and **Shamu Rocks**, which adds a more high-energy, free-form version of the main show, including live music and dramatic lighting. The **Shamu Rocks Dinner Buffet** ($32 adults, $17 children) features an excellent all-you-can eat buffet and reserved seating for the show. Then, over at Sea Lion & Otter Stadium, there is a second evening show, **Clyde And Seamore Present Sea Lions Tonight**, which serves up a fun parody of other SeaWorld shows.

> **BRITTIP**
> Learn more about SeaWorld's conservation and environmental efforts at **seaworld.org**.

It all leads up to the big **Mistify** finale on the Waterfront lagoon. This is a neat mix of pyrotechnics and special effects, invoking giant sea creatures with stunning laser images. The show dazzles with towering fountains (up to 100ft/30m high), mist sprays, flames, unique fireworks (including some that burn under water) and an epic soundtrack. By far the largest and most spectacular evening show SeaWorld has yet produced, it doesn't quite rival Disney pyrotechnics, but it shouldn't be missed. AAAA.

Kraken

Discovery Cove

Fancy a day in your own tropical paradise, with the chance to swim with dolphins, encounter sharks, snorkel in a coral reef and dive through a waterfall into a tropical aviary? Well, Discovery Cove is all that and more. The only drawback is the price. This mini theme park comes at a premium because it is restricted to just 1,000 guests a day, creating an exclusive experience that is reflected in the admission fee.

The weather can get distinctly cool in the winter months, but the water is always heated (apart from the dolphin lagoon, which remains at 72ºF/22ºC) and full wetsuits are available to keep out the chill. The attention to detail is superb and guest satisfaction ratings are extremely high (it is hugely popular with British visitors – up to 40% of the daily attendance at times). However, if any element falls below expectations, it's worth bringing it to the attention of a manager as they are always keen to rectify any oversights.

The costs

In 2008, the flat-rate entrance fee was $269 off peak and $289 in peak season, increasing to $289 and $309, we believe, in 2009. The only reduction is $100 off for those not wishing to do the Dolphin Swim and for 3–5s (under-3s free). So, just what do you get for your money? Well, as you would expect, it's a supremely personal park. You check in at the beautiful entrance lobby as you would for a hotel rather than a theme park, and you have a guide to take you in and get you set for the day. All your basic requirements – towel, mask, snorkel, wet-jacket, lockers, beach umbrellas, food and drink – are included, and the level of service is excellent. A valuable week's pass for SeaWorld or Busch Gardens is also included (valid for 7 consecutive days before or after your Discovery Cove visit), or you can upgrade to the excellent value **Ultimate Ticket**, which adds 14 consecutive days at SeaWorld, Busch Gardens AND Aquatica for an extra $35. Continental breakfast, snacks and beverages (including Anheuser-Busch products) as well as lunch at the buffet-style **Laguna Grill** are all included. But the gift shop and photographic prices reflect the entrance fee – expensive.

Therefore, for all its style and dolphin appeal, Discovery Cove will take a BIG bite out of your holiday budget. A family of 4, with children old enough to do the Dolphin Swim, would pay $1,156 for the day in peak season. Even with a free 7-day SeaWorld pass included, it's a massive outlay. The charge for ages 3–5 is also pretty steep, in our opinion. Your sundries can add up, too. An 8 x 10 photo is $26.99; then there are various photo packages at $31.99, $65.99 and $105.99, while the video of your experience (which includes 30 minutes of park highlights) costs $64.99 ($74.99 for a DVD). A CD with 5 images is $105, 11 images is $155 and 22 images is $210. There are 3 digital packages, too: an interaction DVD with 5 images on CD for $150; the DVD with 11 images for $200; and the DVD with 22 images for $250. Poster-size photos (24 x 36) are available for $49.99. However, the feedback we get is almost unfailingly positive and most people are totally captivated by the whole experience.

Key West's Dolphin Cove

Ray Lagoon

There is also an additional programme that adds a great deal of appeal to the basic day, but at more cost, too. **Trainer for a Day** is an exciting opportunity to go behind the scenes into the training, feeding and welfare of the park's animals. You get to work with the experts as they interact with dolphins, birds, sharks, stingrays and tropical fish. The programme includes a behavioural training class, the chance to experience a double-foot push (ride on the front of two dolphins), souvenir shirt, dolphin book and waterproof camera, and participants must be at least 6 and in good health.

The price? A heavy $488 ($468 non-peak season). For all Discovery Cove bookings, call 407 370 1280 (freephone 0800 33 44 1818 in the UK) or visit **discoverycove.com**.

Location

Situated on Central Florida Parkway, almost opposite the SeaWorld entrance (open year-round 9am–5.30pm; parking free), the whole 30 acre/12ha park is magnificently landscaped, with thatched buildings, palm trees, lush vegetation, white-sand beaches, gurgling streams – even hammocks to chill out in. The overall effect is of being transported to a tropical paradise.

The usual tourist hurly-burly is left far behind. The 5-star resort feel is enhanced by a high staff-to-guest ratio (at times the lifeguards seem to outnumber guests) and there are no queues (though the restaurant may get busy at lunchtimes), while the highlight Dolphin Encounter is world class. Visitors with disabilities are well catered for, with special wheelchairs that can move across the sand and into shallow water, and an area of the Dolphin Lagoon to allow those who can't enter the water still to be able to touch the dolphins. The essence of a day here involves close encounters with all the animals and the ultimate feeling is total relaxation, a holiday from your holiday.

A close encounter at Discovery Cove

The main attractions

Coral Reef: A huge rocky pool, filled with several thousand tropical fish, offers the most amazing man-made snorkelling experience you'll find. The water teems with silverjacks, angelfish and yellowtail snapper and, even if the 'coral' is hand-painted concrete, it's a very clever environment. Some of the larger stingrays inhabiting the bottom are fascinating to watch. Swimmers also come within inches of sharks and barracuda – all safely behind a Plexiglass partition – which adds another novel element. If you stay reasonably still in the water, many of the tropical fish will crowd around to inspect their latest pool-mate! AAAA.

Ray Lagoon: Another carefully sculpted pool provides the opportunity to paddle among several dozen southern and cownose rays – harmless, but with a hint of menace to the fascination. AAAA.

Tropical River: This 800yd/732m circuit of gently flowing bath-warm water is a variation on the lazy river feature of many of the water parks, though with a far more naturalistic aspect and none of the inner tubes. It is primarily designed for snorkellers and features rocky lagoons, caves, a beach section, a tropical forest segment, sunken ruins and an underwater viewing window into the Coral Reef. The lack of fish makes it seem a bit bland after the Coral Reef and Ray Lagoon, but it is as much about relaxing as having fun. It is up to 8ft/2.4m deep at points, so non-swimmers are advised to use a flotation vest. It finishes in the freeform Resort Pool, which provides more idyllic relaxation. AAA.

Aviary: This 3-part adventure is both an area in its own right and a 40yd/37m section of the Tropical River. You can walk in off the beach or swim in through the waterfall from the Tropical River, which is a beautifully scenic touch and fun for snorkellers. Some 250 tropical birds (plus tiny Muntjac deer) fill the main enclosure and, if you stand still, they are likely to use you as a perch. An expansion in 2002 effectively doubled the size of the aviary by adding a small-bird sanctuary – full of finches, honeycreepers and hummingbirds – and a large-bird enclosure, featuring toucans and the red-legged seriema. Guides will introduce you to specific birds (which you can hand-feed) and tell you about their habitats and conservation issues. AAAAA.

Dolphin Swim: The headline attraction at Discovery Cove is the encounter with the park's Atlantic bottlenose dolphin community. A 20-minute orientation programme in one of the 4 thatched beach cabañas, with a film and instruction from 2 of the animal trainers, sets you up for this thrilling experience. Groups of 6–8 go into the lagoon with careful supervision from the trainers and, starting off standing in the waist-deep (slightly chilly) water as one of the dolphins comes to you, you gradually become more adventurous until you are swimming with them. Timid swimmers are catered for and there are flotation vests for those who need them. The lagoon is up to 12ft/3.6m deep so there is a real feeling of being in the dolphins' environment. You will learn how trainers use hand signals and positive reinforcement to communicate with them, and get the

Ray Lagoon

chance to stroke, feed and even kiss your dolphin. The encounter concludes dramatically as you are towed ashore by one of these awesome animals, which can weigh up to 600lb/272kg, though the activities vary according to the dolphins' attention span. You spend around 30 minutes in the water and it is totally unforgettable. Under-6s are not allowed into the lagoon. TTTTT+.

Special occasions

For that special birthday or anniversary or for somewhere completely different to propose marriage, Discovery Cove has a range of options that involve dolphin interaction and private beach cabañas. The **Platinum Ring** (an extra $474.95/couple) includes sharing your special moment with a dolphin, who delivers a specialised message buoy, a private cabaña, a bottle of champagne with souvenir champagne chiller and 2 crystal flutes, a dozen roses, assorted chocolates, safe and secret storage of the engagement ring and a video of the occasion. The **Golden Ring Package** ($224.95/couple) and

Dolphin Swim

Sweetheart Package ($149.95) are scaled-down versions of the same. The **Birthday Package** ($74.95) includes dolphin activity, cake, photo and souvenir buoy, while a **Premium** version ($174.95) adds a disposable underwater camera, T-shirt and a video of the occasion.

You are advised to book at least 3 months in advance as it does sell out in peak periods. There is also a 10% advance discount periodically for online bookings. For more info, visit **discoverycove.com**.

Discovery Cove

Busch Gardens

When is a zoo not a zoo? When it is also a theme park like 335 acre/136ha Busch Gardens in Tampa. The second big Anheuser-Busch park in the area started life as a mini-menagerie for the wildlife collection of the brewery-owning Busch family (makers of Budweiser). In 1959, it opened a small, tropical-themed hospitality centre next to the brewery and now it is a major, multi-faceted family attraction, the biggest on Florida's west coast and just an hour from Orlando. It is rated among the top 4 zoos in America, with more than 2,700 animals representing over 320 species of mammals, birds, reptiles, amphibians and spiders. But that's just the start. It boasts a safari-like section of Africa spread over 65 acres/26ha of grassy veldt, with special tours to hand-feed some of the animals. Interspersed among the animals are more than 20 bona fide theme park rides, including the mind-numbing roller-coasters **Kumba, SheiKra, Montu** and **Gwazi**, with guaranteed fun for coaster addicts, plus plenty of scaled-down rides for younger children. Then there are the animal shows, comedians, musicians, strolling players and *KaTonga*, a family show extravaganza that takes place in the impressive Moroccan Palace Theater.

The overall theme is Africa, hence the park is divided into areas like Nairobi and Congo, and dining and shopping are equal to most of the other theme parks. It doesn't quite have the pizzazz of *Epcot* or Universal, and the

Busch Gardens at a glance

Location	Busch Blvd, Tampa; 75–90 minutes' drive from Orlando
Size	335 acres/136ha in 11 themed areas
Hours	9 or 10am–6 or 7pm off peak; 9am–8pm Easter, Thanksgiving, Christmas; 9 or 9.30am–10.30pm summer
Admission	Under-3s free; 3–9 $57.95 (1-Day Ticket), $69.95 (2-Park Ticket inc Adventure Island water park), $89.95 (2-Park Ticket inc SeaWorld), $124.95 (3-Park Ticket inc Aquatica and SeaWorld), $234.95 (Orlando FlexTicket Plus); adult (10+) $64.95, $79.95, $99.95, $134.95, $279.95.
Parking	$10
Lockers	$5, in Morocco, Congo, Egypt and Stanleyville
Pushchairs	$10 and $15
Wheelchairs	$10 and $35, with pushchairs
Top Attractions	Congo River Rapids, Gwazi, Kumba, Montu, Pirates 4-D, Rhino Rally, SheiKra, Tanganyika Tidal Wave
Don't Miss	Jungala, Edge of Africa, Animal Keeper talks, Ka Tonga, Myombe Reserve, Mystic Sheikhs band
Hidden Costs	**Meals** Burger, chips and Pepsi $9.38 3-course meal $17.99–23.95; family-style diner $13.95 and $7.95 (Crown Colony House) Kids' meal $6.79 **T-shirts** $12.99–34.99 **Souvenirs** $1–1,500 **Sundries** Ride photos $14.99–21.99 (add frame for $5–10)

Morocco
1 Zagora Café
2 Marrakesh Theater
3 Moroccan Palace Theater
4 Gwazi
5 Myombe Reserve

Egypt
6 Crown Colony House Restaurant
7 Edge of Africa
8 Clydesdale Hamlet
9 Show Jumping Hall of Fame
10 Skyride Station
11 Montu
12 Tut's Tomb

Nairobi
13 Curiosity Caverns
14 Elephant Habitat
15 Rhino Rally
16 Jambo Junction

Timbuktu
17 Scorpion
18 Cheetah Chase
19 Phoenix
20 Carousel Caravan
21 Timbuktu Theater: Pirates 3D
22 Desert Grill

Congo
23 Kumba
24 Congo River Rapids
25 Ubanga-Banga Bumper Cars

Jungala
26 Jungle Flyers
27 The Wild Surge
28 Treetop Trails
29 Tiger Lodge
30 Orang Overlook
31 Orang Café
32 Bengal Bistro

Stanleyville
33 Stanley Falls Log Flume
34 Tanganyika Tidal Wave
35 SheiKra
36 Stanleyville Theater
37 Skyride Station
38 Zambia Smokehouse

Bird Gardens
39 Garden Theater
40 Lory Landing
41 Aviary
42 Hospitality House
43 Land of the Dragons
44 Gwazi Pavilion
45 Train Stations

staff are a bit more laid back, but it has guaranteed, 5-star family appeal, especially with its selection of rides just for kids, and it is a big hit with British visitors. In a way, it is like the big brother of Chessington World of Adventures in Surrey, though on a much grander scale (and in a better climate). Busch Gardens is the only park to offer 1-Day Tickets with a **rain guarantee**, which means if you get rained out on your visit, you can return FREE within 7 days. Look for self-serve ticket machines to the right of the park entrance to save time waiting for an attended booth.

Location

Busch Gardens can be a hard place to locate on the sketchy local maps as the signposting is not as sharp as it could be but, from Orlando, the directions are pretty simple. Head west on I-4 for almost an hour (it's 55mls/88km from I-4's junction with Highway 192) until you hit the intersecting motorway I-75. Take I-75 north for 3½mls/5.5km until you see the exit for Fowler Avenue (Highway 582). Continue west on Fowler for another 3½mls/5.5km, then just past the University of South Florida on your right, turn LEFT into McKinley Drive. A mile/1.6km down McKinley Drive, Busch Gardens' car park is on your left, where it costs $10 to park.

Those without a car can use the **Busch Gardens Shuttle Express** bus, which makes several $10 round trips a day from Orlando (FREE if you have a multi-day ticket). You board at SeaWorld, Goodings Shopping Plaza (I-Drive), Orlando Premium Outlets, Universal Studios, Ramada Maingate West, Best Western Lakeside or Old Town in Kissimmee and pick-up times range from 8.30 to 9.40am, returning at 6 or 7pm. Book at the **Guest Services** window at SeaWorld or call 1800 221 1339.

You may think you'll have left the crowds behind in Orlando but, unfortunately, in high season you'd be wrong. It's still advisable to be here in time for opening, if only to be first in line to ride the amazing Rhino Rally or the dazzling roller-coasters, which all draw major queues (especially SheiKra). The Congo River Rapids, Stanley Falls Log Flume ride and Tanganyika Tidal Wave (all opportunities to get wet!) are also prime draws in peak season. The queues do take longer to build up here, though, so for the first few hours at least you can enjoy a relatively crowd-free experience.

On your left through the main gates is the **Adventure Tour Centre**, and you should go there straight away (better still, book in advance on 1888 800 5447 or online at **buschgardens.com**) if you'd like to do the wonderful Serengeti Safari or one of its other Adventure Tours (see pages 217–18). Busch Gardens is divided into 11 main sections, with the major rides all a bit of a hike from the main entrance. Check the back of your park map for times and locations of various organised animal encounters throughout the park – then watch out for passing flamingos as they take the first of their twice-daily promenades through the main courtyard!

Rhino Rally, which opened in summer 2001, is one of the prime attractions, so you should head here first (especially as the animals are more evident early in the day). Bear right through Morocco, turn left into Nairobi, pass the train station, and the Rally entrance is next to the elephant habitat. Coaster fans flock in serious numbers to **SheiKra**, the world's highest and fastest dive

Elephants at Rhino Rally

coaster, and queues can hit 3 HOURS by mid-afternoon so, if you are tempted by this first, bear left through Morocco past the Zagora Café, through the Bird Gardens and up into Stanleyville. **Gwazi**, the rattlin' wooden coaster, is another to draw a crowd relatively quickly, and you could do this en route. Then continue through Stanleyville to Congo for **Kumba**, and retrace your steps to do **Congo River Rapids** and the other 2 water rides. Here is the full layout of the park in a clockwise direction (usually the optimum route):

Morocco

Coming through the main gates brings you into Morocco, home of all the guest services and a lot of good shops. *Epcot*'s Moroccan pavilion sets the scene better, but the architecture is still impressive and this version won't tax your wallet as much as Disney's does! Turning the corner brings you to the first animal encounter, the alligator pen. Morocco is also home to 2 of the park's biggest shows.

Marrakesh Theater: In summer 2008, this live venue presented **Rock A Doo Wop**, a song and dance show offering a host of rock 'n' roll classics from the 1950s and 60s, with period costumes and lively singalong numbers. With faithful reproductions of numbers by the likes of Frankie Valli, Johnny Rivers, Frankie Lymon and The Coasters, it's a musical walk down memory lane. AAA.

KaTonga

KaTonga: A lavish Broadway-style spectacle featuring an 18-strong cast of singers, dancers, acrobats and puppeteers and subtitled *Musical Tales from the Jungle*, this 35-minute theatrical extravaganza celebrates African animal folklore with an ingenious mix of live actor presentation and the award-winning larger-than-life puppets of Michael Curry (who helped create Disney's *The Lion King* show in London and New York). With 57 costumes, 45 puppets and a troupe of stunning acrobats, it makes for a truly eye-catching performance, up to 5 times a day, that is way above usual theme park standards. It is also air-conditioned, a welcome relief in summer. Arrive a little early as the Moroccan Palace Theater doors close right on showtime. AAAAA.

Myombe Reserve: One of the largest and most realistic habitats for the threatened highland gorillas and chimpanzees of Central Africa, this 3 acre/1.2ha walk-through has a superb tropical setting where the temperature is kept high and convincing with the aid of lush forest landscaping and water mist sprays. Take your time, especially as there are good, seated vantage points, and be patient to catch these magnificent creatures on their daily routine. It is also highly informative, with attendants usually on hand to answer any questions. AAAAA.

Gwazi: Busch's second largest roller-coaster is a massive 'duelling' wooden creation in the classic style (i.e. no going upside-down). The 2 sets of cars, the Gwazi Lion and Gwazi Tiger, each top 50mph/80kph and generate a G-force of up to 3.5 as they career around nearly 7,000ft/2,134m of track with 6 fly-by encounters. You get to choose your ride in the intricately themed 8 acre/3ha village plaza and then you are off up the 90ft/27m lift for a breathtaking 2½ minutes. The shake, rattle 'n' roll effect of a classic wooden coaster is much in evidence and the Lion and Tiger rides are slightly different, so you need to do both. Restrictions: 4ft/122cm. TTTTT.

Gwazi Gliders: This gentle circling 'hang-gliding' ride is purely for the pre-school crowd. T (TTT under-6s).

Other entertainment: The marvellous musical fun of the marching, dancing, 8-piece brass band **Mystic Sheikhs** can be found in Morocco at regular intervals, along with **Men of Note**, a strolling 4-piece a cappella group with Motown specialities, and **park characters** like TJ the Tiger, Gina the Giraffe and Hilda Hippo. Basketball fans can also try the **Hoops Challenge** ($7 a play, $10 for 2) next to Gwazi.

Shopping and dining: Take your pick from 7 different shops, with **Anheuser-Busch Trading Co, The Emporium** and **Marrakesh Market** the pick of the bunch. For a quick meal, try **Zagora Café**, especially at breakfast. Alternatively, the enticing **Sultan's Sweets** serves coffee and pastries.

Bird Gardens

The most peaceful area and the original starting point of the park in 1959, it is possible to unwind here from the usual theme park hurly-burly. The exhibits and shows are all family-orientated, too, with live shows, an elaborate kids' playground and more animal exhibits.

BRITTIP

The Bird Gardens area is a good place to revisit in mid-afternoon when most of the rides are busy.

Garden Theater: Here you will find the amusing 25-minute *Critter Castaways* show, which features numerous animals (almost 80 in all) in a light-hearted desert island romp. Dogs, cats, birds and even kangaroos all get in on the act with their human co-stars. AAA.

Lory Landing: Walk through this tropical aviary featuring lorikeets, hornbills, parrots and more, with the chance to become a human perch and feed the friendly lorikeets. A cup of nectar costs $3.25, but makes for a great photo opportunity. AAA. Other animal encounters include the lush, walk-through **Aviary**, **Flamingo Island**, the **Living Dragons** and **Eagle Canyon**, plus the **Backyard Wildlife Habitat**.

Land of the Dragons: Parents will want to know about this large, wonderfully clever area of activities, entertainment, rides and attractions devoted purely to the young ones. It features a 3-storey treehouse complete with towers and maze-like stairways, a rope climb, ball crawl and outdoor *Dragon's Tale Theater*, which presents the 15-minute show *Friends Forever* – with the resident cuddly dragon, a knight and a beautiful princess teaching a gentle message of friendship. It's all good, family-friendly, well-supervised stuff, and some of the kiddie rides are superbly inventive, as well as offering plenty of opportunity to get wet. TTTTT (under-10s only).

Other entertainment: A free taste of Anheuser-Busch products is on offer in **Hospitality House**, where you can also enrol for **Beer School**, a 40-minute lesson in the process of beer-making. It offers a fascinating glimpse into the brewery world, and is excellently explained, with the

Lory Landing

bonus of some tasting! You will also receive a Brewery Master certificate. The 30-minute **Brewmaster's Club** offers a more in-depth sampling of 7 Anheuser-Busch products and their ideal chocolate, cheese and fruit pairings. Reservations are required (ages 21 and over only, with valid photo ID; registration located just inside the admission turnstiles). **Hospitality Patio** features the resident piano-player, serving up a mix of musical favourites, past and present. **Gwazi Park** here is used for the free open-air concerts during the Summer Nights programme.

BRITTIP
While mum and dad try the Brewmaster's Club, youngsters may utilise the children's area, with colouring books, free soda, water and crackers.

Shopping and dining: A real novelty here is the eye-catching **Xcursions** environmentally themed gift shop. Its live frog and gecko displays, Animal Fun Facts and Conservation info on interactive touch-screens make it worth visiting whether or not you intend to buy (but all proceeds contribute to the Busch Gardens Conservation Fund). **Wild Creations Too** is another imaginative shop. For a quick bite, try **Hospitality House Pizza** (with your free beer sample!).

Sheikra

Stanleyville

This brings you back into true ride territory, with the park's biggest coaster, as well as several water rides and shows. You will also find one of the 3 **Train Stations** here (next to SheiKra), for the gentle 35-minute journey around the park.

SheiKra: The park's outstanding big-thrill attraction is the giant steel structure of this monstrous coaster. A world first at 200ft/62m tall and hitting 70mph/112kph, this is the ride to put Alton Towers' fearsome Oblivion in the shade. Higher, longer and faster, it features an initial drop at an angle as near vertical as makes no difference (with a delicious moment of stop-go balance as you teeter on the edge!), a second drop of 138ft/42m into an underground tunnel, an Immelman loop (an exhilarating rolling manoeuvre) and a water splashdown over 0.6mls/1km of smooth-as-silk track. As if all that isn't enough, a 2007 modification removed the coaster's *floor*, so there is nothing between you and track but air! The whole ride lasts less than 3 minutes and is almost as much fun (or terror, depending on your point of view) to watch as to ride. It also draws crowds like nothing else in the park, so get here early or expect a LONG wait. You can buy the video of your ride for $24.99, or a 6 × 8 photo for $14.99. Restrictions: 4ft 6in/137cm. TTTTT+.

Stanley Falls: Almost identical to Log Flume rides at Chessington, Legoland, Thorpe Park and Alton Towers, this guarantees a good soaking at the final 40ft/12m drop. Restrictions: 3ft 10in/116cm. TTT.

Tanganyika Tidal Wave: A distinctly more scenic ride, this takes you on a journey along 'uncharted' African

BRITTIP
Don't stand on the bridge by Tanganyika Tidal Wave or by the SheiKra splashdown unless you want to get seriously wet!

waters before tipping you down a 2-stage drop that really does land with tidal-wave force. Restrictions: 4ft/122cm. TTTT.

Stanleyville Theater: A good place to put your feet up as you watch the resident entertainers turn on the style. This varies seasonally and includes musical acts, acrobats and family-style comedy, plus occasional animal encounters. AAA½.

Skyride: Take the one-way cable-car ride from here back to Egypt (by Crown Colony House) to save a long walk back to the park exit. However, it closes when it's windy and has long queues late in the day. AA.

Shopping and dining: The **Kariba Marketplace** has the best of the shopping here, while, for a hearty meal (and a great view of SheiKra), you should try the **Zambia Smokehouse**, where its wood-smoked ribs platter is a delight among a heavily BBQ-orientated menu (also with salads, sandwiches and kids' meals).

Jungala

The park's newest 'land,' this 4 acre/1.6ha 'village' opened in spring 2008 and adds a couple of small-scale rides, some superb animal habitats and a hugely elaborate children's play area, designed with older children in mind (where Land of the Dragons is primarily for under-6s). It also gets busy quite quickly, so visit here either early on or late in the day.

Jungle Flyers: This kids' ride (6–13s) is a junior-sized zipline journey over part of the Jungala area, a one-seat there-and-back trip from the upper level of Treetop Trails. Great fun for kids, but a rather short ride, and queues build up quickly and move slowly for much of the day. *Maximum* height 4ft 8in/145cm. TTT.

The Wild Surge: Get ready to 'surge' 4 storeys into the air on this tower ride from inside a giant waterfall providing a (brief!) glimpse over Jungala before bouncing back down again. Queues are also long and slow-moving as the ride takes just 14 at a time. Restrictions, 3ft 6in/106cm to ride solo (3ft 2in/96cm with a parent). TTT (TTTTT under-12s).

Treetop Trails: Climbing nets, elaborate bridges, crawl tubes and a multi-level maze are the basis of this fabulous 3-storey playground for children of all ages, with smaller-scale adventures at ground level, including squirt fountains and other watery fun (swimsuits or a change of clothes are highly advisable!). It is also cleverly mixed in with two different animal habitats, for the fun-loving gibbons, flying fox-bats and the rare tomistoma (an Asian crocodile). TTTT (young 'uns only).

BRITTIP

It's worth knowing for parents with younger children that the toddler play area in Treetop Trails is very thoughtfully in the shade.

Tiger Habitat: One of the park's most creative animal environments is this multi-level tiger exhibit (including its rare white tigers). It is divided into *Tiger Lodge*, an air-conditioned overlook including conservation info and issues, and *Tiger Trail*, a walk-through section with various close-up opportunities, including a unique

Tiger Habitat

pop-up turret (which has a separate queue) in the main enclosure and a rope-pull for guests to 'test their strength' against the big cats (available periodically). Huge windows provide maximum viewing of the animals at play, especially in their plunge pool. AAAA.

Orang Outpost: Another brilliant animal habitat, this showcases the park's orangutans, who love to look in on guests viewing them as much as vice versa. A series of close-up windows (including a glass floor over the hammock play area and a kids' tunnel) provide superb observation of the specially designed forest canopy environment. AAAA.

Other entertainment: Look out for colourful **stilt-walkers** around the village area periodically.

Shopping and dining: Shop for gifts at **Tiger Treasures** (organic cotton T-shirts and conservation-related items) and **Cubs Closet** (kids' clothing), and then stop to eat at **Bengal Bistro** (fish, smoked turkey, veggie wraps, salads and sandwiches) or the more snack-orientated **Orang Café** (chicken strips, sandwiches and cookies).

Congo

As you continue into the Congo, this is primarily about just 3 rides, plus a stop on the Serengeti Railway.

Kumba: Another of the park's signature coasters, with this unmistakable giant turquoise structure looming over the area. It's one of the largest and fastest in south-east USA and, at 60mph/97kph, features 3 unique elements: a diving loop that plunges a full 110ft/33m; a camel-back, with a 360-degree spiral; and a 108ft/33m vertical loop. For good measure, it also dives underground! It looks terrifying close up but is absolutely exhilarating, even for non-coaster fans. Restrictions: 4ft 6in/137cm. TTTTT.

Kumba

Congo River Rapids: These look pretty tame after Kumba, but don't be fooled. The giant rubber rafts will bounce you down some of the most convincing rapids outside of the Rockies, and you will end up with a fair soaking for good measure. Restrictions: 3ft 6in/106cm. TTTT.

Ubanga-Banga Bumper Cars: Typical fairground dodgems (restrictions: 3ft 6in/106cm), and you won't miss anything if you pass these by. TT.

Shopping and dining: There is just the **Congo River Rapids** gift shop here, plus 3 refreshment kiosks.

Timbuktu

Passing through Congo brings you to another heavily ride-dominated area. Here in a North African desert setting you will find many typical funfair elements, with a couple of brain-scrambling rides and 2 good shows.

Pirates 4-D: This thoroughly fun 3-D film romp will appeal to children of all ages, as the story centres on a band of hapless pirates lead by an incompetent captain (Leslie Nielsen) and blundering first mate (Eric Idle). Treasure and mutiny cue a riot of 3-D visuals plus many clever (and hilarious) special effects; think water – and lots of it! The film lasts 15 minutes, with full surround-sound, and draws a good crowd through the main part of the day, so go early or leave it until later when you need to cool down. AAAA.

Cheetah Chase: This family-orientated 'Crazy Mouse' style coaster is surprisingly energetic, rising as it does some 46ft/14m and adding tight turns and swift drops. Top speed is only 22mph/35kph, but it *seems* faster and will thrill younger kids. TTT (TTTTT under-10s).

The Phoenix: A positively evil invention that involves sitting in a gigantic, boat-shaped swing that eventually performs a 360º rotation in dramatic, slow-motion style. Don't eat just before this one! Restrictions: 4ft/122cm. TTTT.

Scorpion: A 50mph/80kph roller-coaster, this features a 62ft/19m drop and a 360° loop that is guaranteed to dial D for dizzy for a while! It lasts just 120 seconds, but seems longer. Queues build here from late morning, and you must be at least 3ft 6in/106cm to ride. TTTT.

Sandstorm: A fairly routine whirligig contraption that spins and levitates at high speed (hold on to your stomach). Restrictions: 3ft 6in/106cm. TTT.

Carousel Caravan: This offers the opportunity to ride a genuine Mary Poppins-type carousel. TT.

Other entertainment: As well as the big rides, there is a series of scaled-down **Kiddie Rides** geared to the under-10s. There is also the **Electronic Arcade** and a **Games Area** of side shows and stalls that require a few extra dollars ($2–10), or buy the Games Pass (it can be loaded and reloaded in the Games Area) and simply swipe your card each time you play.

Shopping and dining: Desert Grill is a themed buffet-diner (serving great sandwiches, salads, pasta and kids' meals in souvenir buckets) that also offers live musical entertainment in air-conditioned comfort (the lively **American Beat** show, a song-and-dance cabaret featuring pop music from the 1950s to the 70s), while Timbuktu also has 2 snack kiosks.

Nairobi

It's back to the animals as we enter this area of Busch Gardens, with 5 different habitats, plus one of the park's top rides, which also includes an animal adventure.

Rhino Rally: This wonderfully dramatic and scenic ride starts out as an off-road jeep safari and changes into an innovative raft adventure as your 17-passenger vehicle gets caught in a flash flood. The 8-minute whirl through the wilds of Africa includes encounters with elephants, rhinos, crocodiles, antelope and more, as the off-road part of the ride is just about as real as they can make it. Your driver adds to the fun with some amusing spiel about the rally and your Land-Rover vehicle, but it soon becomes clear that your navigator (the front seat passenger) has led you into a blind gully. An unused pontoon bridge is the only way out, but fate has a unique twist in store, opening the way to part 2 of the ride and the raging river section that is unlike any attraction we've experienced to date. Terrific fun, but arrive early to beat the queues. Restrictions: 3ft 3in/99cm. TTTT/AAAAA.

Serengeti Plain: A 49 acre/20ha spread of African savannah, this is home to buffalo, antelope, zebras, giraffes, wildebeest, ostriches, hippos, rhinos and many exotic birds, and can be viewed for much of the journey on the Serengeti Railway, a full-size, open-car steam train that chugs slowly from its main station in Nairobi to the Congo, Stanleyville and back. AAA.

Congo River Rapids

BRITTIP

Take the Serengeti Railway from Nairobi (or Congo or Stanleyville) in mid-afternoon to give your feet a rest when it's busy elsewhere.

Jambo Junction: The park's field hospital (or nursery) is an interesting animal encounter, with some friendly flamingos outside and a series of critters (lemurs, sloths, possums and various babies needing extra care) inside waiting to be viewed through the large windows. Some animal interaction is encouraged periodically, with feeding, lessons in husbandry and behaviour training. AA.

Other entertainment: Look out here for the **Elephant Habitat** and periodic sessions with animal staff (notably for the afternoon Elephant Wash), while you can see more of the park's inhabitants at the **Reptile House**, **Curiosity Caverns** (nocturnal animals) and **Tortoise Habitat**.

Shopping and dining: Caravan Crossing (safari apparel and hats) has the best shopping here while **Kenya Kanteen** offers drinks and snacks.

Egypt

The final area of Busch Gardens is somewhat tucked away, so it's best visited either first thing or late in the day. It sits in the park's bottom right corner and much of it is carefully re-created pharaoh country, dominated by the roller-coaster Montu, named after an ancient Egyptian warrior god. Here, you can take the **Skyride** cable car on a one-way trip to Stanleyville (providing a great look at Rhino Rally en route).

Jambo Junction

Edge of Africa: This 15 acre/6ha 'safari experience' guarantees a close-up almost like the real thing. The walk-through attraction puts you in an authentic setting of native wilds and villages from which you can view giraffes, lions, baboons, meerkats, crocodiles, hyenas and vultures, and even an underwater inspection of a hippo habitat. Look out for the abandoned jeep – you can sit in the cab while the lions lounge in the back! Wandering naturalists offer informal talks, and the attention to detail is superb. AAAAA.

BRITTIP

Edge of Africa offers some fantastic photo opportunities but, in the hot months, come here early in the day as many animals seek refuge from the heat later.

Tut's Tomb: This re-creation of the Tutankhamen discovery by archaeologist Howard Carter is now missing most of its clever lighting and audio effects, hence is pretty unremarkable. A.

Montu: You cannot fail to see the area's main attraction, another breathtaking creation and one of the world's tallest and longest inverted coasters, covering nearly 4,000ft/1,219m of track at speeds topping 60mph/97kph and peaking with a G-force of 3.85! Like Kumba, it looks terrifying, but really is an absolute 5-star thrill as it leaves your legs dangling and twists and dives (underground at 2 points) for almost 3 minutes of brain-scrambling fun. Restrictions: 4ft 6in/137cm. TTTTT.

Other entertainment: The **Clydesdale Hamlet** is also here but, if you've seen the massive dray horses and stables at SeaWorld, the set-up is pretty similar. Next door is the rather out-of-place **Show Jumping Hall Of Fame**. Youngsters can also make their own excavations in the **Shifting Sands**, a neat sand play area.

Edge of Africa

Shopping and dining: The high-quality **Golden Scarab** offers hand-blown glass items and authentic cartouche paintings, while you can grab more souvenirs at **Edge of Africa Gift Shop** and **Montu Gifts**. For dining, look no further than the **Crown Colony Restaurant**, a large Victorian-style building overlooking the Serengeti Plain. It offers counter-service salads, sandwiches and pizzas downstairs or a full-service restaurant upstairs, with magnificent views of the animals roaming the plain. For a memorable meal (11.30am until an hour before park closing), head here for lunch (it don't take bookings) or, even better, come back for dinner in the early evening and see the animals come down to the waterhole.

Special tours

Busch Gardens features a wide range of behind-the-scenes animal tours and adventure expeditions that add an extra dimension to the park. For all tours, book at the Adventure Tour Center in Morocco or, better still, book in advance on 1888 800 5447 or online at **buschgardens.com**.

Serengeti Safari, a 30-minute excursion (5 times a day, taking 20 people at a time) aboard flat-bed trucks, takes you to meet some of the Serengeti Plain's residents and hand-feed the beautiful giraffes while learning more about the park's environmental efforts. Places tend to fill up quickly and it costs $33.99/person (children must be at least 5, and 5–15s must be accompanied by an adult); the **Guided Adventure Tour** takes just 15 at a time on a 4½-hour VIP trek, with your own guide, reserved seating at KaTonga, front-of-line access for rides like Gwazi and Rhino Rally, counter-service lunch at Crown Colony and up-close encounters with many of the animals and staff, including the Serengeti Safari ($94.99 adults, $84.99 children); **Thrill Seekers Tour** is similar, but substitutes more rides – including the water rides – for the animal encounters ($74.99 and $64.99); **Elite Adventure Tour** is a personal, exclusive park tour with front-of-line access to all rides, feeding a giraffe on the Serengeti Safari, reserved seating at shows, free bottled water throughout and lunch at the Crown Colony Restaurant ($199.99/person, 5 and over); **Animal Adventure Tour** is a 2-hour personal animal experience for 7–10 people a day. The next best thing to being a park zookeeper, it provides close encounters with the Clydesdales, black rhinos, hippos, giraffes and elephants, plus animal behaviour sessions ($119.99/person, no under-5s); **Saving a Species** is a 45-minute meet and greet with various animal

Montu

Halloween screams

The other notable annual extra is the **Howl-O-Scream** extravaganza at Halloween (late Sept–Oct). It is a separately ticketed event (c.$60/person) offering a 'new spin on horror', with various grisly goings-on and themed haunted houses, as well as the chance to ride all the big coasters at night (7.30pm–midnight or 1am). It features some imaginative shows along with all the mock-horror effects but is not advised for young children. It is similar in many ways to Universal's Halloween Horror Nights programme, with the same kind of elaborate set-piece haunted houses and 'scare zones,' but the Busch Gardens version is more spread out and less frenetic. See more at **howl-o-scream.com**.

specialists (notably getting close-up with the rhinos), learning about their work and conservation issues, including how Busch Gardens is involved with various wildlife projects worldwide ($44.99, $2 of which goes to the World Wildlife Fund; no under-5s); the 45-minute **Sundowner Safari** begins at the Crown Colony Brewmaster's Club with samplings of Anheuser-Busch beers, then heads out on the Serengeti Plain to hand-feed giraffes, meet the wildlife and enjoy more premium lager as you tour ($39.99/person, 21 and over only, with valid photo ID); **Keeper for a Day** is an exclusive behind-the-scenes tour where you become the zookeeper, join the animal keepers as they feed, train and care for giraffes and antelope, then move on to assist the Avian team on the Serengeti ($350/person, including park admission; 13 and over only); finally the **Heart of Jungala Tour** is the latest offering, a 30-minute walking journey behind the scenes in the new Jungala area of the park to see more of the orangutans, the tigers, and their keepers ($33.99/person).

Water Play Area at Jungala

Special programmes

Busch Gardens is open until 10pm for the **Summer Nights** programme (June–Aug), which features festive food and drink, live entertainment, music (including veteran rock bands like Guess Who and Grand Funk Railroad) and DJs. There is also a huge **fireworks spectacular** 2–4 July.

For a full family day out, you can also combine Busch Gardens with the next-door water park **Adventure Island** (on McKinley Drive), which is particularly welcome when it hots up. The 25 acres/10ha of watery fun, in a Key West theme, offer a full range of slides and rides, such as the **Wahoo Run** raft ride, a 210ft/64m plunge on the body slide **Gulf Scream**, the exciting 4-lane mat slide **Riptide** and spiralling tube ride **Calypso Coaster**. Adventure Island is open mid-Mar to late Oct (weekends only in Sept and Oct) 10am–5pm (8pm in summer). Tickets are $36.95 (adults) and $34.95 (3–9s), while a Busch Gardens–Adventure Island combo ticket is $79.95 and $69.95.

Well, that's the lowdown on all the main theme parks, but there is still more to discover…

7 The Other Attractions

or One Giant Leap for Tourist Kind

If you think you can 'do' Orlando just by sticking to the main theme parks, think again! There is still a LOT more to discover, starting with the new-look Kennedy Space Center, which we rate as an essential place to visit these days. It will easily demand a day of your attention after its huge upgrade in 2007.

Then there are Silver Springs, Bok Tower Gardens and Cypress Gardens, all of which offer a taste of the more natural Florida, while Gatorland provides another great-value experience with its alligators and shows. Then you have fun venues like WonderWorks, Orlando Science Center and Ripley's Believe It Or Not. For more individual attractions, you have the unique aviation museum Fantasy of Flight, the amazing 'sky-dive' experience of SkyVenture, plus some magnificent water parks. The choice is yours, but it's an immense selection. Let's start with One Giant Leap for Mankind.

Kennedy Space Center

Welcome to the past, present and future of NASA's space programme, and one of the most enjoyable, fun and downright fascinating places in Florida. The KSC has undergone huge redevelopment in recent years, culminating in 2007 with the opening of the stunning **Shuttle Launch Experience**, part of a complete overhaul of the main Visitor Complex. This has really put the KSC among the front rank of local attractions and there is even more now to justify an all-day visit. There are 5 continually running shows (including 2 splendid IMAX films and a live theatre presentation for kids), 6 static showcases, a new children's play area, an art gallery, the captivating Astronaut Encounter and moving Astronaut Memorial, and a bus tour of the Space Center, which add up to great value. Plus there are 2 additional guided tours, the **Astronaut Training Experience** and **Family Astronaut Experience** (with overnight stay), which provide outstanding extras.

You enter through the futuristic ticket plaza and can spend several hours just wandering around the exhibits and presentations of the Visitor Complex itself. But, with the huge draw of its latest attraction, you should head here first and save your meandering for later on.

Susan at Kennedy Space Center

Orlando's Other Attractions

Kennedy Space Center at a glance

Location	Off State Road 405 in Titusville
Size	Visitor Complex 70 acres/28.3ha
Hours	9am–5 or 6pm) year-round (except Christmas Day or launch days)
Admission	Under-3s free; 3–11 $28; adult (12+) $38. Prices do not include tax but include admission to US Astronaut Hall of Fame.
Parking	Free
Lockers	No
Pushchairs	Available on a complimentary basis (with photo ID as deposit) inside the Information Center
Wheelchairs	Available on a complimentary basis (with photo ID as deposit) inside the Information Center
Top Attractions	Shuttle Launch Experience; IMAX films; Astronaut Encounter; KSC Bus Tours
Don't Miss	Apollo-Saturn V Center on Bus Tours; Astronaut Memorial; Rocket Garden; Space Shuttle Plaza
Hidden Costs	**Meals** Burger, chips and coke $8.50 Kids' meal $4.99 **T-shirts** $12.99–19.99 **Souvenirs** 95c–$9,000! **Sundries** Lunch with an Astronaut $15.99 children, $22.99 adults

Shuttle Launch Experience: This is the BIG one in every sense, a dramatic presentation into a real-life shuttle launch – with you on board! You enter the huge building along a life-like gantry and there is then a clever pre-show, with dry ice (for launch 'smoke'), atmospheric lighting and some clever sound and vibration effects to provide the feel of a launch. Then you enter the high-tech 'ready room' to prepare for your own blast-off into space. There are 4 'capsules' of 44 passengers each, designed to look like crew cabins in the cargo hold of the Shuttle, and, once aboard you go through the full launch procedure as the vehicle moves into a near-vertical position for take-off. On the command 'Go for engine start' the fun really begins as you are at the heart of an awesome 5-minute simulation that provides all the features of a realistic launch, with the use of massive vibration generators, sound effects, cabin and seat movements and screen visuals. You get a real taste of the G-forces involved, the Rocket Booster and External Tank separations, and a moment of 'weightlessness' as you enter the earth's orbit. Finally, the cargo hold doors open above you to provide a truly awe-inspiring view. To make sure you don't get your breath back for a while, you exit the Shuttle to 'walk' back to earth via a spiral walkway surrounded by the stars and more satellite views of the planet.

Shuttle launch

BRITTIP

All of the Shuttle Launch Experience is fully wheelchair-accessible, and there is a seat outside for potential riders to test their comfort level. For anyone wary of the full ride experience, there is a customised by-pass room where you can experience the attraction without the motion.

Don't miss the plaques to mark every Shuttle flight – and the memorials to the tragic Challenger and Columbia missions. Even the Gift Shop is a cut above average! TTT and AAAAA.

Bus tours: The KSC's signature air-conditioned coaches depart every 15 minutes from 10am and are fully narrated throughout to provide the full overview of the Space Center. They make 3 important stops in addition to driving around much of the working areas (including the massive Vehicle Assembly Building). The first stop is the **LC39 Observation Gantry**, just 1ml/1.6km from shuttle launch pad 39A, a combination 4-storey observation deck and exhibition centre. The exhibits consist of a 10-minute launch preparation film, models and videos of a countdown and touch-screen info on the shuttle programme.

International Space Station Center: Here you can discover the full story of this orbiting station and the many experiments being conducted there, as well as see new components being put together. A brief film tells the story of the ISSC to date, and you can walk through some full-scale replicas of the modules to feel how it is to live and work in space. Finally, you stop at the **Apollo/Saturn V Center**, one of the KSC's great exhibits, where you can easily spend 90 minutes. It highlights the Apollo missions and first moon landing with 2 impressive theatrical presentations on the risks and triumphs, a full-size 363ft/111m Saturn V rocket and a hands-on gallery that brings space exploration into sharp focus. Allow 2–3 hours to do the tour justice, but be aware that the last bus leaves the Visitor Center at 2.20 or 2.50pm, depending on time of year. AAAAA.

Kennedy Space Center

IMAX films: Back at the Visitor Complex are the IMAX cinemas – 55ft/ 17m screens that give the impression of sitting on top of the action. New in 2006 was the 40-minute film **Magnificent Desolation: Walking on the Moon**, featuring rare NASA footage and narrated by Tom Hanks, that takes the audience to the lunar surface to walk alongside the astronauts. **Space Station 3-D** (narrated by Tom Cruise) is a breathtaking slice of science fact, living with the crew of the International Space Station and affording a truly heart-stopping look at the construction process (no extra charge for either film). AAAA.

Astronaut Encounter: This engaging feature is a daily talk and Q&A session, along with personal observations and anecdotes from various veterans of the Mercury, Gemini and Apollo programmes, plus several Space Shuttle astronauts. It is an insightful and engrossing programme, up to 3 times a day at the Universe Theater. AAAA.

Robot Scouts: This walk-through display-and-show is done in the company of Starquester 2000, your 'robot host', who explains the history of NASA's unmanned space probes in a surprising and amusing style. AAA.

Lunch with an astronaut

For another fully engrossing feature at the Kennedy Space Center, book its special Lunch With An Astronaut, where a small group gets to dine with the star of the daily Astronaut Encounter. The featured person gives their own special briefing, adding extra insight into their space missions, plus answers individual questions, gives autographs and poses for photos. It is $22.99 for adults and $15.99 for children at 12.15pm daily, and tickets may be bought online or by calling 321 449 4400. It's a highly worthwhile opportunity and one we strongly recommend. The buffet-style lunch is pretty good, too!

Shuttle Explorer: This exhibit allows you to inspect a full-scale replica Space Shuttle, while the recently renovated **Launch Status Center** displays shuttle and rocket history boards and rocket scale models, plus live mission briefings of upcoming launches. Free tours are available several times a day. AA.

Early Space Exploration: A clever and coherent walk-through trip into the space programme's recent past, including the Hall of Discovery, the Mercury Mission Control Room – the original consoles from America's first manned space flights – and the Hall of History. AAA.

Exploration in the New Millennium: This futuristic exhibit provides more appeal for youngsters, with an educational but fun element from the spaceship – like *Exploring Gallery*, the *Mars Rock* exhibit and various interactive panels. AAA.

Mad Mission To Mars 2025: Children of 7–14 should enjoy this lively show, a mix of education and pure fun theatricals with special effects, audience participation and even its own hip-hop song, The Newton Rap. AAA (children only).

Other exhibits: Try **Nature and Technology** (which showcases the unique balance the Center maintains with the local environment), the **Center for Space Education** (an interactive learning and teacher resource centre), the **Space Walk of Honor**, and **NASA Art Gallery** (space exhibits and artwork).

Youngsters have their own playground, the **Children's Play Dome**, which has also been upgraded recently with an exciting new range of climbing/crawling/sliding elements.

Finally, head out to see some of the hardware of space flight in the completely revamped **Rocket Garden**, which has a kids' splash fountain and an Apollo space capsule gantry, to give you the feel of that last earthbound walk before the astronauts boarded the Saturn V rocket. Free guided tours are given twice a day. Don't forget to stop at the **Astronaut Memorial**, a sombre but moving tribute to the men and women who have died in the cause of the space programme. AAA.

Shopping and dining: The Visitor Complex has an excellent **Space Shop** (the world's largest store for space memorabilia and gifts – enter at your peril!), the smaller **Space Shop II** by the main exit and **The Right Stuff Shop** at the Apollo/Saturn V Center.

Stop for a bite to eat at the newly enhanced **Orbit Food Court**, a cafeteria-style diner serving a fresh range of salads, burgers, pasta, pizza

Astronaut Training Experience

and sandwiches. You will also find the **Moon Rock Café** at the Apollo/Saturn V Center on the bus tour. There are 4 snack kiosks around the Visitor Complex, including **Space Dots** ('ice cream of the future'), and **New Frontier**, for drinks and sandwiches, near the entrance to the Universe Theater.

Cape Canaveral: Then and Now: If you want to learn more about NASA past and present, here is a 2-hour-plus guided journey (daily at noon) into the early days of space exploration around the older part of the facility. Highlights include the Air Force Space and Missile Museum, Mercury launch sites and Memorial, original astronaut training facility and several active launch pads, all of which are otherwise off-limits. Photo ID is required for all visitors on this tour.

NASA Up Close: The 90-minute guided tour (offered between 10am and 2pm daily) in the company of a space programme expert takes visitors along the astronaut's launch-day routine, including a look at both launch pads, the landing facility, VAB and the gigantic crawler transports, as well as the International Space Station Center. Both tours cost $59 for adults, $43 for 3–11s, inclusive of KSC admission. Book online (see opposite) or call 321 449 4400.

Astronaut Training Experience (ATX): Away from the main attractions, you have the choice of the thrilling, full-day programme into the training required for a Shuttle mission. You progress through a sequence of simulated and hands-on preparations, with the input of various NASA veterans. The training provides a range of activities, from the multi-axis trainer and one-sixth gravity chair, to operating a full-scale Shuttle mock-up and taking the helm in Mission Control. There is an exclusive Space Center tour, with stops at the Launch Pads, International Space Station Center and NASA's Press Site. The ATX is limited to a few participants each day and you must be at least 14 (under-18s must be accompanied by a parent). Hard-wearing clothes and athletic shoes are advised, and 'recruits' should be free of neck and back injuries. It costs $225/person (including lunch and ATX gear), but it guarantees a memorable day for 'space cadets'.

Astronaut Hall of Fame

BRITTIP

Reader Les Watson advises: 'Head to Port Canaveral, and there is a recreation area called Jetty Park. It has a wooden jetty about 100yd/91m long, brilliant for watching Shuttle launches. What an experience.'

Family Astronaut Training Experience: A chance for children as young as 8, with a parent, to participate in a 2-day course (with an overnight stay at a nearby hotel). The days are spent building and launching rockets, riding realistic simulators, getting to meet some of NASA's astronauts and touring the Space Center in a unique way designed around the Family Training Experience. Finally, families will train and work together on a realistic shuttle mission to the International Space Station in the full-scale orbiter mock-up and Mission Control. The Family ATX includes hotel lodging, a 12-month pass for the Space Center, a special logo item, breakfast, dinner and lunch. It's $675 for an adult and one child ($275 for an additional child

Shuttle launches

Despite the magnificent presentations at the Kennedy Space Center, the greatest thrill of all is still witnessing an actual Shuttle launch – an awe-inspiring experience. You can call 321 449 4400 for info and Launch Transportation Tickets to a viewing area just 6mls/10km from the launch pad (or buy online via the Center's website). Adult tickets cost $50 ($40 for children), including admission to the Visitor Complex. There is also viewing from the Visitor Complex and nearby Astronaut Hall of Fame ($38 and $28, including KSC admission, or $17 and $13 without). But, in the event of a launch cancellation, there are NO refunds and tickets cannot be transferred to another mission. The traffic in the area is usually horrendous, too, taking anything up to 3 hours to drive from Orlando. Alternative viewing sites are available along Highway 1 in Titusville and Highway A1A through Cape Canaveral and Cocoa Beach. Call 1877 893 6272 for launch status.

or adult staying in the same room). Book in advance on 321 449 4400 or online (see below).

Getting there: Take the Beachline Expressway out of Orlando (Route 528, and a toll road, see map on page 220) for about 45 minutes, bear left on SR 407 (don't follow the signs to Cape Canaveral or Cocoa Beach at this point) and turn right at the T-junction on to SR 405. The Visitor Complex is located 9mls/14km along on the right. The tours and IMAX presentations start at 10am (**KennedySpaceCenter.com**).

US Astronaut Hall of Fame

While the Space Center tells you primarily about the machinery of putting men and women in space, the US Astronaut Hall of Fame (on SR 405, just before the main entrance to the KSC) gives you the lowdown on the people involved, with fascinating memorabilia, exhibits and engaging explanations. A chronological approach divides it into 5 sections. The **Entry Experience** introduces the visions of space flight, with an 8-minute video of the astronauts as modern explorers, and leads into **Race to the Moon**, the stories of the *Mercury, Gemini* and *Apollo* missions (where you can see how incredibly *small* the first space capsules were). The Museum's heart and soul is the new **Space Shuttle: The Astronaut Experience** exhibit, a unique collection of astronaut testimonials, personal experiences and authentic artifacts, which create a personal connection for visitors with the enduring stories and endeavours of the Space Shuttle men and women honoured in the Hall of Fame. The **Astronaut Adventure** room then features a G-force simulator and space-walk 'chairs', moon exploration, interactive computers (try to 'land' a Shuttle) and Mars Mission experience.

Admission: Included with Kennedy Space Center, or $17 adults, $13 3–11s on its own. Open 9am–6 or 7pm (depending on season). If you enjoyed the KSC, try to spend a couple of hours here (it is busiest towards the end of the day). AAA½.

Cypress Gardens Adventure Park

Florida's original theme park, in Winter Haven and dating back to 1936, this has undergone a major transformation since an 18-month closure in 2003/04. The park was reborn as a fully family-friendly experience with plenty of rides, shows and even a water park. It now makes for a really full day out (about 45 minutes south of Kissimmee),

Paradise Sky Wheel

especially for families with children aged 2–14. Further enhancements are planned, with equal emphasis on shows, the gardens, new food offerings and a backstage animal tour.

Jubilee Junction: You enter into a mini-village of 16 shops, restaurants and cafés, plus a gazebo where you can relax, enjoy a drink and listen to some live music. The shops are an eclectic bunch and include Christmas-themed **Kringles Christmas Shop**, **Myrtle's Candle Co**, **Jubilee Mercantile** and butterfly-themed **Longwings Emporium**. Newest arrival is **Simply Florida Wines**, with an array of unique wines and other local goodies – stop in to sample its award-winning citrus, tropical and berry wines! The **Junior Belles** emporium allows young girls to dress up in the beautiful ante-bellum gowns that all the park's signature lovely ladies wear (including hair, makeup and a photo for $24.95). Main dining options are the barbecue flavours of **Backwater Bill's**, down-home **Aunt Julie's Country Kitchen**, the food court choice of **Jubilee Market** and the snacks of **Gator Bites**. This is a good place to revisit when it's hot to take in its live entertainment, including a new Chinese Acrobat show in the **Royal Palm Theater**.

BRITTIP

Cypress Gardens is a beautiful choice of wedding location, and it offers a range of packages for that special day, from a simple 'I do' to full ceremonies. Call 863 324 2111 or look up **cypressgardens.com**.

Topiary Trail

Nature's Way: Wander down to a natural animal exhibit featuring more than 150 mammals, reptiles and birds, including Tarzan (a 75-year-old alligator that once starred with Johnny Weissmuller in the *Tarzan* movies), a rare albino wallaby, Sheba (a female jaguar), an aviary and a petting zoo, plus the daily **Swamp Critters** educational shows (2 reptile, 2 birds of prey, and 2 mammal shows). **Treasure of Cypress Cove** is the area's fun-themed kids' show, full of nautical slapstick and pirate high jinks. You can also sign up for a **Backstage Tour** (at $10/person) into the animal department, which starts with a close-up look at the park's reptiles, then moves behind the scenes to explain the functions of the care team and meet some of those who live permanently there, like Julian, a ring-tailed lemur, and Josey, the blind wallaby. Then you can take the **Sunshine Sky Adventure**, a massive circular arm that rises 150ft/46m for a bird's-eye view of the park.

Plantation Gardens and Topiary Trail: The park's formal gardens are split into two areas, Plantation Gardens, with more traditional settings, including vegetable, herb, and rose gardens, plus the ultra family-friendly **Wings of Wonder** butterfly house, and **Topiary Trail**, which includes some monumental topiary figures (notably for the Festival of Flowers) and superb flower arrangements. The sparkling waterfall, fountains and wonderfully eye-catching backdrop of Lake Eloise make this an enchanting place to visit at any time of day. Passing the Trail brings you to the park's signature **Water Ski Show**, with a long-standing tradition of spectacular water-ski jumps and stunts (including barefoot skiing, kite-flying and the traditional pyramid) several times daily split between 2 arenas on the edge of the lake. You can also grab an open-air bite to eat here during the day from **Cypress Landing**, with fish and chips, chicken tenders, corn dogs, brownies and smoothies.

Botanical Gardens: The 30 acre/12ha heart of the old-style park, these feature a host of exotic plants and trees (including a massive banyan tree) and the beautiful Gazebo, where you will usually find one of the park's signature **Southern Belles** adding to the old-fashioned grace and style. The Gardens reward the casual wanderer with a myriad different paths and trails, all with a secluded feel. Boat tours of the Gardens were due to restart late in 2008 (water levels permitting), while there are free **guided tours** twice a day (noon and 2pm Mon–Fri) starting at the entrance to the Botanical Gardens opposite the ski stadium.

Bugsville: Turn right out of Jubilee Junction and you come to the start of the park's exciting new area of rides and games. More than 30 rides, split into 2 areas, means guaranteed fun for all ages, from the youngest children to their grandparents. Much of Bugsville is dedicated to younger children, with 12 scaled-down rides and the comedy Wild West antics of the *Shenaniguns* show. There are also 3 of the bigger rides for older children: classic steel coaster **Okeechobee Rampage**; the wooden coaster thrills of the **Triple Hurricane**; and the **Starliner**, a vintage wooden coaster, rebuilt after being salvaged from a now defunct park in Panama Beach. Then there are 2 serious water rides, the family (spinning!) raft ride **Storm Surge** and the single-rider **Wave Runner**, with 2 separate tubes to slide down. You will also find the **Adventure Grill** and **Grove Snacks** counter-service cafés, along with some handy lockers.

Adventure Grove: The more funfair-style section, this is connected to the Gardens area via the indoor **Adventure Arcade** of video games, which also boasts **Big Daddy's Pizza**. The Grove's more traditional rides include the **Paradise Sky Wheel**, bumper cars, a carousel, the **Pharaoh's Fury** pirate ship and another 4 small-scale rides for the younger set. There are then the more unusual (and hugely enjoyable) **Disk'O**, a spinning, whirling platform; the upside-down thrills of **Inverter**; the 120ft/36.6m tower ride **Thunderbolt**; **Swamp Thing**, a fast-turning suspended coaster; and **Galaxy Spin**, a dipping, swooping 'crazy mouse'-type coaster.

Splash Island: Finally, at the furthest end of the park is the new 9 acre/4ha water park, complete with **Paradise River**, a 1,000ft/33m lazy river feature and beach area. It boasts a 20,000sq ft/1,856sq m wave pool called **Kowabunga Bay** (inner tubes available to hire), 5 water speed slides (**Tonga Tubes**, a 40ft/12m tall twin flume complex, and **VooDoo Plunge**, a choice of 3 highly contrasting body slides; restrictions: 4ft/1.2m for all 5), and **Polynesian Adventure**, an amazing interactive children's water adventure area with a Tiki-inspired wet-play structure. All included in the one admission price (see overleaf). When hunger strikes, you can visit **Volcano Jim's Snack Shack & Tiki Bar** for good food and frosty drinks.

Special events: In addition, Cypress Gardens plays host to a variety of concerts (all included with admission), from rock to jazz and country and western. Check out **cypressgardens.com** for the line-up. Spring, 4 July and Christmas add extra

Storm Surge

fun to the entertainment options, with a special **Old-Fashioned Christmas** theme for the festive season featuring dazzling lights and animated displays. There is also the **Festival of Flowers** (Feb–Apr) and a series of themed weekend events, like the **Chili Cook-off** and **Car & Truck Show**, which all combine to make an impressive programme for this lovingly restored park.

Getting there: From Orlando, go west on I-4 to exit 55 for Highway 27 (Haines City) and south for 20mls/32km. Turn right on to SR 540 (look for signs to Cypress Gardens) and the park is 4mls/7km along SR 540 on the left. Parking is $7.
Admission: 10am–6, 7, 8, 9, 10 or 11pm (depending on season); $39.95 adults, $34.95 seniors (60-plus) and children (3–9). Ask at Guest Services for Second Day Free offer (within 6 days of your first visit), while an annual pass is only $79.95 for adults and $59.95 for children. AAAA/TTTT.

Bok Tower Gardens

For those wishing to experience the genuine peace, tranquillity and floral ambience of Florida, there is no better recommendation than this national monument and natural garden centre at Lake Wales, 50mls/80km to the south-west of Orlando (continue past the Cypress Gardens turn-off on Highway 27). With one of the most extraordinary attractions in the state – a majestic 205ft/62.5m pink-and-grey marble carillon tower – set in 250 acres/101ha of unique parkland, this is a feast for the eyes and soul. Called the Singing Tower, the 1920s-built carillon is the centrepiece of the park and recitals are given every day at 1 and 3pm. A carillon is a series of cast bronze bells played by a keyboard or clavier. There are only around 500 in the world, and this one consists of 60 bells (crafted in Loughborough, UK) ranging from 16lb/7.2kg to nearly 12 tons. The park has its own resident player, or carilloneur, and his daily recitals are a real highlight. The tower is also a work of art, a neo-Gothic and art deco mix crafted from coquina stone and marble, with some stunning sculptures. It is wonderfully photogenic and quite stunning on a cloudless day.

Bok Tower Gardens

Gardens: Around the tower are a wide moat, a pond and semi-formal gardens. At the highest point on Florida's peninsular (all of 298ft/90m above sea level), the view is uncluttered and inspiring, and retains an inherent peace and solitude that persuaded the founder, philanthropist Edward Bok, to grant the estate to the community in 1929. The gardens also provide a wildlife observatory (the **Window by the Pond**, where you can often see up to 126 species of birds, plus reptiles, butterflies, squirrels, turtles, rabbits and armadillos, as well as the endangered gopher tortoise), nature trails, an endangered plant exhibit, butterfly and woodland gardens and pine forests. The acres of ferns, palms, oaks and pines create a lush backdrop for the seasonal bursts of azaleas, camellias, magnolias and other flowering shrubs. There is even a children's play area, plus brass rubbing and art classes.

Education and Visitor Center: The award-winning centre illustrates the story of Edward Bok (don't miss the orientation film about him and his impact on American society), his vision for the gardens, the carillon and architecture (with a close-up of the bells themselves), the landscape design and the ecology of Florida. The

Carillon Café adds a pleasant opportunity for a light lunch and snacks (in the open air when it's not too hot – and there's often a pleasant breeze here), while the **Tower & Garden Gift Shop** offers gift and souvenir items.

Pinewood Estate: For an additional fee ($6 adults, $5 5–12s, noon and 2pm daily), you can tour one of the finest examples of Mediterranean revival architecture in Florida. The 20-room mansion was built as a winter retreat for a Pennsylvania steel tycoon in the early 1930s, and has been lovingly maintained to show a slice of period opulence.

Getting there: Located off US Highway 27 on Burns Avenue. Take I-4 west to exit 55, then go south on US 27 for 25mls/40km, turn left on Mountain Lake Cutoff Road (2 traffic lights past Eagle Ridge Mall) and follow the signs. **Admission:** $10 adults, $3 5–12s (under-5s free), apart from occasional specially ticketed events (mainly carillon festivals and recitals). Open 8am–6pm daily (last entry 5pm; Visitor Center 9am–5pm only; 863 676 1408, **boktowergardens.org**). AAA½.

Lake Wales

Continue on around the Lake Wales area after Bok Tower Gardens and you encounter some other local gems.

Chalet Suzanne: A wonderfully eclectic yet classy country inn and restaurant, quietly famous throughout Florida, this family-run (since 1931) delight is a 100 acre/40.5ha estate featuring 30 individual and quite charming guest rooms, a tropical sunken wedding garden, a swimming pool and private lake, plus – wait for it – a soup cannery (which sent its produce to the moon)! In fact, the Chalet is such a sought-after hideaway, it has its own airstrip. Its other claim to fame is its restaurant, voted one of Florida's Top 20 for more than 30 years, and a truly amazing venue. Made up of various cast-off buildings (a wing of stable here, a chicken house there), lovingly restored and melded together, the dining rooms are built on no fewer than 14 levels! The food is another highlight – gourmet cuisine but with a semi-set menu, with specialities including broiled grapefruit, baked sugar-cured ham, Chicken Suzanne, and its own Romaine Soup – such a favourite of Apollo 15 pilot James Irwin that he persuaded NASA to take it on the mission with them, hence it became known as Moon Soup. The set lunch is $29–46 a head ($15 under-12s), while dinner varies from $59 to $96 ($20 under-12s), depending on your main course selection (which includes filet mignon, lobster and King Crab thermidor). Even if you don't dine or stay in one of its remarkable Swiss-style cottage rooms ($169–229/night), it's well worth a visit for the unique charm and to learn the story of the Hinshaw family.

Getting there: Chalet Suzanne can be found just outside Lake Wales, off Highway 27 on Chalet Suzanne Road. Call 1800 433 6011 to book (always essential) or visit **chaletsuzanne.com**.

Lake Wales: Head into the quaint town of Lake Wales itself and you will discover **Spook Hill** (where cars mysteriously roll uphill!), **Grove House Visitor Center** (home of Florida's natural fruit juice products – as fresh as it gets; 10am–5pm Mon–Fri, 10am–2pm Sat) and the quaint **Museum and Cultural Center** (set in

Chalet Suzanne

a restored 1928 Atlantic Coast Line railroad station; 9am–5pm Mon–Fri, 10am–4pm Sat). The **National Historic District** of the downtown area is also being restored, building by building, to its original 1920s appearance, while you can check out the exhibitions and workshops of the **Lake Wales Arts Council**, which is set in a beautiful Mission-style 1920s church. This is also known as the world's sky-diving capital, from Lake Wales airport, with every kind of parachuting known to man. For more info, call Lake Wales Chamber of Commerce on 863 676 3445 or visit **lakewaleschamber.com**.

Silver Springs

Continuing the theme of natural attractions, we have Silver Springs, just under 2 hours' drive to the north of Orlando. This peaceful 350 acre/ 142ha nature park surrounds the headwaters of the crystal-clear Silver River. Glass-bottomed boats take you to watch the world's largest artesian springs, along with plenty of wildlife.

> **BRITTIP**
>
> Silver Springs and Wild Waters are both busy at weekends, but you shouldn't encounter many queues on weekdays, especially in summer. NB: The park was experimenting with new autumn/winter hours in 2008, closing Mon–Thurs for many weeks. Check **silversprings.com** for the full opening hours.

Expect close encounters with alligators, turtles, raccoons and lots of waterfowl, while the park also contains a collection of more exotic animals such as bears, panthers and giraffes. Five animal shows, an alligator and crocodile encounter, one of the world's largest bear exhibits, a petting zoo, kids' adventure playground, a tower ride and a white alligator exhibit complete the attractions. To destroy a few more illusions of the film industry, this was also the setting for the 1930s and 40s *Tarzan* films starring Johnny Weissmuller (a long way from Africa!). In all, you'd probably want at least half a day here.

Susan at Silver Springs

Tours and shows: The park's main attraction (dating back to 1878) is the **Glass-bottomed Boat Ride**, a 20-minute tour that goes down well with all the family and gives a first-class view of the 7 different springs and a host of water life. Similarly, the **Lost River Voyage** is another 20-minute boat trip down one of the unspoilt stretches of the Silver River, with a visit to the park's wildlife outpost. The third boat trip, the **Fort King River Cruise**, takes you back to pioneer Florida, the Seminole wars and a reconstruction of Fort King. With sightings of native wildlife, an archaeological dig, movie set and Florida Cracker Farm, it is another gentle 20-minute historical perspective, with some storytelling from the boat captain as a bonus. The **Wilderness Trail** features a tram ride towed behind a Wrangler Jeep into a wilderness area populated by assorted local wildlife (including gators!). Then there are the 2 **Ross Allen Island Animal Shows**, each lasting 15 minutes and featuring an entertaining – and occasionally hair-raising – look at the worlds of reptiles and non-venomous snakes and **Wings of the Springs**, a 25-minute bird show, with dramatic free-flight demonstrations that showcase a diverse collection of parrots, ducks, hawks, owls, falcons and vultures.

Animal Attractions: On Ross Allen Island, take time to wander **Big Gator Lagoon** and the **Crocodile Encounter**

in a cypress swamp habitat, viewed from a raised boardwalk. See the largest American crocodile in captivity, the 16ft/5m, 2,000lb/900kg Sobek, as well as a collection of alligators, turtles and Galapagos tortoises (with gator feeding daily at 2.30pm). The **Florida Natives** attraction features snakes, turtles, spiders, otters and other local denizens. Other large-scale exhibits are the **World of Bears**, an educational presentation including conservation information in a 2 acre/ 0.8ha spread devoted to bears of all kinds, from grizzly to spectacled and black bears; **Panther Prowl**, with a unique look at the endangered Florida panther and Western cougar; and **Giraffe Barn**, for a close-up encounter with these lovely creatures, which you can hand feed (for a few extra dollars). All 3 also have educational presentations several times daily. Petting zoo **Kritter Korral** (with sheep, rabbits, donkeys, llamas, pot-bellied pigs, ponies, turkeys and goats) is a big draw for the little 'uns.

Rides: In addition to its boat tours, Silver Springs also boasts a child-friendly **Carousel**, next to the imaginative **Kids Ahoy** playland, with its centrepiece riverboat featuring slides, rides, air bounce, ball crawl, 3-D net maze, bumper boats and games. Older children will gravitate to the **Lighthouse Ride**, a combined carousel and gondola lift rising almost 100ft/30m above the park (and magnificently lit at night). By contrast, the **Floral Gardens** provide a peaceful haven in which to sit and watch the world go by.

Shopping and dining: The **Springside Mall** provides an array of shops and eateries, with the **Deli** offering some pleasant sandwich choices and the **Springside Café** also above average, while **Swampy's Emporium** and the **Silver Bells Holiday Store** are the best of the shopping.

Special events: Silver Springs also offers a regular concert series at the **Twin Oaks Mansion** stage (included with admission) through the spring and autumn, with artists like the Spinners, Bobby Vinton and well-known country and western acts. Other special events include 4 July celebrations, themed weekends (International Food Festival, GM Auto Show, Oktoberfest and Native American Festival) Sept–Nov, and its annual Christmas **Festival of Lights** (late Nov–30 Dec, dusk–8.30pm), which features more than a million twinkling lights throughout the park, dozens of neon displays, local choirs, strolling carollers, musical stage shows, a lighted boat parade, a holiday buffet with all the trimmings, and, of course, Santa.

Wild Waters: Worth at least a couple of hours, the neighbouring 9 acre/4ha water park offers slides such as the new Alligator Ambush (a daring tube ride into a 35ft bowl with water-spraying gator!), Bunyon's Bend (a winding body slide), the 220ft/67m Silver Bullet and the helter-skelter Osceola's Revenge, as well as a 400ft/122m tube ride on the turbo-charged Hurricane, a huge wave pool, and various kid-sized fun in Cool Kids Cove and Tad Pool for tots.

BRITTIP

Buy a Silver Springs ticket in advance from **Attraction Tickets Direct** – 0800 975 0002 or **attraction-tickets-direct.co.uk** – and receive FREE entry to the Wild Waters park as well from May to Sept.

Silver Springs

Getting there: On SR40 in Ocala, 72mls/116km north of Orlando. Take the Florida Turnpike (a toll road, see map page 8) until it turns into I-75. 28mls/45km further north, go east on SR40 for 10mls/16km, just past Wild Waters on your right. **Admission:** $33.99 adults, $30.99 seniors (55+), $24.99 3–10s (under-3s free); parking $7; 10am–5pm daily (to 8.30pm for Festival of Lights season; also, closed Mon–Wed parts of Jan and Feb, and Mon–Thurs late Aug to early Dec); Wild Waters is $24.99 for adults and $21.99 for children (under 48in/122cm). A joint Silver Springs/Wild Waters ticket is $36.99 and $27.99; 352 236 2121, **silversprings.com**. AAAA.

Gatorland

For another taste of 'real' Florida wildlife, this is as authentic as it gets and is popular with children of all ages. Gatorland will also be celebrating its **'Cheers to 60 Years'** anniversary in 2009, with prize and ticket giveaways online at **gatorland.com**. Check its details also for a number of 'surprise announcements' in the course of the year.

'The Alligator Capital of the World' was founded in 1949 and is still family-owned, hence it possesses a home-spun charm and naturalism few of its big-name rivals can match. And, when the wildlife consists of several thousand menacing alligators and crocodiles in various natural habitats and 5 fascinating shows, you know you're in for a different experience. Overall, Gatorland is something you're unlikely to get anywhere else, though encounters with these living dinosaurs may not be everyone's cup of tea.

Tree porcupine at Gatorland

BRITTIP

If you have an evening flight home from Orlando International Airport, Gatorland is handy to visit on your final day. Conveniently located about 20 minutes' drive from the airport, it is the ideal place to soak up half a day.

Tours and attractions: Start by taking the 15-minute **Gatorland Express** railway around the park to get an idea of its 110 acre/45ha expanse. This costs an extra $2 but is good for multiple rides, is fully narrated (usually in amusing style) and is especially fun for kids. You also get a good look at the native animal habitat, which features whitetail deer, wild turkey and quail. Wander the natural beauty of the 2,000ft/610m **Swamp Walk**, as well as the **Alligator Breeding Marsh Walkway**, where a 3-storey observation tower gives a close-up view of these reptiles. Ask yourself: are they hanging around the walkway in the hope someone might 'drop in' for lunch?

BRITTIP

If you are at Gatorland first thing in the morning, take the Swamp Walk straight away. There will be far more wildlife activity then and the peaceful ambience is quite invigorating.

Breeding pens, baby alligator nurseries and rearing ponds are also situated throughout the park to provide an idea of the growth cycle of the gator and enhance the overall feeling that it is the visitor behind bars here, not the animals. **Jungle Crocs** features some of the deadliest animals of Egypt, Australia and Cuba, with authentic lairs and brilliant presentation (look out for Sultan and his 'harem' of lady crocs from the Nile). Many of the small-scale attractions have been designed with kids in mind and there is plenty to keep everyone amused. **Allie's Barnyard** is a petting zoo, while you can feed some friendly lorikeets at the **Very Merry Aviary**, and view the pink inhabitants of **Flamingo Lagoon**. Other animals to see include bats, iguanas, turtles, turkey vultures, tortoises, snakes, emus and deer. The park is also home to hundreds of herons and egrets, providing a fascinating close-up of the nests during Mar–Aug. Gatorland is actually central Florida's largest wading-bird sanctuary and it adds an extra aspect to this user-friendly park. However, the gators and crocs are the main attraction and the shows are the real draw (though you will never find yourself on the end of a queue here).

Shows: The 800-seat **Wrestling Stadium** sets the scene for some real cracker-style feats (a 'cracker' is a Florida cowboy) as Gatorland's resident 'wranglers' catch themselves a medium-sized gator and proceed to point out the animal's features, with the aid of some daredevil stunts that will have you questioning their sanity. The **Gator Jumparoo** is another eye-opening spectacle as some of the park's biggest creatures use their tails to 'jump' out of the water and be hand-fed tasty morsels, like whole chickens! **Upclose Animal Encounters** is another amusing showcase of various creatures, from the expected snakes to less obvious cockroaches and scorpions. Great photo opportunities for brave children! **Critters On The Go** is a new roving opportunity for children to meet some cuddlier creatures (like baby goats, porcupines – and even a de-scented skunk!) in the company of Miss Vera and Trail Boss Gabe.

Gator Gully: New in 2007 was this superb little water park featuring numerous ways for kids to cool down, get wet and generally have lots of fun. The ½-acre/0.2ha park features 5 different elements, including a giant jalopy with water jets for spokes and a fountain radiator, an old shack that 'explodes' with water, and giant gators with squirt guns. There is a neighbouring dry play area and chairs and tables for parents to sit back and watch their offspring expend some energy, perhaps with a drink from one of the kiosks.

Shopping and dining: In addition to 3 different gift stores around the park and the amusing **Gator & Snake photo opportunity**, you should visit the newly rebuilt (after a 2006 fire) **Gift Shop** complex at the entrance, which incorporates the trademark Gator Mouth entryway. You can grab a bite or drink at 3 snack bars, try **Gator Jake's Fudge Kitchen** or dine on smoked gator ribs and fried gator nuggets (as well as burgers and hot dogs) at Pearl's Smokehouse, with excellent kids' meals at $4.99.

Special events: Three unique options if you really want to get to know your gators are: **Trainer for a Day**, with the chance to work behind the scenes at the park 8am–10am, finding out what it takes to handle such dangerous animals, behavioural training and novice gator wrangling ($125 for 12s and over, max 5 people; includes park admission); **Gator Night Shine**, which takes guests into the Breeding Marsh after dark for a 1-hour tour with one of the park's senior gator experts, with torches and gator food to lure the local denizens. You can then marvel at how gator eyes shine like red beacons

Gator Gully

in the torchlight and learn more about the habits of these amazing animals – a real family treat, which kids seem to love (8.15pm summer, 6.30pm autumn and winter; $19 adults, $17 under-13s; bug spray provided; reservations required); and **Adventure Hour**, a chance to go truly 'behind-the-scenes' in the Breeding Marsh to feed and pose for photos with the gators here ($10/person).

Getting there: Gatorland is on the South Orange Blossom Trail, 2mls/3km south of the Central Florida Greeneway and 3mls/5km north of Highway 192 (see map on page 13). **Admission:** $22.99 adults, $14.99 3–12s, 9am–5pm (6pm summer), parking free. Annual passes are only $43.99 and $29.99 if you plan more than one visit (407 855 5496, **gatorland.com**). AAAA.

BRITTIP

For photographers and bird-watchers there is a special **Photo Pass** for entry to the Boardwalk rookery section of Gatorland from 7.30am to dusk, Tues–Sat, Mar–July, for $29.99.

Fantasy of Flight

Another wonderful and fresh alternative on the central Florida scene – voted No 1 Best Kept Secret by the locals – is this aviation attraction, which offers a 5-part adventure featuring the world's largest private collection of vintage aircraft. Even those not usually interested in aviation or the glamour of the golden age of flying should find it fascinating.

Fantasy of Flight

You start by entering the **History of Flight**, a series of expertly re-created 'immersion experiences' into memorable moments in aviation history. The entrance alone is eye-opening – along the fuselage of a DC-3 Dakota as if for a parachute drop, stepping out into a moonlit night. Then you visit set-pieces that include a dogfight over the trenches in World War I and a bomber mission with a Flying Fortress in World War II. The latter includes a walk-through of an actual B-17 as it prepares for its bombing run! Audio-visual effects and film clips enhance the experience and give everything an awe-inspiring feeling of authenticity. You exit into the **Vintage Aircraft** displays in 2 huge hangars, with the exhibits ranging from a replica *Spirit of St Louis* to a Ford Tri-Motor, a Mk-XVI Spitfire and the world's only fully airworthy Short Sunderland flying boat, which you can actually board. One aircraft is selected from the collection of more than 40 vintage planes each day for an **Aerial Demonstration** (weather permitting), with the pilot holding a Q&A session about that plane before going on to perform a series of manoeuvres over Fantasy of Flight.

More family-orientated entertainment is provided by **Fun with Flight**, a hands-on interactive area where guests can test their paper aeroplane-making skills in The Fly Zone and learn about the principles of lift with Bernoulli's Ball. There are thrills galore in **Virtual Flight Explorer** (for an extra fee), a full-motion simulator that takes riders back to the battle for Iwo Jima or Desert Storm Strike. A variety of **guided tours** is given each day, with a tram tour of the restricted areas (including the Maintenance Hangar and Wood Shop, where specialists restore and rebuild wooden aircraft), a walking tour of the Backlot, and a visit to the Restoration Shop, highlighting in detail what it takes to restore and maintain these magnificent machines. Finally, **Fightertown** features 8 realistic fighter simulators that take you on a World War II aerial battle. You get a pre-flight briefing on how to handle your 'plane' (a Vought Corsair), and then climb into the enclosed cockpit to do battle with the Japanese Air Force. It's difficult, absorbing, fun and totally addictive. The whole experience is crafted in 1930s' art deco style and includes a full-service diner (the excellent **Compass Rose**; 11am–3pm) and an original gift shop. There is strong Brit appeal, too, with the exhibits of both World Wars. Then there is Fantasy of Flight's 3-hour **balloon ride** for $175 (up to 4 passengers; seasonal operations and reservations required).

Fantasy of Flight is the brainchild of American entrepreneur and aviation whiz Kermit Weeks – who still shows off his pilot skills occasionally for the Aerial Demonstration – and we have yet to encounter an attraction put together with more genuine affection. In fact, it is as much a work of art as a tourist attraction, and the masses have yet to discover it.

Getting there: 20 minutes west of Walt Disney World on I-4 at exit 44 (Polk City), turn first right then left on SR 559 for ½ml/800m to the entrance on the left. **Admission:** $28.95 adults, $14.95 6–15s (under-6s free); 10am–5pm (closed Thanksgiving and Christmas Day), parking free (863 984 3500, **fantasyof flight.com**). AAAA.

Waldo Wright's Flying Service

Flying daily from the Fantasy of Flight airfield is this wonderfully authentic biplane experience. If you ever fancied yourself as a silk-scarf-and-leather-jacket-wearing flying ace, this is definitely the place for you (even if you don't, try it anyway – it's terrific fun). There are 2 distinct rides: in an open-cockpit 1929 **New Standard D-25** biplane (where the front seats can hold up to 4) for $64.95/person; or the more daring, hands-on, 2-seater 1942 **Boeing Stearman PT-17** biplane trainer, where your pilot takes you up and then lets *you* take the controls! The 30-minute experience costs $229. Both rides are fairly gentle (and just a little thrilling) as you get a slow, bird's-eye view of this pretty part of central Florida. The way the planes seem able to turn on a wingtip gives you a deep respect for the pilots of these wonderful machines (863 873 1339, **waldowrights.com**).

INTERNATIONAL DRIVE

The 14½ml/23km tourist corridor of I-Drive (see maps pages 86, 220 and 339) continues to be a ever-changing source of hotels, restaurants, shopping and, more importantly, fun. There are more than 33,000 hotel rooms, 150 restaurants and 500-plus shops, as well as 14 attractions, including 6 mini-golf courses. The **I-Ride Trolley** links it together in

Waldo Wright's Flying Service

transport terms and **InternationalDriveOrlando.com** highlights all the options. Its Official Visitors Guide has an I-Ride map and valuable money-off coupons, which you can download to get you started. There is also a hotel booking facility. Here's a look at the area's top attractions (see also Chapter 10, Orlando By Night, and Chapter 12, Shopping to get the complete picture).

BRITTIP

Ripley's, Festival Bay and WonderWorks are all handy retreats to keep in mind for a rainy day.

Ripley's Believe It Or Not

You can't miss this particular attraction and its extraordinary tilted appearance as it's designed to appear as though it's falling into a Florida 'sinkhole'. However, once inside you soon get back on the level and, for an hour or two, you can wander through this quirky museum dedicated to the weird and wonderful. Robert L Ripley was an eccentric explorer and collector (a real-life Indiana Jones) who for 40 years travelled the world in his bid to assemble a collection of the greatest oddities known to man. The Orlando branch of this chain features 8,900sq ft/830sq m of displays, including authentic artefacts, interactive exhibits, video presentations, illusions and music. The elaborate re-creation of an Egyptian tomb showcases a mummy and 3 rare mummified animals, while the Primitive Gallery contains artefacts from tribal societies around the world (some quite gruesome). There are then Human and Animal Oddities, Big and Little galleries, Illusions and Dinosaurs, plus extra interactive elements. The collection of miniatures includes the world's smallest violin and a single grain of rice hand-painted with a tropical sunset. Larger-scale exhibits include a portion of the Berlin Wall, a two-thirds scale 1907 Rolls-Royce built out of matchsticks and a 26ft/8m tall 'painting' of Vincent Van Gogh made out of postcards!

Ripley's Believe it or Not

Admission: $18.95 adults, $11.95 4–12s; 9am–1am daily (last admission midnight; 407 363 4418, **ripleysorlando.com**). AAA.

Titanic – The Experience

Go back in time (from Jan 2009) at the new location of this fascinating attraction (formerly in the old Mercado Centre and at Orlando Science Center) just north of Sand Lake Rd. Weave through the re-designed Experience featuring full-scale re-creations of the *Titanic*'s famous rooms, including her grand staircase, first class parlour suite, Veranda Café and the newly added Marconi Room, third class cabin and bridge. Actors in period costume portray such notables as Captain Smith and Molly Brown, sharing stories of passengers and crew during a 1-hour guided journey of the famous ship. The 18-room attraction features an interactive Underwater Room, including a 15ft/4.5m 'iceberg' and a detailed replica of the vessel as she appears on the bottom of the Atlantic today. More than 200 artefacts and treasures, including movie memorabilia from James Cameron's blockbuster film *Titanic* are also on display.

Admission: $19.95 adults, $12.95 4–12s (under-4s free); 10am–9 pm daily (**titanictheexperience.com**). AAAA.

Fun Spot Action Park

Here's another choice for full-scale, family-sized fun, just off I-Drive on Del Verde Way (look for the 100ft/31m Big Wheel past the junction with Kirkman Road). The main focus is the go-karts, with 4 challenging tracks, including the max thrills of the 1,600ft/488m *Quad Helix*, the 1,000ft/305m *Conquest*, with its triple level corkscrew, the fiendish 800ft/244m *Thrasher* and the multi-level *Commander*. Then there are also bumper cars and boats, 4 daring fairground-type rides (including the whizzy **Scrambler** and **Paratrooper**), an impressive 2-storey video arcade (one of the largest in Florida), 7 Kid Spot rides and a Cadet track for the little ones. This 4.7 acre/2ha park promises hours of fun! The Oasis Snack Bar serves hot dogs, pizza, nachos, popcorn and ice-cream and the arcade games include some of the latest. Passes are geared around children's height (above and below 4ft 4in/1.32m), with younger children getting free run of all the rides (and as a passenger on the 2-seater go-karts with an adult) and older children (and grown-ups!) having unlimited access to all the rides, go-karts and games.

Admission: Free; then Go-Kart Armband (all day on all 4 tracks, plus all rides and unlimited Free Play arcade) $34.95, Rides Armband (all day on all rides plus unlimited Free Play arcade) $24.95, Kid Spot Armband (all day on Kid Spot rides plus unlimited Free Play arcade) $14.95 and Free Play Armband (unlimited play in upstairs Free Play arcade $4.95. Go-kart rides $6, ride tickets $3. Height requirements: over 4ft 4in/1.32m for Quad Helix, Conquest and Commander; 4ft 6in/1.37m for Thrasher. Open daily 10am–midnight, noon–midnight Mon–Fri in low season (407 363 3867, **fun-spot.com**). TTTT.

Magical Midway

In a similar vein, **Magical Midway** back on I-Drive (just north of Sand Lake Road) offers more go-karts, games and thrill rides, including the **Space Blast Tower** (0–180ft/55m in 3 seconds!) and the amazing **StarFlyer**, a 230ft/70m tower with chair swings that lift and rotate up the full height for a dizzying view of the surrounding area at 54mph (the only ride of its kind in America). The 2 elevated kart tracks, the double uphill corkscrew of *The Avalanche* and the sharply banked *Alpine Jump* are its signature rides (you must be at least 12 and 4ft 8in/147cm tall to drive, at least 16 to drive a passenger, and at least 5 and 3ft/91cm to be a passenger). *Fast Track*, a flat concrete track with a 25° bank turn (riders must be 12 and 4ft 8in/147cm to drive; single cars only) finishes the line-up. And then there are bumper cars, bumper boats, 4 more fairground-type rides and a large arcade, a pizza parlour and ice-cream counter.

Admission: Free, then $27.95 for All Day Armband (includes unlimited go-karts and midway rides); $22.95 3-hour Armband (unlimited go-karts and midway rides for 3 hours); $15.95 Midway Armband (unlimited rides all day but not StarFlyer go-karts, plus 10 tokens for arcade games); individual ride tickets are $7 (StarFlyer), $6 (go-karts), $5 (Space Blast) and $3 (other rides); must be 4ft/121cm for Space Shot, Tornado and Bumper Cars, and

Super Trucks at Fun Spot Action Park

3ft 6in/106cm for Bumper Boats, Kiddie Track. 2–10pm Mon–Thurs, 2pm–midnight Fri, 10am–midnight Sat, 10am–10pm Sun (407 370 5353, **magicalmidway.com**). TTTT.

BRITTIP

Book tickets online for Magical Midway and save $3.95 on the 3-Hour Armband and $4.95 on the All-Day Armband. Click on the 'Buy Tickets here' link.

WonderWorks

This interactive entertainment centre is I-Drive's most unmistakable landmark, a 3-storey chamber of family fun with a host of novel elements. Unmistakable? How many upside-down buildings do you know? That's right, all the 82ft/25m edifice is constructed from the roof up! The basic premise (working on the theory that every attraction must have a story behind it) is that WonderWorks is a secret research facility into unexplained phenomena that was uprooted by a tornado experiment and dumped in topsy-turvy fashion in the heart of this busy tourist district (yeah, right!). Well, you have to give full marks for imagination and, with various enhancements since it opened in 1998, there's a lot here, especially for 6–12s.

BRITTIP

WonderWorks, Fun Spot and Magical Midway are open until midnight in high season, long after most theme parks are shut, so you can have a day at the park, then let the kids loose here for a while to tire them out!

WonderWorks

You enter through an 'inversion tunnel' that orientates you the same way round as the building (look out of the window to check!) and then progress to various chambers of entertaining and mildly educational hands-on experiences that demand several hours to explore fully. Without ever using the words 'science' or 'museum', WonderWorks steers you through various 'labs' of interactive activities, including **natural disasters** (earthquakes, hurricanes, famous disasters and the new Global VR – a virtual reality trek into the Desert War); **physical challenges** (virtual basketball and soccer, virtual 'swim with the sharks', Bed of Nails and the chance to make an impression of your entire body in 40,000 plastic nails at Wonderwall!); **illusions** (with a computer ageing process and 'elastic surgery', ethnicity changer and a 'couple's morph' that combines 2 faces to see what the resulting children would look like!); and **The Control Room**, where you have *Jet Fighters* (virtual reality F18 fighter jet), *Shuttle Landers* (your chance to pilot the Discovery Space Shuttle), a Mercury capsule mock-up, an astronaut spacesuit and *Wonder Coaster* (a pair of enclosed 'pods' that let you design and ride your own coaster). Recent additions include the amazing artwork of the Far Out Gallery, a redesigned Bubble Room, a Titanic exhibit, Fog screen and some active video games for cycling and snow-boarding. Plus there is the **WonderWorks Gift Shop and Café**. A **Lazer Tag** game on the top floor adds even more appeal for youngsters. If you have already seen *DisneyQuest*, WonderWorks may seem tame, while it isn't as educational as the Orlando Science Center, but it also offers a fun dinner-show option, **The Outta Control Magic Comedy Dinner Show** (see pages 310–11), with a good value combo ticket.

Admission: $19.95 adults, $14.95 seniors (55+) and 4–12s; $4.95 for Lazer Tag; $24.95 and $16.95 for The

Outta Control Dinner Show; $38.95 and $28.95 for WonderWorks/dinner show combo; $22.95 and $17.95 for WonderWorks/Lazer Tag combo; and $39.95 and $29.95 for all 3; 9am–midnight (407 351 8800, **wonderworks online.com**). AAA/TTT.

SkyVenture

At the junction with I-Drive and Kirkman Road is this unmistakable blue and yellow funnel that houses one of the most fun 'rides' in town. SkyVenture is billed as a 'freefall skydiving adventure' but it is much more than that – a fun, addictive, difficult but exhilarating 'flying' experience, with the bonus of being a great spectator sport! The basic premise is it's a huge vertical wind tunnel, which provides the feeling of a freefall parachute jump without the hassle of having to leap out of a plane, wrestle with a parachute and possibly hit the ground too hard. The standard 1-hour programme provides a full briefing of this kind of skydiving, with a fully qualified instructor to get you suitably inspired. Then you are provided with all the equipment, including helmet, pads, goggles, earplugs and flight suit, and your group of 8–12 returns to the flight deck, where you get 2 1-minute 'flights' (which seem a lot longer!) with your instructor helping you all the way. Just watching makes it seem all too easy but, as soon as you hit the tunnel, you discover how fiendishly tough it is to just 'hang' in this 125mph/200kph column of air. However, before long it becomes an immensely fun and absorbing experience and it's almost guaranteed to make you want to try again. There is no fee for non-participating members of your group to watch from the observation deck, and you can also turn up to see for yourself at any time (you might even see sky-dive groups practising at this popular venue).

Admission: Standard flight, which includes a special certificate, is $44.95/person; add a DVD and photo CD of your flight for $25. There are discount coupons and gift certificates on its website, with $8 off if you register online. You can even book a Family Package for up to 5 flyers at $229.95 or a Sports Package (double your actual flight time and a T-shirt) for $99.95. 11.30am–9pm Sun–Thur, 11.30am–10pm Fri and Sat; reservations recommended (407 903 1150, **skyventureorlando.com**). TTTT.

Helicopter rides

These are another local staple, and you can go for any one of 7 tours with **Air Florida Helicopters** at 8990 International Drive (just north of the big Convention Center). A minimum of 2 people is required, and then it's just a question of whether you want the local 8-mile tour, a trip over Universal and SeaWorld, the chance to see Disney from the air or a mega 30ml/48km grand journey that includes flying over Windermere and the homes of the rich and famous (like Tiger Woods). Prices vary from $25 for the short flight to $355 for the longest ($20–325 for children). There's no need to book; you just turn up and go. They fly 10am–6pm Sun–Thurs, 10am–7pm Fri and Sat (407 354 1400, **airfloridahelicopters.com**).

Mini-golf

For those in need of more holiday fun, don't miss the 7 mini-golf outlets along International Drive (see pages 273–4).

SkyVenture

The Holy Land Experience

Not so much a conventional attraction but right in the heart of the tourist mainstream (just outside the main I-Drive corridor) is this 15 acre/ 6ha 'living Biblical museum', which aims to re-create in detail the city of Jerusalem and its religious significance from 1450BC to AD66. Its intent is also to provide an explanation and celebration of the Christian faith.

BRITTIP

Arrive at The Holy Land Experience in time for park opening Mon–Fri and you can join a free 30-minute tour with one of its Biblical Archaeologists, beginning in the Jerusalem Street Market.

All the staff are in period costume, the architecture and landscaping are impressive and the background music is a combination of original and inspirational, as well as being suitably atmospheric (perhaps not surprising when some of the designers of Universal's Islands of Adventure park also worked here). From the **Jerusalem Street Market** entrance to the **Dead Sea Qumran Caves, Calvary's Garden Tomb** and on to the impressive **The Great Temple** (destroyed by the Romans in AD70), everything is portrayed in literal Biblical terms and with no little style by its presenters. **Theater of Life** shows a 25-minute film, *Seed of Promise*, which 'communicates God's master plan for redeeming mankind', and a selection of films with Biblical themes, while the **Wilderness Tabernacle** is a theatrical portrayal of the ancient biblical ritual, featuring the Holy Ark with lasers and pyrotechnics. The **Shofar Auditorium** houses a huge model of **Jerusalem**, which took more than a year to build and is explained in great detail several times a day. The **Scriptorium** centre for Biblical antiquities is another themed environment showcasing various rare artefacts in a 55-minute narrated walk through 4,500 years of history in fascinating fashion. At the end, **A Day in The Life of a Monk** provides a look at those who transcribed the Bible during the Middle Ages.

The Holy Land Experience

BRITTIP

Reader Peter Crumpler suggests: 'The Holy Land is an unusual cross between a theme park and an educational tour, but I'd say British Christians would find it fascinating – both for learning more about the Bible and for seeing their livelier American cousins in action.'

Live performances include musical dramas *Moses* and *Praise Through The Ages*, dramatic vignette *The Ministry of Jesus*, and *Centurion*, another highly theatrical musical, showcasing the park's high-quality performers. There is also an increased kids' zone ('Smile of a Child') with a rock-climbing wall, a lively 20-minute skit of *David & Goliath*, a walk through the whale in 'Jonah & the Whale' photo ops at 'Sampson's Column' and 'Jesus Walking on the Water', plus Biblical handicrafts and Hebrew writing and a Christian cartoon and film theatre. There are 5 eateries, the **Oasis Palms Café** (featuring Goliath Burgers and healthier Mediterranean and Middle Eastern fare), the **Royal Portico** for turkey legs and ice-creams, **Simeon's Corner** for hot dogs, snacks and drinks, **The Centurion** for snacks and drinks, and the **TBN Stagecoach** for snacks in the kids' area. There are also 3 major gift shops with different themes. All in all, it is a really unusual 'attraction' (though it doesn't call itself that), a lively and literal celebration of the Christian faith and, though it sits a little awkwardly among the main tourist offerings, it is gaining popularity and interest

Getting there: The Holy Land Experience is off exit 78 of I-4, at the junction of Conroy and Vineland Roads (just north of Universal Orlando). **Admission:** $35 adults, $30 seniors (55+), $23 6–12s (save $5 if you advance book online), parking $5; 10am–5pm Mon–Sat (closed Sundays, Thanksgiving and Christmas Day; 407 872 2272 or 1866 872 4659, **holyland experience.com**). AAA.

Old Town, Kissimmee

In the heart of tourist Highway 192 in Kissimmee is the shopping and entertainment attraction of Old Town. The shopping part is covered in Chapter 12, but there are many associated attractions worth noting. Old Town itself features 15 out-and-out rides, from the standard and rather tame **Happy Days bumper cars**, **Happy Days go-karts** and large **Ferris Wheel** to the **Windstorm** roller-coaster, the **Super Shot** (a free-fall style ride of over 140ft/43m), the **Bull**, and the immense **Old Town Human Slingshot** (a 365ft/110m bungee catapult!). There is a **Fun Town** area of junior rides, plus a **Laser Tag** game, and tickets are sold separately for most rides ($1 each), but if you plan to do several, go for the Valuepak at $20 for 22 tickets or $30 for 35. There is also an All You Can Ride Wristband at $25, and a Family Day Sunday Wristband (noon–6pm Sun) for $15. There are separate fees for Slingshot ($25; ride video $15), bumper cars ($5), The Bull ($10 adults, $5 children), Laser Tag ($5) and go-karts ($6 single rider; $8 adult with a child). For a different kind of fun, you can also try the 2-storey **Grimm Haunted House** ($10 adults, $6.75 children). The Old Town rides are open noon–11pm (later at peak periods; 407 396 4888, **old-town.com**). TTTT.

BRITTIP

Old Town offers a Birthday Party package for up to 12 children at a time, consisting of 3 hours of unlimited rides, meal vouchers for any of their restaurants and use of its party room for 2 hours. E-mail **party@old-town.com** for more info.

Fun Spot USA

Right next door to Old Town (but not connected in any way) is another area of rides and fun owned by Fun Spot of International Drive. There are 4 go-kart tracks, a good selection of thrill rides, a Kid Spot of junior-sized rides and 2 high-adrenalin signature rides, which are real one-offs. Top of the lot is the amazing **SkyCoaster**, a 300ft/90m tower that sends up to 3 riders at a time on a free-fall plunge (for the first 120ft/37m) that turns into a giant swing – at 85mph/136kph! Its partner ride is speed demon **G-Force**, an air-powered dual dragster car race that blasts riders 0–110mph/176kph in just 2 seconds and hits a top speed of 120mph/ 192kph. The ride lasts for a grand total of 11 seconds and the intense thrill costs $20 for the driver and $10 for the passenger. The more down-to-earth rides consist of 2 flat concrete go-kart tracks, *Slick* and *Road Course*, and

SkyCoaster at Fun Spot USA

two multi-level concrete tracks, the labyrinthine *Chaos* and the *Vortex*, with its hugely challenging banked bowl section. The other rides are almost as much fun – check out the **Extraordinary Bike** (pedal your way upside-down!), the **Double Ferris Wheel**, the more fairground style of **Flying Bobs** and the **Paratrooper**, the giant swing of the **Hot Seat** and the tower-ride **Screamer**. Also part of Fun Spot USA are the indoor **Full Speed Race & Golf**. The Race features 6 full-motion NASCAR motor-racing simulators, while the latter is a racing-themed, and quite challenging, 18-hole black-light mini-golf course. There is a well-stocked Snack Bar (with free soft drinks) in the outdoor rides section, drinks and snacks at SkyCoaster and a shop for gifts and snacks at Full Speed Race & Golf, plus pizza, hot dog and candy floss kiosks throughout the park. Oh, and look out for the giant-wheeled **Bigfoot 7** truck here – it featured in the films *Road House* (Patrick Swayzee) and *Tango & Cash* (Sylvester Stallone and Kurt Russell).

Admission: Free, then Go-Kart Armband $34.95 (unlimited go-karts and other rides), Rides Armband (unlimited rides) $14.95 and Track Sampler $20 (4 goes on go-karts or rides); regular tickets $2 each or 20 for $36. SkyCoaster, single rider $40 ($65 for 2 flights), $70 for 2 riders and $90 for 3. Full Speed Race $14.95, $6.95 Race Again, $4.95 passengers; Black-Light Golf, $9.95 adults, $7.95 under-13s, $4.95 Play Again; combo Race & Golf $19.95; All-Day Race & Golf $34.95; noon–midnight Mon–Fri, 10am–midnight Sat and Sun; G-Force 4pm–midnight Mon–Fri, noon–midnight Sat and Sun (407 397 2509, **fun-spotusa.com**).

Orlando Science Center

BRITTIP

See the Fun Spot USA website (see above) for a $2.50 coupon off its Ride Armband, or save your armband from one Fun Spot location to save 20% off the other.

DOWNTOWN ORLANDO

The last couple of years have seen a significant move towards regenerating Orlando's city centre – the downtown area – with new offices, apartments, shops and restaurants. This has also enhanced some notable tourist attractions.

Orlando Science Center

Because this is Orlando, there is no such thing as a simple museum or science centre. Everything must be all-singing, all-dancing just to compete. Hence, the Orlando Science Center is more than a mere museum and far more fun than the average science centre. Here you are given a series of hands-on experiences and habitats that entertain as well as inform, and school-age children in particular will benefit greatly from it.

The Science Center has 9 main permanent exhibits, plus an inviting café, a night sky observatory and a giant screen cinema. Until January 2009, it is also the temporary home of **Titanic – The Experience**, and the fascinating walk-through story with costumed guide that this attraction (relocated from International Drive) consists of.

NatureWorks is an immersion-style exhibit creating 6 typical Florida habitats, complete with native plants and animals (with field stations such as how sea turtles make their nests and a live beehive); **KidsTown** is for those a bit too young for the educational element, with plenty of junior-sized fun and games for under-6s (you'll be amazed at how much they learn in the course of having fun!); **DinoDigs** was a gift from the Walt Disney Company of its former Dinosaur Jubilee exhibit in *Disney's Animal Kingdom*, re-created in the OSC as a palaeontological excavation site, complete with 8 full skeleton replicas and some genuine fossils; **TechWorks** is a hands-on adventure into the worlds of physical science and technology, including a hurricane simulator and Dr Dare's Laboratory; and **Xperience Factory** offers a variety of different live science shows (notably *Cool Science* – fun with frigid temperatures and chemical reactions). There are sure to be more regular exhibits in 2009 when the space taken up by Titanic – The Experience opens up again (consult its website for future details). You will also find a handy **Café** and a large **Science Store** here. In addition, the centre has 2 separate programmes in **Dr Phillips CineDome**, a 310-seat cinema that practically surrounds its audience with large-format films and digital planetarium shows. It also boasts a 28,000-watt digital sound system that makes the experience unforgettable.

BRITTIP

Visit the Crosby Observatory (6–9pm Fri and Sat) on top of the Science Center to gaze through the region's largest publicly accessible refractor telescope.

Getting there: On Princeton Street in downtown Orlando, just off exit 85 of I-4 (go east on Princeton, the Center is on your left but the multi-storey car park is on the RIGHT, see map on page 220). **Admission:** $23 adults, $21 seniors (55+), $18 3–11s (NB: Prices will be adjusted in Jan 2009; check website for details); parking $4. 10am–6pm Sun–Thurs, 10am–9pm Fri and Sat (closed Easter Sunday, Thanksgiving, Christmas Eve and Christmas Day; **osc.org**) AAA.

Orange County History Center

This relatively recent addition offers an imaginative journey into central Florida history, from the wildlife and Native Americans to today's tourist issues and the space programme. Again, the accent is on the interactive, with hands-on exhibits and audio-visual presentations, and it is very much a journey through time, starting outside in renovated Heritage Square, complete with cypress trees and fountains. The Center itself is in the former 1927 Orange County Courthouse, with the foyer converted into a dome featuring more than 150 icons unique to central Florida (see how many you can identify before and after your tour).

The 4-storey adventure starts at the top with the Orientation Theater's 14-minute multimedia presentation as you sit in rocking chairs on the 'front porch'. Then you visit the Natural Environment and First Peoples exhibits (12,000 years ago), before First Contact brings in the European element. Jump into the 1800s and visit a Seminole settlement, a pioneer cracker (the first true cowboy) home, hear tales of the old ranching days, the Seminole wars and learn about the citrus industry. The early 20th century brings the story of transportation, tourism, aviation and the great land boom, Selling Central Florida. Witness how the region fared during World War II and then

Orange County History Center

dramatically altered with the development of the Space Programme and the arrival of a certain Walter Elias Disney in The Day We Changed. From there, you move on to the beautifully restored Courtroom B for some more real-life Orlando history.

BRITTIP

Combine a visit to the History Center with lunch at the wonderfully eclectic Globe restaurant on the corner of Heritage Square nearby.

Finally, you reach the newest permanent exhibit, **Orlando Remembered** – a journey from the 19th century to the edge of the 21st. This tells the story beyond the theme parks and is an inclusive history of Orlando's people, uncovering secrets of the past, including significant artefacts from the Historical Society of Central Florida. Find out about events like the Big Freeze of the 1890s and the area's contribution to World War II (with a replica Flying Fortress). An exhibit on African American history, featuring the achievements and tragedies of central Florida's African American community and a series of travelling exhibits (like NASA's Early Years) round things off, while a visit to the **Historium** gift shop completes your visit. Special large-scale exhibits scheduled for 2008 include *National Geographic Greatest Portraits* (21 Nov 2008–18 Jan 2009) and *Jim Henson's Fantastic World* (6 Feb–3 May).

Getting there: Off Central Boulevard and Magnolia Avenue downtown (exit 82C off I-4, Anderson Street, left on to Magnolia, right on to Central Boulevard, see map on page 220). Park at the Public Library multi-storey car park on Central Boulevard (History Center admission includes 2 hours' free parking if you show your ticket). **Admission:** $9 adults, $7 seniors (60+), $6 5–12s; 10am–5pm Mon–Sat, noon–5pm Sun (407 836 8500, **thehistorycenter.org**). AAA.

More downtown attractions

A subsidiary of the History Center is the 1926 **Orlando Fire Museum**, at 814 Rollins Avenue in Loch Haven Park. This pays homage to the professional and volunteer firemen who have served the local community, with artefacts – from helmets, lanterns and other fire-fighting apparatus to original newspaper stories about historic city fires – dating back to 1885. 9am–3pm Thurs–Sat, free admission and car parking (407 898 3138). Staying downtown, the free **Lymmo** bus service connects the central stretch along Magnolia Avenue, from South Street to the **Amway Arena** for sports and concerts on Amelia Street, the **Downtown Arts District and Arts**

Orlando Fire Museum

Market (on Wall Street, off Orange Avenue, every Sat 11am–9pm Oct–Apr), seasonal concerts and firework shows, plus new shops and restaurants around **Lake Eola**. The Lake itself is a beautiful area to explore, with a park, children's play area and a very peaceful ambience. Children can feed the birds and fish or take a swan paddleboat ride ($12 for 30 minutes), plus there are regular free open-air concerts and storytelling at the Disney Amphitheater (**cityoforlando.net**; click on Departments, then Families, Parks & Recreation).

The **Cultural Corridor** links the Downtown Arts District (which includes the Bob Carr Performing Arts Center and the Centroplex) with the Loch Haven area (where you find the Orlando Museum of Art, Mennello Museum of American Folk Art, Orlando Philharmonic Orchestra and the Orlando-UCF Shakespeare Festival), via the **Dr Phillips Performing Arts Center**, which is home to the Orlando Opera and Orlando Ballet. The 33-year-old **Orlando Ballet** is central Florida's only full-time ballet company, with national and international dancers, plus a Family Series that accommodates children (407 426 1733/1739, **orlandoballet.org**).

The Sunday **Farmers Market** (at Lake Eola, 10am–4pm) is another downtown focal point with vendors now including local artisans such as glassblowers and dressmakers, as well as wonderful fresh produce. The **Thornton Park** area is currently the most happening part of Orlando, with Thornton Park Central (at the junction of Summerlin Avenue and Central Boulevard, just south-east of Lake Eola) offering a mix of unique boutiques and trendy restaurants. For more info, visit **downtownorlando.com** (click on Things To Do, and then the *Downtown Historic Walking Tour* link to download a neat self-guided tour of the city's more historic buildings).

THE WATER PARKS

Florida specialises in elaborate water parks, and Orlando boasts the very best. Predictably, Disney has the 2 most elaborate ones, but the opening of SeaWorld's Aquatica park in 2008 provided some real competition, while Universal-owned Wet 'n Wild is also adept at providing hours of watery fun. They adopt a variety of styles that owe much to the flair of the theme park creators, and are truly imaginative for both the rides and the imagery around them. All require at least half a day of splashing, sliding and riding to get full value from their rather high prices. Lockers are provided for valuables and you can hire towels.

Disney's Typhoon Lagoon Water Park

When *Typhoon Lagoon* opened in 1989, it was the biggest and finest of Florida's water parks. And, although it has since been superceded, in high season it is still the busiest, so be prepared for more queues. *You should definitely arrive ½ hour early if possible as entry often begins before the official opening hour.* The park's 56 acres/ 23ha are spread out around the 2½ acre/1ha lagoon fringed with palm trees and white-sand beaches. It is extravagantly landscaped and the walk up Mount Mayday, for instance, provides a terrific overview as well as adding scenic touches such as rope bridges and tropical flowers. Sun

Shark Reef at Typhoon Lagoon

loungers, chairs, picnic tables and even hammocks are provided to add to the comfort and convenience of restful areas like Getaway Glen. However, you need to arrive early to bag a decent spot.

BRITTIP
While water parks provide a great way of cooling down, it is easy to pick up a 5-star case of sunburn. So don't forget the high-factor *waterproof* sun cream.

To avoid the worst of the summer crowds (when the park's 7,200 capacity is often reached), Monday morning is the best time (steer clear of weekends at all costs), and, on other days, arrive either before opening or in mid-afternoon, when many decide to dodge the daily rainstorm. Early evening is also pleasant when the park lights up. The park is overlooked by Mount Mayday, on top of which is perched the luckless Miss Tilly, a shrimp boat that legend has it landed here during the typhoon that gave the park its name. Watch for the water fountains that shoot from Miss Tilly's funnel at regular intervals, accompanied by the ship's hooter, which signal another round of 6ft/1.8m waves in the **Surf Pool** (you can hire inner tubes to bob around on or just try body-surfing). Circling the lagoon is **Castaway Creek**, a 3ft/1m deep, lazy flowing river that offers the chance to float happily along on rubber tyres.

Disney's Typhoon Lagoon

BRITTIP
Want to learn to surf? Typhoon Lagoon now offers Surfing School 2 hours before park opening every day. Call 407 939 7529 in advance to book at $140/person.

Slides and rides: These are all clustered around Mount Mayday and vary from the breathtaking body slides of **Humunga Kowabunga**, which drop you 214ft/65m at up to 30mph/48kph down some pretty steep inclines (make sure your swimming costume is securely fastened!) to **Ketchakiddee Creek**, which offers a selection of slides and pools for youngsters under 4ft/122cm. In between, you have the 3 **Storm Slides**, body slides that twist and turn through caves, tunnels and waterfalls, **Mayday Falls**, a wild 460ft/140m single-rider inner-tube flume down a series of banked drops, **Keelhaul Falls**, a more sedate tube ride that takes slightly longer, and **Gangplank Falls**, a family ride inside rafts that take up to 4 people down 300ft/90m of mock rapids.

The newest area is **Crush 'n' Gusher**, a fabulous trio of 'water-coaster' tube rides, plus a large heated pool with zero-depth entry (great for toddlers). It also has an extensive sandy beach, which makes it a great place to bag a spot in the sun. The 3 different slides feature tubes for 2 or 3 riders at a time that whoosh you down and UP several inclines before dropping you into the pool with a significant splash. This is also busy from midday on. The imaginative (but chilly) **Shark Reef** is an upturned wreck and coral reef, which you can snorkel through among 4,000 tropical fish and a number of real, but harmless, nurse sharks. Those who aren't brave enough to get in can still get a close-up through the underwater portholes of the sunken ship. The Reef is closed during the coldest months. Substantial queues build up from late morning, so do this early.

Keeping out of the sun can also be a problem as there's not much shade, but a quick plunge into Castaway Creek usually prevents overheating. There are health and 4ft/122cm height restrictions on Humunga Kowabunga and Crush 'n' Gusher (not suitable for anyone with a bad back or neck, or expectant mothers).

BRITTIP

'Buy a disposable waterproof camera to tie around your wrist when you visit the water parks. We bought one cheap at Wal-Mart and have some lovely photos from Typhoon Lagoon,' says reader Judith Bingham.

Shopping and dining: If you have forgotten a sunhat or bucket and spade for the kids, or even your swimsuit, they are all available at **Singapore Sal's**. You CAN'T bring your own snorkels, inner tubes or rafts, but snorkels are provided at Shark Reef and you can hire inner tubes for the lagoon. For snacks and meals, **Lowtide Lou's** and **Let's Go Slurpin'** both offer a bite to eat and drinks, while **Typhoon Tilly's** and **Leaning Palms** serve a decent mix of sandwiches, burgers, salads and ice-cream. Avoid main mealtimes here if you want to eat in relative comfort. You can bring your own picnic (unlike the main theme parks), which you can eat in special scenic areas (but no alcohol or glass).

BRITTIP

As the busiest of the water parks, Typhoon Lagoon can hit capacity quite early in the day in summer. Call 407 824 4321 in advance to check on the crowds.

Getting there: On Buena Vista Drive, ½ml/800m from Downtown Disney (see map on page 73). Admission: $39 adults, $33 3–9s (under-3s free); included with Premium and Ultimate tickets; parking free; 9am (10am off-season)–dusk daily. TTTT/AAAAA.

Disney's Blizzard Beach Water Park

Ever imagined a skiing resort in the middle of Florida? Well, Disney has, and this is the wonderful result. This water park opened in 1995 and is still the largest, with all 66 acres/27ha arranged as if it were in the Rocky Mountains rather than the subtropics! That means snow-effect scenery, Christmas trees and waterslides cunningly converted to look like skiing pistes and toboggan runs.

Slides and rides: Main features are **Mount Gushmore**, a 90ft/27m mountain down which all the main slides run. A ski chair-lift operates to the top, providing a magnificent view of the park and surrounding areas. Don't miss the outstanding rides here, including the world's tallest free-fall speed slide, the terrifying 120ft/37m **Summit Plummet**, which rockets you down a 'ski jump' at up to 60mph/97kph. For those not quite up to the big drop, the wonderfully named **Slush Gusher** is a slightly less terrifying body slide. Then there is **Teamboat Springs**, a wild family inner-tube adventure and arguably the best of all the water rides; **Runoff Rapids**, a choice of three tube plunges; the **Snow Stormers**, a daring head-first 'toboggan' run; and **Toboggan Racers**, which gives you the chance to speed down the 'slopes' against 7 other head-first daredevils.

Slush Gusher

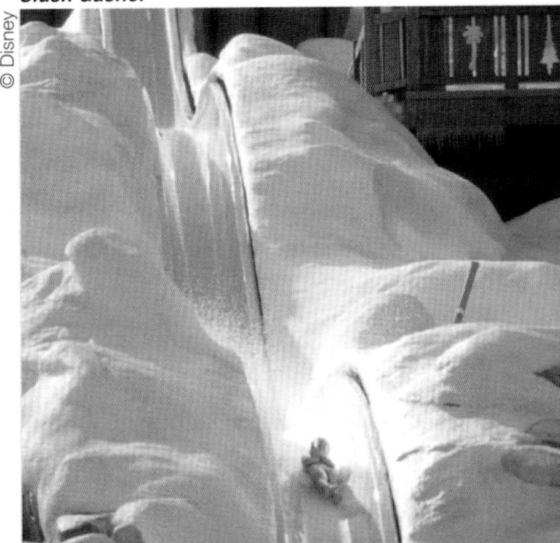

All 4 provide good-sized thrills without overdoing the scare factor. The **Downhill Double Dipper** is 2 side-by-side slides that send you down 230ft/70m tubes in a race timed on a big clock at the bottom, with a real jolt half-way down!

Tike's Peak is a kiddie-sized version of the park's slides and a mock snow-beach, and **Ski-Patrol Training Camp** is a series of slides and challenges for pre-teens. **Melt-Away Bay** is a 1 acre/ 0.4ha pool fed by 'melting snow' (actually blissfully warm), and **Cross Country Creek** is a lazy-flowing ½ml/800m river round the whole park that also floats guests through a chilly 'ice cave' (look out for the ice-water waterfalls!).

Shopping and dining: There is a 'village' area with a **Beach Haus** shop and **Lottawatta Lodge** fast-food restaurant (pizzas, burgers, salads and sandwiches), offering diners a grandstand view of Mount Gushmore. Snacks are also available at **Avalunch** (ouch!), the **Warming Hut**, **Polar Pub** and **Frostbite Freddie's Frozen Refreshments**.

Getting there: Just north of *Disney's All-Star Resorts* off Buena Vista Drive (see map on page 73). **Admission:** $39 adults, £33 3–9s (under-3s free); included with Premium and Ultimate tickets; parking free; 9am (10am off-season)–dusk daily. TTTTT/ AAAAA. Adjacent to Blizzard Beach are the amazing **Winter Summerland Miniature Golf Courses** (where Santa's elves hang out!), with 2 wonderfully elaborate courses that provide children with a great diversion. Watch out for a riot of visual gags, as well as some tricky golf.

Wet 'n Wild

If Disney scores highest for scenic content, Wet 'n Wild, the world's first water park in 1977, goes full tilt for thrills and spills of the highest quality, with its 2 newest rides also being highly sophisticated. This park will certainly test your swimsuit material to the limit!

Wet 'n Wild is one of the best-attended water parks in the country, and its location in the heart of I-Drive makes it a major draw. Consequently, you will encounter some crowds here, though the 15 slides and rides, **Lazy River** attraction, elaborate kids' park (with mini versions of many of the slides), **Surf Lagoon**, restaurant and picnic areas absorb a lot of punters before queues develop. Waits of more than ½ hour at peak times are rare, but it is busy at weekends and throughout July.

BRITTIP

The Kids Park at Wet 'n Wild was built especially for those under 4ft/122cm tall – right down to having the only junior wave pool in the world.

Brain Wash

Slides and rides: You are almost spoilt for choice of main rides, from the highly popular group inner-tube rides of **Surge** and **Bubba Tub**, to the more demanding **The Flyer**, **The Blast** and **Mach 5** (head-first on a mat-slide). For body slides, try the high-energy plunge of **The Storm** and the sheer terror of **Der Stuka** and **Bomb Bay**. The latter duo are definitely not for the faint-hearted. Basically, they are 276ft/23m body slides with drops as near vertical as makes no difference. Der Stuka is the straightforward slide, while Bomb Bay adds the extra terror of being allowed to free-fall on to the top of the slide. For some reason, only a minority of the park's visitors pluck up the courage to try it! There are 4ft/122cm height restrictions on Bomb Bay and Der Stuka, while older kids can enjoy the huge, inflatable **Bubble Up**, which bounces them into 3ft/1m of water. The newest enhancement is to the old Black Hole tube ride, which is now **Black Hole: The Next Generation**, a pulsating 2-person ride down a fully enclosed flume, with the addition of an explosive lighting package and other dynamic special effects.

Our favourites? We like the thrilling toboggan-like **Flyer**, which takes 4 passengers in 8ft/2m in-line tubes down more than 450ft/137m of banked curves and straights, and **The Blast**, with its 1- or 2-passenger tubes that surprise you with sudden twists and turns, explosive pipe bursts and drenching waterspouts, leading to a final waterfall plunge. And don't miss **The Storm**, a pair of identical circular slides billed as 'body coasters' – the enclosed tubes (complete with storm sound and light effects) send the rider plunging into a circular bowl, around which they spin at high speed before landing in the splash-pool below. Possibly the funniest, though, is **Disco H2O**, a superbly themed family raft ride that plunges down an enclosed tube into a wildly swirling 'disco bowl' (featuring lights and a mirror ball!) before spitting you out through a waterfall. It is all accompanied by 1970s-style music and commentary to add to the fun (big queues from midday to late afternoon). Equally, **Brain Wash** is a 65ft/ 20m funnel ride that sends riders on 2-, 3- or 4-person tubes down a long, enclosed flume into a huge swirling funnel that washes the tube wildly backwards and forwards before setting it up for the final splashdown.

For those under 4ft/122cm, the **Kids Park** has a full range of junior-sized slides, plus a sandcastle structure with 2 semicircular waterslides and a giant bucket that fills and tips up at regular intervals. Uniquely, the children can use tubes, beach chairs and tables designed specifically for their height. The neighbouring lake is also part of the fun (though not in chilly winter and spring), adding the options for cable-operated **Knee Ski**, **Wake-Boarding** and (for a nominal fee) the **Wild One** (large inner tubes tied behind a speedboat). Or take a breather in the slow-flowing **Lazy River** as you float past palms and waterfalls, or abandon the water altogether for one of several picnic areas (though they can be crowded). The energetic can play beach volleyball. Lockers, showers and tube and towel rentals are all available; if you bring your own floating equipment, you must have it checked by the lifeguards.

KIds' Park Lazy River

Shopping and dining: Sportswear, swimwear, sunglasses, hats and more can all be found at **Breakers Beach Shop**. For food, **Bubba's Bar-B-Q** serves chicken, ribs, fries and drinks, the **Surf Grill** features burgers, hot dogs, chicken and sandwiches, and another 7 snack bars offer similar fast-food fare, including a pizza bar. You can also bring your own picnic, but not alcohol or glass containers.

BRITTIP

For all the water parks, it's a good idea to bring a pair of deck shoes or sandals that can be worn in water. All the local supermarkets sell them cheaply.

Getting there: Wet 'n Wild is ½ml/800m north of I-Drive's junction with Sand Lake Road at the intersection with Universal Boulevard (see map on page 13), and just off exit 75A and 74B of I-4.

Admission: $39.95 adults, $32.95 seniors (60+), $33.95 3–9s (under-3s free; also included with Orlando FlexTickets). Tube rentals are $4 ($2 deposit), towels $2 and lockers $5 ($2 deposit), or $9 for all 3 ($4 deposit); parking $9; open year-round from 9am in peak periods (9.30 or 10am at other times) until 5, 6, 7, 9 or 11pm (**wetnwildorlando.com**). TTTTT/AAA.

Dolphin Plunge

Aquatica by SeaWorld

Orlando's newest and most eye-catching water park opened in March 2008, and has quickly become a firm family favourite for its wonderful range of children's attractions and facilities. With the benefit of some vivid, colourful styling (inspired by the tropical Pacific cultures of the South Seas) the 59 acre/24ha park features innovative rides, iconic architecture, animal encounters and unique features (like private cabanas and an all-you-eat buffet meal option), this appeals to the widest possible audience.

Slides and rides: Aquatica's signature attraction is the **Dolphin Plunge**, a twin body slide that sends riders down 300ft/91.5m of tubes and through a lagoon of playful, black-and-white Commerson's dolphins (it's a touch gimmicky as you catch only the briefest of glimpses of them on the way down, but it is an exhilarating slide). You can then view the **Dolphins** at the end of the ride through the huge lagoon window, where the inhabitants often hang out to look at their human visitors! **Whanau Way** is a quadruple raft ride with 2 distinct variations that twist and turn before landing with a resounding splash, while **Tassie's Twisters** are double bowl rides that send riders down 1- and 2-person tubes into giant bowls before splashing back into the **Loggerhead Lane** lazy river (which also incorporates a cool coral reef viewing section). **Taumata Racer** is a fast-paced mat slide set up like an 8-lane racing toboggan run, partly enclosed and then with a double drop into daylight (queues can look long here but they usually move quickly). Family raft rides **Walhalla Wave** and **HooRoo Run** offer contrasting experiences, with the longer Wave featuring a winding, enclosed section before a big splash finale, while the latter is a shorter and straighter ride – with a couple of distinctly sudden drops on the way! That is followed by not 1 but 2 wave pools, side-by-side lagoons that operate independently to create a variety of different wave patterns. **Big Surf Shores** offers the bigger, more dynamic waves, while **Cutback Cove** features gentler rolling surf (and a total of 860,000 gallons of water!). The pools front the huge, wide sandy **Beach**, which offers most of the large array of sun loungers and umbrellas, and the private cabañas (which rent for a rather exorbitant $175 per day).

BRITTIP

Head for the Beach area when you first arrive to stake out a place to base yourselves and try to grab one of the bigger fixed umbrellas that offer the most shade.

As well as the gentle Loggerhead Lane, you will certainly want to try out the distinctly dynamic **Roa's Rapids**, which provides a helter-skelter whirl along this river feature, with a series of fountains, jets and other watery boosts to keep you bobbing along with no effort at all. Free life vests are on offer here and it is worth trying one on for the feeling of floating along in high style! Height restriction for Taumata Racer is 3ft 6in/107cm; Walhalla Wave and HooRoo Run (guests under 4ft/122cm must wear a life vest); Dolphin Plunge 4ft/122cm; Roa's Rapids under 51in/129cm must wear a life vest, under 4ft/122cm on Loggerhead Lane.

Kids features: The big success of the park, though, is its extensive features for children, from the youngest to young teens. **Kata's Kookaburra Cove** is an exclusive area for those under 4ft/1.2m tall, with a whole range of scaled-down slides, rides, pools and fountains to provide a gentle experience for the young 'uns. By contrast, **Walkabout Waters** is a vast and frenzied 60ft/18m-high water play structure with every kind of climb and slide and all manner of water eruptions and outpourings, including 2 giant buckets that constantly fill and dump their contents in spectacular fashion over those below. You may lose the kids in here all day! The park's **small animal encounters** are also designed to appeal to children, too, so keep an eye out for the resident macaws, kookaburra, tortoises and tamanduas (a type of anteater).

Shopping and dining: The imaginative **Kiwi Traders** is the biggest of the 4 shops in the park, but both **Adaptations** and **Beachies** are worth a look. The food offerings are pretty inventive, too. **Waterstone Grill** offers a fine mix of salads and sandwiches, while **Mango Market** is a fresh offering of pizza, chicken tenders and wraps and speciality coffees. Perhaps the most novel feature, though, is the **Banana Beach Cookout**, which serves up a buffet you can sample on a one-off basis (for $12.95 adults, $7.95 3–9s) or with an all-day pass ($19.95 and $9.95) that allows you to visit as often as you like through the day. The food choice is a bit more limited but still features salad, burgers, chicken, hot dogs, macaroni and cheese, fresh fruit, corn on the cob, baked beans and desserts, and non-alcoholic drinks are all included. Add another 4 snack/drinks kiosks and it's a truly impressive spread of watery fun that guarantees a full day out in high style.

Aquatica Beach

BRITTIP

Like the other water parks, Aquatica will close to new arrivals when it reaches capacity, which can be as early as 11am in peak season, and it may not re-open again until 4pm. We advise being here for opening time and chilling out on the Beach when it gets busy later on.

The only drawbacks we noticed in its first couple of months of operation were a distinct lack of shade in parts of the park (pretty important in summer months), though SeaWorld has said it intends to address this, and long, slow-moving queues at Tassie's Twisters and the Dolphin Plunge. Long lines can develop at the car park entrance at peak times from around 9.30–11am, and the shower facilities could be more extensive. But features like Roa's Rapids and Walkabout Waters give Aquatica elements no other water park currently has. And, if you take advantage of the new 2-park ticket with SeaWorld, it's great value as, in summer, you could spend much of the day in Aquatica and then hop over to SeaWorld for the evening entertainment.

Getting there: Just across the road from SeaWorld on International Drive, exit 71 or 72 off I-4. **Admission:** $38.95 adults, $32.95 3–9s; 2-Park Ticket (with SeaWorld) $89.95 and $79.95; 3-Park Ticket (inc Busch Gardens) $134.95 and $124.95; parking $10, locker rental $10 and $8, towels $4 ($2 refundable); 9am–10pm (summer season), 9am–7pm (Easter) or 10am–5 or 6pm (407 351 3600, **aquaticabyseaworld.com**) TTTT/AAAAA.

BRITTIP

Buy Aquatica tickets online or in advance and enjoy an 'Hour-Early Exclusive' at the weekend in summer months, providing access to the park an hour before official opening.

That sums up the large-scale attractions on offer, but next let's explore some alternatives to the mass-market experience…

Walkabout Waters

8 Off the Beaten Track

or When You're All Theme-Parked Out

Orlando's main attractions are undoubtedly a lot of fun, but they can also be extremely tiring and you may well need a break from all the hectic theme park activity. Or you may be visiting again and looking for a different experience. If either is the case, this chapter is for you.

Hopefully, you will already have noted the relatively tranquil offerings of Silver Springs and Bok Tower Gardens in the previous chapter but, to enhance your view of the area further, the following are all guaranteed to take you off the beaten tourist track. This chapter could easily be subtitled 'A Taste of the Real Florida', as it introduces the towns of Winter Park, Disney-inspired Celebration and Mount Dora, plus the natural delights of Central Florida's different counties, the state parks, day-trips, eco-tours and sports.

ORLANDO/Orange County

Foremost among the 'secret' hideaways is the elegant northern suburb of **Winter Park**, little more than 20 minutes' drive from the hurly-burly of I-Drive yet a whole world away from the relentless commercialism. It offers museums and art galleries, fabulous shopping, numerous restaurants, walking tours, a delightful 50-minute boat ride around the lakes and, above all, a chance to slow down. You could easily spend a full day here with the range of attractions on offer. To get there, take exit 87 from I-4, Fairbanks Avenue. Turn right on Fairbanks and head east for 2mls/3km and turn left where it intersects with Park Avenue.

Albin Polasek Museum and Sculpture Gardens: Worth a look for culture buffs and for the serene setting devoted to this Czech-American artist (10am–4pm Tues–Sat, 1–4pm Sun; gardens open only July and Aug; $5 adults, $4 seniors, $3 students, under-12s free; **polasek.org**).

Kraft Azalea Gardens: Another Winter Park highlight is on Alabama Drive (off Palmer Avenue at the north end of Park Avenue), 11 acres/5ha of shaded lakeside walkways, gardens and hundreds of magnificent azaleas. The main focal point, the mock Grecian temple, is a beautiful setting for weddings.

Leu Gardens: Midway between Winter Park and downtown Orlando is this 50-acre/20ha retreat featuring formal gardens, peaceful walks and a boardwalk overlooking Lake Rowena. The **Leu House Museum** is open 10am–4pm (closed in July) with tours

Albin Polasek Museum

every 30 minutes (last tour 3.30pm). It's on the corner of Forest and Nebraska Avenues, via Mills Avenue and Princeton Street from exit 85 on I-4 (9am–5pm, 8pm in summer, daily; $7 adults, $2 children; plus free 9am–noon Mon; **leugardens.org**).

Morse Museum of American Art: A must for admirers of American art pottery, American and European glass, furniture and other decorative arts of the late 19th and early 20th centuries, as it includes one of the world's foremost collections of works by Louis Comfort Tiffany. The dazzling chapel restoration from the 1893 Chicago World Expo is now on display in its original form for the first time since the late 19th century and is alone worth the entrance fee, as are its special Christmas exhibitions and periodic family programmes (9.30am–4pm Tues–Sat, 1–4pm Sun; 9.30am–8pm Fri Sept–May; adults $3, students $1, under-12s free, plus free 4–8pm every Fri Sept–May; **morse museum.org**).

Park Avenue: The heart of Winter Park is a classy street of restaurants, fine shops and a wonderfully shaded park. At one end is Rollins College, a small but highly respected arts education centre that houses the beautiful **Cornell Fine Arts Museum**, with the oldest collection of paintings, sculpture and decorative arts in Florida (10am–5pm Tues–Sat, 1pm–5pm Sun, closed Mon and main holidays; $5 adults; **rollins.edu/cfam**). You should also take the **Park Avenue Walking Tour**, with free maps provided by the Chamber of Commerce (on New York Avenue). The shops of Park Avenue are a cut above most and, while you may find the prices equally distinctive, just browsing is an enjoyable experience with the charm of the area highlighted by the friendliness hereabouts. For shops both unique and fun, look for **Park Promenade Jewelers**, **Ten Thousand Villages** (international arts and crafts), Bebe's (children's clothes), the wonderfully eclectic **Bullfish** (a combination petshop and gourmet Mediterranean food store), **Siegel's** (men's clothing) and **Nicole Miller** (for women), plus **Peterbrooke Chocolatier**. Regular pavement craft fairs and art festivals add splashes of colour to an already inviting scenario, plus live jazz in Central Park once a month on Sundays in summer. Street parking allows 3 hours free, but there is a multi-storey car park on the corner of Comstock and Park Avenue, which is a better ½-day option. Keep an eye out for the **Sidewalk Art Festival** in March and **Autumn Art Festival** in October (**winterpark.org** and **parkave-winter park.com**).

Maitland Art Center

Scenic Boat Tour: Started in 1938, this is located at the east end of Morse Avenue and offers a charming, narrated 12ml/19km tour of this beautiful area. It takes you around the lakes and canals, giving a fascinating glimpse of some stunning houses, boat houses and lakeside gardens (property prices in the area start at around $1m and several top $10m!). Tours run 10am–4pm daily and cost $10 for adults and $5 for children 2–11, and it is one of the most relaxing hours you can spend in Orlando (**scenicboattours.com**).

Maitland Art Center: Further north from Orlando brings you to the city of Maitland and its delightful arts centre, which features periodic travelling exhibitions as well as its own regular displays of modern American art, sculpture gardens and a good range of art classes, notably for children. There is also a guided

A Dining Delight

Winter Park boasts some of the very best dining in Orlando, with a wonderful array of chic, contemporary choices. The trendy, upmarket range includes French, Italian and even Turkish restaurants, highlighted by the **Park Plaza Gardens**, which specialises in a modern mix of American and Continental cuisines, as well as a wonderful Sunday brunch. **Rocco's Italian Grille & Bar** is an exceptional authentic Italian choice, created by well-known restaurateur Rocco Potami, while **310 Park South** offers the epitome of elegant, European café culture. **Beluga** – 'Seafood, Martinis, Music!' – gets rave reviews for its fresh fish and fine steaks and you can also try the pavement bistro of **Briarpatch**, the 5-star French fare of **Jardins du Castillon** (wonderfully romantic) or Italian style of **Pannullo's**. We are big fans of **Luma on Park**, which is a 'gastropub' featuring fresh, daily specials from simple burgers to elaborate gourmet offerings and a fantastic range of wines (**lumaonpark.com**). Equally, **The Ravenous Pig** has a similar wide-ranging and upscale pub choice, from its fine micro-brewery to wonderful steaks and seafood. **Palmano's Roastery & Espresso Bar** is a great place to stop just for coffee.

history tour of the grounds, gardens and exhibitions on the third Monday of each month (9am–4.30pm Mon–Fri, noon–4pm Sat and Sun; adults $3, seniors $2, children free; history tour $3/person, reservations required; 407 539 2181, **maitlandartcenter.org**).

Lake Tibet-Butler Preserve: For a more natural view of Florida, head to this small reserve just north of *Walt Disney World* on SR535 (Winter Garden-Vineland Rd). The 440 acre/178ha park features 4mls/6.5km of trails and elevated boardwalks where the cypress swamps, freshwater marshes and scrub and pine flatwoods are home to a variety of gopher tortoises, turtles, armadillos and especially birds (it is on the Great Florida Birding Trail). Stop by the Visitor Center to pick up a map and see its wildlife exhibits (notably the 'pig-frog'!) and enjoy an hour or two of peace and quiet (10am–5 or 6pm daily, **http://myfwc.com/viewing/sites/site-c07.html**).

MOUNT DORA/ Lake County

Immediately to the west and north of Orlando is this large, rural county that is home to some genuinely unspoiled Florida charms and several small-scale attractions, including a notable state park and a well-known winery.

Mount Dora: This lovely town on beautiful Lake Dora is one of Florida's real hidden gems and a day here is a genuine breath of fresh air as you enjoy its unique mix of pleasant shops, restaurants, bars, inns and boat tours. Mount Dora is also renowned as a festival city, with 17 main annual galas. Visit **mountdora.com** to see if there is one during your visit (**4 July** and **Christmas** celebrations are especially notable, while the **Antique Boat Show & Heritage Festival** each March is one of Florida's finest). Start by taking the **Mount Dora Trolley** from the Lakeside Inn, a 1-hour narrated trundle around the streets (11am, noon, 1 and 2pm Mon–Sat, $12 adults, $10 2–13s; 352 385 1023), giving you a good feel for one of the 'Top 100 Great Towns of America', and a former key stop on the now-defunct Florida railroad. Then take a stroll round the compact centre, which is full of quaint shops, cafés and bars. Antique hunters are spoiled for choice but should

Downtown Disney marina

definitely check out **Pak Ratz** and the extensive **Village Antique Mall**, with more than 80 individual vendors. **Uncle Al's Time Capsule** is a must for all fans of movie and celebrity memorabilia (owner Al Wittnebert also features regular celebrity signings), while other unique stores include a **Walk in the Woods** (for clothing and Crocs shoes), **Li'l Guys and Dolls** and **The Clockmaker Shoppe**. The town even boasts **Ridgeback Winery**, which offers tastings of its handcrafted fruit wines. Other stops of interest include **Mount Dora Historic Museum** (the former town jail!), which displays more (free) local history, and the **Museum of Speed**, a constantly changing homage to high-powered American sports cars of yesteryear (plus other memorabilia such as vintage juke boxes and Coca-Cola® machines; 10am–5pm Mon–Fri; $9/person, no under-14s; 352 385 1945, **classicdreamcars.com**).

Another Mount Dora feature is its fine selection of B&B inns (a more upmarket, boutique choice than in the UK). Award-winning **Magnolia Inn** is worth a look (347 East 3rd Avenue), along with the **Grandview Bed & Breakfast** (442 East 3rd Avenue). The **Heron Cay Lakeview B&B** (495 Old Highway 441) is another good choice, but you certainly shouldn't leave without visiting the **Lakeside Inn**. On the National Register of Historic Places, this 124-year-old hotel embodies the South's genteel charm and rewards a stroll of its grounds and public rooms. A favourite retreat of US President Calvin Coolidge in the 1930s, it retains an air of refined quality, notably in the distinctive **Tremain's Lounge** and distinguished **Beauclaire Dining Room** (great Sunday Brunch). If nothing else, you should stop at the lovely coffee lounge, **La Cremerie Inc**, for a drink, pastry or ice-cream (352 383 4101, **lakeside-inn.com**).

Magnolia Inn

You can explore this area further with **Premier Boat Tours** by picking up the *Captain Doolittle* from the Lakeside Inn for a fascinating eco-tour of the lakes and renowned Dora Canal. As well as the inevitable gators, you may see raccoons, turtles, otters, birds of prey, waterfowl and other nesting birds along this unique and stunningly beautiful waterway. Narrated 2-hour tours go twice daily (10am and 2pm Mon–Fri, 11am and 2pm Sat and Sun; $22 adults, children reduced prices; Sunset Tours $12.50/person Fri and Sat; reservations recommended on 352 434 8040). Premier also operates some lovely lunch cruises and adventure outings with **Heritage Eco Tours** from the Tale Chaser Grille in the neighbouring town of Tavares (11am and 2pm Mon–Sat, 2pm Sun; $16 adults, children reduced prices for 90-minute narrated wildlife cruises including Dora Canal; 352 343 5608 or **florida-secrets.com/lake_county_tours. htm**). Another way to explore this area is with **Inland Lakes Railway**. Choose from the 75-minute *Mount Dora Champion* from Mount Dora to Tavares, Wed–Sun (1pm and 3pm, plus 11am Sat; $12 adults, $8 3–12s); the *Magnolia Sun Lunch Train*, a 2-hour journey from nearby Eustis to Tavares, every Sat at 12.45 with a set lunch ($35/person; reservations required); and the fine *Orange Blossom Dinner Train* every Fri and Sat at 5.15pm, a 3-hour round trip from Eustis with a 4-course dinner in a vintage 1948 dining car ($65/person; reservations required) and the 2-hour Italian Star Dinner Train from Eustis to Tavares every Thursday at 5.15pm ($35; to book, call 352 589

Mount Dora dining

You should definitely stop for a meal in Mount Dora, as it offers a wide range of temptations. Try a leisurely lunch at **Palm Tree Grille, The Gables** (with its Victorian garden setting), the charming **Goblin Market** or **5th Avenue Café**. For great pastries and cheesecake, call in at **Sunshine Mountain Bakery**, while **Mount Dora Coffee House** is the place to stop for coffee and the **Windsor Rose** is a genuine English tearoom. For something stronger, **Maggie's Attic** is a fabulous wine bar (and an equally good gift shop) and there are several notable pubs – try **Retro Winery & Bistro** or the unusual Icelandic flavour of **The Frosty Mug**. All the above also offer dinner, but our choice – especially if you get here before the sun goes down – is **Pisces Rising**, a beautiful Key-West-themed restaurant, with fresh, stylish decor, a charming outside Tiki-bar, another even more authentic interior bar – and a grandstand view of sunsets over Lake Dora. The food is excellent, too, with fresh Florida seafood and great steaks, plus an impressive wine list (352 385 2669, **piscesrising dining.com**).

4300 or visit **inlandlakes railway.com**).

Getting there: On US Highway 441 north-east of Orlando, take the (toll) Florida Turnpike to exit 267A for the (toll) Western Beltway (429), and the Beltway north to its junction with 441, from where Mount Dora is 10ml/16km further north. For more info, call the excellent **Mount Dora Chamber of Commerce** on 352 383 2165 or visit **mountdora.com**. The visitor centre is at 341 Alexander Street.

Lake Louisa State Park: Another local gem in Lake County just off Highway 27 (at the west end of Kissimmee's Highway 192), here you can enjoy some beautiful countryside, with 6 lakes, rolling hills (a Florida rarity!) and scenic landscapes. The park has more than 20mls/32km of hiking trails, a picnic pavilion, swimming in Lake Louisa (with lifeguards on duty end May–Aug) and offers 20 cabins (sleeping up to 6), if you fancy staying 'out in the wild'. Lake Louisa is also on the **Great Florida Birding Trail** (a 2,000ml/3,200km route linking 446 major bird-watching sites in the state) and is therefore great territory for a huge variety of birds. (8am–dusk daily, entry $4/car; 352 394 3969, **floridastateparks.org**).

Take half a day to explore further into Lake County along Highway 27 and you will discover the landmark **Citrus Tower**, built in 1956 with panoramic views from its glass observation deck 22 storeys high (9am–6pm Mon–Thurs, 7pm Fri and Sat; $4 adults, $2 3–11s; 352 394 4061, **citrustower.com**); **Lakeridge Winery**, a 127 acre/51ha estate producing some award-winning wines (free tours and tastings, 10am–5pm Mon–Sat, 11am–5pm Sun; 1800 768 WINE, **lakeridge winery. com**); and the unique **Presidents Hall of Fame**, a mix of waxworks and replica miniatures of presidential life and other Americana (9am–5pm daily, $9.95 and $4.95; 352 394 2836 or visit **presidentshallof fame.com**).

OSCEOLA COUNTY

The Kissimmee area is home to much more than just hotels, motels and Mickey Mouse. You'll find some of the most scenic and nature-orientated attractions in Central Florida here – you just need to know where to look!

Leu Gardens

Balloon trips

Florida is one of the most popular areas for ballooning and, if you are up early in the morning, you will often see several, especially in Osceola County. It's a majestic experience; the utterly smooth way in which you lift off into the early morning sky is breathtaking in itself, but the peace and quiet of the ride, not to mention the stunning views from 2,000ft/600m, are quite awesome. It's not a cheap experience, but it is equally appealing to all but the youngest children or those with vertigo or a fear of heights. It can also be a highly personalised ride, with basket capacity starting at just 4 people.

BRITTIP

Dresses are not advisable for balloon trips and hard-wearing shoes for the set-up and landing areas are essential.

Orlando Balloon Rides: The main operator in central Florida, this company was created from the merger of 2 of Orlando's most well-established and respected companies, Orange Blossom Balloons and Blue Water Balloons. Still under British ownership (led by Ian and Fiona Swift), it flies daily (weather permitting), meeting up in the restaurant at **Best Western Lakeside** on Highway 192 (by Marker 4) at 6am (the best flying winds are nearly always early in the morning) and then transferring to the take-off site. Here you can help the crew set up one of the balloons (for 4, 8, 10, 12 or 18 passengers in compartmentalised baskets, one of which is also disabled-accessible). All balloons are brand new and specially designed for passenger comfort and safety. The friendly team sets you up for a leisurely but exciting experience, and you are soon up, up and away in awe-inspiring style, floating serenely up into the sky or sinking to skim the surface of one of the many lakes (disturbing the occasional gator or deer). After about an hour, you come back to earth for a traditional champagne landing ceremony and return to the Best Western for a full breakfast and your balloonist's certificate. The full experience lasts 3–4 hours and costs $175/person (inclusive of tax). Children 10 and under fly free with their parents (additional children $95). Hotel pick-up is available at $10/person for the round trip, or for $20 you can be part of the chase crew and just enjoy the champagne landing and breakfast. Call 407 894 5040 or visit **orlandoballoonrides.com** for reservations (flights book up well ahead).

Thompson Aire balloon ride

Thompson Aire: This is another operator worth noting, with top local pilot Jeff Thompson, a ballooning veteran with more than 30 years' experience. He also flies every day (weather permitting), meeting at the **Black Angus Steakhouse** on Highway 192 (by Marker 5), and returning there for a hearty breakfast. Fares are $185 ($105 10–15s; 1 child under 10 can fly free with a paying adult; discounts for 4 or more adults travelling together). Call 407 421 9322 or visit **thompsonaire.com**. Hotel pick-ups can also be arranged at $15/person.

Airboat rides

The thrill of airboat rides can be experienced on many of Florida's lakes, rivers and marshes, but especially in Osceola County. An airboat is totally different to any boat ride you will have had – it's more like flying at ground level. As much a thrill as a scenic adventure, it has the bonus of exploring areas otherwise inaccessible to boats. Airboats simply skim over and through the marshes, to give you an alternative, close-up and highly personal view. Travelling at up to 50mph/80kph means it can be loud (hence you will be provided with headphones) and sunglasses are also a good idea to keep stray flies out of your eyes. It is NOT the trip for you, however, if you are spooked by crickets, dragonflies and similar insects that occasionally land in the boat! In summer months, a good insect repellent is essential.

BRITTIP

Look out for discounts on Boggy Creek's website, **bcairboats.com**, for either $1.50 off if you book online or for a $1 discount coupon.

Boggy Creek Airboat Rides: Several operations offer airboat rides in the area, from 'you-drive' boats that do barely 5mph/8kph to much bigger ones, but for the most quality-conscious (and downright friendly) operation, our vote goes to Boggy Creek. Its airboats can be found at its main site on Lake Toho at peaceful **Southport Park** (all the way down Poinciana Boulevard, off Highway 192 between Markers 10 and 11, and across Pleasant Hill Road into Southport Road – about a 35-minute drive) and at **East Lake Toho** (either take exit 17 off Central Florida Greeneway – 417 – and go 3mls/5km south on Boggy Creek Road, then right into East Lake Fish Camp, or take Osceola Parkway east until it hits Boggy Creek Road. Go left and then turn right at the Boggy Creek T-junction, then right into East Lake Fish Camp after about 2mls/3km). Boggy Creek's ½-hour ride features the most modern 18-passenger airboats in Florida, skimming over the local wetlands for a close-up of the majestic cypress trees and wildlife including eagles, ospreys, snakes and turtles, as well as the ever-present gators. The Southport Park site tends to be quieter, with more wildlife – especially in spring – but is a longer drive than to East Lake Fish Camp.

East Lake Fish Camp is itself a little gem, offering a variety of boating and fishing options (407 348 2040, **eastlakefish camp.net**) as well as the wonderfully authentic rural Florida charm of the restaurant and gift shop (8am–9pm daily). If you are heading for a morning airboat ride, consider arriving early for a huge all-day breakfast at the fish camp, where the more adventurous will want to try the local delicacies – catfish, frogs' legs and gator tail. For another great slice of local eating, the all-you-can-eat Friday 'home-style' buffet and Saturday night seafood buffet are fabulous value at $10.95 and $12.95.

BRITTIP

The best time for an airboat ride is first thing on a weekday morning when the wildlife is not hiding from the weekend boaters.

You don't need to book, just turn up, as boats go every ½ hour (9am–5.30pm daily); $22.95 adults, $17.95 3–12s). Don't forget the sunscreen as you can really burn on the water (just look at the unusual red colour Boggy Creek captain Chad has acquired over the years!). It also does a 1-hour Night Tour ($34.95 adults, $29.95 3–12s, mid-Mar–mid-Nov only; Mon–Thurs at Southport Park, Fri and Sat at East Lake) for a completely different and exhilarating experience (gator eyes

Boggy Creek Airboat Rides

glow red in the dark!), but you must book up to 2 weeks in advance. Finally, it offers a 45-minute private tour in its 6-passenger boat ($45/ person), which provides an even more personal view of this amazing area. Boggy Creek Airboats make a worthwhile and enjoyable ½-day adventure by the time you stop on its covered picnic terrace for a drink or ice-cream (407 344 9550 or **bcairboats.com**).

BRITTIP

For Celebration, don't stop at the first set of shops and services you come to off Highway 192. Keep going until you find Market Street and the centrepiece lake that lets you know you have found the proper downtown area.

Celebration

In 1994, the Walt Disney Company set out to build a 'new urban' neighbourhood, a model community with a friendly, welcoming spirit and strong traditional values. The result was Celebration, where picture-perfect Victorian homes mingle with smart, well-kept townhouses surrounding a charming array of shopping, dining and entertainment options. Today, it is a fully self-sufficient, bustling town with a hospital, schools, a cinema and 2 distinctive hotels. Located just minutes from Disney's southern border, Celebration is easily found off Highway 192. Enter at the landmark water tower via Celebration Ave, then follow signposting to Celebration Hotel, in the centre of town.

The town of Celebration

Once in the downtown area itself you are spoiled for choice when it comes to shopping. Market Street shops are open 10am–9pm Mon–Sat, noon–6pm Sun, with delightful boutique shopping at the likes of **Market Street Gallery** (featuring Disney collectables, Swarovski crystal, Lladro, and other fine gifts), **Hopskotch** (classic women's clothing, shoes and accessories), **Downeast – An Orvis® Shop** (Orvis clothing, housewares – and fly fishing equipment!) and **Lollipop Cottage** (children's clothing and gifts). Besides having a wonderfully whimsical name, **Soft as a Grape** is the place to find casual wear for the whole family, while the old-timey **Village Mercantile** carries collections such as Tommy Bahama, Oakley, Roxy and Quiksilver. Other speciality shops include **Jewel Box** for jewellery, and **Day Dreams Collectible Dolls & Bears**. Think it would be fun to scoot around in one of the many smart zero-emission vehicles you see parked around town? Hire one for the day from **Family Fun Station** on Front Street. More traditionally minded? Family Fun Station also has bicycles for hire and a video arcade, plus some new tours on the unique 2-wheeled Segway transporters (407 566 9846, **familyfunstation.com**). You can even get a traditional shave or haircut at the modern-yet-old-fashioned **Carr's**. There are also miles of bike and walking paths to take advantage of here, with the pretty lakefront setting, children's play area and periodic festivals. **4 July** is a huge event, with picnics, street entertainment and face-painting plus Disney-inspired fireworks over the lake (parking is laid on at the entrance to Celebration, with a park-and-ride bus for visitors), while the **Christmas** period sees festive events and nightly snow on Market Street (**celebration.fl.us.com**).

A cause for Celebration

Dining in celebration is another highlight. Stop in at **Main Street Café**, a funky 50s-style diner serving down-home American favourites such as turkey dinners, meat loaf and hearty sandwiches. Or try *Zagat* award-winning **Café D'Antonio**, authentic Italian cuisine in a sleek, family-friendly atmosphere (407 566 2233, **antoniosonline.com**); Spanish-Cuban **Columbia** creates unique combinations of authentic ingredients to create some mouth-watering dishes (407 566 1505, **columbiarestaurant.com**); **Celebration Town Tavern**, a casual ambiance, specialising in New England seafood dishes; **Seito Japanese Restaurant**, the place to go for contemporary sushi and fusion dishes; or **Boston Garden**, which serves up 'flown in fresh' seafood and lobster. You should also consider the fine dining of the **Plantation Restaurant** at the gracious Celebration Hotel, with contemporary American cuisine in old-world Florida charm. However, the main *Brit Guide* thumbs-up goes to **Sherlock's of Celebration** for its warm, welcoming atmosphere, intimate patio area and fabulous selection of pastries, beers, wines and traditional afternoon tea served without pretence – no chintz and ruffles here, just a comforting cup of tea in its proper vessel and a light lunch done right. Stop by for a meal (soup, salads, quiche, ploughman's lunch; you can even get Heinz beans on toast!), a pint of the finest imported brews (Italian, British, Irish and Belgian; 22 to choose from), premium Illy coffee and a fresh scone, or browse the extensive selection of 80 bottled wines available for purchase. Look for the familiar red phone box outside, then enjoy a comforting sense of home in the heart of Celebration (8am–9pm Mon–Thurs, 8am–10pm Fri, 9am–10pm Sat, 9am–9pm Sun; on Bloom Street just off of Front Street). Sherlock's can also be found at a smart new location at Cagan Crossings on Highway 27 (407 566 1866, **sherlocksgroup.com**).

Disney's Wilderness Preserve: This authentic slice of Florida is run by the Nature Conservancy (the world's leading private international conservancy group) in Poinciana, south of Kissimmee. The restoration of a 12,000 acre/4,860ha preserve is a work in progress and allows visitors in for various (well-marked) hiking trails. The preserve's pine and scrubby flatwoods, dry and wet prairies, freshwater marshes and forested wetlands are home to more than 300 wildlife species, including bald eagles, Florida scrub-jays and sandhill cranes, Sherman's fox squirrels, eastern indigo snakes and gopher tortoises, plus more than 50 butterfly species. Come here for a chance to unwind and enjoy the peace and quiet of the Florida countryside. Located at the end of Pleasant Hill Road (CR531; follow Hoagland or Poinciana Boulevard south off

A Brit of all right!

When **Sherlock's** owners Mark and Penny made the move to Celebration, they brought with them an innate knowledge of what people look for in a tea room and how to make guests feel like family from the moment they walk through the door. They also proudly display a wealth of memorabilia on the walls. Best of all, their dedication to doing things the proper way shows, down to the smallest touches. Sherlock's even blends its own teas, so you know you're getting impeccable quality and full, satisfying flavour. Be sure to inquire about their selection of fine wines or try what they like to call a 'conversational beer' (ask about your selection and the staff will strike up a knowledgeable conversation). And don't miss their signature Afternoon Champagne Tea!

Sherlock's

Highway 192, then turn right on Pleasant Hill; open 9am–5pm Mon–Fri; $3 adults, $2 6–17s). Trails may be closed due to flooding or conservancy work, so call 407 935 0002 in advance or visit **http://nature.org/wherewework/northamerica/states/florida/**.

Florida Eco-Safaris

Genuine eco-tourism is still in its infancy hereabouts, but Florida Eco-Safaris at Forever Florida is well worth visiting and is, for our money, one of the most outstanding non-theme-park attractions. It is both a 4,700 acre/1,900ha wilderness preserve and a working ranch. As well as a close-up of Florida's flora and fauna and its conservation issues, you get a taste of the original cracker-style life ('crackers' were the original cowboys, pre-dating their Western counterparts by 50 years), which is a fascinating slice of history. Eco-safaris, horseback safaris, nature walks and, for the kids, pony rides and a petting zoo, are the highlights, as well as the magnificent **Cypress Restaurant and Visitor Center**, which offers an essential 30-minute orientation programme into the conservancy's creation.

Beginning as a dream of gifted young biologist and ecologist Allen Broussard, Forever Florida was completed after his death (from complications of Hodgkin's disease) by his parents, Dr William and Margaret Broussard. They continue to give their time and energy to developing the wilderness as a non-profit-making memorial to their son. The education element here alone is awesome, and tours feature a strong conservation message in this tranquil, untouched corner of Florida. The 2-hour **Guided Eco-Safaris** is its stock-in-trade, a tranquil trundle in a large-wheeled, open-sided buggy round much of the woods, swamp and prairie that make up the Crescent J Ranch and Conservancy. Your tour guide gives the low-down on the fascinating history and environmental issues of the countryside, as well as some real insights into local life long before the tourists arrived. A boardwalk along Bull Creek affords the chance to get up close with a typical cypress 'dome' and breathe the amazingly pure air it gives out. You are likely to encounter alligators (at a safe distance), turtles, whitetail deer, armadillos and a host of bird life – including bald eagles and wild turkeys – as well as the native cracker cattle and horses (which make a great story in their own right), and you'll leave with a good understanding of the *real* Florida. Eco-Safaris cost $28 ($22 6–12s) and depart daily at 10am and 1pm. **Horseback Safaris** is another feature of Forever Florida (ages 12 and over; 10 and 11 only with proven riding experience), with the chance to enjoy its Western trail rides for 1, 2 or 3 hours with a native cracker guide, who offers his own observations on the local flora and fauna. Horseback Safaris cost $40, $60 or $80 (reservations needed 24 hours in advance on 1866 854 3837).

Horse riding

BRITTIP

Wearing long trousers and closed-toed shoes is essential for Florida Eco-Safaris' Horse Safaris. An early morning ride here was one of the most enjoyable hours we've spent in Florida.

If you want to go further into cowboy country, **Rawhide Round-up** is a half-day experience with cattle on the Crescent J Ranch, including lunch ($99). The **Horseback Safaris** can also be extended to 2 and 3 days ($199 and

$299), staying in bunk-house-style accommodation. The ranch **riding school** (which is working to bring back the genuine Florida Cracker breed of horse) is also adjacent to the Visitor Center, where you can see some amazing horse-training feats at first hand under the tutelage of experts Dean van Camp and Sandra Wise. They are happy to demonstrate and explain their work (for free!), and they also offer roping and cow-working skills classes (experienced riders only; call for prices). Forever Florida is a good 80-minute drive out of Orlando, 40mls/64km east on Highway 192, through St Cloud as far as Holopaw, then 7½mls/12km south on Highway 441, but is well worth the journey to experience the charm and tranquillity on offer (1866 854 3837, **floridaeco-safaris.com**).

Green Meadows Petting Farm

From one extreme to another, this is guaranteed fun for kids aged 2 to about 11 and their parents. It's the ultimate hands-on experience as, on the 2-hour guided tour, kids get to milk a cow, pet a pig, cuddle a chick or duckling, feed goats and sheep, meet a buffalo, chickens, peacocks and donkeys and learn what makes a farm tick. There are pony rides and a play area for the young ones, tractor-drawn hay rides, and the Green Meadows Express train tour. Don't forget your camera!

The shaded areas, free-roaming animals and peaceful aspect all contribute to another pleasant change of pace, especially as Green Meadows is barely 10 minutes from the tourist hurly-burly of Highway 192. Allow 3–4 hours for your visit. Drinks, snacks and gifts are available, but it is also the ideal place to bring a picnic (on Poinciana Boulevard; 9.30am–5.30pm daily, last tour 4pm; $21/person, $15 seniors, under-2s free; 407 846 0770, **greenmeadows farm.com**).

BRITTIP

Reader Lynda Letchford says: 'My 2-year-old really enjoyed Green Meadows. When you are in the pens with the animals, they nibble your toes and you step in all sorts, so wear enclosed shoes! Also, take some hand wipes for extra hygiene.'

Osceola County Pioneer Museum

Only just off the beaten track in Kissimmee, but a delightful discovery, is this small-scale homage to 19th-century Florida life, with a preserved 'cracker' (cowboy) homestead portraying how the original settlers lived in the 1890s. This fascinating little museum traces the history of Osceola County, and includes a cattle camp, nature walk, school house, country store and information centre with library. A recent addition is an 1890 citrus-packing operation from nearby Narcoossee, which was originally started by a family from the UK! But the real bonus is the volunteers who take you round, providing a fascinating view of life here more than 100 years ago. Situated on N Bass Road (turn off Highway 192 by the Wal-Mart Supercenter next to Medieval Times between markers 14 and 15. 10am–4pm Thurs–Sat, noon–4pm Sun; $2 adults, $1 children, under-5s free; 407 396 8644).

Florida Eco-Safaris

Reptile World Serpentarium

Another throwback to an earlier time in Florida is this wonderfully kitsch roadside halt in St Cloud. Florida is actually home to a wide variety of both venomous and non-venomous snakes, and all of them can be seen here. In all, there are more than 60 species of worldwide reptile featured in the clean, indoor exhibits (including the Australian taipan – rated the world's deadliest snake), but the main feature is the twice-daily (noon and 3pm) 'milking' of venom from some of the more hazardous residents (cobras and vipers) for snake research. Snakes are its stock-in-trade, but you will also meet turtles, gators and iguanas. Out on the eastern stretch of Highway 192, just past St Cloud, it's open 9am–5.30pm Tues–Sun (closed Sept); $5.75 adult, $4.75 6–17s, $3.75 3–5s; 407 892 6905.

BRITTIP

If you are brave enough to volunteer during the venom show, you won't actually be asked to help in this genuinely dangerous activity, but you will get the chance to stroke a boa.

Scenic Lake Tours

For a more sedate view of the local flora and fauna, try this company in downtown Kissimmee. Under the expert guidance of a local captain, you will head out on to Lake Tohopekaliga for a 1½-hour circuit in its 24ft/7.5m pontoon boat, taking in Makinson Island and the Shingle Creek waterway (with soft drinks, water and snacks included). Your guide will point out all the wildlife, from gators and turtles to ospreys and eagles, and you will gain a valuable insight into the local ecosystems. Once again, it's an opportunity to step into the real Florida, leaving the tourist version behind. Scenic Tours leaves the Toho Marina dock (on Lakeshore Boulevard; take Ruby Avenue off Broadway in downtown Kissimmee; 10am, noon, 2pm and 4pm Mon–Fri, 9am, 11am, 1pm and 3pm Sat and Sun; $25 adults, $15 6–12s, 5 and under free). There is also a special sunset cruise on request, while a new 2-hour Makinson Island Nature Tour, a combined cruise and guided tour of the island, is available daily ($50 adults, $30 children). Alternatively, try its fishing excursions on Lake Toho, some of the surrounding lakes or even inshore in the Fort Myers-Sanibel Island area. Fishing is from $250 for 2 anglers for 4 hours to $450 for a full 8-hour day, and saltwater inshore fishing is $350–550 (1800 244 9105, **fishingchartersinc.com**).

Dora Canal in Mount Dora

Warbird Adventures & Kissimmee Air Museum

Anyone even slightly interested in World War II aviation should certainly consider a trip to Warbird Adventures. *This is the best ride in town, bar none – guaranteed.* Not only do you get to fly in one of its 3 1945 T-6 Harvard fighter-trainers, but also, after a period of getting used to the front seat of this vintage 2-seater… you get to fly it! And you don't just handle the controls; your instructor will get you doing all manner of aerobatics. This is simply the most exhilarating ride we have ever tried, enhanced by in-flight video and wingtip camera to record every moment. It's the only place we know of where, 20 minutes after walking in off the street and with no previous experience, you can be flying a warplane. Roller-coasters? They're for wimps! Mind you, this is not cheap – a 15-minute flight costs

$220, a 30-minute trip is $390 and an hour $670. Aerobatics (on 30- or 60-minute flights only) cost $35, while the DVD is $50 and photos $25. Nevertheless, the memory of this would last a lifetime, and just the thought of it is still thrilling. Maximum weight is 18 stone/115kg and minimum height is 4ft/122cm. New here in 2008 was the **Kissimmee Air Museum**, a combination warplane showcase and restoration centre where you can get up close with the exhibits, which include a Bell 47 helicopter, an open-cockpit Ryan PT-22, a Boeing Stearman biplane, its 3 T-6 Harvards and the amazing one-off Aerocar, plus small-scale offerings like a WWII rifle collection and Luftwaffe memorabilia. Peer into the corners of the main hangar and you'll find the incredible Focke-Wulf 190 restoration project (**white1 foundation.org**), where the keen-as-mustard volunteer mechanics will happily explain the painstaking intricacies of their work to other enthusiasts. It can all be found just off Hoagland Boulevard, ½ml/1 km south of Highway 192, on the left (Air Museum open 9am–5pm Tues–Sat, $5/person, under-12s free; 407 870 7366, **warbirdadventures.com**, **ww11fighteraircraftfoundation.org** and **kissimmeeairmuseum.com**).

SEMINOLE COUNTY

You may well have arrived in the heart of Seminole County – with its historic town of Sanford – without realising it if you flew into Orlando Sanford International Airport. But it's worth pointing out the possible diversions here that get you well off the beaten track. In fact, if you wanted to finish your Orlando holiday with a day or two in the area, there are now several decent hotel choices, too, and you will get the chance to catch your breath after all the hectic theme-parking!

Altamonte Springs: Seminole County's second city (right off exit 92 of I-4) is now the area's brightest development of shops, restaurants, parks and lakeside walks, highlighted by the chic **Uptown** area. This ultra-modern and pedestrian-friendly urban scene is set around Cranes Roost Lake and features numerous small shopping plazas (as well as neighbouring Altamonte Mall – see page 350), with free open-air concerts at the Eddie Rose Amphitheater, karaoke, children's activities and other live entertainment (notably on Fri and Sat), plus the nightly Dancing Fountain Show at 8 and 9pm (not Tues). Some 19 restaurants and bars are added to the overall mix, notably the lively Elephant Bar Restaurant, Gina's Lakeside Grill and Volcano's Coffee Bar. Look up more at **uptownaltamonte.com**.

Black Hammock Fish Camp and Restaurant: One of the most fun and entertaining of the area's airboat rides is to be found off exit 44 on the Central Florida Greeneway (take SR 434 east, turn left on Deleon Street and left on to Black Hammock Road). This quiet backwater on beautiful **Lake Jesup** is home to Captain Joel Martin, a Frenchman who enjoys his Florida boating, and his ½-hour tour will take you into every nook and cranny of either the east or west lake (and this really is a great lake to explore, positively crammed with gators, including some of the biggest we've seen in the wild). It's an eye-opening adventure, and Captain Martin even keeps his own gators, large and small, back at the Fish Camp. The standard rides leave every ½ hour (no reservation required) and are $23.95 and $19.95 (under-11s),

WWII Fighter Aircraft Foundation, Kissimmee

but there are then 45-minute ($45/person), 1-hour ($39.94 and $34.95) and 45-minute night-time rides ($35.95/person), for which reservations are required (minimum 4 people; 407 365 1244, **theblackhammock.com**). Then you can grab lunch or dinner at the **Black Hammock Restaurant** (fine local delicacies, especially the catfish and gator tail, plus other dishes and a kids' menu; 11am–9pm Sun–Thurs, 11am–10pm Fri and Sat; 407 365 2201) or visit the **Lazy Gator Bar** (from 3pm Mon–Thurs, 2pm Fri, noon Sat and 11am Sun), with nightly drink specials and Happy Hour 3–6:30pm. You can rent canoes or fishing boats and enjoy another view of this unspoilt corner.

Bill's Airboat Adventures: This is a 90-minute tour on the St John's River east of Sanford in the company of river historian and conservationist Captain Bill Daniel for $45 ($30 under-13s) on his 6-person boat, subject to a $160 minimum (407 977 3214, **airboating.com**).

Central Florida Zoological Park: This private, non-profit organisation puts a pleasant, natural accent on the zoo theme, set in a wooded 116 acres/47ha of unspoilt Florida countryside with boardwalks and trails around all the attractions. These include more than 100 species of animal, weekend feeding demonstrations, educational programmes, a picnic area, pony rides and a butterfly garden, plus the Zoofari Outpost gift shop and a new water play area. It's good value at $9.95 for adults, $7.95 for seniors (60+) and $5.95 for 3–12s and is open 9am–5pm daily (not Thanksgiving Day or Christmas Day). Recent updates have enlarged several exhibits and added new habitats, including an Australian section with emus and kangaroos, while the Tropical Splash Ground is a great way for kids to cool down, with various animal 'fountains', raining trees, water tunnel and bucket dump (off exit 104 of I-4; 407 323 4450, **centralfloridazoo.org**).

Central Florida Zoo

BRITTIP

Visit Central Florida Zoo at the weekend and you will be offered a series of educational and enjoyable animal encounters (ranging from gators and snakes to hedgehogs).

Dana's Fishing and Scenic Tours: Brilliant bass fishing or guided scenic tours on Seminole County's lakes and waterways (by appointment only, call 407 645 5462 or **fishingincentralflorida.cc**).

Rivership Romance: For a lower-key approach, this is a great choice (daily out of downtown Sanford), especially for the lunch cruises on the wildlife-rich St John's River. The old-fashioned steamer can take up to 200 in comfort and adds a fine meal, live entertainment and a river narration, as well as providing a relaxing alternative to the tourist rush. Choose from the 3-hour lunch cruise (11am–2pm Mon, Wed, Fri, Sat and Sun; $38/person), 4–hour lunch cruise (11am–3pm Tues and Thurs; $48.50), or Moonlight Dinner Dance (7.30–11pm Sat; $53.75, all drinks extra). On Sundays see the **Special Event Show**, a themed dinner show that might feature a haunted holiday, a madcap wedding or something equally offbeat to entertain you while you eat (4–6.30pm, $46.25). To book, call 407 321 5091 or visit **rivershipromance.com**. Its dock can be found off exit 101A of I-4, east into Sanford, then left on Palmetto Ave.

Sanford: A fascinating city (more like a town by UK standards) on the south shore of Lake Monroe, Sanford is a historic centre, full of brick-paved streets, antique shops and an artists' colony at the heart of a major regeneration project. It's very much small-town America, having lost the growth battle with Orlando years ago, but it makes a peaceful diversion with some lovely walks, notably along the **Riverwalk**. Head for **Sanford Museum** (520 East 1st Street) to get an overview of how the city grew from incorporation in 1877, under the patronage of pioneering lawyer and diplomat Henry Sanford, as a hub on the St John's River, the 'Nile of America'. The free museum (11am–4pm Tues–Fri, 1–4pm Sat) illustrates the life and times of the city's founder, its growth into the 'celery capital of the world' and its modern history as a US naval base. From there, head on to **First Street** and check out the many restored turn-of-the-century buildings, stopping for a bite at **Morgan's Gourmet Café** or **The Hart Sisters Café, Tea Room and Catering**, a wonderful tea room with a sophisticated Victorian touch. It's one of the prettiest settings for a meal in Florida, serving some mouth-watering soups, sandwiches, quiches and soufflés, as well as a fabulous selection of tea trays. This little gem (11am–3pm Tues–Fri, 11am–4pm Sat) is on Park Avenue, 13 blocks out of the town centre (407 323 9448, **hartsisters.com**). Or you could try the equally stylish and Victorian **Higgins House** (on South Oak Ave and 5th Street; 407 324 9238, **higginshouse.com**).

State Parks: You could, of course, just head for one of Seminole County's splendid parks and follow the well-marked trails. **Wekiva Springs State Park** offers bike rentals, hiking, canoeing, swimming, picnic areas and shelters, and **Little Big Econ** state forest has 5,048 acres/2,045ha of scenic woodlands and wetlands. **Spring Hammock Preserve** offers 1,500 acres/607ha of wilderness to explore and the **Lake Proctor** area has 6mls/10km of equestrian, hiking and biking adventures. There are more trails along the Econlockhatchee River at the **Econ River Wilderness Area**, while **Chuluota** has 625 acres/253ha and the **Geneva Wilderness** Area 180 acres/73ha, including the **Ed Yarborough Nature Center** (407 665 7352, **co.seminole.fl.us/trails**).

St John's River Cruise: At Blue Spring State Park, there's an immensely personable 2-hour nature tour of this historic waterway, with interactive narration of the flora, fauna (including manatees in winter) and history. $20 adults, $18 seniors (60+), $14 3–12s. It leaves from Orange City marina at 10am and 1pm daily (not Thanksgiving or Christmas Day; take Highway 17/92 north from Sanford to French Avenue and head west for 1ml/1.6km; 407 330 1612 to check times, **sjrivercruises.com**).

Where to stay: At Altamonte Springs, look for the new **Embassy Suites Orlando North** (407 834 2117), while the Lake Mary area (right off exit 98 of I-4, closest to downtown Sanford) offers 5 smart, newly built hotels, the **Courtyard by Marriott** (407 444 1000), **La Quinta Inn & Suites** (407 805 9901), **Hampton Inn Suites** (407 995 9000), **Homewood Suites** (407 805 9111) and **Candlewood Suites** (407 585 3000).

BRITTIP

The Visit Seminole website (see overleaf) offers a '3rd night free' with many of its hotels with a weekend stay Mar–Dec.

Wekiva Springs State Park

More info: Look up **visitseminole.com** or go to one of the **Visitor Centers** at Orlando Sanford International Airport (in the Welcome Center as you exit the main building) or at 1230 Douglas Avenue in Longwood (a block west of exit 94 on I-4; 407 665 2900).

CITRUS COUNTY

If you enjoy the Seminole County experience, you may want to travel a little further, in which case the 2 state park delights of Citrus County, on the Gulf Coast north-west of Orlando, are well worth seeking for a day out.

Crystal River Preserve State Park: Head to this park, just north of Homosassa Springs, to find another wildlife fiesta. The Crystal River is home to the endangered manatee and it is possible to go swimming with these wonderful creatures, either on a self-guided or an organised tour. Winter and spring are ideal times for manatee sightings, but the park offers year-round outdoor adventure, with hiking and biking trails, kayaking, canoeing and fishing – or just pack a picnic lunch and enjoy a relaxing afternoon amid the natural beauty.

Getting there: Take the (toll) Florida Turnpike north to I-75, then, almost immediately, take SR44 west to Crystal River. **Admission:** Free (8am–dusk; 352 563 0246, **floridastateparks.org/crystalriverpreserve**).

Tubing on the Crystal River

BRITTIP

Never touch or disturb a wild manatee. They are protected animals and there are heavy fines, strictly enforced, for harassing them.

Homosassa Springs Wildlife State Park: Another major venture into Florida nature, this park also showcases the manatee (via their underwater observatory), plus whooping cranes, Key deer, bobcats, black bear and even a hippopotamus among an active display of rehabilitating animals. There are daily educational programmes on its wildlife (10.30 am, 11.30am, 12.30pm, 1.30pm, 2.30pm and 3.30pm), notably Florida's snakes and birds of prey, plus a hands-on children's education centre. The park's 210 acres/85ha encompass some of the state's loveliest landscape as well as the headwaters of the Homosassa River and this is extremely popular in the spring.

Getting there: As for Crystal River, but turn left on to CR490 just after Lecanta on SR44. **Admission:** $9 adults, $5 3–12s (9am–5.30pm, last entry 4pm; 352 628 5343, **homosassasprings.org**).

Excursion operators

For those without a car (or anyone just looking to put their feet up for a day or two), there is an increasing number of tours and day trips offered in and around Orlando, visiting as far afield as the Everglades, Miami, Florida Keys and even the Bahamas. And, if you are prepared to put up with a long day out (up to 16 hours), you can see a lot this way. However, if the main attraction of a trip to the Everglades is the airboat ride, you are better off going to Boggy Creek Airboats (see page 259) and avoiding the journey.

Florida Dolphin Tours: Make this first on your list to check as it offers an increasingly diverse range of memorable excursions, notably its swim-with-dolphins trips to the

Florida Keys and manatee swim adventure. More to the point, as a *Brit Guide* partner, it offers readers a *12½% discount* on all tours (see inside back cover). Choose from: **Sun, Sand and Scales**, an excellent-value all-day trip to Cocoa beach for an afternoon of fun in the sun, then a hands-on interactive animal show and an exciting night airboat ride in search of gators, all with a wonderful evening barbecue with unlimited beer, wine and soft drinks ($109 adults, $79 3–9s); the **Kennedy Space Center** trip, with transportation to both the Space Center and Astronaut Hall of Fame. Ask about options such as including an airboat ride, Lunch with an Astronaut, or even the Ultimate Kennedy Experience (prices from $89 and $79; there are also separate excursions for Shuttle and Rocket Launches); **Swim with the Manatees**, another all-day adventure (and the No 1 Florida attraction), featuring an all-you-can-eat breakfast buffet and 2-hour boat trip on the picturesque Crystal River (with snorkel and mask to check out at close quarters where the manatees swim). There is also a picnic lunch, airboat ride and trip to Homosassa State Wildlife Park, plus an educational briefing on manatees and a chance to see them being fed from the underwater viewing area ($119 and $89); **Swim with the Dolphins**, 2 trademark tours: a 1-day excursion to the beautiful Florida Keys with a 2-hour dolphin programme (and the choice of an organised or unstructured dolphin swim), or the grand 2-day trip, including accommodation, dolphin swim, buffet-style evening meal, Everglades airboat ride, alligator and snake-handling show (interactive!), and ½ a day to see Miami with shopping at Bayside or a boat tour along the inland waterways. The dolphin programme includes a full briefing and then about 30 minutes in the water, with dolphin contact guaranteed ($199–349); **American Football**, where high-energy action is up for grabs with an all-day excursion to see the Jacksonville Jaguars of the National Football League ($109/person, Aug–Dec); **NBA Basketball**, more sporting excitement with the Orlando Magic ($99/person, Nov–Apr); **Disney limo trips** give you the Grand Floridian character breakfast, Chef Mickey's dinner buffet or Planet Hollywood VIP (from $79); **The Fast & The Furious**, a day-trip to Daytona International Speedway followed by a Florida nature adventure at an airboat outpost, with animal encounters and a full barbecue ($109 and $79); **Clearwater Paradise**, a day-trip to the Gulf Coast for a beach adventure, including a ride on the huge Sea Screamer speedboat (or other optional boat excursions) and a chance to see the local dolphins in their natural environment AND work on your tan! (from $65 and $59 to $110 and $85); and a **Shopping Extravaganza**, an all-day retail adventure with stops at the top Malls and outlets like Wal-Mart and Lake Buena Vista Factory Shops ($45 and $35).

BRITTIP

More info on all tours on 407 352 5151 or visit **floridadolphintours.com**. To enjoy our special discount, just call and say '12½% off with the *Brit Guide*, please'!

Gator Tours: This company offers a wide range of more than 30 tours and sight-seeing around Orlando but specialises in day trips to the Kennedy Space Center and Daytona Race Speedway. The company also features Space Shuttle launches and landings, a wide range of sporting event tours (including golf, Orlando Magic

Swimming with the manatees

basketball and major motorsport), shopping excursions and even a unique **Orlando City Tour** ($59 adults, $49 2–11s). Its **Kennedy Space Center** trips go daily and can mix and match with the full range of opportunities, including Lunch with an Astronaut, the Astronaut Hall of Fame, NASA Up Close Tour and an airboat ride ($87–129 adults, $77–99 2–11s). It offers tickets and round-trip transportation to the Pepsi 400 at the world-famous **Daytona Speedway**, while the **Shoppers Paradise** ($39 and $29) excursion visits the Florida Mall and several of the discount outlets in one go. Other notable tours include transportation to the **Beaches** at Clearwater ($49); an **Everglades and Miami** adventure ($119 and $99); an all-day trip to all the fun of Miami ($69 and $59); and even transport (with or without tickets) to **Gatorland** ($35–49). For full pricing, call 407 522 5911 or visit **gatortours.com**.

Of course, a great day-trip can also be just jumping into your hire car and heading for one of Florida's superb Beaches (see Chapter 9, The Twin Centre Option).

SPORT

In addition to virtually every form of entertainment known to man, central Florida is one of the world's biggest sporting playgrounds, with a huge range of opportunities to either watch or play your favourite sport.

Golfing in Citrus County

Golf

Without doubt, the No 1 sport in Florida is golf, with almost 200 courses in the central Florida area. The weather makes it a popular pastime, but some spectacular courses, many designed by famous names like Greg Norman, Tom Watson, Arnold Palmer and Jack Nicklaus, add to the attraction, and there are numerous packages geared to golfers of all abilities. With an 18-hole round, including cart hire and taxes, from as little as $40 (average around $75), it's an attractive proposition and quite different from British courses. If you go in for 36-hole days, it's possible to save up to $30 by replaying the same course, while it is cheaper to play Mon–Thurs than Fri–Sun. Sculpted landscapes, manicured fairways and abundant water features and white-sand bunkers add up to some memorable golf. Winter is the high season, hence the most expensive, but many courses are busy year-round. Be aware that some courses pair golfers with little thought given to age, handicap etc., so, if 2 of you turn up, you may be paired with 2 strangers.

BRITTIP

Golf balls are inexpensive in Florida, so there's no need to bring your own. Good-quality clubs are usually available for hire, including top brands.

Virtually every course will offer a driving range to get you started, plus lockers, changing rooms and showers, while the use of golf carts is universal (many include the amazing GPS system, which gives the yardage for every shot). They all feature comforts like iced water stations and drinks carts that circulate the course (don't forget to tip the trolley drivers). Some have swimming pools, and all offer a decent bar and restaurant afterwards!

Your best starting point is one of the 5 **Edwin Watts** golf shops around Orlando for a free copy of the *Golfer's*

Guide or the *Guide to Golf* for a handy introduction to most of the courses available (and perhaps buy some new clubs at the Watts National Clearance Center just south of Wet 'n Wild on I-Drive; 407 352 2535, **edwinwatts.com**). **Tee-Times USA** (1888 465 3356, **teetimesusa.com**) offers excellent advice and a reservation service. **Daytona Beach** has an excellent website, **golfdaytonabeach.com**, devoted to the sport in its area (1800 881 7065), while **Visit Florida** also has its own golf section (**visitflorida.com/golf**).

Professional Golf Guides of Orlando: For a unique and personal touch, you can't beat this all-in-one instruction service, led by owner/operator and PGA member Phillip Jaffe, who is a mine of golf lore and knowledge, as well as great company. The guides take up to 3 golfers at a time around some of the finest courses, and can supply transport and clubs if required. The playing lesson is of the highest quality and includes full on-course instruction, course management strategies, game analysis, improvement suggestions, shot-making demos and a wrap-up lesson to leave you with the knowledge and skills to take your game to the next level. It is an eye-opening experience to play alongside Phillip and his staff of PGA professionals and well worth it for the keen golfer who wishes to improve their game in 1 round (407 227 9869 for rates or **progolfguides.com**). Alternatively, the **Nick Faldo Golf Institute** on the lower portion of I-Drive (1888 463 2536) is a great place just to hit a few balls.

BRITTIP

An early-morning tee-off in the summer can provide some peaceful and scenic golf.

Walt Disney World: Quick to attract the golf fanatic, Disney has 4 high-quality courses, including the 7,000yd/6,400m **Palm**, rated by *Golf Digest* in its top 25 (the 18th hole is reputedly one of the toughest in America), plus a 9-hole par-36 course, **Oak Trail**. Fees are $89–135 for Disney resort guests and $99–145 for visitors ($38 at Oak Trail), with 50% off after 3pm. Call 407 938 4653 for tee-times. Private and group lessons are available under PGA professional guidance, with video analysis and a range of club rentals.

BRITTIP

Some of the best tee-times at the *Walt Disney World Resort in Florida* golf courses are reserved for those staying at a Disney resort.

Champions Gate: Challenging and eye-catching, the 2 magnificent Greg Norman-designed courses to the south of Disney (exit 58 off I-4) are the International (a British-style links course) and the National (a more traditional style). The practice facilities, clubhouse, service and coaching (this is the HQ of the renowned David Leadbetter Academy) are world class, and there are stay-and-play packages with the superb Omni Orlando Resort (407 787 4653, **championsgategolf.com**).

Falcon's Fire: An outstanding course in Kissimmee, featuring the ProShot digital caddy system carts. Plenty of water around the course assures a testing 18 holes, but it is highly picturesque (407 239 5445, **falconsfire.com**; $77–147).

Grande Lakes Orlando: This wonderful resort complex just off

Champions Gate Golf Club

John Young Parkway is another Greg Norman masterpiece, offering 18 holes of Florida nature with a caddie-concierge service (call for rates, 407 206 2400, **grandelakes.com**).

Hawk's Landing: At the Orlando World Center Marriott, this beautiful course boasts extensive practice facilities, an award-winning shop, resort exclusivity and the world class teaching skills of Bill Madonna's Golf Academy (1888 305 9236, **marriott worldcenter.com**; from $89).

Hyatt Grand Cypress: A luxury experience on Winter Garden-Vineland Road (407 239 1904, **grandcypress.com/golf/**; $120–190), with 3 elegant 9-hole courses and a superb 18-hole links-style offering (all designed by Jack Nicklaus).

Kissimmee Oaks: Some majestic moss-draped oaks as well as 18 holes of memorable lakeside golf, all just 3½mls/6km south of Highway 192 in the Oaks Community off John Young Parkway (407 933 4055, **kissimmeeoaks golf.com**; $55–85).

Legends Golf and Country Club: Just 25 minutes from Disney on Highway 27 towards Clermont, this has a pleasant layout with rolling hills (unusual for Florida) in an ultra-peaceful location (352 243 1118, **legendsgolforlando.com**; $71–85).

Magnolia Plantation: Up in Seminole County, this wooded haven feels miles from the theme park world yet is just ½ hour away up I-4 among the lakes of the Wekiva River basin. Phillip Jaffe rates it a 'must-play' course (407 833 0818, **magnoliaplantationgolf club.com**; $45–90).

Magnolia Plantation Golf Club

MetroWest Country Club: On South Hiawassee Road, north of Universal Orlando (407 299 1099, **metrowest golf.com**; $90–130), this is a 7,051yd/ 6,447m masterpiece designed by Robert Trent Jones Snr, featuring elevated tees and greens, with rolling fairways and expansive bunkers.

Mystic Dunes: Just off Highway 192 near the Disney entrance, this course winds through native oaks and other vegetation and is a real test. The club-house features a wonderful menu plus the latest equipment (407 787 5678; **mysticdunesgolf.com**; $45–95).

Orange Lake Country Club: A huge vacation resort just 4mls/6km from Disney, with 2 18-hole courses, a 9-hole course and a par-3 floodlit 9 (407 239 1050, **orangelake.com**; $60–120).

Reunion Resort and Club: This extravagant club (in Davenport, just south of Disney, exit 54 off I-4) has 3 courses – a Watson, Palmer and Nicklaus collaboration, with 18 holes designed by each. Watson's 7,257yd/ 6,636m Independence Course is the most challenging, with a style not dissimilar to Augusta National (1888 300 2434, **reunionresort.com**; $50–85). Golf here is restricted to those who own property in the resort or are staying here (highly recommended; see page 95) but, with the 5-star clubhouse, it is well worth it.

Shingle Creek: A beauty from great local architect Dave Harman, set in dense oaks and pines along historic Shingle Creek. Within a mile of the Convention Center, it is a world-class

BRITTIP

The Reunion Resort hosts the annual **Ginn Open**, one of the top-paying tournaments on the women's golf circuit and a wonderful spectator event every April. Visit **ginnopen.com** for the full details in 2009. If you've never been to a golf tournament before, this is the ideal place to start.

facility with some amazing features, at the heart of this 5-star resort. The Brad Brewer Golf Academy is highly rated by Golf magazine and features a private teaching range with state-of-the-art technology (407 996 3306, **shinglecreekgolf.com**, $65–110).

Sugarloaf Mountain: This new club, the first in Florida from the respected team of Bill Coore and Ben Crenshaw, is carefully sculpted to follow the natural features of the land and offers 18 holes of the finest golf in the state (407 544 1104, **themountain.cc**; from $89).

Timacuan Golf Club: A stunning 7,047-yd championship course in Lake Mary (near Sanford), the front 9 resembles a Scottish links layout while the back 9 is all pineland and natural wildlife (407 321 0014, **golftimacuan.com**; from $85).

Victoria Hills: Rolling and aptly named, you'll find this in DeLand (midway between Orlando and Daytona Beach, exit 116 off I-4). It gets a big thumbs up from Phillip Jaffe ('A great track, very challenging!'), with a par-72 course and superb practice facilities (386 738 6000, **stjoegolf.com**; $40–80).

There are dozens of other courses, so this is only a sample. Don't be afraid to ask if green fees are negotiable as they can often be reduced at quiet times of the year or even on a quiet day. There are also often reductions for seniors. When you book, check on the club's dress code, as there are differences from course to course. Typically, you need a collared shirt, Bermuda shorts and no denim.

Spectating: For those just looking to see golf stars in action, Orlando has several big annual events. The **Arnold Palmer Invitational** at the Bay Hill Club off Apopka-Vineland Road in west Orlando (23–29 Mar 2009) is a major tournament (see Tiger Woods, Vijay Singh *et al.*; 1866 764 4843, **bayhillinvitational.com**). The **Children's Miracle Network Classic** is another big PGA date each Nov, held over Disney's superb Palm and Magnolia courses (407 835 2525, **childrensmiraclenetworkclassic.com**).

Mini-golf

Not exactly a sport, but definitely for fun, Orlando's many quite extravagant mini-golf centres are a big hit with kids and good fun for all the family (if you have the legs after a day at the parks!). Several attractions and parks offer mini-golf as an extra but, for the best, try out the self-contained centres, of which there is a large variety. Typically, Disney has some terrific courses of its own.

Disney's Fantasia Gardens Miniature Golf: Next to the *Swan* hotel just off Buena Vista Drive is a 2-course challenge over 36 of the most varied holes of mini-golf you will find. Fountains leap, hippos dance, and broomsticks march on the 18-hole crazy-golf-themed **Fantasia Gardens** – its style is taken from the classic film *Fantasia*, meaning lots of cartoon fun and a riot of visual gags as well as some diabolically difficult mini-golf. Watch out for *Toccata and Fugue in D Minor*, where good shots are rewarded with musical tones, and *The Nutcracker Suite*, where obstacles include dancing mushrooms! **Fantasia Fairways** is a cunning putting course, complete with rough, water hazards and bunkers to test even the best golfers. The 18 holes range from 40ft/12m to 75ft/23m, and it can take more than an hour to play a full round. Each course is $11.75 for adults, $9.75 for children (10am–11pm daily).

Disney's Winter-Summerland Mini-golf

Winter-Summerland Mini-Golf: The 36-hole courses are at the entrance to *Disney's Blizzard Beach* water park. Divided into 2 18-hole courses, these mini works of art feature a 'summer' setting of surf and beach tests (watch out for squirting fish) and a 'winter' variety of snow and ice-crafted holes, all with a welter of visual puns as befits the vacation resort of Santa's elves (yes, that's the theme, and kids love it – you can even see the marks where Santa landed his sleigh!). An adult round is $11.75 ($9.75 3–9s), a double round is half price. Open 10am–11pm. *Blizzard Beach* admission is not needed for the mini-golf.

International Drive: Mini-golf is a staple part of the scene here, with no fewer than 7 courses in the vicinity. Check out the 18-hole **Congo River** set-up in front of the Sheraton Studio City hotel and its 36-hole course just south of Wet 'n Wild; $10.45 adults, $8.45 under-10s, both courses for $14.50 and $12.50 – visit **congoriver.com** for a money-off coupon; 10am–1pm Sun–Thurs, 10am–midnight Fri and Sat); the 36-hole **Tiki Island Golf** behind the Salt Island restaurant north of Sand Lake Road, where a hole-in-one at the last hole sets off the volcano (10am–11.30pm; $10 adults, $9 children, or $13 and $12 for both courses); **Hawaiian Rumble** has 36 holes next to WonderWorks on I-Drive (and in Lake Buena Vista); 10am–11pm Sun–Thurs, 10am–midnight Fri and Sat; $9.95 adults, $7.95 4–10s for 18 holes and $14.95 and $11.95 for 36; see **hawaiianrumble orlando.com** for a discount coupon); the unusual indoor, glow-in-the-dark 18 holes of the **Putting Edge** at Festival Bay, at the top of I-Drive (11am–9pm Mon–Thurs, 11am–10.30pm Fri, 10am–10.30pm Sat, 11am–7.30pm Sun; $9.35 adults, $8.35 7–12s, $6.85 5–6s, $3 extra for a second game); **Pirates Cove**, next to the new The Square development, remains the original I-Drive set-up, with caves, waterfalls and rope bridges to test your skills over 2 18-hole courses (the Captain's Course and the harder Blackbeard's Challenge; 9am–11.30pm daily; $9.95 adults, $8.95 children, or $13.95 and $12.50 for all 36 holes). There is a near-identical Pirates Cove set-up at Lake Buena Vista at the back of the Crossroads shopping plaza.

Congo River Golf

New in 2007 was the amazingly detailed **Gator Golf and Adventure Park**, just past Carrier Drive, next to Murphy's Arms Pub. Here you can watch gator shows and gator wrestling, and sink your teeth into a round of surprisingly challenging mini-golf (10am–11pm Sun–Thurs, 10am–midnight Fri and Sat; $12 adults, $10 under-12s).

Kissimmee: Here you'll find the wonderfully scenic 36-hole **Congo River Golf & Exploration Co** set-up on Highway 192 (just south of the junction with Highway 535, between mile markers 12 and 13) (10am–midnight daily). Then there is the 18-hole **River Adventure** just north of Medieval Times (markers 14–15; 9am–11pm; $8, second game $4); and the 2 imaginative cowboy-themed mini-golf courses of **Bonanza Golf** (also on Highway 192 by marker 5) 9am–midnight; $7.95/person. **Pirates Cove** is a 36-hole course next to Old Town (behind the Red Lobster restaurant, between markers 9 and 10; 9am–11.30pm); as is **Jungle Golf** (Highway 192 at mile markers 4 and 5; 9am–11:30pm; $9.95 adults, $8.95 4–12s, all-day play for $11.95).

Freshwater fishing

Freshwater fishing on central Florida's abundant rivers and lakes (St John's River, Kissimmee Chain of Lakes, and Lake Tohopekaliga, for example) attracts enthusiasts worldwide. In addition, many visitors find a quiet day's angling provides an enjoyable and welcome change of pace. The primary draw for most out-of-towners is the opportunity to catch giant Florida bass – which often grow to record sizes in the area's grassy waters – and view some of the wildlife in its natural environment.

To fish in a freshwater lake, river, or stream you need a Florida Freshwater Fishing License, available from the Florida Fish and Wildlife Commission (**http://myfwc.com/license/index.html** to purchase online at a $2.25 surcharge – have your credit card handy). You'll be issued with a temporary licence number within minutes, enabling you to fish right away. A permanent licence will be mailed within 48 hours. A 3-day licence costs $17. It is also advisable to book your reservation at least 2 weeks in advance, especially in holiday periods.

AJ's Freelancer Bass Guide Service: The oldest continuously operating guide service in central Florida specialises in trophy bass fishing on Lake Toho in Kissimmee. Toho is rated the best big bass lake in the USA, and AJ's holds the record for largemouth bass here – 16lb 10oz! Saltwater guide trips are also offered. *The Freelancer* is owned and operated by Captain A James Jackson, one of the top fishing guides in the country, providing a highly personalised service to both regular and novice fishermen. All guides are experienced, full-time professionals and run trips of 4, 6 and 8 hours. Rates start at $250 for a ½-day (4-hour) guided trip. For other services, photos, testimonials and fish reports, visit the excellent website **orlandobass.com**. For reservations call 407 348-8764 or email **capjackson@aol.com**.

Kissimmee fishing: For other opportunities, try **Scenic Lake Tours** (see page 264) or visit the Outdoor Recreation section of **floridakiss.com**. Go bass fishing (catch-and-release) at *Walt Disney World* (from any of 11 of its resort hotels, plus the Marketplace at *Downtown Disney*) for $225 or $250 for 2 hours for a boat with up to 5 people.

Water sports

Florida is mad keen on water sports of all types. So, on any area of water bigger than your average pond, don't be surprised to find the locals water-skiing, jet-skiing, knee-boarding, canoeing, paddling, windsurfing, boating or indulging in many other watery pursuits.

Buena Vista Watersports: This is the place to come for jet-skiing ($55/½ hour), water-skiing, wakeboard and tube rides ($85/½ hour) on Little Lake Bryan by the Holiday Inn Sunspree on Highway 535 (**bvwatersports.com**).

Orlando Watersports Complex: Just off the Beachline Expressway (528) near Orlando International Airport, this is an elaborate teaching facility featuring wakeboarding and water-skiing, by boat and suspended cable, for both novices and experts. It has a huge range of classes for individuals, groups and birthday parties. (407 251 3100 or visit **orlandowatersports.com**).

Slider Spectacular at Orlando Water Sports

Walt Disney World: Disney offers all manner of boats (from catamarans to canoes and pedaloes) and activities (from water-skiing to parasailing) on the main **Bay Lake**, as well as the smaller **Seven Seas Lagoon**, **Crescent Lake** and **Lake Buena Vista**. Parasailing (from *Disney's Contemporary Resort* – see pages 68–9) comes in 2 price categories: a Regular flight, which goes to 450ft/137m for 8–10 minutes, and a Premium flight to 600ft/183m for 10–12 minutes. It costs $95–120 solo or $160–185 tandem, while boat rentals vary from $33/½ hour (21ft pontoon boat) to $125/hour (personal watercraft and wave runners), and can be found at 11 Disney resorts, plus The Marketplace at *Downtown Disney*. To book, call 407 939 0754.

Horse riding

For a more peaceful and scenic way to see some of Florida, take a tour on horseback. Several locations feature it, and we thoroughly recommend giving it a try.

Grand Cypress Equestrian Center: One of the foremost equestrian centres in America, this is part of the 1,500 acre/608ha Grand Cypress Resort, and all its rides and facilities are open to non-residents. This stunningly equipped equine haven offers a dazzling array of opportunities for horse enthusiasts of all abilities. A full range of clinics, lessons and other instructional programmes is available, from ½-hour kids' sessions to all-summer academies, plus a variety of trail rides. Serious horse riders will note that this was the first American equestrian centre to be approved by the British Horse Society, and it operates the BHS test programme. Inevitably, this 5-star facility does not come cheap but it is a valuable experience, especially for children. Private lessons are $55/½ hour or $100/hour; a package of 8 1-hour group lessons is $280. Western Trail Rides (4 different 45-minute excursions for riders of all abilities, minimum age 10) are $45–85; 8.30am–6pm Mon–Fri, 8.30am–5pm Sat and Sun. Take exit 68 on I-4 on to Route 535 north, turn left at the traffic lights after ½ml/1km, then go north for 1ml/1.6km past the Grand Cypress Hotel and it's on the right (407 239 1938, **grandcypress.com/equestrian**).

Horse World Riding Stables: On a smaller scale but no less charming, this is on Poinciana Boulevard, just 12mls/19km south of Highway 192. This gets you further out into the wilds and you can spend anything from 1 hour to a full day enjoying the rides and lessons. The 3 main rides through 750 acres/304ha of untouched Florida countryside are the Nature Trail ($39 adults, $16.95 5 and under riding double with parent), a walking-only tour of 45–50 minutes for beginners aged 6 and over; the

Grand Cypress Equestrian Center

Intermediate Trail (10 and over) for nearly 1 hour ($47); and the Advanced Private Trail, a 75–90 minute trip with a private guide for advanced riders ($69). There is also a picnic area with fishing pond, playing fields, pony rides for under-7s ($7) and farm animals to pet. Riding lessons are $49/hour for group or private lessons. A 3-hour Children's Horse Camp (8–14s) is available at 9am on Saturdays (call for prices). There is no charge for just looking, and the stables are open 9am–5pm daily (407 847 4343, **horseworldstables.com**).

Spectator events

When it comes to spectator events, Orlando is not quite as well furnished as other big American cities, but there is always something for the sports fan who would like to see a local game. There are no top-flight American football or baseball teams, but there is an indoor version of gridiron (American football) and Arena Football, plus Spring Training (pre-season) for several baseball teams (notably Atlanta in *Disney's ESPN World of Sports*™).

Basketball: The main sport is basketball with the **Orlando Magic** of the National Basketball Association (NBA). The season runs Nov–May (with exhibition games in Oct), and the only drawback is that the 16,000-seat **Amway Arena** where they play (on Amelia Street, exit 83B off I-4, turn left, then left again) is often fully booked. Contact the Center's box office (407 649 3245) to see if there are any tickets, though you'll have to call in person to buy them (from $12 in the upper seats to $250 for the best seats courtside), or try TicketMaster on 407 839 3900 for credit card bookings. **Florida Dolphin Tours** (407 352 5151, **floridadolphintours.com**) also offers Orlando Magic packages for $99 with transport. See more on **nba.com/magic/**.

American football: For the real thing, the nearest teams in the **National Football League** are the **Tampa Bay Buccaneers**, 75mls/120km to the west, the **Miami Dolphins**, 3–4 hours' drive south, down the Florida Turnpike, or the **Jacksonville Jaguars** way up the east coast past Daytona, a 3-hour drive up I-4 and I-95. Again, TicketMaster can give you ticket prices ($40–120) and availability (Sept–Dec; and the Buccaneers sell out early these days). Once again, *Brit Guide* partner **Florida Dolphin Tours** (see pages 268–9) runs a limited number of trips to Jacksonville each season, and these are worth seeking out.

Arena football: The **Orlando Predators**, one of America's top teams, is also popular at the Amway Arena (Mar–June, $15–130). Call several days in advance to see one of its home games that feature lively entertainment as well as its fast, hard-hitting version of indoor gridiron (407 447 3300, **orlandopredators.com**).

BRITTIP

We rate the local sports experiences very highly if you want to partake in some real Americana. You don't need to understand the details of the game, just turn up and enjoy the genuine fan-friendly atmosphere and enthusiastic excitement.

Baseball: A spring training opportunity can be seen at Osceola County Stadium in Kissimmee, where the **Houston Astros** take up home each Mar. Being part of the audience here is to experience real local colour. Call 321 697 3201 for more info, or

Orlando Magic

© OCVB

TicketMaster for tickets on 407 839 3900. In fact, the best opportunity is a **Tampa Bay Rays** game in St Petersburg; tickets are nearly always available and the indoor stadium is superb (see page 277).

Disney's ESPN World of Sports™

Inevitably, the best all-round sports facility in the area is a Disney project, though there is only a handful of genuine spectator events here. *Disney's ESPN World of Sports*™ is a 220 acre/86ha state-of-the-art complex, featuring 30 sports and just wandering round even when there's no game is awesome. The complex's main features are a 9,500-seater baseball stadium, a softball quadraplex, an 11-court tennis complex, athletics track and extensive sports field.

The Ballpark: Top of the crop for a must-see visit, this is home for spring training of baseball's **Atlanta Braves**, where the crowds flock for 16 pre-season games in late Feb and Mar (highly recommended; tickets $15–30, 407 839 3900). This is a big deal for American sports fans and games do sell out. The complex is also home for a month from mid-July to the NFL's **Tampa Bay Buccaneers** for their pre-season training, and watching these amazing athletes in action is an eye-opening experience, even if it is only in practice (available FREE on a daily basis). The centre's extensive fields also cater for soccer, lacrosse, baseball and softball, and you can often see some keen sporting action just with college and high school teams. **Disney's Soccer Showcase** (late Dec) is a fine example of this, with some 400 teams competing under the eye of various scouts. The level of skill is bound to surprise you. Standard admission is $11.75 for adults, $9 for 3–9s, but it is also an optional extra with all Premium and Ultimate tickets (excluding special events like baseball). *Disney's ESPN World of Sports*™ is off Osceola Parkway, on Victory Way. Call 407 939 4263 for events and prices or visit **disneyworldsports.com**.

Extreme Bulls at Silver Spurs Rodeo

Walt Disney World Marathon: A major annual event, its 15th running will be on 11 Jan 2009. Some 13,500 runners take part – including some of the world's leading athletes – drawing huge crowds and taking in all 4 Disney theme parks. Be aware that the parks face some serious disruption but, as with the London Marathon, the Disney version is a great spectacle. The annual half-marathon takes place the same weekend.

Rodeo

An all-American pursuit straight out of the Old West, the **Silver Spurs Rodeo** is staged twice a year at the brand new, 8,300-seat Silver Spurs Arena. The biggest event of its kind in the south-east, it is held in early Oct and mid-June (in 2008; check its website for 2009 dates). However, it sells out fast so book in advance on 407 677 6336 (**silverspurs rodeo.com**).

The event features classic bronco and bull riding and attracts top competitors from as far away as Canada. The arena is part of **Osceola Heritage Park**, which includes Osceola County Stadium (for baseball) and the Kissimmee Valley Livestock Show and Fair Pavilion. The **Silver Spurs Arena** is a state-of-the-art facility that can be used for concerts too, and there isn't a bad seat in the house.

Motor sport

Richard Petty Driving Experience: For the guaranteed ultimate in high-speed thrills, *Walt Disney World* has its own racetrack (next to the car park for the *Magic Kingdom*). Here on the 1-mile oval, you can experience one of its 650bhp stock cars as either driver or passenger at up to 145mph/233kph, with programmes devised by top NASCAR driver Richard Petty. Choose from the 3-lap **Ride-Along Experience**; the 3-hour **Rookie Experience** (with tuition and 8 laps of the speedway); the **Kings Experience** (tuition plus 18 laps); and the **Experience of a Lifetime** (an intense 30-lap programme). The Ride-Along Experience will probably appeal to most (16 and over only) – 3 laps of the circuit with an experienced driver lasting just 37 seconds a lap but an unbelievable blast all the way. Your start from the pit lane takes you from 0 to 60mph/97kph in a couple of seconds and you are straight into Turn One with your brain some distance behind – it's a bit like flying at ground level! It's hot and noisy and you must wear sensible clothes (you have to climb in through the window), but it is definitely the real thing in ride terms and a huge thrill.

You don't need to book for the Ride-Along Experience, which is available daily, and there is no admission fee, so you can come along just to watch (8am–1pm). The 3 driving programmes (not Tues or Thurs) all require reservations, while the track is sometimes closed Oct–Apr for race testing. However, wait for the prices: $109 for Ride-Along; $399 for Rookie; $799 for Kings; and $1,249 for the Experience of a Lifetime. You must be 18 or over for the last 3 (407 939 0130, **1800bepetty.com**).

Daytona International Speedway: Just up the road in Daytona (take I-4 east, then I-95 and Highway 92), race fans will find lots more big-league car and motorcycle thrills. It hosts more than a dozen race weekends a year, including stock car, sports car, motorcycle and go-kart, and highlights are the **Rolex 24** (a top 24-hour sports car event, 24–25 Jan 2009), the world famous **Daytona 500** (15 Feb), **Pepsi 400** (4 July) and **Bike Week** (27 Feb–8 Mar). The big events attract audiences of some 200,000 devotees and provide some of the most exciting sport anywhere in the world (386 254 2700, **daytona internationalspeedway.com**).

And don't forget to visit the fun, interactive **Daytona USA** attraction as well, and the chance to tour the Speedway (see pages 283–4). The **Richard Petty Driving Experience** is available here too (but only for 16s and over) and the $135 fee for 3 laps of the world-famous, steeply banked 2½ml/4km tri-oval includes entrance to Daytona USA as well. There is also a Daytona Highbanks 8 ($525), Daytona Super 16 ($1,249) and grand Daytona Experience ($2,099).

Okay, that's the local area sorted out; now let's take you further afield…

Daytona USA

9 The Twin Centre Option

or To Orlando – and Beyond!

While Orlando and its surroundings continue to get bigger and better year by year, it is equally true that there's a LOT more to see in the rest of Florida, with some magnificent twin-centre options. From St Augustine in the north-east to Key West in the extreme south (the 'Floribbean'!), it's easy to find wonderful resorts, glorious beaches and more family-friendly attractions.

The beaches of the Gulf (west) coast, the Atlantic coast from Ormond Beach all the way down to Miami, and the fabulous Florida Keys all feature some of the best and most inviting seaside escapes in the world, while the cities of St Augustine, West Palm Beach, Daytona, Tampa, Fort Lauderdale and Miami provide another fascinating facet of the Sunshine State. Two-centre (or fly-drive) options are common with most tour operators, but it is also easy to arrange your own stays away from Orlando, be they for a week, 2 weeks or just a night. A cruise-and-stay holiday is also a great choice these days, with the cruise ports of Tampa, Port Canaveral, Port Everglades (Fort Lauderdale) and Miami all within easy distance of Central Florida.

BRITTIP

The Florida Turnpike (toll) is the main route south-east from Orlando, but it is a seriously dull drive. If time is not a factor, try taking the Beachline Expressway (528) east and then I-95 or, better still, Highway 1, south. The journey will be far more rewarding

So, with the idea that you can head out from Orlando in almost any direction in search of a great twin-centre experience: to the **east**, Cocoa Beach, New Smyrna Beach, Ormond Beach and the famous Daytona Beach all have terrific appeal and are barely an hour's drive. The sea is a degree or so cooler on the Atlantic side, and the surf and currents are more noticeable, hence this is good surfing territory; **north-east** you have the historic city of St Augustine about 2 hours away; go **west** for the city of Tampa and miles of pristine sands, from Clearwater Beach all the way south to Naples and lovely Marco Island. This tends to be slightly better for families with younger children, while the Clearwater-St Pete Beach area is a perfect combination with Orlando (about 1½–2 hours' drive); go **south-east** and you hit Vero Beach, West

BRITTIP

Spanish adventurer Ponce de Leon was searching for the Fountain of Youth when he arrived at the site of St Augustine in 1513. The modern day Archaeological Park tells the full story of his arrival and the discovery of the continent of America – and offers the chance to drink the famous waters. Visit **www.fountainofyouthflorida.com**

Palm Beach, Fort Lauderdale and incomparable Miami (about a 4-hour drive); continue **south** and there are the Keys, a magnificent 110ml/177km chain of islands linked by roads and bridges, culminating in eclectic Key West. So, heading north-east first, here's what you find:

St Augustine

A 2-hour drive up I-4 and then I-95 brings you to America's oldest city. Founded by Spanish conquistadores in 1565, St Augustine is a genuine historic relic, full of authentic buildings and signs of the original settlement around the imposing Castillo de San Marcos. Much of the original walled city still remains and 'old' is a much-revered term here, as the 18th- and 19th-century Mediterranean influences are seemingly everywhere. Walk the narrow, uneven streets of the **Restoration Area** to discover a host of colonial architectural treasures, now home to gift shops, restaurants, pubs, ice-cream parlours, antiques shops, quaint B&Bs and other historic attractions. Golf fans should head for nearby Ponte Vedra, where the **World Golf Hall of Fame** is located.

To see as much as possible, you can hop on a horse-drawn carriage, the **St Augustine Sightseeing Train** or the **Old Town Trolley Tours** for a narrated ride round the city. For a spookier experience, try walking the streets with **Ghost Tours of St Augustine**, with your guide in period costume. Other tours reveal St Augustine's rich architectural heritage (also the product of British and colonial American rule). Florida railroad mogul Henry Flagler was another big influence here, building some magnificent hotels for his 'passengers to paradise'. The **Lightner Museum**, formerly Flagler's Hotel Alcazar, is home to his turn-of-the-century treasures, including Tiffany and other glass works of art. Don't miss the hotel's remarkable indoor swimming pool – considered a wonder in its day.

Other attractions include a modern theatre, art galleries, **Potter's Wax Museum**, **Ripley's Believe It Or Not Museum** and a local chocolate factory. Restaurants range from **The Spanish Bakery** and the famous, family-owned **Columbia Restaurant**, where recipes have been handed down for more than a century, to a modern microbrewery, **A1A Aleworks**.

BRITTIP

Festivals are an integral part of St Augustine's routine, from monthly art walk nights to annual costumed torchlight re-enactments of British occupation and the City Birthday on 8 September.

Where to stay: The city's premier hotel is the historic **Casa Monica** (904 827 1888, **casamonica.com**), but there are also numerous B&Bs, plus chain hotels like Best Western and Hampton Inn. The boutique **St George Inn** (904 827 5740; **stgeorge-inn.com**) is also a good choice.

More info: Dept of Heritage Tourism, 904 825 1000, **historicstaugustine.com**.

Volusia County

Travel south from St Augustine and you arrive in one of Florida's most famous beach areas that has much tourist appeal.

Daytona Beach: Only an hour from Orlando along I-4 east, this area is undergoing something of a transformation to a more

Ponce de Lion Inlet lighthouse

sophisticated seaside resort with all mod cons, including new hotels and restaurants, but it is still extremely family-friendly (see **familybeach break.com**). It gets busiest at spring break (the weeks leading up to Easter) but there is something for everyone. The prime attraction is the array of good **beaches** (some of which you can drive on – for a $5 toll, speed limit 10mph/16kph). From these open expanses of sands, you can go boating, parasailing, biking, jet-skiing and fishing, while there is also plenty of sight-seeing. Base yourself in the **Oceanfront** area and you are at the heart of all things beach-related, with the **Pier**, the historic **Bandshell**, **Boardwalk** and the shops and restaurants of **Ocean Walk Village**.

BRITTIP

Look out for Speeding Through Time, a series of memorials and plaques along Daytona's Boardwalk, highlighting the world speed records set on the beaches, including those of Britons Sir Henry Segrave and Sir Malcolm Campbell.

Here you have **RC Theatres' Ocean Walk Movies 10 Cineplex**, the fun of the **Mai Tai** bar, seafood emporium **Backwater Fresh Grill & Tavern**, **Johnny Rockets** diner, **Adobe Gila's Cantina** (check out a near-lethal range of cocktails!), **Starbucks**, and some unique shopping at **Maui Nix Surf Shop**, **Candle Gallery**, **Bath Junkie** and market-style **Shoppes Bazaar**. When you want to eat, our recommendation is the film-themed offerings of **Bubba Gump Shrimp Co.** (based on the film *Forrest Gump*). With fun decor, a wonderfully casual style and an excellent menu (food that lives up to its surroundings), it is ideal for a quick lunch or more leisurely dinner.

Daytona Lagoon

BRITTIP

Spend the day on Daytona beach, then try some water park fun at Daytona Lagoon after 4pm, when admission is only $14.99.

Right opposite Ocean Walk Village is **Daytona Lagoon**, a combination water park, go-kart track, mini-golf course, arcade and laser tag centre, plus an exciting new thrill ride, The Phoenix, which propels riders on a 210° arc to experience 4Gs of force at 55 mph. The water park consists of a wave pool and lazy river, 10 different flumes and an area purely for toddlers (adults $27.99, children under 4ft/122cm $19.99). The 3 9-hole mini-golf courses ($7 for 18 holes), single and double go-karts ($7–9), laser tag (must be above 3ft 6in/108cm, $7), The Phoenix ($7–12) and classic carousel ride ($1) are all separate items. Find out more at **daytona lagoon.com**.

Historic **Downtown Daytona Beach** on Beach Street is the heart of the city, with a museum of local history, restaurants, nightclubs, coffee bars and a performing arts theatre, all in a riverside setting. The **Angell & Phelps Chocolate Factory** is another notable curiosity. Head to the Riverfront in early evening when the street takes on a café society style. There are plenty of worthwhile places to eat, but for something different try the lively **Loggerhead Club & Marina** (right on the river at Ballough Road) or sophisticated **Rain Supper Club** (on Seabreeze Boulevard). Similar upmarket choices are **Martini's Chophouse Restaurant** (on S Ridgewood Avenue) and **The Cellar** (on Magnolia Avenue).

Other local highlights include a variety of ways to enjoy the waterways. Cruising the intra-coastal Halifax River to see the sights, including dolphins at play, is highly worthwhile. Check out a **tiny cruise line** (at Halifax Harbor Marina on S Beach Street; 386 226 2343) for 4 different cruises ($12.44–23.24), which include a lovely Sunset/City Lights tour Apr–Oct. Head south along S Atlantic Avenue and you find even more choice of beaches and attractions, including **Sun Splash**, **Frank Rendon Park** and especially **Lighthouse Point Park**, a 52 acre/21ha stretch of nature trails, fishing, observation deck, swimming and picnicking (8am–9pm; $3.50/vehicle). The tide here can retreat by up to 500ft/150m and the beaches, open to the public year-round, tend to be quieter, though there can also be some serious rip-tides. At the southern end of the beaches is the wonderful **Ponce de Leon Inlet Lighthouse**, with a formidable 203 spiralling steps to the top. This well-preserved national monument is a magnificent re-creation of 19th-century Florida maritime life and the view from the top of America's second tallest lighthouse is superb (10am–5pm, 9pm Jun–Aug; $5 adults, $1.50 children). It also has a lovely gift shop. Ponce Inlet has some great deep-sea fishing, too – visit **http://inletharbor.com/fishing.html** for more info.

BRITTIP

Try lunch or dinner at Lighthouse Landing in Lighthouse Point Park for an eclectic piece of Floridian restaurant life.

More family-orientated fun can be found at the **Marine Science Center** (just round the corner from the lighthouse), which showcases mangrove, manatee and sea turtle exhibits, a seabird sanctuary and a turtle rehab facility. It has a 5,000 gallon/22,750 litre artificial reef aquarium, as well as static and interactive educational displays. A boardwalk and nature trail extend through the Center, which also has a gift shop (10am–4pm Tues–Sat, noon–4pm Sun, closed Mon; $3 adults, $1 under–13s; **echotourism.com/msc**). New in 2008 was the **Aqua Safari**, a combined 4-hour coastal eco-tour and entry to the Marine Science Center and Ponce de Leon Inlet Lighthouse. Climb aboard its red double-decker bus at Daytona Lagoon and head south to pick up its boat for an eco-tour of the Inlet waterway (11am–3pm most days but call to check times). Led by a licensed captain and marine biologist, the tour provides a hands-on overview of the region's ecosystem (casting and pulling up fishing nets and crab traps), with refreshments provided. You are then free to visit the Lighthouse and Marine Center ($50 adults, $30 under-13s, reduced prices available for non-all-inclusive admission; 386 405 3445, **daytonabeachaquasafari.com**).

Of course, one of the biggest draws is the Daytona racetrack (see page 279), while the accompanying **Daytona 500 Experience** is well worth trying even if you're not a race fan. This interactive centre offers a series of hands-on exhibits, rides and films to give you a taste of the high-speed action. Change tyres in the *Ford 16-Second Pit Stop Challenge*, design and video test a racing car, check out the technology involved, commentate on a race and experience the Daytona 500 film. Other elements include *Acceleration Alley* (for an additional fee), with full-size NASCAR simulators to capture the thrills of head-to-head racing at more than 200mph/322kph, and *Daytona Dream Laps*, another elaborate motion simulator to put riders inside the Daytona 500 itself. The history of speedway is well detailed in *Heritage of Daytona* and there is a good gift shop. A ½-hour *Tram Tour* of the Speedway stops on the track, in Pit Road and Victory Lane, giving a real close-up of this stunning arena. The **Pepsi IMAX Theater** features the unique 45-

minute *NASCAR 3-D: The IMAX Experience* and 14-minute *Daytona 500: The Movie* (9am–7pm, not Christmas Day; $24 adults, $19 seniors and 6–12s, under-6s free with adult; Speedway tour on its own $8.50/person; 386 947 6800, **daytona500experience.com**).

Continue south on Highway 1 and you come to up-and-coming (but still largely undiscovered) **New Smyrna Beach**, with 13mls/20km of pristine white sands, great surfing, shell collecting and boating at any of the many marinas hereabouts (386 428 1600, **nsbfla.com**).

Where to stay: You'll find two of our favourite resorts in Daytona Beach. The **Wyndham Ocean Walk Resort** is a huge ultra-modern complex right on the beach at Ocean Walk Village, with versatile accommodation in luxurious 1-, 2- and 3-bed condos (all with kitchens and fab views). With 3 outdoor pools, waterslide and lazy river, plus a kids' water play area, 2 indoor pools, a 9-hole indoor mini-golf, daily kids' programmes, a spa and an excellent lounge and food court, it is hugely family-friendly (386 323 4800, **oceanwalk.com**). The **Shores Resort & Spa** is a real boutique choice on a quieter stretch of the beaches, with an elegant, refined ambience, beautiful rooms, charming bar and signature fine-dining Azure restaurant. It also boasts an excellent pool, kids' pool and fitness centre, plus a heavenly Spa with a range of Balinese and Thai treatments (386 767 7350, **shoresresort.com**).

More info: Call 01737 643 764 in the UK, 1800 854 1234 in the US or visit **daytonabeach.com**.

Ormond Beach: Immediately to the north is another up-and-coming area where you find more smart resorts and great beaches, notably at **Bicentennial Park** (with a nature walk, fishing dock, tennis courts and playground) and **Birthplace of Speed Park** (which commemorates the first automobile race on the beach here in 1903). Just west of Daytona Beach is **DeLand** and St Johns River Country. Located in the western half of the region, this is home to several nature preserves (**riveroflakesheritage corridor.com**).

The Space Coast

Further south on the Atlantic seaboard is the area known as the Space Coast, because of its proximity to the Kennedy Space Center (see pages 219–25).

Cocoa Beach: Closest to Orlando, barely 50 minutes east (on the Beachline Expressway 528, then south on Highway A1A), this area has 2 excellent public beaches plus trademark shopping at the unmissable **Ron Jon's Surf Shop**, a massive neon emporium of all things water related. As it's the Atlantic, the sea can be chilly Nov–Apr, but its resort style ensures good facilities (**cocoabeach.com**). Cocoa Beach is also home to the excellent **Astronaut Memorial Planetarium & Observatory**, which holds daily shows in its large-screen cinema and world-class planetarium, plus an exhibition hall, art gallery and gift shop, all on Brevard Community College Campus (321 433 7373, **brevardcc.edu/planet**).

Titusville: Head here for attractions like the **US Space Walk of Fame** (a riverwalk with displays of memorabilia, plaques and public art depicting America's history in space), **Merritt Island National Wildlife Refuge** (a 6ml/9km driving tour adjacent to the Kennedy Space Center) and the fascinating and rather moving **American Police Hall of Fame & Museum**, with all you ever wanted to know about the history of crime and law enforcement, a tribute to police officers who have died in the line of duty, plus an indoor shooting centre and helicopter rides (**aphf.org**). Aviation fans may want to check out the **Valiant Air Command Warbird Museum**, with more than 35 vintage

Breakfast with a difference!

Just north of DeLand in DeLeon Springs State Park is the unique **Old Spanish Sugar Mill** grill and griddle house, one of Florida's little restaurant treasures. Famous for its hearty cook-it-yourself breakfasts (9am–4pm; 8am at weekends), each table has an inset griddle, and you choose your ingredients and get cracking. Pancakes are its speciality (pitchers of batter provided), with all manner of fillings, but it also has bacon, eggs, ham, sausage, home-made breads, French toast, sandwiches and salads. You'll struggle to pay more than $8 per person and it's great fun, as well as a local institution. However, as it is inside the State Park, there is a $5/car entry fee (386 985 5644, **planetdeland.com/sugarmill**). You can then enjoy the park facilities, which include canoes and kayaks, boat tours and hiking trails (**floridastateparks.com**).

war planes and guided tours through the history of military aviation (**vacwarbirds.org**).

Where to stay: Try **Four Points by Sheraton Cocoa Beach** (321 783 8717, **starwoodhotels.com**) or **Holiday Inn Oceanfront Resort** (321 783 2271, **hicocoabeachhotelsite.com**).

More info: Call 321 637 5483 or visit **space-coast.com**.

Tampa

Turning west from Orlando brings you down I-4 to the bright city of Tampa, right on a major sea bay and with some excellent attractions of its own.

Dinosaur World: Right on I-4 as you head to Tampa (and a nice stopping point by exit 17) is this family-run attraction ideal for 3–8s. With more than 150 life-sized dinosaurs in a lush, natural setting, plus walking trails, a picnic area, playground and gift shop, it makes a pleasant diversion for an hour or two. There are no rides or audio-animatronics, just set-piece models with explanatory signs, plus a cave-themed video theatre, small-scale fossil dig, museum and large 'boneyard' sand pit, while The Skeleton Garden features 6 replica dino skeletons. It's mildly educational, very laid back and a nice change of pace from the main parks. There is no food service, but it does have picnic facilities and there are fast-food locations nearby, including a pizza delivery service (9am–6pm; $9.75 adult, $8.95 seniors, $7.75 3–12s, under-3s free; 813 717 9865, **dinoworld.net**).

Florida Aquarium: In the heart of Tampa (right next to the port area) is this superb 5-part journey into Florida's waterways, coast and deep-sea elements, beautifully presented and ultra child-friendly. It starts with the *Wetlands*, then moves on to *Bays & Beaches, Coral Reef* the new *Ocean Commotion* section (full of interactive modules, including touch-screens, videos and podcasts) and the outdoor *Explore A Shore* water-play area, which boasts squirt pools, fountains, a pirate ship and more, plus an excellent Caribbean-themed Bar & Grill. Highlights include the amazing Leafy Sea-dragons, the daily Penguin Promenade (where a couple of the centre's penguins are brought out for a personal meet-and-greet), the Touch Tank, the amusing River Otters and Shark Bay, where anyone who is scuba-certified can take part in the daily dive into the huge lagoon ($150/person, advance reservations

Shark Dive at Florida Aquarium

required on 813 2713 4015). There is even a daily **Wild Dolphin Eco-Tour** (twice a day at weekends), leaving from the aquarium to explore the Bay where more than 500 dolphins live, along with the occasional manatee (9.30am–5pm daily, closed Thanksgiving and Christmas Day; parking $5; $17.95 adults, $14.95 seniors, $12.95 under-12s; with Dolphin Eco-Tour $32.05, $29.95, $22.95; 813 273 4000, **flaquarium.org**).

The Aquarium is right next to the **Channelside Bay Plaza** centre of shops and restaurants, which is well worth exploring for unique stores like Sports City, Surf Down Under, White House Gear and Quachbal Chocolatier and some great dining and entertainment options. Choose from Bennigan's, Hooters, Oishi Sushi, Gallagher's Steakhouse, Margarita Mama, Thai Tani and Stumps Supper Club, plus Coldstone Creamery (great ice-cream and milkshakes). Like Ybor City, this is where Tampa parties – hence the restaurants and bars, many featuring live music, are hopping at weekends. You will also find the **Official Tampa Bay Visitor Center** here (**channelsidetampa.com**).

Museum of Science and Industry: More family-friendly fun (especially for 4–12s) can be found at this highly entertaining science centre, with 3 floors of education-tinged exhibits, activities and large-screen IMAX films. Highlights include the huge *Kids In Charge* science play area (under-13s), *The Amazing You* (a tour of the human body), *Disasterville* (an interactive look at natural disasters – feel a hurricane in close-up!) and the *High-Wire Bicycle* (ride a bike on a steel cable 30ft/9m up). The permanent exhibits include Demystifying India and the Saunders Planetarium, while the IMAX Dome theatre offers a range of films daily on its 82ft hemispherical screen and there are periodic travelling exhibits. Outside are the Butterfly Gardens and Historic Tree Grove, providing more insight into Florida's natural wonders (9am–5pm Mon–Fri, 6pm Sat and Sun; $20.95 adults, $18.95 seniors, $16.95 2–12s, includes 1 IMAX film; additional films $7.95, $6.95 and $5.95; 813 987 6100, **mosi.org**).

Channelside Bay Plaza

Ybor City: Tampa's other entertainment district can be found in the rejuvenated Cuban quarter of the city, where a fine mix of shops and restaurants provide a lively vibe both by day and at night. Shop at **The Silver Edge** for jewellery; **Stogie Castillo's**, where you can see its cigars being made; **Urban Outfitters** for trendy apparel and accessories; **Ybor Ybor** for visitor merchandise; **Sunglass Hut** and more. Then stop for a meal at any of **Adobe Gila's** (Mexican cantina style), **Fresh Mouth** (tempting burgers), **Rock-N Sports Bar & Grille**, **Samurai Blue** (fine sushi and sake), or (our favourite) the **Tampa Bay Brewing Co**, a British-run brewpub with an inviting, varied menu, a great range of beers, multiple TV screens and pool table (**tampabaybrewing company.com**). More fun can be had at **Gameworks**, a 'grown-up' arcade of games, bars and restaurant, and the **Improv Comedy Theatre**. Again, it is busiest on Fridays and Sundays but lively most evenings (**centroybor.com**). Much of downtown Tampa, including Ybor City and Channelside, is linked by the handy **TECO Line Streetcar**, replicas of authentic electric trams, with one-way fares of $2 and just $4 for an all-day card.

More info: Call the Visitor Center on 813 223 2752 or **visittampabay.com**.

Florida's Beach

Continue west and you have the gorgeous **Gulf Coast**, which is a 2-hour drive down I-4 from Orlando and through Tampa on I-275 south to **St Pete Beach** (105mls/169km) or **Clearwater Beach** (110mls/177km), with a string of equally beautiful resorts in between, all of which feature stunning white-sand beaches, great fishing, water sports and far fewer crowds than you would think. The sea is a touch warmer and calmer on this side of Florida so is more suitable for small children. The 35ml/56km stretch from St Pete Beach to Clearwater represents the heart of the Sunshine State seaside experience, hence it is known as 'Florida's Beach,' and is one of the most popular twin-centre options for British visitors. It has a wonderful array of attractions and an average 361 days of sunshine a year.

St Petersburg: This city, just across the Howard Frankland Bridge from Tampa, is a wonderful mix of developments, both recent and historic. Take time here for the **Dali Museum** (9.30am–5.30pm Mon–Wed, Sat, 9.30am–8.30pm Thurs, 9.30am–6.30pm Fri, noon–5.30pm Sun; $15 adults, $13.50 seniors, $10 students, $4 5–9s), and the **Bay Walk** complex of shops, restaurants and a 20-screen cinema. An additional mix of museums, notably the elegant **Museum of Fine Arts**, with its new Hazel Hough Wing (**fine-arts.org**), the recently expanded **St Petersburg Museum of History** right on the Pier, the exceedingly child-friendly International Museum and the fascinating **Great Explorations Children's Museum** (**stpete.org/art.htm**). Pedestrian-friendly streets and the Pier provide plenty of interest, while fan-friendly Tropicana Field hosts the **Tampa Bay Devil Rays** baseball team (Apr–Sept) for another slice of highly recommended local fun ($8–85; **devilrays.com**). For a tour with a difference, try the **Bayside Tours** from the Museum of History on the Pier approach on the amazing 2-wheeled Segways – 'the ride technology of the future'. They are easy to master and provide a wonderful way to see much of the city's miles of waterfront parks, beaches and residences with your knowledgeable guide. Suitable for ages 12 and over (max 275lb/125kg), choose from its standard downtown tours or the offroad/beach tours at Bilmar Beach Resort on Treasure Island (Mon 12.30, 2.30 and 4.30pm; Tues–Sat 10.30am and 2pm, Sun 12.30 and 2.30pm; 1-hour tour $35, 1½-hour $50; call for reservations on 727 896 3640, **gyroglides.com**).

Weedon Island Preserve: Enjoy the rich cultural history of this 3,700 acre/1,500ha seaside nature park in St Petersburg. Start at the Natural History Center (the main entrance, confusingly, is at the back) and learn about the prehistoric and Native American settlements here (plus periodic exhibitions), then go up to the 3rd floor observation deck. There are several miles of boardwalks and trails around these tidal wetlands, which are home to a wide variety of wildlife, including ospreys, spoonbills, turtles, mangrove crabs, raccoons and gopher tortoises, and guided hikes at 9am on Saturdays (10am–4pm Wed–Sun, free entry; 727 453 6500, **weedonislandcenter.org**). The more energetic may want to try a paddle round the shallow waters with **Sweetwater Kayaks**. This wonderfully peaceful close encounter with nature (stingrays, jumping mullet and the occasional manatee) takes 2–3 hours on the self-guided tour (9am and 12.30pm Sat and Sun; $40 for a ½-day single-kayak rental, $56 for double, or $17 and $25 hourly; 727 570 4844 or **sweetwaterkayaks.com**).

BRITTIP

Insect repellent is essential for any visit to Weedon Island Preserve as it is not sprayed for mosquitoes, and the little pests will feed on tourists!

Beaches: Head out to the beaches themselves and you have a magnificent choice, from the 1,100 acre/445ha **Fort De Soto Park** (voted America's No 1 beach in 2005) in the south to stunning **Caladesi Island** in the north (voted No 1 in 2008). There is plenty to do, too, with the likes of Treasure Island, Sand Key and St Pete Beach all receiving the Blue Wave Award for cleanliness and safety. Fort De Soto Park offers free walking tours of its Spanish-American War-era fort, while **John's Pass Village and Boardwalk** is an unusual shopping district and marina full of art galleries and restaurants (and home to the fun **Pirate Cruise** – a replica sailing ship that offers a 2-hour party cruise 3 times daily around the waters of Treasure Island; $33 adults, $23 under-20s, inclusive of beer, wine and soft drinks; 11am, 2pm and sunset Mon–Sat; 727 423 7824). Parasailing, jet-skiing and fishing are also popular here.

BRITTIP

Most public beaches will have toilets, changing facilities and picnic tables, but there is usually a parking fee.

You definitely shouldn't miss **Dolphin Landings** in St Pete Beach. Its 7-vessel fleet includes 2 51ft yachts that sail on 2-hour trips on the calm inland waterway 2 or 3 times a day for guaranteed close-up dolphin-watch cruises and sunset sailings, plus Shell Island day trips and fishing excursions ($33 adults, $23 children; 727 367 4488, **dolphinlandings.com**). Further north at Indian Shores is America's largest wild bird hospital, the **Suncoast Seabird Sanctuary**, usually caring for more than 500 injured birds including birds of prey, pelicans, spoonbills and egrets. There is no charge to visit this non-profit-making rehabilitation centre, but it does ask for donations (727 391 6211, **seabirdsanctuary.org**).

Continuing north, you find **Clearwater Beach**, and more expanses of clean, white sands. This is home to the **Marine Aquarium**, a wonderful non-profit organisation that rescues and rehabilitates injured animals, from dolphins to turtles, river otters and more. The dolphins are the star attraction (see Brit Tip below) but there are also regular animal presentations and lively exhibits. Try its VIP behind-the-scenes tour, with access to all the rehab areas and a close-up of the dolphins, or the Sea Life Safari (especially good for children) that goes out on the intracoastal waterway (9am–5pm Mon–Sat, 10am–5pm Sun; $9 adults, $6.50 3–12s; add $10/person for behind-the-scenes tour; Sea Life Safari $21.35 and $13.75; $35.95 and $26.75 for all 3; 727 441 1790, **cmaquarium.org**). **Pier 60** is where the daily sunset celebration (complete with craft stalls and music) is held, and you can also catch the 2-hour **Captain Memo's Pirate Cruise** from the Marina (10am and 2pm daily; $35 adults, $30 seniors and teens, $25 under-13s) or the Sunset Champagne Cruise (at 5, 6 or 7pm, $38, $30, $25). Going further north brings you to **Caladesi Island** and another of the world's most picturesque beach spots.

BRITTIP

Don't leave Clearwater Beach without visiting the Marine Aquarium's headline attraction, a dolphin called **Winter**, who was rescued from a crab trap as a youngster. Her tail had to be amputated and she was not expected to survive but, happily, she not only lived but learned a new way to swim.

For those wishing to take it easy rather than drive, the **Suncoast Beach Trolley** is the perfect transport link (5.05am–10.10pm daily) both along the beaches and into St Petersburg for $1.50/ride, $3.50 for an all-day pass and $15 for a week pass (727 530 9911, **psta.net**). The area also boasts 2,000 restaurants, of which the Key West bistro style of **Frenchy's Rockaway Grill** and **Frenchy's South Beach Café** (both in Clearwater Beach), the **Daiquiri Deck/Oceanside Grill** (Madeira Beach), **Crabby Bill's Seafood** (Indian Rocks, Clearwater Beach and St Pete Beach) and the **Moon Under Water** (St Petersburg) are all well worth visiting. The smart new **Parkshore Grill** in downtown St Pete is also worth seeking out for a relaxing lunch or elegant dinner (727 896 9463, **parkshoregrill.com**).

Where to stay: There's a wide choice of accommodation here. A range of **Superior Small Lodgings** combine beachfront locations with small-scale, personalised service. Check out **Beach Side Palms** in Treasure Island as an ideal example, with weekly rates from $725 for a 3-room apartment (727 367 2791, **floridassl. com**). There are upmarket hotels, too – witness the family-friendly **Tradewinds Island Resort** on St Pete Beach, a 774-room complex of 2 resorts with a wide range of facilities, including a huge inflatable beach slide and excellent restaurant choice in this blissful location (1800 360 4016, **tradewinds resort.com**) and the hugely impressive **Sheraton Sand Key Resort** at Clearwater Beach, a 10-storey edifice with 10 acres/4ha of private beach and facilities including floodlit tennis courts, a fitness centre, children's pool and playground (with supervised programmes in summer), plus the excellent Rusty's Bistro restaurant (727 595 1611, **sheratonsandkey.com**). The newest hotel is the superb **Sandpearl Resort**, a truly upscale choice right on Clearwater Beach with a mix of stylish standard rooms and ultra-spacious junior suites. The pool, bar and grill are a true beachfront sanctuary, while the modern spa boasts a magnificent array of treatments. If nothing else, Caretta on the Gulf is one of the area's great restaurants, with an inventive fusion cuisine from South American, Caribbean and other sources, plus ceviche, sushi and a raw bar (727 441 2425, **sandpearl.com**). **Sunset Vistas Beachfront Suites** on Treasure Island, with grand 1- and 2-bed suites and fully equipped kitchens, is another smart new choice for a week or more (727 360 1600, **sunsetvistas.com**).

More info: Call 0208 651 4742 in the UK, 727 464 7200 in the US, or visit the excellent **floridasbeach.com**.

BRITTIP

During Easter and the summer months, the beaches are extremely popular with the locals at weekends, so the main stretches tend to get very crowded.

The South-West

Bradenton/Sarasota: Around 2 hours' drive from Orlando is this artsy area (take I-4 then I-75), which features the superb beachfronts of **Anna Maria Island** (charming and secluded beaches), **Longboat Key** and **Venice** ('the shark tooth capital of the world' and great for fossil hunters). Sarasota is year-round home to the **Ringling Circus**, and there are many circus-influenced offerings hereabouts, including the Ringling Estates museum, gardens and theatre. There is superb shopping at **St Armand's Circle** in Lido Key, and the **Mote Aquarium** is also worthy of note. In Bradenton, look out for the Village of Arts, and the sophisticated South Florida Museum, with its manatee mascot. Good seafood is always on the menu here, and you should check

Sandpearl Resort

out the Spanish/Cuban style of the **Columbia Restaurant** in Sarasota (941 388 3987, **columbiarestaurant.com**) and lively beachfront **Siesta Key Oyster Bar** (941 346 5443, **skob.com**).

Where to stay: Anna Maria Island is full of small-scale B&Bs and cute beachfront inns. The **Hyatt Sarasota** is one of the top resorts in the area (941 953 1234, **sarasota.hyatt.com**), while the **Ritz-Carlton** is a Gulf Coast landmark (941 309 2000, **ritzcarlton.com**).

More info: Sarasota, call 941 957 1877 or visit **sarasotafl.com**; Bradenton (and Anna Maria Island), 941 729 9177 or **http://floridasgulfislands.com/**.

Charlotte Harbor: Go further south (170mls/272km from Orlando) and you have Florida's second-largest bay after Tampa Bay, and home to the lower-key destinations of **Punta Gorda, Port Charlotte, Englewood** and **Boca Grande**. From here, the **Fort Myers/Sanibel** area is only a short drive. This is part of the mini tropical paradise of the **Lee Island Coast**, south of Charlotte Harbor, featuring history- and nature-rich **Fort Myers** and funky **Pine Island**.

BRITTIP

Don't miss the big local festival, MangoMania, on Pine Island in celebration of the local fruit in July each year.

Shores Resort

Among the many highlights of the barrier islands are **Fort Myers Beach**, a bustling family-orientated beach town, **Sanibel Island**, centred around its famous shell-strewn beaches, and the bird-watching Mecca at the **Darling National Wildlife Refuge**, the quirky jumble of shops and restaurants in **Captiva Island**, and **Bonita Beach**, where the **Great Calusa Blueway** paddling trail heads north for some 90mls/145km. Sanibel is also home to the unique **Bailey-Matthews Shell Museum**, plus a historic village and several wildlife attractions. Canoeing, kayaking and nature tours are all featured among these truly beautiful beaches.

Where to stay: You will find a good mix of vacation homes and cottages in Fort Myers Beach and Sanibel, while the top hotels are **Lovers Key Resort** (239 765 1040, **loverskey.com**) and the **Sanibel Harbor Resort & Spa** (1866 283 3273, **sanibel-resort.com**).

More info: Call 239 338 3500 or visit **fortmyers-sanibel.com**.

Paradise Coast: Continue south for about 230mls/368km and you have the magnificent 'Paradise Coast' of **Naples** and **Marco Island**, 2 of Florida's lesser-known seaside treasures. Naples is both a fresh, modern city with plenty of attractions (notably the **Museum of Art**, **Naples Nature Center** and **Corkscrew Swamp Sanctuary**, plus great shopping) and a major beach destination. Its art-tinged ambience is well-evidenced in **Fifth Avenue South**, with boutique stores, sidewalk cafés and art festivals, while **Third Street** and the **Avenues** offer more of this street life and café society atmosphere. **Gallery Row**, the **City Dock**, the **Waterside Shops at Pelican Bay** and **Venetian Village** are other notable shopping districts. The beaches are mere steps away; at the municipal beach, **Naples Pier** juts into placid Gulf waters, while **Lowdermilk Beach** is fully family-friendly, with volleyball and other

Seminole Central

Head west out of Fort Lauderdale and you find the rewarding **Ah-Tah-Thi-Ki Museum**, home to the Seminole tribe of Florida. Here you can learn about Native American culture, from its customs to the bitter 19th century Seminole Wars and its modern face as 'guardians' of the Everglades. See the Living Village and walk the 1ml/1.6km Boardwalk over the Cypress Swamp. Then try the nearby **Billie Swamp Safari**, a 2,200 acre/1.6ha Cypress Reservation featuring close-ups of the wildlife (including snakes and gators) via its giant-wheeled buggy, airboat rides and swamp critter shows. You can even stay overnight in its Chickee huts (1800 683 7800 or **seminoletribe.com**).

facilities. Marco Island is the largest of the Ten Thousand Islands, consisting of 2 main communities: **Marco**, known for its wide-coved beach and fine resorts, plus a multitude of fishing charters, and **Goodland**, with its eclectic collection of fish house restaurants, plus fishing charters into the Everglades backwaters.

BRITTIP

The Naples/Marco Island area is the perfect base from which to explore the amazing **Florida Everglades** themselves, though you can also reach them from Fort Lauderdale on the east coast.

Where to stay: Take your pick from some high-quality resorts, like **Hilton Marco Island Beach Resort** (239 394 5000, **marcoisland.hilton.com**), the **Marco Beach Ocean Resort** (239 393 1400, **marcobeachoceanresort.com**) and **Naples Grande Resort & Club** (239 597 3232, **naplesgranderesort.com**).

More info: Call 1800 688 3600 or visit **paradisecoast.com**.

Treasure Coast

Returning to the Atlantic Coast, and heading out of Orlando for 2 hours on the Beachline Expressway (528) and Highway 1 brings you to another often-overlooked Florida jewel, **Vero Beach**. Nicknamed the Treasure Coast (for its history of shipwrecks), it boasts the intriguing **McLarty Treasure Museum** and the **Pelican Island National Wildlife Refuge**. Vero Beach itself is located on the barrier island of North Hutchinson but spreads to the mainland, with an array of art galleries, smart shops, restaurants, small resorts and beach parks, including a boardwalk atop the dunes. Head south for another hour and you reach **Palm Beach** and the mainland city of **West Palm Beach**, foremost among Florida's chic communities. A traditional playground of the rich and famous, Henry Flagler's **Whitehall** mansion is a highlight, while the many upscale restaurants are places to go celebrity-watching. Also here is **Lion Country Safari**, with lions, elephants and giraffes among many other animals.

Where to stay: Disney's Vero Beach Resort doesn't always have availability (it is a Disney Vacation Club property first and foremost), but it is 71 acres/24ha of true Disney fantasy and the perfect family resort on this coast (772 234 2000, **dvcresorts. com**). In Palm Beach there is really only one place to stay (or visit) – the truly opulent **The Breakers**, one of America's legendary resort destinations (561 655 6611, **thebreakers.com**).

More info: Call 561 233 3000 or visit **palmbeachfl.com**.

Miami and Fort Lauderdale

From Palm Beach, your enjoyable coast drive brings you through increasingly built-up resort territory as you go through Delray Beach, chic Boca Raton, Deerfield Beach and Pompano Beach to **Fort Lauderdale**. This latter has become one of Florida's most upmarket and enjoyable destinations in recent years, with a great mix of resorts, shopping, attractions and the fabulous beachfront. It also has a canal and waterway network that makes it the 'Venice of America', with **water taxis** being more plentiful than the wheeled variety. Top things to see are the **Museum of Discovery & Science** (one of the state's finest), **Bonnet House Museum & Gardens**, **Old Fort Lauderdale Village & Museum** and the unmissable **Las Olas Boulevard** area, full of eye-catching shops and mouth-watering restaurants. Do shop at **Sawgrass Mills**, Florida's largest mall, which has around 350 outlet-style stores with some of the big-name designers, plus the Wanadoo City role-playing park for kids. Fort Lauderdale is also a perfect stay for a few days before or after a cruise, as both Port Everglades and Miami are only a short distance away.

Where to stay: Look for their **Superior Small Lodgings** or the many high-class resorts now dotting the beachfront, like **Sheraton Yankee Clipper Hotel** (954 524 5551, **starwoodhotels.com**) and the 5-star **St Regis Resort** (954 465 2300, **starwood hotels.com**).

More info: Call 954 765 4466 or visit **sunny.org**.

If you have taken the full 4-hour drive south from Orlando, you will finally arrive in the state's biggest and most glamorous city, **Miami**. With superb high-rise resort developments, miles of open, accessible beaches, the ultra-chic South Beach area (with its atmospheric **Art Deco District**), fantastic shopping, great sports, scintillating restaurants and nightlife,

Captain Memo's Pirate Cruise

and an array of outstanding attractions, you could spend 2 weeks here and still not see it all. The city is actually 5mls/8km from the main Beaches area, which runs north for almost 15mls/24km along the sprawling corridor of Collins Avenue, where you have most of the resorts and nightlife. High style is almost everywhere, and a narrated boat tour (from the **Bayside Marketplace**) will show off the mansions of the rich and famous, while you should also tour **Coral Gables** and the older, neater **Coconut Grove** (with its CocoWalk shopping district and superbly ornate **Vizcaya Museum**). Other attractions include **Miami Seaquarium** on the island of Key Biscayne, the amazing **Venetian Pool** at Coral Gables, and **Parrot Jungle Island**, especially for children. You are spoiled for choice for shopping, with some of the best at the fashion-conscious **Bal Harbor Shops**, massive **Aventura Mall** and funky **Lincoln Road** in South Beach.

Where to stay: There are boutique hotels and dazzling resorts aplenty here; the iconic **Fontainebleau** has reopened following its $1b renovation (305 538 5000, **Fontainebleaumiami beach.com**); the beautiful **Mandarin Oriental** is about as upmarket as it gets (305 913 8288, **mandarin oriental.com/miami**); more modest but still decent is the **Best Western Atlantic Beach Resort** (305 673 3337, **bestwestern.com**).

More info: Call 305 539 3000 or visit **miamiandbeaches.com**.

Florida Keys

Leaving Miami behind on Highway 1 brings you to the unique realm of the Keys, a loose archipelago of 1,700 islands that arc down into the Caribbean. If you thought mainland Florida was easygoing, just try the laid-back 'Conch Republic', where shoes and flip-flops are official wear and the mix of Floridian and Caribbean influences merge into a 'Floribbean' culture. Scuba divers are

Miami nice

If you see nothing else in Miami, do spend some time in South Beach (or SoBe as it is known) and the über-cool **Ocean Drive**, full of open-air cafés, art galleries and pulsating nightclubs. Tranquil during the day, non-stop at night, this is where the beautiful people hang out, or just cruise in their Ferraris and Hummers. Here the restored Art Deco gems twinkle at night and will use up plenty of film!

in their element here, with some of the world's best coral reefs, with renowned **John Pennekamp Coral Reef State Park** the highlight of the many miles of National Marine Sanctuary. The first city you encounter is **Key Largo**, closely followed by **Islamorada**, where you should stop to see **Theater To The Sea**, with its dolphin and sea-lion interaction programmes. If you're looking for fishing, some of the best charters can be found at Islamorada, **Marathon** and **Big Pine Key**.

BRITTIP

Don't miss the opportunity to feed the hungry giant tarpon that hang around the docks by Robbie's boat rentals in Islamorada.

Marathon is the starting point of the amazing **Seven Mile Bridge**, the unofficial 8th wonder of the world, which connects the biggest gap between the islands, while Big Pine Key is home to **Bahia Honda State Park**, one of Florida's finest beaches. Finally, the 375ml/600km drive from Orlando brings you to the southernmost city in the US (just 90mls/145km from Cuba). **Key West** is possibly the most eclectic city in the US, a mixture of laid-back and outrageous, of street performers, sidewalk artists, cafes and bars (LOTS of bars!), plus the former home of **Ernest Hemingway**, whose residence and museum are essential viewing. You should also see **Key West Aquarium** and **Shipwreck Historeum**, and the wonderfully diverse array of shops. You must be on the harbour front, though, for the daily **Sunset Celebration**, when Key West's party spirit is in full force. The other great feature of Key West is its myriad of ways to get around – you can try the **Conch Tour Train**, **Old Town Trolley Tours**, **pedicabs** and **bicycles**. Just don't expect your stay to be sedate!

Where to stay: Guest houses, inns and B&Bs are plentiful in the Keys, like **Old Customs House Inn** (305 294 8507, **oldcustomshouse.com**) in Key West's Old Town or the utterly charming **Banyan Resort** (305 296 7786, **thebanyanresort.com**).

More info: Call 1800 352 5397 or visit **fla-keys.com**.

Cruise-and-Stay

The options for twin-centre holidays don't end just because Florida does. Taking a cruise is fast becoming a popular option with an Orlando stay and, with the introduction of *Disney Cruise Line* in 1998, there's much publicity for these well-priced 3-, 4-, 5- and 7-day sailings out of Port Canaveral, Tampa, Fort Lauderdale's Port Everglades and Miami.

Disney has 2 breathtaking ships, the 83,000-ton *Disney Magic* (1998) and *Disney Wonder* (1999), with a dedicated Port Canaveral cruise

Disney Cruise Line

© Disney

terminal. Classic design plus the usual Disney Imagineering have produced 2 vessels that incorporate special features for kids, teenagers AND adults. Both are a destination in their own right, each having 4 restaurants, a 977-seat theatre, cinema, nightclub complex, choice of bars and a gorgeous spa, while they sail to the Bahamas, the Caribbean and Disney's stunning private island, Castaway Cay. It's not a cheap option and the 3- and 4-night cruises can feel a bit frenzied, but the 7-night Caribbean voyages offer a genuinely relaxing style that is hard to beat. They boast novel touches with their on-board entertainment, Disney character interaction and wonderful features like the adults-only champagne brunch. Book with many of the tour operators or direct with Disney on 1800 511 9444 (**http://disney cruise. disney.go.com**).

Other Port Canaveral options (**portcanaveral.org**) include the glitzy **Carnival Cruise Lines** (all-modern hardware, party atmosphere; call 1888 2276 4825 in the US or 020 7940 4466 in the UK, **carnivalcruise.co.uk**) with 3- and 4-day Bahamas voyages on the *Carnival Sensation*, and 7-night cruises alternating to the east and west Caribbean on one of its biggest ships, the *Carnival Glory*. From autumn 2009, the new *Carnival Dream*, the company's largest ship, will also be based here. **Royal Caribbean International** (also 2 modern, glamorous ships; call 1866 562 7625 in the US or 0845 165 8414 in the UK, **royalcaribbean.co.uk**) has similar 3- and 4-day trips to Nassau and its private island of Coco Cay on *Sovereign of the Seas* and alternating 7-day Caribbean cruises on mega-ship *Mariner of the Seas* (to the Bahamas, St Thomas and St Maarten, or Jamaica, Grand Cayman and Cozumel).

Fort de Soto

Carnival and Royal Caribbean, plus upmarket **Holland America** (1877 724 5425, **hollandamerica.com**) offer 4–14-day Caribbean cruises from the port of **Tampa** (**tampaport.com**), while there is a huge choice if you venture further south to **Miami** or **Fort Lauderdale**. Rather congested Miami boasts the largest cruise ships in the world (Royal Caribbean's amazing 160,000-ton trio *Freedom, Liberty* and *Independence of the Seas*), as well as other cruises from Carnival, and **Celebrity Cruises** (0845 456 1520, **celebritycruises.co.uk**), **Norwegian Cruise Line** (0845 658 8010, **ncl.co.uk**), upmarket **Oceania Cruises** (1800 531 5619, **oceaniacruises.com**), the Italian style of **Costa Cruises** (1800 445 8020, **costacruises.co.uk**) and 6-star **Crystal Cruises** (1888 722 0021, **crystal cruises.com**). Sail from **Fort Lauderdale** (**broward.org/port**) and the choice is Carnival, Celebrity, Costa, Holland America, Royal Caribbean, 6-star **Regent Seven Seas Cruises** (023 8068 2280, **rssc.co.uk**), **MSC Italian Cruises** (0870 850 4883, **msccruises. co.uk**) and glamorous **Princess Cruises** (0845 075 0031, **princess cruises.co.uk**).

For more advice, consult *World of Cruising* magazine (0870 429 2686, **worldofcruisingmagazine.com**) or specialist travel agent The Cruise Line Ltd (0870 112 1102, **cruiseline.co.uk**). In Orlando, try Cruise Planners on 1877 772 7847 or **gocruiseplanner.com**.

Well, that represents pretty much the full range of holiday choices. Now we need to tell you about how to enjoy all the night-time entertainment...!

10 Orlando by Night

or Burning the Candle at Both Ends

If Orlando and the parks are hot during the day, they positively sizzle at night, with yet more diverse and thrilling entertainment, much of it also extremely family-friendly. Inevitably, Disney and Universal lead the way, but there is much to enjoy in the live music scene generally.

The full range runs from purpose-built entertainment complexes and an amazing range of dinner shows to a unique array of bars and nightclubs. The choice is suitably widespread and almost always high quality. Disney raised the bar for the big evening entertainment concept in 1987 by opening *Pleasure Island*, an imaginative range of clubs, discos and restaurants, and it continues to refine the formula to keep it fresh. **Disney's BoardWalk Resort**, which opened its doors in 1996, has added more to its night-time options.

> **BRITTIP**
> Photo ID is essential for most bars and clubs, and especially *Pleasure Island*, even if you happen to be the 'wrong' side of 30. No ID equals no alcohol, and there are no exceptions.

International Drive (I-Drive) caught up with this process in 1997 when **The Pointe Orlando** opened. Although its prime focus is shopping and restaurants, it now has a strong evening entertainment component with a magnificent array of exceptional restaurants, BB King's Blues Club and the big Regal Cinemas 20+ IMAX multiplex. Finally, Universal Orlando got with the beat in 1998 with the opening of **CityWalk**,

CityWalk

possibly the most elaborate and sophisticated centre of the lot. They all represent yet another slick opportunity for you to be dazzled and relieved of your cash all in the name of holiday fun. However, you should try to experience at least one.

DOWNTOWN DISNEY

The large-scale development of what is now *Downtown Disney* has evolved into a 3-part complex (The Marketplace, *Pleasure Island* and West Side) doubling the size of the old site (in 1998) to 120 acres/48.5ha and providing world-class entertainment. A 2007 redevelopment of *Pleasure Island*, followed by a complete 're-imagining' of the former nightclub complex in 2008 has led to some big changes, but this is still Night-Time Central for Disney's non-theme park entertainment, and you will find the whole area a very different prospect by night than by day.

Pleasure Island

Prior to 2007, this used to be Disney's only real 'grown-ups' area, with 7 contrasting nightclubs, from high-energy discos to the elaborate Adventurers Club and Comedy Warehouse. However, in June 2008, Disney management decided this was no longer what their customers wanted and announced that ALL the clubs would close down for good on 28 September (to much wailing and gnashing of teeth from fans of the hugely inventive live venue of the Adventurers Club in particular). The 2007 refurbishment had already prepared the way for this by opening up the Island more to through-traffic (actually changing the 'Island' emphasis) and providing more in the way of all-day attractions. Now, from 2009 onwards, we can expect a drastically different area, characterised more by restaurants and unique shopping with a 'global village' outlook. Gone, therefore are the Rock 'n Roll Beach Club, BET Soundstage Club, Mannequins Dance Palace, Motion and 70s-themed disco 8Trax, as well as the Adventurers Club and Comedy Warehouse. In their place will come entertainment of the shopping and dining variety, plus 'a number of one-of-a-kind, immersive experiences for guests'. The first new development, for spring 2009, will be a big South and Central America-themed restaurant featuring regional cuisine, speciality drinks and live music in a waterfront setting.

Raglan Road

However, though the clubs will be left in the dark while Disney's Imagineers come up with some more appropriate ideas for their usage (or other developers offer alternative 'unique' opportunities), some of *Pleasure Island*'s existing elements will remain. These include the chic cigar lounge **Fuego by Sosa Cigars**, the iconic **Orlando Harley-Davidson** store, hip beach/surf clothing emporium **Curl by Sammy Duval** and the outdoor food and drink kiosks. Also still here is one of our *Downtown Disney* favourites, **Raglan Road**, an Irish-themed pub with lively musical entertainment, food to match and a genuine Emerald Isle style, where you really can enjoy the craic (11am–2am). Much of the restaurant's interior was shipped over from Ireland (including no fewer than 4 reclaimed 130-year-old bars, plus 9 European beers on draft), establishing an authentic backdrop to an original menu created by celebrity master chef Kevin Dundon. Fresh, simple ingredients combined with an imaginative twist make the likes of shepherd's pie, planxty and bread pudding (the best we have tasted!) a real wake-up call for the senses. Live traditional Irish music in its Grand Room is another feature from 9pm nightly, plus Irish dancing. Stop in at the gift shop for all your Guinness souvenirs and be sure to check out Kevin Dundon's *Full On Irish* cookbook to create a taste of Raglan Road at home (407 938 0300, **raglan roadirishpub.com**).

BRITTIP

Raglan Road has established itself as one of Orlando's must-do venues, as much for its genuine pub charm as its fabulous food.

Other restaurants: To one side of Raglan Road is **Cooke's of Dublin**, a chippie serving up a taste of home with real chips, beer-battered fish, gourmet battered sausages and 'Do bars' (deep-fried Snickers bars!). For a full-scale meal, the neighbouring **Portobello Yacht Club** has also undergone a recent transformation (in summer 2008) to a Tuscan Country Trattoria, featuring family-style dishes and a complete redesign both inside and out, adding more outdoor seating. Next door, **Fulton's Crab House** offers some of the best seafood in Orlando (see also page 333), though this will also undergo a major refurbishment in spring 2009 to update its interior fixtures and furnishings as well as the exterior.

Of course, you can also visit the other eateries nearby, including **Planet Hollywood**® (the largest and busiest of this chain) and the fun new animatronic restaurant **T-Rex: A Prehistoric Adventure** should also be open in 2009 immediately adjacent to the *Pleasure Island* area in The Marketplace. For advanced dining reservations at any Disney restaurant, call 407 939 3463.

Later in 2009 you should also look out for the signature **Tethered Balloon** ride, which will be added to the *Pleasure Island* area (similar to the wonderful Panoramagique balloon in the Disney Village area of *Disneyland Resort Paris*). This will offer 20-minute 'flights' over the *Downtown Disney* area (weather permitting) at heights up to 300ft/91.5m, providing a wonderful panorama of much of the huge extent of *Walt Disney World* itself.

The Marketplace

While The Marketplace is largely the shopping heart of *Downtown Disney* (see page 338), it still offers some evening entertainment possibilities. For dining fun, there is the elaborately-themed **Rainforest Café**, with its safari-style 'adventures' under a volcano-topped exterior, while **Cap'n Jack's Restaurant** serves up great chowder, crabcakes, shrimp and its trademark 'fishbowl' margaritas. The **Ghirardelli Soda Fountain & Chocolate Shop** is a great location for dessert or just a soda or milkshake while you wander, and the recently-refurbished **Earl of Sandwich** is an excellently-priced café for a quick bite or a lighter meal. Finally, the **Marketplace Stage** was due to be completely replaced in late 2008, with a larger, covered stage to provide more live musical entertainment, including Disney's Magic Music Days for school and community groups.

T-Rex: A Prehistoric Adventure

West Side

This is the other big night-time draw at *Downtown Disney*. Here you will find the **AMC® Pleasure Island 24 Theaters Complex**, with 24 screens and 6,000 seats in state-of-the-art surroundings, plus an excellent mix of live entertainment that includes the Cirque du Soleil® theatre company, more fine dining, unique shopping and *DisneyQuest*, the ultimate in interactive game arcades. As a bonus, the whole of West Side is characterised at night by some outstanding lighting effects and a vibrant, almost intoxicating atmosphere.

BRITTIP
Save $2 on adult tickets at the AMC® cineplex by visiting before 6pm each weekday.

Bongos Cuban Café™: Co-owned by Gloria and Emilio Estefan, the sights, sounds and tastes of Old Havana come to this imaginative setting, with red-hot Latin music and some excellent Cuban fare (11am–2am).

House of Blues®: This cavernous combination live music venue and restaurant in backwoods Mississippi style is a must for anyone even vaguely interested in blues, rock 'n' roll, R&B, gospel and jazz – and some top-name bands play here (407 934 2583, **hob.com**), while its trademark Gospel Brunch on Sundays serves up some fab food with a full gospel show

Wolfgang Puck Café

BRITTIP
If you need to escape the *Downtown Disney* hurly-burly, head upstairs to the Virgin™ Megastore, where its coffee/sandwich shop is a relative oasis of (usually queue-free) calm offering a good range of snacks and drinks.

(10.30am and 1pm; $33.50 adults, $17.25 3–9s). 'Praise the Lord and pass the biscuits' is the slogan, and it's a lot of fun. The 500-seat restaurant next door to the concert hall (11am–11pm) also offers some fine fare, including jambalaya, catfish and a host of other Cajun delicacies, with more good, foot-stompin' live music (free) in the **Blues Kitchen** (Thurs–Sat). The inevitable gift shop also stocks quality merchandise.

Wolfgang Puck® Café: A rich experience from the renowned Californian chef, with no fewer than 4 options: the Café, gourmet food in a casual setting; Wolfgang Puck Express, the fast-food version; the Sushi Bar for seafood, pizzas and micro-brew beers; and the Dining Room, an upscale restaurant featuring the best of the group's international cuisine (407 938 9653, **wolfgangpuck.com**; see also page 332). It caters for just about every taste (the sushi is to die for) and is highly family-friendly, with excellent kids' menus and games (11.30am–11pm, 6–10.30pm in the Dining Room). NB: This is another venue due for updates to its interior décor and outdoor patio in 2009.

Shopping: Original and engaging, from the basic sweet shop **Candy Cauldron**, which resembles a fairytale dungeon, through the one-off outlets such as **Sosa Family Cigars**, **Sunglass Icon** and the stylish art of **Hoypoloi Gallery**, to the predictable souvenir stores and truly mega **Virgin™ Megastore**, the largest music store in Florida, with more than 100 listening stations, a café, hydraulic outdoor stage and a mean sound system!

DisneyQuest

The most unusual element to *Downtown Disney, DisneyQuest* is described variously as 'an immersive, interactive entertainment environment', the latest in arcade games, a series of state-of-the-art adventure rides or, as one Cast Member said, 'a theme park in a box'. It houses 11 major adventures, such as *CyberSpace Mountain* (design and ride your own roller-coaster), *Invasion – An Alien Encounter* (a fun virtual-reality rescue mission), *Ride the Comix!* (a virtual-reality battle, this time with super-villains), *Virtual Jungle Cruise* (shooting the rapids, prehistoric style) and *Aladdin's Magic Carpet* (more virtual-reality fun in best cartoon fashion), a host of old-fashioned video games in *Replay Zone*, the latest sports games, a test of imagination in *Animation Academy* and 2 cafés – Wonderland Café, with computers and internet tables, and Food Quest, straight out of a space-age comic book.

BRITTIP

You can buy a combined annual pass for *DisneyQuest* and Disney's water parks at $137.39 for adults and $105.44 for 3–9s that can work out good value for multiple visits.

Two more interactive experiences are *Pirates of the Caribbean: Battle for Buccaneer Gold* (an amazing 3-D immersion in a swashbuckling, cannon-shooting quest for pirate treasure) and *Buzz Lightyear's Astro Blasters* (inter-galactic bumper cars with cannonball action! Restrictions: 4ft 3in/129cm). You enter via the clever Cybrolator to Ventureport and then have 4 main areas to explore: Score Zone (for most of the game-playing); Explore Zone (a mix of role-playing and virtual-reality games); Create Zone (hands-on activities to be your own 'Imagineer'); and Replay Zone (a 'moonscape' of classic games and rides). Admission: 10.30am– 11pm Sun–Thurs, 10.30am–midnight Fri and Sat. But, if you want to avoid the queues (the building admits only 1,500), go during the day. A 1-day ticket costs $39.41 ($33.02 3–9s). It's a bit too elaborate for most youngsters but teenagers will absolutely love it.

Cirque du Soleil® – La Nouba

Saving the best for last here, the most eye-catching part of West Side is home to the greatest show on earth (or at least, the greatest we've seen anywhere), the Cirque du Soleil® production *La Nouba*™. Twice a day, 5 times a week, the company's purpose-built, 1,671-seat theatre stages the most stupendous combination of dance, circus, acrobatics, comedy and live music in a 90-minute show that involves more than 60 performers. Anyone familiar with the unique styling, outrageous costumes and captivating sounds of the world-famous Cirque company will have an idea of what to expect, but even they will be left in awe by this stunning multi-dimensional assault on the senses.

The show title comes from the French phrase *faire la nouba*, to party or live it up, and this *La Nouba* does in grand style. It features trampolines, trapezes, balancing acts and even mountain bikes, woven with comedy (watch out for the inspired clowns), innovative dance routines and

La Nouba

spellbinding music, all with the most magnificent staging. Some of the stunts are truly jaw-dropping, notably the Chinese diabolo acrobats and the final act *Power Track/Trampoline*, which is worth the entry price alone. But the overall effect of the constant flow of movement, sublime timing and multitude of different characters (almost to the point where you hardly know where to look at any one time) is a masterpiece of modern theatre.

Words alone do not do it justice – go and see it. It is not cheap, but we believe it is worth every cent and a highlight of any visit to Orlando. Booking is vital and can be done up to 6 months in advance on 407 939 7719 (or **cirquedusoleil.com**). Shows are at 6pm and 9pm Tues–Sat, but try to be early for some excellent pre-show fun. **Admission:** there are 5 pricing groups, Category Front and Center at $114 for adults and $91 for 3-9s; Cat 1 at $99 and $79; Cat 2 at $81 and $65; Cat 3 at $65 and $52; and Cat 4 at $52 and $42 (but there is hardly a bad seat in the house). We've seen it multiple times and still look forward to going again!

Disney's BoardWalk

Disney's other big evening entertainment offering is part of its impressive Disney's B*oardWalk Resort*, where the waterfront entertainment district contains several notable venues (not counting the excellent micro-brewery and restaurant of the Big River Grille and Brewing Works, the thrilling ESPN Club for sports fans and the 5-star Flying Fish Café). **Jellyrolls** is a variation on the duelling piano bar, with the lively pianists conjuring up a humorous and often raucous evening of audience participation songs (7pm–2am; $10 cover charge; 21 and over only). The **Atlantic Dance** club features mainly modern dance music (it started life as a classic 1930s dance club and also moved through a Latin phase) with both house and guest DJs, plus occasional live music, all with a huge dance floor and a great bar service and ambience. It's especially popular on Fri and Sat nights, perhaps because there's no longer a cover charge (9pm–2am; closed Sun and Mon). It's strictly 21 and over, so remember your ID (no ID, no entry here). *Disney's Boardwalk Resort* also features some amusing stalls and live entertainers, which add to the carnival atmosphere, while the **ESPN Club** features regular celebrity (American) sports guests.

Bubba Gump's Shrimp Co.

UNIVERSAL'S CITYWALK

As part of the big Universal Orlando development – and in direct competition with *Downtown Disney* – this 30 acre/12ha spread has just about everything in the world of entertainment. The resort's hub is a busy, bustling expanse of shops, restaurants, snack bars, open-air events and nightclubs. It offers a huge variety of cuisines, from fast food to fine dining, an unusual blend of speciality shops and a truly eclectic nightclub mix, from reggae and rock 'n' roll to salsa, jazz and high-energy disco, plus the Blue Man Group show and a new karaoke theatre. There's a $7 entry fee at the 6 clubs but you can buy a **CityWalk Party Pass** ($11.99) or **Party Pass with Movie** (1 free film at the 20-screen **Universal Cineplex**; $15.00) for entry to all of them, while

BRITTIP

Park in Universal's multi-storey car park (no charge after 6pm) for all the CityWalk venues. For more info on the complex, call 407 363 8000 or visit **citywalkorlando.com**.

most multi-day tickets include a Party Pass. The area splits into 3, the Main Plaza (shopping and dining), Lagoon Front (dining, live music and theatre) and the Promenade (dining and nightclubs).

Main Plaza

Shopping: Among the most original (and amusing) of the 10 shops are **Endangered Species**, with products designed to raise eco-awareness; **Quiet Flight**, for radical surf and beachwear; the retro-American decor of **Fossil** for leather goods, watches and sunglasses; **DAPY** for trendy gifts; the large **Island Clothing Store** (for Tommy Bahama clothing and merchandise); and **Hart & Huntington Tattoo Company** with an astonishing array of permanent tattoos, as well as clothing and accessories.

Restaurants: Take your pick from a wide dining choice. **Bubba Gump's Shrimp Co** has a full *Forrest Gump* theme, from the Southern-inspired menu offerings to the decor and the little flip-sign on your table to tell your server whether you need something (Stop Forrest Stop!) or not (Run Forrest Run!). The menu is predictably heavy on seafood – with prawns done every possible way – but also includes chicken, ribs, sandwiches, salads and more, with catchy names like Bubba's After the Storm 'Bucket of Boat Trash'. The gift shop carries Shrimp beanies, Gump

BRITTIP

Mention you are celebrating a birthday at Bubba Gump's and you'll find you quickly become the centre of attention!

Gear clothing, lots of miscellanea and, of course, A Box of Chocolates. Open 11am–12am.

Emeril's: At the 5-star end of the range, this is a sophisticated and vibrant journey into the cuisine of New Orleans with master chef Emeril Lagasse. Fine wines and a cigar bar both enhance Emeril's Creole-based gourmet creations, and if you don't try the Louisiana oyster stew you'll have missed a real treat (lunch 11.30am–2pm; dinner 5.30–10pm Sun–Thurs, 5.30–11pm Fri and Sat). It gets booked up well in advance at weekends, so try for a weekday (407 224 2424).

Jimmy Buffet's Margaritaville: An island homage to Florida's laid-back musical hero, with 'Floribbean' cuisine (a mixture of Key West and Caribbean), live music and 3 bars (11am–2am), including the Volcano Bar, which 'erupts' margarita mix (!) when the blender needs filling. There is a cover charge ($7) after 10pm when the live band hits the stage.

NASCAR Sports Grill: A must for motor-racing fans (11am–late), with full-size stock cars and racing memorabilia, tableside plasma

Jimmy Buffet's Margaritaville

screens, videos and interactive games while you dine on burgers, ribs, steaks, pasta and grilled shrimp. The interior has been completely revamped and now has a smart, sophisticated look, with a balcony and patio seating for a taste of the 'Tailgating' experience (that uniquely American 'picnic in the car park' phenomena).

Pastamore: A delightful indoor/outdoor Italian diner, with the choice of full-service dining (5pm–midnight) for pizza, pasta, grilled chicken and steaks, or try the **Marketplace Café** (8am–2am) for panini, pastries and ice-cream.

Lagoon Front

Blue Man Group: The newest element of CityWalk and the most entertaining descended on the Sharp AQUOS Theatre (the old Nick Studios building) in 2007 with its unique brand of comedy, music and multi-media theatrics, adding something completely novel to the Universal line-up. In the hands (or mouths!) of the Blue Men, mundane items like pipes, paintballs, cereal and even audience members become the instruments of wild creativity with sometimes stunning, occasionally somewhat gross but always hilariously gratifying outcomes. There is a strong live music element to the show and it can feel like a rock concert at time – to such an extent one of their acts is all about how to be a proper rock star audience, with suitably comical results. Their penchant for percussion is another recurring theme and their ability to drum up a tune on various bits and pieces is truly amazing. The wild finale, involving the whole theatre, is a real corker, and don't worry if you're seated in the 'poncho section'; the Blue Men will make sure you have adequate protection. It all adds up to an unforgettable evening of family entertainment for just $59–74 adults, $49–64 3–9s. Tickets are available online at **universalorlando.com** or from the theatre box office.

Pat O'Brien's

Hard Rock Café and Hard Rock Live: Of course, you can't miss the world's largest example of this worldwide chain, with its collection of rock 'n' roll memorabilia (including a pink 1959 Cadillac) and concert venue. It remains hugely popular, so try to get in early for lunch or dinner (11am–late) to sample its classic diner fare. Collectors of Hard Rock souvenirs will also find prices in the excellent gift shop friendlier than in the UK. **Hard Rock Live** is the massive mock-Coliseum architecture, a 2,500-seat theatre with high-tech staging and sound. Big-name bands and performers are on stage several times a week (both Robbie Williams and Oasis have played here) in this slightly retro rock 'n' roll venue (407 351 LIVE, **hardrocklive.com**).

NBA City: Across the CityWalk waterway is the 2-storey Lagoon Front location of NBA City, another huge dining experience that is sure to thrill basketball fans with its Cage dining room, interactive playground area and Club lounge where you can watch live and classic games (11am–10.30pm Sun–Thurs; 11am–11.30pm Fri and Sat).

BRITTIP

CityWalk too crowded? Can't get in any of the restaurants? Jump on one of the boats to the Hard Rock Hotel or Portofino Bay Hotel and you can usually dine without a wait at The Kitchen (Hard Rock), Trattoria del Porto or Mama Della's (Portofino Bay).

Promenade

Finally, you come to the Promenade area, which offers a choice of nightclubs and some more fine dining, plus the ubiquitous **Starbucks** coffee house.

Bob Marley – A Tribute to Freedom: A clever re-creation of Marley's Jamaica home is turned into a courtyard live music venue, restaurant and bars. The bands are excellent, the atmosphere authentic and the place really comes alive at night (4.30pm–2am, 21 and over only after 9pm; cover charge $7 after 8pm).

Latin Quarter: South America is the vibe for this wonderful venue/ restaurant that serves up a genuine slice of Latin style in its atmosphere, music, dance, decor and cuisine. The food is outstanding – a combination of beef, fresh fish and poultry with tangy fruit sauces, spicy salsas and mouth-watering marinades (don't miss its version of rack of lamb) – the ambience is mesmerising and the sounds are so wonderfully vibrant and alive, you can't help dancing, even in your seat. Drop in for a meal or just check out the music (open 5–10pm). There's even a Latin Quarter Express dining window if you'd like a quick bite on the go.

Pat O'Brien's: This is a faithful reproduction of the famous New Orleans bar and restaurant (4.30pm–1am), with its Flaming Fountain courtyard, main bar and special duelling piano bar (5pm–2am, with a $7 cover charge; 21 and over only). Excellent Cajun food and world-famous Hurricane cocktails are the order of the day, but if you have too many don't expect to walk back!

Rising Star Karaoke: It's karaoke taken to the next level, with a live band, back-up singers and a host who makes every volunteer singer feel like the latest, greatest star (Tues–Sat; back-up singers and host only on Sun and Mon). There is also a full bar with speciality cocktails, appetisers and a large list of songs to choose from (21 and over; 18 and over on Thurs only; 8pm–2am; $7 cover charge, no additional charge to sing).

Red Coconut Club: For a slightly older generation, this is a retro dance club with a trendy, tropical vibe. With live music, signature cocktails, tapas-style menu, a cool bar and eclectic South Seas decor, it is a popular CityWalk venue (8pm–2am Sun–Thurs; 6pm–2am Fri and Sat; cover charge $7, free admission for ladies on Thurs). Free valet parking 6–8pm, with validated receipt.

the groove: For younger, club-minded visitors is the next generation in disco entertainment – a vivid, pounding, high-energy dance venue designed like a Victorian theatre but with the latest in club music, lighting and special effects (9pm–2am; 21 and over only; cover charge $7).

Not breathless yet? Well, there's still the 20-screen **Universal Cineplex** cinema complex with a capacity of 5,000 and the latest in movie comfort.

Bob Marley's at CityWalk

THE POINTE ORLANDO

This eye-catching development on I-Drive, almost opposite the Convention Center, is a mix of unique shops, cinema multiplex, restaurants, live entertainment and the **WonderWorks** fun centre (with its magic-themed dinner show). The Pointe is open all day but has notable evening appeal, especially with the completion of a $30m redevelopment that added 10 new restaurants, bars and clubs. The shops (10am–10pm Mon–Sat, 11am–9pm Sun) are all upscale and include some imaginative touches (see pages 343–4). Here is the full night-time entertainment choice, starting with the clubs:

Adobe Gila's: On the upper level you have a fine Mexican *cantina*, home of the 64oz margarita and more than 70 tequilas (!), plus some south-of-the-border dining delicacies – try the signature Gila Wraps. Adobe Gila's is especially popular with locals and is often packed at weekends as it stays open late and features live outdoor music and DJs several days a week. On Fridays and Saturdays the place should be kicking from 6.30pm: on weekdays, it's more likely to be 8.30pm (11.30am–2am; 407 903 1477; **adobegilas.com**).

Maggiano's Little Italy

BB King's Blues Club: Live jazz and blues make this a fine choice for a meal or drinks and a show in this imaginative venue, which features a main 2-storey concert hall, a variety of bars, an open-air terrace and a gift shop. It's not quite the place if you're looking for a quiet meal, especially when the band is playing, but if what you want is a real party, BB King's takes some beating. A Southern comfort-food menu features items such as Fried Green Tomatoes, Fried Shrimp Po Boy, Lip Smacking Ribs and (Simon's favourite) Southern Fried Catfish. Soups, salads and desserts round out the menu, and a full bar is available. There is live music nightly from 7pm with one of its 2 excellent house bands, plus special guest performers (11am–midnight Sun–Thurs, to 2am Fri and Sat; 407 370 4550 or **http://orlando.bbkingclubs.com**).

Restaurants: Capital Grille adds an elegant dining option with an extensive wine menu, dry-aged steaks, chops and seafood, with complimentary valet parking; **Hooters** is the local party place, with its famous 'Hooter Girl' waitresses and 'soon to be relatively famous' wings, burgers and seafood; **Johnny Rockets** provides a 1950s diner-style, with an indulgent burger-and-milkshake menu; **Maggiano's Little Italy** is a journey into family-style Italian dining in a relaxed, friendly atmosphere; the **Oceanaire Seafood Room** offers a classic 1930s ocean liner vibe and a heavenly range of fresh fish and shellfish, ideal for a special night out; **Taverna Opa** is a chance to go Greek and enjoy some lively taverna society, where impromptu table dancing may erupt all around you with paper napkins thrown at all and sundry (cheaper than breaking plates!); and **Tommy Bahama's Tropical Café**, a laid-back Island setting for an impressive array of food, wine and cocktails, for both lunch and dinner (plus a huge emporium of home furnishings, accessories and clothing).

Cuba Libre: The newest arrival to the Pointe (due late 2008), this bar/club/restaurant adds a touch of 1940s Havana to the local scene, with Latin floorshows, salsa dancing – and some wicked cocktails! The energetic tropical open-air atmosphere should lend itself to the party spirit, with the architecture, music and art to match. It promises genuine Latin-inspired cuisine, combining beef, pork, seafood and chicken with exotic fruits, vegetables, herbs and seasonings, plus a signature Tropical Brunch at weekends 10.30am–2.30pm (11.30am–11 pm Mon–Thurs, 11.30 am–1 am Fri, 10.30 am–1 am Sat, 10.30 am–11 pm Sun; **cubalibrerestaurant.com**).

The Grape: Settle in for an evening of wine, music and tapas-style nibbles at this Orlando outpost of a growing national chain that has become a notable gathering spot (11am–11pm Sun–Thurs, 11am–midnight Fri and Sat; 407 351 5815; **yourgrape.com**).

Tommy Bahama's Tropical Café and Emporium: Dining in a laid-back, tropical setting, Tommy Bahama's also carries home furnishings, accessories and men's and women's clothing with a casual Island flair (11am–11pm Sun–Thurs, 11am–midnight Fri and Sat; 321 281 5888, **tommybahama.com**).

BRITTIP

Be aware that American cinema popcorn is almost invariably of the SALTED variety!

Also here is the **Regal Cinema**, a 21-screen movieplex (one an IMAX) with a vast and cleverly themed entrance foyer, state-of-the-art stadium seating and sound systems, where you can often see a new film several months before it arrives in the UK. Look for the ticket office on the ground level (407 248 9228).

For more on The Pointe Orlando, call 407 248 2838 or visit **pointeorlando.com**. For more on the restaurant choices, see page 331 in Dining Out.

THE SQUARE

This is the long-awaited development in the place of the old Mercado Center. And, while is it not due to open its first phase until summer 2009, it should be worth waiting for. The basic line-up includes restaurants, bars and shops, plus 2 boutique-style hotels and a central plaza area staging live entertainment and state-of-the-art multi-media shows. The developers promise Las Vegas glitz and South Beach glamour to make this a hub of evening entertainment, with a lively, open-air dining choice and a trademark lights-and-lasers spectacular periodically 9pm–2 am. These latter will focus on the 1 acre/ 0.4 ha courtyard at the heart of The Square (a 4-storey edifice stretching from I-Drive right back to Universal Boulevard), with a huge water feature incorporating mist screens, fountains, elaborate lighting and music. Add in high-tech screens and pyrotechnics and this should be a truly eye-catching venture.

Capital Grille

Confirmed tenants include restaurants **Ra Sushi**, Venetian-themed **Carnevale**, the gourmet seafood **Truluck's**, **The Butcher Shop**, Roman-style **Dolce Vita**, Brazilian steakhouse **Fogo de Chao** and **Guy Harvey's Island Grill**, plus several Asian and UK-specific boutiques. Other plans, for 2010, include the amazing entertainment of San Francisco cabaret-and-circus group **Teatro Zinzanni**, the **Red Door Spa**, the hip 10-pin bowling extravaganza of **Lucky Strike**, a **SeaLife Aquarium**, **Madame Tussaud's** waxworks and some more upscale shops in the neighbouring Goodings Plaza. There will be a multi-storey car park and big festivals for New Year's Eve and other occasions (**thesquareorlando.com**).

Great Orlando Wheel: A sneak preview of this enormous project due to open in 2010, this will be a 400ft/ 122m observation wheel with 24 slowly revolving glass capsules. It will be one of the best vantage points for the nightly fireworks with views of Disney, SeaWorld and Universal.

DINNER SHOWS

Another source of evening entertainment comes in the many and varied dinner shows that are a major Orlando phenomenon. From murder mysteries to full-scale medieval battles, it's all wonderful, imaginative fun, even if the food is usually quite ordinary. As the name suggests, it is live entertainment coupled with dinner and unlimited free wine, beer and soft drinks in a fantasy-type environment, where even the waiters and waitresses are in costume. They always have a strong family appeal and you are usually seated at large tables where you get to know other people, too, but, at $35–50, they are not cheap (especially with taxes and tips). Be aware, too, of the attempts to extract more dollars from you with photos, souvenirs, etc.

Disney shows

Walt Disney World's offerings are often overlooked by visitors unless they are staying at one of the hotel resorts, but they are well worth considering.

Disney's Spirit of Aloha: For an excellent night of South Seas entertainment, go to Luau Cove at *Disney's Polynesian Resort.* It's a bit expensive at $59.99 for adults (Category 1 seating, including tax and tip) and $30.99 for under-10s; or Cat 2 $54.99 and $26.99; Cat 3 $50.99 and $25.99 but good value all the same as the 2-hour show features some splendid entertainment, from the fun to the thrilling (Hawaiian sounds, singers, dancers and other Polynesian acts, including the amazing Samoan fire juggler, all with a strong family story). You need to come hungry as the food is plentiful, with salad, roast chicken, ribs, vegetables and rice, plus a Kilauea Volcano Dessert (or peanut butter and jam sandwiches, chicken fingers, macaroni cheese and hot dogs for kids). Beer, wine and soft drinks are included, and shows are at 5.15 and 8pm Tues–Sat. You can make reservations up to 180 days in advance, with full payment to be made when booking.

Hoop-Dee-Doo Musical Revue: At *Disney's Fort Wilderness Resort & Campground* is an ever-popular nightly dinner show that maintains the resort's impressive cowboy theme, and has great food (all-you-can-eat ribs, fried chicken, corn-on-the-cob, baked beans and strawberry shortcake, plus unlimited beer, wine, sangria and soft drinks). Especially loved by children, it features the amusing song and dance of the Pioneer Hall Players in a merry American hoedown-style show. Okay, it's corny and a tad embarrassing to find yourself singing along with the hammy action, but it is performed

Hoop-Dee-Doo Musical Revue

with great gusto – and you're on holiday, remember! The Revue plays nightly at 5, 7.15 and 9.30pm at the Pioneer Hall, Category 1 seating is $59.99 for adults (inclusive of tax and tip), $30.99 for under-10s; Cat 2 $54.99 and $26.99; Cat 3 $50.00 and $25.99 (under-3s free) and the show lasts almost 2 hours. Reservations are ALWAYS necessary (can be made up to 180 days in advance; full payment due when booking).

Mickey's Backyard Barbecue: If you can't get enough of the Disney characters, try this twice-weekly dinner show, usually Thurs and Sat, Mar–Dec at 6.30pm and 8pm, at *Disney's Fort Wilderness* resort. It features Mickey and the gang in a country buffet-style dinner at picnic tables under an open-air pavilion with live music, line dancing, rope tricks and other entertainment, and plenty of character interaction (great for younger children). The all-you-can-eat buffet offers barbecued pork ribs, baked chicken, hot dogs, macaroni cheese, salads, watermelon and ice-cream. Like all Disney dining, this is a no-smoking environment. The show may be cancelled if bad weather threatens ($44.99 adults, $26.99 3–9s). To make a reservation for a Disney show, call 407 939 3463.

Electrical Water Pageant: An alternative is the nightly (and free!) pageant that circles Bay Lake and the Seven Seas Lagoon, passing by each of the *Magic Kingdom* resorts in turn. It lasts just 10 minutes so it's easy to miss, but it's almost a waterborne version of the SpectroMagic parade, with thousands of twinkling lights on a floating cavalcade of boats and mock sea creatures. The usual schedule is 9pm at *Disney's Polynesian Resort*, 9.15 at *Disney's Grand Floridian Resort & Spa* (get a grandstand view in Narcoosee's restaurant), 9.35 at *Disney's Wilderness Lodge*, 9.45 on the shores of *Disney's Fort Wilderness Resort* and 10.05pm at *Disney's Contemporary Resort*. It can also be seen from the boat jetties outside the *Magic Kingdom*.

BRITTIP

Most dinner shows can be quite chilly, especially those with animals such as Arabian Nights and Medieval Times, so bring a jacket or sweater to beat the air-conditioning.

Pirate's Dinner Adventure

Arabian Nights

This lovingly maintained, family-owned attraction, which celebrated its 20th anniversary in 2008, is a real large-scale production and one of the most popular with locals as well as tourists. It's a treat for horse lovers but you don't need to be an equestrian expert to appreciate the spectacular stunts, horsemanship and marvellous costumes as some 70 horses, including Arabians, Andalusians, Belgians and Walter Farley's famous black stallion, perform a 20-act show. The storyline features Abra Kadabra, the sultan's genie, acting as mentor to the brash young Hocus Pocus, genie to the Princess. The show is staged in the huge arena at the centre of this 1,200-seat 'palace'. Daring gypsy acrobats, magical genies, square-dancing cowboys, exotic Latin Garrocha riding, and a thrilling chariot race all add up to a memorable show that kids, especially, adore. A special **Christmas Holiday Show** takes over for the winter season (Nov–Jan), and there is also some impressive pre-show entertainment, featuring star magician Michael Baron. The food – salad, a choice of New York Strip Steak, grilled chicken breast, Pasta Primavera (which can also be requested without cheese for

Arabian Nights

vegans), chicken tenders or chopped steak, and dessert – is above average, too, with hot tea available on request. Located just ½ml/1km east of I-4 on Highway 192 (on the left, just to the side of the Parkway shopping plaza, at Marker 8), Arabian Nights runs every evening at 6 or 8.30pm (often both), with occasional matinees. It lasts almost 2 hours, and you can buy tickets ($56.60 adults, $31.03 3–11s; VIP experience $73.72 and $46.01) at the box office 8am–10pm or by credit card on 407 239 9223 (visit **arabian-nights.com** for a saving offer or free upgrade or $10 discount per ticket). A 'VIP' upgrade adds a souvenir poster, pre-show drink in the VIP area, priority seating (in the first 3 rows) and the chance to meet the stars pre-show.

Medieval Life at Medieval Times

Medieval Times

Spain in the 11th century is the entertaining setting for this 2-hour extravaganza of medieval pageantry, sorcery and robust horseback jousts that culminate in furious hand-to-hand combat between 6 knights. It's worth arriving early to appreciate the clever mock castle design and the staff's costumes as you are ushered into the pre-show hall before being taken into the arena itself. The Knights of the Realm show features fast-paced skills tests, loosely centred on a treacherous plot within the king's inner circle. But honour and bravery ultimately prevail, restoring order to the Kingdom, and it's all set to a dramatic musical score played by the Prague Symphony Orchestra. The weapons are all real and used with great skill, and there are some neat special effects. You need to be in full audience participation mode as you cheer on your knight and boo the others, but kids (not to mention a few adults) get a huge kick out of it and they'll also love eating without cutlery (don't worry, the soup bowls have handles!). The elaborate staging is backed up by an excellent chicken dinner and the serfs and wenches who serve you make it a fun experience. Prices, which include the **Medieval Life** exhibit (see below), are $56.95 for adults and $35.95 for 3–12s (check its website for discounts). A Royalty Package upgrade for $10/person includes preferred seating, knight's cheering banner, a commemorative programme and behind-the-scenes souvenir DVD. Doors open 90 minutes prior to show time. Times vary with the season, so call 1888 935 6878 or visit **medieval times.com** for details and reservations. The castle is on Highway 192, 5mls/8km east of the junction with I-4 and has recently undergone an $8m renovation that makes the whole place fresh and inviting. If you have 45 minutes to spare before the show, the **Medieval Life** exhibit is an interesting diversion. This mock village portrays the life and times of people living 900 years ago, with artisans demonstrating pottery and tool-making, glassblowing, spinning and weaving, plus a wonderfully gruesome dungeon and torture chamber (definitely not for young children!). Stay on after the show (the 2nd show only on busy nights) for **The Knight Club**, with bar service, music, dancing and the chance to meet royalty and knights for autographs and photo opportunities.

Pirate's Dinner Adventure

This show (which has been revamped several times since it opened in 1997) features one of the most spectacular settings, with the Spanish galleon pirate ship centrepiece being 150ft/46m long, 60ft/18m wide, 70ft/21m tall and 'anchored' in a 300,000 gallon/1,365,000 litre lagoon. It also delivers good value with its pre-show elements, plentiful (if ordinary) food and drink, and the imaginative after-show Buccaneer Bash disco until 10.30pm. Coffee is also served at the Buccaneer Bash, and there are kids' meals (chicken fingers and vegetarian) if the main choice of pork, shrimp and chicken with rice and mixed veg doesn't appeal. The basic premise of the audience being 'hijacked' by the wicked pirates is a clever one, even if the story is hard to follow occasionally. Chaos and mayhem ensue, with the local princess abducted by the villainous crew of Captain Sebastian the Black. Swashbuckling abounds, with sword fights, acrobatics, trapeze artists and boat races. There are plenty of energetic stunts and special effects – plus audience participation, which the kids love ($57.95 adults, $37.95 3–11s; see website for discounts).

BRITTIP

When there are 2 or more shows of The Pirate's Dinner Adventure in one night, opt for the last one if you want the disco bash afterwards.

Pirate's Dinner Adventure

There is also a **Governor's VIP Upgrade** ($25 extra) with an exclusive pre-show lounge and bar, front row seating, guaranteed audience participation, special appetiser buffet, champagne toast and one-on-one cast photo opportunity; **Treasurer's Upgrade** ($12), with enhanced seating (row 2), pirate hat and beads; and **Pirate's Upgrade** ($10) row 3 seating, hat and beads. The show is located on Carrier Drive between I-Drive and Universal Boulevard, and runs daily at 6pm, 7.30pm or 8.30pm (additional shows in peak periods), with appetisers served for 45 minutes until it's time to be seated (407 248 0590, **orlando pirates. com**). There is also a special **Pirates Christmas Dinner Adventure** show, which adds suitable festive theming.

Sleuth's Mystery Dinner Shows

This is a real live version of Cluedo acted out before your eyes in hilarious fashion while you enjoy a substantial meal (with a main course choice of honey-glazed Cornish hen, prime rib or lasagne) and unlimited beer, wine and soft drinks. You can choose between 3 theatres and no fewer than 13 different plot settings (several of which have amusing British settings), including *Joshua's Demise, Roast 'Em, Toast 'Em* and *Lord Mansfield's Fox Hunt Banquet* (mayhem at an English banquet), that add up to some elaborate murder mysteries. The action takes place all around you and members of the audience can take some cameo roles. The quick-witted cast keep things moving and keep you guessing during the theatrical part of the 2½-hour show, then during the main part of dinner you think up questions for interrogation (but be warned, the real murderer is allowed to lie!). Solve the crime and you win a prize, but that is pretty secondary to the overall enjoyment and this is a show we enjoy a lot. Prices are $49.95 adults, $23.95 3–11s and times vary (407 363 1985 or **sleuths.com**). Purely for children is **Sleuth's Merry Mystery Dinner Adventure**, with a special kids' dinner, dessert and unlimited soft drinks. Designed primarily for 6–12s (mainly Sat afternoon), it features one of two adventures, *The Faire of the Shire* and *The Magical Journey of Juniper Junior* ($28 adults, $16 3–12s, reservations required). Sleuth's is located in the Goodings Plaza on International Drive, with 3 different theatres, a smart pre-dinner bar area and expanded gift shop.

Sleuth's

WonderWorks: Outta Control Magic Comedy Dinner Show

On a smaller scale but no less fun, this show is at WonderWorks on I-Drive (on one corner of The Pointe Orlando). A novel mixture of improvised comedy and clever, close-up magic, the show is accompanied by all-you-can-eat pizza, salad and dessert, plus beer, wine and coke. Set in the intimate Shazam Theater, it features live music, special lighting effects and some slick magic tricks from illusionist Tony Brent. The tricks are all fairly routine, but the show is served up in style and involves plenty of audience participation. There are a couple of terrific running gags throughout the fast-paced show, but beware of sitting too close to the stage – you WILL end up as part of the act! Performed twice nightly at 6pm and

8pm, it costs a reasonable $24.95 for adults and $12.95 for 4–12s and seniors. Alternatively, a Magic Combo ticket for the show and access to WonderWorks afterwards (open until midnight, see pages 238–9) is $38.95/ $28.95 (407 351 8800, **wonderworks online.com**).

Capone's Dinner & Show

The setting is 1930s gangland Chicago and, although prohibition is still in full swing, the drinks flow freely at Al's speakeasy. More importantly, in 2008 Capone's introduced an all-new comedy show with song-and-dance acts, loosely fitted around Bugs Moran's sinister plot to take over the club. Ditzy Bunny-June (the real star of the show, with a voice worth paying to hear!) and her new husband, Fingers Salvatorio, keep the snappy one-liners coming, along with perfectly-timed commentary from the wait-staff. Although it leans slightly toward the risqué, the show still remains in family-friendly territory, while an Italian-American buffet offers 3 types of pasta, ham, turkey, pot roast and side dishes; basic fare, but sure to keep everyone happy. Unlimited Bud Light draughts, a selection of wines and cocktails, plus soft drinks, juice, Kiddie Cocktails and Mama Capone's 'dessert surprise' round out the all-you-can-eat-and-drink menu. Tickets $47.98 adults, $29.98 4–12 (3 and under free). See its website for money-off coupons (407 397 2378 or **alcapones.com**)

THE NIGHTCLUB SCENE

Orlando is blessed with a huge variety of nightlife, from regular discos to elaborate live music clubs and 'duelling piano' bars. The majority are situated in the downtown area, away from the main tourist centres. The *Orlando Sentinel* has a Friday supplement, *Calendar*, which has all the local entertainment listings, while **orlandocitybeat.com** details the nightspots, events, happy hours and other essential info. The free *Orlando Weekly* (available from supermarkets and tourist centres) is also a valuable guide, or visit **orlandoweekly.com**.

Bars and discos come and go at an amazing rate, so don't be surprised if you try to revisit a nightclub and find it has had a complete change of name and personality. The basic distinctions tend to be live music clubs; mainstream nightclubs, with the occasional live band; and bars with evening entertainment.

Live music clubs

The following should give you a taste of the most popular venues (in most cases for those aged 21 and over only).

Bosendorfer Lounge: For pure, relaxed jazz and other live music, have a look at this venue at the Grand Bohemian Hotel (see page 92) on South Orange Avenue. Usually 6–10pm every evening (plus Sunday Jazz Brunch 10.30am–2.30pm), the sounds of its $250,000 Bosendorfer piano are well worth travelling to hear.

Capone's

Sak Comedy Lab: As a complete alternative to the music scene (on West Amelia Avenue in the Theater Garage), this is like a live version of the TV show *Whose Line Is It Anyway?*. Fast-paced and funny (and with a 'no obscenity' rule for concerned parents), the Sak performers do a mix of competitive ad lib comedy, with every show offering something different and the young performers living on their wits. Consistently voted Florida's best live comedy, see it for yourself Tues–Sat (with 2 different shows Fri and Sat), admission $5–15. Its Lab Rats show (Tues) features Sak's 'students' and is just $2. Booking is advised on Fri and Sat nights (407 648 0001, **sak.com**).

The Social: While Hard Rock Live at CityWalk and House of Blues at *Downtown Disney* are the 2 main regular live music venues in town, this is the next best option in size terms, and offers a far more intimate and 'clubby' atmosphere, along with a great range of local bands, up-and-coming acts and the occasional bigger name (The Killers, Supergrass and Billy Bragg among others) looking for a more offbeat venue. Situated in the heart of the city's downtown area (on North Orange Avenue, right next to Tabu nightclub), The Social features the full spectrum of blues, rock, jazz and Latin sounds, with great house and guest DJs in between. The small main auditorium and bar holds up to 400, and the secondary bar provides an excellent hideaway at the back of this well-run club. Its website (**thesocial.org**) offers the chance to listen to some of the forthcoming acts and buy tickets in advance (generally $8–25; 407 246 1419). Check out the local hangout of the **Bar BQ Bar** next to The Social for cheap drinks.

Mainstream nightclubs

The Club at Firestone: Hard to categorise, this scores well with the alternative/progressive crowd. It ranges from mainstream disco to acid jazz lounge, with something different each Fri, Sat and Sun. Separate rooms inside the club feature Reggaeton salsa, house, electronic and hip-hop, with its Latin Ladies Night on Fri and special guest DJs on Sat. North of Church Street on the corner of Orange Avenue and Concord Street. Cover charge $5 (407 872 0066; **clubat firestone.com**).

The Independent: On Orange Avenue on the corner of Washington Street, offering alternative and new wave music, this has more of a techno-dance sound, but features various retro-progressive, old wave, goth and indie college rock. The club has 3 contrasting levels, including an area with pool tables. Doors open at 10pm; cover charge $5 (407 839 0457; **independentbar.net**).

The House of Blues

© OCVB

Tabu

Tabu: In addition to the mainstream DJ dance centres at *Downtown Disney's Pleasure Island* and Universal's CityWalk, Tabu (46 North Orange Avenue, just up from Church Street) appeals widely to the young, trendy crowd with regular nightly line-ups, guest DJs and special events, usually of a fairly raucous nature! (Wed–Sun, 21 and over only Sat; $7–12; 407 648 8363 **tabunightclub.com**).

Gay scene: For the gay scene, **Parliament House** (on North Orange Avenue) and **Southern Nights** (Bumby Avenue and Anderson Street) remain the most happening venues in the area, while the **Cactus Club** (on North Mills Avenue), **Studz Bar** (on Edgewater Drive) and **Wylde's** (on South Orange Avenue) are also popular.

Bars

Orlando also has a vast array of night hot spots. With live entertainment, extrovert barmen, sports-themed bars and raw bars (seafood, often by the bucket!), the choice is wide-ranging. Bars of all types simply abound in downtown Orlando.

Church Street: Newly opened after a long refurbishment, Church Street is making a comeback with a decent range of restaurants and bars. Seek out the stunningly ornate **Cheyenne Saloon & Opera House**, where live country music, a nightly Happy Hour with generous food and drink specials and Nickel Beer Wednesdays (5–7pm) add to the Wild West dance saloon atmosphere. The menu includes salads, sandwiches, ribs, pulled pork and chicken, plus the World's Smallest Sundae (4pm–2am Tues–Sat; $5 admission after 7pm; 407 839 3000 or **cheyennesaloonandoperahouse.com**). Just a few doors down is **The Dessert Lady**, where cakes, pies, cobblers and a light Bistro Menu are sure to appeal (**dessertlady.com**). The tempting Spanish tapas style of **Ceviche** (with a truly beautiful bar area) is another popular and elegant choice (321 281 8140, **http://ceviche.com**).

Also worth noting are **Big Belly Brewery**, with a micro-brewery and an impressive range of other beers (as well as an outrageous collection of wall art), also featuring roof-top bar **Latitudes**, and **The Orlando Brewing Co**, creators of hand-crafted organic beer, with 21 beers on tap, 6 of which are its own, brewed on-site and served by the pint in a 100-seat tasting room. Brewery tours are

Cheyenne Saloon and Opera House

available, as is Wi-Fi access, live entertainment and a gift shop, 3–10pm Mon–Thurs, noon–late Fri and Sat, noon–9pm Sun. Find it at 1301 Atlantic Ave (next to the Amtrak train station) or visit **orlandobrewing.com**.

Orange Avenue, Pine Street and Wall Street: Travel out past Church Street and you are into real locals' territory with the likes of **One-Eyed Jack's** and the **Loaded Hog**, the eclectic duo of **Slingapour's** and **The Globe** (the latter an off-the-wall diner), worth seeking out for a lively drink or three. **Urban Flats** is a tempting casual dining and wine bar-style venue, while **Corona Cigar Co** is a totally modern cigar bar, shop and lounge.

Sports bars

Finally, among the multitude of sports bars (another particularly American speciality), **Friday's Front Row Sports Grill** on I-Drive (just south of the Sand Lake Road junction) is a major landmark that even the locals enjoy. Here you can catch all the action on 84 TV screens, plus enjoy 100 beers from around the world (the bar features $1.99 domestic 12oz draughts and half price on some appetisers during Ecstatic Happy Hour!). Try out its basketball nets, shuffleboard and pool tables, and rub shoulders with local sports stars from time to time. The food is the regular TGI Fridays menu but there is plenty to keep the kids amused too (paper tablecloths for drawing and colouring, and video games). The atmosphere varies according to the time of day and event (pretty rowdy for Orlando Magic basketball games), so call 407 363 1414 for latest info (11am–2am daily; **frontroworlando.my fridays.com**).

Best of British Soccer World

Our favourite is the **Orlando Ale House** group, with a fine example on Kirkman Road, opposite Universal Studios (407 248 0000) and at Lake Buena Vista on Highway 535 (407 239 1800). It features more than 30 TVs, a raw bar, good seafood, its signature spicy 'chicken zingers' and an above-average range of beers (**millersale house.com**). Another chain worth noting is **Buffalo Wild Wings**, with 3 Orlando locations (notably on I-Drive just south of Wet 'n Wild, 11am–1am Mon–Thurs, 11am–2am Fri and Sat, noon–midnight Sun; 407 351 6200), where masses of chicken-orientated dishes (including signature wings with 14 sauces; watch out for the Blazin' – it's seriously hot!) are served up in a casual, lively atmosphere, highlighted by its Buzztime Trivia System at each table and multiple big-screen TVs (**buffalowildwings.com**).

Walt Disney World boasts the excellent **ESPN Club** at *Disney's BoardWalk Resort*, a full-service restaurant with sports broadcast facilities, video games, more than 70 TV monitors, giant scoreboards and even a Little League menu for kids. No sports fan should miss it. Equally, **NBA City** (for basketball fans) at Universal's CityWalk, and the **Cricketers' Arms** in Festival Bay (noon– 2am) and **Orlando George & Dragon** next to Wet 'n Wild (for British sport) should not be overlooked, especially for TV addicts (**cricketers armspub.com** and **britanniapubs.com**). There is also the signature **Best of British Soccer World** on I-Drive (see pages 326–7).

Now you'll want to know a lot more about where, when and how to tackle that other holiday dilemma – where to eat. Read on…

11 Dining Out

or Man, These Portions are HUGE!

America takes the concept of dining out VERY seriously. Consequently, the restaurant scene is an essential component of its tourism business. Going out for meals is second nature as it is usually much cheaper and better value than in the UK, while it has an extra element of convenience that is extremely family-friendly. The options for dining out are therefore seemingly omnipresent and large scale.

This is all excellent news for us Joe Tourists as it means it's impossible to go hungry and easy to feed the family without breaking the bank (though you will find some restaurants tend to rush the diners through meals – they are not the focal point they usually are in Europe).

Variety

The variety, quantity and quality of restaurants, cafés, fast-food chains and snack bars is in keeping with the local tradition of convenience and value. At first glance, the choice is overwhelming. Cruising along I-Drive or Highway 192 will reveal a bewildering array of eateries.

As a general rule, food is plentiful, relatively cheap, available 24 hours a day and nearly always appetising and filling. You will encounter an increasing number of fine-dining possibilities, but the basic emphasis is still on value for money. Put simply, portions will be large! Service is also efficient and friendly, and it's usually hard to come by a bad meal. The one real exception is if you like fresh veg. Many restaurants seem to overlook this staple but, if you look up the vegetarian options or visit outlets like **Sweet Tomatoes**, you will find a more balanced choice.

Exceptional deals

In keeping with the climate, most restaurants tend towards the informal (T-shirts and shorts are usually acceptable) and cater readily for families (you will always find a kids' menu, for example, and many have activity packs). This also leads to 2 great deals for budget-conscious tourists, especially those with a large tribe. Many hotels and restaurants offer 'kids eat free' deals, provided parents are also dining. The age limits vary from under-10 to under-14, but it obviously represents good value. The

Red Rock Canyon Grill

all-you-can-eat buffet is another common feature. This means you can probably eat enough at breakfast to keep you going until dinner! Some places also offer early-bird specials – a discount to dine before 6pm. Be aware that 5.30–7.30pm is rush hour for many restaurants and you may have to wait for a table. Try to arrive by 5pm or after 8pm.

BRITTIP

As portions are so large, you can save money by sharing a main course. Your waiter or waitress will be happy to oblige (provided you keep their tip up to the full rate).

Don't be afraid to ask for a doggy bag if you have leftovers (even if you haven't brought the dog!). Just ask for the leftovers 'to go'. And don't hesitate to speak up if something isn't right. Americans will readily complain if they are not happy, so restaurants are keen to ensure everything is to their diners' satisfaction. And, please, don't forget to **tip**. The basic wage for waiters and waitresses is low. They rely heavily on tips as part of their income and are taxed on an assumed level of tips. Unless service really is shoddy (in which case you should mention it), the usual rate for tips is 10% of your bill at buffet-style restaurants and 15% at full-service restaurants. It is worth checking to see if service is already added to your bill, though this is not common in the US.

With Orlando being such a worldwide holiday favourite, you will encounter a huge array of food types. Florida is renowned for its seafood, which comes much cheaper than in Mediterranean countries. Crab, lobster, shrimp (what we know as king prawns), clams and oysters can all be had at decent prices, as well as several dozen varieties of fish, many of which you won't have come across before. Latin-influenced cuisines, notably Cuban and Mexican, are common (especially for the delicious citrus-marinated seafood called ceviche) but there is also plenty of Asian fare, from Chinese and Indian to Japanese, Thai and Vietnamese. The big shopping malls offer a good choice in their food courts, which are often particularly good value. 'Cracker' cooking is original Floridian fare, and the speciality is alligator, either stewed, barbecued, smoked, sautéed or braised. Fried gator tail 'nuggets' are a local favourite. And you must try Key Lime Pie – a truly wonderful dessert.

How to order

Ordering food can be an adventure in itself. The choice for each item is often the cue for an inquisition! You can never order just 'toast' – it has to be white, brown, wholewheat, rye, muffin or bagel; eggs come in a baffling variety (order them 'sunny side up' for a traditional British fried egg; 'over easy' is fried both sides but still soft); an order of tea or coffee often brings the response 'Iced, lemon, green, herbal or English? Regular or decaff?'; and salads have more dressings than the NHS. Ask to see a menu if it isn't displayed.

Vegetarian options

In a country where beef is culinary king, vegetarians often find themselves hard done by. However, there are some bright spots. First, there are several largely veggie restaurants, like **Blue Bistro & Grill** on Mills Ave in downtown Orlando (407 898 5660), the Indian cuisine of **Woodlands** on S Orange Blossom Trail (407 854 3330; **woodlandsusa.com**), **Black Bean Deli** on S Orlando Ave in Winter Park (406 628 0294), trendy **Ethos Vegan Kitchen** on N Orange Ave, just north of downtown (407 228 3898, **ethosvegankitchen.com**) and the well-established Chinese of **Garden Café** on West Colonial Drive downtown (407 999 9799). The tapas-style **Café Tu Tu Tango** on I-Drive also serves a good variety of vegetarian dishes. However, most upscale restaurants can offer a veggie option and will be happy for you to ask in advance. *Walt Disney World* is more enlightened in that the **California Grill** (in **Disney's Contemporary Resort**), **Citricos** (*Grand Floridian Resort and Spa*), **Le Cellier** (Canada pavilion in *Epcot*) and **Spoodles** (*Disney's BoardWalk*) feature good vegetarian choices, while the seafood-orientated **Flying Fish** (*Disney's Boardwalk*) and **'Ohana** (*Disney's Polynesian Resort*) also serve up decent veggie fare if asked. Most full-service restaurants (notably **Bongos Cuban Café™** and **Wolfgang Puck® Café** in *Downtown Disney*) and even some counter-service outlets can cater for non-menu requests. It's always worth asking.

BRITTIP

An excellent section of the All Ears Net website run by Deb Wills lists places that cater for special diets, including veggie, at **allearsnet.com/din/special.htm**.

However, **Sweet Tomatoes** (on I-Drive by the Kirkman Road junction) is notably the most popular vegetarian-friendly outlet in Orlando. A buffet restaurant with some great meal deals, it has an all-you-can-eat lunch for $7.29 ($8.99 at dinner, after 4pm) that includes a vast salad spread, a choice of soups, pizza, pasta, bread and pastries, plus fruit and frozen yoghurt. Drinks are $1.89 (refills free) and kids' meals are $1.99 3–5s and $4.99 6–12s (10.30am–9pm Mon–Thurs, 11.30am–10pm Fri and Sat, 9am–9pm Sun; **soupplantation.com**). **Chamberlin's Market & Café** (with 8 Orlando outlets) is another more enlightened choice, with home-made soups, vegetarian chilli, salads, sandwiches and fruit smoothies (**chamberlins.com**). The **Panera Bread** chain also offers some decent veggie options (plus free wireless internet).

BRITTIP

American bacon is always streaky and crisp-fried and sausages are chipolata-like and slightly spicy.

Eating 24/7

It's not unusual to find restaurants that never close – you can eat around the clock, or '24/7' as the Americans say. So, for those who can't sleep on their first night in the US (plus those who just like to eat!), here is where you can go for a snack or even a full-scale meal at 4 in the morning. **Chain restaurants:** Denny's, Waffle House, Steak & Shake, some McDonald's; **Individuals:** B-Line Diner (Peabody Hotel, I-Drive), Planet Java (Gaylord Palms Resort), Sundial 24-7 (Regal Sun Resort) and Mainstreet Market (Hilton at *Walt Disney World Resort*).

BRITTIP

If there are several of you drinking beer, ordering a pitcher will work out cheaper than buying it by the glass.

Drinking

A big complaint from Brits on holiday in the US is about the beer. With the exception of a handful of English-style pubs and micro-breweries, American beer is always lager, either bottled or on draught, and ice cold. It goes down great when it's hot but is generally weaker and fizzier than our

There are opportunities from formal to casual

own. Of course, there are exceptions (try Killian's Red, Michelob's Amber Bock, Bare Knuckle Stout or Sam Adams beers for a fuller flavour), but if you are expecting a good, old-fashioned British pint, forget it (though the **Cricketers Arms** at Festival Bay has introduced a new chilling process for some of its ales, which serves them closer to the proper temperature). You should also look out for **The Big River Grille** at *Disney's Boardwalk Resort*, **Big Belly Brewery** in downtown Orlando or any of the **Hops Bar & Grill** chain, which are all micro-breweries. Spirits (always called 'liquor' by Americans) come in a typically large selection, but beware of ordering just 'whisky' as you'll get bourbon. Specify if you want Scotch or Irish whiskey and demand it 'straight up' if you don't want it with a mountain of ice. Also, when you order a Coke or similar from a counter-service outlet, ask for 'no ice' or 'light ice' unless you want a drink that is 50% ice.

BRITTIP

Most Orlando supermarkets don't sell spirits, just beer and wine (and some liqueurs, like Kahlua). If you want whisky, gin etc., you need to seek out a 'liquor store' like the ABC chain.

If you fancy a cocktail, there is a massive choice and most bars and restaurants have lengthy happy hours with good prices. Good-quality Californian wines are better value than European. If you are sticking to soft drinks ('sodas') or coffee, most bars and restaurants give free refills. You can also run a tab in the majority of bars and pay when you leave. But please note that US licensing laws are stricter than ours and **you must be 21 or over to drink alcohol in a bar or lounge**. You will often be asked for proof of age before you are served (or allowed into a club), and this means your passport or photo driving licence. Don't bother to argue – no photo ID, no beer!

BRITTIP

Tourist brochures often include money-off coupons for certain restaurants, and you can make useful savings here.

Cricketers Arms

Where to eat

That gives you the inside track on HOW to eat and drink like the locals. Now you need to know WHERE, so here's a guide to that profusion of choice. There are 4,000-plus restaurants in greater Orlando, so it would be a tall order to list each one. However, the following selection covers the main areas. We group them into: Fast Food, Family Favourites, International Flavours, Home from Home, Seafood Specials, and Deluxe Dining. You'll find the Fast Food and Family Favourite type in all the main areas. We also indicate a budget:

$ = most main courses under $10

$$ = most main courses $10–15

$$$ = most main courses $15–20

$$$$ = most main courses $20–$30

$$$$$ = most main course $30-plus

And we have a special section on each of the three main areas of International Drive, Highway 192/ Kissimmee and Lake Buena Vista.

It's McDonald's, Jim, but not as we know it!

McDonald's is not renowned for its healthy options – until you come to Orlando and find the restaurants owned and operated by Oerther Foods, which pioneered the chain's Bistro Gourmet menus. Oerther has 19 McDonald's outlets, all of which are themed, while 12 are open 24 hours and 7 feature the new bistro offerings – an amazing deviation from the fast-food norm. As well as the usual Big Mac and fries, they feature fresh pasta selections, hand-made pizza, gourmet sandwiches, veggie wraps, mountainous salads, gourmet coffees and eye-catching desserts. You order in the normal way, then watch your meal being created for you at the deli counter. Portions are generous, freshly made and quite delicious. Bistro breakfast selections (7am–10.30pm) include Eggs Benedict, Belgian Waffles and French Toast. The 19 themed locations vary from 1950s (at 5890 S Orange Blossom Trail) to Motorbikes (5400 S Kirkman Road) and an African Safari (2944 S Kirkman Road). The finest examples, though, are the Sand Lake Road duo – The World's Largest Entertainment McDonald's & PlayPlace (6875 Sand Lake Road) and Sand Lake Too (7344 Sand Lake Road), an ultra-modern venue. The former features a huge games arcade and vivid themed areas, plus a Kids' Club and toddler area, with animatronics and other fun features (bistro hours 7am–11pm Mon–Thurs, to 3am Fri–Sun; regular McDonald's menu available 24 hours). Look up more at **mcfun.com**.

FAST FOOD

This section is reserved primarily for all the counter-service fast food outlets and all will be in the $ category.

The big names: If you are a fan of **McDonald's**, there are around 70 outlets in the area, from small drive-through types to a mega, 24-hour establishment on Sand Lake Road (near the junction with I-Drive) that also has the biggest Play Place for kids of any McDonald's in the world. **Burger King** is well represented, as is that other burger bastion, **Wendy's**. **KFC** also has outlets throughout the area, and you'll find plenty of **Pizza Huts** and **Domino's Pizza**, both of which deliver locally – even to your hotel room.

Local variations

Check out **Checkers** or **Hardees** for burgers, **Popeye's Famous Fried Chicken & Biscuits** or **Chick-fil-A** as a KFC alternative, **Taco Bell**, if you'd like the cheap and cheerful Mexican option, or **Arby's** for a range of hot roast beef sandwiches that make a nice change from burgers. **Dairy Queen** offers a mix of burgers, hot dogs, pork sandwiches and ice-cream dishes, while **Papa John's**, **Little Caesar's** and **Hungry Howie's** make a decent alternative to Pizza Hut. The 'sub', or torpedo-roll sandwich, is what they serve at **Subway, Sobik's, Quiznos** and **Miami Subs**. An even better bet is the health-conscious **Tijuana Flats** chain, which started in central Florida and now has 17 local outlets, notably in Winter Park and on the S Orange Blossom Trail. Its Tex-Mex style is geared around fresh, hand-made products in a lively, convivial atmosphere. Check out its burritos, quesadillas, enchiladas, tacos and salads, and you'll struggle to spend more than $10/person (**tijuanaflats.com**).

Drive-through

Many fast food options also have a drive-through window, which is fun to try at least once. Simply drive around the side of the building where indicated and there is a take-away menu and voice box to take your order. Carry on around the building (don't wait by the voice box!) and you pay and receive your food at a side window. You will probably find your car has a slide-out tray from the dashboard area that will take a cup. A neat variation on this theme is **Sonic**, a modern version of the old American drive-in diner, where you stay in your

Susan's choice

A relatively recent chain that provides a good balance between tasty and healthy is the **Panera Bread** counter-service option (dine in or takeaway). As well as a wonderful range of pastries and fresh-baked breads, it serves some terrific sandwiches, soups and salads, including vegetarian options. Open 7am–10pm; visit **panerabread.com** for more info.

car and the 'carhop' waiter or waitress comes to take the order. The fare – burgers, hot dogs, wraps, salads and sandwiches – won't win any awards, but the style is fun. Check out its I-Drive location just north of Kirkman Road (7am–11pm; **sonicdrivein.com**).

FAMILY FAVOURITES

After all the fast food choices, there is a huge selection that specialise in more regular fare, still with an all-American flavour but with greater variety and ultra family friendly. They vary from the buffet kind to fairly sophisticated, and you will find them in multiple locations.

The breakfast specialists

Need to start the day by stoking up with a big breakfast? Look no further than this selection.

Cracker Barrel: Delightful old country store style, with mountainous breakfasts, well-balanced lunch and dinner menus, Kid's Stuff choices and an old-fashioned charm that's a nice change from the usual tourist frenzy ($; 6am–10pm Sun–Thurs, 6am–11pm Fri and Sat; **crackerbarrel. com**). **Bob Evans:** Also notable for its friendly, country-style, hearty menus (plus low-carb options) and delicious desserts. It also offers a good takeaway and country store selection ($; 6 or 7am–10pm; **bobevans.com**). **International House of Pancakes** (or IHOP) and **Waffle House:** You will struggle to spend more than $7 on a full meal, whether it be one of its huge breakfast platters or a hot sandwich with fries. Waffle Houses are open 24 hours a day ($; **wafflehouse.com**) and IHOPs 6am–midnight ($; **ihop.com**). **Denny's:** Another traditional 24-hour restaurant, its wide selection makes a traditional bacon-and-egg breakfast seem ordinary, and it does an excellent range of toasted sandwiches and dinner meals, like grilled catfish, as well as a Senior Selections menu, with smaller portions at reduced prices for over-55s ($; **dennys. com**). **Perkins:** Also a great breakfast choice; for a really hearty meal try Perkins Eggs Benedict (2 eggs and bacon on a toasted muffin with hash browns and fresh fruit), while its bread-bowl salads are equally satisfying (some branches open around the clock; **perkinsrestaurants.com**). **Friendlys:** Another cheerful diner, with a typical array of American fare, plus delicious ice-cream-based desserts ($; 7am–11pm; **friendlys.com**).

Buffet style

The unarguable value of the all-you-can-eat restaurants is very much in evidence here.

Ponderosa Steakhouse and **Sizzler:** These two popular, identikit, consistent but unspectacular big-chain offerings feature huge breakfast, lunch and dinner buffets. You order and pay as you enter and are then seated, before being unleashed on the help-yourself serveries. You'd be hard pushed to tell whose food was whose but there IS a difference in price depending on location, with I-Drive tending to be a dollar or two dearer than elsewhere. Standard dinner fare includes chicken wings, meatballs, chilli, ribs, steaks (for a small extra supplement) and seafood, while their immense salad bars are also a big draw ($–$$; 7am–late evening, **ponderosasteakhouses.com** and **sizzler. com**). **Golden Corral**, **Black Angus** and **Shoney's:** The breakfast buffet theme is served rather better by these 3, where you may pay a bit more

Simon's fave

If you are hooked on burgers and similar fare, we suggest you try the classic diner-style option of **Steak 'n Shake**. Open round the clock, it cooks everything to order, with counter service, table service and a drive-through. It also serves proper hand-dipped milkshakes and malts that on their own are worth going in for! Check them out at **steaknshake.com**.

but the extra quality is undeniable. Golden Corral impresses for its fresh style and Carver's Choice of roast meats plus an excellent vegetable selection and terrific dessert bar (usually at least 20 choices, plus ice-cream and various toppings!). There is a weekend supplement at some outlets as they add steak to the main choices ($–$$; 7.30am–10pm; **goldencorral.com**).

BRITTIP

A buffet breakfast at Golden Corral or similar should keep you going until tea-time and is a good way to start a theme-park day.

Shoney's has an à la carte menu as well as excellent buffets, all with a Southern accent ($; 7am–11pm; **shoneys.com**). Black Angus is the odd one out in that it becomes a full-service (i.e. with a bar) steakhouse after breakfast ($–$$; 7am–11.30pm; **blackangusorlando.com**). **CiCi's Pizza:** A real hit with us, it features an extensive pizza buffet (up to 16 types), plus salad and desserts all for a bargain $5.49 ($; under-3s eat free; 11am–10pm; **cicispizza.com**).

The big chains

Moving up into the next price category (and with a greater range of facilities) are the following choices.

Applebee's: Calling itself the 'neighborhood bar and grill', this offers a rather more health-conscious menu with good salads and weight-watchers' choices as well as a tempting array of steaks and chicken dishes ($–$$; 11am–midnight; **applebees.com**). **Bahama Breeze:** Step forward into the Caribbean with this lively chain that boasts food as good as the surroundings. Try West Indies Patties, Fresh Ahi Tuna or the Jerk Chicken Pasta. Service is in keeping with its personable style, there is a pleasing individual touch and you will struggle to get better value just about anywhere else in Orlando. The decor is refreshing and entertaining, and it's worth just popping in for a drink ($$–$$$$; 4pm–2am Mon–Sat, 4pm–midnight Sun; **bahamabreeze.com**).

BRITTIP

The Bahama Breeze restaurants don't take reservations and are extremely popular in the evening. Try to arrive before 5.30pm to avoid a wait or try the Lake Buena Vista location, which can be a bit quieter.

Bennigan's: This chain is a *Brit Guide* favourite for its friendly, efficient service, smart decor and tempting menu, especially for lunch. Its bar atmosphere is straight out of TV's *Cheers*, and the Irish flavour comes into its own on St Patrick's Day ($–$$; 11am–2am; **bennigans.com**). **Boston Market:** These restaurants set their store by typical home cooking, café-style. They specialise in fresh-carved meats, rotisserie chicken, decent vegetables (praise be!) and excellent value if you have a hungry brood to

Delicious food at Bahama Breeze

feed ($–$$; 11am–10pm; **bostonmarket.com**). **Buffalo Wild Wings:** A huge bar and grill, featuring chicken wings, tenders, wraps, salads, burgers and ribs. Simple but tasty, and very popular for big sports events with its multiple large-screen TVs ($–$$; 11am–1am Mon–Fri, to 2am Fri and Sat, noon–midnight Sun; **buffalowildwings.com**). **Café Tu Tu Tango:** Another chain (like Bahama Breeze) high on style and quality, the accent is artist-colony Spanish, with an original tapas-style menu, live entertainment and artwork on the walls that changes daily. Vegetarians are well catered for, and you can try some succulent pizzas, seafood, salads and paella. Mexican and Chinese dishes are also on offer, along with a well-thought-out kids' menu (11.30am–midnight; **cafetututango.com**). **Cattleman's Steak House:** With a neat saloon bar, early bird specials (4–6pm) and the Little Rustlers' Round-up menu for kids, this goes for the cowboy approach. Steaks are the order of the day, but you can also try chicken, seafood and pork ($$–$$$; 5pm–10pm Mon–Fri, 12:30–10pm Sat, 12:30–9pm Sun). **Cheesecake Factory:** While its prime feature is desserts (including more than 30 cheesecakes), the rest of the huge menu is impressive in an eclectic, high-tech setting. Mexican dishes jostle with pizza, pasta, seafood, burgers, steaks and salads, plus it offers a great brunch, so come here hungry! ($$–$$$; 11am– 11pm; **thecheesecakefactory.com**). **Chevy's:** A healthy slice of Mexicana while still providing reassuring American selections, its salsa is freshly made every hour, and the tortilla chips, guacamole and tortillas are equally appetising ($–$$; 4–11pm Mon–Thurs, 4pm–midnight Fri, 11am–midnight Sat, 11am–11pm Sun; **chevys.com**). **Chili's:** Also in Tex-Mex territory (an American version of Mexican cuisine that originated in Texas), it places the emphasis more on steak and ribs and less on tortillas and spices. Service is usually frighteningly efficient and, if you're looking for a quick meal, you'd be hard pushed to find a speedier turnaround ($–$$; 11am–1am Mon–Sat, 11am–11pm Sun; **chilis.com**). **Don Pablo's:** A fairly elaborate Mexican offering with clever theming, a lively atmosphere (especially round the Cantina bar) and classic, well-explained menus, making for a fun experience ($$; 11.30am–10pm Sun–Thurs, 11.30am–11pm Fri and Sat; **donpablos.com**). **Fazoli's:** You'd have to try hard to get better value anywhere; its fresh Italian market style is served up with a menu featuring 20 main course items at $6 or less, either dine in or drive through, plus unlimited breadsticks and drinks when you dine in ($; 10.30am–10pm Sun–Thurs, 11pm Fri and Sat; **fazolis.com**). **Fuddruckers:** Purely and simply some of the best burgers you'll find, with a huge choice (including veggie and ostrich) and a real kid-friendly style. Make your selection, find a table and wait for your burger to be cooked fresh, or choose from the salad and sandwich options, plus tempting shakes, cookies and desserts ($; 11am–10pm Sun–Fri, 11pm Sat; **fuddruckers.com**). **Hooters:** A lively place that makes no bones about its style – 'delightfully tacky yet unrefined'. This is a relatively simple establishment, popular with the younger, beach-party crowd – and for the famous Hooter Girl waitresses. The entertaining menu features seafood, salads and burgers, plus Hooters

Café Tu Tu Tango

Pop into our 'local'

The nearest thing to a typical pub in these parts is the **Orlando Ale House** chain. Hugely popular with the locals, it features pool tables, multiple TV screens for all the sports action and a friendly, efficient style with a surprisingly varied menu. Check out its spicy Chicken Zingers, barbecue ribs and fish sandwich for some great tastes. It can be a bit rowdy on big-game days at the weekends, but is still a great place to hang out with friends, bring the family or just pop in for a drink. The Ale House in Lake Buena Vista on Winter Garden-Vineland Road is also our 'local'! ($–$$; 11am–2am; **millersalehouse.com**).

Nearly World Famous Chicken Wings in eight strengths – beware of the Samurai! ($; 11am–midnight Mon–Thurs, 11am–1am Fri, Sat, noon–11pm Sun; **hooters.com**).

Hops: With the accent on its in-restaurant breweries (there are 4 standard 'house' beers, all worth trying) and seasonal specials, plus a good selection of steaks, chicken, pastas and seafood in its own signature sauces and marinades, this is a pleasant, airy choice ($–$$; 11am–11pm; **hopsrestaurants.com**). **Houlihan's:** Another classic bar-restaurant with plenty of style, cheerful service, an extensive and appetising menu (look out for its Down Home Pot Roast) – and seriously large portions (but also a mini-dessert option; $–$$; 11am–1am; **houlihans.com**). **Logan's Roadhouse:** A fun and, rustic atmosphere includes masses of peanuts in their shells (which end up all over the wooden floor!), plus a menu featuring burgers, chicken, steaks and ribs, while it also offers an express lunch selection ($$; 11am–10pm Sun–Thurs, 11am–11pm Fri and Sat; **logansroadhouse.com**). **Lone Star Steakhouse:** Head to Texas for its mesquite-grilled steaks, ribs, chicken and fish, with a friendly welcome and roadhouse ambience (plus huge portions!). Kids eat free with parents on Tues ($–$$; 11am–11pm; **lonestarsteakhouse.com**). **Olive Garden:** One of America's big successes, bringing Italian food into budget, mass-market range. The light and airy dining rooms create a relaxing environment and, while it doesn't offer a huge choice, what it does, it does well and in generous portions. Pasta is the speciality, but it also offers chicken, veal, steak, seafood and great salads, plus unlimited refills of salad, garlic breadsticks and non-alcoholic drinks ($$; 11am–10pm Sun–Thurs, 11am–11pm Fri and Sat; **olive garden.com**). **Outback Steakhouse:** An Australian slant, some of the best fare – and biggest portions. Its thick, juicy, well-seasoned steaks, ribs and seafood selections are all above average, while its trademark is the Bloomin' Onion, a large fried onion with a special dipping sauce. It also features a good kids' menu ($$–$$$; 4–10.30pm Mon–Thurs, 4–11.30pm Fri, 3.30pm–11.30pm Sat, 3.30–10.30pm Sun; **outback.com**). **Smokey Bones:** With a rustic, log-cabin touch and some succulent, deep-smoked barbecue, it serves up fish, chicken, burgers and salads, but we recommend the barbecue platters. Sports fans are well served with a huge array of TVs ($–$$$; 11am–11pm; **smokeybones.com**). **Sonny's Real Pit Bar-B-Q:** A national chain with no great pretensions, just masses of food of the barbecue persuasion served up in friendly, let's-get-messy style. The good kids' menu makes it ideal for families, and you should definitely try the ribs and its own-recipe coleslaw ($–$$; 11am–10pm; **sonnysbbq.com**). **Steak and Ale:** A popular, basic diner that does some good steaks and ribs, plus tempting seafood and chicken dishes, with early-bird specials of a 3-course set meal 4–7pm (4–6pm Nov–Mar), and 2-for-1 drink specials ($–$$; 11.30am–10pm Mon–Thurs, 11.30am–11pm Fri, noon–11.30pm Sat, noon–10pm Sun; **steakandale.com**). **TGI Fridays:** Anyone familiar with this international chain will know what to expect from its lively, eclectic style, and Orlando boasts multiple offerings (notably on I-Drive just north of The Pointe Orlando). The drinks menu is the size of a book and the main menu is heavy on wings, ribs, burgers and steaks ($–$$; 11am–2am; **tgifridays.com**). **Tony Roma's:** A place that rightly pronounces itself 'famous for ribs', the airy decor and ambience, clever kids' menu, junior meals and melt-in-the-mouth ribs are a winning combo. You can still get chicken, burgers and steaks, but why ignore a dish that's done this well? ($$–$$$; 11am–midnight Sun–Thurs, 11am–1am Fri and Sat; **tonyromas.com**). **Uno Chicago Grill:** The place to go if you're bored with Pizza Hut, it specialises in deep-dish pizzas plus pastas, chicken dishes, steaks and salads, ($–$$; 11am–midnight; **unos.com**); **Urban Flats:** An upmarket new chain of flatbread grills, specialising in creative dips, salads, wraps and a wide variety of toppings for its flatbreads ($–$$; 11am–10pm Mon–Wed, 11am–11pm Thurs–Sat, 11am–10pm Sun; **urbanflats.net**).

INTERNATIONAL FLAVOURS

Your restaurant choice extends beyond the obvious to an array of international cuisines, notably Chinese and Indian but also Thai, Japanese and Italian. Some are still chains, others are one-offs.

Asian extravaganza

Kobe: This brings a touch of Americana to its Japan-themed dining, but still achieves individuality with the chef preparing the food at your table ($$$; 11.30am–11pm; **kobesteakhouse.com**). **Ran-Getsu:** This does for Japanese cuisine what the Ming Court does for Chinese – it's stylish, authentic, as much an experience as a meal, and reasonably priced ($$–$$$$; 5pm–midnight; **rangetsu.com**). **Red Bamboo:** Wonderfully authentic Thai flavours and clean, contemporary decor. Its soups and curries are to die for, while house speciality Smokey Pot is a stew of marinated prawns, vegetables and glass noodles in chilli – heavenly! ($$–$$$$; 11am–2.30pm Tues–Fri, 5–10pm Sat, noon–10pm Sun, closed Mon; 407 226 8997; **redbamboothai.com**). **Seito Sushi:** Another great Japanese offering from this local chain, with a formal sushi bar and a more inviting, small-scale approach ($$–$$$$; 11.30am–2.30pm, 5–10pm; 407 644 5050; **seitosushi.com**). **Shogun Steakhouse:** This national chain, which is ideal for those a little unsure whether to go for the full Japanese experience, opts for the full Teppanyaki-style service, at long, bench-like tables with the chef cooking in front of you. But you can still order a no-nonsense steak or chicken ($$$–$$$$; 6–10pm Mon–Thurs, 6–10.30pm Fri–Sun; 407 977 3988).

Indian & Chinese

There's a wide range of Chinese restaurants, from the ordinary to 5-star, but the Indian choice is harder to pin down as there is a lot of fluctuation.

Aashirwad: A decent Indian choice, with an excellent lunch buffet and some seriously spicy Mughlai dishes ($–$$$; 11am–10.30pm; 407 370 9830); **Bill Wong's Famous Super Buffet:** This I-Drive buffet (yes, they really do call it that) offers a cross between Chinese and diner-type fare. The all-you-can-eat 100-item buffet features jumbo shrimp, as well as crab, prime rib, fresh fruit and salad. Think cheap and cheerful ($–$$$; 11am–10pm). **Dragon Court Buffet:** This locals' favourite in Lake Buena Vista serves a magnificent spread of fresh, appetising dishes at a terrific lunch price. With more than 50 items on offer, including a sushi selection, this is well worth trying ($$–$$$; 11am–midnight; 407 238 9996). **India Palace:** An unassuming location tucked in a small shopping plaza in

The Cream of America

Orlando boasts a number of outstanding ice-cream parlours, many of which offer some truly heavenly concoctions. Check out **Carvel**, **Baskin Robbins**, **Dairy Queen** and **Marble Slab Creamery** for good examples. However, our award for the crème de la crème in this area goes to **Cold Stone Creamery**, which has new outlets at Winter Garden Village and Dr Phillips Boulevard. Its amazing range of ice-creams can be combined with a range of wonderful ingredients and mixed into cups and cones that are sheer heaven. It also mixes some of Simon's favourite milkshakes (**cold stonecreamery.com**).

Lake Buena Vista, this serves good food in large amounts and with family-friendly service ($–$$$; 11.30am–11pm Tues–Sun, 5–11pm Mon; 407 238 2322). **Memories of India:** Arguably the best of the local Indian selections, this is also a good choice for vegetarians. Its Goan fish curry is a particular speciality but it also offers a great range of biryanis and tandoori dishes ($$–$$$; 11.30am–10pm Mon–Sat, 11.30am–9pm Sun; 407 370 3277). **Ming Court:** While there are plenty of Chinese outlets, the Rolls-Royce version is this beautiful place on I-Drive, opposite The Pointe Orlando. With its magnificent setting and live entertainment most evenings, you can easily convince yourself you have been transported to China itself. The menu is extensive and beautifully presented by friendly servers, who make you feel at home the moment you walk in. Many dishes can be had as a side order rather than a full main course, giving you the chance to sample more. The basil chicken is one of our true favourites ($$–$$$; 11am–2.30pm, 4.30pm–midnight; **ming-court.com**).

Mughlai Indian Cuisine: This recent offering out at the west end of Highway 192 picks up rave reviews from the locals for its traditional style and authentic flavours, notably the tandoori choice, with the head chef

BRITTIP

Check out the Ming Court's recently revamped website for a valuable 10% money-off coupon that you can print out at home (click on 'View our menus').

from a famous Bombay restaurant ($$–$$$; 5–11pm daily; 863 424 6969, **mughlaidinner.com**). **New Punjab:** Another fine Indian choice, this is suitably authentic, with excellent tandoori dishes and a memorable vegetable platter ($–$$$; 5.30–11pm Mon, 11.30am–11pm Tues–Sun; 407 352 7887; **http://punjabindian restaurant.com**).

BRITTIP

Visit Mughlai Indian Cuisine online for a 10% discount coupon off your total bill.

Passage to India: A long-standing Indian choice on International Drive, this reliable 'old favourite' mixes the standard range of dishes with regular specials ($$–$$$; 407 396 6957). **PF Chang's China Bistro:** This mixes classic Chinese fare with an American bistro style that makes fans of virtually all who sample it. You should try the spicy ground chicken and eggplant, Cantonese roasted duck or Oolong marinated sea bass for dishes

Ming Court

with real distinction. There is also a good veggie selection ($$–$$$$; 5–11pm; **pfchangs.com**). **Sizzling Wok:** A similar offering to Bill Wong's on Sand Lake Road (by the Florida Mall), it offers a massive Chinese buffet at a very reasonable price ($–$$; 11am–10pm Sun–Thurs, 11am–10.30pm Fri and Sat).

The Italian job

Good Italian family-style dining has some excellent chains here, too.

Antonio's: This impressive local chain goes distinctly upmarket, with 3 restaurants (including one with a café, deli and superb wine shop) that all feature an individual, exclusive style as well as outstanding cuisine – sensational risottos are a signature dish, while veal and New York strip steak are equally wise choices ($$$–$$$$$; 5–10pm Mon–Sat; **antonios online.com**). **Brio Tuscan Grille:** Equally stylish and a real slice of Italy with some superb taste sensations. The menu emphasis is on prime steaks and chops, pasta specialities and flatbreads prepared in an authentic wood-burning oven. The interior decor is well above average, but it is also on the pricier side ($$$–$$$$; 11am–10pm Sun–Thurs, 11am–11pm Fri and Sat; **brio italian.com**). **Carrabba's:** Direct from Sicily, here's casual-but-elegant dining in a warm, festive atmosphere. House specialities include crispy calamari, chicken marsala, fabulous pasta dishes and hand-made pizzas in a wood-burning oven. The kids' menu is one of the best and the style is very child-friendly ($$–$$$; 4–10pm Sun–Thurs, 3–11pm Fri and Sat; **carrabbas.com**). **Macaroni Grill:** Another wonderful slice of Little Italy, its spacious restaurants are stylish, comfortable and well served, with excellent à la carte and family-style menus (serving 8–10). The pasta and wood-oven pizzas are first class and the wine list is impressive ($$–$$$$; 11.30am–10pm Sun–Thurs, 11.30am–11pm Fri and Sat; **macaronigrill.com**).

HOME FROM HOME

Having extolled the virtues of the all-American choices, there is an array of British-style pubs appealing to UK visitors. All offer a predictable array of pub grub and beers and you can happily take the kids into any of them.

Best of British Soccer World: This fresh choice (opposite Ripley's Believe It Or Not on I-Drive) goes for a full footy-themed style, with 12 flat-screen TVs, plus a giant theatre-style screen for all the big games. It boasts 8 British beers on tap, plus pool and darts, Curry Nights, a traditional roast on Sundays, karaoke, live music and even 2 internet terminals. Typical menu items include shepherd's pie, fish 'n' chips, ploughman's, burgers, steaks and kids' specials, while its full breakfast really is the Best of British (8am–midnight; 407 264 9189, **bestofbritishpub.com**). **Cricketers Arms:** This is the area's oldest-established British pub (having moved to Festival Bay in 2007) and is a favourite haunt of visitors. This is due to the large selection of beers (up to 17, including real ales), a Happy Hour, appetising food, live evening entertainment, stylish indoor and outdoor seating and (soccer fans take note) live Premiership and other domestic matches. It gets busy in the evenings, its live music is usually good, and many of the staff are Chelsea fans – but we don't hold that against them! NB: There is sometimes a cover charge for footy ($$–$$$; 9am–1am; 407 354 0686, **cricketers armspub. com**). **Frankie Farrell's:** Brand new in 2007 inside the Lake Buena Vista Resort Village & Spa, there's nothing especially Irish about this offering, but it does still serve up good pub style with an imaginative menu, excellent range of beers and live entertainment ($$–$$$; 9am–2am daily; 407 597 0214). **Orlando George & Dragon:** This is another all-British operation that serves a hearty traditional breakfast as well as typical pub fare. It stocks Guinness, Boddingtons, Stella, Fosters,

International Drive

The majority of restaurants in this busy tourist area are of the Fast Food or Family Favourite type, but there are several individuals.

The **North** section (from Prime Outlets International to Sand Lake Road) features *Fast Food:* Baskin Robbins, Burger King, Cold Stone Creamery, Dairy Queen, Dunkin' Donuts, KFC, McDonald's, Quiznos, Pizza Hut, Popeye's Chicken, Sonic, Starbucks, Subway and Taco Bell. *Family Favourites:* Bennigan's, Black Angus, Buffalo Wild Wings, Chili's, CiCi's Pizza, Denny's, Fuddruckers, IHOP, Perkins, Sizzler, Sweet Tomatoes, TGI Fridays. *International Flavours:* Aashirwad, Bill Wong's, Passage to India, Punjabi Indian Restaurant, Red Bamboo, Shogun Steakhouse. *Home from Home:* Cricketers Arms, Orlando George & Dragon. *Seafood Specials:* Red Lobster. *Deluxe Dining:* Salt Island Chophouse, Texas de Brazil. Plus, **Bergamo's:** at Festival Bay, an Italian restaurant that features fine dining – and singing waiters! Opera and pasta are served up in equal measure and quality, plus a great Italian wine list ($$$–$$$$$; 5–10pm; 407 352 3805, **bergamos.com**); **Wild Jack's:** the magnificent wood-smoked aroma of this restaurant hits you as you walk in. The huge interior features an open-pit barbecue where you watch your food being cooked. Steaks, ribs, chicken and turkey represent the main choices, all served with panache ($$–$$$; 11.30am–11pm; 407 352 4403).

The **South** section (from Sand Lake Rd to Orlando Premium Outlets) has *Fast Food:* McDonald's, Pizza Hut, Subway. *Family Favourites*: Bahama Breeze, Café Tu Tu Tango, Cattleman's Steakhouse, Denny's, Don Pablo's, Friday's Front Row Sports Grille, Friendlys, Golden Corral, Houlihan's, IHOP, Olive Garden, Outback Steakhouse, Ponderosa, TGI Fridays, Tony Roma's Uno Chicago. *International Flavours:* Kobe Steakhouse, Ming Court, Ran-Getsu. *Home from Home:* Best of British Pub, Sherlock's. *Seafood Specials:* Boston Lobster Feast, Crab House, Red Lobster. *Deluxe Dining:* Charley's Steakhouse, Vito's Chophouse. Plus, **B-Line Diner:** inside the Orlando Peabody Hotel is a fab art deco homage to the traditional 1950s diner. You sit at a long counter or in one of its booths, with a good view of the chefs at work and a rolling menu that changes 4 times a day. The food is way above usual diner standards, but the prices aren't. Desserts are displayed in a huge glass counter and you just can't ignore them! ($$; 24 hours; 407 352 4000).

Newcastle Brown, Bass and Carlsberg (among others), and also features darts, pool, karaoke, Sky Sports and live entertainment on its outdoor patio. This is a good option for a traditional Christmas turkey dinner, while St George's Day (23 April) is celebrated in style ($–$$$; 9am–2am; 407 351 3578). **Stage Door:** Another friendly, family-run pub and restaurant, this has also been a local fixture for many years and still draws a good crowd of locals and tourists, with typical fare and a good range of beers, plus live entertainment or karaoke most nights ($–$$$; 4pm–1am Tues–Sat, 4pm–midnight Sun, closed Mon; 863 424 8056, **stagedoorpub.com**). **The Pub:** Out on Highway 27 in Davenport (just at the junction with I-4, exit 55), this has a great range of beers, excellent food (from a wonderful US-UK crossover menu), multiple TVs and another genuine family-friendly touch ($–$$$; 11am–2am Mon–Sat, 11am–midnight Sun; 863 424 4242, **thepubb.net**).

Stage Door

SEAFOOD SPECIALS

The choice of seafood eateries is equally wide and features some fun chains and excellent individuals.

Boston Lobster Feast: The place for a real blowout on an unlimited lobster and seafood buffet. There are excellent early-bird specials (4.30–6pm Mon–Fri, 2–4.30pm Sat and Sun), and, while it is not gourmet fare, its 40-item Lobster Feast is guaranteed to stretch the stomach ($$–$$$$; 4.30–10pm Mon–Fri, 2–10pm Sat and Sun; **bostonlobster feast.com**). **The Crab House:** Self-explanatory: garlic crabs, steamed crabs, snow crabs, Alaskan king crabs… you could try its prime rib, pasta or other seafood, but it would be a shame to ignore the house speciality ($$–$$$$; 11.30am–11pm Mon–Sat, noon–11pm Sun; **crabhouseseafood.com**). **Flying Fish:** At *Disney's Boardwalk Resort*, the menu of this superb seafood experience is not overburdened with choice, but what it does is wonderfully presented. Its Chardonnay-steamed Mussels starter is a taste sensation, while the Potato-wrapped Red Snapper and Citrus-zest Yellowfin Tuna are also outstanding. Steak and beef short ribs, plus a vegetarian option, are also available (4–11pm Mon–Sat, 4–10pm Sun; 407 939 3463). **Joe's Crab Shack:** Part of Crab House chain but more fun and inventive and less seafood-based (despite the name). Distinctly family-friendly with its Sand Lot play area, this is ideal if you don't want the whole shellfish thing ($–$$$; 11am–10pm Sun–Thurs, 11am–11pm Fri and Sat; **joescrabshack.com**). **Landry's Seafood:** From the same company but with a more elegant touch, there is a fresh catch of the day, seafood platters and an excellent salad bowl with each dish, while the staff really know the menu ($$–$$$$; 11am–10pm Sun–Thurs, 11am–11pm Fri and Sat; **landrysseafoodhouse.com**). **McCormick and Schmick's:** Easily the most quality-conscious of the seafood chains, there is nothing mass-produced about its offerings. The chef creates a daily menu based on product, price and availability (with a prominent list of what's fresh). Oysters are a speciality, along with soups and salads, and you will be hard pushed to find better prawns, scallops and salmon ($$–$$$$$; 11am–11pm Mon–Thurs, 11am–midnight Fri and Sat, 11am–10pm Sun; **mccormickand schmicks.com**). **Red Lobster:** Part of the Olive Garden chain and for the family market, with a varied menu, lively atmosphere and one of the best kids' menu/activity books. While lobster is the speciality, the steaks, chicken, salads and other seafood are equally appetising, and it does a variety of combination platters ($$–$$$$; 11am–10pm Sun–Thurs, 11am–11pm Fri and Sat; **redlobster.com**).

Flying Fish

DELUXE DINING

This is where you can really go to town with your dining choice, especially when it comes to a fine array of steakhouses.

Boheme Restaurant: A quite magnificent (and regularly changing) menu can be found in this tucked-away gem at the Grand Bohemian hotel in downtown Orlando. Fine seafood mixes with exquisite lamb and duck, with some eclectic twists from master chef Robert Mason ($$$–$$$$; 5.30–11pm, 407 313 9000). **Cala Bella:** At the stylish Rosen Shingle Creek Resort is this superb Italian-

Sand Lake Road

This new area, just off International Drive (west of I-4 and including Dr Phillips Marketplace) boasts arguably the best concentration of fine dining in Orlando. Here's the full array. *Fast Food:* Coldstone Creamery, McDonald's, Panera Bread, Pizza Hut, Starbucks, Subway. *International Flavours:* Antonio's. *Seafood Specials:* Bonefish Grill. *Deluxe Dining:* Moonfish, Morton's, Samba Room, Season's 52, Roy's, Ruth's Chris Steakhouse, Timpano Chophouse. Plus, **Amura Sushi:** fine dining, Japanese style, with some of the best sushi in Florida ($$$; 11.30am–2.45pm and 5–10.15pm Mon–Fri, 5–10.45pm Sat, noon–2.45pm and 5–10.15pm Sun; 407 370 0007); **Christini's:** a lovely, formal Italian restaurant, with regional specialities as well as prime aged steaks, chops and Maine lobster ($$$$–$$$$$; 6pm–midnight; 407 345 8770, **christinis.com**); **Press 101:** this trendy wine bar offers some great light bites as well as a fuller menu featuring sandwiches, salads and delicious pastries ($$; 11am–10pm Mon–Thurs, 11pm Fri, Sat; 407 351 2101).

influenced restaurant, with overtones of Tuscany, heavy on pasta and seafood, but with signature dishes like its sensational Cala Bella Lamb, Veal Piccata and Mediterranean Pork. Save room for dessert, too – the pastry chefs are among of the finest in America ($$$–$$$$; 5.30–10.30pm; 407 996 3663, **callabellarestaurant.com**).

Charley's Steak Houses: Cooking over a specially built wood-fire pit earns high marks from US meat-lovers. All the meat is specially aged, hand-cut and seasoned, making for a superb array of steaks and chops and, while it also offers fine seafood, you'd be foolish to overlook its stock-in-trade ($$$–$$$$$; 5–11pm; **charleyssteak house.com**). **Del Frisco's:** Locals consistently rate this (on Lee Road in north Orlando) their favourite steakhouse and the more formal dining experience is enhanced by prime steaks and lobster, beautifully cooked and presented ($$$$–$$$$$; 407 645 4443; **delfriscosorlando.com**). **Moonfish:** Another great place for seafood, this is truly individual in both decor and menu. You could make a feast of its appetisers alone, while its sushi and sashimi are inspired and it has a superb raw bar. Many restaurants that go for the avant-garde look often fail to deliver the goods, but Moonfish doesn't fall into that trap. It also makes a good romantic choice ($$–$$$$; 11.30am–10pm; 407 363 7262, **fishfusion.com**). **Morton's of Chicago:** A more upmarket (sometimes pretty smoky) style, with a lively ambience that adds to the enjoyment of its trademark steaks, which are cooked on an open range. It doesn't come cheap, especially as vegetables are extra, but eating here is always memorable ($$$$; 5pm–midnight Mon–Sat, 5–11pm Sun; **mortons.com**).

BRITTIP

American restaurant terminology calls a starter an 'appetizer' and a main course an 'entrée'.

Old Hickory Steakhouse: A hotel-based offering (in the Gaylord Palms Resort), the elaborate Everglades theme gives it an extra dimension, but the steak needs few gimmicks as the house speciality of certified Black Angus beef is aged for 21–35 days and cooked to perfection. Side dishes are extra, but the attentive service and alternatives such as oven-roasted swordfish and Maine lobster provide a memorable experience ($$$–$$$$$; 5–10.30pm Mon–Fri, 5–11pm Sat, 5–10pm Sun; **gaylordhotels.com**).

Porterhouse: A recent discovery at the Orlando Airport Marriott just off Semoran Boulevard and a hidden gem. Under British chef Tony Hull, it has a relaxed, intimate ambience that perfectly sets off its prime cuts of beef, chops and grilled seafood, plus a good wine list and dreamy desserts ($$$$; 5.30–10pm Mon–Sat; 407 851

9000). **Roy's:** Go upscale Hawaiian at this grand choice, where the Asian-Pacific fusion cuisine is as spectacular as the decor and service. Celebrity chef Roy Yamaguchi is the creator of this chain, and his sense of grand style is well served ($$$$–$$$$$; 5.30–10pm; **roysrestaurant.com**). **Ruth's Chris Steak House:** Another major chain, this also offers prime beef in a mouth-watering variety of choices. It isn't cheap, but you'll be hard pushed to get a better steak. Simply seared, seasoned and served, they are the reason it has more than 80 locations worldwide ($$$$–$$$$$; 5–11pm Mon–Sat, 5–10pm Sun; **ruthschris.com**). **Salt Island Chophouse and Fish Market:** Not only an unusual name, it's also an unusual place, from its tiki-torch outdoor terrace to the eclectic aquatic interior decor (complete with large aquariums) and live jazz lounge. The comprehensive wine list superbly offsets the heavily steak and seafood dominated menu, while service is suitably refined. All the dishes are well explained and even demonstrated, and you'll find it hard to choose between the oak-grilled steaks and trademark daily seafood specials. ($$$–$$$$; 5–11pm; 407 996 7258, **saltislandrestaurant.com**). **Samba Room:** Try this if you like a memorable Cuban experience in an elegant lakefront restaurant with a Latin ambience. The menu exhibits a wonderfully exotic touch, with the likes of Mango-barbecued Ribs, Cachaca-smoked Boneless Chicken and Sugar Cane Beef Tenderloin, and its range of cocktails is suitably Cuban-laced. Extremely popular, so reservations are advised, and a touch pricier than the rest ($$$–$$$$; 11am–midnight Mon–Sat, noon–10pm Sun: 407 266 0550; **sambaroom.net**). **Shula's Steak House:** Expansive (on your waistline) and expensive, the porterhouse and prime rib steaks are outstanding, and this chain (owned by famous ex-American football coach Don Shula) is highly popular with locals at the *Walt Disney World Dolphin Hotel* ($$$$$; 5–11pm; 407 934 1362; **donshula.com**). **Texas de Brazil:** An unusual but delicious Brazilian-style steakhouse, or *churrascaria*, with a wonderfully upscale touch. Its variety of meats – every one carved at the table off sword-like skewers – is quite superb, all beautifully cooked over its open-flame grill ($$$–$$$$$; 12–3pm for lunch, 5–10pm Mon–Thurs, 5–10.30pm Fri, 4–10.30pm Sat, 4–9.30pm Sun; 407 355 0355, **texasde brazil.com**). **The Palm Restaurant:** The opening of Universal's Hard Rock Hotel brought with it this upscale nationwide chain. Founded in New York in 1926, it is famous for prime-aged steaks and jumbo lobsters, served in spacious, elegant surroundings. The house speciality, Jumbo Nova Scotia Lobster, is truly spectacular. Its steaks are special, too, plus you can choose swordfish, crab, salmon, pork, veal and pasta. All this is reflected in the prices, and vegetables are extra, but the lunch menu is more modest, while maintaining the quality ($$$$–$$$$$; 11am–11pm Mon–Sat, noon–10pm Sun; 407 503 7256, **thepalm.com**). **Timpano Italian Chophouse:** Step back in time at this richly decorated upscale diner, with cuisine and service to match. The dark, elegant interior is bustling and convivial and the 1950s' New York accent is carried through with panache. And, from its trademark Martini Bar to the tiramisu dessert, everything is served with style and taste. Menu highlights include filet mignon, pork chops and Maine lobster ($$$–$$$$; 11am–10pm Mon–Fri, noon–11pm Sat, noon–10pm Sun; 407 248 0429, **timpanochophouse.com**). **Village Tavern:** This new chain (notably next to Mall at Millenia) offers a surprisingly chic and varied choice, from simple but satisfying salads, pizza, flatbreads and sandwiches to mouth-watering specialities like pan-seared scallops, shrimp risotto, grilled meatloaf, Maryland crabcake and filet mignon. The elegant decor helps set the scene for a memorable culinary

Try it all at The Pointe!

Dining choice doesn't come much better or more varied than at The Pointe Orlando after its complete rebuild from 2007/08. *Fast Food:* **Johnny Rockets** 1950s-style diner for burgers and shakes ($; 11am–9pm Sun–Thurs, 11am–11pm Fri and Sat; 407 903 0762, **johnnyrockets.com**); **Hooters; Pizza Valdiano**, for café-style pizza, salads, subs and panini ($–$$; 11am–10pm Sun–Thurs, 11pm Fri and Sat; 407 903 5855, **pizzeriavaldiano.com**); **Redrock Canyon Grill** appeals to hearty appetites with wood-fired rotisserie chicken, hearty chicken pot pie, steaks and succulent barbequed ribs ($$–$$$$; 11am–10.05pm Sun–Thurs, to 11.05pm Fri and Sat; 407 363 3933; **rrcanyongrill. com**). *International Flavours:* **Maggianos Little Italy** serves exceptional family-style Italian dining in a relaxed, friendly atmosphere with vintage 1940s Chicago decor and ambience. Portions are huge (even by Orlando standards!). The Bombalina appetiser platter will feed a family of 4, while the Family Style meals feature all-you-can-eat refills – and no one leaves hungry ($$–$$$$; 11am–10pm Sun–Thurs, to 11pm Fri and Sat; 407 241 8660; **maggianos. com**); **Taverna Opa** is a lively Greek option, with a thoroughly traditional and appetising menu, from hot and cold meze to moussaka, souvlaki and stewed lamb, but much more besides, like fine steaks and fresh seafood ($$–$$$$; 11am–2am; 407 351 8660, **opaorlando.com**). *Deluxe Dining:* **Capital Grille**, a wonderfully upscale and elegant restaurant featuring dry-aged steaks, seafood and tantalising desserts ($$$$–$$$$$; 11.30am–3pm Mon–Fri, 5–10pm Sun–Thurs, 11pm Fri and Sat; 407 370 4392, **thecapitalgrille.com**); **The Oceanaire** (see Top 10, page 334); **Tommy Bahama's Tropical Café** offers inspired dining in a laid-back, tropical setting (plus an Emporium of home furnishings, accessories and casual Island clothing). The menu is tropical and refreshing, too, for lunch or dinner, with highlights being its Loki Loki Tuna appetiser and mouth-watering shrimp entrées, plus sandwiches, chicken, fresh fish and fabulous salads ($$–$$$; 11am–11pm Sun–Thurs, to midnight Fri and Sat; 321 281 5888, **tommybahama.com**).

Other options here include **BB King's Blues Club**, which adds a Louisiana-tinged menu with some excellent options (chicken, ribs, catfish, Cajun pasta carbonara and steak) as well as standard burgers and salads ($–$$$$; **http://orlando.bbkingclubs.com/**); chic wine bar **The Grape**, with a tempting range of easy-drinking wines plus a Bistro-style menu offering bite-size appetisers, salads, quiches and cheese plates ($–$$; 11am–11pm Mon–Thurs, 11am–midnight Fri and Sat, noon–9pm Sun; **yourgrape. com**); and lively bar-restaurant **Adobe Gila's**, Mexican style, with a killer range of margaritas! ($–$$; **adobegilas.com**). The Pointe's very latest dining and entertainment spot, **Cuba Libre Restaurant and Rum Bar**, was due to open in late 2008 featuring traditional Cuban cuisine with an exciting twist, from tasty ceviche to pan-seared sugarcane-skewered jumbo shrimp ($$$–$$$$$; **cubalibrerestaurant.com**).

journey, with an extensive and award-winning wine list and its own range of cocktails. It's ideal for a romantic evening out, an upscale family meal or a quick casual lunch or dinner. Or you can just stop by the bar for Martini Night (Thurs), Wine Down Wednesdays, 9 draft beers and its organic sangria ($–$$$$; 11am–midnight Mon–Thurs, 11am–1am Fri and Sat, 10–1am Sun; **village tavern.com**). **Vito's Chop House:** Another meat-eater's paradise, here its choice beef cuts (notably the Tuscan T-Bone) are aged for 4–6 weeks and cooked over wood fires.

Village Tavern

Pork chops, seafood and pasta are also on offer, as well as an extensive wine list ($$$–$$$$; 5–10.30pm Sun–Thurs, 5–11pm Fri and Sat; **vitoschophouse.com**). **Wolfgang Puck's:** At *Downtown Disney*, you'll find this unusual mix of styles and restaurants – 4 under one roof – but it represents some of the best family dining in *Downtown Disney,* with a great upscale option in the **Dining Room**. The main Café is smart enough, but head upstairs and you are in seriously romantic territory, with a great view of *Pleasure Island* and service to match. The contrast with the fun hubbub below is striking, while the menu is well thought out and varied – try the Chinois-style Lamb Rack or Pan-seared Salmon for a taste sensation ($$$–$$$$ Café 11.30am–11pm; $$$$–$$$$$ Dining Room 6–10.30pm; 407 938 9653; **wolfgang puck.com**).

BRITTIP

Dining at the Village Tavern? Don't miss its Braised Short Ribs – a true taste sensation and definitely one of Simon's favourites.

Our Top 10

Finally, if you fancy really splashing out, here are some suggestions for where both the food and the ambience are distinctly special. Fine dining is on the increase in Orlando, and this selection is always popular, so you should certainly book in advance. For a romantic evening out, you also can't go wrong with any of these.

A Land Remembered: Quite simply, this is the best steakhouse we've ever visited. Located in the golf clubhouse of the Rosen Shingle Creek Resort (but open to non-residents), it is a superbly refined venue boasting exquisite service and an outstanding wine list. The menu oozes class from top to bottom and features local specialities like Frog Legs, Gator Stew, a fresh fish selection and Key Lime Pie. But, while the lamb, chicken and short ribs are outstanding, the steak choice is out of this world (featuring all-natural prime Black Angus beef from the Harris Ranch in California). Filet Mignon, New York Strip, Ribeye, Porterhouse, Prime Rib, Chateaubriand and a Surf and Turf (with lobster) are among the most succulent meat dishes you will find anywhere and, while it is suitably pricey, it is worth every cent ($$$$–$$$$$; 5.30–10pm; 407 996 3663; **landrememberedrestaurant.com**).

bluezoo: When it comes to one of the hippest places in town (at the *Walt Disney World Dolphin Hotel*), bluezoo not only looks the part, it also serves up some of the finest food in the Disney realm. Celebrity chef Todd English has made a name for himself by creating individual and contrasting restaurant experiences and bluezoo is another gem. With an under-the-sea theme that benefits from superb lighting (dine here later rather than earlier for the full effect), it has a wonderfully soothing feeling, whether you are just at the bar or in one of the 3 main areas of the restaurant. Both the service and the waiting staff's knowledge of the cuisine and

A Land Remembered

Kissimmee/Highway 192

The long stretch of this tourist corridor offers the greatest density of restaurants in Central Florida. Here's how they line up, starting with the **East** section from the junction with I-4 to John Young Parkway. *Fast Food:* Arby's, Burger King, Chick-Fil-A, Domino's, Dunkin' Donuts, KFC, McDonald's, Pizza Hut, Quiznos, Subway, Taco Bell, Wendy's. *Family Favourites:* Applebee's, Bennigan's, Bob Evans, Cattleman's Steakhouse, Chevys, Chili's, CiCi's Pizza, Cracker Barrel, Denny's, Fazoli's, Friendlys, Golden Corral, IHOP, Logan's Roadhouse, Longhorn Steakhouse, Olive Garden, Perkins, Ponderosa, Ruby Tuesday, Shoney's, Smokey Bones, TGI Fridays, Uno Chicago, Waffle House. *International Flavours:* Kobe's Steakhouse, Punjab Indian Restaurant. *Seafood Specials:* Boston Lobster, Joe's Crab Shack, Red Lobster. *Deluxe Dining* Charley's Steakhouse. Plus, **Pacino's:** a well-established and family-friendly Italian choice, offering suitably healthy portions in a themed setting. Highly traditional and with an emphasis on pasta and seafood, plus some good steaks ($$–$$$$; 4–11pm; 407 396 8022; **pacinos.com**).

In the **West** section (from I-4 all the way to Highway 27) you have, *Fast Food:* Burger King, Chick-Fil-A, Dunkin' Donuts, McDonald's, Pizza Hut, Subway, Taco Bell, Wendy's. *Family Favourites:* Bennigan's, Black Angus, Bob Evans, Carabba's, Cracker Barrel, Denny's, Golden Corral, IHOP, Outback Steakhouse, Perkins, Ponderosa, Shoney's, Sizzler, TGI Fridays, Waffle House. *International Flavours:* Mughlai Indian Cuisine, Passage to India. *Home from Home:* Stage Door. *Seafood Specials:* Red Lobster. Plus, **Colorado House of Beef:** an excellent, more budget steakhouse choice but still high on quality, this features a good range of steaks, ribs, veal, prime rib and fresh seafood, plus burgers and a good kids' menu ($$–$$$; 4–11.30pm; 407 396 1170); **Key W Kool's Open Pit Grill:** another fine choice (by marker 4) with mouth-watering steaks, daily specials, a succulent, inviting aroma and a good atmosphere ($$–$$$$; 4–11pm; 407 396 1166, **kwkools.com**).

extensive wine list are impeccable, so feel free to let them steer you around a mouth-watering menu, which includes ceviche and a raw bar. Fish is the signature dish (though rotisserie chicken, beef filet and pork loin are also on offer) and seafood lovers will struggle to narrow down the choice here: Miso-glazed Chilean Sea Bass, Berbere Spiced Swordfish, Bacon-wrapped Tuna, Cantonese Lobster and more, or just opt for bluezoo's Dancing Fish – your choice of freshly caught fish, whole-roasted over its special rotisserie ($$$$–$$$$$; 3.30–11pm; 407 934 1111; **thebluezoo.com**).

Fulton's Crab House: Good seafood is not hard to come by, but great seafood is the preserve of a handful – like Fulton's in *Downtown Disney*'s Marketplace. This mock riverboat has 6 different dining rooms (albeit each with the same menu), plus the Stone Crab Lounge, which features a busy raw bar. The interior is filled with nautical props, photos and lithographs, giving it an eclectic, period atmosphere, but the real attraction is the food – some of the freshest and most tempting fish, crab and lobster dishes in Florida. The Alaskan king crab is a rare treat, the snow crab claws and tuna filet mignon are as succulent as they come, but there are fresh specials every day (the air shipping bills for which are posted in the main hall), as well as a children's menu. The Stone Crab Lounge serves lunch and dinner 11.30am–11pm, while the restaurant is open for dinner only ($$$–$$$$$; 4–11pm; 407 394 2628; **levy restaurants.com**).

Fulton's Crab House

Jiko: This great favourite of ours is at *Disney's Animal Kingdom Lodge* and is possibly Disney's most imaginative and impressive culinary offering to date. Maintaining the hotel's African theming with its decor and lighting, Jiko ('the cooking place') features twin wood-burning ovens, a masterful menu and an exclusive selection of South African wines. The menu has Indian, Asian and African influences, with dishes like Swahili Curry Shrimp, Berbere Braised Lamb and Broiled Filet of Arctic Char, plus a couple of excellent vegetarian choices and a cheese plate that can be ordered as a main course or dessert. Its flatbreads are also a speciality and the full dessert selection is truly decadent. The personal service and ethnic ambience underline the adventure of eating here, and it's also the perfect venue for a romantic meal (5–11pm; 407 939 3463).

Luma on Park: Head to Winter Park for this ultra-trendy 'gastropub', where the cuisine can be as simple as a well-cooked burger or pizza or a truly gourmet salad or fabulous filet mignon. The mix of outdoor patio, lounge bar and restaurant makes this a chic and lively venue, with a fresh contemporary cuisine from chef Brandon McGlamery that is wonderfully imaginative and constantly changing. Fine lamb, duck and fish are among the many highlights, along with a wine cellar that lists almost 190 varieties and serves many by the glass, half-bottle and even the half-glass, if you'd like to try a good sampling! It also features a 3-course *prix fixe* menu at $35 a head ($45 with wine pairings) Sun–Tues, and a special Chef's Table that should be booked in advance ($$–$$$$$; lounge bar 4.30–midnight, dining room 5.30–10.30pm; 407 599 4111; **lumaonpark.com/home.html**).

The Oceanaire

The Oceanaire: Step back in time at this beautifully relaxed and stylish seafood room at The Pointe Orlando. The decor, reminiscent of a classic 1930's ocean liner, and mood music lead you into a fish and shellfish wonderland, complete with superb oyster bar. Shrimp, crab, scallops, clams, lobster and as many as 15 types of fish all jostle for attention on a sumptuous menu that also offers great salads, steaks and chicken (though you'd be crazy to ignore the seafood here). The selection varies daily according to the freshest produce available but typical examples include 'Black & Bleu' Hawaiian Swordfish, Cioppino (a delightful fish and shellfish stew), Pan-roasted Key West Snapper and Maine Lobster Thermidor, as well as a Surf & Turf option and a dozen types of oyster. Its Grand Shellfish Platter (at $55 or $105) is an eye-opening extravaganza of shrimps, crab, lobster, mussels and oysters and there is an equally impressive wine list. The service is top-notch ($$$$–$$$$$; 5–10pm Sun–Thurs, 11pm Fri and Sat; 407 363 4801; **theoceanaire.com**).

Portobello Yacht Club: Back in *Downtown Disney* (next to Fulton's) is another of our favourites. It's easy to miss in its tucked-away location but don't, for this is an Italian experience of great richness. From the complimentary glass of Italian sangria and fresh bread with oven-baked garlic to the classically elegant menu and full wine list, this is a

Lake Buena Vista

The third main tourist area, this features the broadest range of choice. Looking first at the area **East** of I-4. *Fast Food:* Subway, Wendy's. *Family Favourites:* Bahama Breeze, Bennigan's, Carraba's, CiCi's Pizza, Golden Corral, Lone Star Steakhouse. *Home from Home:* Frankie Farrell's. *Seafood Specials:* Landry's Seafood. To the **West** of I-4 (in the Crossroads area, SR 535 and Palm Parkway) there is: *Fast Food:* Pizza Hut, Quiznos, Steak 'n Shake, Subway, Taco Bell. *Family Favourites:* Black Angus, Buffalo Wild Wings, Chevys, CiCi's Pizza, Denny's, Hooters, Macaroni Grill, Olive Garden, Perkins, Shoney's, Sizzler, TGI Fridays, Uno Chicago, Waffle House. *International Flavours:* Dragon Court Buffet; India Palace, Kobe Steakhouse. SFS: Joe's Crab Shack.

Downtown Disney completes the picture for this area. *Fast Food:* McDonald's. *Family Favourites:* Earl of Sandwich (see page 000). *Seafood Specials:* Cap'n Jack's Oyster Bar (see page 297). *Deluxe Dining:* Fulton's Crabhouse, Portobello Yacht Club, Wolfgang Puck Cafe. Plus, **Planet Hollywood:** pure fun can be found here. The food is fairly predictable, but it's all served with pizzazz and the cavernous interior provides a party atmosphere, complete with film clips and movie memorabilia. Some great cocktails, too, but visit mid-morning or mid-afternoon to avoid the queues ($$–$$$$; 11am–2am; 407 939 3463, **planet hollywood.com**); **Raglan Road:** there are plenty of Irish-themed pubs in town, but none comes close to this for style and cuisine. From the decor – much of it imported from Ireland – to the eye-catching bars and fabulous beers and whiskeys, this is a real taste of the Emerald Isle. Live music adds to the ambience and there are 3 separate, spacious bar areas, 2 outdoor terraces and even a neighbouring chippie (Cooke's of Dublin). You could treat it just like a pub and enjoy a drink at the bar, but we recommend finding a table and sampling the superb modern-Irish cuisine of master chef Kevin Dundon. For starters, try the Drunk Chicken (a whiskey-glazed kebab) or Dalkey Duo (battered sausages), while the Sesame-coated Haddock, Posh Pan Chicken, Kevin's Heavenly Ham (his signature dish – oven-roasted loin of ham) and It's Not Bleedin' Chowder (!) are all first class. If nothing else, try Kevin's version of bread pudding and you'll be in holiday heaven ($$–$$$$; 11am–2am; 407 938 0300, **raglanroadirishpub.com**); **Rainforest Café:** the *Downtown Disney* version of this big chain is topped by a huge 'volcano' – and you don't dine, you go 'on safari' in a rainforest setting amid audio-animatronic animals (including elephants and gorillas), thunderstorms, tropical birds, waterfalls and aquariums. It's great for kids and the food is above average. Unless you arrive before midday, you'll have a wait, but that's no hardship given its locations. Beware the huge gift shop! ($$–$$$$; 11am–11pm; 407 939 3463, **rainforestcafe.com**).

restaurant to be savoured in relaxed style. You can choose from something as simple as pizza or a classic Caesar salad to prosciutto and sage-wrapped yellowfin tuna, with fine steaks, veal, rack of lamb and great pastas. The Portobello Mushroom is a superb starter, while another signature dish is the Spaghettini Frutti di Mare (a heavenly seafood pasta). It all adds up to one of the most enjoyable dining options anywhere in *Walt Disney World* – and reservations are not always necessary ($$–$$$$; 11.30am–midnight; 407 934 8888; **levy restaurants.com**).

Seasons 52: A trendy and growing national chain (in the Plaza Venezia

Luma

on Sand Lake Road and next to the Altamonte Mall here in Orlando), this presents some of the best fine dining in the state. The name refers to the fact that different fresh produce comes into season each week, and this is reflected in the menu; new items feature weekly, with some seriously creative cuisine. It's also highly health-conscious, with a balanced approach to carbohydrate and fat content. All appetisers, salads and soups range from 100–250 calories, the majority being either grilled or oven-roasted, and all entrées are less than 475 calories. Its fish and seafood are a real highlight but lamb, chicken and steaks are equally tempting and vegetarians are offered some good choices. The 'mini indulgences' desserts (individual servings in small glasses) are ideal to finish a meal in style but without over-eating. Your server will be able to offer bags of advice – not least with an extensive wine list, while the bar area and outdoor terrace are equally stylish – ideal for a romantic occasion ($$–$$$$; 11.30am–2.30pm and 5–10pm Mon–Fri, 11.30am–11pm Sat, 11.30am–10pm Sun; 407 354 5212; **seasons52.com**).

Zen: Find a fine hotel and you will find a fine restaurant these days, and that is true of the Omni Orlando resort at Champions Gate, where Zen is a wonderful Asian-themed restaurant with a tempting menu. With a sake bar, sushi bar and its elegant main restaurant, this is an oasis of Oriental charm and style – with food to match. Highlights are the mouth-watering Beijing Spare Ribs and Sautéed Shrimp with Chile Pepper Sauce and Glazed Walnuts, or just opt for the stunning Zen Experience, a multi-course sampler feast – beware your waistline! (6–10pm; 407 390 6664; **omnihotels.com**).

Seasons 52

And our No 1…

While it's practically impossible to single out one restaurant from this vast wealth of culinary delight, if pushed we would have to plump for what we consider the most amazing restaurant experience in central Florida, at Universal's Royal Pacific Resort. **Tchoup-Chop** (pronounced 'chop chop'), from the gourmet stable of New Orleans master chef Emeril Lagasse, offers Asian-Pacific fusion cuisine in the most eye-catching setting. Service is a team effort at each table and the superb menu is well presented and explained. And oh, that menu! Taking some of the most aromatic and flavoursome elements of Thai, Chinese, Japanese, South Seas and other Pacific Rim cuisines, Lagasse has conjured up a delectable array of dishes. Start with Homemade Dumpling Box (with a fresh port and ginger filling, hand-rolled, steamed and served with sake-soy dipping sauce) or Polynesian Crabcake (with mango-habanero butter sauce and papaya salsa), then graduate to Macadamia-nut Crusted Atlantic Salmon (with ginger soy butter sauce, steamed rice and stir-fried vegetables), Asian Pepper-grilled Kurabota Pork Tenderloin or Chicken Hawaiian-style (rotisserie-roasted with spicy peanut fried rice, pineapple soy glaze and stir-fried vegetables). Dinner here is always busy, so try lunch if it can't squeeze you in ($$$–$$$$$; 11.30am–2pm and 5.30–10pm Sun–Thurs, 5.30–11pm Fri and Sat; 407 503 2467; **emerils.com**).

And now on to another of our favourite topics – shopping…

12 Shopping

or How to Send Your Credit Card into Meltdown

As well as being a theme park wonderland, this vast area of Florida is a shopper's paradise, with a dazzling array of specialist outlets, malls, flea markets and discount retailers. New centres also spring up all the time, from smart malls to cheap gift shops – and you can't go a few paces in the tourist areas without a shop insisting it has the 'best bargains' of one sort or another.

With the exchange rate in recent years being so favourable for UK visitors, shopping has become as much of an attraction as the theme parks. The only danger is seriously exceeding your baggage allowance for the flight home – or your duty free allowance. From 1 December 2008 your limit in the catch-all duty category of 'gifts and souvenirs' rises to £290 per person (from £145), but it's still only too easy to go beyond that! If you do, you need to keep your receipts and go through the 'goods to declare' channel (though paying the duty and VAT can still be cheaper than buying the same items at home).

You pay duty (which varies depending on the item) on the total purchase price (i.e. inclusive of Florida sales tax) once you have exceeded £290, plus VAT at 17.5%. You CANNOT pool your allowances to cover one item that exceeds a single allowance. Hence, if you buy a camera that costs £300, you have to pay the duty (at 6.6%) on the full £300, taking the total to £319.80, and then VAT on that figure. However, if you have several items that add up to £290, and then another that exceeds that, you pay the duty and VAT only on the excess item (and customs officers usually give you the benefit of the lowest rate on what you pay for). Duty rates are updated regularly and vary from 2.7% (e.g. golf clubs) to 15% (e.g. mountain bikes). For more info, contact the Customs and Excise National Advice Service on 0845 010 9000 or visit **hmrc. gov.uk**. Your ordinary duty-free allowances from America include 200 cigarettes and 1 litre of spirits or 2 litres of sparkling wine and 2 litres of still wine. Alligator products, which constitute those of an endangered species (to UK authorities), require an import licence, and you should consult the Department of the Environment for more info.

Prime Outlets International

BRITTIP

Pick up the *Orlando Sentinel* newspaper on a Sunday and you will get the full local lowdown on all the great sales for the coming week.

When it comes to the fun part of shopping (and American stores are genuinely fun to just browse, let alone splash out in), you can expect to pay roughly the same in dollars as you do in pounds for items like clothes, books and CDs, and real bargains are to be had in jeans, trainers, shoes, sports equipment and cosmetics. Virtually everywhere offers free, convenient parking, while American shop assistants couldn't be more polite and helpful. Be aware, though, of the hidden extra costs of shopping. Unlike our VAT, Florida sales tax is NOT part of the displayed purchase price, so you must add on 6% or 7% (depending on the county) for the final price. Also, some shops will ask for photo ID with credit card purchases, so if you have a new UK card driving licence it is useful to have it with you. That's the mechanics of it; here's a rundown of the main shopping fun to be had.

Downtown Disney

In many ways the heart of *Walt Disney World* is its *Downtown Disney* district, split into 3 linked sections: *Disney Marketplace, Pleasure Island* and *West Side*. This is typical Disney, a beautiful location, imaginative architecture and a host of one-off elements that make shopping a pleasure, with no fewer than 48 shops and dining opportunities. A water-taxi links the 3 main elements of this 120 acre/ 48.5 ha plaza, making for easy movement around the whole area.

Downtown Disney can be found off exits 67 and 68 of I-4 and is well signposted (exit 68 can be congested at peak periods). You can also rent boats at **Cap'n Jack's Marina** (Marketplace), including the fun new 2-person Sea Raycers ($25/½ hour) and the 21ft Sun Tracker pontoons, which take up to 10 people ($40/½ hour).

Disney Marketplace: When you are here (9.30am–11pm), don't miss the **World of Disney** store, the largest of its kind, which now includes **Bibbidi Bobbidi Boutique** (where young girls can have hair, make-up and nails done in true Princess style, or opt for

World of Disney at Downtown Disney

© Disney

BRITTIP

Don't buy electrical goods in the US – they won't work in the UK without an adapter. Some games systems (notably the Nintendo Gamecube) are NOT compatible with UK players. Hand-held games are fine, though.

the Hannah Montana-inspired Disney's Secret Star Makeover), the **Lego Imagination Center** (an interactive playground and shop), the amazing **Art of Disney** and **Team Mickey's Athletic Club. Once Upon A Toy** is a gigantic toy emporium complete with a host of classic games, many with a Disney theme, for kids to try. Other worthwhile one-offs are the blissful **Basin** (for hand-carved soaps, bubble baths and shampoo bars) and **Disney's Wonderful World of Memories** (for all scrapbook fans, plus the only place to get a Disney postmark for your postcards home!). **Arribas Brothers** is another big, attractive store of gifts (including hand-blown glass) and collectibles. Those keen on the Disney hobby of pin trading should check out **Pin Traders**, while **Summer Sands** offers excellent swimwear and casual clothing. For bargain-hunters, the aisle next to **World of Disney Kids** and **Disney Tails** offers **Mickey's Mart** – everything for $10 or less. Dancing fountains and squirt pools (where kids tend to get seriously wet), the lakeside setting and boating opportunities all add to the appeal here.

The restaurants here include the superbly themed **Rainforest Café, McDonald's, Wolfgang Puck Express** and the casual waterfront setting of **Cap'n Jack's Restaurant**, while ice-cream and chocolate fans should check out **Ghirardelli's** for cool sundaes and super shakes. For a British touch, opt for one of the range of speciality hot sandwiches and salads at the **Earl of Sandwich**, which start at $5.75 (some will feed 2!), making them some of Disney's best-priced fare. For an upmarket touch, we rate **Fulton's Crab House** and **Portobello Yacht Club** (see Chapter 11, Dining Out) very highly. The new **T-Rex: A Prehistoric Family Adventure** was due to open in November 2008, with another innovative restaurant from the people who run Rainforest Café, offering dining with dinosaurs and plenty of interactive features! There will be a Build-A-Dino workshop in its gift shop, and an extensive menu featuring the likes of Pterodactyl Wings, Gigantosaurus Burgers, Triassic Tortellini and Paleo Shrimp, along with soups, salads, pizza, sandwiches, chicken and steak. A full kid's menu will be available and the desserts are set to be dino-rific (try the Chocolate Extinction – big enough for sharing!).

BRITTIP

Parents beware! The Bibbidi Bobbidi Boutique hair and make-up shop is hideously expensive. Packages range from $35 to $175, so you may want to steer your Princesses gently away!

Pleasure Island: This area is still being revamped with new shops and restaurants being added to make it more lively during the day as well as by night. You can check out the cornerstone **Harley-Davidson** store as well as **Curl by Sammy Duvall**, a surfing, apparel and accessories shop with the latest trendy clothing, and **Fuego Cigars by Sosa** to enjoy a

Downtown Disney

© Disney

Orlando's Shopping Centres

Raglan Road

premium range of cigars. Although not confirmed at the time of writing, we believe a new South American café and Tequileria is due to open along one side of Pleasure Island, offering beautiful lakeside views. However, the one unmissable element is wonderful **Raglan Road**, an Irish-themed pub and restaurant, with live music every evening (see pages 296 and 335). The entire area is now a more continuous part of *Downtown Disney*, with a large bridge to the West Side, wider walkways and a water-taxi dock.

West Side: Continuing into West Side (10.30am–11pm) gives you the superb **AMC 24** cinema complex and the world's largest **Virgin Megastore**, plus another 18 retail and dining outlets. The **Hoypoloi Gallery** is one of our favourites for an eclectic range of artwork from metal to glass, while **Magic Masters** (a wide variety of tricks and souvenirs, with demonstrations), **Mickey's Groove** (exclusively Mickey-related items), **Pop Gallery** and **Starabilias** are also highly original. The dining choice is superb, with **Planet Hollywood, House of Blues, Bongo's Cuban Café** and our favourite, **Wolfgang Puck** – an ultra-versatile family-friendly restaurant.

International Drive

This core tourist area is simply awash with shopping of all kinds, from the cheapest and tackiest plazas, full of tourist gift shops, to 3 clever, purpose-built centres. Some of the shops just north of the Sand Lake Road junction are best avoided, while the northern end of I-Drive has undergone a major redevelopment.

This area has been renowned for discount outlet shopping – a local speciality – offering name brands at heavily reduced prices to clear.

Prime Outlets International: At the top of I-Drive, this has completely replaced the sprawling old Belz Discount Outlet World that used to be here following an extensive $250m, two-stage rebuild to make it a more coherent 'village' design. Now an attractive 100-shop 'lifestyle centre', Prime has gone all out for the big, semi-open-air style that encourages people to wander the long interior promenades full of welcoming shop fronts and big-name brands. Boasting a landscaped canal running through the centre, outdoor seating, cafés, a Market Place food court and a free-standing Guest Services centre, it provides a wealth of shopping opportunity with a luxury tinge. Major brands include the **Neiman Marcus Last Call Clearance Center**, which will certainly attract the fashion-conscious, as will the **Hugo Boss Factory Store, White House/ Black Market, Esprit** and **Jones New York Outlet**. Other familiar names include **Nike Super Store, Tommy Hilfiger, Crabtree & Evelyn** and the inevitable **Starbucks**. Phase 2 completed the impressive picture in May 2008, adding more international brands such as **Banana Republic, Bath & Body Works, BCBG/MaxAzria** and **Brooks Brothers**, while you should also look for designer stores from **Eddie Bauer, J Crew** and menswear specialist **Hickey Freeman**. Add in the attractive **food court**, which includes Chicken Now, Jack's Steakery, China Max and Sbarro, and you have one of the brightest shopping centres in the area (10am–9pm; 407 352 9600; **primeoutlets.com**).

Festival Bay: Also at the top end of I-Drive is this unique indoor mall. Its mix of shops and entertainment is quite unusual, and many of the stores will be unfamiliar to Brits; but don't let that put you off as there are some interesting shops to discover here and some very good value (though up to a third of the units remain empty, which can be off-putting). The emphasis here is as much on entertainment as shopping, and the village street style is aimed at the casual wanderer. The main entrance is graced by a huge fountain and multi-coloured tiling, while it also features **Ron Jon's Surf Shop** battling for prominence with **Fuddruckers** diner (superb burgers) and **Bergamo's** Italian restaurant. Pub fans will want to know the popular **Cricketers Arms** has relocated here from the now demolished Mercado. Step inside the mall doors and you discover a huge water feature and another 60-plus stores and restaurants, plus **Vans Skatepark** and the superb **Cinemark 20-screen Movie Complex**. The massive **Bass Pro Shops Outdoor World** is worth checking out for its range of outdoor clothing and equipment (fishing, boating, hunting and hiking) as well as the amazing themed decor, while **Shepler's Western Wear**'s range of apparel, boots and other footwear has to be seen to be believed (all at great prices, too).

Festival Bay

BRITTIP

Visit Bass Pro Shops at the weekend and watch the amazing in-store fishing demonstrations in its huge fish tank!

Steve & Barry's University Sportswear is another unusual clothing store, especially for the value-conscious – there are some serious bargains to be had here – while the **Universal Orlando Store** was new in 2007 (good for discounted merchandise). Other standouts are **Kasper** (women's attire), **Nine West** (women's shoes and accessories) and **Jones New York, Charlotte Russe** (trendy women's clothing), **Zirbes Emporium** (an eclectic gift-and-furniture store) and **Swim Smart**, plus a unique, glow-in-the-dark mini-golf course, the **Putting Edge**, which is a great place to occupy the kids for a while. The huge **Monkey Joe's** play centre is another ideal opportunity to let the youngsters (3–8s) run free (with a Parent Area including TVs and

Festival Bay

relaxing seating), while there is also the **Fantasy Arcade** for video games. **Vans Skate Park** is perfect for anyone with a skateboard or roller-blade obsession (visit **vans.com**, then Skateparks, then Orlando), offering 6 2-hour sessions a day (10am–midnight) as well as a full range of safety equipment and board rentals, plus a chill-out lounge.

BRITTIP

International visitors can go to the Guest Services booth, with photo ID, and pick up a free advantage card offering $200 in savings throughout Festival Bay.

There is no food court, but there are small dining outlets dotted around, notably **New York Deli**, **Asian Café**, **Auntie Anne's**, **Sandella's Café**, **Cold Stone Creamery** (superb ice-cream), **Smoothy Bee** and **Villa Pizza Cuccina**. The 3 feature restaurants up front are all great choices for a meal or just a post-shopping snack. **Fuddruckers** is a highly tempting counter-service diner offering all manner of burgers (including ostrich, turkey, salmon and vegetarian options), salads, soups and desserts; **Bergamo's** has long offered good-quality Italian dining (pasta, seafood, veal and prime Angus steaks), plus its signature singing waiters, who range from grand opera to folk songs; and **The Cricketers Arms** offers typical pub grub, plus a terrific range of local and imported beers, as well as live entertainment and the all-important footie on the TV! It even has a private function/ dining room (see also page 326) (10am–9pm Mon–Sat, 11am–7pm Sun, later at the restaurants; 407 351 7718; **shopfestivalbaymall.com**).

BRITTIP

The new-look Cricketers Arms features one of the biggest ranges of beers in Florida, with 17 on tap, including 4 hand-drawn ales. It even has a special Sampler Platter on its own 'cricket bat' server!

The Pointe Orlando: This is another I-Drive complex to have undergone a major change, completing a massive redevelopment in 2007/08. The dramatic rebuild has opened a new entrance plaza directly from I-Drive, as well as adding a wealth of new shops and especially restaurants, making this a great choice for an evening out as well as retail therapy. Among some 30 smart stores, you can indulge your passion for fashion at **Victoria's Secret**, **Armani Exchange**, **Image Leather**, **Chico's**, **Gray Fifth**

Avenue and the **Everything But Water** swimwear store, or stock up on gifts and souvenirs at **Bath & Body Works**, eclectic **Artsy Abode**, **SGH sunglass hut** and the excellent **Tharoo & Co** jewellery. Don't miss **L'Occitane en Provence** for French body care, skin care and fragrances, while **Footlocker**, **Bimini Shoes** and **Boardwalk Surf & Sport** all offer more options. The dining choices at The Pointe are its real attraction, though, from the upscale **Capital Grille** (dry-aged steaks, seafood and tantalising desserts) and **The Oceanaire**, whose menu changes daily to highlight some of the best seafood from round the world, to **Johnny Rockets** American diner, **Pizzeria Valdiano**, **Starbucks** and **Hooters** (wings, ribs, chicken and the famous Hooters girls!). Read more about The Pointe's fabulous dining choice on page 331, and you will also find plenty of entertainment by night here, too, at **BB King's Blues Club** and the **Regal Cinemas Stadium 20 + IMAX Cineplex**, which shows first-run movies in large screen format. Parking is at The Pointe's multi-storey car park, but several stores and restaurants will redeem your parking ticket if you shop there. It's open 10am–10pm Mon–Sat, 11am–9pm Sun, but later at the bars and restaurants (407 248 2838, **pointe orlando.com**).

Old Town Kissimmee

BRITTIP

Brit Guide readers receive FREE Pointe Orlando coupons by turning in the ad on the back flap of this book. Take advantage of this exclusive opportunity for added savings on your holiday shopping.

Kissimmee

Down along the tourist territory of Highway 192, you will again find a complete mix of outlets, with a profusion of the cheap and cheerful (some of which you probably wouldn't want if they were giving it away!), but also several highly enticing possibilities.

Old Town: This is Kissimmee's version of the purpose-built tourist shopping centre, an antique-style offering with an eclectic mix of shops, restaurants, bars and fairground attractions, all set out along brick-built streets. The 50 shops range from standard souvenirs, novel T-shirt outlets and Disney merchandise to sportswear, motorbike fashions and other collectables (check out the **Old Town General Store** for a step back in time, or the **Old Town Portrait Gallery** for period style photographs). The individual style of **Out Of This World Embroidery** offers a 'you name it, we'll stitch it' service, while **Black Market Minerals**, **Kandlestix**, **Andean Manna** and **Magic Max** are also great for novel gift ideas. There are 16 restaurants or snack bars, plus **The British Store** when the craving for familiar foods from home strikes (this is the place to get Walker's crisps, Mr Kipling cakes and Cadbury's chocolates). Those in need of some pampering or a massage should head for the **Time For Pleasure Day Spa** (10am–10pm daily). **Kool Katz Grill & Pub** features American favourites in a casual atmosphere reminiscent of the Friday and Saturday Nite car cruises, while the **Blue Max Tavern** is a fun alternative. **Jam Rock Caribbean Café** and **Old Town Chippy** (British-style fish 'n' chips) are also worth trying,

A Kissimmee tradition

Old Town is home to some weekly events that appeal to locals and tourists alike and are well worth catching if possible. The **Saturday Nite Cruise** at 8.30pm is a drive-past of 300-plus vintage and collector cars (the biggest in America) that has become a real trademark here. A **Friday Nite Cruise** features cars built between 1973 and 1987, while every Thursday is **Motorcycle Nite** from 6pm. There is live music, fairground-type stalls and prizes, and it can get fairly raucous later on, with plenty of alcoholic libations (witness the **Sun on the Beach** bar!).

while there are other snack outlets, with offerings from popcorn to candy. Parking is free (10am–11pm daily; rides open noon–11pm; 407 396 4888; **old-town.com**).

Downtown Kissimmee offers the more local, authentic face of shopping in Florida, with the charming Main Street area featuring a range of tempting antique shops, one-off boutiques, cafes and restaurants. You should certainly look into the likes of local landmarks **Lanier's**, **Cee Jay's Collectibles** and **Gallery One Artists**, while Italian restaurant **Tarantino's** is something of a local institution. The authentic Mexican family style of **Azteca's** is also worth trying. Every Thursday (7am–1pm) you can also sample the local **Farmers' Market** on the corner of Pleasant St and Darlington Ave.

Kissimmee itself is short of quality shopping otherwise, as the Kissimmee Manufacturers' Outlet Mall and Osceola Square Mall are in urgent need of refurbishment. But head up to the Osceola Parkway (at the junction with John Young Parkway), which runs parallel to Highway 192, and you find the extensive developments of **The Loop** and the recently added **Loop West**, which help redress the balance. This double open-air plaza offers a unique mix of shops and restaurants, plus a 16-screen **Regal Cinema**, in a pedestrian-friendly setting, with the shops grouped around 2 large car parks. Many of the shops may not mean much to UK visitors but are well worth visiting. Of note at The Loop are **Ross** (a huge discount warehouse of clothes, shoes, linens, cosmetics and more), **Kohl's** (a well-priced department store), **Bed, Bath & Beyond** (an amazing range of household wares), **Pacific Sunwear** (beach and casual wear), **Old Navy** (clothing), **Michaels** (arts and crafts), **Sports Authority** and **Famous Footwear** (discounted shoes and trainers). In addition, there is a hairdresser, nail salon, chemist (**CVS**) and a superb line-up of 10 restaurants and cafés. Look out in particular for **Johnny Rockets**, the excellent Italian style of **Macaroni Grill**, **Red Brick Pizza**, the gourmet offerings of **Chipotle Mexican Grill**, **Shane's Rib Shack** and the hearty fare of **Panera Bread** (great soups, salads and

Tarantino's

sandwiches). At The Loop West, look for the 2 big department stores of **JC Penney** (clothing and housewares) and **Belk** (home goods), plus **Circuit City** (electronics) and **DSW** (shoes) plus 15 additional shops and another 4 restaurants – **BJ's Restaurant and Brewhouse**, the Asian style of **Pei Wei**, **Tropical Smoothie Café** and the upmarket **Bonefish Grill**. In all, The Loop and Loop West boast 65 shopping and dining outlets and this has quickly become a major proposition, especially for the extensive dining choice (open 10am–9.30pm Mon–Sat, 11am–6pm Sun, later at the restaurants and cinemas; 407 343 9223; **attheloop.com**).

Lake Buena Vista

The Lake Buena Vista area has 2 of the best discount outlet centres, with a range of goods to make even the most jaded shopper salivate – and prices to match!

Orlando Premium Outlets: High on your list of 'must visit' shops, this is a huge hit with UK visitors – and it's still growing! With a fresh look and style, and a legion of big-name designers (from Nike, Adidas and Gap to Polo Ralph Lauren, Dior, Hugo Boss, Coach and Zegna), it can be found on Vineland Avenue between I-Drive and I-4 (just south of SeaWorld; or exit 68 off I-4).

In all, it offers 110 stores of well-known brand names (like Timberland, Reebok, Diesel, Fossil, Banana Republic, French Connection and Calvin Klein) in a semi-covered

The Food Court at Orlando Premium Outlets

BRITTIP

Don't try to battle with the crowds in the main open-air car park at Orlando Premium Outlets. Instead, head towards the back of the centre where you will find the new 1,600-car multi-storey car park.

pedestrian plaza, with free parking and the added convenience of being at the south end of the I-Ride Trolley (main line). Other significant signature shops are **Samsonite Company Store**, **Ecko** (upscale T-shirts, jeans and sportswear), **Fendi** (stylish women's clothing and signature handbags), **OshKosh B'Gosh** (baby/toddler clothes), **Le Gourmet** (kitchen items), **Factory Brand Shoes** (a mini-warehouse of footwear fashion) and **KB Toys** (a huge discount choice for kids of all ages). Watch out also for big Disney bargains at the **Character Premiere**.

BRITTIP

Brit Guide **Itinerary Planner Service** clients will receive Orlando Premium Outlets' special Premier Platinum VIP Passport voucher, for significant extra savings at many shops (see page 49).

The food court is quite tempting, too, with 11 outlets, from **JR's Steakery** and **Max Orient** to **Starbucks** and **Subway**. In addition, 39 new luxury outlets will be opening at the main centre on 13 November 2008, as part of a major 2-stage expansion plan. Part 2 (starting in 2009) will see Orlando Premium Outlets taking over the former Dixie Stampede property next door and adding a further 60-plus upscale new stores, linked by a bridge from the existing centre, for completion in 2010. For those without a car, there is a daily free shuttle service from 15 hotels in the Lake Buena Vista area, but it costs $10/person from Highway 192 in Kissimmee. Call 407 390 0000 for reservations, which are required

(2 hours in advance highly advised). The **Lynx** bus service also stops here (407 841 2279) or you can try **Star Taxi** (407 857 9999). Premium Outlets is open daily from 10am–11pm (to 9pm Sun; 407 238 7787; **premiumoutlets.com**).

BRITTIP

After shopping at Orlando Premium Outlets, look to grab afternoon tea, with home-made scones, or a glass of wine or speciality beer at the new **Sherlock's** tearoom and wine bar, all with a proper British touch (near the Outback Steakhouse on the north side of the centre).

Lake Buena Vista Factory Stores: Get ready for more big-name products at discount prices here, from Fossil, Sony, Reebok, Liz Claiborne and London Fog to a budget-priced **Disney Character Outlet**, **OshKosh B'Gosh** superstore and (the better-priced) **Carter's For Kids**. It is another open-air plaza, with almost 50 stores spread over 6 acres/2.5ha and with plentiful, convenient parking. It's slightly off the beaten track and therefore not quite as busy as some of the others. New shops are opening all the time, and recent additions include stylish **Tommy Hilfiger**, funky **Aeropostale**, **Bass Shoes**, **Hard Rock Outlet Store**, **Converse** and **Rawlings Factory Store** for sporting goods. There is also a decent food court and a kids' playground. Some of the stores and brand names may not be well known to us, but the likes of **Old Navy** (excellent value casual clothing), **Perfume Outlet** (heavily discounted fragrances and cosmetics), **SAS Shoes** (think Hush Puppies, only cheaper!), **Travelpro** (luggage) and **Rack Room Shoes** (big names at serious savings) are worth discovering. **Borders Books Outlet** offers great bargain books, **Camera Outlet** carries a large selection of European PAL systems, and **World of Coffee** is both an internet café and one of the best places you could find to sip a latte and enjoy a cake or pastry, with its outdoor terrace and bird cages.

Worth noting at the neighbouring Lake Buena Vista Resort Village and Spa are the luxurious **Reflections Spa** for a bit of pampering after your day of shopping, and the new **Frankie Farrells Irish Pub & Grill**, an excellent choice for lunch or dinner in an authentic pub atmosphere (with lots of TVs showing UK sport!). Its 32 brews on tap (including Boddingtons,

Orlando Premium Outlets

Guinness, Bass and Magners) complement a traditional Irish and American menu.

BRITTIP

If you are into scrapbook hobbies or other arts and crafts, you should seek out one of Orlando's 8 **Michaels** stores, which are a scrapbooking heaven!

Other services here include the welcome lounge and off-site airline check-in for **Travel City Direct**. The Factory Stores are on SR 535 (2miles/3km south off exit 68 on I-4) and are open daily 10am–9pm (to 6pm Sun). Its shuttle service picks up at hotels and condo units in a 10ml/16km radius (407 238 9301, **lbvfs.com**).

BRITTIP

Go to lbvfs.com for up to $400 in discount coupons.

Malls

Head out slightly beyond the main tourist territory and you will discover the further choice and style of the area's many malls, several of which are well worth adding to your holiday agenda. They contain a huge range of shops and, if you take advantage of their periodic sales, you will be firmly back on the bargain trail. The top 2 locally are the Florida Mall and the Mall at Millenia, and both offer a contrasting shopping experience.

BRITTIP

Need a good book? Make a beeline for **Barnes & Noble**, on West Sand Lake Road in the Venezia Plaza, on the South Orange Blossom Trail opposite the Florida Mall, or at the new Winter Garden Village shops. Each has a great coffee shop, too.

Florida Mall: The largest in central Florida, this features more than 250 shops, with 6 large department stores and a 22-counter food court, plus a children's play area, the lively bar-restaurant **Ruby Tuesday**, the smart Mexican-influenced **Salsa Taqueria and Tequilla Bar, California Pizza Kitchen** and hearty **Buca di Beppo**. Located on the South Orange Blossom Trail, on the corner of Sand Lake Road, this spacious and extremely smart mall is open 10am–9pm Mon–Sat, noon–6pm Sun). Highlights are the department stores, led by the upmarket (but expensive) **Saks Fifth Avenue** and **Macy's**, plus **JC Penney**, **Nordstrom** (which also has a sit-down café), **Sears** and **Dillard's**. Other shops worth looking out for are **Bath & Body Works, Williams-Sonoma** ('the place for cooks' – and how!), **PacSun** (beachwear and more) and, for kids, the **Build-a-Bear Workshop**, **KB Toys**, **Game Stop** and the wonderfully fun **M&M World** store. The new **Adrenalina The Extreme** store features a huge range of extreme sports gear and apparel,

The Florida Mall

plus a fun FlowRider surfing pool – also great for spectators! You can benefit here from a discount coupon packet (from Guest Services) that includes a handy international size chart to help deal with American sizing. Extra services include free wheelchair use, pushchair rental and foreign currency exchange. There are even spa and beauty treatments in the Lancôme Institut de Beauté in Dillard's, the JC Penney styling salon and day spa, and the Elizabeth Arden salon at Saks Fifth Avenue (407 851 6255; **simon.com**). The Mall also benefits from the integral **Florida Hotel**, with Cricket's Grille & Bar. Nearby on Sand Lake Road, you will find the warehouse-like **Old Time Pottery**, which is a vast emporium of home goods of all kinds, from crockery to linens (look up **oldtime pottery.com**).

BRITTIP

Kids – let your parents take you to the Florida Mall, then insist on visiting the huge Toys R Us store at the front and then M&M World inside the mall!

Mall at Millenia: If the Florida Mall is the biggest shopping venue in town, this is the smartest. Opened in October 2002 and located just off I-4 to the north of Universal Orlando (exit 78), it is the most upmarket, dramatic and technologically advanced shopping complex in Florida, with New York's most famous department stores – Bloomingdale's, Neiman Marcus and Macy's – among a select number of other top-name boutiques such as Tiffany & Co and Louis Vuitton. The entrance features a 60ft/18m glass rotunda with a flowing water garden theme and a helpful concierge desk (valet parking is also available). Then you can head out in one of 4 directions over the marble and terrazzo floors or go upstairs to the refreshing, high-quality 13-outlet food court, **Orangerie Cafés**, where the only difficulty is deciding which of the tempting (and health-conscious) eateries to choose. Look out for **Bistro Sensations** (wonderful salads, pastas, pittas and wraps), the authentic Mandarin-style of **Chinatown**, the fresh **Greek Jalapeno** (tacos, burritos, but nothing Greek!) and the **Southwest Grill** (succulent chicken, barbecue beef and salads), plus **Tony's & Bruno's** for Italian specialities (pasta, pizza, salads, cheesecake).

BRITTIP

Visit the concierge office at Mall at Millenia, fill out its marketing questionnaire and receive a free gift.

The grand architecture is also focused on 5 separate courts along a flattened, serpentine S-shape, topped by a flowing, arched glass roof like some gigantic conservatory. On 2 airy levels (3 in Bloomingdale's and Macy's) and with 8 Juliet balconies connecting the 2 sides, the mall consists of a colossal amount of glass, plus a stunning Grand Court, featuring a dozen 20ft/6m columns capped by curved plasma video screens. And, while around 20% of the 150 outlets are upscale and exclusive (Cartier, Chanel, Lacoste, Jimmy Choo, Dior, Coach etc., plus the luxury of Neiman Marcus for brands like Gucci and Swarovski), the other 80% comprise more mainstream shops like Gap,

The Mall at Millenia

Banana Republic and Victoria's Secret. Several outlets provide a distinctive experience – **Metropolitan Museum of Art**, **Z Gallerie** and **Rocks Fine Jewellery** – without the price tag to go with it. The 4 main restaurants are also first class: heavenly **Cheesecake Factory**, gourmet seafood **McCormick & Schmick**, **PF Chang's China Bistro** and **Brio Tuscan Grille**. On top of that (AND the Orangerie Cafés), there is the excellent fresh sandwich style of **Panera Bread**, the **California Pizza Kitchen** and a **Johnny Rockets** diner. This is also the only mall with a US post office inside (NB: Standard postcards to the UK cost 94c). A currency exchange is available, as are international phone cards. The chic **Blue Martini**, a speciality martini bar, sushi-tapas restaurant and music venue, is well worth trying for something a bit special. With more than 32 unique martinis, plus an extensive wine list, premium cigars and a tapas-style menu, this is the current trendy hangout, with an outdoor terrace and indoor stage room. There's live music (8–11.30pm Mon–Thurs, 7.30–11.30pm Fri and Sat), then dance music with the house DJ (4pm–2am Mon–Fri, 1pm–2am Sat and Sun, Happy Hour 4–7pm Mon–Fri; **bluemartinilounge.com**). All in all, this takes the Florida shopping experience to a new level (10am–9pm Mon–Sat, 12am–7pm Sun; 407 363 3555; **mallatmillenia.com**).

Blue Martini

Brio Tuscan Grille

There are 4 alternatives to these popular (and busy – especially at weekends) malls: the **Altamonte Mall**, on Altamonte Avenue in the suburb of Altamonte Springs (take exit 92 off I-4 and head east for ½ml/800m on Route 436, then turn left); **Seminole Towne Center**, just off I-4 to the north of Orlando on the outskirts of Sanford (exit 101C off I-4); **Oviedo Marketplace**, to the east of Orlando (right off exit 41 of Central Florida Greeneway, 417); and **West Oaks Mall**, on West Colonial Drive (SR50), in the suburb of Ocoee, west of downtown Orlando (take the Florida Turnpike to exit 267A with SR50, and go back east on 50 for 1½mls/2.5km). The Altamonte Mall is the best of the bunch and well off the beaten tourist track, featuring 160 speciality shops, 4 major department stores – Macy's, Dillard's, JC Penney and Sears – and 19 eateries, including the fun **Bahama Breeze**, upmarket **Seasons 52** and pub-style **Orlando Ale House**. An 18-screen cinema and children's soft-play area round out the offerings. Open 10am–9pm Mon–Sat, 11am–6pm Sun, it offers a VIP savings book to visitors at the Customer Service Center (**altamontemall.com**). Shop during the week and you'll feel as if you have the place to yourself!

Our shopping tips

As we live locally, shopping is very close to our hearts, and we would recommend the following as an essential slice of the Orlando shopping scene:

Outlet shopping: Orlando Premium Outlets or Prime Outlets International

Mall: Mall at Millenia

Open-air centre: Winter Garden Village

Supermarket: Whole Foods Market

Chemist: Walgreens

Electronics: Best Buy

Clothing: Marshalls and Steve & Barry's

Home goods: Old Time Pottery

Bookshop: Barnes & Noble

Specialist store: Shepler's Western Wear

One last major shopping recommendation is the more offbeat **Winter Garden Village**, 5mls/8km north of *Walt Disney World* on Highway 535 at the junction with toll road 429, which is primarily a new locals' centre but still has a lot of visitor appeal. The expansive open-plan design, set around key stores like **Target**, **Best Buy**, **Sports Authority** and **Beall's**, features a mix of the big names and smaller boutiques, as well as a tempting array of 21 cafes and restaurants sprinkled throughout. Look for the upmarket seafood choice of Bonefish Grill, the elegant Longhorn Steakhouse, family-style

Orlando Premium Outlets

The Mall at Millenia

Chili's, Cracker Barrel, UNO Chicago Grill and Mimi's Café, or the counter-service options like Urban Flats, Quiznos, Panda Express, Coldstone Creamery and Chick-Fil-A (look up more at **wintergardenvillage.com**).

Flea markets

Flea World: The locals also have a passion for flea markets, highlighted by America's largest covered market, with 1,700 stalls spread over 104 acres/42ha, including 3 massive (air-conditioned), themed buildings and a 7 acre/2.8ha amusement park, **Fun World** (several multi-ride wristbands available). Flea World is open 9am–6pm Fri, Sat and Sun (Fun World 9am–6pm Sat and Sun only), and can be found a 30-minute drive away on Highway 17/92 (best picked up from exit 90 on I-4) between Orlando and Sanford (to the north). The stalls include all manner of market goods (nearly all new or slight seconds), from fresh produce to antiques and jewellery, while there is a full-scale food court and a 300-seat pizza and burger eatery, the **Carousel Restaurant**, plus free entertainment on the Fun World Pavilion stage (407 330 1792; **fleaworld.com**).

Osceola Flea and Farmers' Market: On a smaller scale at the east end of Highway 192 in Kissimmee (8am–5pm Fri–Sun), this offers food, clothing, household and kitchen supplies, electronics, sporting goods, collectables and handicrafts (407 846 2811).

Supermarkets: High on many people's lists is **Wal-Mart**, the warehouse-like American supermarket that sells just about everything. There are no fewer than 21 Wal-Marts in central Florida, 16 of which are the 24-hour Supercenter kind. The main tourist area stores are on Highway 27 (just north of 192); Highway 192 by Medieval Times (between markers 14 and 15); Osceola Parkway (at Buenaventura Lakes); John Young Parkway (at Sand Lake Road); on Kirkman Road (north of Universal Boulevard); by Highway 535 and Osceola Parkway; and on Turkey Lake Road.

BRITTIP

Wal-Mart offers 1-hour photo processing at great savings on UK prices, as do branches of Walgreens.

There is plenty of supermarket choice, though, and you will find better-quality produce at the likes of **Publix** (throughout the main tourist areas, notably on Highway 192 and 27); **Goodings** (on I-Drive and the Crossroads plaza near Downtown Disney); **Winn-Dixie** (a major south-east US chain) and **Albertson's** (mainly Orlando and to the north – the store at Dr Phillips Boulevard is close to I-Drive). The real Rolls-Royce of food stores was due to open a new Orlando branch on Turkey Lake Road late in 2008 – **Whole Foods Market** is a superb fresh produce emporium, with plenty of chances to sample as you go, plus a hot-food counter to grab a meal at the end (**wholefoodsmarket.com**). For clothes, DIY, home furnishings, electrical goods, household items, gifts, toys and groceries, visit **Target** (its new superstores on Highway 192 just west of Highway 535 and near Mall at Millenia are fine examples). The big chemists ('drug stores') of **Walgreens** and **CVS** also carry a surprisingly wide range of goods and almost resemble mini-supermarkets in their own right.

Outdoor World at Festival Bay

© OCVB

BRITTIP

If you shop at any US Wal-Mart store, you can return faulty or wrong-size goods to your local Asda for a refund, as long as you present the receipts.

Specialist shops

Keen shoppers will want to check out other individual outlets that might not mean much at first glance. **Ross** (10 in Orlando, see **rossstores.com**) carries a huge range of discounted brand-name clothes, shoes, linens, towels and other goods (9.30am–9.30pm Mon–Sat, 11am–7pm Sun), while **Marshalls** (5 in Orlando, **marshallsonline.com**) and **TJ Maxx** (also 5, **tjmaxx.com**) are similar. For jeans and more, **World of Denim** (and **Denim Place**) has 6 shops in the main tourist areas (good for Tommy Hilfiger, DKNY, Calvin Klein, Polo, Lee and more), while **The Sports Authority** and **Sports Dominator** offer all manner of sporting goods and apparel. Golfers should visit the **Edwin Watts Golf** shops (including the I-Drive clearance centre, **edwinwatts.com**), or any of the **Special Tee Golf & Tennis** shops. You can pick up some great deals on golf clubs in particular. By the same token, anglers can stock up on the latest gear at bargain prices at **Bass Pro Shops Outdoor World** (Festival Bay).

However, now the shopping is done, it's time to think about the journey home…

13 Going Home

or Where Did the Last Two Weeks Go?

And so, dog-tired, lighter in the wallet but (hopefully) blissfully happy and with enough memories to last a lifetime, it's time to deal with that bane of all holidays – the journey home.

If you have come through the last 2 weeks relatively unscathed, here's how to avoid any last-minute pitfalls.

The car

Returning the hire car can take time if you had to use an off-airport car depot, so allow ½ hour. The process is much slicker with the firms that operate directly from the airports. Most airlines require you to arrive 3 hours before an international flight, so don't be tempted to leave your check-in until the last minute. The off-airport check-in facilities for Virgin, Travel City Direct and Airtours (at *Downtown Disney*, Lake Buena Vista Factory Stores and International Drive respectively) are a major bonus in making this aspect smoother for their passengers. Now you'll have time to kill, so here is a guide to the 2 main airports.

Orlando International Airport

Orlando International is 46mls/74km from Cocoa Beach and 54mls/87km from Daytona Beach on the east coast, 84mls/135km from Tampa and 110mls/177km from Clearwater and St Petersburg to the west, 25mls/40km from *Walt Disney World* and 10mls/16km from Universal Orlando; so always allow enough time for the return journey plus check-in. The Beachline Expressway (528) can get quite congested in the afternoon, for example, and the Central Florida Greeneway (417) is often better.

This modern airport is the 4th largest in size in the USA, the 10th for number of passengers (No 1 in Florida) – and the top rated for passenger satisfaction. It hit a record 36.4 million passengers in 2007 (some 100,000 a day), busier than Gatwick and San Francisco. It can get busy at peak times, but its 854 acre/345ha terminal complex usually handles crowds with ease, and this is one of the most comfortable airports you could ever hope to find. It boasts great facilities, and its wide, airy concourses make it feel more like an elegant hotel (one end is actually the airport-owned Hyatt Hotel). Ramps, restrooms, wide lifts and large open areas ensure easy wheelchair access, and there are features like TDD and amplified telephones, wheelchair-height drinking fountains, Braille lift controls and companion-care restrooms to assist any travellers with disabilities. In keeping with the area, this airport is always engaged in staying a step ahead, and it is often engaged in an enhancement project or two. It boasts a major food court, extra restaurant options and some superb shops. There is even a 'green' aspect to Orlando International, as its latest

BRITTIP

You are advised to leave all luggage unlocked (no combination locks or padlocks) when you check in for your return flight as the TSA security staff open a LOT of bags during its screening process and have the right to access any case, locked or unlocked.

fleet of shuttle buses are hydrogen powered, with zero emissions.

Should you have more than 3 hours to spare, it's worth taking the 15-minute taxi ride to the Florida Mall, or checking in early, keeping the car and visiting Gatorland about 20 minutes away (see pages 232–4).

Landside

As with all international airports, there is a division between LANDSIDE (for visitors) and AIRSIDE (where you must have a ticket). There are 3 levels at Orlando's Landside.

- **1** is for ground transportation, tour operator desks, parking, buses and car rental agencies.
- **2** is for Baggage Claim (which you negotiated on your arrival) and private vehicles meeting passengers.
- **3** is where you enter on your return journey as it holds the check-in desks, shops and restaurants.

Orlando International Airport

Level 3: This divides into 5 interconnected sections: **Landside A** is the check-in for **Gates 1–29** and **100–129**. Here you'll find American Airlines, Air Canada, Continental, Aer Lingus, Southwest, JetBlue and Virgin (though Virgin departs from Gates 60–99). **Landside B** has check-in desks for **Gates 30–99** and the likes of Air France, BA, Delta, Northwest, United, Spirit, US Airways, AirTran.

Once you've checked in, you can explore both the **East** and **West** sections of the main concourse on Level 3. These house a good mix of shops and restaurants, plus currency exchange, information desks and ATM machines, while the Hyatt Hotel is also in the East Hall. The East and West Halls are then linked by the restaurants, shops and services of the **North** and **South Walks**. In total, there are 40 places to shop and eat, plus a handy food court, and it's almost like being in a smart shopping mall. There's a games arcade, a Suntrust bank, post office and even the relaxing **D-parture Spa and Salon** (have a massage before your flight!). Many shops feature outstanding design and even photo opportunities: see the 2 **Disney** stores, **Harley-Davidson**, **Universal, SeaWorld/ Busch Gardens** and **Kennedy Space Center**. Other notable shops are the blissful bath products of **Lush**, the natural cosmetics of **L'Occitane**, the unique apparel of **Del Sol**, **Borders Books** (with its **Seattle's Best** coffee bar), **Ron Jon Surf Shop**, **Perfumania, Florida Market**, the fashion accessories of **Bijoux Terner** (everything $15) and **Hudson News**.

Dining: Another pleasure! The 8-counter food court features **McDonalds**, **Sbarro**, **Carvel** ice-cream, **Krispy Crème** and **Nathan's Hot Dogs**, as well as the healthier options of **Zyng's Asian Noodlery**, **Fresh Attractions Deli** and **Chick-Fil-A. Macaroni Grill** is a tasty Italian option, while **Fox Sports Sky Box** adds a multi-screen TV set-up plus

Take to the AirTran

To really make the most of your American adventure, *Brit Guide* can thoroughly recommend exploring some other key cities direct from Orlando with **AirTran Airways**, who we fly with regularly and which is one of the most reliable operators in the US. It offers low fares – especially if you book well in advance (sign up for its email sale alerts and special offers) – and a route network that includes San Diego (southern California's hidden secret), New York, Washington and Buffalo/Niagara, all non-stop from Orlando. In all, it covers 65 US destinations, also using a major hub at Atlanta to cities like Las Vegas, Los Angeles and San Francisco, plus the Bahamas, with a modern fleet of Boeing 717 and 737 aircraft (including live XM satellite radio). Other major US gateways include Detroit, Philadelphia, Raleigh-Durham, Boston, Chicago and Dallas, which all provide connecting flights to the UK for alternative transatlantic routes. For a low-cost carrier it is rare in offering a business upgrade at less than business-class prices; in fact, it puts many scheduled services to shame. Book online (**airtran.com**) for the best bargains, or call 1800 247 8726 in the US (001 678 254 7999 from the UK). If you are staying on the Florida coast, AirTran also flies from Tampa, Miami, Sarasota/Bradenton, Fort Myers, Fort Lauderdale, West Palm Beach, Daytona Beach and Jacksonville, making it one of the Sunshine State's most user-friendly airlines.

counter and table service; and upstairs at the West Hall is **Chili's Too**, a cheerful, quick-service Tex-Mex bar-diner.

The **East Hall** tends to be quieter and more picturesque as it is dominated by the 8-storey Hyatt Hotel atrium. Up the escalator is the main entrance, and to see out your visit in style, **McCoy's Bar and Grill** (up and turn right) is a smart bar-restaurant with a grandstand view of the runways. To go really upmarket, take the lift to the 9th-floor **Hemispheres** (breakfast and dinner only). You'll have an even more impressive view, and its superb Continental cuisine and wine-tasting evenings offer some of the best fare in the city. It's pricey, but the service and food are 5-star.

Airside

Once it's time to move to your departure gate, be aware of the 4 satellite 'arms' that make up the airport's Airside. This is where you will probably need to queue as the security screening takes time, and you should allow AT LEAST 30 minutes (though the airport is also bringing in new queuing methods and extra screening stations in 2008 to speed things up). The arms are divided into Gates 1–29 and 30–59 at the west end, and 60–99 and 100–129 (all American domestic flights) at the east. All the departure gates are here, plus duty-free shops and more cafés.

BRITTIP

Save some film (or card space) for the excellent photo opportunities at the airport: outside the Disney stores, the 2 Harley-Davidson shops and the Kennedy Space Center outlets.

The 4 satellites are each connected to the main building by an automated tram, so you need to be alert when it comes to finding your departure gate. There are no tannoy announcements for flights, so you should check your departure gate and time when you check in. However, there are new, large monitors in the terminal with all the departure information. The usual gates are:

- Aer Lingus, American and Continental: 1–29.
- Air Canada, Northwest, Spirit, United and US Airways: 30–59.
- AirTran, British Airways, Delta and Virgin: 60–99.
- JetBlue and Southwest: 100–129.

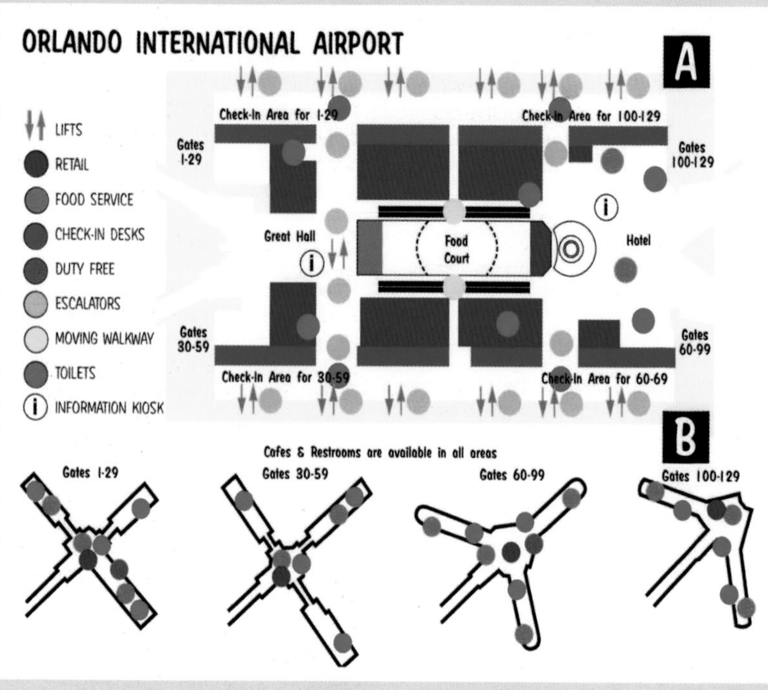
ORLANDO INTERNATIONAL AIRPORT
A
LIFTS
RETAIL
FOOD SERVICE
CHECK-IN DESKS
DUTY FREE
ESCALATORS
MOVING WALKWAY
TOILETS
INFORMATION KIOSK
Check-In Area for 1-29
Check-In Area for 100-129
Gates 1-29
Gates 100-129
Great Hall
Food Court
Hotel
Gates 30-59
Gates 60-99
Check-In Area for 30-59
Check-In Area for 60-69
B
Cafes & Restrooms are available in all areas
Gates 1-29
Gates 30-59
Gates 60-99
Gates 100-129

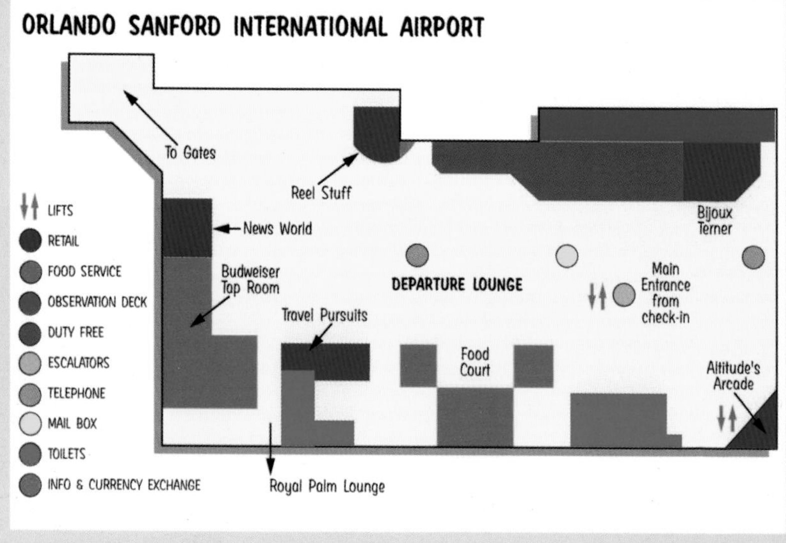
ORLANDO SANFORD INTERNATIONAL AIRPORT
To Gates
Reel Stuff
News World
Bijoux Terner
Budweiser Tap Room
DEPARTURE LOUNGE
Main Entrance from check-in
Travel Pursuits
Food Court
Altitude's Arcade
Royal Palm Lounge
LIFTS
RETAIL
FOOD SERVICE
OBSERVATION DECK
DUTY FREE
ESCALATORS
TELEPHONE
MAIL BOX
TOILETS
INFO & CURRENCY EXCHANGE

Although there isn't as much choice as at the main terminal, you should find the Airside areas just as clean and efficient, with the bonus of 2 duty-free shops (your purchases are delivered to the departure gate for you to collect as you board). Both stores have been significantly upgraded, with merchandise expanded to include designer sunglasses, jewellery, handbags, fashion watches, new perfumes and a selection of travel retail exclusives.

At **Gates 1–29**, you will find the first duty-free shop, a newsagents (the **Keys Gift Shop**), 2 **Café Azalea** lounge bars, **Pepito's Cuban Café**, and a mini food court featuring **Starbucks**, **Burger King**, **Cinnabon** and **TCBY** ('The Country's Best Yogurt'). **Gates 30–59** have **Café Azalea**, **Pepito's Cuban Café**, the **Floribbean Court** (with **Miami Subs**, **Villa Pizza**, **Freshens Treats** and the **Manatee** bar/lounge) and Hudson News. **Gates 60–99** (the main satellite for UK flights) offer another good duty-free shop, a currency exchange, **Stellar News & Gifts**, the speciality **Mindworks** shop, **The Grove** snacks and candy and a mini play area. A food court contains **Burger King**, **Nathan's Hot Dogs**, **Carvel**, **Starbucks** and **Fresh Attractions** deli, plus the excellent table service of the **Outback Steakhouse Outpost** and bar. **Gates 100–129** offer 2 **Johnny Rivers Smokehouse Express** outlets, a food court with **Freshens Treats**, **McDonald's** and **Sbarro Pizza**, plus **Seattle's Best** coffee shop, **Au Bon Pain** café, **Kafe Kalik** bar/lounge and 4 shops. For more details, visit **orlandoairports.net**, which features live departure and arrival info.

Orlando Sanford International Airport

Returning to what is now the main Orlando gateway for British charter flights should be a relatively simple experience, providing you retrace your route on the Central Florida Greeneway (following signs for Orlando Sanford Airport, NOT Orlando International) and come off at exit 49. Turn first right at the lights, then first right again on to Lake Mary Boulevard and follow it to the airport. The efficiency of Alamo and Dollar's car return adds to the simplicity. NB: The airport turn-off sign is immediately after the toll plaza before exit 49 and is easy to miss, so be aware once you go through that toll plaza that you need the very next turn-off.

Orlando Sanford was created as a full international airport in 1996, as an initiative between the airport authorities and several British tour operators. And so Thomson, Monarch, Thomas Cook and XL

Airside 4 at Orlando International

Orlando Sanford Airport

Airways, plus the new Sanford operations of Icelandair and Scotland's flyglobespan, all now go for this simpler option. Of course, you are further north, so your journey time is 45 minutes longer and you have to pay an extra $3 in tolls compared with the journey to and from Orlando International but, providing you follow the simple directions, you should have no problem retracing your steps here.

And, while this charter gateway is smaller than Orlando International, it boasts a spacious check-in area and works hard to make the departure as painless as the arrival, especially with its Royal Palm Lounge (formerly the Guest House) facility. Icelandair and flyglobespan usually use **Terminal B** for check-in: the other UK airlines check in at **Terminal A**. But all passengers use the same international departure lounge in Terminal A. It continues to grow with both domestic and international traffic, and has recently finished a major facility upgrade, notably in Terminal B.

There are no food or beverage outlets at the check-in level at Terminal A, but you can walk across to Terminal B where there is a **Ritazza Café** and food court. Once checked in, you need to pass through security (again, allow a minimum of 30 minutes) to reach the International Departure Lounge. Here you have the **Budweiser Tap Room**, which serves a decent selection of international beers, and the handy **Food Court**. The 4-part outlet offers American Grill (burgers and fries), Daily Specials (shepherd's pie, chicken pot pie, lasagne and more), Sweet Endings (baked goods and pastries) and the aptly named Grab-N-Go (soft drinks, snacks and bottled water). There is then an extensive **Duty Free** store (also with an increased range of merchandise), a new **Bijoux Terner** shop (fashion accessories – everything $10!), **Reel Stuff** character gifts from the likes of Disney, TV and film, and entertainment shop **Travel Pursuits**, featuring travel games, electronic toys, soft toys, Lego and K'Nex sets and novelty sweets, as well as **News World** for souvenirs, confectionery, books and magazines (including UK newspapers). **Altitudes Arcade** (neatly located in a corner) is guaranteed to appeal to the kids,

Your chance to give something back

After hopefully having the holiday of a lifetime, you might like to know about 2 charities helping children with serious illnesses to have a memorable time here. Give Kids the World Village is an amazing organisation in Kissimmee, providing a week's holiday in central Florida for children with life-threatening illnesses. GKTW works with over 250 wish-granting foundations worldwide to provide an unforgettable Wish Vacation for children and their families. It is set up as a resort and includes meals, accommodation, transportation, whimsical venues, donated theme park tickets and many other thoughtful touches in a magical setting. It's a charity we are happy to support ourselves, and we hope you will too. You can make a donation through its website – **gktw.org** – or send it to: Give Kids The World, 210 South Bass Road, Kissimmee, Florida 34746, USA.

Equally, Dreamflight is a registered UK charity taking seriously ill children (aged 8–14) to Florida annually, often with the help of British Airways. It costs around £3,000 per child and, while many people generously donate their time to help, cash donations are essential. You can contribute by post: Dreamflight, 7C Hill Avenue, Amersham, Bucks HP6 5BD (01494 722733), online at **justgiving.com**, or by email to **office@dream flight.org**. Look up more at **dreamflight.org**.

Thanks for any contributions to these worthwhile organisations.

while there is also an **Information and Currency Exchange** kiosk. Smoking is not allowed inside the Lounge, but there is an extensive outdoor deck for smokers.

The big extra here, though, is the **Royal Palm Lounge**, a premium space available to all passengers for a modest fee. It's in a separate annexe from the main lounge and is an oasis of comfort and quiet, perfect for relaxing for the last few hours of your holiday (the only things they don't have here are beds and shower facilities!). Split into 2 distinct halves, it boasts a pleasant café bar, where you can enjoy unlimited tea, coffee, soft drinks and snacks (plus 2 glasses of beer or wine per over-21). It also provides 2 home theatre lounges, with widescreen TV and surround-sound, for recently released films; 2 quiet reading rooms; 11 computer terminals for internet access and email; a youth entertainment centre, with 14 Sony PlayStation 2 consoles; a separate toddlers' playroom with soft toys and games; a smoking lounge; and a left-luggage area. The Royal Palm Lounge is billed as an airport lounge with the comforts of home and it is well worth the $25 each extra ($20 for children) to while away the last few hours on US soil. Most tour operators offer it in advance at a discount, or you can book on arrival or through your reps at the resort. With its increased capacity and facilities, this is a very satisfying way to conclude a holiday. See the Royal Palm Lounge (and more information on airport facilities) at **OrlandoSanford Airport.com**.

Whether you are using Orlando International or Orlando Sanford, you can also expect the return flight to be about an hour shorter than the journey out thanks to the Atlantic jetstreams that provide tail-winds to high-level flights. Nevertheless, you'll land back at Gatwick, Manchester, Glasgow or wherever rather more jet-lagged than on the trip out because the time difference is more noticeable on eastward flights, and it may take a day or so to get your body clock back on local time. It is very important not to indulge in alcohol on the flight if you will be driving when you land. And, much as it may seem like a good idea, the best way to beat Florida jet-lag is NOT to go straight out and book another holiday to Orlando!

But, believe us, the lure of this theme park wonderland is hard to resist – you WILL be back!

14 Your Holiday Planner

Example: 2 weeks with Disney's 5-Day Premium Ticket and Orlando FlexTicket

(Disney's 5-Day Premium Ticket gives 5 days at their 4 main theme parks, plus 4 visits to *Blizzard Beach, Typhoon Lagoon, DisneyQuest* and/or *Disney's ESPN World Of Sports*™, valid for 14 days from first use. The Orlando FlexTicket is valid for Universal Orlando's 2 parks, plus SeaWorld, Wet 'n Wild and CityWalk for 14 days from first use.)

Day	Our Example	Your Planner
ONE (Sun)	Arrive 2.40am local time, Orlando Sanford airport; transfer to resort – check out local shops and restaurants	
TWO (Mon)	Attend tour operator Welcome Meeting; rest of day at UNIVERSAL STUDIOS	
THREE (Tues)	Chill-out day at *Disney's Blizzard Beach* water park	
FOUR (Wed)	All day at MAGIC KINGDOM PARK (Wishes fireworks at 9pm)	
FIVE (Thurs)	All day at DISNEY'S HOLLYWOOD STUDIOS (Fantasmic! show at 8.30pm)	
SIX (Fri)	All day at EPCOT Park (IllumiNations at 9pm)	
SEVEN (Sat)	Have a lie-in, then try some shopping at Orlando Premium Outlets and Lake Buena Vista Factory Shops	
EIGHT (Sun)	DISNEY'S ANIMAL KINGDOM PARK Eve: Medieval Times Dinner Show (8pm)	
NINE (Mon)	ISLANDS OF ADVENTURE Eve: CityWalk and dinner at Hard Rock	
TEN (Tues)	KENNEDY SPACE CENTER Eve: International Drive	
ELEVEN (Wed)	All day at SEAWORLD ADVENTURE PARK (Mistify at 10pm)	

Day	Our Example	Your Planner
TWELVE (Thurs)	Have a chill-out day; head for the new Aquatica water park	
THIRTEEN (Fri)	Enjoy a UNIVERSAL ORLANDO highlights day. Eve: Sleuth's Mystery dinner show	
FOURTEEN (Sat)	Have a lie-in, then head for MAGIC KINGDOM PARK (Wishes fireworks at 9pm)	
FIFTEEN (Sun)	GATORLAND/Back to airport; return flight at 5.30pm	

Busy Day Guide

NB: These days can change on a month-by-month basis; for the most up-to-date info, please check our website, **www.askdaisy.net/orlando**.

Day	Busiest	Average	Lightest
Mon	*Magic Kingdom; Disney's Animal Kingdom*	*Disney's Hollywood Studios*	*Epcot;* Universal Studios; Islands of Adventure; Busch Gardens; Kennedy Space Center; SeaWorld; water parks
Tues	*Epcot; Magic Kingdom*	*Disney's Animal Kingdom*; Universal Studios	*Disney's Hollywood Studios;* Busch Gardens; IoA; Kennedy Space Center; SeaWorld; Water Parks
Wed	*Disney's Hollywood Studios* (high season)	*Disney's Animal Kingdom*; Islands of Adventure; SeaWorld; water parks	*Magic Kingdom; Epcot*; Busch Gardens; Kennedy Space Center; Universal Studios
Thurs	*Magic Kingdom*; Universal Studios	*Epcot*; Busch Gardens; SeaWorld; water parks	*Disney's Hollywood Studios*; *Disney's Animal Kingdom*; IoA; Kennedy Space Center
Fri	*Disney's Hollywood Studios* (high season) SeaWorld; Water Parks	*Disney's Animal Kingdom*; IoA; Busch Gardens; Kennedy Space Center	*Magic Kingdom*; *Epcot* Universal Studios
Sat	*Disney's Animal Kingdom*; Busch Gardens; IoA; Kennedy Space Center; SeaWorld; Universal Studios; water parks	*Magic Kingdom*; *Epcot*	*Disney's Hollywood Studios* (high season)
Sun	*Epcot*; *Magic Kingdom*; IoA; Kennedy Space Center; SeaWorld; water parks	*Disney's Hollywood Studios*; Busch Gardens; Universal Studios	*Disney's Animal Kingdom*

Index

Page numbers in *italics* refer to maps or tables. Those in **bold** refer to major references. (A) = Animal attraction, (D) = Dinner show, (R) = Restaurant, (T) = Tour company, (W) = Water park

Copyright notices

The author and publisher gratefully acknowledge the provision of the following photographs.
Cover: Universal Orlando. Disney.
Advantage Vacation Homes 100; AirTran 33; Albin Polasek Museum and Sculpture Gardens (Wendy Murray) 253; Arabian Nights 308; Astronaut Hall of Fame 224; Bahama Breeze 321; Best of British Soccer World 314; Best Western Lake Buena Vista 74; Blue Heron Beach Resort 97; Blue Martini 350 bottom; Boggy Creek Airboat Rides 259; Bok Tower Gardens 228; Brio Tuscan Grille 350 top; British Homes Group 104 bottom; Bubba Gump's Shrimp Co. 300; Busch Gardens 29, 38, 39, 209, 210, 211, 212, 213, 214, 215, 216, 217, 218; Café Tu Tu Tango 322; Capone's 311; Chalet Suzanne 229; Champions Gate Golf Club 271; Channelside Bay Plaza 286; Cheyenne Saloon and Opera House 313; Citrus County, Florida 268, 269, 270; Cricketers Arms 318; Cypress Gardens 225, 226, 227; Daytona Beach 17, 278, 279, 282, 290; Fantasy of Flight 234; Festival Bay Mall 342, 343; Florida Aquarium 16, 285; Florida Eco-Safaris 263; Floridays Resort 85; Fulton's Crab House 333; Fun Spot Action Park 237; Fun Spot USA 241; Gatorland 232, 233; Gaylord Palms Resort 91; Grand Cypress Resort 47, 276; Hawaiian Rumble 274; Holiday Inn Maingate East 80; Holy Land Experience 240; Hyatt Regency Grand Cypress 89; I-Ride 53; Kennedy Space Center 219, 221, 222, 223; LakeView Restaurant at the Regal Sun Resort 75; Land Remembered 332; Leonardo.com 76, 94, 101; Luma 335; Magnolia Inn 256; Magnolia Plantation Golf Club 272; Maitland Art Center 254; Mall at Millenia 351; Mears Transportation 56; Medieval Times 308; Ming Court 325; Oceanaire 334; Omni Orlando Resort at Champions Gate 93; Orange County History Center 243; Orlando Fire Museum 244; Orlando Marriott World Center 84; Orlando Premium Outlets 346, 347; Orlando Science Center 242; Orlando Sentinel 90; Orlando Watersports Complex 275; Orlando/Orange County Convention and Visitors Bureau, Inc. 35, 40, 45, 50, 92, 257, 260, 262, 277, 298, 304, 305, 312, 317, 344, 348, 349, 351, 352; Overlook at Lake Louisa 103; Pat O'Brien's 302; Portofino Bay Hotel 83; Preconstructionconnection.com 88; Prime Outlets International 337; Raglan Road Irish Pub 296, 341; Redrock Canyon Grill 305; Reunion Resort 95; Ripley's Believe It or Not 236; Rosen Shingle Creek Hotel 87; St Pete's and Clearwater Tourist Office 21, 25, 28, 37 top, 43, 104 top, 281, 292, 294; Sandpearl Resort 289; Seasons 52; SeaWorld, Discovery Cove and Aquatica 19, 24, 48, 193, 194, 195, 196, 197, 198, 199, 200, 201, 202, 203, 204, 205, 206, 251, 252; Seminole County Visitors Bureau 266; Sherlock's 261; Silver Springs 230, 231; SkyVenture 239; Sleuth's 310; Stage Door 327; Sun Villas Florida Direct 102; Tabu 313; Tarantino's 345; Thompson Aire 258; Universal Orlando/Islands of Adventure 18, 20, 22, 23, 26, 32, 37, 42, 82, 165, 166, 169, 170, 171, 172, 173, 174, 175, 176, 177, 178, 181, 182, 183, 184, 185, 186, 187, 188, 189, 190, 295, 301, 303; Village Tavern 331; Waldo Wright's Flying Service 235; Wekiva Springs State Park 267; Wet 'n Wild 248, 249, 250; Windsor Palms Resort 96; Wonderland Inn 98; WonderWorks 227; WW11 Fighter Aircraft Foundation, Kissimmee (Chuck Gardner) 265.

Page 34 Downtown Disney © Disney
Page 15 Cinderella Castle © Disney
Page 36 Guests at the Magic Kingdom © Disney
Page 41 Disney's Boardwalk Resort © Disney
Page 44 Cinderella wedding at Walt Disney World Resort © Disney
Page 63 Disney's Beach Club Resort © Disney
Page 65 Woody at Disney's All-Star Movie Resort © Disney
Page 67 Disney's Port Orleans Resort © Disney
Page 68 Disney's Animal Kingdom Lodge © Disney
Page 69 Disney's Grand Floridian Resort and Spa © Disney
Page 70 Wilderness Lodge © Disney
Page 71 Disney's Yacht and Beach Club Resort © Disney
Page 72 Fort Wilderness Resort and Campground © Disney
Page 105 Mad Tea Party © Disney
Page 106 Magic Carpets of Aladdin © Disney
Page 108 Guests at the Magic Kingdom © Disney
Page 109 It's a Small World © Disney
Page 111 Main Street USA with Cinderella's Castle © Disney
Page 113 Space Mountain © Disney
Page 114 The Jungle Cruise © Disney
Page 115 Big Thunder Mountain Railroad © Disney
Page 116 Liberty Square Riverboat © Disney
Page 117 Mickey's PhilharMagic © Disney
Page 118 Cinderella's Golden Carousel © Disney
Page 119 Barnstormer at Goofy's Wiseacre Farm © Disney
Page 120 Buzz Lightyear's Space Ranger Spin
Page 121 SpectroMagic Parade © Disney
Page 122 Wishes Firework Show © Disney
Page 123 Fireworks at the Magic Kingdom © Disney
Page 125 Test Track © Disney
Page 127 Epcot monorail © Disney
Page 128 'Honey, I Shrunk the Audience' © Disney
Page 129 Soarin'™ at Epcot © Disney
Page 130 The Seas with Nemo and Friends
Page 131 Cinderella Meet and Greet at Epcot © Disney
Page 132 Germany pavilion © Disney
Page 133 China pavilion © Disney
Page 134 Morocco pavilion © Disney
Page 135 Italy Pavilion © Disney
Page 136 Spaceship Earth © Disney
Page 137 International Food and Wine Festival © Disney
Page 139 Rock 'n' Roller Coaster starring Aerosmith © Disney
Page 141 The Hollywood Brown Derby restaurant © Disney
Page 143 Lights, Motors, Action! Extreme Stunt Show © Disney
Page 144 Catastrophe Canyon © Disney
Page 145 Toy Story Mania © Disney
Page 146 top Lights, Motors, Action! Extreme Stunt Show © Disney
Page 146 bottom Disney Playhouse Live on Stage! © Disney
Page 147 top Rock 'n' Roller Coaster Starring Aerosmith © Disney
Page 147 bottom Hollywood Tower of Terror © Disney
Page 148 Fantasmic! © Disney
Page 149 Jedi Training Academy © Disney
Page 152 top Kilimanjaro Safaris © Disney
Page 152 bottom Expedition Everest © Disney
Page 153 Primeval Whirl © Disney
Page 154 It's Tough to Be a Bug © Disney
Page 155 The Tree of Life at Disney's Animal Kingdom © Disney
Page 156 Kilimanjaro Safaris © Disney
Page 157 top Festival of the Lion King © Disney
Page 157 bottom Kilimanjaro Safaris: the Trail © Disney
Page 158 top Expedition Everest © Disney
Page 158 bottom Maharajah Jungle Trek © Disney
Page 159 Kali River Rapids © Disney
Page 160 Finding Nemo – the Musical © Disney
Page 161 The Boneyard at Disney's Animal Kingdom © Disney
Page 162 top TriceraTOP Spin at Disney's Animal Kingdom © Disney
Page 162 bottom Primeval Whirl © Disney
Page 163 top Mickey's Very Merry Christmas Parade © Disney
Page 163 bottom Dinosaur! © Disney
Page 164 Mickey's Jammin' Jungle Parade © Disney
Page 245 Shark Reef at Disney's Typhoon Lagoon © Disney
Page 246 Disney's Typhoon Lagoon © Disney
Page 247 Disney's Blizzard Beach © Disney
Page 255 Downtown Disney marina © Disney
Page 273 Disney's Winter-Summerland Mini-golf © Disney
Page 293 Disney's Cruise Line © Disney
Page 296 Downtown Disney © Disney
Page 297 T-Rex: A Prehistoric Adventure © Disney
Page 299 La Nouba at Cirque du Soleil © Disney
Page 307 top Hoop-Dee-Doo Musical Revue © Disney
Page 307 bottom Pirate's Dinner Adventure © Disney
Page 309 Pirate's Dinner Adventure © Disney
Page 328 Flying Fish Café at Disney's Boardwalk Resort © Disney
Page 338 World of Disney at Downtown Disney © Disney
Page 340 Downtown Disney © Disney

Acknowledgements

The authors wish to acknowledge the help of the following in the production of this book:

The authors wish to acknowledge the help of the following in the production of this book: The Orlando/Orange County Convention and Visitors' Bureau, Travel Industry Association, Visit Florida, The Kissimmee/St Cloud Convention & Visitors' Bureau, St Petersburg/Clearwater Area Convention and Visitors' Bureau, Daytona Beach Area Convention & Visitors' Bureau, Seminole County Convention & Visitors' Bureau, Tampa Bay and Company, Mount Dora Chamber of Commerce, Walt Disney Attractions Inc., Universal Orlando, The Busch Entertainment Corporation, The British-American Chamber of Commerce, The Greater Orlando Aviation Authority, Orlando-Sanford International Airport and Alamo Rent A Car.

In person: Danielle Courtenay, Susan Greer and Donna Taliercio (Orlando CVB), Larry White, Sylvia Oliande, Chris Long (Kissimmee CVB), Sharon Sears, Patrick Harrison (Seminole County CVB) Mary Haban, (St Petersburg/Clearwater CBV), Tangela Boyd, Georgia Turner (Daytona Beach CVB), Brooke Maynard (Tampa Bay and Company), Tom Bartosek (Florida's Space Coast), Andrea Farmer (Kennedy Space Center), Cathy Hoechst (Mount Dora Chamber of Commerce), Sarah Hodson, Nikki Palmas, Jason Lasecki, Geoff Pointon (Walt Disney Co), Tom Schroder (Universal), Carolyn Fennell, Rod Johnson (Orlando Aviation Authority), Alyson Gernert, Nancy Daley, Haley Kish (Cypress Gardens), John Stine (Baker Leisure Group), Lorraine Ellis (Get Married In Florida), Andy James, James Brown (Florida Dolphin Tours), Susan Flower, Christine Haughney (Discovery Cove), Oliver Brendon, Chris Bradshaw (Attraction Tickets Direct), Lauren Skowyra (SeaWorld), Janeche Petrou, Gerard Hoeppner, (Busch Gardens), Jackie Vazquez (WonderWorks), Laura Richeson (Bennett & Company), Lisa Earnhardt, Aida Talaber (Unicorp Developments), Michael Caires, Greg Dull (Orlando Sanford International Airport), Allan Oakley (Alexander Homes & Associates), Nigel Worrall (Florida Leisure), Bill Cowie (BACC), Wrenda Goodwyn (International Drive), Judy Graham-Weaver (AirTran Airways), Jeff Stanford (Orlando Science Center), Michelle Harris, Bret Chism (Gatorland), Terry Lynn Morris (Lake Buena Vista Factory Stores), Jessica Zuniga (Medieval Times), Billy Seay (Arabian Nights), Lance Lancaster (Sleuths), Phillip Jaffe (Pro Golf Guides of Orlando), Mary Deatrick (Deatrick PR for Shingle Creek Resort), Sally March (Mall at Millenia), Leigh Jones (Orlando Premium Outlets), Shannon Clayton (The Pointe Orlando), Deborah Detweiler (Festival Bay), Shani Jefferson (Tampa MOSI), Tom Wagner (Florida Aquarium), Michele Palmer (Sandpearl Resort), Margie Long, Michele Peters (Boggy Creek Airboats), John Cooke (Raglan Road), Phil Coppen (Cricketers Arms), Wayne Gray (FRO Group), Jennie and Paul Skingley (Best of British Soccer World) and Laurie Babb.

Special thanks to Pete Werner and all at the DIS – you know who you are!

Got a red-hot Brit Tip to pass on? The latest info on how to beat the queues or the best new restaurant in town? We want to hear from YOU to keep improving the guide each year. Drop us a line at: Brit's Guide (Orlando), W. Foulsham & Co. Ltd, The Oriel, Thames Valley Court, 183-187 Bath Road, Slough, Berkshire SL1 4AA. Or e-mail **britsguide@yahoo.com**.